Studies in Adolescence

Studies in Adolescence

A Book of Readings in Adolescent Development

SECOND EDITION

SELECTED AND EDITED BY

Robert E. Grinder

University of Wisconsin

The Macmillan Company

Collier-Macmillan Limited, *London*

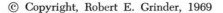

First Printing

Earlier edition, entitled *Studies in Adolescence,*
© 1963 by Robert E. Grinder

Library of Congress catalog card number: 69–11182

THE MACMILLAN COMPANY
COLLIER-MACMILLAN CANADA, LTD., TORONTO, ONTARIO

Printed in the United States of America

Preface to the Second Edition

THE perfectibility of man seemed imminent at the turn of the century. Optimism flowed effusively from faith in the theory of evolution, and the outpouring led the scientists who were founders of child study to believe that in the study of adolescence they had a vehicle that would elevate men to lofty status. The harsher aspects of reality soon dashed this dream, but enthusiasm for the task of improving the lot of man did not disintegrate. Instead, it shifted to an enthusiasm for achieving for the youth of every generation a harmonious adjustment between adolescence and adulthood. Many educators, psychologists, and others interested in adolescence have struggled since then to define adjustment norms, to describe and standardize the socialization experiences that culminate in maturity, and to compare growing adolescents against these criteria.

Judging or analyzing youth from the viewpoint of preconceived adjustment and maturity norms has become a prominent practice. Those who are keenly aware of the urgency and magnitude of their responsibility for socializing adolescents have contributed proportionately more to the literature, but have been inclined to emphasize what they believe adolescents *ought* to be doing rather than to urge dispassionate analyses of why adolescents function as they do. The orientation has hardly advanced the scientific understanding of adolescents. To avoid the contradictions so often apparent in exhortations, adolescent adjustment is usually described in trifling abstractions. The common approach has been to assume, for example, that youths should acquire the personality traits necessary for sustaining themselves as adults in terms of intimate and persistent social relationships, vocational and economic responsibilities, societal customs, and religious and philosophical convictions. In short, youths should acclimate themselves for living in adulthood happily ever after.

Studies in Adolescence suggests that contemporary theory and research data illuminate several pathways to life-adjustment and happiness. Adults differ tremendously in their maturity. Some are urbane, others are uncouth; some are vivacious, others are reserved; some are retiring, others are ruggedly individualistic. In their growth, rather than converging toward an ideal personality, adolescents progressively diverge from one another. Passage through adolescence involves a highly particularistic sampling of the advantages and shortcomings of numerous different aspects of life; it is a time during which individuals become relatively differentiated from one another on the basis of physical characteristics, cognitive skills, and personality traits. They may or may not become wholly adjusted persons, but certainly, given even slight impetus from their culture, they become wholly distinct persons. This new revision of *Studies in Adolescence*, therefore, is comprised predominantly of papers focusing on the relations between socialization experiences and the myriad characteristics of adolescents. The text offers theoretical discussions, empirical tests of propositions and hypotheses, and importantly, substantive bases for deriving predictions of adolescent behavior in contemporary society.

The book shares with its first edition an attempt to introduce students to a series of exploratory investigations concerning the nature of adolescence. During the past decade, research has burgeoned independently and more vigorously than ever in several disciplines—anthropology, education, medicine, psychology, social work, and sociology. An interdisciplinary approach is necessary to draw the insights from these diverse sources together; *Studies in Adolescence* aims to meet this requirement. Its forty-two selections, for example, have been compiled from twenty-seven sources, only seven of which are wholly psychological in orientation.

The revision reveals that new emphases in the study of adolescence have emerged in recent years. Research on youth culture has accelerated notably; therefore, included here are investigations of youth culture in relation to school and parental activities as well as substantive analyses of language, clique, crowd, and dating systems. Also represented in the text are studies of ancillary youth-culture functions and problems, such as young marriages, runaways, delinquents, changing interests, drugs, smoking, automobile driving, and sexual exploitation and sex education. Further, in the important area of vocational development, the book encompasses recent research exploring antecedent vocational aspirations and school achievement.

Studies in Adolescence strongly emphasizes traditional areas of research on adolescent development as well. Such issues as sex-role identification, family power structure, achievement motivation, child-rearing consistency, parent-peer cross pressures, and religious and moral development are covered in detail. Several "dimensions" of cognitive growth—growth in concepts, egocentrism, orientation to the future, and political ideas—complement the major emphases on socialization. Although new investigations supplant many of the papers that represented traditional areas in the first edition, the new materials are often direct outgrowths of the studies they replace. Certain investigations in the first edition, however, prove to be as timely now as before—those pertaining to G. Stanley Hall, adolescent initiation rites, psychoanalytic theory, stability of achievement motivation, physical growth, and cross-cultural perspectives on sexual behavior are retained.

Parts 1, 2, and 6 of the second edition correspond closely to their counterparts in the first. The portions on peer and school influences (in Parts 2 and 3 in the earlier volume) have been revised and now constitute Part 3, "Youth-Culture Involvement," Part 4, "Value Commitments," and Part 5, "High-School Achievement and Vocational Orientation." "Physical and Cognitive Growth" (Part 4 in the first edition) has been renumbered Part 6.

Studies in Adolescence collates the scholarship of nearly sixty researchers, and I am grateful to them and to their publishers for permitting me to reprint their materials here. A footnote included on the introductory page of each article formally acknowledges their contribution. I am especially indebted to Gary L. Carlson, Sue A. Porter, and Mary L. Stelly, whose secretarial and editorial skills, augmented by their perseverance, good humor, and critical acumen, greatly facilitated the preparation of the manuscript.

R. E. G.

Madison, Wisconsin

Preface to the First Edition

S*tudies in Adolescence* has been compiled with the aim of introducing students to a series of exploratory investigations concerning the nature of adolescence. The book brings together current, substantive studies, of both a theoretical and empirical nature. On the whole, the hypotheses offered and the findings presented stem from objective, behavioral analyses rather than clinical or case study methods. In addition to contributing to an understanding of adolescence, the selected papers have another significant feature in common: all are highly provocative, stimulating treatises that raise as many questions as they answer. This is as it should be, for the psychology of adolescence while being one of the more ancient domains of psychology is indeed one of its least charted. Therefore, the student of adolescent behavior who searches for definitive conclusions in this volume will eventually forsake its pages in disappointment. If he should seek, however, perspective, insight, and information as bases for his hypotheses and his appraisals, he will swiftly realize his expectations.

Two general assumptions furnish the rationale for the selection of papers that are included in this volume. First, it is assumed that with the advent of adolescence, persons and institutions of society-at-large become increasingly important as agents of socialization while parents and family diminish in status and influence. Second, it is assumed that the adolescent must extinguish many childhood habits and roles as he simultaneously masters several new patterns of behavior, which must be appropriate not only for his sex and age but also for his apprenticeship of the adult positions that he will eventually occupy. Hence, a study of development during adolescence necessitates an analysis of theory and research from several branches of the social sciences, especially psychology, sociology, and anthropology, and a focus upon the specific developmental, sociocultural, familial, peer, and school issues affecting the socialization process.

Social scientists have long affirmed that cultural conditions affect socialization during adolescence; nonetheless, in the past half-century, viewpoints about the effect of this influence have changed markedly. The papers in Part 1, which draw both upon historical precedents and contemporary trends, are presented specifically to acquaint the student with a variety of viewpoints about the ways in which the adolescent and his society interact upon one another. The interdisciplinary approach is attested to by the fact that the section is comprised of the deliberations of a historian and several psychologists, sociologists, and anthropologists.

Parts 2 and 3 are similarly eclectic. The first selection in Part 2 subjects the pronouncements of psychoanalytic theorists to critical analysis; the second paper offers an imaginative new behavioral theory to account for the socialization process. Following these papers, a series of studies demonstrates the relationships of such variables as family background, socioeconomic status, changing interests, delinquency behavior, religious experiences, and ethnic attitudes to development during adolescence. Finally, the last paper in this section comprehensively reviews the empirical research on these theories and variables. Part 3 brings together experimental studies of peer and high school influences upon socialization. Popularity, peer-status, and extracurricular activities are given special attention.

Part 4 departs from the socialization theme in order to describe the physical and intellectual characteristics that develop during the adolescent period. These growth factors may influence socialization by imposing limitations upon an individual's development. Moreover, even when certain aspects of growth may be functionally insignificant, societal standards place a premium on the attainment of attributes related to athletic prowess, physical attractiveness, and intellectual aptitude. The first papers in this section describe how adolescents grow physically and how this growth is associated with their personality development. Subsequent articles discuss the development of cognitive and intellectual abilities in adolescents and the influence of home and high school variables upon superior scholastic performances.

I am deeply grateful to the authors and publishers who generously granted permission to reprint their materials. I have acknowledged their contributions in appropriate footnotes throughout the volume. I am particularly indebted to those authors who either prepared original papers or revised earlier versions of their papers for inclusion in this collection.

In preparation of the manuscript I was aided immensely by the editorial

suggestions of Wendy S. Spotts and by the secretarial assistance and counsel of Dorothy B. Ratcliff. I am very much pleased that I may express my
appreciation to them here.

R. E. G.

University of Wisconsin

Contents

Part 6   Physical and Cognitive Growth During Adolescence: Relationships Between Maturational and Societal Factors   429

Studies in Adolescence

Socialization: Adolescence and Society

Robert E. Grinder
Charles E. Strickland

G. Stanley Hall and the Social
Significance of Adolescence

No other psychologist has written more about adolescence than G. Stanley Hall. His famed two-volume treatise on adolescence was actually an encyclopedia. His interests ranged on the one hand from embryology to education and religion, and on the other, from gynecology to counseling techniques. For all his genius, enthusiasm, and energy, however, his efforts to establish recapitulation theory as the all-explanatory principle of psychological development aborted early in the twentieth century. The anonymity into which he has fallen, as a consequence, has rendered his assumptions about adolescence relatively inaccessible and misunderstood. In the following paper, the authors show how Hall's nineteenth-century Darwinism and his ideas for social reform merge to yield a strikingly unusual interpretation of the adolescent years.

IF the influence of historical personages in psychology were to be appraised by contemporary status, the names of Sigmund Freud, William James, Ivan Pavlov, and Edward L. Thorndike would be included in any serious listing. The theoretical formulations of these pioneers have survived rigorous investigations; today they underpin conceptual scaffolds for innumerable systems of learning and personality. But absent from the list would be the name of G. Stanley Hall (1844–1924), the man earning America's first Ph.D. in psychology, the father of the child study movement in the United States, the founder of the American Psychological Association, and the author of some 350 papers, articles, and books, including an enormously comprehensive two-volume treatise on the psychology of adolescence.[1] Lecturer at Harvard, professor at Johns Hopkins, and president of Clark University from its inception until his retirement, Hall enjoyed a thoroughly productive professional career. Most of the institutions fathered by him are now nationally prominent, but from its peak at the turn of the century, the influence of his

FROM *Teachers College Record,* LXIV (February, 1963), 390–399. Reprinted by permission of the authors and the publisher.

[1] G. Stanley Hall, *Adolescence: Its Psychology and Its Relation to Physiology, Anthropology, Sociology, Sex, Crime, Religion and Education* (2 vols.; New York: D. Appleton and Co., 1904).

theory and research has ebbed continuously. Even as early as 1928, it was declared in the preface of a highly regarded text on adolescence that "students of Dr. G. Stanley Hall will miss this extensive reference to his voluminous pioneer works on adolescence . . . such reference would seem of historic value primarily, rather than of scientific or practical value today." [2]

Although Hall's *magnum opus* on adolescence has been taken as the starting point for discussions of the adolescent phenomena for decades, the majority of psychologists who have worked in this area, except for a small clique of first-generation devotees, have renounced his theoretical formulations unequivocally. Specifically, Hall has been impugned for (a) ignoring the influences of culture and overly emphasizing the importance of physiological functions in the adolescent's development, (b) conceptualizing adolescence as a period of intense storm and stress which arises from instinctual upheavals, and (c) regarding physical growth of adolescents as saltatory rather than as continuous and gradual. These interpretations of Hall's views have had a telling effect upon contemporary thinking in adolescent psychology and have caused him to appear, in his historical role, somewhat like an antichrist.

G. Stanley Hall differs from most psychologists, past or present, in the degree to which he attempted to apply Charles Darwin's evolutionary view of man to both psychology and social philosophy. His most important adaptation of Darwinian or evolutionary biology was the theory of recapitulation. He argued that every phase of a person's growth represents one of the different levels at which the human race was once mature; hence, every person recapitulates or repeats the history of the race in his development. Whereas the human fetus reveals a very remote stage of evolution, some adult behaviors are the actual cutting edges of a new stage. Hall reasoned that the phylogeny of the human race could be reconstructed by research not only in human psychology, but also in biology, anthropology, sociology, history, and comparative psychology. On the one hand, Hall literally envisaged himself to be the prophet of a new social order. In Hall's opinion, evolution pointed to the development of a super-race, and to this end, a collective society should be organized under the control of an elite who could direct mankind toward its goal of evolutionary perfection. On the other hand, Hall enjoyed being honored as a "Darwin of the mind." [3] His ambition was to construct the history of the psyche, from the lowly amoeba to man himself.[4] He believed that possession of this knowledge would reveal the complexities of human development, accelerate evolutionary processes, and unlock even the purpose and destiny of life itself. Primarily, these twin ambitions turned Hall toward the adolescent phenomena.

[2] Leta S. Hollingworth, *The Psychology of the Adolescent* (New York: D. Appleton and Co., 1928), p. ix.

[3] G. S. Hall, *Life and Confessions of a Psychologist* (New York: D. Appleton and Co., 1923), p. 360.

[4] G. S. Hall, "Evolution and Psychology," *Fifty Years of Darwinism,* American Association for the Advancement of Science (New York: Henry Holt and Co., 1909), p. 252.

Although G. Stanley Hall hoped to gain a better understanding of adolescence and to improve education and psychology, his aims were obviously more grandiose. Interpreting adolescence within the context of his particular Darwinian and utopian premises, Hall made judgments never fully acceptable to many psychologists. His opponents often have attempted to subject his pronouncements to *reductio ad absurdum,* and the resulting misunderstandings doubtless have contributed in part to the decline of his influence in the twentieth century. But even more important, Hall's Darwinian assumptions gave his views of adolescent phenomena a turn-of-the-century air that may be strange to many contemporary students of adolescence. Therefore, this paper presents: (a) a clarification of his basic assumptions, and (b) in terms of them, the essential features of his views about adolescence.

SOCIAL REFORM [5]

Accustomed as we are to Darwin's evolutionary view of life, it is difficult to imagine the intellectual upheaval occasioned by the theory during Hall's formative years. Within three decades after *The Origin of Species* appeared in 1859, the influence of Darwinism had reached every branch of the social sciences. Although Hall began his career as a divinity student, his interests were also rapidly drawn to Darwinian theory. Toying with this dangerous but fascinating new idea while attending Union Theological Seminary in the 1860's, Hall became disillusioned with theological orthodoxy. The fate of the keen young intellect balanced precariously for a time until Henry Ward Beecher, the famed clergyman, convinced that philosophical studies abroad would do no harm to a young man's piety, secured the funds necessary for Hall's journey to Berlin University.[6] German society fascinated Hall to such an extent that he returned to America only with reluctance, and he later confessed to planning several "unpractical ways" of spending the rest of his life abroad.[7] Events during the Gilded Age convinced Hall that laissez-faire individualism would no longer answer the needs of a complex, civilized society, and in his judgment, Germany was leading the civilized world in social reform legislation. As Hall saw it, Germany took seriously the admonitions of her philosopher, Johann Fichte, who early in the century had called for an educational state, governed by an elite and dedicated to the cultural perfection of mankind. The German social order had "actualized the Platonic Republic." [8]

When he condemned laissez-faire individualism and materialism, Hall marched in step with a hardy band of nineteenth-century American intellectuals and reformers. But when he began to formulate his own brand of utopia he broke the cadence. To the ideas of Plato and Fichte, he added

[5] The authors are greatly indebted to Charles O. Burgess for insight into Hall's social philosophy.
[6] Hall, *Life,* pp. 177–181.
[7] *Ibid.,* p. 222.
[8] G. S. Hall, "The Moral and Religious Training of Children," *Princeton Review,* N. S., IX (1882), 27.

elements drawn from the thought of Darwin and the German philosopher, Friedrich Nietzsche. The result was a collectivistic utopia based on a profound distrust of reason, individualism, and democratic egalitarianism.

Darwinism provided scientifically respectable support for Hall's pessimism about the intellectual qualities of the average man. Surveying the course of evolutionary development, Hall belittled the rational powers as determinants of behavior. They were a relatively late development in evolution. "Instincts, feelings, emotions and sentiments were vastly older and more all-determining than the intellect," Hall asserted; moreover, they were basically right.[9] Awed by what he perceived to be the perfect social organization of the insect, Hall believed that the "superiority of instinct over reason is that it regulates conduct in the interest of the species at every point." [10] While science in general was affirming that nature could be controlled for service to man's purposes, Hall was contending that man should be controlled in deference to the expressions of nature.[11]

Hall distrusted not only reason but also individualism and democratic forms of government. Here the influence of Nietzsche—as Hall understood him—is apparent. G. Stanley Hall observed that the mediocrity of most men testified to the fact that they lacked the "push" necessary to move them upward on the evolutionary scale,[12] and that democracy "everywhere thus, tends to the dead level of the average man and to the dominance of . . . incompetence and mediocrity." [13] In a paper written for an audience of German educators in 1915, he declared that America was the home of men suffering from "overstimulation." "Our very schoolboys are told that they may possibly become presidents or millionaires, that theirs is a land of boundless opportunity." [14] Hall thought "the peril of democracy is that it has aroused so large a body of hopes that are utterly unrealizable. . . ." Inevitably democracy would experience a "gospel of renunciation." [15] Perhaps the most serious evil of democracy, as he saw it, was its encouragement of concern for individuals, and on one occasion he turned the generally accepted definition of pity on its head. Hall argued that "pity" must not be extended to the downtrodden "because by aiding them to survive it interferes with the process of wholesome natural selection by which all that is best has hitherto been developed. . . . Its work is no longer the salvage of the wreckage of humanity. . . . Pity has its highest office then in removing the handicaps from those most able to help man to higher levels—the leaders

---

[9] Hall, *Life*, pp. 361–362.

[10] G. S. Hall, "A Glance at the Phyletic Background of Genetic Psychology," *American Journal of Psychology*, XIX (April, 1908), 211.

[11] Charles O. Burgess, "The Educational State in America: Selected Views on Learning as the Key to Utopia, 1800–1924" (unpublished Ph.D. dissertation, Dept. of Education, University of Wisconsin, 1962).

[12] G. S. Hall, "The Ideal School Based on Child Study," *Proceedings*, National Education Association (1901), p. 484.

[13] Hall, *Life*, p. 440.

[14] G. S. Hall, "Recreation and Reversion," *Pedagogical Seminary*, XXII (1915), 510.

[15] G. S. Hall, "Can the Masses Rule the World?" *Scientific Monthly*, XVIII (May, 1924), 466.

on more exalted plains who can be of most aid in ushering in the kingdom of superman." [16]

G. Stanley Hall's longing for a superanthropoid utopia bore a significant relation to his view of the adolescent because Hall believed that youth would play an important role in bringing about the new society. Needed were persons who would realize that the destiny of human beings collectively was more important than the welfare of an individual. Needed were persons who would subordinate themselves to the nurture of that "elite youth" who are harbingers of the future.[17] Hall felt that adolescents were well equipped with the collectivistic sentiments necessary to bring about the super-race, and to nourish these sentiments, he called for an educational program that would stress the development of sound body and sound emotions rather than the cultivation of intellectual abilities. He scorned teachers who would "allow or even encourage callow classes to debate, discuss and weigh evidence or regurgitate the matter of the textbook." [18] Early in adolescence, he would have the sexes separated, girls to be prepared for marriage and motherhood, boys to be trained for service and citizenship.[19] For boys, Hall placed particular emphasis on instruction in body culture, patriotism, military discipline, and industrial education.[20] Perhaps the most striking characteristic of Hall's educational plan for adolescents was his belief that intellectual training should be reserved for comparatively few. "Many gather at the foot of the mount, some ascend a little way, but only a chosen few can scale the summit above the clouds and bring down the tables of the law for those who wait below. . . . The few hundred picked and ripened adolescents who could and would live solely for research and the advancement of the kingdom of man and of truth in the world are too often lost in the growing academic crowds." [21]

RECAPITULATION THEORY

To a democratic nation that was realizing equality in public schooling for all children, the social significance of G. Stanley Hall's concept of adolescent education probably seemed offensive. But Hall believed that his views rested on scientifically respectable grounds, and that the theory of recapitulation provided the psychological justification he needed. Before Hall fully endorsed this new biological interpretation of psychological data, however, he passed through an interlude of enthusiasm for the experimental psychology of Wilhelm Wundt. After completing his doctorate at Harvard in 1878, Hall journeyed to Germany to study at Wundt's newly established laboratory in

---

[16] G. S. Hall and F. H. Saunders, "Pity," *American Journal of Psychology*, XI (1900), 590–591.

[17] *Ibid.*, p. 591.

[18] G. S. Hall, "Certain Degenerative Tendencies among Teachers," *Pedagogical Seminary*, XII (1905), 459.

[19] Hall, *Adolescence*, II, Chap. 17.

[20] *Ibid.*, I, Chap. 3.

[21] Hall, *Adolescence*, II, 559.

Leipzig. Convinced that muscle sensations were the bedrock of the psyche, Hall hailed Wundt as the "coming philosopher in Germany," [22] whose experiments on muscle reactions would settle major epistemological controversies. To Hall the laboratory technique represented an "independent look at nature" that "has opened new impulses and enthusiasm for me such as nothing else has." [23] During the 1880's, however, Hall slowly turned his back on the psychological laboratory. He found it too confining for his ambitions, which were nothing less than to "unlock the past history of the race," [24] namely, to construct the origin and development of the psyche, not merely the conscious intellect, but the unconscious emotions and instincts as well. Wundt had erred in ignoring Darwin, and G. Stanley Hall resolved not to make the same mistake.[25]

The heart of G. Stanley Hall's grand design was the theory of recapitulation—an imaginative corollary of Darwin's evolutionary theory. By observing species in their natural habitats, Darwin had ordered his data on a scale from lower to higher complexity. But his effort was more than mere description and classification, for in denoting the lower forms as "earlier" and the higher forms as "later," he told a story of the origin and development of life. Nonetheless, how on the basis of observation and hypothesis could Darwin know that simpler forms of life were also earlier? Paleontological evidence was as yet scanty, and archeology and anthropology were still highly speculative; so Darwin and others interested in the validity of his argument turned to the relatively advanced science of embryology. In 1864, a German biologist, Fritz Mueller, published a study showing that in its development the embryo of higher animals recapitulates the forms through which its species had evolved. In 1868 the idea achieved prominence in the popular lectures of Ernst Haeckel, who extended the notion to include postnatal psychic development, and who coined the phrase by which the theory became widely known: "ontogeny is a brief and rapid recapitulation of phylogeny." [26] Haeckel's "bio-genetic law" gave impressive support to Darwin's hypothesis that complex living forms had descended from more simple beginnings. In embryonic development lay the record of evolution for all to see.[27]

Bolstered by Haeckel's biogenetic law, Darwin's view of natural history swept through the field of biology and on into psychology. The great pioneer, Darwin himself, led the way. In *Expression of the Emotions in Man and Animals* Darwin described phenomena such as fear, anger, and joy as inherited remnants of similar expressions in "earlier" forms, e.g., the sneer

[22] G. S. Hall, "The Philosophy of the Future," *Nation*, XXVII (Nov. 7, 1878), 283.
[23] Letter from G. S. Hall to William James, Ralph Barton Perry (ed.), *The Thought and Character of William James* (2 vols.; Boston: Little, Brown and Co., 1935), II, 20–21.
[24] Hall, "Evolution and Psychology," *op. cit.*, p. 263.
[25] *Ibid.*, p. 254.
[26] Ernst Haeckel, *Evolution of Man* (2 vols.; London: C. Kegan Paul and Co., 1879), II, Chap. 26.
[27] See Erik Nordenskiold, *The History of Biology: a Survey* (New York: Tudor Pub. Co., 1935), pp. 516–517; and Loren Eisely, *Darwin's Century: Evolution and the Men Who Discovered It* (Garden City, N.Y.: Doubleday and Co., 1958), p. 5.

invoked in human social situations was reminiscent of the canines who bared their teeth in rage. Inspired by Darwin's analyses, Hall praised him as "standing almost alone" in the investigation of emotional expression.[28] Darwin's bold manner of applying to the psyche the methods which he had applied so successfully to physical form and function completely won Hall's admiration. Speaking in 1909 before an assemblage honoring the contributions of Darwin, Hall demonstrated his indebtedness. He assured the group that "psychic rudiments and recapitulatory traces" are "as recognizable as the rudimentary gill-slits in the embryo" for "the child is vastly more ancient than the man." The child is, in fact, "his very venerable and, in his early stages, half-anthropoid ancestor."[29] Impending was a "well-established embryology of the soul," which would provide the necessary basis for a "true mentally, esthetically, and morally orthopedic education."[30]

G. Stanley Hall's enthusiasm for the theory of recapitulation propelled him from the laboratory to the leadership of the child study movement in America. After Hall became President of Clark University, men and women flocked there to work under his direction, and the literature about children increased rapidly. From the beginning Hall's interests were less in the development of the child and adolescent per se than in "coordinating childhood and youth with the development of the race . . . and also to establish criteria by which to both diagnose and measure arrest and retardation in the individual and the race."[31] Because Hall argued that study of the history of the race would provide the "true norms" for human development, he held that the psychologist must study the past, not merely traditional history with its concern for war and politics, but also cultural, social, and economic history. Above all, Hall proclaimed the relevance of anthropology, for he believed that some of the more psychologically significant aspects of human nature emerged before the rise of civilization and the advent of written records.[32]

Hall's belief that the psychologist must look to the past for norms of psychological development may appear unorthodox to modern investigators, but it offers an essential key to understanding his view of the adolescent years. The theory of recapitulation gave him confidence that anthropology and other historical data were indeed relevant, and his interpretations of these data provide the broad framework for his evaluations. In anthropology, the idea that human culture, like the animal world, evolved from simple beginnings had developed even before Darwin won acceptance for his theory of biological evolution. In America, the most influential representative of the "evolutionary" school of anthropology was Lewis Henry Morgan, whom Hall cited on several occasions. Morgan, in his epoch-making *Ancient*

[28] G. S. Hall and Theodate Smith, "Curiosity and Interest," *Pedagogical Seminary,* X (September, 1903), 315.

[29] Hall, "Evolution and Psychology," *op. cit.,* pp. 260–262.

[30] *Ibid.,* p. 263.

[31] Hall, *Adolescence,* I, viii.

[32] See G. S. Hall, *Educational Problems* (2 vols.; New York: D. Appleton and Company, 1911), II, 292, 306–310.

Society (1877), sketched the development of mankind in three broad stages
—savagery, barbarism, and civilization. Particularly noteworthy is the fact
that Morgan contended the stages exhibited respectively the following patterns of social organization: collectivism, individualism, and collectivism
again. On the basis of his findings, Morgan predicted that the individualism
characteristic of the nineteenth century would prove only to be a transient
stage peculiar to barbarism, and that eventually it would give way to a
civilized collectivism.[33] Although Morgan's idea of a collective civilization
bore little resemblance to Hall's notion of a totalitarian utopia governed by
an elite, nevertheless, the essential pattern—individualism giving way to
collectivism—matched Hall's social philosophy. Since Hall believed that
every individual retraced the history of the race in his development, he
fully expected everyone to exhibit stages resembling the three that Morgan
had outlined.

The parallel between Morgan's evolutionary scheme and Hall's description of the course of human development is striking. Although Hall remained extremely vague about the relation of evolution to early childhood,
ignoring infancy and dismissing summarily the "kindergarten" stage as a
"sentimental" period, he showed considerable concern for the "juvenile"
or "prepubescent" stage, which ranged from eight or nine to twelve or
thirteen years of age. The child's entry into this second stage is marked by
"a decreased rate of growth, so that the body relatively rests," and the next
four years represent "on the recapitulation theory, a long period in some
remote age, well above the simian, but mainly before the historic period." [34]
The child's eagerness to throw, run, dodge, hit, chase, wrestle, box, fish,
and hunt are all lingering vestiges of ancient times when these activities
were necessary for survival.

More significant for Hall's total scheme, however, were the social attitudes expressed by the juvenile. The child at this age represents a mature
barbarian, who is healthy, vigorous, selfish, and totally unsentimental. While
he is responsive to his peers, tending to form "barbaric associations . . .
pirates, robbers, soldiers . . . and other savage reversionary combinations," [35] he is indifferent to the adult, civilized world. "The wisest requirements seem to the child more or less alien, arbitrary, heteronomous, artificial,
falsetto." [36] "Reason, true morality, religion, sympathy, love, and esthetic
enjoyment are but very slightly developed. Everything, in short, suggests
the culmination of one stage of life as if it thus represented what was once,
and for a very protracted and relatively stationary period, the age of maturity in some remote, perhaps pigmoid, stage of human evolution." [37] According to Hall, the school should introduce these children into the

[33] Carl Resek, *Lewis Henry Morgan: American Scholar* (Chicago: University of Chicago Press, 1960), pp. 139–143.

[34] Hall, "The Ideal School," *op. cit.*, p. 477.

[35] G. S. Hall, *Youth: Its Education, Regimen and Hygiene* (New York: D. Appleton
and Co., 1904), pp. 226–227.

[36] *Ibid.*, p. 4.

[37] Hall, *Adolescence*, I, ix–x.

necessities of learning "as intensively and quickly as possible with a minimal strain and with the least amount of explanation or coquetting for natural interest." [38]

G. Stanley Hall's pessimism about human development gave way to an exhilarating optimism when he saw the individual reach the adolescent years, from fourteen to twenty-four. As early as 1896 Hall observed that, although "the child has been selfish" during a long period of "complete individual development," the adolescence years signal "a second birth." Now one witnesses the "birth of love in the largest Christian sense, psychologically free from all selfish motives." [39] In *Adolescence*, Hall elaborated this point of view further. As Hall put it, the adolescent "must conquer a higher kingdom of man for himself, break out a new sphere, and evolve a more modern story to his psycho-physical nature." [40] "Adolescence is a new birth, for the higher and more completely human traits are now born." [41] "Individuation is suddenly augmented and begins to sense its limits and its gradual subordination to the race which the Fates prescribe." [42] "In some respects, early adolescence is thus the infancy of man's higher nature, when he receives from the great all-mother his last capital of energy and evolutionary momentum." [43] And in a most significant passage, Hall remarked, "at any rate, for those prophetic souls interested in the future of our race and desirous of advancing it, the field of adolescence is the quarry in which they must seek to find both goals and means. If such a higher stage is ever added to our race, it will not be by increments at any later plateau of adult life, but it will come by increased development of the adolescent stage, which is the bud of promise for the race." [44]

THE ADOLESCENT YEARS

Hall's distrust of democracy and individualism and his aspirations for a utopian super-race merged in his thinking to yield a concept of the adolescent phenomena that other psychologists, from his time onward, have found generally unpalatable. Recapitulation theory persuaded G. Stanley Hall that the outgrowth of plasticity at adolescence was the best hope for mankind's evolutionary progress, and he and his students recognized this period as "the focal point of all psychology." [45] As a result of the controversial nature of his views, and as a consequence of the ensuing confusion, Hall

[38] Hall, *Youth*, p. 5.
[39] G. S. Hall, "Discussion," *Proceedings*, National Education Association (1896), pp. 193–195. The concept of adolescence as a second birth was first given prominence in modern thought by Jean Jacques Rousseau, *Emile* (originally published in 1762; New York: E. P. Dutton and Co., 1911), pp. 172–173.
[40] Hall, *Adolescence*, II, 71.
[41] *Ibid.*, I, xiii.
[42] *Ibid.*, II, 58.
[43] *Ibid.*, II, 71.
[44] *Ibid.*, I, 50.
[45] E. G. Lancaster, "The Psychology and Pedagogy of Adolescence," *The Pedagogical Seminary*, V (1897), 119.

has been misunderstood in this major respect: it has been said that "the work of G. Stanley Hall set the theme for emphasis upon the physiology of adolescence. . . . Hall, and the writers who studied his works, attributed many of the peculiarities of adolescence to the facts of puberty," [46] and "he ignored the effects of cultural setting." [47] Actually Hall's views were unequivocally and diametrically opposite to these contentions. Although Darwinism committed Hall to an emphasis on the genetic determinants of behavior, he believed firmly that at adolescence the process of recapitulating instincts gave way to the primacy of cultural influences. "No age is so responsive to all the best and wisest adult endeavor. In no psychic soil, too, does seed, bad as well as good, strike such deep root, grow so rankly, or bear fruit so quickly or so surely." [48] To show that phylogenetic recapitulation now abated, he said: "Young children grow despite great hardships, but later adolescence is more dependent upon favoring conditions in the environment, disturbances of which more readily cause arrest and prevent maturity." [49] "The whole future of life depends on how well the new powers now given suddenly and in profusion are husbanded and directed." [50] "There is nothing in the environment to which the adolescent nature does not keenly respond." [51] "The processes last to be attained are least assured by heredity and most dependent upon individual effort, in aid of which nature gives only propulsion, often less defined the later it can be acquired." [52]

To show that *Adolescence* was a product of his concern for cultural influences, he said: "Hence there is need of the most careful study of consummate practical wisdom, in providing the most favorable environment and eliminating every possible cause of arrest or reversion. This is indeed the practical problem of this book." [53] Part of the confusion regarding Hall's views may stem from his attitudes toward the child as opposed to his attitudes toward the adolescent. Hall did disregard the effects of cultural factors upon the former, but he certainly did not do so with respect to the latter. It was, in fact, the very plasticity of adolescence that bolstered Hall's hopes for creating an improved society based on continued evolutionary progress.

Perhaps the most controversial of Hall's views of the adolescent years has been his statement that the period was "suggestive of some ancient period of storm and stress when old moorings were broken and a higher level attained." [54] In physical growth, therefore, Hall observed the presence of instinctual remnants. "Early adolescence brings sudden spring freshets

[46] Harold W. Bernard, *Adolescent Development in American Culture* (Yonkers-on-Hudson, N.Y.: World Book Co., 1957), p. 8.
[47] Dorothy Rogers, *The Psychology of Adolescence* (New York: Appleton-Century-Crofts, 1962), p. 26.
[48] Hall, *Adolescence*, I, xviii–xix.
[49] *Ibid.*, I, 47.
[50] *Ibid.*, I, xv.
[51] *Ibid.*, II, 453.
[52] *Ibid.*, II, 94.
[53] *Ibid.*, I, 49.
[54] *Ibid.*, I, xiii.

of growth impulse in all directions, and these initial momenta . . . are at first more or less uncoordinated in all." [55] "Different organs and tissues or determinants compete for the available nutritive material in the blood, and some for a time get ahead of others in this internal struggle for survival." [56]

In the ensuing decades several psychologists and anthropologists, notably Margaret Mead,[57] have attempted to show that instead the adolescent stresses are largely a product of cultural pressures. These investigators have judged Hall correctly in assuming that he conceptualized adolescence as a period of great storm and stress, but in anticipation of contemporary thinking, Hall attributed considerably more influence to cultural factors than he did to instinctual processes. Even in the biological aspects of behavior, Hall noted the permeability of adolescence to the influences of environmental pressures, and he saw that "the great influx of muscular vigor that unfolds during adolescent years . . . seems to be a very plastic quantity." [58] Speaking of the evils of "city life, modern industrialism, and mixture of distinct ethnic stocks," he said "under these provocations, some instincts spring into activity with a suddenness that is almost explosive." [59] "Civilization is so hard on the body that some have called it a disease." [60] "Our vast and complex business organization that has long since outgrown the comprehension of professional economists, absorbs ever more and earlier the best talent and muscle of youth . . . but we are progressively forgetting that . . . youth needs repose." [61]

Within the framework of the social reforms that Hall was seeking, however, storm and stress approached turgid proportions. The adolescent was free of the past and responsive to the present, but above all, he felt the pull of the future. The contemporary student of psychology generally regards adolescence as a period of transition from childhood to adulthood,[62] and the usual criterion marking an individual's successful passage is his achievement of satisfactory physiological and social adjustment in his here and now society, but Hall was much less parochial. Adolescence was a time when "henceforth the race, not the self, must become supreme." [63] Doggedly pursuing a super-race, Hall juxtaposed his concept of what he believed the environment could do for the adolescent with his concept of what it was doing to the adolescent, and the resulting hiatus suggested intensive storm and stress. His notion of adolescent transition extended far beyond the best that

[55] *Ibid.*, I, 309.

[56] *Ibid.*, I, 241.

[57] Margaret Mead, *Coming of Age in Samoa* (originally published in 1928; New York: Mentor Books, 1949), p. 11.

[58] Hall, *Adolescence*, I, 157.

[59] *Ibid.*, I, 322.

[60] *Ibid.*, I, 169.

[61] *Ibid.*, I, xvi–xvii.

[62] See, for example, Raymond G. Kuhlen, *The Psychology of Adolescent Development* (New York: Harper and Bros., 1952), p. 4; Arthur T. Jersild, *The Psychology of Adolescence* (New York: The Macmillan Co., 1957), p. 4.

[63] Hall, *Adolescence*, II, 303.

he saw in his civilization, and he believed that adolescence, "and not maturity as now defined, is the only point of departure for the superanthropoid that man is to become." [64] To his way of thinking, it was "a colossal assumption that what we call civilization is the end of man, or the best thing in the world." [65] Therefore, Hall not only anticipated recent investigators in attributing primary stress during adolescence to interaction of environmental and genetic factors, but in his zeal to rearrange things and produce a superanthropoid, he surpassed them.

Another persistent issue facing those who study the adolescent years is whether physical growth is gradual or whether it is saltatory, that is, sudden and abrupt. Impregnated with the theory that every man recapitulates history until at his adolescence the racial instincts exhaust themselves in a new birth of human malleability, Hall perceived adolescent growth to be saltatory.[66] As with most of Hall's views, opinions became differentiated sharply. By the sheer magnitude of their output and prestige, Hall and his students were able to polarize the early balance of scientific opinion in their "cataclysmic" camp.[67] But there were others, namely Edward L. Thorndike and Leta Hollingworth, who disagreed radically. "It is a favorite dictum of superficial psychology and pedagogy that instincts lie entirely dormant and then spring into full strength within a few weeks. At a certain stage, we are told, such and such a tendency has its 'nascent period' or ripening time. . . . These statements are almost certainly misleading . . . what data we have show nothing to justify the doctrine of sudden ripening." [68] Today the preponderance of scientific evidence continues to increase the substance of Thorndike's position. Doubtless Hall's inadequate statistical techniques contributed partly to his analyses; if his studies and those of his students had been more analytical and precise, the saltatory growth phenomena probably would have seemed less apparent. Even so, Hall's saltatory theory retains some of its descriptive merit. For, as was recently observed, "physical growth . . . does *not* occur in a series of jumps, but continuously . . . except in so far as one might consider the rapid change at adolescence as the achievement of a new, and mature, stage." [69]

Stormy in his role as a social prophet and zealous in his exposition of Darwinism, G. Stanley Hall created an image of the adolescent years that always aroused controversy. Convinced by his interpretation of recapitulation theory that the democratic system was little more than barbaric, he sought to achieve social and educational reforms in the face of democratic individualism. On the adolescent he focused his aspirations for a super-race,

[64] *Ibid.,* II, 94.
[65] *Ibid.,* II, 717.
[66] *Ibid.,* I, xiii.
[67] Frederick E. Bolton, *Adolescent Education* (New York: The Macmillan Co., 1931), pp. 76–79.
[68] Edward L. Thorndike, *The Original Nature of Man* (New York: Teachers College Publications, Columbia University, 1930), pp. 260–261.
[69] J. M. Tanner, *Education and Physical Growth* (London: University of London Press Ltd., 1961), p. 63.

and by the force of his ambitions, he neglected the educability of the child, overestimated the potential of the adolescent as an agent of social reform, and consequently, exaggerated the magnitude of storm and stress. Had G. Stanley Hall studied adolescence to test recapitulation theory rather than to justify it, he might never have lost stature in the field he did so much to establish.

Albert Bandura

The Stormy Decade: Fact or Fiction?

Long before the earliest surveys and experiments in developmental psychology, the belief prevailed that adolescence marked a time fraught with emotional stress, frustration, and anxiety. G. Stanley Hall augmented this view when he likened adolescence to the late eighteenth-century period of Sturm and Drang, *during which time young German romanticists stirred widespread ideological fomentation. The impact of the storm-and-stress hypothesis dampened after Margaret Mead, in* Coming of Age in Samoa, *revealed the tranquility with which Samoan adolescents passed through the "storm." The tide again turned, however, when adherents of Freudian theory argued persuasively that endogenous, genetic factors inevitably foster during adolescence urgency, fear, panic, fragmentation, and rebelliousness. In this paper, Bandura shows that contemporary research fails to sustain the venerable notion. The review suggests that the stresses of adolescence are largely products of difficulties begun in pre-adolescent social experiences. Why then the persistence of the storm-and-stress hypothesis? Bandura identifies seven sources of the "myth," and in pointing out the weaknesses of each, hastens, we may hope, the eventual demise of this highly misleading and distorting belief.*

IF you were to walk up to the average man on the street, grab him by the arm and utter the word "adolescence," it is highly probable—assuming he refrains from punching you in the nose—that his associations to this term will include references to storm-and-stress, tension, rebellion, dependency conflicts, peer-group conformity, black leather jackets, and the like. If you then abandoned your informal street corner experiment, and consulted the professional and popular literature on adolescence, you would become quickly impressed with the prevalence of the belief that adolescence is, indeed, a unique and stormy developmental period.[1]

FROM *Psychology in the Schools,* I (1964), 224–231. Reprinted by permission of the author and the publisher.

[1] J. R. Gallagher and H. I. Harris, *Emotional Problems of Adolescents* (New York: Oxford University Press, 1958); Elizabeth B. Hurlock, *Adolescent Development* (New York: McGraw-Hill Book Co., 1955); Irene M. Josselyn, *Psychosocial Development of Children* (New York: Family Service Assoc. of America, 1948); G. S. Mohr and Marian A. Despres, *The Stormy Decade: Adolescence* (New York: Random House, Inc., 1958); T. Parsons, "Psychoanalysis and Social Structure," *Psychoanal. Quart.,* XIX (1950), 371–384; G. H. S. Pearson, *Adolescence and the Conflict of Generations* (New York: W. W. Norton and Co., 1958).

The adolescent presumably is engaged in a struggle to emancipate himself from his parents. He, therefore, resists any dependence upon them for their guidance, approval or company, and rebels against any restrictions and controls that they impose upon his behavior. To facilitate the process of emancipation, he transfers his dependency to the peer group whose values are typically in conflict with those of his parents. Since his behavior is now largely under the control of peer-group members, he begins to adopt idiosyncratic clothing, mannerisms, lingo, and other forms of peer-group fad behavior. Because of the conflicting values and pressures to which the adolescent is exposed, he is ambivalent, frightened, unpredictable, and often irresponsible in his behavior. Moreover, since the adolescent finds himself in a transition stage in which he is neither child nor adult, he is highly confused even about his own identity.

The foregoing storm-and-stress picture of adolescence receives little support from detailed information that Dr. Walters and I obtained in a study of middle class families of adolescent boys.[2] Let us compare the popular version of adolescence with our research findings.

PARENTAL RESTRICTIVENESS

At adolescence, parents supposedly become more controlling and prohibitive. We found the very opposite to be true. By the time the boys had reached adolescence, they had internalized the parents' values and standards of behavior to a large degree; consequently, restrictions and external controls had been lightened as the boys became increasingly capable of assuming responsibility for their own behavior, and in directing their own activities. The parents were highly trustful of their boys' judgment and felt that externally imposed limits were, therefore, largely unnecessary. The following interview excerpts provide some typical parental replies to inquiries concerning the restrictions they placed on their boys:

M. (Mother). I don't have to do anything like that any more.
I think he's getting so mature now, he's sort of happy medium.
I don't have to do much with him.

I. (Interviewer). What are some of the restrictions you have for him? How about going out at night?

F. (Father). We trust the boy. We never question him.

I. Are there any things you forbid him from doing when he is with his friends?

F. At his age I would hate to keep telling him that he mustn't do this, or mustn't do that. I have very little trouble with him in that regard. Forbidding I don't think creeps into it because he ought to know at 17, right from wrong.

I. Are there any friends with whom you have discouraged him from associating?

[2] A. Bandura and R. H. Walters, *Adolescent Aggression* (New York: Ronald Press, 1959).

F.   No, not up to now. They are very lovely boys.

I.   How about using bad language?

F.   Only once, only once have I; of course I'm a little bit hard of hearing in one ear, and sometimes he gets around the wrong side and takes advantage of that.

The boys' accounts were essentially in agreement with those given by the parents. In response to our questions concerning parental demands and controls, the boys pointed out that at this stage in their development parental restraints were no longer necessary. An illustrative quotation, taken from one of the boys' interviews, is given below:

I.   What sort of things does your mother forbid you to do around the house?

B.   Forbid me to do? Gee, I don't think there's ever anything.
The house is mine as much as theirs. . . Oh, can't whistle, can't throw paper up in the air, and can't play the radio and phonograph too loud. Rules of the house; anybody, I mean, it's not just me. . .

I.   Are you expected to stay away from certain places or people?

B.   She knows I do. I'm not expected; I mean, she figures I'm old enough to take care of myself now. They never tell me who to stay away from or where. Well, I mean, they don't expect me to sleep down on Skid Row or something like that. . .

Since the boys adopted their parents' standards of conduct as their own, they did not regard their parents and other authority figures as adversaries, but more as supportive and guiding influences.

DEPENDENCE-INDEPENDENCE CONFLICTS

The view that adolescents are engaged in a struggle to emancipate themselves from their parents also receives little support from our study.

Although the boys' dependency behavior had been fostered and encouraged during their childhood, independence training had begun early and was, therefore, largely accomplished by the time of adolescence. A similar early and gradual decrease in dependency upon adults is reported by Heathers,[3] who compared the dependency behavior of two-year-old and of five-year-old children. He found that, even over this small age range, dependency on adults had declined, whereas dependency on other children had increased.

For most of the boys that we studied, the emancipation from parents had been more or less completed rather than initiated at adolescence. In fact, the development of independence presented more of a conflict for the parents, than it did for the boys. Some of the parents, particularly the fathers, regretted the inevitable loss of the rewards that their sons' company had brought them.

[3] G. Heathers, "Emotional Dependence and Independence in Nursery School Play," *J. Genet. Psychol.*, LXXXVII (1955), 37–57.

I. Do you feel that you spend as much time with Raymond as other fathers do with their sons, or more?

F. I would say about average, but perhaps I should spend more time with him, because as the years go by, I see that he's growing into manhood and I'm losing a lot of him every year. When he was younger, I think I was with him more than I am now. I think, as he gets older, he's had a tendency to get his pleasures from people his own age, this is fine as long as he makes home his headquarters. That's all I want.

Although the boys devoted an increasing amount of time to peer-group activities, they, nevertheless, retained close ties to their parents and readily sought out their help, advice, and support when needed.

PARENT PEER-GROUP CONFLICTS

The boys' primary reference groups were not selected indiscriminately. Since the adolescents tended to choose friends who shared similar value systems and behavioral norms, membership in the peer-group did not generate familial conflicts. In fact, the peer-group often served to reinforce and to uphold the parental norms and standards of behavior that the boys had adopted. Consequently, the parents were generally pleased with their sons' associates because they served as an important source of control in situations where the parents could not be present.

An essentially similar picture of adolescence, based on an intensive study of middle class families, has been presented by Elkin and Westley.[4] They summarize their findings as follows:

Family ties are close and the degree of basic family consensus is high. The parents are interested in all the activities of their children, and the adolescents, except for the area of sex, frankly discuss their own behavior and problems with them. In many areas of life, there is joint participation between parents and children. . . In independent discussions by parents and adolescents of the latters' marriage and occupational goals, there was a remarkable level of agreement. The adolescents also acknowledged the right of the parents to guide them, for example, accepting, at least manifestly, the prerogatives of the parents to set rules for the number of dates, hours of return from dates, and types of parties. The parents express relatively little concern about the socialization problems or peer group activities of their children.[5]

SOURCES OF THE ADOLESCENT MYTHOLOGY

What are the origins of the mythology about adolescence, and why does it persist?

[4] F. Elkin and W. A. Westley, "The Myth of Adolescent Culture," *Amer. Sociol. Rev.*, XX (1955), 680–684; W. A. Westley and F. Elkin, "The Protective Environment and Adolescent Socialization," *Social Forces*, XXX (1956), 243–249.

[5] Elkin and Westley, "The Myth of Adolescent Culture," *op. cit.*, p. 682.

Overinterpretation of Superficial Signs of Nonconformity

The view that adolescence is a period of rebellion is often supported by references to superficial signs of nonconformity, particularly adolescent fad behavior.

It is certainly true that adolescents frequently display idiosyncratic fashions and interest patterns. Such fads, however, are not confined to adolescent age groups. Several years ago, for example, coon skin caps and Davy Crockett apparel were highly fashionable among pre-adolescent boys. When Davy Crockett began to wane a new fad quickly emerged—every youngster and a sizeable proportion of the adult population were gyrating with hoola-hoops. The hoola-hoop also suffered a quick death by replacement.

If pre-adolescent children display less fad behavior than do adolescents, this difference may be primarily due to the fact that young children do not possess the economic resources with which to purchase distinctive apparel, the latest phonograph records, and discriminative ornaments, rather than a reflection of a sudden heightening of peer-group conformity pressures during adolescence. The pre-adolescent does not purchase his own clothing, he has little voice in how his hair shall be cut and, on a 15-cent a week allowance, he is hardly in a position to create new fads, or to deviate too widely from parental tastes and standards.

How about adult fad behavior? A continental gentleman conducts a fashion show in Paris and almost instantly millions of hemlines move upward or downward; the human figure is sacked, trapezed, chemised, or appareled in some other fantastic creation.

Fashion-feeders determine the styles, the colors, and the amount of clothing that shall be worn. It would be rare, indeed, to find an adult who would ask a sales clerk for articles of clothing in vogue two or three years ago. As long as social groups contain a status hierarchy, and tolerance for upward mobility within the social hierarchy, one can expect imitation of fads and fashions from below which, in turn, forces inventiveness from the elite in order to preserve the status differentiations.

Mass Media Sensationalism

The storm-and-stress view of adolescence is also continuously reinforced by mass media sensationalism. Since the deviant adolescent excites far more interest than the typical high-school student, the adolescent is usually portrayed in literature, television, and in the movies as passing through a neurotic or a semi-delinquent phase of development.[6] These productions, many of which are designed primarily to generate visceral reactions or to sell copy, are generally viewed as profound and sensitive portrayals of the *typical* adolescent turmoil. Holden Caulfield, the central character in *The Catcher in the Rye*,[7] has thus become the prototypic adolescent.

[6] N. Kiell, *The Adolescent through Fiction* (New York: International University Press, 1959).
[7] J. D. Salinger, *The Catcher in the Rye* (Boston: Little, Brown and Co., 1945).

Generalization from Samples of Deviant Adolescents

Professional people in the mental health field are apt to have most contact with delinquent adolescents, and are thus prone to base their accounts of adolescence on observations of atypical samples. By and large, the description of the modal pattern of adolescent behavior fits most closely the behavior of the deviant 10 per cent of the adolescent population that appears repeatedly in psychiatric clinics, juvenile probation departments, and in the newspaper headlines.

Our study of the family relationships of adolescents also included a sample of antisocially aggressive boys. In the families of these hyper-aggressive adolescents there was indeed a great deal of storm-and-stress for many years. The boys' belligerence and rebellion, however, were not a unique product of adolescence. The defiant oppositional pattern of behavior was present all along, but because of their greater size and power the parents were able to suppress and to control, through coercive methods, their sons' belligerence during the early childhood years. By the time of adolescence, however, some of the boys had reached the stage where they were almost completely independent of the parents for the satisfaction of their social and physical needs. Moreover, they had developed physically to the point where they were larger and more powerful than their parents. With the achievement of the power reversal and the decrease of the parents' importance as sources of desired rewards, a number of the boys exhibited a blatant indifference to their parents' wishes about which they could now do little or nothing.

I. What sort of things does your mother object to your doing when you are out with your friends?

B. She don't know what I do.

I. What about staying out late at night?

B. She says, "Be home at 11 o'clock." I'll come home at one.

I. How about using the family car?

B. No. I wrecked mine, and my father wrecked his a month before I wrecked mine, and I can't even get near his. And I got a license and everything. I'm going to hot wire it some night and cut out.

I. How honest do you feel you can be to your mother about where you've been and what things you have done?

B. I tell her where I've been, period.

I. How about what you've done?

B. No. I won't tell her what I've done. If we're going out in the hills for a beer bust, I'm not going to tell her. I'll tell her I've been to a show or something.

I. How about your father?

B. I'll tell him where I've been, period.

The heightened aggression exhibited by these boys during adolescence primarily reflected response predispositions that became more evident following the power reversal in the parent-child relationship, rather than an adolescence-induced stress.

Inappropriate Generalization from Cross-cultural Data

It is interesting to note that many writers cite cross-cultural data as supporting evidence for the discontinuity view of child development in the American society. The reader suddenly finds himself in the Trobriand Islands, or among the Arapesh, rather than in the suburbs of Minneapolis or in the town square of Oskaloosa.

In many cultures the transition from child to adult status is very abrupt. Childhood behavior patterns are strongly reinforced, but as soon as the child reaches pubescence he is subjected to an elaborate initiation ceremony which signifies his abrupt transformation into adult status. Following the ceremonial initiation the young initiate acquires new rights and privileges, new responsibilities and, in some cultures, he is even assigned a new name and a new set of parents who undertake his subsequent social training in the skills and habits required to perform the adult role.

In our culture, on the other hand, except for the discontinuities in the socialization of sexual behavior, there is considerable continuity in social training. As was mentioned earlier, independence and responsibility training, for example, are begun in early childhood and adult-role patterns are achieved through a gradual process of successive approximations. This is equally true in the development of many other forms of social behavior.

It should be mentioned in passing, however, that cross-cultural studies have been valuable in demonstrating that stresses and conflicts are not inevitable concomitants of pubescence, but rather products of cultural conditioning. Indeed, in some societies, adolescence is one of the pleasant periods of social development.[8]

Overemphasis of the Biological Determination of Heterosexual Behavior

With the advent of pubescence the adolescent is presumably encumbered by a powerful biologically determined sexual drive that produces a relatively sudden and marked increase in heterosexual behavior. The net result of the clash between strong physiological urges demanding release and even more substantial social prohibitions, is a high degree of conflict, frustration, anxiety and diffuse tension. In contrast to this widely-accepted biological drive theory, evidence from studies of cross-species and cross-cultural sexual behavior reveals that human sexuality is governed primarily by social conditioning, rather than endocrinal stimulation.[9]

The cross-species data demonstrate that hormonal control of sexual behavior decreases with advancing evolutionary status. In lower mammalian species, for example, sexual activities are completely regulated by gonadal hormones; among primates sexual behavior is partially independent of physiological stimulations; while human eroticism is exceedingly variable

---

[8] M. Mead, "Adolescence in Primitive and in Modern Society," *The New Generation*, eds. V. F. Calverton and S. D. Schmalhausen (New York: Macauley, 1930).

[9] C. S. Ford and F. A. Beach, *Patterns of Sexual Behavior* (New York: Harper and Bros., 1951).

and essentially independent of hormonal regulation. Humans can be sexually aroused before puberty and long after natural or surgical loss of reproductive glands. Thus, one would induce sexual behavior in a rodent Don Juan by administering androgen, whereas presenting him lascivious pictures of a well-endowed mouse would have no stimulating effects whatsoever. By contrast, one would rely on sexually-valenced social stimuli, rather than on hormonal injections for producing erotic arousal in human males.

The prominent role of social learning factors in determining the timing, incidence and form of sexual activities of humans is also clearly revealed in the wide cross-cultural variability in patterns of sexual behavior. Sex-arousing properties have been conditioned to an extremely broad range of stimuli, but the cues that are sexually stimulating in one culture would, in many instances, prove sexually repulsive to members of another society. A similar diversity exists in the timing of the emergence of sexual interest and in the choice of sexual objects. In cultures that permit and encourage heterosexual behavior at earlier, or at later, periods of a child's development than is true for American youth, no marked changes in sexual behavior occur during adolescence.

It is evident from the foregoing discussion that "sexual tensions" are not an inevitable concomitant of pubescence. Furthermore, any significant increase in heterosexual activities during adolescence is due more to cultural conditioning and expectations than to endocrinal changes.

Stage Theories of Personality Development

Until recently, most of the theoretical conceptualizations of the developmental process have subscribed to some form of stage theory. According to the Freudian viewpoint,[10] for example, behavioral changes are programmed in an oral-anal-phallic sequence; Erickson[11] characterizes personality development in terms of an eight-stage sequence; Gesell[12] describes marked predictable cyclical changes in behavior over yearly or even shorter temporal intervals; and Piaget[13] delineates numerous different stages for different classes of responses.

Although there appears to be relatively little consensus among these theories concerning the number and the content of stages considered to be crucial, they all share in common the assumption that social behavior can be categorized in terms of a relatively prefixed sequence of stages with varying degrees of continuity or discontinuity between successive developmental periods. Typically, the spontaneous emergence of these elaborate age-specific modes of behavior is attributed to ontogenetic factors. The seven-year-old, for example, is supposed to be withdrawn; the eight-year-old turns into an exuberant, expansive and buoyant child; the fifteen-year-old becomes remote

[10] S. Freud, *An Outline of Psychoanalysis* (New York: W. W. Norton and Co., 1949).

[11] E. H. Erickson, *Childhood and Society* (New York: W. W. Norton and Co., 1950).

[12] A. Gesell and F. Ilg, *Infant and Child in the Culture of Today* (New York: Harper and Bros., 1943).

[13] J. Piaget, *The Moral Judgement of the Child* (Glencoe, Ill.: The Free Press, 1948); J. Piaget, *The Construction of Reality in the Child* (New York: Basic Books, 1954).

and argumentative; parents are finally rewarded at sweet sixteen.[14] In truth, all seven-year-olds are not withdrawn, all eight-year-olds are not exuberant, expansive and buoyant, nor are all fifteen-year-olds aloof and argumentative. I am also acquainted with sixteen-year-olds who are anything but sweet. The withdrawn five-year-old is likely to remain a relatively withdrawn eight-, nine-, and sixteen-year-old unless he undergoes social-learning experiences that are effective in fostering more expressive behavior.

Although the traditional stage theories of child development are of questionable validity,[15] they have nevertheless been influential in promoting the view that adolescence represents a form of stage behavior that suddenly appears at pubescence, and as suddenly disappears when adulthood is achieved.

Self-fulfilling Prophecy

If a society labels its adolescents as "teen-agers," and expects them to be rebellious, unpredictable, sloppy, and wild in their behavior, and if this picture is repeatedly reinforced by the mass media, such cultural expectations may very well force adolescents into the role of rebel. In this way, a false expectation may serve to instigate and maintain certain role behaviors, in turn, then reinforce the originally false belief.

In discussing our research findings with parents' groups I have often been struck by the fact that most parents who are experiencing positive and rewarding relationships with their pre-adolescent children are, nevertheless, waiting apprehensively and bracing themselves for the stormy adolescent period. Such vigilance can very easily create a small turbulence at least. When the prophesied storm fails to materialize, many parents begin to entertain doubts about the normality of their youngster's social development.

In closing, I do not wish to leave you with the impression that adolescence is a stress- or problem-free period of development. No age group is free from stress or adjustment problems. Our findings suggest, however, that the behavioral characteristics exhibited by children during the so-called adolescent stage are lawfully related to, and consistent with, pre-adolescent social behavior.

---

[14] F. L. Ilg and L. B. Ames, *Child Behavior* (New York: Harper and Bros., 1955).

[15] A. Bandura and F. J. McDonald, "The Influence of Social Reinforcement and the Behavior of Models in Shaping Children's Moral Judgements," *J. Abnorm. Soc. Psychol.*, LXVII (1963), 274–281; A. Bandura and W. Mischel, "The Influence of Models in Modifying Delay-of-Gratification Patterns," (unpublished manuscript, Stanford Univer., 1963); A. Bandura and R. H. Walters, *Social Learning and Personality Development* (New York: Holt, Rinehart and Winston, Inc., 1963).

Robert J. Havighurst

The Educationally Difficult Student:
What the Schools Can Do

*Advances in technology and changes in social systems are displacing tra-
ditions and demanding of the adolescent increasingly stringent attitudes
and standards for effective living. He must master a bewildering variety
of familial, social, and vocational roles before he is accepted on an equal
footing by adults. Not every adolescent is equal to the task. In the following paper, Havighurst describes three classes of persons—"socially disadvantaged," "mentally handicapped," and "privatist non-conformer"—for
whom school life may be particularly rigorous. After identifying the
general characteristics of each of the three and explaining the tribulations
each faces, he offers an informative, provocative, and sobering appraisal
of how educational programs might be implemented for these youth.*

W HEN we are confronted by a baffling phenomenon, our first impulse
is to name it. During the past five years, educators have been baffled
by a substantial number of pupils who do not learn in spite of instruction
by reasonably well-trained teachers in well-equipped schools.

We suppose that these pupils come to school under some kind of handicap that makes it difficult to teach them. We have given them a variety of
names—"culturally deprived," "intellectually deprived," or "socially disadvantaged." These names imply our belief that these children are not innately
dull, but that they have been denied some experiences that other "normal"
children have had. If the schools can discover what these mind-building
experiences are, perhaps the schools can compensate for the handicaps
which the pupils have suffered. Hence we speak of "compensatory" education.

The title of this paper—the difficult student—gives a different name to
the phenomenon and suggests a deeper perspective which can include other
types of pupils as well as those with social handicaps.

There are three visible and bothersome groups of "difficult" students
which are especially important today. They are:

FROM *The Bulletin of the National Association of Secondary-School Principals*, XLIX
(1965), 110–127. Reprinted by permission of the author and the National Association
of Secondary School Principals, Washington, D. C.

1. The Socially Disadvantaged.
2. The Mentally Handicapped.
3. The Privatist Non-Conformer.

THE SOCIALLY DISADVANTAGED

The socially disadvantaged pupils may be defined and described in three ways: in terms of certain family characteristics relating directly to the child; in terms of their personal characteristics; or in terms of the social group characteristics of their families.

Family Characteristics

Compared with other children whose families give them average or better advantages for getting started in modern urban life, the socially disadvantaged child lacks several of the following:

1. A family conversation which: answers his questions and encourages him to ask questions; extends his vocabulary with new words and with adjectives and adverbs; gives him a right and a need to stand up for and to explain his point of view on the world.
2. A family environment which: sets an example of reading; provides a variety of toys and play materials with colors, sizes, and objects that challenge his ingenuity with his hands and his mind.
3. Two parents who: read a good deal; read to him; show him that they believe in the value of education; reward him for good school achievement.

Bernstein [1] has studied the language behavior of families that relate to the intellectual development of their children. He distinguishes between two *forms* or *types* of language. (These language types are statistically related to social class, as will be pointed out later.) One form of language is called *restricted* and the other form is called *elaborated*. A family which employs restricted language gives a child a language environment characterized by:

1. Short, grammatically simple, often unfinished sentences with a poor syntatical form stressing the active voice.
2. Simple and repetitive use of conjunctions (so, then, because).
3. Little use of subordinate clauses to break down the initial categories of the dominant subject.
4. Inability to hold a formal subject through a speech sequence; thus a dislocated informational content is facilitated.
5. Rigid and limited use of adjectives and adverbs.

[1] B. Bernstein, "Language and Social Class," *British J. Sociol.*, XI (1960), 271–276; B. Bernstein, "Social Class and Linguistic Development. A Theory of Social Learning," *Economy, Education and Society*, eds. A. H. Halsey, J. Floud, and C. A. Anderson (New York: The Free Press, 1961), pp. 288ff.; B. Bernstein, "Social Class, Linguistic Codes and Grammatical Elements," *Language and Speech*, V (October–December, 1962), 221–240; B. Bernstein, "Elaborated and Restricted Codes: Their Origins and Some Consequences" (Committee on Human Development: The University of Chicago, 1964).

6. Constraint on the self-reference pronoun; frequent use of personal pronoun.
7. Frequent use of statements where the reason and conclusion are confounded to produce a categoric statement.
8. A large number of statements/phrases which signal a requirement for the previous speech sequence to be reinforced: "Wouldn't it? You see? You know?" etc. This process is termed 'sympathetic circularity.'
9. Individual selection from a group of idiomatic phrases or sequences will frequently occur.
10. The individual qualification is implicit in the sentence organization; it is a language of implict meaning.

On the other hand, a family which employs an *elaborated* language gives the child a language environment characterized by:

1. Accurate grammatical order and syntax regulate what is said.
2. Logical modifications and stress are mediated through a grammatically complex sentence construction, especially through the use of a range of conjunctions and subordinate clauses.
3. Frequent use of prepositions which indicate logical relationships as well as prepositions which indicate temporal and spatial contiguity.
4. Frequent use of the personal pronoun 'I'.
5. A discriminative selection from a range of adjectives and adverbs.
6. Individual qualification is verbally mediated through the structure and relationships within and between sentences.
7. Expressive symbolism discriminates between meanings within speech sequences rather than reinforcing dominant words or phrases, or accompanying the sequence in a diffuse, generalised manner.
8. A language use which points to the possibilities inherent in a complex conceptual hierarchy for the organising of experience.

A child who has learned a restricted language at home is likely to have difficulty in school, where an *elaborate* language is used and taught by the teacher; and the difficulty of the child is likely to increase as he goes further in school, unless he learns the elaborate language that is expected in the school. On the other hand, the child who had had experience with an elaborate language from his earliest years has a relatively easy time in school, because he must simply go on developing the kind of language and related thinking which he has already started.

Personal Characteristics

The family environment with the characteristics just cited tends to produce children with certain personal deficits. Martin Deutsch [2] has studied such children with techniques of the experimental psychologists, and he finds them to have inferior auditory discrimination, inferior visual discrimi-

[2] M. P. Deutsch, "The Disadvantaged Child and the Learning Process," *Education in Depressed Areas*, ed. A. H. Passow (New York: Bureau of Publications, Teachers College, Columbia University, 1963).

nation, inferior judgment concerning time, number and other basic concepts. He finds that this inferiority is not due to physical defects of eyes and ears and brain, but is due to inferior *habits* of hearing and seeing and thinking. Presumably, the family environment of these children did not teach them to "pay attention" to what was being said around them, or to the visual scene. Then, when they came to school, their school performance suffered because they had not learned to "listen" to the teacher and other important people or to "see" the things they are shown in the school.

Social Group Characteristics

We introduce the social group characteristics of socially disadvantaged children last so as to avoid giving the impression that there is a hard-and-fast relation between socio-economic status, or some other group characteristic, and social disadvantages for the child. While there are statistical relations and very important ones between socio-economic status and social disadvantages of children, there are so many individual exceptions to the statistical generations that any educational policy aimed at identifying socially disadvantaged children should avoid reliance upon general socio-economic characteristics as the decisive criteria.

Above all, it is important to avoid the error of saying that all children of working-class families are socially disadvantaged. Approximately 65 per cent of the children of this country are living in working-class homes. That is, their fathers or mothers do manual work for a living. The great majority of these families give their children a fairly good start for life in an urban industrial democratic society. Their children are adequately fed and clothed. They are loved and protected by their parents. They learn to respect teachers and to like school. They do fairly well or better than that in school.

While working-class children as a group are somewhat different from the children of white-collar workers, it would not be reasonable to say that the working-class children are socially disadvantaged or culturally deprived. Working-class children as a group score slightly below children of white-collar families in intelligence tests; they fall slightly below on tests of school achievement; they attain somewhat less formal education. But the differences are relatively small, and become even smaller when the socially disadvantaged children are removed and the majority of working-class youth who remain are compared with white-collar children.

Most working-class families participate fully in the American mass or core culture. This is certainly not a culture of deprivation. While the differences between the upper working class and the lower middle class are real and they are interesting, these differences should not be described in terms of social advantage or social disadvantage. The great amount of movement of people across the boundary between these two classes as they grow up is evidence that the differences between these two classes are not fundamental ones.

Who, then, are the socially disadvantaged when we attempt to describe them in terms of observable social groups? They are groups with the following characteristics:

1. They are at the bottom of the American society in terms of income.
2. They have a rural background.
3. They suffer from social and economic discrimination at the hands of the majority of the society.
4. They are widely distributed in the United States. While they are most visible in the big cities, they are present in all except the very high income communities. There are many of them in rural areas, especially in the southern and southwestern states.

In racial and ethnic terms, these groups are about evenly divided between whites and non-whites. They consist mainly of the following:

1. Negroes from the rural south many of whom have migrated recently to the northern industrial cities.
2. Whites from the rural south and the southern mountains many of whom have migrated recently to the northern industrial cities.
3. Puerto Ricans who have migrated to a few northern industrial cities.
4. Mexicans with a rural background who have migrated into the west and middle west. Also rural Spanish-Americans in the southwestern states.
5. European immigrants with a rural background, from east and southern Europe.

Altogether, these groups make up about 15 per cent of the United States population. Since they tend to have large families, their children make up as much as 20 per cent of the child population. Not all socially disadvantaged children come from these groups, but the great majority do. Not all children in these groups are socially disadvantaged, but the great majority are.

How Many Are Socially Disadvantaged?

There is an infinite gradation of social advantage-disadvantage, and therefore any quantitative estimate of the number of socially disadvantaged children and youth must be a personal rather than a scientific statement.

The writer would place the number of socially disadvantaged children at about 15 per cent of the child population. One basis for this estimate is the proportion of unemployed, out of school youth between the ages of 16 and 20. These young people have been relatively unsuccessful in school and in the labor market. The great majority of them come from the social groups listed above. There are about 11 per cent of boys and 17 per cent of girls in this group. The boys are clearly maladjusted to society. Some of the girls are not; they are simply doing what girls have done for a long time, helping out at home while waiting to get married. But these figures place a minimum on the numbers of socially disadvantaged youth. There are a few others who have jobs which are below their capacity or are disadvantaged in other ways—enough to bring the total up to about 15 per cent.

Since these children and their families tend to concentrate in the large cities, while upper-income people tend to move out from the cities to the suburbs, the socially disadvantaged children are in big cities in larger proportions than 15 per cent. Probably *30 per cent of the children* in such cities as New York, Chicago, Philadelphia, Washington, Detroit, Cleveland, and Baltimore fall into the socially disadvantaged category.

The Mentally Handicapped

The truly mentally handicapped child is one with inborn mental deficiency, indicated by an IQ below 75 or 80, depending on the definition adopted by the state or the school system. Some of these children have clearly marked physical signs of mental deficiency, but others do not. The number of mentally handicapped children is estimated by various authorities to be about 2 per cent of the age group.

However, it is not an easy matter to distinguish a truly mentally handicapped from a socially disadvantaged child. Mental retardation is no longer regarded as a condition easily diagnosed. It appears that a considerable fraction, perhaps as many as half, of the school age children now treated as mentally retarded could have developed normal intelligence if they had had expert treatment in their pre-school years.

Thus we may expect to see school programs designed for young children who appear to be mentally retarded with the aim of bringing some of them into the range of normal intelligence.

The Privatist Non-Conformer

An entirely different kind of "educationally difficult student" is found mainly in the economically favored communities and schools. This is a youth of average or superior intelligence, who has done well in school until he reaches high school age, and then seems to lose his drive and direction. Some observers would identify this kind of youth as a "beatnik," but this is not a thoroughly satisfactory name for the youth of high school age whom we shall call the *privatist non-conformer.*

This kind of boy or girl has such doubts about the quality of his society that he refuses to commit himself to supporting the political and business and educational institutions around him, but prefers to lead a life of private or asocial activity.

At the coming of adolescence, a person must commence to achieve his own self-esteem and his social fidelity. This is a part of his achievement of his *identity* as a person in his own right. It comes about normally as a part of his adolescent experience in school, work, play with his age-mates, and association with adult citizens and workers. The youth as he achieves identity narrows and focuses his personal, occupational, sexual, and ideological commitments by getting started in one occupation, getting married and starting a family, and beginning to take part in community civic life.

Apparently this process of growth toward identity is more difficult today than it was a generation or more ago. The evidence for this statement comes from the testimony of high-school counselors and teachers, from parents of intelligent and sensitive children, and from psychologists and sociologists who have studied youth culture. A discussion of this form of deviancy is given by Erikson, Keniston, Parsons, and others in a special issue of the journal, *Daedalus.*[3]

Privatism has always been present, but has not been so noticeable formerly as in the most recent years. The tendency in former years has been to attribute youth problems to poverty. Therefore it is a shock to discover a problem group who are not poverty-stricken. Parsons and Keniston, especially, concern themselves with middle-class youth.

Talcott Parsons sees young people generally learning the dominant American value pattern of *instrumental activism,* in which responsibility, autonomy, and individualism are motives, and achievement is best demonstrated through work. The American youth is oriented toward control or mastery of the human condition by working at the task. But as work opportunities for youth have decreased, the demands on youth have become more complex. A young person must learn more than ever before in order to become an effective citizen, worker, and husband or wife in a society where many marriages break up. There is a rising general level of expectation of performance by youth in comparison to previous decades or generations. Also, youths have the opportunity and the responsibility of making more choices—such as the increasing range of vocational choices for boys and especially for girls.

Inevitably there is some strain for many young people in this complex situation, and some lose their nerve. Youth has some right to complain that he has been brought into "a world I never made." But Parsons takes an optimistic view.

Kenneth Keniston is less optimistic about the situation of youth. He sees the "youth culture" as a culture which is *non-adult,* if not *anti-adult.* He says it has roles, values, and ways of behaving all its own; it emphasizes disengagement from adult values, sexual attractiveness, daring, immediate pleasure, and comradeship in a way that is true neither of childhood nor of adulthood. Eventually a young person must leave this youth culture and enter adult life, but Keniston believes that in this process few young people are becoming deeply involved as citizens and workers. Instead, they tend to be alienated, refusing to accept the adult world with positive feeling, and retreating to a world of private and personal satisfactions. He calls this attitude *privatism.* Such a person declines to become involved with political and social problems, and prefers to spend his time with music and art. He feels powerless to affect the great society, and turns to the things closer

[3] K. Keniston, "Youth: Change and Challenge," *Daedalus,* XCI (Winter, 1962), 158–166.

home that he feels able to control. He may value family closeness above meaningful work because he can control things within his family, but not in his occupation. Leisure activities may be more important to him than work because he can control what he does in his free time. "Many young people expect to find in leisure a measure of stability, enjoyment, and control which they would otherwise lack. Hence their emphasis on assuring leisure time, or spending their leisure to good advantage, or getting jobs with long vacations, and on living in areas where leisure can be well enjoyed. Indeed, some anticipate working at their leisure with a dedication that will be totally lacking in their work itself." But Keniston does not believe this will be satisfactory. He thinks this will cause a fatal split in a person's life. "The man who spends his working day at a job whose primary meaning is merely to earn enough money to enable him to enjoy the rest of his time can seldom really enjoy his leisure, his family, or his avocations. Life is of a piece, and if work is empty or routine, the rest will inevitably become contaminated as well, becoming a compulsive escape or a driven effort to compensate for the absent satisfactions that should inhere in work. Similarly, to try to avoid social and political problems by cultivating one's garden can at best be only partly successful. . . . Putting work, society, and politics into one pigeonhole, and family, leisure and enjoyment into another creates a compartmentalization which is in continual danger of collapsing."

The mood of our society includes frankness in formerly taboo areas, self-criticism, and skepticism. Youth are exposed to this mood very directly through the mass media (television, cinema, paper-back literature, etc.). They read such books as Salinger's *Catcher in the Rye* and Golding's *Lord of the Flies,* and they are encouraged to read such literature by high school teachers of literature who represent the mood of society. These books are true portrayals of a part of human nature—an unpleasant part, and not the whole truth, by any means. Perhaps these are more accurate than the literature adolescents read a generation or more ago—*Rebecca of Sunnybrook Farm, Strive and Succeed* (Horatio Alger). Furthermore, the sober and realistic writing about the dangers of nuclear war and the difficulties of international control of armaments give young people an ample picture of the immorality of national policies.

Boys and girls are shown the seamy side of personal and political life and then asked to commit themselves to social loyalty.

At the same time boys and girls are confronted with the tasks of making good in school, of choosing an occupation, of establishing themselves with the opposite sex, and these tasks are set for them a year or two earlier than they were a generation or two ago, due to the social forces making for social precocity in the middle-class part of society.

Under the circumstances it is not surprising that contemporary middle-class youth show a considerable degree of self-doubt and lack of confidence in the political and economic structure of modern society. It is not surprising that a *privatistic* life is perferred to one of greater social commitment. Boys find it difficult to make up their minds what occupation they will prepare for. Some of them engage in a kind of sit-down strike against the academic demands made on them by school or college. Their fathers wonder why sons are so in-grown and uncertain, as compared with the greater assurance and task-orientation they remember as normal for their generation. There is not so much concern about girls, since they are not expected to show the degree of *instrumental activitism* expected of boys. With them there is more concern about their sex-role, and about the place of sexual activity in the life of a teen-age girl.

The number of privatistic non-conformers is hard to estimate because we know no measure of this quality and because a great many youths show this quality only to a limited extent. But the number who show it in such an acute form that they are recognized by their teachers and age-mates to be in a special category is probably no more than 2 or 3 per cent of an age-group.

EDUCATIONAL PROGRAMS FOR DIFFICULT STUDENTS

The first two groups of students have been observed and studied with enough research to serve as a basis for educational programs. The third group is only just beginning to receive special educational attention.

For the socially disadvantaged and for the mentally handicapped there is emerging a program of "compensatory" education with something for every age level from pre-school to the end of the teens.

Preschool Classes

There are strong indications, based both on scientific data and experimental programs, that the earlier the child can be reached, the more effective the program will be. J. McVicker Hunt of the University of Illinois and Martin Deutsch [4] of the New York Medical College are among the scholars who have marshalled impressive evidence for the thesis that the nature and extent of experiences in the years from 1 to 5 have much to do with school achievement. Bloom has published a study [5] supporting the proposition that variations in the environment can produce changes in human characteristics and that such variations have the greatest effect at the period when the particular characteristic is changing most rapidly. This bears out Hunt's thesis (which was also that of Mme. Montessori) that different age levels are crucial for different kinds of learnings, and that children go through various phases of learning, with each phase lending support to those which follow.

Bloom has also assembled the results of research indicating the extent

[4] M. P. Deutsch, J. McV. Hunt *et al.*, "Selected Papers from the Arden House Conference on Pre-School Enrichment of Socially Disadvantaged Children," *Merrill-Palmer Quarterly* (July, 1964).

[5] B. Bloom, *Stability and Change in Human Characteristics* (New York: John Wiley and Sons, 1964), p. 89.

of educational growth experienced by children at various age levels. Results indicate that at least one-third of the learnings which will determine later levels of school achievement have already taken place by age 6, and at least 75 per cent by age 13. These findings point to the most important periods for school programs directed to raising achievement levels of children. Based on the estimate that 33 per cent of educational growth takes place before age 6, Bloom suggests that "nursery schools and kindergartens could have far-reaching consequences on the child's general learning pattern." The approximately 17 per cent of growth which takes place between ages 6 and 9 suggests that elementary grades one to three are also crucial. Tending to support this suggestion in another way are the rather disappointing results reported of the Higher Horizons program in New York, which has not attempted to reach any children below the third grade. On the other hand, experimental programs at the prekindergarten level in Baltimore, New York, and elsewhere have already shown gratifying results in better performance on IQ tests and other measures of readiness and achievement.

A final quotation from Bloom sums up the situation:

> A conservative estimate of the effect of extreme environments on intelligence is about 20 IQ points. This could mean the difference between a life in an institution for the feeble-minded or a productive life in society. It could mean the difference between a professional career and an occupation which is at the semi-skilled or unskilled level. . . . The implications for public education and social policy are fairly clear. Where significantly lower intelligence can be clearly attributed to the effects of environmental deprivations, steps must be taken to ameliorate these conditions as early in the individual's development as education and other social forces can be utilized.[6]

Primary Grades

The effect of successful compensatory education at the preschool level is to get children ready for reading in the first grade. In 1963, 45 per cent of Chicago first-graders scored "below average" in the Metropolitan Reading Readiness Test. This meant that they would have difficulty in first-grade work and would not learn to read unless they were given a good deal of individualized help. In two of the city's twenty-one districts, two thirds of the first graders were in the "difficult" category. For these children, an expert on the teaching of reading comments,

> Tried and true traditional approaches are not working. In Chicago, in those districts with the largest percentage of culturally disadvantaged families, standardized reading tests indicate one and a half to two years' retardation. A highly visual and tactile approach to words growing from students' experiences should be explored in the early grades. These students should not meet typical basal readers and other books until they have more familiarity with the con-

[6] *Ibid.* .

cepts attached to the printed symbols. This early approach might capitalize on audio-visual approaches, manipulative materials, and very brief booklets.[7]

In the primary grades the "non-graded" form of organization is now being widely used. If this method is used skillfully, it may be good for disadvantaged children. Skillful use with disadvantaged children means, among other things, that they should have materials adapted to them, that teachers should be trained to work with them in small groups, and that their reading and arithmetic work groups should be organized separately.

Intermediate Grades

In the intermediate grades the difficult pupils are just beginning to emerge as behavior problems. A few become aggressive and hostile to school and to authority. Others become apathetic. This is the period in which least is now being done for such pupils. Sometimes they are given remedial instruction; sometimes they are put in low ability classes. Nobody seems to know how to help them, and they are not yet big enough to be a threat to order in the school and community, thereby forcing the schools to pay special attention to them.

Junior High School Level

By the seventh or eighth grade these boys and girls are a clear threat to the smooth running of the school. In slum schools they may constitute 50 per cent of the enrollment. The hostile aggressive ones make it difficult for the teacher to really teach because he is so busy merely controlling behavior. The apathetic ones become a dead weight on the class. These pupils have given up on school, and come to class merely because they have to or because their friends are there.

There is a good deal of experimentation with educational programs for this group. One kind of program is a remedial academic one. They are given extra drill in reading and/or arithmetic, with a variety of remedial methods. Sometimes they are set aside in special classes or special "upper grade centers." Some improvement has been claimed for such programs. Even as much as a two- or three-year gain of reading level has been claimed for a six-month remedial program. However, the writer does not know of any carefully designed research with a control group which substantiates these claims.

It is reasonable to suppose that, with sympathetic and realistic counseling and direction, some of these boys and girls would make a serious effort to overcome their academic deficiencies at this age. The basic question is whether their earlier disadvantages and deficiencies are so deep and damaging that they can no longer learn the mental skills they would have

[7] R. J. Havighurst, *The Public Schools of Chicago* (Chicago: Board of Education, 1964), p. 119.

learned at a much earlier age if they had been taught more effectively in earlier years.

The only alternative program which has been extensively tried is a work-experience program. This has generally been used with boys, though girls have been included in some projects. Work-study programs fall into three general groups: (a) those which are part of a regular vocational high school program, and for which alienated or marginal youth cannot qualify; (b) those which are for youth aged 16 or 17, who are about to drop out or have dropped out of school; (c) those which are for junior high school youth, aged 13 or 14 and up.

Experience to date with work experience programs for difficult youth has given equivocal results. Some youth profit from this kind of program, while others drop out or are expelled after they have proven to themselves and their teachers that they are not meeting the requirements or getting satisfaction from the program.

The best estimate the writer can make now is that about half of the boys who are identified as socially disadvantaged are likely to learn the habits and attitudes and skills of a work-study program well enough to get and hold steady work at the age of 18.

Since there are as many girls as boys, if not more, in the marginal group, it is important to note that very little has been done of an experimental nature for girls. They do not show as much delinquency, and consequently tend to be ignored by society, though their performance as mothers of the next generation is perhaps more dangerous, potentially, to society than the actual delinquency of their sociological brothers.

Programs for Youth After 16

Nearly all of the socially disadvantaged youth drop out of school at age 16 or 17. Most of the girls get married within a year or two. Most of the boys have a period of three to five years in which they are idle most of the time, employed fitfully but unable to keep a steady job, and a few of them have a brief and unsatisfactory experience in the armed services. The numbers of this group will increase during the next five years, due to increased birthrates after World War II combined with the disappearance of juvenile jobs from the labor force.

Schools have begun to serve these young people in recent years, under programs supported by the federal government through the Manpower Development Training Act, and under the Economic Opportunities Act of 1964. There are also some possibilities for experimental vocational programs under the Vocational Education Act of 1963.

We may look ahead to a substantial program under public school auspices of work experience for youths aged 16–21. This will tax the ingenuity of secondary school personnel, both in the vocational education and the general education fields. An important part of the program will be work-related schooling. Some of the young people in the program will want to get credits toward a high-school diploma, and the high schools will be under pressure to offer some basic English and mathematics courses for these boys and girls.

Another element in such a program will be the placement of youth in jobs and the counseling necessary for helping youth who are marginal to the labor force to adapt themselves to the requirements of a steady job.

The secondary schools are just at the beginning of a tough and challenging experience of providing personally and socially useful educational experience to young people over 16 who have consistently failed in their earlier school work. It will require imagination, ingenuity, and perseverance on the part of secondary school administrators and staff to measure up to this new kind of responsibility.

Differentiation Between Socially Disadvantaged and Mentally Retarded

It has been noted that the true "mentally retarded" cannot be readily distinguished from those who are learning poorly because of social disadvantages, especially in the early years. This seems to argue for similar forms of compensatory education in preschool classes, except for the children for whom a diagnosis of true mental retardation has been made. These exceptional children will generally show certain physical characteristics and they will come from homes where the emotional and intellectual environment is average or better.

By the age of 8 or 9, however, the child who is clearly retarded in the judgment of a clinical psychologist will generally be placed in a special class of "educable mentally handicapped" or "trainable mentally handicapped," with a specially trained teacher. This teacher can generally do more for such a child than an ordinary teacher in a regular classroom. But provision should be made for transfer of some of these children to regular classes as they improve.

At the high school level there is need for classes for retarded children—that is, for children who read at the fourth grade level or below. Such classes should have work-experience programs, since a large number of retarded pupils can become self-supporting workers if trained suitably.

EDUCATIONAL PROGRAMS FOR THE PRIVATIST NON-CONFORMIST

What can the schools do about the difficult student who is a privatist nonconformist? If the analysis of the preceding pages is reasonably correct, boys and girls of average or superior intelligence need an educational program during the high-school period that is designed to build self-esteem and social fidelity. The characteristics of the youth who tend toward the privatist position are the following:

1. Lack of self-esteem based on their own achievement in school and society.
2. Uncertainty about vocational choice.
3. Cognitive development more advanced than personal autonomy.
4. Lack of naive faith in society.
5. Discontent with school.

The educational program should be designed to build social fidelity as well as self-confidence. It might contain the following elements:

1. Opportunity for service to society. A variety of projects during the school year and during the summer for improvement of the school, the local community, and the wider community. This will lead to a commitment to social welfare and a faith in the improvability of society.

2. Positively oriented study of society. Stress in courses in social studies on the achievement of modern society in solving problems of public health, poverty, educational and economic opportunity, and the building of an interdependent world.

3. Use of adult models who demonstrate both self-esteem and social fidelity. Choice of teachers who are socially optimistic, active, and oriented toward the improvement of society. There is a greater chance in the future for the selection of teachers with appropriate personalities for certain age groups, as the teacher shortage decreases and opportunity increases to select the better ones. The use of biography in literature and the social studies could stress heroes with these positive qualities. A set of biographical films produced by Elizabeth Drews of Michigan State University centers on the lives of contemporary people who are making positive contributions to the life of society, who have faith in the improvability of this society, and who lead personal lives that can serve as models of youth.

Good education strikes a balance between analysis and affirmation. Perhaps the education of middle-class children in recent years has been too strong on analysis and too weak on affirmation.

DANGERS AND CAUTIONS

So much attention is being paid to the socially disadvantaged pupil that we are in danger of organizing a large section of our educational program around his problems, especially in the big cities. While certainly it is necessary to give major attention to this type of pupil, he only represents some 12 to 15 per cent of youth, and secondary education cannot be structured primarily around him.

A major problem in connection with this type of youth is found in some of the high schools in low income areas of the big cities. Table 1 illustrates this problem, by comparing the students of such a high school with those in a high achievement suburban-type high school in Chicago.

School A differs from School B in being about twice as large, and containing many more low achieving, socially disadvantaged pupils. Note that the ratio of ninth to twelfth grade students is 4 to 1 for School A and 1.5 to 1 for School B. The "basic courses" in Chicago high schools are for pupils who are three years or more retarded, while the "essential courses" are for pupils who are between one and three years retarded. School A has two thirds of its ninth graders in these two categories, while School B has one eighth in the "essential courses" and none in the "basic" level. On the other

Table 1 Comparison of Two Contrasting High Schools (Schools A and B)

	Grade 9		Grade 10		Grade 11		Grade 12	
	A	B	A	B	A	B	A	B
AGE	PERCENTAGE DISTRIBUTION OF AGES							
11-9 to 12-8	2	0						
12-9 to 13-8	6	16	0	0				
13-9 to 14-8	31	53	2	10	0	0		
14-9 to 15-8	39	23	25	58	4	14	0	0
15-9 to 16-8	18	7	43	23	35	56	10	14
16-9 to 17-8	3	1	24	7	38	28	35	69
17-9 to 18-8	1	0	5	2	18	2	38	16
18-9 to 19-8			1	0	4	0	15	1
19-9 and over								
Number	2,039	668	1,246	549	676	524	503	443
	PERCENTAGE ENROLLMENTS IN BASIC, ESSENTIAL, AND HONORS COURSES							
Basic course								
English	35	0	23	0	—	—	—	—
Mathematics	19	0	0	0	—	—	—	—
Essential course								
English	30	12	36	0	42	0	31	0
Mathematics	56	14	44	0	—	—	—	—
Honors course								
English	1	12	2	5	4	5	7	6
Mathematics	2	12	0	23	0	10	0	18

SOURCE: Havighurst, Robert J. *The Public Schools of Chicago.* Chicago: Board of Education, 1964, p. 42.

hand, School B has many more pupils in "honors courses," which are for students at least one year advanced.

School A is in a position to specialize in the adaptation of curricula and methods to socially disadvantaged pupils. School B might specialize in gifted pupils. But this might be bad for the goodly number of above average pupils in School A.

There is much to be said for the "mixed school"—that is, mixed in socioeconomic status and mixed in achievement of its students. Ideally, this kind of school can challenge its best students and also use their performance as a model for other students while at the same time being realistic about their lesser ability. But there are major problems of discipline, of school climate, and of curriculum adaptation in School A.

One way to get around these problems and others as well is to adopt the Educational Plaza or Educational Park plan, which is now being discussed widely. Essentially, this is a plan which brings a mixed group of pupils in terms of ability and vocational interest and socio-economic status together on a particular school campus, but organizes their work so that a part of it is done in common and a part in subgroups of similar ability and life-expectation. Additionally, the Educational Park idea may include a wide age range of students, certainly from grades seven to fourteen, and possibly from the first to fifth grade on through junior college.

Such a program is especially desirable in a self-contained or cross-sectional community of 50 to 150 thousand population. However, it can also be adapted to a section of a big city with 100 to 400 thousand population.

The American ideal of a comprehensive high school may only be realizable under urban conditions by the Educational Park.

The Privatist Non-Conformist Needs Leeway

Another danger lies in too naïve and didactic an approach to the complexity of the privatist non-conformist. This kind of person has much to contribute to the social welfare if he acquires a social conscience and a social commitment while retaining his faculty for criticism and non-conformity. There is danger of "brain-washing" him with over-simple and over-optimistic and over-patriotic teaching during his high school years. Perhaps he needs these years to grow in his powers of analysis and social criticism, even though he may be somewhat unhappy and he may make his family uncomfortable.

The art of teaching this kind of boy or girl is to combine experiences of basic affirmation of democratic social values with experiences of analysis and criticism of social reality, so that the youth discovers and works out for himself his identity both as a conformer to some social values and a non-conformer to some social practices.

Lee G. Burchinal

Trends and Prospects for
Young Marriages in the United States

Despite the fact that in recent years youth has accelerated in social devel-opment, independence, peer affairs, and sexual intimacy, the rate of young marriages has remained relatively stable for nearly a generation. In the paper presented below, Burchinal thus contradicts the belief that a trend toward younger marriages exists. He shows that every year only a small proportion of noncollege youth under 19 do indeed marry. He describes cogently and exhaustively a variety of social factors favoring or operating against young marriages, and concludes that the balance of counter-vailing forces may encourage later instead of earlier marriage. Burchinal points to such demographic characteristics of early marriage as wives being younger than husbands, premarital pregnancies, conventional wed-dings, partners being of lower intellectual, educational, and social-class attainment, and on the basis of these data, offers hypotheses "for fore-casting the probable success of young marriages with different kinds of premarital and postmarital characteristics."

MARRIED adolescents represent a small but conspicuous segment of the adolescent population. How small, of course, depends upon the age definitions used; how conspicuous, in large part, depends upon the criteria used to evaluate youthful marriages. Considerable variation for both defi-nitions and assessment of young marriages exists in the literature.[1] Lack of precise agreement in defining young marriage is not too serious, however, because nearly all of the studies on the subject pertain to marriages in-volving females who are 18 years of age or less. In this discussion, therefore, young marriages are defined as those involving at least one partner, typically a female, who is not yet 19 years of age. Specifically excluded are studies of married college students. Aside from the fact that only a small proportion of college marriages are entered into before the age of 19, the two popula-

FROM *Journal of Marriage and the Family,* XXVII (1965), 243–254. Reprinted by per-mission of the author and the publisher.

[1] Lee G. Burchinal, "Research on Young Marriage: Implications for Family Life Edu-cation," *Family Life Coordinator,* 9 (September–December, 1960), 6–24; reprinted in *Sourcebook in Marriage and the Family,* ed. by Marvin B. Sussman, 2nd Ed. (Boston: Houghton-Mifflin, 1963), pp. 508–529. This report contains an annotated bibliography of 39 popular and technical publications related to youthful marriages.

tions probably differ greatly in many respects, including their economic resources, interests, and experiences, and the capacities of couples for solving problems and relating to others.[2]

In the following discussion, data on young marriage are organized around a historical review of rates; consideration of factors affecting young marriage decisions; review of characteristics of such marriages; an assessment of their outcomes; and, finally, discussion of some implications, based on present research.

YOUNG MARRIAGE RATES

From the marriage rates listed in Table 1 by single years of age from 15–18 for the decennial censuses from 1910 through 1960, it is clear that:

1. Young marriage rates increased consistently for males and females, white and nonwhite alike, from 1910 through 1950.

2. For the most part, young marriage rates remained substantially unchanged between 1950 and 1960.

3. Among nonwhite females, the largest increases in young marriage rates occurred between 1910 and 1930, with little further change after 1930; whereas among white females, rates remained relatively constant from 1910 to 1940, with the big increases coming between 1940 and 1950, and with virtually no changes occurring between 1950 and 1960.

4. With few exceptions, young marriage rates among nonwhites were higher than and sometimes almost double those among whites.

5. A possibly important exception to difference in marriage rates between whites and nonwhites occurred among 18-year-old females in 1960. In 1950, 23.2 per cent of white females as compared with 29.3 per cent of nonwhite females aged 18 were married. In contrast, by 1960 a smaller percentage of 18-year-old nonwhite females (23.6) than white females (24.5) were married.

6. Young marriages predominantly involve females. In 1960, for instance, percentages for marriage among males 17 and 18 years of age ranged from about 2 to slightly over 5 per cent. Corresponding rates for females ranged from 12 to 24 per cent.

Not shown in Table 1 are the absolute numbers of young marriages. Much confusion exists between the absolute numbers and rates of young marriages. In 1910, for example, 296,293 females aged 15 through 18 were married; in 1960, 589,508 females in this age group were married, but the rate of marriages among these females rose only slightly, from 8 to almost 11 per cent. Although only 1 per cent of males aged 15 to 18 were married in 1910, and only 2 per cent were married in 1960, the number of married men in this age group increased ten-fold, from 19,026 to 119,223 in 1960.

[2] Clyde Foreman, "Levels of Aspiration and Marital Status on the College Campus," unpublished dissertation, Seattle: University of Washington Library, Doctoral Dissertation Series, Publication #22, 1957; also, Chilman's study of marriages among students at Syracuse University found that students married late in their college careers: Catherine S. Chilman, "Undergraduate Marriages and Higher Education," unpublished manuscript.

Table 1   Per Cent of Any Age Level, Among the 15–18 Year-Old Population
Who Were of the Married Status During the Given Year by Sex and Color *

	Females											
AGE	WHITE						NONWHITE					
	1910	1920	1930	1940	1950	1960	1910	1920	1930	1940	1950	1960
15	1.1	1.3	1.1	1.0	1.0	2.3	2.1	2.7	2.9	2.6	2.8	2.9
16	3.4	3.8	3.9	3.4	5.6	5.6	6.6	7.8	8.8	7.6	8.1	6.8
17	8.1	9.1	9.1	8.0	12.7	12.0	13.0	17.9	18.7	16.4	17.3	13.6
18	15.9	17.9	17.7	16.2	23.2	24.5	24.4	32.2	32.7	28.9	29.3	23.6
	Males											
15	0.1	0.2	0.1	0.1	0.6	0.6	0.1	0.3	0.2	0.3	0.4	0.7
16	0.1	0.3	0.2	0.3	0.6	0.9	0.2	0.6	0.4	0.6	0.4	1.1
17	0.3	0.8	0.6	0.6	1.2	1.9	0.9	1.6	1.4	1.4	1.8	2.1
18	1.2	2.4	1.9	1.9	3.4	5.4	3.0	5.3	4.2	4.2	4.8	5.3

* Adapted from Bureau of Census, Population Characteristics, for the respective years.

Further increases in the frequencies of young marriage will occur, largely because the population base of youth aged 15 to 18 is expanding each year. In 1964, one million more adolescents will become 17 years old than in 1963. In this year's crop of 3,700,000 17-year-olds, approximately 258,000 will be married, based on the 1960 rate of 12 per cent for girls and 2 per cent for boys.[3]

Current population survey data provide the only estimates for young marriage rates since 1960. Unpublished data from the Bureau of Census indicate that for the two youngest age groups for which data are reported, 14 to 17 and 18 and 19, marriage rates for both males and females in 1963 are slightly less than comparable rates for 1960.[4]

In summary, young marriage rates, contrary to widely circulated assertions, are not going up, up, and up. Young marriage rates have remained stable or have declined slightly since 1950, and only a small proportion of high-school-age students are married.[5]

FACTORS AFFECTING YOUNG MARRIAGE RATES

The attention of sociologists generally has been focused on "explaining" the long-term trend toward younger ages at marriage in the United States. With this trend now apparently arrested, consideration must be given to why young marriage rates have remained relatively stable despite rapid social

[3] Based on data reported in "Rising Tide of the 17-Year-Olds Presents Major Social Problems," *Population Profile* (September 7, 1964).

[4] *Current Population Reports*, p. 20.

[5] For details, see Burchinal, *op. cit.*, p. 10; Vladimir de Lissovoy and Mary Ellen Hitchcock, "High School Marriages in Pennsylvania: Problems and School Board Policies," *Pennsylvania School Boards Association Bulletin*, 28 (June, 1964), 31–35; and Vladimir de Lissovoy and Mary Ellen Hitchcock, "Student Marriage Rates Remain Low in Pennsylvania," *Pennsylvania School Journal*, 112 (April, 1964), 374–375.

changes that have included acceleration of the psycho-social development of youth, earlier adoption of adult roles, and greater emancipation of young people.

Consider, for instance, the vast difference in the sociological conditions that influenced the socialization processes for youths who became 16 to 18 years of age in 1950 as compared with 1964. The former cohort was born in 1932–1934, felt the pinch of the depression, and entered adolescence during World War II. The latter cohort was born between 1946 and 1948 and grew up during the postwar boom. The two groups of youths grew up in much different social worlds, yet marriage was about as attractive at age 16 through 18 for members of the one group as for those of the other.

Obviously, available data are not adequate for "explaining" the recent stability in young marriage rates. Information is needed on changes or stability in young marriage rates for various status, regional, residential, color, and ethnic groupings of youth, because the general pattern of stability may hide marked increases for some subgroups and equally marked decreases for others.

Especially needed is research in various subgroupings on the relative saliency of factors that promote or restrain movement toward young marriages. For now, however, available information is used to assess the impact of selected factors upon young marriage rates; and beyond the limits of these data, suggestions are made regarding the probable influences of broad societal developments upon young marriage decisions.

In a previous overview of research on young marriage, the author examined the support for ten factors believed to contribute to young marriage decisions.[6] The first four factors, previously dismissed as spurious, remain questionable in light of the recent stability in youthful marriage rates. These are:

1. The insecurity of our times, which has created needs among young people to find someone with whom they can have unquestionable loyalty and love.

2. The cult of personal happiness and the rejection of intellectualism and achievement.

3. The bandwagon effect: one marriage contributes to another, and soon "everybody is doing it."

4. The impact of World War II, the Korean War, and the continuation of the draft.

The following two "explanations" are stressed by popular writers; however, the research data bearing on these conditions is inconclusive and contradictory.[7]

5. An escape from an unhappy home, school, or community situation.

6. An attempt to resolve personal or social adjustment problems.

[6] Burchinal, *op. cit.*
[7] *Ibid.;* see also Robert J. Havighurst *et al., Growing Up in River City* (New York: John Wiley, 1962), p. 185.

Another factor that is widely acclaimed as a "cause" of young marriages is:

7. The reduction of economic risks in marriage as a result of current prosperity.

As an instrumental factor in most marriage decisions, reduction of economic risks no doubt contributes to young marriage decisions as well, but this factor has limited value in accounting for youthful marriage decisions. Historically, marriage rates in general, including young marriage rates, have risen with prosperity and have declined in periods of depression or recession (see Table 1). Assurance of employment, often recently obtained, was a commonly cited factor in marriage decisions reported by young brides interviewed in Iowa and Nebraska.[8] Although it is hard to say to what degree the general affluence of American society serves to promote young marriages, without question, high rates of unemployment among young men are not conducive to young marriages. Unemployment rates of young people between the ages of 16 and 24 are more than twice the average for workers of all ages. School dropouts and nonwhites are particularly disadvantaged.[9] Thus, even in the midst of general affluence, widespread employment among young workers may serve as an impediment to young marriages.

Factors That May Favor Young Marriage

Very likely, the most probable explanation for the maintenance of present levels of young marriages lies in the balance of influences stemming from the American dating and courtship process and images of married life which in some cases favor but which in other cases discourage young marriages. Among important conditions that promote young marriage decisions are:

8. Encouragement from romantic and glamorous images of marriage and the corresponding unrealistic overevaluation of marriage.

9. Acceleration of adult status as reflected in advanced levels of heterosexual interaction at younger ages.

10. Stimulation of sexual drives by sex appeals and intense physical expressions of affection in mass media, with the result that premarital pregnancy becomes a precipitating factor in many if not most youthful marriage decisions.

Idealized images of marriage, though perhaps intensified and more unrealistic among adolescents, are held by many young adults as well. The higher rates of disillusionment, unhappiness, separation, and divorce among

[8] Lee G. Burchinal, "Comparisons of Factors Related to Adjustment in Pregnancy-Provoked and Non-Pregnancy-Provoked Youthful Marriages," *Midwest Sociology*, 21 (July, 1959), 92–96; J. Joel Moss and Ruby Gingles, "The Relationship of Personality to the Incidence of Early Marriage," *Marriage and Family Living*, 21 (November, 1959), 373–377.

[9] "Younger Workers," *Manpower Report of the President and a Report on Manpower Requirements, Resources, Utilization, and Training*, Washington, D.C.: U.S. Government Printing Office, March, 1964, pp. 123–132.

young than among other marriages (described later), however, probably reflect the greater degree or prevalence of glamorized and naïve views of marriage among adolescents who marry at younger ages. Other indications of the impulsiveness of many young marriages include the brief period of acquaintanceship or engagement preceding most young marriages,[10] their meager economic bases (also described later), the fact that such marriages often occur despite parental opposition,[11] and their greater degree of departure from religiously endogamous norms.[12]

Acceleration of adult relationships, especially through younger ages of dating, appears to be linked with younger marriage. In contrast with those who had not married by the time they would have graduated from high school, an Iowa study found that girls who were married had started dating younger, begun going steady earlier, gone steady more often, been "in love" more frequently, dated more frequently at younger ages, had a larger number of close friends who also married young, and more frequently dated men older than themselves.[13] Results of studies in Nebraska and in Columbus, Ohio, confirmed the Iowa findings.[14]

Early and serious dating generally promotes movement toward increased physical involvement, with the result that premarital pregnancy often becomes the precipitating factor in marriage decisions. Estimates of premarital pregnancy rates among young marriages range from over 30 per cent to nearly 90 per cent when both spouses are of high-school age in comparison with approximately 20 per cent of all brides.[15]

Idealization of marriage, earlier and more serious dating, and increased intimacy among youths, however, have not led to an increase in young marriage rates. Operating against these and related factors that should increase young marriage rates are other factors that should discourage young marriages.

Factors That May Operate Against Young Marriages

Within middle-class society, dating and courtship norms generally have the effect of discouraging rather than encouraging movement toward young marriage. Evidence from a number of studies provides little support for the "Hollywood" notion of dating and courtship for most youths. Student prefer-

[10] Burchinal, "Comparison of Factors . . .," *op. cit.*

[11] Lee G. Burchinal, "How Successful Are School-Age Marriages?" *Iowa Farm Science*, 13 (June, 1962), 8–9.

[12] Lee G. Burchinal and Loren E. Chancellor, *Factors Related to Interreligious Marriages in Iowa, 1953–1957*, Ames, Iowa: Iowa Agricultural and Home Economics Experiment Station, Research Bulletin 510, November, 1962; Lee G. Burchinal and Loren E. Chancellor, "Ages at Marriage, Occupations of Grooms and Interreligious Marriages," *Social Forces*, 40 (May, 1962), 348–354.

[13] Lee G. Burchinal, "Adolescent Role Deprivation and High School Age Marriage," *Marriage and Family Living*, 21 (November, 1959), 380–382.

[14] Moss and Gingles, *op. cit.*; Rachel M. Inselberg, "Social and Psychological Factors Associated with High School Marriages," *Journal of Home Economics*, 53 (November, 1961), 766–772.

[15] Burchinal, "Research on Young Marriage . . .," *op. cit.*

ences for dates and mates are more consistent with mature and realistic conceptions of marriage than with the frivolous trivia assumed to go with dating today.[16] These norms, however, apply much less to lower-status youths, particularly those who drop out of school and to whom young marriage is most attractive. Yet diffusion of middle-class norms to lower-class youths and increased saliency of these norms among middle-class youths, especially as these norms are reinforced by increased educational requirements and the upward drift in job requirements, should serve to lengthen the dating period and forestall some impulsive youthful marriages.

There also are countervailing influences against young marriages resulting from earlier ages at dating and other indications of acceleration of heterosexual behavior. Most youths who begin dating early, at ages 13 or 14, for example, do not marry by age 17 or 18, and it is unlikely that ages for initial dating will decline much below their present levels. Furthermore, it seems clear that dating among adolescents becomes an enjoyable end in itself rather than only a means to the end of marriage. Research is needed to specify the conditions under which early dating leads to early marriage, as seems to be typical for the small proportion of youths who marry young; and, on the other hand, to specify what other conditions and processes accompany early dating which does not lead to early marriage, as seems to be the case for the majority of adolescents.

Although premarital pregnancy probably is the single most compelling factor affecting the timing of a young marriage, it is probable that movement toward marriage generated by heavy petting, intercourse, and pregnancy may be offset by further development and diffusion of those dating patterns described by Lowry, Blood, Hill, and others,[17] and by changes in values and norms for degrees of sexual behavior appropriate to differing levels of affection. Greater permissiveness, with the assurance of affection, reflects the emerging equalitarian and personal-centered dating, courtship, and marriage system in the United States. For middle-class youth particularly, emerging sexual norms allow for varying degrees of physical expression of affection as part of the dating relationship itself, quite separate from expectations of moving toward engagement or marriage.[18] Widespread availability and increased use of contraceptives also permit intercourse without pregnancy among those who wish to move their affectional relationship to that level, and when pregnancies occur, alternatives to marriage are more readily available and accepted by the girl, the couple, and their parents.

Increased school and post-high-school attendance should be associated with a reduction in young marriage rates. Among 17-year-olds, school dropout rates declined from 32 per cent in 1950 to 24 per cent in 1960. Post-high-school attendance rates continue to climb. As the value of education diffuses

16 For a view of dating and courtship norms and values, see Lee G. Burchinal, "The Premarital Dyad and Love Involvement," in *Handbook on Marriage and Family,* ed. Harold T. Christensen (Chicago: Rand-McNally, 1964), pp. 626–641.

17 *Ibid.*

18 Ira L. Reiss, *Premarital Sex Standards in America* (Glencoe, Ill.: Free Press, 1960).

further through lower-class subcultures, marriage rates among 16- and 17-year-olds may decline. Changes in marriage rates among 18-year-olds due to increased school enrollment are more difficult to forecast, because 18 is the modal age at first marriage among females and, for most, represents the year of high-school graduation. Marriage rates for 18-year-olds may also decline due to post-high-school education plans; however, it is possible that marriage rates among 18-year-old females will edge upward as lower-status youth defer marriage until after high school but, following subcultural norms for earlier marriage, marry soon after graduation. Also, with increased post-high-school education among lower-status youths, part of whose subcultural expectation is for earlier marriage, college marriage rates may be expected to climb. Again, more precise research, based on large samples with longitudinal designs, is needed.

Increased employment among women, including the mothers and older sisters of today's adolescent girls, has undoubtedly contributed to the enhanced status of women and to expectations among adolescent females of enjoying a period of young adult independence before marriage. Many young females want to work a few years after high school, enjoy independent living, travel, and other aspects of young adulthood before "settling down" to marriage. In short, their norms are increasingly similar to those of young men. In this pattern, young marriage would appear less attractive and marriage plans would be moved into the early twenties.

Rising levels of expectation for marriage, in the interpersonal sense as well as materially, are hardly conducive to young marriages. The female's increased status, her potential financial contribution to the family, the personal qualities expected in a spouse by both parties, the need for assurance of a steady income, mainly based on the husband's education, work history, and initiative, all point to caution in movement toward marriage during high school years or immediately thereafter.

One additional development should be noted: the influence of counseling and guidance programs and family life parental education and related education programs conducted by high schools, community organizations, and churches. Although the influence of these programs is largely limited to upwardly mobile lower-class and middle-class youths and their parents, such programs probably have contributed to more serious consideration of marriage at younger ages, and, consequently, to the decreased likelihood of impulsive young marriages.

In summary, factors believed to encourage young marriages are offset by others that prompt youths to postpone marriages until their early twenties.[19] Taken together, however, it is suggested that the balance of these countervailing developments may be toward support of conditions that encourage later instead of earlier marriage for some groups of youths.

[19] In discussing the influence of selected trends upon young marriage rates, there has been no attempt to develop cross-national comparisons. For such a discussion, see J. Joel Moss, "Teenage Marriage: Cross-National Trends and Sociological Factors in the Decision of When to Marry," *Acta Sociologica*, 8 (Fasc. 1–2, 1964), 98–117.

CHARACTERISTICS OF YOUNG MARRIAGES

In addition to information about factors believed to influence young marriage decisions, some information is available for selected characteristics for the small minority of youths who marry young. Among the generalizations concerning characteristics of young marriage and young spouses are the following:

1. As shown in Table 1, youthful marriages predominantly involve young females and their slightly older husbands. Not shown in Table 1, however, is the fact that the age difference between spouses is inversely related to the age of the bride. For 15-year-old brides, the average groom is 5.5 years older; for 18-year-old brides, he is 3.6 years older; the difference is 2.3 years at age 21, and falls to 1.6 years at age 28.[20]

2. Approximately one third to over one half of all young marriages involve premarital pregnancies. Premarital pregnancies are highest among couples in which both spouses are still of school age, and such pregnancies are lower among couples represented by older husbands. Data already have been presented on this point.

3. Young marriages are not elopements: instead, they reflect the characteristics of conventional weddings. In Iowa in 1956, Burchinal and Chancellor found that about 73 per cent of all marriages involving brides who were under 19 years of age occurred in the county in which the bride lived, and 92 per cent of the weddings were performed by clergymen.[21]

4. Educational levels of young husbands and wives are lower than those for single persons of comparable ages. As shown in Table 2, school dropout rates are particularly high among 16- and 17-year-old married persons and remain higher among 18- and 19-year-old married persons. Estimates of school dropout rates for married girls range from about half to over 90 per cent and from about 35 to 45 per cent for married boys. Few married students who drop out ever re-enter school.[22]

5. Students who marry before they have graduated from high school generally have lower measured intelligence scores and have lower grades than unmarried students.[23]

6. Young marriages disproportionately involve persons from lower- or working-class backgrounds (see Table 3).[24] The occupational status of

[20] Paul H. Jacobson, *American Marriage and Divorce* (New York: Rinehart, 1959), p. 63.

[21] Lee G. Burchinal and Loren Chancellor, "What About School-Age Marriage?" *Iowa Farm Science*, 12 (June, 1958), 12–14.

[22] Lee G. Burchinal, "School Policies and School Age Marriages," *Family Life Coordinator*, 8 (March, 1960), 45–46; Havighurst *et al., op. cit.*, p. 119; de Lissovoy and Hitchcock, *op. cit.*

[23] Havighurst *et al., op. cit.*, pp. 120–121.

[24] Exceptions to this family established generalization may occur among marriages involving youths from small town and rural areas: see Moss and Gingles, *op. cit.*; and de Lissovoy and Hitchcock, "High School Marriages in Pennsylvania," paper presented at the National Council on Family Relations annual meeting, Miami, Fla., October, 1964.

*Table 2   Marital Status and Educational Levels Among Males and Females, Aged 14–19, 1950 ***

		14 and 15		16 and 17		18 and 19	
		Single	*Married*	*Single*	*Married*	*Single*	*Married*
		MALES					
No school years completed		1.1	2.1	0.9	1.7	0.8	0.7
Elementary	1–4 years	5.8	4.2	4.1	9.5	3.5	6.2
	5–7 years	38.1	16.6	13.3	18.3	9.5	16.8
	8 years	30.4	17.5	13.2	14.5	9.5	15.1
High School	1–3 years	22.6	15.3	63.1	37.4	33.5	33.8
	4 years	0.1	1.7	3.5	4.6	32.7	22.5
College	1–3 years			0.2	0.6	8.4	2.5
	4 or more					0.1	0.2
Not reported		1.9	42.6	1.7	13.4	2.0	2.2
		FEMALES					
No school years completed		0.9	1.7	0.7	0.6	0.6	0.6
Elementary	1–4 years	3.4	8.4	2.2	4.8	1.8	3.2
	5–7 years	30.1	35.3	7.7	19.2	4.7	11.8
	8 years	34.3	26.3	9.1	18.8	5.5	12.7
High School	1–3	29.5	20.8	73.0	49.7	28.1	39.1
	4 years	0.2	0.7	5.5	4.7	45.2	28.7
College	1–3 years			0.4	0.2	12.2	2.2
	4 or more					0.2	0.1
Not reported		1.6	6.8	1.4	2.0	1.7	1.6

* Adapted from the United States Census of Population: 1950, Report P.E. No. 5B, Volume IV, Part 5, Chapter B, Table 8, p. 5B–63.

Table 3   First Occupational Status Distributions of Grooms by Ages of Brides and Grooms, Iowa, White Marriages, 1953–1957

Occupational Status of Grooms*	Ages of Brides				
	17 OR UNDER	18	19–22	23–29	30 OR OVER
N	11,088	15,736	37,019	10,394	2,198
High	26.1	28.8	43.9	51.1	46.1
Middle	19.3	21.5	20.9	24.4	29.2
Low	42.8	36.4	23.9	18.6	22.6
Armed Forces	11.8	13.3	11.3	5.9	2.1
	Ages of Grooms				
N	2,580	4,404	35,951	28,771	4,727
High	34.4	27.7	34.4	45.8	49.2
Middle	16.3	19.6	19.4	24.1	26.6
Low	40.2	38.7	30.2	24.6	22.3
Armed Forces	9.1	14.0	16.0	5.5	1.9

* High occupational status occupations include professionals, managers, farm operators and owners, officials, and proprietors; middle-status occupations include clerks, sales, and operatives; and low status occupations include domestics, farm laborers, and other laborers.

grooms entering first marriages in Iowa from 1953 to 1957 is shown by ages of brides and grooms. As the ages of the brides or grooms increased, the proportion of marriages involving high-status grooms increased, and the proportion of marriages involving lowest-status grooms decreased.[25]

7. With lower levels of education and with employment largely limited to unskilled and semiskilled jobs, young marriages generally are established and maintained on a meager economic basis. In two studies, mean annual incomes of young couples were approximately $3,000 to $3,800.[26]

8. Parental financial assistance represents an important contribution to the economic livelihood of the young couples.

A minority of young couples always maintain their own residences; most must double-up with relatives; and most report receiving other forms of family assistance as well, including payment for rent if they are not living with relatives, cash for food, furniture, car payments, and other bills.[27]

Outcomes of Young Marriages

Two sets of data can be used to examine the outcomes of young marriages. One set consists of objective standards such as divorce and separation rates; the other includes subjective ratings or evaluations of marriage. Both point to greater stresses encountered in young marriages.

Divorce rates are between two and four times greater among young marriages than among marriages begun by persons in their twenties.[28]

Additional data for combined divorce and separation rates are reported for 1950 and 1960 in Table 4 for white and nonwhite marriages by the ages of males and females involved. (Separation represents legal separation or living apart due to marital discord, and not separations imposed because of military service, illness, or employment.) The combined rates were highest for youngest spouses and declined consistently for all groups from age 15 through 18. For both sexes, nonwhite rates generally exceeded those for whites, often being twice as large. In general, rates for given age-sex-color groupings were approximately the same in 1960 as in 1950.

Even when some of the effects associated with status are controlled, marriages begun at younger ages in contrast to those begun by persons in their twenties still have higher divorce rates. For instance, survival rates for Iowa marriages from 1953 to 1957 varied among the three status levels used, but survival rates were always lower in each status level for the marriages

[25] Burchinal and Chancellor, "Factors Related to Interreligious Marriages in Iowa," *op. cit.*, and "Ages at Marriage, Occupations of Grooms and Interreligious Marriages," *op. cit.*

[26] Burchinal, "Research on Young Marriages . . .," *op. cit.*; Rachel M. Inselberg, "Marital Problems and Satisfactions in High School Marriages," *Marriage and Family Living*, 24 (February, 1962), pp. 74–77.

[27] Burchinal, "Comparisons of Factors . . .," *op. cit.*, pp. 94–95.

[28] See Thomas P. Monohan, "Does Age at Marriage Matter in Divorce?" *Social Forces*, 32 (October, 1963), 81–87.

Table 4 Percentages for Divorce, Legal Separation, and Separation Due to Marital Discord by Sex, Color, and Age, 1950 and 1960*

| | MALE | | | | | | FEMALE | | | | | |
| | WHITE | | NONWHITE | | TOTAL | | WHITE | | NONWHITE | | TOTAL | |
AGE	N	%	N	%	N	%	N	%	N	%	N	%
						1960						
15	7,845	8.5	1,246	22.4	9,091	10.4	26,607	6.8	4,927	14.2	31,534	7.9
16	11,621	7.3	1,834	17.6	13,455	8.7	68,465	5.6	11,380	12.0	79,845	6.6
17	24,338	7.0	3,544	14.6	27,882	8.0	148,698	5.6	22,701	11.2	171,399	6.3
18	59,726	4.9	7,815	11.0	67,541	5.6	268,037	4.9	35,628	11.6	303,665	5.7
						1950						
15	7,330	28.0	655	19.1	7,985	27.1	16,805	5.8	4,160	14.5	20,965	7.5
16	7,810	19.8	925	11.4	8,735	18.9	50,920	5.5	12,305	15.0	63,225	7.4
17	12,965	8.9	3,005	12.6	15,970	9.6	112,655	5.1	23,980	13.6	136,635	6.6
18	34,890	5.6	7,380	11.8	42,270	6.6	226,920	4.8	42,175	14.3	269,095	6.3

* From "Detailed Characteristics," United States Census of Population, 1960, Series PC (1), 1D, Table 176, pp. 1–424–427; and from 1950 United States Census of Population, U. S. Summary, "Detailed Characteristics," Table 104, pp. 182–183.

involving the brides 19 or younger in comparison with brides who were 20 or older.[29]

Various self-assessments of marriages point to more difficulties associated with younger ages of marriage. Persons who married in their teens generally rated their marriages as being less satisfactory than persons who married later in life. Most of these differences hold for early- and later-married couples who have been married for ten to 15 years.[30]

At least two studies have focused on self-assessment of satisfaction among young couples. According to these two investigations in different localities, from approximately one-third to over one-half of young husbands and wives reported they regretted that they married when they did.[31] Regret was reported by a greater proportion of premaritally pregnant wives than by those who did not marry under such circumstances.[32]

The preceding uniform negative assessments of the outcomes of young marriage apply to the youthful married population as a whole. It is important not to overgeneralize findings of comparatively greater disillusionment, discord, and divorce among many youthful marriages to all young couples. Not all young marriages are doomed to failure or unhappiness. There are many successful and competent youthful marriages. In addition to describing the greater probability of discord among young marriages, it is equally important to identify correlates of success in young marriages. Yet this important research problem goes virtually untouched.

In the absence of adequate data, however, some hypotheses can be advanced for forecasting the probable success of young marriages with different kinds of premarital and postmarital characteristics. In Table 5, 14 conditions are related to the general outcomes of young marriages. Some factors are directly based upon research results; others are based upon inferences from general knowledge of correlates of marital competency. All are presented tentatively, as suggestions for discussion or hypotheses for further research.

The forecast is gloomiest for marriages with the characteristics listed in the left-hand column of Table 5 and is most optimistic for those having characteristics listed in the right-hand column. Of course, both the positive and negative factors are interrelated and combine into clusters. With the presence of an increasing number of negative factors, forecasts for competent or satisfying marital relations would become more doubtful; whereas with the presence of an increasing number of positive factors, more com-

[29] Lee G. Burchinal and Loren E. Chancellor, *Survival Rates Among Religiously Homogamous and Interreligious Marriages,* Ames, Iowa: Iowa Agricultural and Home Economics Experiment Station, Research Bulletin 512, December, 1962; and Lee G. Burchinal and Loren E. Chancellor, "Survival Rates Among Religiously Homogamous and Interreligious Marriages," *Social Forces,* 41 (May, 1963), 353–362.

[30] For a review of relevant studies, see Burchinal, "Research on Young Marriage . . .," *op. cit.*

[31] Burchinal, "How Successful Are School-Age Marriages?" and "Comparisons of Factors . . .," *op. cit.;* and Inselberg, "Marital Problems and Satisfactions in High School Marriages," *op. cit.,* p. 77.

[32] Burchinal, "Comparisons of Factors . . .," *op. cit.*

Table 5 Hypothesized Relationships Between Selected Characteristics and Outcomes of Young Marriages

	Forecast of Marital Competence and Satisfaction		
CHARACTERISTIC	POOREST	INTERMEDIATE	BEST
Ages at Marriage	Both 17 or younger	Female 17, male 20 or older	Female at least 18, male 20 or older
Educational attainment	Both school dropouts	Female dropout, male high school graduate	Both high school graduates, male, at least, with some post-high school education
Pregnancy	Premarital pregnancy	No premarital pregnancy, pregnancy immediately following marriage	Pregnancy delayed until at least one year following marriage
Acquaintance before marriage	Less than six months, no engagement period, formal or informal	One year, at least, with at least six months engagement or understanding to marry	Several years, with at least six months engagement or understanding to marry
Previous dating patterns	Limited number of dating partners, went steady immediately, or short period between first date and first date with fiancé	Some dating experience before first dating fiancé	Numerous different dates, played the field, some previous experience with going steady
Personality dynamics	Generally poor interpersonal skills, lacking maturity, limited interests, poor personal and social adjustment	Mixed	Generally competent in interpersonal relations, flexible, mature, maintaining healthy and pleasurable relations with others
Motivation for marrying	Drift into marriage, because of pregnancy, seemed like the thing to do, just wanted to, or other impulsive reasons with no strong emphasis on marital and parental roles	Mixed, marriage as preferred to career, though had previous post-high-school educational aspirations and for females perhaps tentative plans to work, etc.	No post-high-school educational aspirations and, for females: marriage, family, and homemaking preferred as career over working, living independently; positive emphasis upon role as wife and mother
Status of families of orientation	Both lower	Mixed, lower, and middle or high	Both midde or high
Parental attitudes before marriage	Strongly opposed	Mildly opposed or resigned acceptance	Supportive once the decision was clear
Wedding	Elopement and civil ceremony		Conventional, hometown, and church-sanctioned

Forecast of Marital Competence and Satisfaction

CHARACTERISTIC	POOREST	INTERMEDIATE	BEST
Economic basis	Virtually completely dependent upon relatives	Low dependence upon relatives, mostly independent income, even if near hardship level	At least assured income above self-perceived hardship level
Residence	Always lived with in-laws or other relatives	Doubled up with relatives some of the time, independent other periods of time	Always maintained own independent place of residence
Post-marriage parental views	Rejecting or punitive, assistance provided as a method of controlling the marriage	Cool	Psychologically supportive, sincerely want to help the young couple, assistance provided with no strings attached

petent or successful marital and parental interaction could be expected. Factors listed in Table 5 are also useful for assessing possible outcomes of young marriages that reflect a mixture of conditions, some of which are positively related to socially desired marital outcomes and others of which are not. Consider, for instance, the common mixed type which occurs when a school-aged girl who had not planned for any post-high-school education becomes pregnant and marries before graduation, with only mild parental support, and whose husband is in his early twenties and is employed with a steady, modest income. In such cases, problems typically associated with pregnancy-provoked young marriages would be less serious.[33]

Forecasts of marital outcomes for various other types are not necessary. Research is needed to determine what mixtures of conditions produce what kinds of marital outcomes. Until these data are available, we are left with documentation for somewhat greater risks of young marriage in general and with hypotheses for how risks vary by characteristics of young married couples.

IMPLICATIONS

It is not necessary to reiterate various implications of young marriages for family life education, marriage counseling, and related programs that have been discussed in a previous review of young marriages.[34] Instead, several general observations are offered:

1. Age per se is not an adequate criterion for predicting the degree of marital competence of couples. Numerous factors related to readiness for marriage are correlated with age, but these relationships are not immutable; for some categories of youths, marriage may not entail any greater risk than

[33] *Ibid.*
[34] Burchinal, "Research on Young Marriages . . .," *op. cit.*

for the population as a whole, but for other categories of youths, marital forecasts are extremely pessimistic. One of the goals of family life education and counseling should be to decrease the relationship between age and competency for marriage, given at least a minimum age of 18 or 19.

2. Behind age at marriage are numerous confounding influences which increase the risks for achieving marital success at age 16 or 17 and possibly even at age 18. A general index of many conditions that are negatively related to competency in marriage is the lower-status background of a predominant number of youths who marry before the age of 18. Competency in marriage and family relationships today requires a set of values, personality characteristics, and interpersonal skills associated with middle-class society. At the risk of overgeneralizing, data from numerous studies indicate that child-rearing and family relationship patterns of lower-status families are in direct contrast to those that research shows are associated with emotional health, school achievement, goal setting and attainment, social success, and reasonably competent interpersonal relations—all required for competent marital relationships.[35] Under these conditions, attempts to alter high risks associated with young marriages require education, counseling, social services, and related programs, including attempts to change values, role expectations, and behavioral patterns among lower-class families toward middle-class values and goals. To contribute even modestly to better preparation for marriage and adult living, programs will have to exceed anything that is currently envisioned.

3. Another factor standing behind young marriages, both in promoting decisions to marry and in eroding the basis for marriage, is premarital pregnancy. Also disruptive to young marriages are unexpected pregnancies during the first year of the marriage. Greater and more vigorous educational efforts are needed to prevent both circumstances. For newly married youths, requested instruction in birth control and family planning may be an important contribution to the satisfaction of the couple and to their level of living. Efforts to help pregnant girls, whether single or married, to continue their education, acquire homemaking skills, and become more competent mothers and wives also will greatly assist these marriages.[36]

4. There are justifiable grounds for discouraging young marriages, but a young marriage, no matter what the circumstances are and no matter how injudicious it may seem, is not a crime and, if used as grounds for punitive reactions, probably will only promote the completion of the self-fulfilling prophecy of greater risks of young marriages. Inadequate understanding of the causes of these marriages, however, leads many well-meaning persons

[35] Catherine Chilman, "Child-Rearing and Family Relationship Patterns of the Very Poor," *Welfare in Review,* 3 (January, 1965), 9–19.

[36] Examples of programs for pregnant girls include demonstration or experimental programs such as "School Centered Rehabilitation Program for Pregnant School-Age Girls in Washington, D.C.," being conducted by the Washington, D.C. Public Schools and directed by Mrs. Elizabeth M. Goodman, with support from the Children's Bureau, U.S. Welfare Administration; and the "Interagency Program for Pregnant Girls," being conducted by the Oakland Interagency Project, Oakland, California, with support from the Ford Foundation.

to take actions which only serve to increase the obstacles confronting youthful couples and which put additional burdens on these couples. For instance, some school boards require the withdrawal or suspension of married students. This restrictive policy is intended to prevent additional marriages among high-school students, but the few studies that have been attempted show that restrictive policies have little effect on high-school marriage rates.[37] Instead, such policies only guarantee that married youths will be prevented from acquiring a basic education necessary for employment today. Also, parents are warned against the "hidden dangers" of subsidizing the marriages of their children.[38]

According to the preceding admonition, youths who marry are to be left to flounder if they encounter economic or other difficulties. Actually, the causes leading to young marriages are extremely complex. Attempts to alter young marriage rates must deal with these causes and not with spurious ones. Threats or actual failure to support young marriages which occur probably have little influence on the marriage plans of other youths. Marriage plans grow out of a complex of factors involving previous dating histories, family relationships, personality characteristics, and life goals.[39]

5. Aside from the fact that restrictive school policies, curfews, and other "tough-minded" solutions probably will have little influence on the processes that lead to young marriages, stringent policies such as these cannot be justified in relation to the relatively low and stable or possible declining rates of marriage among 15–17-year-olds.

6. It may be that long-term trends toward younger age at marriage have selected from the young population about as large a proportion of adolescents as possible who, for various reasons, are disposed to marriage; and that now, with countertrends becoming more obvious, continuation of early dating, emancipation of youth, and varying degrees of physical involvement will not result in higher young marriage rates. More likely, it could be argued, a greater proportion of youths are being better prepared and helped to prolong dating experiences, without moving quickly into courtship and marriage. Continued stability or possible slight declines in young marriage rates may be expected, although the absolute number of such marriages will

[37] Burchinal, "School Policies and School Age Marriages," *op. cit.*, pp. 43–48; and Lee G. Burchinal, "Do Restrictive Policies Curb Teen Marriages?" *Overview*, 1 (March, 1960), 72–73. For a recent report describing lack of constructive school policies regarding student marriages, see: John G. Willmarth and Leroy G. Olsen, "Practices and Attitudes of 253 High School Principals Regarding Teen-age Marriages and Unwed Pregnant Girls," *Clearing House*, 39 (November, 1964), 171–175. The Willmarth and Olsen report contains eight references to similar studies of high school policies regarding married students.

[38] Rosalind Russell, as told to Lester David, "I'm Glad I Didn't Marry Young," *Reader's Digest*, 74 (February, 1959), 75–77. See also, David R. Mace, "The Hidden Danger in 'Subsidized' Marriage," *McCall's*, 88 (September, 1961), 36, 157; reprinted in *Reader's Digest*, 80 (January, 1962), 37–39.

[39] In addition to the previous discussion of factors affecting young marriage rates, see Lee G. Burchinal, "Young Marriages," in *Foundations for Christian Family Policy*, eds. Elizabeth S. Genne and William H. Genne, New York: National Council of Churches of Christ in the U.S.A., 1960. Contained in this paper is a diagram relating knowledge, inferences, and value judgments to development of programs to prepare youths for dating, courtship, and marriage decisions.

continue to increase. Also, it well could be that increases in young marriage rates may occur among certain subgroups and that declines in similar rates will occur among other subgroups.

Another result of continuing trends in dating and courtship patterns may be the development of a pronounced modal age for first marriage at 19 or 20 for females and at 21 or 22 for men, with a considerably smaller range in ages at first marriage than has been true. Data from the 1970 census of population will provide a test of the push toward marriage at age 19 or in the early twenties, which is beyond the limits of young marriage as used in this discussion.

Programs to help youths avoid injudicious marriage decisions may well serve best by not focusing on the risks of youthful marriage per se, but, instead, by assisting youths to develop their personalities, interests, and potentials as fully as possible. Socialization experiences in the home and community programs in schools, churches, and other organizations can play a part in this process. Research and demonstration projects are needed to determine in what ways socialization, schools, and community processes influence dating, affectional, sexual, and marriage decisions of youths; and how dating, courtship, and marriage outcomes vary accordingly to types of programs and experiences youths had before marriage. Programs of planned social change may also influence young marriage decisions.

8. Aside from their immediate intended effects, programs to provide for expanded opportunities for youths may operate against young marriages by giving lower-class youths reason for aspiring to middle-class norms and values, one of which is to defer marriage until the twenties. Programs that might have this added consequence include the various methods now being developed to make education more meaningful to lower-class youths, to prevent school dropouts, to expand educational and job opportunities, to reduce the effects of racial discrimination, and, in general, to provide challenge to youths and to increase their sense of significance. For all youths, the Peace Corps, community development projects, and the developing VISTA program as part of the war on poverty, offer opportunities for service, enriched growth and development, and exciting participation in the larger society. By providing attractive alternate roles to marriage, these national service programs also might encourage postponement of marriage during or immediately following high school.

Judith K. Brown

Adolescent Initiation Rites Among
Preliterate Peoples

In many preliterate societies a phenomenon occurs at adolescence that must seem strange to citizens of literate, Western societies. Generally labeled the "initiation rite," it provides a formal, institutionalized procedure for inducting youth into adulthood. The initiation may be of short or prolonged duration, and it lays stress upon external and outwardly impressive ceremonials. Nevertheless, a completely acceptable explanation for the necessity of initiation rites is still lacking. In the following paper, Brown discusses several hypotheses based, respectively, upon the Oedipal complex, sex identity conflict, and stabilization of sex role. Interpretations of the rite notwithstanding, Brown and the anthropologists whom she cites affirm that usually it makes men of boys and women of girls.

W HEN is an adolescent ready to accept the rights and duties of adulthood in our own society? Although each state sets certain legal requirements for the right to vote, to drive a car, to have a job, and to get married, no specific event marks the transition from adolescence to adulthood. Gradually, with the passage of successive birthdays and commencements, adulthood is reached. No commonly accepted definition for this stage of life exists, and it is possible for us to say even of a thirty-year old, "He is too immature for marriage."

Many preliterate societies are as vague as we ourselves are in their criteria for adulthood. Many others, however, celebrate a definite rite to mark the end of adolescence. In these societies, all those who have been initiated have the privileges and responsibilities of adults, and those who have not been initiated do not. Those who have been initiated are adults by definition; those who have not been initiated are not.

Adolescent initiation rites have presented a difficult area for study due to their great variety, and due to the fact that no analogous observances exist in our own society. The ceremonies are generally different for each sex. They are celebrated some time between the eighth and the twentieth

FROM Paper prepared especially for this volume from "A Cross-Cultural Study of Female Initiation Rites" (unpublished Ed.D. dissertation, Harvard University, 1961).

year, and are absolutely mandatory.[1] However, some ceremonies are elaborate and take years to complete. Others are relatively simple observances
that take only part of a day. In some ceremonies the initiate is treated
harshly and subjected to great pain. Others are joyous events that are eagerly
anticipated. Some ceremonies are observed under great secrecy. In others,
the whole community participates, and guests arrive from afar. Such variety
is not surprising considering the wide geographic distribution of initiation
rites. They have been reported in every continent except Europe.

Early travellers and missionaries were puzzled and intrigued by the
initiations they found in far away lands. They registered strong disapproval
of those rites in which the initiate was treated harshly, ritually deflowered,
or subjected to a genital operation. Such observances were regarded as
needlessly cruel or as immoral. No discernible purpose seemed to be served
by the rites, for no analogous celebrations existed in our own society. The
tribes themselves, however, ascribe very definite functions to their rites.
Among the Bemba of Africa, female initiation is practised to make the girl
"a woman as we are" and "to teach her." Richards writes:

> . . . The chisungu [initiation rite] teaches, not the technical activities of the
> wife, mother and housewife, but the socially approved attitudes toward them.
> The women themselves see this point and, in fact, made it to me. An intelligent
> *nacimbusa* [mistress of ceremonies] will admit that the girls know how to cook
> and grind but will say that after her chisungu a girl does her work in a different
> way.[2]

Although much has been written about both male and female initiation
rites, only a limited review of this literature is possible here. One of the older
works on the subject, which is still highly regarded is Arnold Van Gennep's
Les Rites de Passage.[3] In this book, Van Gennep placed initiation rites in
context with other events in the life cycle of the individual. Societies arrange
their members in certain categories, e.g., infants, children, adolescents,
adults. As the individual passes from one category to another various rites
serve to mark this transition. There are rites which mark the end of one
period of life, rites which mark the fact that the individual is in a stage of
transition, and rites which mark his admission into the new category. Rites
celebrated at adolescence are but one of a series of such observances.

Numerous studies of initiation rites have been written from a psychoanalytic point of view. One such recent book is Bruno Bettelheim's *Symbolic
Wounds*.[4] Based on Bettelheim's observations of emotionally disturbed chil-

---

[1] Observances in our own society, such as confirmation, graduation from high school,
initiation into a Greek letter organization and the coming out party do not meet this
definition, and can therefore not be considered as true initiation rites.

[2] Audrey Richards, *Chisungu: a Girl's Initiation Ceremony among the Bemba of
Northern Rhodesia* (New York: Grove Press, 1956).

[3] Arnold Van Gennep, *Les Rites de Passage* (Paris: Librarie Critique Émile Nourry,
1909).

[4] Bruno Bettelheim, *Symbolic Wounds* (Glencoe, Ill.: The Free Press, 1954).

dren and on a very limited sampling of the ethnographic literature, this book proposes that an unconscious desire for the genitals of the opposite sex underlies those initiation rites characterized by genital mutilation. Bettelheim suggests that this desire is universal, however, such initiation rites are not. Although Bettelheim's hypothesis is an interesting one, it lacks adequate substantiation.

In recent years, a number of cross-cultural studies have been devoted to initiation rites. These ceremonies have come to be regarded as very sensible solutions to specific problems inherent in certain forms of family structure and in certain types of infant and child rearing. In the following, three recent hypotheses concerning the purpose of male initiation rites will be presented. Next several hypotheses dealing with the initiation of girls will be reviewed. The knowledge gained from a study of these ceremonies has been found to have definite relevance to certain problems in our own society. Therefore a final section will be devoted to the application of these findings.

THE FUNCTION OF MALE INITIATION RITES

Published in 1958, Whiting, Kluckhohn and Anthony's paper, "The Function of Male Initiation Ceremonies at Puberty," [5] attempts to explain why some societies celebrate male initiation rites, and why others, such as our own, do not. The authors restrict their definition of these ceremonies to those that contain one or more of the following elements: painful hazing, isolation from women, tests of manliness and genital operations. As an example of a particularly severe rite they cite from an account of the ceremony of the Thonga tribe of Africa recorded by Junod. [6]

> When a boy is somewhere between ten and sixteen years of age, he is sent by his parents to a "circumcision school" which is held every four or five years. Here in company with his age-mates he undergoes severe hazing by the adult males of the society. The initiation begins when each boy runs the gauntlet between two rows of men who beat him with clubs. At the end of this experience, he is stripped of his clothes and his hair is cut. He is next met by a man covered with lion manes and is seated upon a stone facing this "lion man." Someone then strikes him from behind and when he turns his head to see who has struck him, his foreskin is seized and in two movements cut off by the "lion man." Afterwards he is secluded for three months in the "yards of mysteries," where he can be seen only by the initiated. It is especially taboo for a woman to approach these boys during their seclusion, and if a woman should glance at the leaves with which the circumcised covers his wound, and which form his only clothing, she must be killed.
>
> During the course of his initiation, the boy undergoes six major trials: beatings, exposure to cold, thirst, eating unsavory foods, punishment and threat of

[5] J. W. M. Whiting, R. C. Kluckhohn and A. Anthony, "The Function of Male Initiation Ceremonies at Puberty," *Readings in Social Psychology*, eds. Eleanor Maccoby, T. M. Newcomb and E. L. Hartley (New York: Henry Holt and Co., 1958), pp. 359–370.

[6] Henri A. Junod, *The Life of a South African Tribe* (London: The Macmillan Co., 1927).

death. On the slightest pretext he may be severely beaten by one of the newly initiated men who is assigned to the task by the older men of the tribe.[7]

Whiting, Kluckhohn and Anthony's hypothesis is based on the psychoanalytic assumption that very early experiences continue to exert an influence in later life, and that the Oedipal situation exists among mother, father and son. Although the original formulation of the Oedipus complex was based on observations in our own Western society, Whiting, Kluckhohn and Anthony believe that child rearing conditions in certain preliterate societies heighten the "family romance." Thus when the mother-son bond is particularly strong, and when the father-son rivalry is accentuated, initiation rites are celebrated at adolescence in order to prevent the son's incestuous approaches to the mother and his open hostility toward the father.

In certain preliterate societies, mother and infant enjoy an exclusive sleeping arrangement during the first two or three years of the child's life. In many of these same societies there is also a taboo on sexual relations between the father and mother during this same period. The mothers devote themselves to their infants in a manner that would be impossible and deemed improper in our own society. It is under circumstances like these that Whiting, Kluckhohn and Anthony believe a particularly strong bond develops between mother and son.

This relationship is then abruptly terminated when the child is weaned, at age two or three. The exclusive sleeping arrangements are ended, and the mother resumes sexual relations with the father. Under these circumstances Whiting, Kluckhohn and Anthony believe that the young boy is subject to particularly strong feelings of rivalry toward the father. At adolescence both the incestuous feelings toward the mother and the rivalrous feelings toward the father could be dangerously disruptive to the society. The initiation rite serves to counteract such a possibility.

Societies like our own, in which the infant does not enjoy such exclusive possession of the mother during the early years, and in which the rivalry with the father never reaches such intensity, do not need an initiation at adolescence to check the potentially disruptive Oedipal strivings of its adolescent boys. Whiting, Kluckhohn and Anthony tested this hypothesis on a sample of fifty-six societies distributed around the world, and found that a statistically significant number of the cases corresponded to their prediction.

In a recent paper, Young [8] rejects the hypothesis suggested by Whiting, Kluckhohn and Anthony, and sets forth his own explanation of the function of male initiation rites. He expands the definition of the latter also to include observances such as tattooing, tooth filing, fasting, special taboos, gifts,

---

[7] Whiting, Kluckhohn and Anthony, *op. cit.*, p. 360.

[8] Frank W. Young, "The Function of Male Initiation Ceremonies: a Cross-Cultural Test of an Alternate Hypothesis," *The American Journal of Sociology*, LXVII, No. 4 (January, 1962), 379–396.

dances, participation in raids and change of name. Young does not accept the basic psychoanalytic assumption that events in infancy and early childhood determine behavior later in life, and that problems generated in the early years need resolution in the form of an initiation at adolescence. His explanation of these ceremonies is that they serve to stabilize the sex role of the young boy when he enters adult life, and that this stabilization is of particular importance in those societies characterized by a high degree of male solidarity. The latter, Young describes as follows:

> Such solidarity may be defined as the co-operation of men in maintaining a definition of their situation as one which is not only different from that of women, but which involves organized activities requiring the loyalty of all males.[9]

Male solidarity is generally found in conjunction with polygyny, as it seems to take several women to support a man devoting his time to the activities of a cooperating male group. Young suggests that the child rearing factors which necessitate adolescent initiation rites according to Whiting, Kluckhohn and Anthony are actually merely aspects of polygynous family life, and are spurious explanations of the need for male initiation ceremonies. According to Young, it is the presence of a high degree of male solidarity that best explains the initiation of adolescent boys. In societies like our own, where there is a low degree of male solidarity, such rites are not celebrated.

A further criticism of Whiting, Kluckhohn and Anthony's research has been made by Norbeck, Walker and Cohen.[10] They attempted to replicate Whiting, Kluckhohn and Anthony's ratings on seven of the societies in the sample, and found that their own ratings differed. They felt that Whiting, Kluckhohn and Anthony were not specific enough in their definition of the variables they used, that often the ratings were made without regard for their context in the ethnographic accounts, and that Whiting, Kluckhohn and Anthony often reinterpreted ethnographic works that were already interpretative. They also criticized the statistical method Whiting, Kluckhohn and Anthony used. Norbeck, Walker and Cohen concluded that Whiting, Kluckhohn and Anthony's study was overburdened with hypotheses, and that present ethnographic data is inadequate for the kind of research Whiting, Kluckhohn and Anthony attempted.

Norbeck, Walker and Cohen's article is of interest as it points out many of the problems that beset cross-cultural research. The complexity of the ethnographic accounts makes the definition of specific variables difficult. These variables are of necessity treated out of context to some extent. All ethnographic accounts are somewhat interpretative, as the observer is selective in what he reports of a preliterate society. Although replication is an

---

[9] *Ibid.*, p. 381.
[10] Edward Norbeck, Donald E. Walker, and Mimi Cohen, "The Interpretation of Data: Puberty Rites," *American Anthropologist*, LXIV, No. 3, Part 1 (June, 1962), pp. 463–485.

important aspect of research, Norbeck, Walker and Cohen attempted to carry out their work without much of the necessary information. The article by Whiting, Kluckhohn and Anthony was a mere summary and did not contain all the facts that would be needed to make replication possible. Due to the complexity of the material, elaborate instructions would be necessary, embodying all the decisions that the raters have made. The criticism that Whiting, Kluckhohn and Anthony's study was overburdened by hypotheses has some justification. However, the material with which the research dealt was such as to invite numerous conjectures. Ethnographic accounts are never as complete as one would wish for the purposes of cross-cultural research. It is therefore all the more amazing that a hypothesis like that of Whiting, Kluckhohn and Anthony finds the kind of cross-cultural confirmation that it does.

The hypothesis proposed by Whiting, Kluckhohn and Anthony has recently been revised in an article by Burton and Whiting.[11] This revision contains what is probably the most convincing explanation of male initiation rites suggested to date. Burton and Whiting restrict their definition to those ceremonies which contain circumcision as a component. No longer are male initiation rites seen to counteract Oedipal strivings, but rather to counteract a conflict in sex identity. According to Burton and Whiting, "The process of identification consists of the covert practice of the role of an envied status." [12] Envy is in turn based on the distribution of "resources." This is the term by which the authors refer to anything one person wants but over which some-one else has control; e.g., food, water, freedom from pain, love, solace, praise, etc. When a parent withholds a resource from a child, the child envies that parent. According to Burton and Whiting, the envy thus generated will drive the child to wish to be like, and thus to identify with the parent.

The setting in which the young infant spends the greatest part of his time is his bed. It is in this setting that he receives resources or that resources are withheld from him. If he shares his bed with both parents, he will come to envy and to identify with the adult status. If, however, he sleeps with his mother in the exclusive mother-child sleeping arrangements described by Whiting, Kluckhohn and Anthony, the infant will envy and identify with the female status. (Our own society is unique in that the infant usually sleeps in a bed of his own, apart from both parents.)

When the infant grows into a child and enters the world of the family and the household, he is confronted with new possibilities for envy and identification. In those societies in which the married daughters continue to live near or with their mothers (matrilocal societies), women hold a position of power in the household. In those societies in which the married sons continue to live near or with their fathers (patrilocal societies), men hold a position of power in the household. (In our own society, and in several

---

[11] Roger V. Burton and J. W. M. Whiting, "The Absent Father and Cross-Sex Identity," *Merrill-Palmer Quarterly of Behavior and Development*, VII, No. 2 (1961), 85–95.
[12] *Ibid.*, p. 85.

others, the married couple lives away from both the husband's and the wife's family.)

According to Burton and Whiting, sex identity conflict arises in those societies in which the infant experiences the exclusive mother-infant sleeping arrangement, and in which the family structure is patrilocal. In his early years, the infant envies and identifies with the female status, but in childhood, men hold the envied status. Conditions for sex identity are confusing, and the male rite at adolescence serves to force the initiate to relinquish his unacceptable female identification and to identify once and for all with his male initiators. Societies like our own are not characterized by conditions which foster sex identity conflict, and therefore do not practise ceremonies. Burton and Whiting tested this hypothesis on a sample of sixty-four societies distributed around the world, and found that a statistically significant number of the cases conformed to their prediction.

THE FUNCTION OF FEMALE INITIATION RITES

The initiation of girls presents a very different picture. Only very rarely do these rites subject the initiate to harsh treatment or to genital operations. The usual female initiation rites contain one or more of the following elements: bathing, beautification such as a new hair arrangement, isolation in a special place, dietary restrictions, an announcement of the initiate's changed status and instruction in such matters as womanly tasks, etiquette, behavior toward in-laws, menstrual observances, contraceptive devices and observances during pregnancy. The ceremony is often closely related to other events in the young girl's life, such as menarche, betrothal and marriage. Menarche is often prerequisite for initiation, and initiation in turn is often prerequisite for betrothal and marriage.

The following account of the initiation of girls among the Cheyenne Indians of North America contains many of the typical elements:

The passage of a girl from childhood to young womanhood was considered as hardly less important to the tribe than to her own family. She was now to become the mother of children and thus to contribute her part toward adding to the number of the tribe and so to its power and importance.

When a young girl reached the age of puberty and had her first menstrual period, she, of course, told her mother, who in turn informed the father. Such an important family event was not kept secret. It was the custom among well-to-do people for the father of the girl publicly to announce from the lodge door what had happened and as an evidence of his satisfaction to give away a horse.

The girl unbraided her hair and bathed, and afterward older women painted her whole body with red. Then, with a robe about her naked body, she sat near the fire, a coal was drawn from it and put before her, and sweet grass, juniper needles, and white sage were sprinkled on it. The girl bent forward over the coal and held her robe about it, so that the smoke rising from the incense was confined and passed about her and over her whole body. Then she and her grandmother left the home lodge, and went into another small one near by, where she remained for four days.[13]

The few female initiation rites which inflict extreme pain on the young girl are those involving a genital operation or extensive tattooing. Brown [14] found that such rites are practised by societies characterized by those conditions, specified by Burton and Whiting, that foster a conflict of sex identity. The societies that practise painful female initiation rites also practise male rites involving a genital operation and seclusion. It appears that when the conflict in sex identity arises both sexes are subject to dramatic and painful rites in order to compel them to accept their respective roles.

The usual female rite is celebrated in matrilocal societies. Since the young girl lives among the same people throughout her life, the initiation serves to announce her changed status when she reaches adulthood. In non-matrilocal societies the change in residence at marriage seems to serve the same purpose.

Female initiation rites are also characteristic of those societies in which women do a major share of the bread-winning. It seems as if the rite serves to assure the girl and those around her that she will be competent to carry on the vital activities of the society. Thus for example, among the Jivaro Indians of South America, women carry on most of the subsistence activities. At initiation, tobacco medicine is administered to the young girl in order that the spirit of tobacco will give her the strength to carry out her womanly tasks, give her skill with the domestic plants and animals, and make her a successful wife and mother. After the rite, she undergoes a prolonged period of training in womanly activities.

In those societies, like our own, in which women merely share in the subsistence activities, or in which men carry on the major part of these activities, female initiation rites are not celebrated. The hypotheses concerning female initiation rites were tested on a sample of seventy-five societies distributed all over the world, and a statistically significar.t number of cases conformed to each of the predictions.

RELEVANCE OF THE FINDINGS FOR CONDITIONS IN WESTERN SOCIETY

At first glance, the observance of initiation rites at adolescence may appear as an exotic custom far removed from our own experience. Yet the research dealing with these ceremonies has given a new perspective to certain problems in our own society. For example, Burton and Whiting summarize a number of studies in our own society which clearly show that family structure can produce a sex identity conflict which may find its resolution in initiation into the delinquent gang. Brown's findings concerning the initiation cere-

[13] G. B. Grinnell, *The Cheyenne Indians, Their History and Ways of Life* (New Haven: Yale University Press, 1923), Vol. 1, p. 129.

[14] J. K. Brown, "A Cross-Cultural Study of Female Initiation Rites," *American Anthropologist,* in press.

monies of girls have a definite bearing on that controversial subject, the education of women.

The father-absent household is not unknown in our own lower class. Burton and Whiting summarize a number of investigations in which this particular type of family structure had been studied. Although these investigations were concerned with lower class culture and delinquency, rather than sex identity conflict, their data do in effect corroborate the Burton and Whiting hypothesis.

The boy growing up in the "female based" household in our own lower class grows up under conditions very much like those found in certain preliterate societies. As he gets older and moves into the world of the lower class community he finds himself under the domination of the older men and boys who constitute the gang. Often admission into the gang very much resembles the tests of manhood required in male initiation ceremonies. The strongest evidence of sex identity conflict comes from the lower class youth's preoccupation with masculinity and "toughness," and his compulsive rejection of all things feminine. Due to his early experiences femininity is also equated with authority. Delinquent acts appear to serve as part of this reaction against the early feminine identification. Thus although the initiation of boys in preliterate tribes may appear far removed from the problems we encounter in our own society, the study of these ceremonies has shed new light on the delinquent gang in our own lower class culture.

The conditions which Brown found to be present in those preliterate societies which practise the more usual initiation ceremonies for girls (matrilocality and women as the major bread-winners) are not characteristic of our own society. However, the study gives a new perspective to the status of women in our own society and to the type of education they receive.

Female initiation rites are observed in order to make young girls womanly, an attribute for which the society has a clear definition, and one which is highly valued. Among the Bemba tribe of Africa, the womanly role has the following definition:

> Women, unlike men, are admired for industry and for resources in finding food in the bush. They are honoured for bearing and rearing many children and for courage in childbirth which is often, under Bemba conditions, a terrible ordeal. They are expected to be loyal to their own sex and to accept the domination of older women.[15]

Not only do these societies have a definition for the womanly role, but the areas of womanly endeavor are also clearly defined. Competence in these activities is sufficiently valued that definite steps are taken to assure the proficiency of the young girl.

In our own society, the domain of women is not clearly designated, and the few truly feminine occupations are not prestigeful. This condition is reflected by our educational system, in which preparation for womanhood

15 Richards, *op. cit.*, p. 48.

is not undertaken with seriousness. Training in grooming, womanly demeanor, household tasks and child care is usually given informally in the home. When specific instruction is offered in these areas, it is not accorded the same prestige as other subjects. Reflecting the attitudes of our society, our system of education trains girls for what is considered important work, that work in which women compete with men.

The young girl of today finds herself confronted by a perplexing array of opportunities. Unlike her grandmother, she may choose her life work from a vast number of occupations as well as the age-old tasks of the homemaker and mother. The greatest recognition will be accorded to that work in which she competes successfully with men. There is no doubt but that our society has benefited by drawing indiscriminately on both its men and its women to do its work. But this is not necessarily the best way of using women's peculiarly feminine gifts. Also, it is perhaps the lack of societal valuation of specifically feminine endeavors that brings on the penis envy which our psychoanalysts find characteristic of their women patients. Would this phenomenon perhaps be absent in a society in which the work of women was a specific and independent domain, and in which this work was highly valued? On this subject, Margaret Mead makes the following statement:

> . . . This Western experience, which undoubtedly does occur often enough to be a very frequent characteristic of the woman who finds her way to the analyst's couch, occurs . . . in a society that has so over-rewarded male positions that envy for the rôle which is played by the father can coalesce with an experience of the little brother's or boy companion's more conspicuous anatomical equipment.[16]

No attempt will here be made to suggest what would constitute the best possible education for women, or what constitutes the best possible use of their talents within a society. We should be aware, however, that educating women to be successful men is only one of many possible alternatives. The female initiation rite represents the opposite extreme.

[16] Margaret Mead, *Male and Female* (New York: Wm. Morrow and Co., 1949), p. 85.

Part 2

Socialization: Theory and Practice

Gerald S. Blum

Prepuberty and Adolescence

Of the personality theories biased toward a genetic interpretation of personality development, the formulations of Freud and his followers long have commanded the most attention. According to orthodox psychoanalytic theory, personality development proceeds sequentially through oral, anal, phallic, latent, and adolescent stages before adulthood is attained. Although inability to control impulses, curb anxieties, or delay gratifications may initiate crises at any stage, maturation of sexuality at adolescence marks this period as particularly susceptible to psychological turbulence. One psychoanalytic writer (J. C. Gustin, "The Revolt of Youth," Psychoanalysis and the Psychoanalytic Review, XLVIII [1961], p. 83) offers this vivid description of adolescence: "Picture an adolescent now poised at the brink of adulthood. Racked by sexual desire, frustrated by outer prohibitions and inner inhibitions; desperately longing for independence yet fearful of isolation; eager for responsibilities yet fraught with anxieties about inferiority; flooded by irrational impulses yet committed to rules of propriety, he is hopelessly and helplessly confused and an enigma to everyone and himself."

Certain factors mitigate the rather dismal picture of adolescence favored by psychoanalytic theorists: (a) equally plausible alternative explanations of adolescent behavior frequently are available; (b) the majority of the interpretations are based upon nonreplicable subjective observations; and (c) several key inferences appear contradictory. In the paper presented below, Blum presents a review of orthodox and neoorthodox psychoanalytic concepts as they relate to adolescence, and in his excellent commentary, he clarifies the implications of these points of view for adolescent development.

I F there has been relative peace and quiet in the latency period, it comes to an abrupt end with the onset of puberty. Attainment of sexual maturity brings in its wake a wave of disturbance, not only in the sexual area but also in the broader realm of social behavior. According to psychoanalytic theory, the adolescent, flooded by his own resurgent impulses, must regroup the defensive forces of his ego in an attempt to meet this new onslaught.

FROM G. S. Blum, *Psychoanalytic Theories of Personality* (New York: McGraw-Hill Book Co., 1953), pp. 136–155. Copyright, 1953, by the McGraw-Hill Book Company, Inc. Reprinted by permission of the author and the publisher.

ORTHODOX VIEWS

Psychosexual Development

The interval between latency and puberty—known as "prepuberty" or "preadolescence"—is preparatory to physical sexual maturity. There are no qualitative changes, says Anna Freud, but the quantity of instinctual energy has increased (see Note 1). The increase is not confined to the sexual life. There is more libido at the id's disposal and it cathects indiscriminately any impulses which are at hand. In her own words: [1]

> Aggressive impulses are intensified to the point of complete unruliness, hunger becomes voracity and the naughtiness of the latency-period turns into the criminal behaviour of adolescence. Oral and anal interests, long submerged, come to the surface again. Habits of cleanliness, laboriously acquired during the latency-period, give place to pleasure in dirt and disorder, and instead of modesty and sympathy we find exhibitionistic tendencies, brutality and cruelty to animals. The reaction-formations, which seemed to be firmly established in the structure of the ego, threaten to fall to pieces. At the same time, old tendencies which had disappeared come into consciousness. The Oedipus wishes are fulfilled in the form of phantasies and day-dreams, in which they have undergone but little distortion; in boys ideas of castration and in girls penis-envy once more become the centre of interest. There are very few new elements in the invading forces. Their onslaught merely brings once more to the surface the familiar content of the early infantile sexuality of little children (see Note 2).

Deutsch [2] presents a different account of prepuberty in girls. She characterizes it as a period of greatest freedom from infantile sexuality and from aggression. The increased activity is interpreted, not as a manifestation of aggression, but rather as an intensive process of adaptation to reality and mastery of the environment, which precedes the passivity of puberty. Spiegel, [3] in a review of psychoanalytic contributions to adolescence, questions these conclusions on the basis of Deutsch's own materials. He points out that it is difficult to reconcile the supposed freedom from infantile sexuality with evidences of strong interest in the function of the sexual organs, the preoccupation with prostitution fantasies, and sado-masochistic interpretations of intercourse. Also the prepubertal girl is described as being full of rage and hatred as well as of dependent, clinging feelings toward the mother.

With the arrival of bodily sexual maturity (puberty proper), there is, according to Anna Freud, a further change of a qualitative character (see Note

[1] Anna Freud, *The Ego and the Mechanisms of Defence*, trans. by C. Baines (New York: International University Press, 1946), p. 159.

[2] Helene Deutsch, *The Psychology of Women* (New York: Grune and Stratton, 1944), I.

[3] L. A. Spiegel, "A Review of Contributions to a Psychoanalytic Theory of Adolescence," *Psychoanal. Study of the Child*, VI (1951), pp. 375–393.

3). Previously the heightening of instinctual cathexis was general and undifferentiated; now libido, especially in males, is concentrated specifically on genital feelings, aims, and ideas. Pregenital tendencies are relegated to the background, which results in an apparent improvement in behavior. The boorish aggressiveness of preadolescence gives way to the more refined genital masculinity. What seems to be a spontaneous cure of pregenitality is largely deceptive, though. The temporary triumph of genitality over early fixations recedes in adult life, when the pressure of the instinct sinks to its normal level and all the old anxieties and conflicts reappear unchanged.

Heterosexual outlets, however, are limited by the fact that society strongly opposes sexual intercourse during adolescence (see Note 4). According to Fenichel, the conflicts between drives and anxieties are felt consciously by present-day adolescents principally in the form of conflicts around masturbation. The heightened genital strivings sooner or later find expression in masturbatory activity, unless the infantile repressions have been too intense. The fears and guilt feelings originally connected with the accompanying oedipal fantasies are displaced to the masturbation. Adolescents react to these fears and guilt feelings by taking sides with the drive and fighting with anxiety and the parents, or they may more frequently side with the anxiety and the parents and try to fight off instinctual temptations. Often they do both (see Note 5).

For the boy, sexual developments in puberty are said to be a reawakening and continuation of infantile sexuality. He maintains his interest in the penis, whereas for the girl there is a change of direction. During adolescence she becomes aware of her vagina as a source of pleasure, while previously she had been interested solely in her clitoris and the desire to be boyish. At puberty the feminine function and its passive role must be accepted. Where strong penis envy exists, this switch is seriously impeded. The first menstruation, says Spiegel,[4] may play an important role in the process, either by supporting the feminine tendencies with all the fantasies concerning passive-masochistic gratification, pregnancy, and childbirth; or, on the contrary, leading to a rejection of femininity by increasing penis envy and the castration complex (see Note 6). Buxbaum [5] reports that, unconsciously, the first menstruation is experienced as an injury to the genitals, as a castration, and as punishment for masturbation. Deutsch [6] also emphasizes the double sexual role of mother and lover which the girl must ultimately integrate.

Sex differences in narcissism at puberty, originally formulated by Harnick, are summarized in Spiegel's review. The male is said to retain the narcissistic estimation of his own penis to a great extent throughout his life, while the woman, on reaching maturity at puberty, tends to prize the beauty of her face and figure. The basis for this female libidinal shift from the genitals to the body as a whole is found in the wave of repression, occurring at puberty,

---

[4] *Ibid.*
[5] Edith Buxbaum, "Angstäusserungen von Schulmädchen im Pubertätsalter," Z. *psa. Pädagogik,* VII (1933).
[6] Deutsch, *op. cit.*

which relates especially to sexuality associated with the clitoris. The male undergoes a similar but less extreme shift in setting up ideals of bodily strength and manliness.

EGO AND SUPEREGO FORMATION

With the advent of preadolescence, as we have seen, the balanced relationship or truce between the ego and the id in latency is disrupted. Physiological forces stimulate the instinctual processes and upset the balance. The ego, already strengthened and consolidated, struggles desperately to regain the equilibrium by using all the defenses in its repertory. The conflict is translated readily into behavior. While the id is winning out, there is an increase in fantasy, lapses into pregenital sexual gratification, and aggressive or even criminal actions. While the ego is ahead, there are various forms of anxiety, neurotic symptoms, and inhibitions.

In adolescence there are two extremes in which the conflict may possibly end. Either the id, now grown strong, may overcome the ego, in which case no trace will be left of the previous character of the individual and the entrance into adult life will be marked by a "riot of uninhibited gratification of instinct," in Anna Freud's words. Or the ego may be victorious, in which case the character of the individual during the latency period will remain permanently. When this happens, the id impulses of the adolescent are confined within the narrow limits prescribed for the instinctual life of the child. No use can be made of the increased libido and there has to be a constant expenditure on countercathexes, defense mechanisms, and symptoms. The ego generally remains rigid and inflexible throughout life. As a result of these conflicting forces, adolescent personality characteristically manifests such contradictory traits as altruism and selfishness, gregariousness and solitariness, indulgence and asceticism.

The factors which determine whether the outcome will be a one-sided or a happier solution are threefold: (1) the strength of the id impulses, which is conditioned by the physiological process at puberty; (2) the ego's tolerance or intolerance of instinct, which depends on the character formed during the latency period; and (3) the nature and efficacy of the defense mechanisms at the ego's command (see Note 7).

The ego also alienates itself from the superego during adolescence. Since the superego is still intimately related to the parents, it is itself treated as a suspicious incestuous object. The principal effect of this break between ego and superego is to increase the danger which threatens from the instincts. The individual tends to become asocial, since the former alliance of ego and superego is at an end. The defensive measures prompted by superego anxiety become inoperative and the ego is thrown back to the level of pure instinctual anxiety, accompanied by its primitive protective measures (see Note 8). Conditions are then ripe for the development of what Fenichel describes as an "impulsive character." At the other extreme is Spiegel's [7] commentary on

[7] Spiegel, op. cit.

the growing stress which society places upon superego formation during adolescence. This tendency to maximize compliance may be responsible for the frequent appearance of the pseudo-mature adolescent who, although he complies with the serious demands of present-day society, is nevertheless emotionally very close to blind revolt against these demands. The revolutionary type of adolescent, he adds, does not seem to be found so frequently nowadays.

Bernfeld,[8] in a series of papers, has attempted to classify reactions of adolescents to the libidinal changes of puberty and also to the shifting ego-superego relations. With respect to the former, he distinguishes two types: the neurotic and the simple or uncomplicated. The neurotic group tries to deny the pubertal changes and to live as if nothing new has occurred. Anxiety and defense against anxiety characterize their behavior. The simple group, on the other hand, maintains the ideal of being grown up and consequently assumes a positive, welcoming attitude to the signs of sexual maturity. On the ego-superego variables Bernfeld differentiates the adolescent who is extremely compliant to the wishes of the environment, the one who is extremely rebellious, and the one who is mixed in his reactions. Wittels[9] suggests a chronological type of breakdown of adolescent phases into a second phallic period, a second latency, and finally a mature ego stage.

RELATIONSHIPS WITH OTHERS

In the preadolescent phase libido is again directed toward the love objects of childhood. Incestuous oedipal fantasies are prominent. The adolescent ego's first task is to revoke these tendencies at all cost. Typically, the young person isolates himself and behaves like a stranger with members of his own family (see Note 9). He substitutes new attachments to replace the parental ties. Sometimes the individual becomes attracted to young people of his own age, in which case the relationship takes the form of passionate friendship or of actually being in love; sometimes the attachment is to an older person, whom he takes as his leader—clearly a substitute for the abandoned parents. While they last, these love relations are passionate and exclusive, but they are of short duration. Persons are selected as objects and abandoned without any consideration for their feelings, and others are chosen in their place. The abandoned objects are quickly and completely forgotten, but the form of the relation to them is preserved down to the minutest detail and is generally reproduced, with an exactness which almost suggests obsession, in the relation to the new object. Spiegel makes the point

[8] S. Bernfeld, "Über eine typische Form der männlichen Pubertät," *Imago. Lpz.,* IX (1923); S. Bernfeld, *Vom dichterischen Schaffen der Jugend* (Vienna: Verlag, 1924); S. Bernfeld, "Über die einfache männliche Pubertät," *Z. psa. Pädagogik,* IX (1935); S. Bernfeld, "Types of Adolescence," *Psychoanal. Quart.,* VII (1938), 243–253.

[9] F. Wittels, "The Ego of the Adolescent," *Searchlights on Delinquency,* ed. K. R. Eissler (New York: International University Press, 1949).

that the reanimation of the Oedipus complex often does not appear in clear form, especially after adolescence has been under way for some time. Parent substitutes who have less and less in common with the original parent images are chosen with increasing frequency as maturation continues.

According to Anna Freud, these fleeting love fixations are not really object relations, but rather identifications of the most primitive kind. The fickleness characteristic of puberty does not indicate any inner change in the love or convictions of the individual, but instead a loss of personality as a consequence of a change in identification. Fenichel says that in many ways objects are used as mere instruments to relieve inner tensions, as good or bad examples, as proofs of one's own abilities, or as reassurances. Objects are easily abandoned if they lose their reassuring significance.

Anna Freud goes on to state that the adolescent regresses in his libidinal life from object love to narcissism. He avoids complete collapse by convulsive efforts to make contact with external objects once more, even though by a series of narcissistic identifications.

Following this wave of narcissism, orthodox theory describes a normal, temporary phase of homosexual object choices (see Note 10). Fenichel elaborates this topic by maintaining that homosexual preferences are due to social factors as well as a narcissistic orientation. Adolescents prefer to meet in homosexual gatherings so as to avoid the exciting presence of the other sex and at the same time avoid being alone. In this way they hope to find the reassurance they are looking for. However, the friendships that were formed in the hope of avoiding sexual object relationships often assume a sexual character themselves.

In her discussion of the girl's development Deutsch [10] says that object choice changes from homosexual in preadolescence to bisexual in early puberty and to heterosexual in later puberty. The homosexual relationship at times shows a sado-masochistic quality. There are typical crushes on some older girl, as well as very close contacts with another girl of the same age. The bisexuality of early adolescence is emphasized in frequently occurring love triangles. Along with the growing sexual desires come numerous fantasies, the most common concerning pregnancy and prostitution and, to a lesser extent, rape.

Psychologically, there is the appearance of narcissism, which is one of the important parts of the feminine core, along with passivity and masochism. The development of passivity is aided by the fact that women cannot be active and aggressive because of the double standard. Also, the trauma associated with the lack of an active organ, the penis, leads the girl to seek passive means of sexual gratification. Since activity and aggression cannot be expressed toward the outside world, they are turned against the self in a masochistic fashion. Narcissism, the intensification of self-love, serves as a defense against the masochistic urges.

[10] Deutsch, *op. cit.*

MECHANISMS

Prepubertal Defenses

In an effort to regain the equilibrium of the latency period, the prepuberty ego indiscriminately calls upon all the defense mechanisms at its command. Even the breakthroughs of pregenital tendencies, while representing a failure in defense, are considered by Lander [11] to serve as regressive protection against delinquency. Greenacre [12] describes a specific defense of this period—the "prepuberty trauma," in which the young girl provokes or cooperates in a sexual act with an adult. By shifting her feelings of guilt to the adult, she can keep the experience in consciousness and use it as a "real defense" against the demands of puberty. Spiegel [13] cites this illustration as evidence for the fact that external reality may be used primarily for defensive purposes.

Asceticism

A common mechanism in adolescence is the repudiation of all instinctual impulses, so-called "asceticism." The individual mistrusts enjoyment in general, and the safest policy for him is to counter his urgent desires with more stringent prohibitions, similar to those of strict parents in early training. The mistrust of instinctual wishes has a tendency to spread, extending even to the ordinary physical needs. Examples are adolescents who avoid the society of those of their own age, decline to join in any entertainment, and refuse to have anything to do with plays, music, or dancing. More extreme forms of asceticism are exposures to unnecessary health risks, like wearing inadequate clothing, giving up food pleasures, rising very early in the morning, and so on.

Anna Freud [14] differentiates asceticism from repression on two grounds: (1) Repression deals with a specific instinctual relationship and is concerned with the nature and quality of the instinct. Anal-sadistic tendencies may be repressed and oral ones gratified. Asceticism, on the other hand, is concerned with the quantity of the instinct, and all instinctual impulses are regarded as dangerous. (2) In repression there is some form of substitute expression, such as a hysterical symptom, whereas asceticism can be altered only by a sudden switch to instinctual excesses. Generally, asceticism is a more primitive and less complex process.

[11] J. Lander, "The Pubertal Struggle against the Instincts," *Amer. J. Orthopsychiat.,* XII (1942), 456–461.
[12] Phyllis Greenacre, "The Prepuberty Trauma in Girls," *Psychoanal. Quart.,* XIX (1950), 298–317.
[13] Spiegel, *op. cit.*
[14] Freud, *op. cit.*

Intellectualization

A second mechanism in adolescence is intellectualization. The aim of asceticism is to keep the id within limits simply by imposing prohibitions. The aim of intellectualization is to link up instinctual processes closely with ideational contents in order to render them accessible to consciousness and amenable to control. This mechanism has its origin in the increased effectiveness of intellectual functioning. Interests change from the concrete ones of latency to abstractions (see Note 11). There are all sorts of abstract discussions on such topics as marriage, political philosophy, religion, professions, and so on. However, the superiority of intellectual performance at this time makes very little imprint on the adolescent's actual behavior. Despite his lofty views he remains preoccupied by his own mundane personality problems. The intellectualization is not reality oriented, but rather serves as a defense against instincts. Instead of an ascetic flight from instinct, there is a turning toward it, but only in thought. Anna Freud describes the situation as follows: [15]

> The abstract intellectual discussions and speculations in which young people delight are not genuine attempts at solving the tasks set by reality. Their mental activity is rather an indication of a tense alertness for the instinctual processes and the translation into abstract thought of that which they perceive. The philosophy of life which they construct—it may be their demand for revolution in the outside world—is really their response to the perception of the new instinctual demands of their own id, which threaten to revolutionize their whole lives. Their ideals of friendship and undying loyalty are simply a reflection of the disquietude of the ego when it perceived the evanescence of its new and passionate object-relations. The longing for guidance and support in the often hopeless battle against their own powerful instincts may be transformed into ingenious arguments about man's inability to arrive at independent political decisions. We see then that instinctual processes are translated into terms of intellect. But the reason why attention is thus focussed on the instincts is that an attempt is being made to lay hold of and master them on a different psychic level.

Creativity as a Defense

Spiegel [16] summarizes the writings of several psychoanalytic authors who interpret adolescent creativity as a defense against impulses aroused by the reenactment of the oedipal conflict. The most common form of creative endeavor at this time is the diary, which contains in addition to actual events all sorts of reflections, plans, and recollections. Poetry and other literary efforts have also been studied in this connection. Bernfeld states that the incestuous libidinal drives are deflected to other permissible objects, fantasies, values, and ideas, which he calls "also-objects." Creativity in this form is approved by the ego ideal. Rank points out that dramas written in

---

[15] *Ibid.*, pp. 177–178.
[16] Spiegel, *op. cit.*

adolescence concern themselves primarily with problems of incest. The frequent sudden cessation of creative activity toward the end of adolescence is accounted for by the inability to master the incest conflict.

The transformation of defensive into true creativity comes about when the adolescent sacrifices his private needs to the demands of communicability, thus finding his way back from fantasy to reality. The motive for renunciation of gratification derived from private daydreams, as recorded in diaries, is to be found in the ambitious strivings of the adolescent for fame and power gained from impressing a wide audience. The hero of these literary products represents the author's ego ideal, for whom he pleads in order to obtain sympathy, recognition, and love.

Rankian View: Hankins

Blanchard [17] describes Rankian theories of adolescence, as expounded in a paper by Hankins. According to the latter, the period of adolescence brings new developments in the child's continuing struggle for independence and sense of self. The sexual drives appear as generic forces within the individual which offer a threat to this recently increased self-assertiveness and self-differentiation. The adolescent fears and resists his sexual impulses because they might dominate him and force him to renounce his capacity to act as a total self. The reconciliation, provided by our culture, between sexual drives and individual self-expression is in a love relationship with another person. However, the adolescent is reluctant to enter such a relationship because he would have to give up total personal control and to accept partial control from the other person.

Hankins states that the normal outcome of adolescence is an acceptance of the fact that new experiences and relationships enrich the personality, despite some element of self-sacrifice. She criticizes Anna Freud's explanation of adolescent asceticism on the grounds that it serves mainly to promote individuality by denying sexuality or keeping it under strict control. Also sexual promiscuity is to be viewed, not as an uninhibited effort for instinctual gratification, but rather as an attempt to preserve the individual self. This kind of transitory relationship can be used to dominate the other person through his sexual needs, while at the same time refusing to yield any part of the self.

Neo-Freudian Views: Sullivan

In the preadolescent era, according to Sullivan, the capacity to love matures. Love exists only when the satisfactions and security of the loved one are as important as one's own satisfactions and security. Since boys feel more at ease with each other than with girls at this time, the capacity to love first

---

[17] Phyllis Blanchard, "Adolescent Experience in Relation to Personality and Behavior," *Personality and Behavior Disorders*, II, ed. J. McV. Hunt (New York: Ronald Press, 1944), 691–713.

involves a member of the same sex, the chum. When this happens, there is a great increase in the consensual validation of symbols. The preadolescent learns to see himself through the other's eyes, so that there is a consensual validation of one's own personal worth. In Sullivan's words: [18]

> In this period there begins the illumination of a real world community. As soon as one finds that all this vast artistic and somewhat validated structure to which one refers as one's mind, one's thoughts, one's personality, is really open to some comparing of notes, to some checking and counter-checking, one begins to feel human in a sense in which one has not previously felt human. One becomes more fully human in that one begins to appreciate the common humanity of people—there comes a new sympathy for the other fellow, whether he be present to the senses or mediated by rumors in the geography, or the like. In other words, the feeling of humanity is one of the aspects of the expansion of personality which comes in adolescence. Learning at this stage begins to assume its true aspect of implementing the person in securing satisfactions and maintaining his security in interpersonal relations through the rest of life.

Preadolescence, for most people in our culture, is the period closest to untroubled human life (see Note 12). From that time on life's problems reduce them to "inferior caricatures of what they might have been." Difficulties in adolescence center around the maturation of the "genital lust mechanism." Sex finally comes into its own, but conflicts concerning sex are a function of two cultural factors: (1) premarital sexual experience is frowned upon; and (2) early marriage is discouraged, so that the gap between the adolescent awakening of lust and the proper circumstances for marriage is progressively being widened.

Lust cannot be disassociated easily when the sexual impulses collide with the self-system. In most people it cannot be disassociated at all; in some it can, but only at grave risk to effective living. Generally, sexual feelings operate again and again to threaten security and produce anxiety. One method which may or may not work is sublimation, or as Sullivan phrases it, the sublimatory reformulation of interpersonal relations. He describes sublimation as follows: [19] "A motive which is involved in painful conflict is combined with a social (culturally provided) technique of life which disguises its most conflict-provoking aspect and usually provides some representation for the opposing motive in the conflict." An illustration is the young woman with fantasies of prostitution who devotes her time to philanthropic work with fallen women in the city slums. Mullahy [20] claims that Sullivan's use of the term "sublimation" is much broader than the orthodox, since it can refer to any tendency system or drive (see Note 13).

If adolescence can be successfully negotiated, the person emerges with self-respect adequate to almost any situation. Along with this self-respect

[18] H. S. Sullivan, *Conceptions of Modern Psychiatry* (Washington, D.C.: William Alanson White Psychiatric Foundation, 1947), pp. 20–21.
[19] *Ibid.*, p. 62.
[20] P. Mullahy, *Oedipus Myth and Complex* (New York: Hermitage, 1948).

goes respect for others and a freedom of personal initiative which allows him to adapt his personal characteristics to the social order.

SUMMARY

Anna Freud describes the prepuberty phase as one in which impulses once again break through, accompanied by aggression, pregenital symptoms, and oedipal fantasies. Deutsch, on the other hand, says that for girls this is the period of greatest freedom from infantile sexuality and aggression. At the onset of puberty, according to orthodox theory, libido becomes concentrated specifically on genital feelings, aims, and ideas, with an apparent improvement in behavior. Heterosexual outlets, however, are limited by society, so that conflicts around masturbation are common. The adolescent girl is said to become aware of the vagina as a source of pleasure while previously she had been interested solely in the clitoris and the desire to be boyish. At this time she faces the problem of accepting the feminine function and its passive role. Narcissism is high-lighted in both sexes during adolescence.

Conflict between the ego and the id is characteristic. Two possible extremes can result: if the id wins out there is a "riot of uninhibited gratification of instinct," and if the ego is victorious impulses are confined within narrow limits and there has to be constant expenditure of energy on counter-cathexes, defense mechanisms, and symptoms. The ego also alienates itself from the superego in this period, which further increases the danger from instincts and tends to make the individual asocial.

In the area of relationships to others, the adolescent has to fight off the oedipal fantasies stirred up again during prepuberty. He substitutes new attachments to replace parental ties. These love relations, whether to a person of his own age or a parental substitute, are passionate and exclusive but typically of short duration. Others are selected as objects and then abandoned without any consideration for their feelings. Fleeting love fixations of this sort, says Anna Freud, are highly narcissistic and really represent primitive forms of identifications. Following this wave of narcissism is a normal, temporary phase of homosexual relationships. In the case of the girl Deutsch states that there is a change in object choice from homosexual in prepuberty to bisexual in early puberty to heterosexual in later puberty. Significant elements in the feminine core are said to be narcissism, passivity, and masochism.

In prepuberty the ego has to call indiscriminately upon all the defense mechanisms at its command. During adolescence two frequent mechanisms are asceticism, the repudiation of all instinctual wishes, and intellectualization, the linking of instinctual processes to ideational contents. Adolescent creativity, such as the diary, is also interpreted as a form of defense.

The Rankian view of adolescence stresses the continuing struggle for independence and sense of self. The individual fears and resists his sexual impulses because they might dominate him and force him to renounce his capacity to act as a total self. Sullivan describes prepuberty as the most untroubled phase of human life, during which the capacity to love matures. Difficulties in adolescence occur in relation to the "genital lust mechanism." Sex becomes conflict-laden because premarital sexual experience is frowned upon and early marriage is discouraged. If adolescence can be successfully negotiated through the use of sublimation, Sullivan adds, then the person emerges with self-respect adequate to almost any situation.

NOTES

1. Energy Complications Once More

Anna Freud's reference to the increased quantity of instinctual energy in prepuberty seems to be at variance with the orthodox notion of a closed system containing a fixed amount of energy. Perhaps she intends to convey an increase in the amount of energy actively mobilized at this time. In any case, the psychic energy concept, with all its attendant confusions and limitations, stands as something less than a cure-all for what ails personality theory.

2. The Problem of Individual and Class Differences

A difficulty inherent in many psychoanalytic formulations is the unknown extent to which they apply to the population at large. A prime example here is Anna Freud's description of the unruly, boorish behavior of the preadolescent. The issue of how many preadolescents conform to this picture is not treated, so the reader is left with the impression that such characteristics are at least typical. Doubtless there are wide individual differences. The crucial effects, in this connection, of social class membership have been sharply delineated by sociologists. Allison Davis,[21] for example, describes adolescent aggression as an approved, socially rewarded form of behavior in the lower classes. Until adequate normative evidence becomes available, judgments concerning frequency should probably be reserved.

3. Onset of Physical Changes in Adolescence

Kinsey et al.[22] state that the onset of adolescent physical changes in boys is more or less abrupt, usually occurring between eleven and fourteen years of age. In girls adolescent development is said to be more gradual, spread over a longer period of time, and does not reach its peak until a good many years after boys are sexually mature. Stolz and Stolz [23] describe three phases

[21] A. Davis, "Socialization and Adolescent Personality," *Readings in Social Psychology,* ed., T. M. Newcomb and E. L. Hartley (New York: Henry Holt and Co., 1947), pp. 139–150.

[22] A. C. Kinsey, W. B. Pomeroy and C. E. Martin, *Sexual Behavior in the Human Male* (Philadelphia: Saunders, 1948).

[23] H. R. Stolz and L. M. Stolz, "Adolescent Problems Related to Somatic Variations," *Yearb. Nat. Soc. Stud. Educ.,* XLIII (1944), 80–99

of adolescent growth: prepubertal, pubertal, and postpubertal. The first phase takes place sometime before age thirteen in boys and before eleven in girls. Its duration for boys is approximately a year and a quarter and for girls slightly shorter. The pubertal phase, which contains the most noticeable growth spurt, occurs between thirteen and fifteen for males and between eleven and fourteen for females. The third phase in the girl lasts for a year and a half and is somewhat shorter in the case of the boy. The legal definition of puberty, according to Webster's Dictionary, is usually given as fourteen for boys and twelve for girls.

4. Sexual Activities

Surveys of the sexual habits of adolescents confirm the widespread use of masturbatory and homosexual outlets. Kinsey *et al.*[24] report the incidence of masturbation in boys by age fifteen to be 82 per cent. For the period of preadolescence 60 per cent of the boys recalled some homosexual activity, with the average initial contact occurring at 9.2 years, in comparison with 40 per cent who recalled heterosexual activity, beginning typically at 8.8 years. Between the ages of twelve and fifteen the reported frequency of homosexual play ranged from 20 to 29 per cent, of heterosexual play from 16 to 23 per cent. Willoughby's [25] survey of the literature in 1937 revealed adolescent masturbation to be more characteristic for boys than for girls. Concerning homosexuality he inferred that many individuals were so inclined, but for the most part their homosexual activity was a function of restricted heterosexual companionship. In a study of normal and psychotic women Landis and his coworkers [26] noted that masturbation and emotional attachments to other women were frequent in adolescence.

The forms of expression of sexuality are, of course, culturally determined. Malinowski [27] and Mead [28] have described primitive cultures in which adolescents have much more sexual freedom than in our own. In the latter connection Mead stresses the inconsistency of American customs with respect to heterosexual activity. "Dating" now begins as early as the prepubertal period and follows the rules of the game, especially in the middle classes, according to social rather than sexual motives. Later, when sexual urges become dominant, their permitted expression in adolescence is distorted in such a way as to hinder future sexual adjustment in marriage. Cattell [29] points out the differences between Western culture, in which the lack of structure and signposts confuse the adolescent in his new role, and the comfortingly clear expectations and initiation rites among the Arunta, Andamanese, and Kwoma.

[24] Kinsey, Pomeroy and Martin, *op. cit.*
[25] R. R. Willoughby, "Sexuality in the Second Decade," *Monogr. Soc. Res. Child Develpm.*, II, No. 10 (1937).
[26] C. Landis *et al.*, *Sex in Development* (New York: Hoeber, 1940).
[27] B. Malinowski, *Sex and Repression in Savage Society* (New York: Harcourt, Brace, 1927).
[28] Margaret Mead, *Male and Female* (New York: Wm. Morrow and Co., 1949).
[29] R. B. Cattell, *Personality* (New York: McGraw-Hill Book Co., 1950).

5. Adolescent Fantasy

Symonds [30] administered 42 pictures, similar in type to those in the Thematic Apperception Test series, to 20 normal adolescent boys and 20 girls. They were asked to make up stories about each one as a "test of creative imagination." The resulting 1,680 stories revealed, among others, a frequently occurring theme of "Oedipus longing and conflict." In addition, almost everyone in the group gave at least three stories revolving about aggression and love. Other characteristic themes concerned depression, anxiety, ambition, guilt, independence, injury, popularity, appearance, and dominance. While this study cannot itself be considered definitive, on the basis of the limited sample of subjects and the absence of comparative data for other age groups, it offers a fruitful method for further explorations of fantasy.

6. The First Menstruation

Mead [31] emphasizes the significance in primitive cultures of the first menstruation (menarche) as a sharp dividing line between childhood and womanhood. She goes on to describe in detail the variety of customs which have arisen. The puritanical Manus women have an important, festive ceremony for the adolescent girl at menarche, but all later menstruations are concealed with great secrecy. Among the Arapesh, the girl's first menstruation, which takes place several years after she has been betrothed, is also an occasion for ceremony. Her brothers come and build her a menstrual hut, placing it beyond the edge of the village to keep the village safe from the dangerous supernatural strength attached to menstruating women. In contrast the peoples of Iatmul, Tchambuli, Mundugumor, and Samo place little or no social stress on menarche.

Apart from anthropological sources, there are two well-controlled studies by Stone and Barker,[32] who compared the interests and attitudes of pre- and post-menarcheal girls. The latter group showed greater heterosexual interests and activities, regardless of chronological age; indulged in daydreaming more frequently; avoided vigorous physical exercise; and showed more concern over their physical appearance. A similar investigation in boys was conducted by Sollenberger,[33] who separated more and less mature boys on the basis of amount of male sex hormone content in their urine. The sexually mature group proved to be more interested in heterosexual activities, strenuous competitive sports, and personal appearance.

---

[30] P. M. Symonds, *Adolescent Fantasy* (New York: Columbia University Press, 1949).

[31] Mead, *op. cit.*

[32] C. P. Stone and R. G. Barker, "Aspects of Personality and Intelligence in Post-menarcheal and Pre-menarcheal Girls of the Same Chronological Ages," *J. Comp. Psychol.*, XXIII (1937), 439–455; C. P. Stone and R. G. Barker, "The Attitudes and Interests of Pre-menarcheal Girls and Post-menarcheal Girls," *J. Genet Psychol.*, LIV (1939), 27–71.

[33] R. T. Sollenberger, "Some Relationships Between the Urinary Excretion of Male Hormone by Maturing Boys and Their Expressed Interests and Attitudes," *J. Psychol.*, IX (1940), 179–190.

7. Factors Determining Outcome of the Adolescent Struggle

A fourth factor affecting adolescent development, in addition to impulse strength, ego tolerance, and efficacy of defenses, is omitted by Anna Freud. This relates to the degree and type of stress provided by the environment. Presumably two equally equipped adolescents, from the point of view of the three listed attributes, will react differently if one becomes subjected to a malevolent social climate and the other does not.

8. Explanations of Asocial Behavior

An alternative way of looking at asocial behavior, other than the ego-superego split, is in terms of the adolescent's marginal position. Being no longer a child and not yet a man, he is placed in a very tenuous situation by society. One conceivable reaction to this anomalous role is social withdrawal.

9. Adolescent Revolt against Parents

Dollard *et al.*[34] interpret the adolescent's commonly observed rebelliousness, directed against his parents and authority figures in general, as a response to frustration. The source of the frustration lies in the situation described in Note 8. However, according to this group of authors, aggressive reactions are most typical of early adolescence, since substitute satisfactions tend to be worked out gradually by trial and error. Placing the focus of aggression in early adolescence is in disagreement with Tryon's[35] observation that the period of greatest resistance to adults is middle adolescence, when growth is most accelerated. Thus our knowledge of adolescent relationships, if we can generalize from this particular form, seems to be deficient in the facts of actual behavior, to say nothing of underlying reasons.

A few isolated studies have been done in this area, but even the surface has hardly been scratched. Kitay[36] found that the majority of children between eleven and fourteen, responding to a questionnaire, felt that their parents understood them, whereas from age fifteen on there was a much greater feeling of being misunderstood. Stott,[37] averaging ratings on several personality tests, noted poorer adjustment in those adolescents who criticized their parents most. Another suggestion of the connection between disturbance and rebelliousness comes from Watson's study, reported by Cattell,[38] in which those individuals with radical antiauthority views turned out to have been punished more frequently and more severely by their parents.

[34] J. Dollard, L. W. Dobb, N. E. Miller and R. R. Sears, *Frustration and Aggression* (New Haven, Yale University Press, 1939).

[35] Caroline M. Tryon, "The Adolescent Peer Culture," *Yearb. Nat. Soc. Stud. Educ.*, XLIII (1944), 217–239.

[36] P. M. Kitay, "A Comparison of the Sexes in Their Attitude and Beliefs about Women: A Study of Prestige Groups," *Sociometry*, III (1940), 399–407.

[37] L. H. Stott, "Adolescents' Dislikes Regarding Parental Behavior and Their Significance," *J. Genet. Psychol.*, LVII (1940), 393–414.

[38] Cattell, *op. cit.*

10. Homosexual Behavior

See Note 4 for a summary of existing data on homosexuality during adolescence.

11. Interests and Attitudes

This general area is one which has received considerable attention from investigators, though not specifically on the concrete-abstract dimension stressed by Anna Freud. Beginning with the preadolescent period, we have available a foreign study by Zillig [39] (summarized by Cattell [40]), who used recorded spontaneous conversations of a large number of boys and girls ranging from 9 to 12 years of age. The group manifested a boastful and fantastic tone, wishful thinking, and a lack of modesty and ethics. Boys talked mainly about physical strength and daring exploits, whereas girls were concerned with appearance, possessions, and social prominence. In connection with this research, it is interesting to note the congruence with Anna Freud's description of preadolescent behavior, which was based largely on observations of children in Austria. The need for more extensive cross-cultural checks again makes itself felt at this point.

The early adolescent, as portrayed by Tryon,[41] Zeligs,[42] Jones,[43] James and Moore,[44] and others, indulges in like-sex clubs or gang activities. These cliques, formed slightly earlier in the case of girls, emphasize in-group secrets, slang, loyalties, and by and large, tend to suppress individuality. Twelve-year-old boys behave in an active, aggressive, competitive, boisterous manner, whereas girls of the same age are generally neat, docile and prim, though some tomboyishness is acceptable. Interests in boys emphasize political and social questions, personal development, and possessions and pleasures; in girls family welfare. With respect to superego functioning, Buck [45] notes that 12- and 13-year-olds consider about 50 per cent more activities to be morally wrong than do 20-year-olds.

The period of middle adolescence, according to Tryon,[46] features the striving for social conformity. Boys of fifteen become less boisterous and more interested in social poise. Early maturing girls at this age stress sophistication; others attach importance to being "good fellows." Parties are es-

---

[39] M. Zilig, "Prollereien unter Schulkindern," *Z. pädag. Psychol.*, XXXIX (1938), 241–250, 263–270.

[40] Cattell, *op. cit.*

[41] Tryon, *op. cit.*

[42] R. Zeligs, "Social Factors Annoying to Children," *J. Appl. Psychol.*, XXIX (1945), 75–82.

[43] H. E. Jones, *Development in Adolescence* (New York: Appleton-Century-Crofts, 1943).

[44] H. E. O. James and F. F. Moore, "Adolescent Leisure in a Working-Class District," *Occup. Psychol.*, XIV (1940), 132–145.

[45] W. Buck, "A Measurement of Changes of Attitudes and Interests of University Students over a Ten-Year Period," *J. Abnorm. Soc. Psychol.*, XXXI (1936), 12–19.

[46] Tryon, *op. cit.*

pecially attractive. Using the Strong Vocational Interest Blank, Taylor [47] found relatively greater stability of interests during the later rather than the earlier years of mid-adolescence. Subsequently, around the ages of 17 and 18, Tryon reports boys to be concerned with social maturity, athletics, and leadership, whereas girls are absorbed with feminine ideals and security. James and Moore,[48] analyzing leisure activities by keeping diaries, noted increasingly heterosexual and social interests at these ages. Symonds [49] characterizes the older adolescent boy as intrigued primarily by an urge toward success, and the girl as being more passive, receptive, and interested in people.

12. Conflicting Views on Preadolescence

Sullivan's description of preadolescence as the period closest to untroubled human life is in sharp contrast to Anna Freud's. The latter, as we have seen, stresses unruliness, brutality, exhibitionism, and pregenital breakthroughs. Deutsch's portrayal of the preadolescent girl as showing the greatest freedom from infantile sexuality and aggression corresponds to Sullivan's, whereas Spiegel's reinterpretation of Deutsch's data follows Anna Freud. These discrepancies point to the necessity for systematic, reliable observations of behavior.

13. The "Sublimatory Reformulation of Interpersonal Relations."

The merit, if any, in Sullivan's attempt to redefine sublimation obviously requires greater substantiation than Mullahy provides. Broader coverage alone is frequently not a virtue.

---

[47] K. Van F. Taylor, "The Reliability and Permanence of Vocational Interests of Adolescents," *J. Exp. Educ.*, XI (1942), 81–87.

[48] James and Moore, *op. cit.*

[49] P. M. Symonds, "Changes in Sex Differences in Problems and Interests of Adolescence with Increasing Age," *J. Genet. Psychol.*, L (1937), 83–89.

Alfred B. Heilbrun, Jr.

An Empirical Test of the
Modeling Theory of Sex-Role Learning

Simple analyses of socialization processes are complicated by the fact that in some instances several hypotheses may be advanced to account for the same behavior. For example, everybody agrees that children and adolescents acquire the characteristic behavior patterns of adult models, but how does this identification occur? Definitive conclusions are not yet on the horizon, but considerable insight is presently at hand. In this article, Heilbrun contrasts "role-modeling" and "reciprocal-role" interpretations of sex-role identification, and in a thorough discussion of the problems, shows that both hypotheses provide a useful framework for understanding the development of the masculine and feminine sex-roles. In brief, he finds that sex-role distinctions between males and females are maximal given an identification with a highly masculine father. The data strongly support the general contention that fathers are more capable than mothers of differentiating their sex role and of systematically varying it as they relate to their children. It is noteworthy that the findings corroborate earlier studies in showing that for boys, stronger father identification is associated with better adjustment and more masculine sex-role behavior, whereas for girls, strong mother identification is less clearly associated with adjustment and feminine sex-role behavior.

JOHNSON [1] has recently proposed that the crucial factor in learning the masculine sex role for males *and* the feminine sex role for females is identification with the father. She bases her reasoning upon certain basic premises adopted from Parsons' role theory.[2] First, Parsons considers identification as encompassing the behaviors a child learns in the context of a social role with a parent (i.e., the internalization of a reciprocal-role relationship). Accordingly, the learned behaviors need not be those which are typical of the adult

FROM *Child Development,* XXXVI (1965), 789–799. Reprinted by permission of the author and the Society for Research in Child Development.

[1] M. M. Johnson, "Instrumental and Expressive Components in the Personalities of Women," (Unpublished Ph.D. dissertation, Radcliffe, 1955).

[2] T. Parsons, "Social Structure and the Development of Personality: Freud's Contribution to the Integration of Psychology and Sociology," *Psychiatry,* XXI (1958), 321–340; T. Parsons and R. F. Bales, *Family, Socialization and Interaction Process* (Glencoe, Ill.: The Free Press, 1955).

but rather are those which are systematically elicited and reinforced in the course of the child's interaction with the adult. The child is presumed to make a series of successive identifications, both boys and girls making an initial identification with the mother which is not sex typed. The following identification with the father, in which he forms differentiated role relationships with the son and the daughter, provides the basis for sex-role learning in offspring of both sexes.

Second, Parsons regards the essence of masculinity and femininity to be a difference in instrumental and expressive orientation. The feminine-expressive role is distinguished by an orientation of giving rewarding responses in order to receive rewarding responses. Johnson states: "The expressive role player is oriented toward the relationships among the actors within a system. He is primarily oriented to the attitudes and feelings of those actors toward himself and toward each other. . . . By being solicitous, appealing, and 'understanding,' a woman seeks to get a pleasurable response by giving pleasure." [3] The instrumental (masculine) role, in contrast, is defined as a behavioral orientation toward goals which transcend the immediate interactional situation. Since the interaction is viewed primarily as a means to an end, the instrumental-role player cannot be primarily oriented to the immediate emotional responses of others to him. Rather than soliciting positive responses from others like the expressive person, instrumental-role-playing requires an ability to tolerate the hostility which it will very likely elicit.

It is further proposed that the father (but not the mother) is capable of engaging in both instrumental and expressive roles. This follows from the assumption that the early relationship of both boys and girls with their mothers mediates learning of expressive behavior and that later boys, but not girls, learn a new orientation, instrumentalness, so they can deal effectively with the non-familial environment. Thus, boys retain the capacity to respond in either an expressive or instrumental manner, whereas girls can behave only expressively. Ten studies are cited by Johnson [4] that support the conclusion that fathers differentiate their own sex-role behavior toward male and female offspring more than mothers do.

Johnson summarized her hypothesis as follows: "The mother is predominantly expressive toward children of both sexes and uses, intentionally or not, "love-oriented" techniques of control on both. It is in this first identification of both male and female children with the mother in a love-dependency relationship that the basic superego is laid down. Sex-role differentiation then follows the initial mother identification and results from the identification of both sexes with the father in differentiated role relationships. The father adds the specifically feminine element to the female's initial expressiveness by rewarding her, by his appreciative attitude, not simply for being 'good' but for being 'attractive.' With his son as with his daughter

---

[3] M. M. Johnson, "Sex Role Learning in the Nuclear Family," *Child Development,* XXXIV (1963), 320–321.
[4] *Ibid.,* pp. 323–327.

the father is solidary, but with his son he is also demanding, thus giving the extra push that instrumentalness requires." [5]

Although Johnson presents a cogent argument for a reciprocal-role interpretation of sex-role learning, there is no reason, in principle, why a single mode of transmitting sex-role attributes from parents to children must be posited. For example, modeling theory [6] would predict that sex-typed behaviors that are observed in the repertoires of the parents and are modeled after by children represent an important basis for appropriate sex-typing. The major question pursued in the present investigation was whether modeling principles would also prove useful in predicting the sex-role behavior of children granting that fathers are more capable of sex-role differentiation than mothers and that the instrumental-expressive distinction represents a useful basis for defining the masculine and feminine sex roles. The present study did not compare the relative usefulness of the reciprocal-role and the modeling hypotheses, however, since no evidence relevant to the former was collected.

Even though the father typically assumes the instrumental role within the nuclear family, it must be assumed that individual differences in masculinity occur, since many fathers have not learned instrumentalness in the course of their own social development. On the other hand, a very high proportion of fathers have at least been exposed to the conditions under which expressive qualities are presumably learned (early mother-child interaction). The observation that there are at least two classes of fathers—those who are primarily instrumental but retain the capacity for expressive behavior (i.e., can differentiate their roles) and a smaller proportion who are primarily expressive but lack the capacity for instrumental behavior (i.e., are less capable of differentiating their roles)—seems accurate. A similar case can be made for mothers; although most mothers may be regarded as expressive in orientation, some, at least, will have learned instrumental behaviors in their social development. When these four classes of parent-model types are employed, the following prediction would follow from a modeling hypothesis of sex-role learning:

> The greatest sex-role disparity between males and females, commonly identified with a single parent type, will be mediated by identification with (modeling after) the instrumental father. This parent, more than any other single type, is capable of providing an instrumental model for his son and an expressive model for his daughter.

Two logical assumptions implicit in this prediction should be emphasized. First, it is reasonable to maintain that a father's behavior is of a generally instrumental character even though he may behave expressively under special conditions, one such condition being interaction with a female child. Second, the parental behavior that is most likely to be modeled after by a

---

[5] *Ibid.*, p. 324.

[6] R. R. Sears, E. E. Maccoby, and H. Levin, *Patterns of Child Rearing* (New York: Row, Peterson, 1957), pp. 368–376.

child is the behavior that occurs in the context of the parent's interaction with him.

The first of these assumptions allows for the possibility that a girl whose father is legitimately classified as masculine based upon the preponderance of his behavior may still be directly exposed to an expressive model in his dealings with her. This avoids the seeming paradox of a finding that modeling after a masculine parent mediates feminine qualities in a girl. The second assumption is equally crucial to interpretation of father-daughter results. If the masculine father engages in expressive behaviors only in the exceptional circumstance of father-daughter interaction, it must be assumed that the father's behavior at these times has a greater potency to elicit modeling from the daughter than do the more frequently emitted instrumental behaviors that the daughter observes as a bystander and in direct dealings with the father. Since many of the father's expressive behaviors which occur in interaction with the daughter can be described as nurturant in character, the findings of Bandura and Huston [7] strengthen the second assumption. They found that children imitate the behavior of more nurturant adult models more readily than they imitate that of their less nurturant counterparts. Thus, the instrumental father should be especially effective as a model when he directly interacts with the daughter.

METHOD

Subjects

A total of 279 undergraduates at the State University of Iowa, 139 males and 140 females, were employed in this study. These groups were further divided by the particular parent with whom they made their primary identification and the relative instrumental-expressive orientation of that parent. The resultant group sizes were: males identified with instrumental fathers ($N = 47$), with instrumental mothers ($N = 27$), with expressive fathers ($N = 20$), with expressive mothers ($N = 45$); females identified with instrumental fathers ($N = 42$), with instrumental mothers ($N = 31$), with expressive fathers ($N = 21$), with expressive mothers ($N = 46$).

Measures of Developmental Variables

The parental object of identification was indicated by a scale that reflects the relative similarity between the child and his two parents as perceived by the child. Norms for the identification scale have been developed for college students so that a score of $T = 50$ indicates the average similarity between the son or daughter and the same-sex parent along 15 personality dimensions (e.g., nurturance, dominance, aggression). A score of $T > 50$ was used to define identification with the same-sex parent, whereas $T \leq 50$ indicated a cross-sex identification. A detailed description and validity evidence pertaining to this scale are available elsewhere.[8]

[7] A. Bandura and A. C. Huston, "Identification as a Process of Incidental Learning," *J. Abnorm. Soc. Psychol.*, LXIII (1961), 311–318.

[8] A. B. Heilbrun, "The Measurement of Identification," *Child Development* (1965).

Instrumental-expressive orientation of the parents was estimated from behavioral descriptions rated by the subjects and used as part of the identification measure. Each was asked to judge whether certain types of behaviors were descriptive more of his mother or of his father. Nine of the 15 behaviors so rated had been found to be sex-typed based upon the ratings of 400 college students.[9] In this earlier study fathers were rated as more need-achieving, autonomous, and dominant and as showing greater endurance; whereas mothers were judged to be more deferent, affiliative, succorant, abasing, and nurturant. The instrumental character of the "father" traits and the expressive nature of the "mother" traits are clearly evident. In the present study the appropriateness of the parents' sex roles was determined by counting the number of times the appropriate parent was rated as better described by the prescribed instrumental or expressive behavior. A score of 6 or greater was selected as a cutting point for defining instrumental fathers and expressive mothers; 5 or less defined the sex-role reversed expressive fathers and instrumental mothers. These particular cutting scores resulted in classifying about 66 per cent of the male Ss' parents and about 63 per cent of the female Ss' parents as appropriately instrumental or expressive in orientation.[10]

The Personality Measure

The Adjective Check List (ACL) [11] was used as the personality test in this study. Included in the ACL are 300 behavioral adjectives from which the person is asked to select those which are most self-characteristic. There are a large number of studies [12] that demonstrate that ACL self-descriptions obtained from normally functioning persons afford valid predictions of their actual social behaviors.

RESULTS

The ACL self-descriptions of the four sets of male and female comparison groups were analyzed by chi square procedures. Differential endorsement of any ACL adjective as self-descriptive was defined as $p < .05$. The 1,200 x^2 values were obtained by computer analysis which included Yates' correction for continuity.

Although the x^2 analysis provided a basis for establishing patterns of behavior differences between sex groups, evaluation of whether these patterns

[9] A. B. Heilbrun, "Perceived Maternal Attitudes, Masculinity-Femininity of the Maternal Model, and Identification as Related to Incipient Psychopathology in Adolescent Girls," *J. Genet. Psychol.* (in press).

[10] We recognize that the measurement of instrumental or expressive character of parental behaviors employed here represents but one of many possible approaches and involves the same risks as any personal evaluation by a single, ego-involved judge. The congruence between ratings obtained in this fashion and expectancies based upon Parsons' theory, however, makes us confident that their use is justified.

[11] H. G. Gough and A. B. Heilbrun, *Joint Manual for the Adjective Check List and the Need Scales for the ACL* (Palo Alto, Calif.: Consulting Psychologists Press, 1965).

[12] *Ibid.*

reflect instrumental versus expressive orientation differences was still necessary. This was accomplished by using the judgments of four clinical psychologists at the University of California as the basis for defining ACL adjectives as instrumental (I) or expressive (E) in character. All discriminating ACL adjectives were rated as I, E, or indeterminate based upon definitions provided by Johnson.[13] Interjudge agreement was high when only I and E ratings of the four judges are considered; some 93 per cent of these ratings were in accord. Final acceptance of an adjective as I or E required the agreement of at least two judges with no contrary (E or I) judgment ($N = 13$), the agreement of three judges as to I or E ($N = 15$), or the agreement of four judges ($N = 16$).

Table 1   Instrumental and Expressive Behavior Differences between Males and Females who Identified with Sex-Role Appropriate Parents

Instrumental Fathers		Expressive Mothers	
MALES MORE:	FEMALES MORE:	MALES MORE:	FEMALES MORE:
Aggressive [a]	Appreciative [b]	Aggressive [a]	Adaptable
Cruel [a]	Artistic [b]	Conservative	Attractive [b]
Enterprising [a]	Curious	Enterprising [a]	Contented [b]
Forceful [a]	Effeminate	Handsome	Fearful [b]
Foresighted [a]	Emotional [b]	Inventive [a]	Feminine
Frank [a]	Excitable [b]	Masculine	Flirtatious
Handsome	Fearful [b]	Quiet	Frivolous
Hardheaded [a]	Fickle	Shrewd [a]	Mannerly
Logical [a]	Reliable [a]	Strong [a]	Outgoing [b]
Masculine	Self-pitying [b]	Tough [a]	Pleasant [b]
Opportunistic [a]	Sentimental [b]		Poised
Progressive [a]	Sincere [b]		Praising [b]
Reckless [a]	Sympathetic [b]		Selfish
Sharp-witted [a]	Warm [b]		Sympathetic [b]
Shrewd [a]	Wholesome [b]		Talkative
Stern [a]			Unaffected [a]
Strong [a]			Understanding [b]
Tough [a]			Wholesome [b]
Unscrupulous [a]			
Vindictive [a]			

[a] Behaviors judged to be instrumental.
[b] Behaviors judged to be expressive.

The test of the prediction that the clearest instrumental vs. expressive sex-role distinctions would be evidenced by males and females identified with instrumental fathers was based upon data presented in Tables 1 and 2. These four patterns of behavior differences provide rather striking support for the prediction. Comparison of male and female offspring who identified with instrumental fathers provided 35 differences in behavior, 29 of which

[13] Johnson, *op. cit.*, 1963.

Table 2   Instrumental and Expressive Behavior Differences between Males and Females Identified with Sex-Role Inappropriate Parents

Expressive Fathers		Instrumental Mothers	
IDENTIFIED MALES MORE:	IDENTIFIED FEMALES MORE:	IDENTIFIED MALES MORE:	IDENTIFIED FEMALES MORE:
Aggressive [a]	Awkward	Calm	Feminine
Anxious	Confused	Insightful	Mischievous
Deliberate [a]	Feminine	Masculine	
Faultfinding [a]	Outgoing [b]	Mild	
Handsome	Selfish	Opportunistic [a]	
Masculine	Sympathetic [b]	Original	
Opportunistic [a]	Unaffected [a]	Peculiar	
Self-denying [b]		Relaxed [b]	
Self-punishing		Resourceful [a]	
		Robust [a]	
		Sharp-witted [a]	
		Shrewd [a]	
		Silent	
		Steady [a]	
		Tough [a]	

[a] Behaviors judged to be instrumental.
[b] Behaviors judged to be expressive.

were judged to be appropriately instrumental or expressive. This proportion for the remaining three conditions were: expressive-mother identified, 15 of 28; instrumental-mother identified, 7 of 17; and expressive-father identified, 6 of 16. Chi square comparison of these proportions (not considering "masculine," "feminine," and "effeminate") [14] showed them to be significantly different ($x^2 = 13.34$ for 3 df; $p < .01$).

One inferential limitation of a x^2 statistical analysis such as that reported above is that finding male and female offspring who describe themselves as more similar to instrumental fathers are most distinct in their instrumental and expressive role behaviors could be the result of comparing extremely masculine males with females who are not particularly feminine. That is, the distinct instrumental-expressive patterns could be accounted for by extreme instrumentality in the males without assuming expressive qualities in the females. One additional set of comparisons would allow greater clarity here. The ACL indorsement patterns of girls identified with instrumental fathers could be compared with those obtained from girls identified with expressive mothers; boys identified with these two types of models could similarly be compared. The extent and quality of difference patterns which emerged would tell us something of the deviance of instrumental-father identified females from what is presumably the most expressive group of girls and the deviance of expressive-mother identified boys from their

[14] The adjectives "masculine," "feminine," and "effeminate" were not rated because of their similarity in meaning to "instrumental" and "expressive."

highly instrumental counterparts, males identified with instrumental fathers. These comparisons (Table 3) indicate that relatively few differences appear between the two female groups. Those differences which were found suggest that instrumental-father identified females do not assume blatant instrumental qualities relative to very expressive females but rather maintain

Table 3 Behavior Differences between Instrumental-Father and Expressive-Mother Identified Males and Females

MALES		FEMALES	
INSTRUMENTAL-FATHER IDENTIFIED MORE: *	EXPRESSIVE-MOTHER IDENTIFIED MORE	INSTRUMENTAL-FATHER IDENTIFIED MORE:	EXPRESSIVE-MOTHER IDENTIFIED MORE
Adaptive	Appreciative	Self-confident	Considerate
Assertive	Cautious		Fearful
Capable	Conservative		Gentle
Confident	Dependent		Obliging
Dominant	Excitable		Silent
Egotistical	Meek		Submissive
Forceful	Peaceable		Trusting
Frank	Quiet		
Hard-headed	Shy		
Opinionated	Slipshod		
Outgoing	Timid		
Outspoken			
Self-confident			
Self-seeking			

* All adjectives on this table discriminated at the $p < 0.05$ level.

an expressive orientation which lacks the passive character of extreme expressiveness. The male pattern indicates that more extensive personality differences appear as a function of the attributes of the primary parent model than is the case for females. The differentiating behaviors suggest both the strong instrumental qualities of a masculine-father identification and the passive-dependent expressiveness of a feminine-mother identification. Summarily, this additional analysis suggests that the distinct instrumental-expressive behavior differences found when instrumental-father identified males and females were compared can be attributed to the presence of both instrumental qualities in the sons and expressive (but not passive) qualities in the daughters.

DISCUSSION

Males and females who are identified in a modeling (similarity) sense with instrumental fathers show the most extensive and appropriate sex-role differences in personality. Sex-role differences for males and females identified with expressive mothers are somewhat less extensive and appropriate, while male and female differences under the condition of identification with a sex-role reversed instrumental mother or expressive father were restricted and even less appropriate to sex role. These empirical findings suggest that identification with (role-modeling after) the instrumental father is associated with enhanced masculinity in the son and femininity in the daughter, the same relationships predicted by Johnson [15] from Parsons' reciprocal-role hypothesis.

Since the same sex-role outcomes are predictable from two apparently different hypotheses of sex-role "identification," one is led to wonder whether the differences are not semantic. The importance of reciprocal-role practice to the strengthening of sex-role behavior can be granted without abandoning modeling principles of identification-learning. Even though the expressive behaviors of the mother as a model may provide the initial opportunity and instigation for the girl to learn components of the expressive role, the amount of reinforced practice of these behaviors offered by the father or any other person should strengthen the expressive orientation of the girl. If the term "identification" were used to encompass any learning experience that contributed toward the sex-role adoption of the child, such sex-role practice would be legitimately included. However, to broaden the definition of identification to this extent would require inclusion of such divergent experiences as athletic activities and military service for males and dating behaviors and marriage for both sexes. It seems more useful to accept a more restricted conception of parental identification (i.e., as role-modeling behavior) but to consider it as but one contributor to the adult sex-role identity of the person.

It was noted earlier that fathers are presumed by Parsons to be more capable than are mothers of differentiating their sex role. That is, fathers are more capable of responding expressively than mothers are of acting instrumentally. It was also assumed that fathers systematically vary their sex role as they relate to male and female offspring. These suppositions bear considerable explanatory weight in interpreting the present results within the scope of a modeling theory, since the data suggest that employing the generally instrumental father as a model for identification mediates expressive behaviors in the daughter. Data collected from University of Iowa students for a previous study [16] and some currently unpublished data obtained from males at the University of California allow some further light to be shed on these assumptions. Ratings of the degree of parental nurturance provided by instrumental and by expressive fathers were obtained from college males and females, and those data (Table 4) corroborate the proposed tendency of fathers to relate in an equally expressive manner toward daughters whether the father was regarded as more expressive or more instrumental in his general sex-role orientation. Thus, an instrumental father as a model

[15] Johnson, *op. cit.*
[16] A. B. Heilbrun, "Parent Model Attributes, Nurturant Reinforcement, and Consistency of Behavior in Adolescents," *Child Development,* XXXV (1964), 151–167.

Table 4   Perceived Nurturance of Instrumental and Expressive Fathers

| SEX OF CHILD | Instrumental Fathers[a] | | | Expressive Fathers[b] | | | |
	n	MEAN NURTURANCE	SD	n	MEAN NURTURANCE	SD	t
Male:							
Iowa	38	25.2	5.8	18	28.4	5.2	2.00*
California	46	25.1	6.5	18	28.4	6.7	1.79*
Female:							
Iowa	38	30.7	5.3	22	30.4	7.3	—

[a] Rating on Parental Description Survey 6 or more.
[b] Rating on Parental Description Survey 5 or less.
* $p < .05$ (one-tailed test).

does seem to provide expressive qualities for the daughter to emulate. The relationship of fathers to sons, as rated by the sons in both samples, demonstrates the expected difference between instrumental and expressive fathers. Instrumental fathers are, as a group, significantly less nurturant than are expressive fathers.

Since the present study provided identification and sex-role learning results which were interpreted as consonant with a modeling theory, a final point of discussion is called for. How can the trend of parental identification research findings [17] be accounted for within a modeling framework? Specifically, the trend suggests that father-son identification relationships are clearly established, with stronger father identification being associated with better adjustment and more masculine sex-role behavior of the son. In contrast, the female results are almost without exception more equivocal than those for males,[18] usually reported as "not significant but . . ."! Heilbrun has also reported a similar set of findings; [19] maladjusted males were significantly less identified with their fathers than were their adjusted counterparts, but two samples of maladjusted girls demonstrated less clear tendencies to be more identified with their mothers than did adjusted girls. The equivocal findings for females suggest that *additional* variables (perhaps of an interactive nature) must be considered before the relationships among the identification, sex-role, and adjustment variables for females will come into

[17] Johnson, op. cit., pp. 324–331.
[18] A. L. Sopchak, "Parental 'Identification' and 'Tendency toward Disorders' as measured by the MMPI," *J. Abnorm. Soc. Psychol.*, XLVII (1952), 159–165; M. M. Helper, "Learning Theory and the Self Concept," *J. Abnorm. Soc. Psychol.*, LI (1955), 184–194; Johnson, op. cit.; C. Osgood, G. Suci, and P. H. Tannenbaum, *The Measurement of Meaning* (Urbana: University of Illinois Press, 1957); W. Emmerich, "Parental Identification in Young Children," *Genet. Psychol. Monogr.*, LX (1959), 257–308; S. W. Gray, "Perceived Similarity to Parents and Adjustment," *Child Development*, XXX (1959), 91–107; P. Mussen and L. Distler, "Masculinity, Identification, and Father-Son Relationships," *J. Abnorm. Soc. Psychol.*, LIX (1959), 350–356.
[19] A. B. Heilbrun, "Parental Identification and College Adjustment," *Psychol. Rep.*, X (1962), 853–854.

clearer focus. One such variable treated in the present study, but for some reason largely ignored in others, is individual differences in the sex-role behavior of the parents. Despite numerous investigations showing individual differences in sex-role adoption among children of the same biological sex, both fathers and mothers have usually been treated as homogeneous classes as far as their sex-role identity is concerned.

David B. Lynn

The Process of Learning Parental
and Sex-Role Identification

In the following paper, Lynn derives far-ranging implications from the concept of identification. As Heilbrun does, he focuses on the role of parental models; however, in addition to the expressive and instrumental dimensions, Lynn also discusses social learning experiences, rewards, and negative admonishments as influences on both personality development and sex-role identity. He explains that boys acquire relatively stronger sex-role identity than girls because the masculine role is accorded greater prestige, boys are ridiculed more for adopting the opposite sex-role, and girls become increasingly disturbed with their lot, preferring instead the requisites of the masculine role. The analyses presented here and in the preceding paper suggest coherent, plausible hypotheses pertaining to identification during childhood and adolescence, and clearly anticipate certain of the major research trends of the early 1970's.

THE purpose of this paper is to summarize the writer's theoretical formulation concerning identification, much of which has been published piecemeal in various journals. Research relevant to new hypotheses is cited, and references are given to previous publications of this writer in which the reader can find evidence concerning the earlier hypotheses. Some of the previously published hypotheses are considerably revised in this paper and, it is hoped, placed in a more comprehensive and coherent framework.

THEORETICAL FORMULATION

Before developing specific hypotheses, one must briefly define identification as it is used here. *Parental identification* refers to the internalization of personality characteristics of one's own parent and to unconscious reactions similar to that parent. This is to be contrasted with *sex-role identification,* which refers to the internalization of the role typical of a given sex in a particular culture and to the unconscious reactions characteristic of that role. Thus, theoretically, an individual might be thoroughly identified with the role typical of his own sex generally and yet poorly identified with his

FROM *Journal of Marriage and the Family,* XVIII (1966), 466–470. Reprinted by permission of the author and the publisher.

99

same-sex parent specifically. This differentiation also allows for the converse circumstances wherein a person is well identified with his same-sex parent specifically and yet poorly identified with the typical same-sex role generally. In such an instance the parent with whom the individual is well identified is himself poorly identified with the typical sex role. An example might be a girl who is closely identified with her mother, who herself is more strongly identified with the masculine than with the feminine role. Therefore, such a girl, through her identification with her mother, is poorly identified with the feminine role.[1]

Formulation of Hypotheses

It is postulated that the initial parental identification of both male and female infants is with the mother. Boys, but not girls, must shift from this initial mother identification and establish masculine-role identification. Typically in this culture the girl has the same-sex parental model for identification (the mother) with her more hours per day than the boy has his same-sex model (the father) with him. Moreover, even when home, the father does not usually participate in as many intimate activities with the child as does the mother, e.g., preparation for bed, toileting. The time spent with the child and the intimacy and intensity of the contact are thought to be pertinent to the process of learning parental identification.[2] The boy is seldom if ever with the father as he engages in his daily vocational activities, although both boy and girl are often with the mother as she goes through her household activities. Consequently, the father, as a model for the boy, is analogous to a map showing the major outline but lacking most details, whereas the mother, as a model for the girl, might be thought of as a detailed map.

However, despite the shortage of male models, a somewhat stereotyped and conventional masculine role is nonetheless spelled out for the boy, often by his mother and women teachers in the absence of his father and male models. Through the reinforcement of the culture's highly developed system of rewards for typical masculine-role behavior and punishment for signs of femininity, the boy's early learned identification with the mother weakens. Upon this weakened mother identification is welded the later learned identification with a culturally defined, stereotyped masculine role.

(1) * *Consequently, males tend to identify with a culturally defined masculine role, whereas females tend to identify with their mothers.*[3]

Although one must recognize the contribution of the father in the identification of males and the general cultural influences in the identification of

[1] D. B. Lynn, "Sex-Role and Parental Identification," *Child Development*, 33:3 (1962), 555–564.

[2] B. A. Goodfield, "A Preliminary Paper on the Development of the Time Intensity Compensation Hypothesis in Masculine Identification," paper read at the San Francisco State Psychological Convention, April, 1965.

* Specific hypotheses are numbered and in italics.

[3] D. B. Lynn, "A Note on Sex Differences in the Development of Masculine and Feminine Identification," *Psychological Review*, 66:2 (1959), 126–135.

females, it nevertheless seems meaningful, for simplicity in developing this formulation, to refer frequently to *masculine-role identification* in males as distinguished from *mother identification* in females.

Some evidence is accumulating suggesting that (2) *both males and females identify more closely with the mother than with the father.* Evidence is found in support of this hypothesis in a study by Lazowick [4] in which the subjects were 30 college students. These subjects and their mothers and fathers were required to rate concepts, e.g., "myself," "father," "mother," etc. The degree of semantic similarity as rated by the subjects and their parents was determined. The degree of similarity between fathers and their own children was not significantly greater than that found between fathers and children randomly matched. However, children did share a greater semantic similarity with their own mothers than they did when matched at random with other maternal figures. Mothers and daughters did not share a significantly greater semantic similarity than did mothers and sons.

Evidence is also found in support of Hypothesis 2 in a study by Adams and Sarason [5] using anxiety scales with male and female high school students and their mothers and fathers. They found that anxiety scores of both boys and girls were much more related to mothers' than to fathers' anxiety scores.

Support for this hypothesis comes from a study in which Aldous and Kell [6] interviewed 50 middle-class college students and their mothers concerning childrearing values. They found, contrary to their expectation, that a slightly higher proportion of boys than girls shared their mothers' child-rearing values.

Partial support for Hypothesis 2 is provided in a study by Gray and Klaus [7] using the Allport-Vernon-Lindzey Study of Values completed by 34 female and 28 male college students and by their parents. They found that the men were not significantly closer to their fathers than to their mothers and also that the men were not significantly closer to their fathers than were the women. However, the women were closer to their mothers than were the men and closer to their mothers than to their fathers.

Note that, in reporting research relevant to Hypothesis 2, only studies of *tested similarity,* not *perceived similarity,* were reviewed. To test this hypothesis, one must measure tested similarity, i.e., measure both the child and the parent on the same variable and compare the similarity between these two measures. This paper is not concerned with perceived similarity, i.e., testing the child on a given variable and then comparing that finding with a measure taken as to how the child thinks his parent would respond. It is this writer's opinion that much confusion has arisen by considering perceived

[4] L. M. Lazowick, "On the Nature of Identification," *Journal of Abnormal and Social Psychology,* 51 (1955), 175–183.

[5] E. B. Adams and I. G. Sarason, "Relation Between Anxiety in Children and Their Parents," *Child Development,* 34:1 (1963), 237–246.

[6] J. Aldous and L. Kell, "A Partial Test of Some Theories of Identification," *Marriage and Family Living,* 23:1 (1961), 15–19.

[7] S. W. Gray and R. Klaus, "The Assessment of Parental Identification," *Genetic Psychology Monographs,* 54 (1956), 87–114.

similarity as a measure of parental identification. It seems obvious that, especially for the male, perceived similarity between father and son would usually be closer than tested similarity, in that it is socially desirable for a man to be similar to his father, especially as contrasted to his similarity to his mother. Indeed, Gray and Klaus [8] found the males' perceived similarity with the father to be closer than tested similarity.

It is hypothesized that the closer identification of males with the mother than with the father will be revealed more clearly on some measures than on others. (3) *The closer identification of males with their mothers than with their fathers will be revealed most frequently in personality variables which are not clearly sex-typed.* In other words, males are more likely to be more similar to their mothers than to their fathers in variables in which masculine and feminine role behavior is not especially relevant in the culture.

There has been too little research on tested similarity between males and their parents to presume an adequate test of Hypothesis 3. In order to test it, one would first have to judge personality variables as to how typically masculine or feminine they seem. One could then test to determine whether a higher proportion of males are more similar to their mothers than to their fathers on those variables which are not clearly sex-typed, rather than on those which are judged clearly to be either masculine or feminine. To this writer's knowledge, this has not been done.

It is postulated that the task of achieving these separate kinds of identification (masculine role for males and mother identification for females) requires separate methods of learning for each sex. These separate methods of learning to identify seem to be problem-solving for boys and lesson-learning for girls. Woodworth and Schlosberg differentiate between the task of solving problems and that of learning lessons in the following way:

> With a problem to master the learner must explore the situation and find the goal before his task is fully presented. In the case of a lesson, the problem-solving phase is omitted or at least minimized, as we see when the human subject is instructed to memorize this poem or that list of nonsense syllables, to examine these pictures with a view to recognizing them later. [9]

Since the girl is not required to shift from the mother in learning her identification, she is expected mainly to learn the mother-identification lesson as it is presented to her, partly through imitation and through the mother's selective reinforcement of mother-similar behavior. She need not abstract principles defining the feminine role to the extent that the boy must in defining the masculine role. Any bit of behavior on the mother's part may be modeled by the girl in learning the mother-identification lesson.

However, finding the appropriate identification goal does constitute a major problem for the boy in solving the masculine-role identification prob-

---

[8] *Ibid.*
[9] R. S. Woodworth and H. Schlosberg, *Experimental Psychology*, New York: Henry Holt & Co., 1954, p. 529.

lem. When the boy discovers that he does not belong in the same sex category as the mother, he must then find the proper sex-role identification goal. Masculine-role behavior is defined for him through admonishments, often negatively given, e.g., the mother's and teachers' telling him that he should not be a sissy without precisely indicating what he *should* be. Moreover, these negative admonishments are made in the early grades in the absence of male teachers to serve as models and with the father himself often unavailable as a model. The boy must restructure these admonishments in order to abstract principles defining the masculine role. It is this process of defining the masculine-role goal which is involved in solving the masculine-role identification problem.

One of the basic steps in this formulation can now be taken. (4) *In learning the sex-typical identification, each sex is thereby acquiring separate methods of learning which are subsequently applied to learning tasks generally.*[10]

The little girl acquires a learning method which primarily involves (a) a personal relationship and (b) imitation rather than restructuring the field and abstracting principles. On the other hand, the little boy acquires a different learning method which primarily involves (a) defining the goal (b) restructuring the field, and (c) abstracting principles. There are a number of findings which are consistent with Hypothesis 4, such as the frequently reported greater problem-solving skill of males and the greater field dependence of females.[11]

The shift of the little boy from mother identification to masculine-role identification is assumed to be frequently a crisis. It has been observed that demands for typical sex-role behavior come at an earlier age for boys than for girls. These demands are made at an age when boys are least able to understand them. As was pointed out above, demands for masculine sex-role behavior are often made by women in the absence of readily available male models to demonstrate typical sex-role behavior. Such demands are often presented in the form of punishing, *negative* admonishments, i.e., telling the boy what not to do rather than what to do and backing up the demands with punishment. These are thought to be very different conditions from those in which the girl learns her mother-identification lesson. Such methods of demanding typical sex-role behavior of boys are very poor methods for inducing learning.

(5) *Therefore, males tend to have greater difficulty in achieving same-sex identification than females.*[12]

(6) *Furthermore, more males than females fail more or less completely in achieving same-sex identification, but rather, they make an opposite-sex identification.*[13]

[10] Lynn, "Sex-Role and Parental Identification," *op. cit.*
[11] *Ibid.*
[12] D. B. Lynn, "Divergent Feedback and Sex-Role Identification in Boys and Men," *Merrill-Palmer Quarterly*, 10:1 (1964), 17–23.
[13] D. B. Lynn, "Sex Differences in Identification Development," *Sociometry*, 24:4 (1961), 372–383.

Negative admonishments given at an age when the child is least able to understand them and supported by punishment are thought to produce anxiety concerning sex-role behavior. In Hartley's words:

> This situation gives us practically a perfect combination for inducing anxiety —the demand that the child do something which is not clearly defined to him, based on reasons he cannot possibly appreciate, and enforced with threats, punishments and anger by those who are close to him.[14]

(7) *Consequently, males are more anxious regarding sex-role identification than females.*[15] It is postulated that punishment often leads to dislike of the activity that led to punishment.[16] Since it is "girl-like" activities that provoked the punishment administered in an effort to induce sex-typical behavior in boys, then, in developing dislike for the activity which led to such punishment, boys should develop hostility toward "girl-like" activities. Also, boys should be expected to generalize and consequently develop hostility toward all females as representatives of this disliked role. There is not thought to be as much pressure on girls as on boys to avoid opposite-sex activities. It is assumed that girls are punished neither so early nor so severely for adopting masculine sex-role behavior.

(8) *Therefore, males tend to hold stronger feelings of hostility toward females than females toward males.*[17] The young boy's same-sex identification is at first not very firm because of the shift from mother to masculine identification. On the other hand, the young girl, because she need make no shift in identification, remains relatively firm in her mother identification. However, the culture, which is male-dominant in orientation, reinforces the boy's developing masculine-role identification much more thoroughly than it does the girl's developing feminine identification. He is rewarded simply for having been born masculine through countless privileges accorded males but not females. As Brown pointed out:

> The superior position and privileged status of the male permeates nearly every aspect, minor and major, of our social life. The gadgets and prizes in boxes of breakfast cereal, for example, commonly have a strong masculine rather than feminine appeal. And the most basic social institutions perpetuate this pattern of masculine aggrandizement. Thus, the Judeo-Christian faiths involve worshipping God, a "Father," rather than a "Mother," and Christ, a "Son," rather than a "Daughter." [18]

[14] R. E. Hartley, "Sex-Role Pressures and the Socialization of the Male Child," *Psychological Reports,* 5 (1959), p. 458.

[15] Lynn, "Divergent Feedback and Sex-Role Identification in Boys and Men," *op. cit.*

[16] E. R. Hilgard, *Introduction to Psychology,* New York: Harcourt, Brace, and World, 1962.

[17] Lynn, "Divergent Feedback and Sex-Role Identification in Boys and Men," *op. cit.*

[18] D. G. Brown, "Sex-Role Development in a Changing Culture," *Psychological Bulletin,* 55 (1958), 235.

(9) *Consequently, with increasing age, males become relatively more firmly identified with the masculine role.*[19]

Since psychological disturbances should, theoretically, be associated with inadequate same-sex identification and since males are postulated to be gaining in masculine identification, the following is predicted: (10) *With increasing age males develop psychological disturbances at a more slowly accelerating rate than females.*[20]

It is postulated that as girls grow older, they become increasingly disenchanted with the feminine role because of the prejudices against their sex and the privileges and prestige offered the male rather than the female. Even the women with whom they come in contact are likely to share the prejudices prevailing in this culture against their own sex.[21] Smith [22] found that with increasing age girls have a progressively better opinion of boys and a progressively poorer opinion of themselves. (11) *Consequently, a larger proportion of females than males show preference for the role of the opposite sex.*[23]

Note that in Hypothesis 11 the term "preference" rather than "identification" was used. It is *not* hypothesized that a larger proportion of females than males *identify* with the opposite sex (Hypothesis 6 predicted the reverse) but rather that they will show *preference* for the role of the opposite sex. *Sex-role preference* refers to the desire to adopt the behavior associated with one sex or the other or the perception of such behavior as preferable or more desirable. *Sex-role preference* should be contrasted with *sex-role identification,* which, as stated previously, refers to the actual incorporation of the role of a given sex and to the unconscious reactions characteristic of that role.

Punishment may suppress behavior without causing its unlearning.[24] Because of the postulated punishment administered to males for adopting opposite-sex role behavior, it is predicted that males will repress atypical sex-role behavior rather than unlearn it. One might predict, then, a discrepancy between the underlying sex-role identification and the overt sex-role behavior of males. For females, on the other hand, no comparable punishment for adopting many aspects of the opposite-sex role is postulated. (12) *Consequently, where a discrepancy exists between sex-role preference and identification, it will tend to be as follows: Males will tend to show same-sex role preference with underlying opposite-sex identification. Females will tend to show opposite-sex role preference with underlying same-sex identifica-*

---

[19] Lynn, "A Note on Sex Differences in the Development of Masculine and Feminine Identification," *op. cit.*

[20] Lynn, "Sex Differences in Identification Development," *op. cit.*

[21] P. M. Kitay, "A Comparison of the Sexes in Their Attitudes and Beliefs About Women: A Study of Prestige Groups," *Sociometry,* 3 (1940), 399–407.

[22] S. Smith, "Age and Sex Differences in Children's Opinion Concerning Sex Differences," *Journal of Genetic Psychology,* 54 (1939), 17–25.

[23] Lynn, "A Note on Sex Differences in the Development of Masculine and Feminine Identification," *op. cit.*

[24] Hilgard, *op. cit.*

tion.[25] Stated in another way, where a discrepancy occurs both males and females will tend to show masculine-role preference with underlying feminine identification.

Not only is the masculine role accorded more prestige than the feminine role, but males are more likely than females to be ridiculed or punished for adopting aspects of the opposite-sex role. For a girl to be a tomboy does not involve the censure that results when a boy is a sissy. Girls may wear masculine clothing (shirts and trousers), but boys may not wear feminine clothing (skirts and dresses). Girls may play with toys typically associated with boys (cars, trucks, erector sets, and guns), but boys are discouraged from playing with feminine toys (dolls and tea sets). (13) *Therefore, a higher proportion of females than males adopt aspects of the role of the opposite sex.*[26]

Note that Hypothesis 13 refers to *sex-role adoption* rather than *sex-role identification* or *preference*. *Sex-role adoption* refers to the overt behavior characteristic of a given sex. An example contrasting sex-role adoption with preference and identification is an individual who *adopts* behavior characteristic of his own sex because it is expedient, not because he *prefers* it nor because he is so *identified*.

Summary

The purpose of this paper has been to summarize the writer's theoretical formulation and to place it in a more comprehensive and coherent framework. The following hypotheses were presented and discussed:

1. Males tend to identify with a culturally defined masculine role, whereas females tend to identify with their mothers.
2. Both males and females identify more closely with the mother than with the father.
3. The closer identification of males with their mothers than with their fathers will be revealed most frequently in personality variables which are not clearly sex-typed.
4. In learning the sex-typical identification, each sex is thereby acquiring separate methods of learning which are subsequently applied to learning tasks generally.
5. Males tend to have greater difficulty in achieving same-sex identification than females.
6. More males than females fail more or less completely in achieving same-sex identification but rather make an opposite-sex identification.
7. Males are more anxious regarding sex-role identification than females.
8. Males tend to hold stronger feelings of hostility toward females than females toward males.
9. With increasing age, males become relatively more firmly identified with the masculine role.

[25] Lynn, "Divergent Feedback and Sex-Role Identification in Boys and Men," *op. cit.*
[26] Lynn, "A Note on Sex Differences in the Development of Masculine and Feminine Identification," *op. cit.*

10. With increasing age, males develop psychological disturbances at a more slowly accelerating rate than females.
11. A larger proportion of females than males show preference for the role of the opposite sex.
12. Where a discrepancy exists between sex-role preference and identification, it will tend to be as follows: Males will tend to show same-sex role preference with underlying opposite-sex identification. Females will tend to show opposite-sex role preference with underlying same-sex identification.
13. A higher proportion of females than males adopt aspects of the role of the opposite sex.

Charles E. Bowerman
Glen H. Elder, Jr.

Variations in Adolescent Perception
of Family Power Structure

The socialization of childen and adolescents is a joint enterprise. Neither parent can possibly function independently of the other. The conjugal balance of power presumably exerts critical influence on socialization, and in this study, Bowerman and Elder investigate certain aspects of the issue. First, on the basis of adolescents' perceptions of mother-father relations, parental-authority patterns, and parent-child relations, families are represented as matriarchal, equalitarian, or patriarchal. Variations in these perceived structures are then studied with respect to adolescents' age, sex, and social class. Also, the authors assess the effects of the family structural models on adolescents' scholastic motivation and on parental affect. The data reveal that the majority of adolescents perceive their families as equalitarian; however, middle-class boys tend to see their families as father-dominant, and lower-class girls, as mother-dominant. Older youths, in grades 10 through 12, tend to evaluate their same-sex parent as the principal authority figure whereas younger youths, grades 7 through 9, tend to report equality between parents. On the whole, the researchers find little association between dominance in conjugal relations and dominance in parent-child relations. The results also indicate "that parental power in child-rearing relations is not accurately pictured from knowledge of a child's perception of one parent's power over the other." Further, for both boys and girls, in contrast to earlier studies of father-dominance, these findings show that scholastic motivation appears to be strongest when fathers are perceived as head of the family and as democratic in their parent-adolescent relations.

THE decline of paternal authority in the twentieth century is considered by some authorities in the marriage and family field to be one of the major changes in the family.[1] In fact, the relative scarcity of patriarchal

FROM *American Sociological Review*, XXIX (1964), 551–567. Reprinted by permission of the authors and the American Sociological Association.

[1] John Mogey, "A Century of Declining Paternal Authority," *Marriage and Family Living*, 19 (August, 1957), 234–239. (See also William G. Dyer and Richard Urban, "The Institutionalization of Equalitarian Family Norms," *Marriage and Family Living*,

families has restricted study of the effects of extreme types of family structure on personality development.[2] Not only does this evidence suggest that patriarchal rule is relatively uncommon, but recent data indicate that equality between spouses is increasing and that women are more frequently stepping into the primary role in the family.[3] Some of these observed and predicted changes in family structure have been assessed in terms of their effects on family stability and on the personality development and achievement of the child.[4]

A confusing aspect of some descriptive accounts of family structure is that terms are used rather loosely. Families in which the father severely controls the behavior of his children are sometimes considered patriarchal, while in other instances the concept is used to refer to paternal administration of discipline, or to the structure of husband-wife relations. Dominance by the husband and father may characterize any or all of the following relationships: marital, parent-adolescent, and mother-father relations in child rearing. In short, any number of variations can be subsumed under the term patriarchal family, as is true of any blanket description of family structure not accompanied by explicit statements about the specific relationships being described and measured.

This study is organized around three research objectives. The first one involves constructing crude models of family power structure, while the second focuses on variations in these perceived models among adolescents who differ in position as defined by age and sex within middle- and lower-class families. Finally, the behavioral significance of different perceived models of family power structure is examined through an analysis of the relation between an adolescent's perception of family structure and parental roles and his reported educational goals. On the level of family decision making, we wish to determine whether mother, father, or both are seen as most frequently making final decisions. Similar types of role pattern may prevail in child rearing: father, mother, or both may be seen as the authority figure in matters of behavior policy. The third relation is between the adolescent and each parent (see Table 1). We will investigate five structural variations, ranging from strong parental domination to minimal parental control: autocratic, authoritarian, democratic, equalitarian, and permissive.[5]

---

20 (February, 1958), 53–58). When Ogburn and Nimkoff asked "18 experts" in the area of the family to note major changes in the family, 12 of the 18 mentioned a decline in the authority of husbands and fathers. William F. Ogburn and Meyer F. Nimkoff, *Technology and the Changing Family*, New York: Houghton Mifflin, 1955, p. 18.

[2] See Edward C. Devereux, Jr., Urie Bronfenbrenner, and George J. Suci, "Patterns of Parent Behavior in America and West Germany: A Cross-National Comparison," *International Social Science Journal*, 14 (1962), 488–506.

[3] Robert Blood and Donald Wolfe, *Husbands and Wives*, New York: The Free Press, 1960.

[4] Urie Bronfenbrenner, "The Changing American Child," *The Journal of Social Issues*, 17 (1961), 6–18.

[5] Seven child-rearing structures were measured by two items with seven response categories apiece. Each response category represents a type of interdependence as indicated below, and both items are similarly worded with the exception of the referent. "In

*Table 1 Family Structural Patterns and Their Effects on Adolescent Behavior**

	Conjugal Power Structure		
Wife Dominant	Equalitarian	Husband Dominant	
			Effects on behavior
	Parental Role Patterns		
Mother Dominant	Shared	Father Dominant	
			Effects on behavior
	Child-Rearing Structures		
Mother		Father	
Autocratic		Autocratic	
Authoritarian		Authoritarian	Effects on
Democratic		Democratic	behavior
Equalitarian		Equalitarian	
Permissive		Permissive	

* In this diagram, we have traced the possible structural patterns in which mother is perceived as holding more power than father in both family and parental matters. The total number of possible patterns is 225, with 25 variations possible in child-rearing relations alone. Note that the effects of different social structures on adolescent behavior may be examined on three distinct levels. An assessment of the effects of conjugal power structure on adolescent behavior is a research problem quite different from an analysis of the effects of parental power in child-rearing relations. This difference will become more apparent in subsequent pages. Throughout the paper, we shall refer to the perceived structure of husband-wife relations as the *conjugal* or *marital role pattern*, to the structure of mother and father relations in child rearing as the *parental role* or *authority pattern*, to the structure of parent-child relations as the *child rearing structure*, and to structures based on all three relationships as *family structural patterns*. The term "authority figure" denotes dominance in the *parental* role pattern.

A family in which mother is perceived as having the final say on family matters and on child-rearing policy, and in which mother-adolescent relations are autocratic or authoritarian, clearly approximates a matriarchy. Similarly, a patriarchal family is most nearly represented when father is dominant in all three relationships. In an equalitarian family, parents are seen as sharing the power throughout.[6]

---

general, how are most decisions made between you and your (mother/father)? 1. [Autocratic] My (mother/father) just tells me what to do. 2. [Authoritarian] (Mother/father) listens to me, but makes the decision (herself/himself). 3. [Democratic] I have considerable opportunity to make my own decisions, but my (mother/father) has the final word. 4. [Equalitarian] My opinions are as important as my (mother's/father's) in deciding what I should do. 5. [Permissive] I can make my own decision, but my (mother/father) would like for me to consider (her/his) opinion. 6. [Laissez-faire] I can do what I want regardless of what my (mother/father) thinks. 7. [Ignoring] My (mother/father) doesn't care what I do." For purposes of this analysis, responses 6 and 7 are grouped with response 5. For an analysis of the correlates and possible effects of structural variations in parent-child relations, see Glen H. Elder, Jr., "Structural Variations in the Child-Rearing Relationship," *Sociometry*, 25 (September, 1962), 241–262.

[6] The social bases of structural variations in child-rearing relations have been reported in a recent paper. Autocratic and authoritarian parents were most likely to be fathers

First, we shall examine variations in adolescent perceptions of family structure by age, sex and social class of adolescents. Second, we shall investigate interrelations among the three basic relationships and their role patterns, describing them as structural patterns. At this point we shall be able to determine the prevalence of matriarchal, patriarchal, and equalitarian families in our sample. Finally, we shall appraise the effects of the different structural patterns on the perceived supportiveness and affection of parents and on the academic motivation and college plans of adolescents.

Considerable data on various aspects of family structure have recently been obtained from children and adolescents. Since our data are also based on the child's viewpoint, our delineation of different structural patterns and our assessment of some correlates of each should add to prior knowledge of family structure and adolescent socialization. Many different techniques have been used to measure family power structure; we shall discuss the problem of measurement validity at several points in the paper. Let us consider some of the research relevant to our objectives and several hypotheses suggested by these investigations.

HYPOTHESES

Perception of Family Power Structure: The Effects of Age,
Sex and Social Class

Several recent studies indicate that an equalitarian arrangement between husband and wife in family decision making is the most common type of conjugal role structure. In an investigation of marital relations in approximately 900 families in and around Detroit, Blood and Wolfe found that 46 per cent of the wives described decision making in their families as equalitarian, while only 22 per cent reported dominance on the part of the husband and 22 per cent on the part of the wife.[7] Using a modification of Strodtbeck's revealed difference technique, Middleton and Putney found

---

with older sons and daughters, lower class in status, and to possess a high school education or less. Democratic and equalitarian parents were most apt to be mothers, parents of older adolescents, middle class in status and to have had at least some college education. Mothers were more likely than fathers to be permissive. *Ibid.*

[7] Blood and Wolfe, *op. cit.*, p. 23. Like many other studies concerned with perceptions of family power structure, this one is indebted to the conceptual framework outlined by Herbst in the early 1950's. Herbst delineated four regions of activities and decision making: household duties, child control and care, social activities and economic activities. Four basic types of family patterns were constructed on the relative husband-wife involvement in activities and decision making in these areas: Autonomic pattern—husband and wife are active and dominant in different regions: Husband dominance—husband decides and husband and wife act together; Wife dominance—wife decides and husband and wife act together; and Syncratic pattern—a democratic arrangement in decision making and in task performance. See P. G. Herbst, "Conceptual Framework for Studying the Family" in O. A. Olsen and S. B. Hammond (eds.), *Social Structure and Personality in a City*, London: Routledge and Kegan Paul, 1954, pp. 126–137. For a review of the techniques used in measuring family power, see David M. Heer, "The Measurement and Basis of Family Power: An Overview," *Marriage and Family Living*, 25 (May, 1963), pp. 133–139.

in a small sample of 20 couples that the equalitarian pattern in decision making was most common.[8]

Johannis and Rollins analyzed data collected from 1,584 tenth graders in Tampa, Florida, and reported that 63 per cent perceived mothers and fathers as being equal in power. Only 15 per cent saw father as the decision maker and even fewer thought mother was dominant.[9] Working with a sample of similar size, which included children enrolled in grades 2 through 8, Hess and Torney report sizable sex and age differences in perception of the "boss in the family." [10] Equalitarian structure was the most frequently reported only among girls. With the possible exception of the latter study, to which we shall return shortly, these data suggest the following hypothesis:

1. *Adolescents are most likely to report that final decisions are made by both parents, and least likely to perceive mother as the principal decision maker on family matters.*

The Hess and Torney research reveals large age and sex variations in a child's perception of family leadership. If such variations occur in perception of the conjugal role pattern, we should certainly expect variations in adolescent perceptions of parental authority in child rearing. Numerous studies have shown that parents tend to be more involved in rearing children of the same sex—this is particularly true for fathers.[11] Thus, while a portion of the variation by sex in perception of decision making on the family level may be due to a lack of understanding or awareness on the part of children, this is much less likely to be true of child-rearing relations. This is an arena of frequent parent-adolescent interaction in regard to independent and mutual interests, while family decision making is presumably not as familiar a territory for a child. Hess and Torney found that boys are more inclined than girls to see father in the ruling position and girls more apt than boys to see mother as boss.[12] But the data show no sizable sex differences with regard to those checking mother as family leader. Girls were more likely than boys to report an equalitarian pattern. From ages nine to 13 and older, the percentages of children reporting the mother, father and equal patterns changed very little.

Several possible explanations might account for this sex-linked difference in perception of power allocation on the family level. It may reflect parental

[8] Russell Middleton and Snell Putney, "Dominance in Decisions in the Family: Race and Class Differences," *American Journal of Sociology*, 65 (May, 1960), 605–609.

[9] Theodore B. Johannis, Jr. and James M. Rollins, "Teenager Perception of Family Decision Making," *The Coordinator*, 7 (1959), 70–74.

[10] Robert D. Hess and Judith V. Torney, "Religion, Age, and Sex in Children's Perceptions of Family Authority," *Child Development*, 33 (1962), 781–789. See also Edward C. Devereux, Jr., "Children of Democracy: On the Consequences for Children of Varying Patterns of Family Authority in the United States and Germany," a summary of a research report read at the 7th International Seminar on Family Research, Washington, D.C., September, 1962, p. 3.

[11] See, for instance, Urie Bronfenbrenner, "Some Familial Antecedents of Responsibility and Leadership in Adolescents," in Luigi Petrullo and Bernard Bass, eds., *Leadership and Interpersonal Behavior*, New York: Holt, Rinehart and Winston, 1961, pp. 239–271.

[12] Hess and Torney, *op. cit.*, p. 785.

role differentiation in child rearing; as Henry's data indicate, "mothers tend to punish daughters and fathers tend to punish sons."[13] Data on age differences among adolescents are too ambiguous to support any expectation, but on sex differences, we hypothesize that:

2. *Boys are more likely than girls to see father as dominant in both the conjugal parental relations, and girls are more likely than boys to see mother as dominant in both areas. Sex differences will be most pronounced in perceptions of the authority pattern in child rearing.*

These and other studies show that father's power in the family varies directly with the economic rewards and social prestige of his work. Blood and Wolfe, in their Detroit study, found wife-dominance to be more common in blue-collar families, while husband-dominance was more common in white-collar homes.[14] The likelihood that mother is the authority figure was inversely related to father's educational level among the tenth graders in Bronfenbrenner's Ithaca study.[15] In his New Haven sample of 1,151 boys between the ages of 14 and 17, Strodtbeck found that paternal power was directly related to father's occupational status.[16] No class differences were obtained by Hess and Torney; this might well be due, as they suggest, to the gross class categories employed.[17]

On the basis of these results we hypothesize that:

3. *Middle-class adolescents, in contrast to lower-class adolescents, more frequently report father as dominant in conjugal and child-rearing relations, while lower-class adolescents more commonly report mother as dominant in these areas. These differences are independent of age and sex in direction.*

Family Structural Patterns

While there has been considerable research on the structure of particular family relationships and on the effects of different types of structural patterns on children, there is a dearth of information on *patterns of role structure* in the family system. Devereux and Bronfenbrenner investigated the structure of conjugal relations in the families of 400 tenth-grade students by asking them which parent had the final say in four areas of family decisions.[18] Five types of family structure were delineated: extreme father

[13] Andrew F. Henry, "Sibling Structure and Perception of the Disciplinary Roles of Parents," *Sociometry*, 20 (March, 1957), 67–74. In a study of adolescents in Ithaca, New York, Bronfenbrenner found that each parent tends to be more active, unyielding, and demanding with a child of the same sex, and more lenient and indulgent with a child of the opposite sex. The punitive parent is probably more likely to be seen as most powerful. Urie Bronfenbrenner, *op. cit.*

[14] Blood and Wolfe, *op. cit.*, p. 29.

[15] Bronfenbrenner, "Some Familial Antecedents of Responsibility and Leadership in Adolescents," *op. cit.*

[16] Fred L. Strodtbeck, "Family Interaction, Values, and Achievement," in David C. McClelland, Alfred L. Baldwin, Urie Bronfenbrenner, and Fred L. Strodtbeck, *Talent and Society*, New York: D. Van Nostrand, 1958, Ch. 4.

[17] Hess and Torney, *op. cit.*

[18] This study is reported in Devereux *et al.*, "Patterns of Parent Behavior in America and West Germany . . .," *op. cit.*

dominance (patriarchal), father dominance (patricentric), equalitarian, mother dominance (matricentric), and extreme mother dominance (matriarchal). They found that parental role differentiation tended to correspond with these five types of conjugal structure. In patriarchal families, fathers tended to be seen as the principal agents of pressure and discipline in child rearing, and mothers were viewed as the chief source of support. At the other extreme, the matriarchal family, mother was generally reported as the principal agent of both discipline and support, with father dropping into the background as a powerless figure in the family. Parental role differentiation was minimal in equalitarian families. Thus, substantial correspondence between familial and child-rearing structures was obtained in this study.

Although we may find considerable similarity in role patterns across the three relationships, it is unlikely that there is a one-to-one correspondence. Many variants of the three major types are possible *and* probable, as we suggested earlier. In addition, the results of at least two studies, those conducted by Hess and Torney and by Johannis and Rollins, indicate that the perception of wife dominance is much less common than the perception of husband dominance. Thus, a matriarchal family in which mother is perceived as dominant in marital relations, in child rearing, and in mother-adolescent relations, is likely to be extremely rare. To a lesser extent this should also be true of the patriarchal family. The equalitarian family, on the other hand, should be the most common major type of family power structure. Accordingly we hypothesize that:

4. *A moderate degree of correspondence exists among perceived role patterns in marital, parental and parent-adolescent relations, the order of prevalence being the equalitarian, patriarchal and matriarchal types of family structure.*

Some Correlates of Types of Family Structure

In predicting the effects of family structure on a child's perception of his parents as sources of affect, on his motivation to achieve in school, and on his college plans, it is essential to recognize that some power-dependence relations in the family impinge more directly than others on adolescent behavior and socialization. A father's power over his son should have a much more direct bearing on the boy's initiative, decision making competence and aspirations than does the distribution of power in conjugal relations.[19] This assumption will be tested in regard to each of the dependent variables.[20]

---

[19] In a preliminary report of results from an analysis of methods used to measure family power structure, Hess and Torney found relatively little association between conjugal and parent-child power structures. See Robert Hess and Judith Torney, "A Comparison of Methods Used to Measure Family Power Structure," paper read at the Biennial Meeting of the Society for Research in Child Development, April, 1963, University of California, Berkeley.

[20] See Hoffman and Lippitt's discussion of level of variables and their predicted effect on a child's personality. Lewis W. Hoffman and Ronald Lippitt, "The Measurement of

Research by Blood and Wolfe,[21] Straus,[22] and Devereux indicates that wife-dominance in marital relations, in contrast to husband-dominance and the equalitarian pattern, is associated with a greater prevalence of marital conflict and parental rejection. Devereux notes that the father in such families tends to be neither a principal agent of discipline nor a major source of support.[23] Dominance on the part of either mother or father in child-rearing relations is strongly associated with parental rejection.[24] At the positive extreme, in terms of effect on family climate, is the equalitarian family, with families ruled by father tending to be intermediate with respect to home happiness and marital conflict.[25] From the virtually complete unanimity of these results, we hypothesize that:

5. *Adolescents perceive mother as a principal source of support most frequently when she is seen as sharing leadership responsibilities with her husband in marital and parental relations, next most frequently when father is perceived as dominant in these areas, and least frequently when she is perceived as dominant. Perceived supportiveness will vary with parental child-rearing pattern more than with husband-wife structure. The same predictions hold for father as a source of emotional support if we substitute mother for father and father for mother in the above hypothesis.*

The family environment most favorable to the development of high-achieving, ambitious children is not at all clear in current research literature on the subject. A number of studies indicate that youth from wife-dominant families display a generally high level of achievement and aspiration.[26] In his analysis of power allocation and achievement values in Italian and Jewish families, Strodtbeck found that "—the less mother and son are dominated by the father in the power area, the greater the disposition of both to believe that the world can be rationally mastered and that a son should risk separation from his family." [27] The important point here is that dominance relations in the family are negatively related to achievement and independence orientation among sons, not, as some researchers have implied, that a wife-dominated family is a favorable environment for the development of such an outlook in boys. Similar results were obtained by

---

Family Life Variables," in Paul H. Mussen, ed., *Handbook of Research Methods in Child Development*, New York: John Wiley, 1960.

[21] Blood and Wolfe, *op. cit.*

[22] Murray A. Straus, "Conjugal Power Structure and Adolescent Personality," *Marriage and Family Living*, 24 (February, 1962), 17–25.

[23] Devereux, "Children of Democracy," *op. cit.*

[24] Elder, *op. cit.*

[25] See bottom of Table 5 for a description of the index used to measure the adolescent's perception of father and mother's emotional support.

[26] Straus, *op. cit.*, p. 22, and Devereux, "Children of Democracy," *op. cit.*, p. 6. See also Bernard C. Rosen and R. D. D'Andrade, "The Psycho-social Origins of Achievement Motivation," *Sociometry*, 22 (September, 1959), 185–218.

[27] Strodtbeck, *op. cit.*, p. 183.

Morrow and Wilson in a study of the relation between democratic parent-child relations and sons' achievement.[28]

A recent study based on data collected in part from the adolescents in the present sample has disclosed that adolescent achievement is negatively affected by parental dominance in parent-child relations more than by dominance in husband-wife relations.[29] The equalitarian husband-wife structure was more strongly associated with high adolescent motivation to achieve than was either of the other two conjugal structures, though differences between measures were not great. Furthermore, the structure of parent-adolescent relations explained more of the variance in academic motivation than did the conjugal structure. The relation between family structure and adolescent motivation needs clarification and we shall examine it in greater detail in this paper. On the basis of our previous research, we propose the following hypothesis regarding family structure effects on boys of high-school age:

> 6. *High academic motivation is most likely to characterize boys from equalitarian families in which fathers allow them freedom for independent decision making, yet continue to exercise control and guidance over their behavior.*

SAMPLE

The data for the present study were secured from a larger program of research on adolescence in the Institute for Research in Social Science at the University of North Carolina. The objective of the larger research is the delineation of three types of adolescent attitudinal orientation toward mother, father and peers: affectional, associational and value. Analysis of the social bases and behavioral correlates of various patterns is a major part of this project. Of the larger sample of 19,200 white adolescents from unbroken homes, slightly fewer than half were obtained through the public and parochial school systems in central Ohio, and the rest from public schools in the rapidly industrializing central region of North Carolina. The data were collected in April and May, 1960, with a structured questionnaire administered by teachers in the classroom. The research reported in this paper is based on data from a 40 per cent sample of the 7th through 9th graders and a 60 per cent sample of the 10th through 12th graders randomly drawn from the total sample.

[28] William R. Morrow and Robert C. Wilson, "Family Relations of Bright High-Achieving and Under-Achieving High School Boys," *Child Development*, 32 (1961), 501–510. Cf. Elizabeth M. Douvan and Joseph B. Adelson, "The Psychodynamics of Social Mobility in Adolescent Boys," *Journal of Abnormal and Social Psychology*, 56 (January, 1958), 31–44.

[29] Glen H. Elder, Jr., *Adolescent Achievement and Mobility Aspirations*, Chapel Hill, North Carolina: The Institute for Research in Social Science, 1962.

RESULTS [30]

Family Structure: Variations by Age, Sex and Social Class

1. CONJUGAL POWER STRUCTURE. Each respondent was asked the following question on the conjugal role pattern: "When important family problems come up, which parent usually has the most *influence* in making the decision?" Those who felt that mother tended to make these decisions more often than father were classified as adolescents from wife-dominant homes; those who indicated father, as adolescents from husband-dominant homes; and those reporting both parents as equal or about equal in influence in family decisions were placed in the equalitarian category. (This method of measuring influence in family decision making is roughly similar to the one used by Hess and Torney.) [31]

The most commonly reported role structure is the equalitarian pattern (45.6 per cent) with husband-dominance (34.3 per cent) next and wife-dominance (20.1 per cent) least frequent. As hypothesized, the proportion of adolescents seeing no differentiated pattern in family leadership is much larger than the percentage who see mother as having the "final say" on such matters. Substantial variations in perception of conjugal structure by sex, social class, and age of adolescent are shown in Table 2.[32] The older age group includes adolescents in grades 10 through 12; younger adolescents are those in grades 7 through 9.

Older adolescents are more likely to report that father has the final say on family matters, while those of junior high school age are more likely to report equality between parents. No consistent age differences appear for wife-dominance. Perception of the more powerful parent varies by sex of adolescent, especially among older youths, with girls more likely than boys to see mother as dominant. Social class differences consistently support hypothesis 3 in each age and sex group; middle-class adolescents are more

---

[30] Percentage differences and gamma, a measure of association for ordinal variables, are our principal statistics. Since the sample and most subgroups are large, percentage differences of reasonable size represent "real" or significant differences. On gamma coefficient see Leo Goodman and William Kruskal, "Measures of Association for Cross Classifications, I," *Journal of the American Statistical Association*, 49 (December, 1954), 747–754.

[31] Hess and Torney, "Religion, Age and Sex in Children's Perceptions of Family Authority," *op. cit.*

[32] Social class was measured by assigning adolescents and their families to occupational categories employed by the U.S. Census Bureau. (Adolescents with fathers in farm occupations were excluded from the sample used in this study.)

Social Class	U.S. Census Occupational Categories
Middle	Professional, technical, and kindred workers Managers, officials, and proprietors, except farmers Clerical and kindred workers
Lower	Craftsmen, foremen, and kindred workers Operatives and kindred workers Laborers, except farm and mine

Table 2   Perception of Conjugal Power Structure by Age, Sex, and Social Class

CONJUGAL POWER STRUCTURE	Older Boys		Older Girls		Younger Boys		Younger Girls	
	MC [a] %	LC [a] %	MC %	LC %	MC %	LC %	MC %	LC %
Wife Dominant	16.6	22.6	23.7	28.0	14.0	19.9	13.0	21.4
Equalitarian	33.2	40.1	38.7	41.9	48.0	50.0	56.8	56.1
Husband Dominant	50.2	37.3	37.6	30.1	38.0	30.1	30.2	22.5
Total	100.0	100.0	100.0	100.0	100.0	100.0	100.0	100.0
Total N [b]	(897)	(950)	(899)	(970)	(878)	(948)	(821)	(1022)

[a] MC refers to Middle Class, LC to Lower Class.
[b] The difference between Tables 2 and 3 in subgroup totals is due to non-response variations.

likely to consider father as dominant, while lower-class youths are more likely to report mother as dominant. The equalitarian pattern is slightly more prevalent in lower-class families. Several aspects of these observed differences warrant examination in more detail.

The age differences shown in Table 2 are inconsistent with the results of a similar analysis reported by Hess and Torney.[33] The oldest respondents in their sample were in the 7th and 8th grades, while we include these two grades in our younger age group. Comparisons between 7th and 8th graders in their sample showed practically no differences in perception of family authority. When they compared the younger children with those 11 and older, however, perception of father dominance decreased and the equalitarian pattern increased in frequency among the older children. In contrast, our results show that perception of father dominance increases with age of adolescent. Much of the discrepancy between these two studies may be due to differences in the age composition of the samples and in the measurement of the conjugal role pattern. Lack of agreement among self-reports, interviewer ratings, and other techniques used to measure family power structure constitute a serious obstacle to replication.[34]

The largest sex differences appear among middle-class adolescents of high school age. Girls are more inclined to see mother as dominant, and boys are more apt to place father in this position. In the younger age group, sex differences are less marked; girls in this group are more likely to report equal influence for each parent, while the boys tend to check the father-dominant pattern. Social class differences across the four age and sex groups are generally relatively small, but in all sub-groups, father dominance is

[33] Hess and Torney, "Religion, Age and Sex in Children's Perceptions of Family Authority," *op. cit.*

[34] Preliminary research on this measurement problem has been conducted by Hess and Torney, "A Comparison of Methods Used to Measure Family Power Structure," *op. cit.* A preliminary analysis of agreement in perception of family relations between 294 sibling pairs drawn from our study, showed that 7.1 per cent of the pairs attributed dominance to different parents. See George T. Noel, III, "A Comparative Analysis of Siblings' Perception of Objective Events and Subjective Phenomena: A Validation Study," University of North Carolina, September, 1960, unpublished manuscript.

more commonly perceived in middle-class families, dominance by mother in lower-class homes. Dividing the sample into four social classes increases the average percentage difference for husband dominance (the percentage difference between upper-middle and lower-lower is well over 20 per cent for older boys). A smaller increase appears for wife-dominance.

2. PARENTAL AUTHORITY IN CHILD REARING. At points of obvious disagreement power differences become most apparent, but to function effectively as a unit, the family must resolve many of these differences. Each adolescent was asked which parent usually makes the final decision or has the greatest influence in making the decision when parents disagree on behavior limits and demands. As in the case of role relations in family decision making, the largest percentage of adolescents (44 per cent) report the shared pattern, while equal proportions (28 per cent) report mother and father dominance. In view of her traditional involvement in this area, it is surprising that mother is not more often considered the authority on child-rearing issues. Is this lack of difference due to fathers' tendency to assume control over behavior matters relevant to sons, and mothers' tendency to supervise daughters more than sons? The data in Table 3 do reveal large sex differ-

Table 3   Perception of Authority Pattern in Child Rearing by Age and Sex

AUTHORITY PATTERN IN CHILD REARING	Older Boys MC %	Older Boys LC %	Older Girls MC %	Older Girls LC %	Younger Boys MC %	Younger Boys LC %	Younger Girls MC %	Younger Girls LC %
Mother	22.4	24.5	37.8	42.0	15.9	19.2	28.2	31.1
Shared	37.5	40.8	32.8	32.4	52.7	55.4	49.7	47.9
Father	40.1	34.7	29.3	25.6	31.4	25.4	22.1	21.0
Total	100.0	100.0	100.0	100.0	100.0	100.0	100.0	100.0
Total N	(877)	(955)	(883)	(954)	(866)	(938)	(792)	(1009)

ences. As hypothesized, sex affects adolescent perception of the authority pattern in child rearing more strongly than perception of the conjugal structure. Boys tend to report father rather than mother as the principal authority figure, and the reverse is true for girls.

Older adolescents of both sexes are more likely to perceive one parent dominant, while younger adolescents are more apt to report shared decision making. Social class differences consistently support our expectations and parallel the results obtained on the conjugal structure. Father dominance is slightly more prevalent in middle-class families, while maternal dominance is more common in lower-class families. But class differences in maternal dominance, though in the expected direction, are relatively small. Comparison of the distribution of perceptions of the conjugal and parental structures reveals that adolescents of high school age are more likely to report father-dominance in both areas, while younger adolescents are more inclined to see little or no power difference between parents.

Overall, the data indicate that the perception of differentiation in parental power increases with age. Evidence presented earlier indicates that parents tend to be more active and firm with adolescents of the same sex. Thus, primary responsibility for handling sons is likely to be assumed by father, while mother takes charge of adolescent daughters. Many of the problems faced by older adolescent boys are best understood by someone who has gone through the same experience, as illustrated by the no doubt common plea of a perplexed mother to her husband to "please go talk to your son, I can't seem to get anywhere with him."

Dissimilarities between perceptions of the husband-wife and parental role structures suggest that our respondents considered these as two distinct areas of decision making. Parental role patterns vary substantially with sex of child, as we expected. We had less reason to expect as sharp a difference in perception of conjugal structure, and our data tend to confirm this expectation. And the fact that social class has a greater effect on the conjugal pattern than on child-rearing relations also indicates that these are distinguishable areas of decision making. However, power in one area is probably related to power in the other. How much correspondence is there?

Family Structural Patterns

We hypothesized that types of role structure in marital, child-rearing and parent-adolescent relations will be strongly related (hypothesis 4). In this section we shall examine first the association between types of role differ-

Table 4   Perception of the Conjugal Power Structure and the Parental Authority in Child Rearing (in percentages)

CONJUGAL POWER STRUCTURE	Parental Authority Pattern in Child Rearing				
	MOTHER	SHARED	FATHER	TOTAL	(N)
Wife Dominant	55.3	28.0	16.7	100	(1437)
Equalitarian	22.5	58.5	19.0	100	(3278)
Husband Dominant	18.4	32.5	49.1	100	(2480)

Degree of Association Between Role Structures
(gamma coefficients)

AGE AND SEX	MIDDLE CLASS	LOWER CLASS
Older Boys	.52	.42
Older Girls	.46	.46
Younger Boys	.46	.47
Younger Girls	.35	.39

entiation in the marital and parental relations and then the association between these nine structural patterns and types of interdependence in parent-adolescent relations. Is the parent perceived as dominant in family decision making the same parent also reported as dominant in establishing behavior restrictions and demands? Table 4 shows a strong relation between the two role patterns; at least half of the adolescents who report each of the three types of family leadership give the same response for the parental authority structure (gamma = .46). Note that the percentage of adolescents in wife-dominant families who perceive father as the authority figure is almost the same as the percentage in husband-dominant families who see mother as the authority. Among those who indicate that both parents are approximately equal in power in family decision making, mother is cited as the chief authority figure slightly more often than father.

Controlling for age, sex and social class does not change the association appreciably (see the bottom part of Table 4). Regardless of whom they believe rules the family, children of junior high school age are more likely than their older counterparts to report an equalitarian pattern in child rearing. At each age level, adolescents who do not report an equalitarian pattern choose the same-sex parent more often than the other as being in control in child rearing. This sex difference holds consistently regardless of the type of perceived family leadership. Families described by their adolescent sons and daughters as equalitarian in both areas of decision making constitute 27.9 per cent of the total sample; 16.7 per cent report husband dominance in both areas, and 11.3 per cent, wife dominance. In all instances, the proportions attributing dominance to the same parent in both areas are less than the proportion attributing dominance to that parent in only one area.

The power of the lower-class father in conjugal relations tends to be seen as relatively low, but in more cases than not, his son views him as the parent who makes the final decisions concerning his behavior. This result elaborates the oft-noted direct relation between a father's power in the family and his occupational status; lower-class paternal influence in child rearing is directly related to the sex of the child or children. A lower-class father may not rule his family, but at least he may rule his son. No differences worth noting appear among middle-class youths.

Cross-classification of the marital and parental role structures yields nine possible types of family structure. These are shown in Table 5 in relation to the structures of mother- and father-adolescent relations.[35] Inspection of Table 5 reveals that the two types of parental role structure differentially affect parent-adolescent relations. But parental role patterns are much more strongly related to each other (see Table 4) than to the degree of control parents exercise in rearing their children. Thus the hypothesized degree of correspondence in dominance patterns across marital, parental and parent-adolescent relations is not strongly supported by the data (see hypothesis 5). On the other hand, the equalitarian role pattern is, as we expected, more common in all three types of relationship than either maternal or paternal dominance.

[35] In Footnote 5 we described the items used to measure child-rearing structures. In this analysis we shall group the seven response categories into three categories as follows: 1. autocratic and authoritarian, 2. democratic and equalitarian, and 3. permissive, laissez-faire and ignoring, designating these categories as autocratic, democratic and permissive, respectively. Only data on adolescents in grades 10 through 12 are shown in Table 5; points at which the two age groups differ substantially will be noted in the text.

Table 5 Perception of Mother and Father Child-Rearing Structures in Relation to Variations in Parental Role Patterns: Older Adolescents (in percentages)

CONJUGAL POWER STRUCTURE	AUTHORITY PATTERN IN CHILD REARING	CHILD-REARING STRUCTURE BY PARENT	SOCIAL CLASS	Older Boys					Older Girls				
				NUMBER OF RESPONDENTS	AUTOCRATIC OR AUTHORITARIAN	DEMOCRATIC OR EQUALITARIAN	PERMISSIVE, LAISSEZ-FAIRE OR IGNORING	TOTAL	NUMBER OF RESPONDENTS	AUTOCRATIC OR AUTHORITARIAN	DEMOCRATIC OR EQUALITARIAN	PERMISSIVE, LAISSEZ-FAIRE OR IGNORING	TOTAL
Wife Dominant	Mother Dominant	Mother	MC	78	24.3	43.6	32.1	100	132	20.5	52.3	27.2	100
			LC	111	18.9	51.4	29.7	100	175	30.3	47.5	22.2	100
		Father	MC	78	26.9	43.5	29.6	100	132	31.1	40.2	28.7	100
			LC	111	34.2	30.7	35.1	100	175	33.1	40.0	26.9	100
	Shared	Mother	MC	44	9.1	54.5	36.4	100	48	14.6	56.2	29.2	100
			LC	47	17.0	53.2	29.8	100	66	21.2	50.0	28.8	100
		Father	MC	44	15.9	56.8	27.3	100	48	22.9	54.2	22.9	100
			LC	47	31.9	38.3	29.8	100	66	33.3	33.4	33.3	100
	Father Dominant	Mother	MC	24	29.1	58.4	12.5	100	30	23.4	39.9	36.7	100
			LC	57	17.6	47.3	35.1	100	31	16.0	63.4	20.6	100
		Father	MC	24	29.1	66.7	4.2	100	30	36.7	36.6	26.7	100
			LC	57	31.6	43.8	24.6	100	30	53.3	40.0	6.7	100

				N					N				
Equalitarian	Mother Dominant	Mother	MC	60	18.4	53.3	28.3	100	121	14.0	52.4	33.6	100
			LC	72	19.5	48.6	31.9	100	142	15.5	52.1	32.4	100
		Father	MC	60	30.1	46.6	23.3	100	122	31.2	40.2	28.6	100
			LC	72	43.1	30.5	26.4	100	142	26.1	43.7	30.2	100
	Shared	Mother	MC	152	17.8	53.6	28.6	100	139	10.8	59.6	29.6	100
			LC	221	18.1	52.9	29.0	100	174	10.9	47.9	41.2	100
		Father	MC	154	25.4	51.0	23.6	100	140	14.3	57.9	27.8	100
			LC	221	23.0	53.0	24.0	100	175	22.9	48.6	28.5	100
	Father Dominant	Mother	MC	77	19.5	57.1	23.4	100	76	19.8	60.1	20.1	100
			LC	88	21.6	45.4	33.0	100	76	17.1	48.7	34.2	100
		Father	MC	74	37.7	45.5	16.8	100	77	28.6	59.8	11.6	100
			LC	88	34.1	47.7	18.2	100	76	47.4	31.6	21.0	100
Husband Dominant	Mother Dominant	Mother	MC	60	8.4	61.0	30.6	100	75	6.7	60.0	33.3	100
			LC	50	22.0	54.0	24.0	100	84	15.4	56.0	28.6	100
		Father	MC	60	38.4	44.9	16.7	100	75	37.3	41.4	21.3	100
			LC	50	48.0	30.0	22.0	100	84	47.6	49.3	13.1	100
	Shared	Mother	MC	128	14.9	58.1	27.0	100	102	9.8	70.6	19.6	100
			LC	121	18.2	54.6	27.2	100	67	16.4	52.3	31.3	100
		Father	MC	129	33.3	49.6	17.1	100	102	33.3	53.9	12.8	100
			LC	121	36.4	48.8	14.8	100	67	38.8	37.2	24.0	100
	Father Dominant	Mother	MC	245	15.1	54.8	30.1	100	151	15.9	54.3	29.8	100
			LC	183	21.3	45.4	33.3	100	141	22.0	50.4	27.6	100
		Father	MC	247	37.6	48.2	14.2	100	151	48.4	37.7	13.9	100
			LC	183	37.7	46.4	15.9	100	139	57.6	25.1	17.3	100

A boy who reports maternal dominance in both family and child-rearing matters is not likely to describe his mother as autocratic in controlling his behavior—only a fourth of the older middle-class boys in mother-dominated families feel that their mothers make all decisions that concern them and do not take seriously their points of view. In fact, a larger percentage (32.1) report that their mothers are permissive. Among younger boys who see mother as dominant in family matters and in child-rearing, however, 36.2 per cent see mother as autocratic, and 21.3 per cent, as permissive. Comparisons of the percentage autocratic with the percentage permissive among older and younger middle-class girls from mother-dominated homes show similar differences. Among lower-class youth from mother-dominated homes, the percentage differences for maternal control are similar in direction (except for older girls), but larger.

How is father perceived in a wife-dominated home? About one third of the older girls and boys describe their fathers as autocratic and about one third permissive. On the other hand, younger boys and girls are more than twice as likely to report autocratic fathers as they are permissive fathers. Both parents in wife-dominated families are more likely to be permissive than domineering with sons and daughters of high school age, and more likely to be autocratic with younger adolescents. In families in which mother is perceived as more influential than father, dominance in parental relations does not necessarily imply dominance in parent-adolescent relations. Approximately 75 per cent of the older adolescent sons who perceive mother as the power figure in family and child-rearing affairs do *not* see mother as autocratic.

Clearly, a matriarchal family, in which mother is dominant in all three relationships, is rare in our sample. Available data indicate that such a family is likely to be an extremely rejecting, conflict-ridden environment for the child because fathers are seldom perceived as less controlling in child-rearing relations than their wives.[36] A shared or equalitarian arrangement in decision making in either or both marital and parental relations, in contrast to singular leadership in either or both areas, produces comparatively small proportions describing parents as autocratic. When both types of parental relationships are characterized by more power in the hands of one parent, the likelihood of domination in parent-adolescent relations by this parent is usually greater, with the exceptions visible in Table 5.

Though a wife's dominance over her husband is relatively unlikely to be accompanied by dominance over her children, a high degree of correspondence occurs in equalitarian families. More than half the adolescents from this type of family indicate that their parents are either democratic or equalitarian, and generally, larger percentages characterize their parents as permissive than autocratic. Larger proportions of lower-class adolescents tend to report parents as autocratic.

[36] See Elder, "Structural Variations in the Child Rearing Relationship," *op. cit.*, and "Family Structure and the Transmission of Norms and Values in the Process of Child Rearing," unpublished Ph.D. dissertation, University of North Carolina, Ch. 5.

In families in which father is seen as chief decision-maker on family and child-rearing issues, 37.6 per cent of the middle-class boys see their fathers as autocratic, while 14.2 per cent describe them as permissive. In contrast, the percentages of autocratic, democratic, and permissive mothers in this type of family are 15.1, 54.8 and 30.1, respectively. These results do not differ substantially from those obtained from lower-class youth. Turning to older girls in father-dominated families we find that both middle- and lower-class girls are more likely than their male counterparts to report father as either autocratic or authoritarian, but are less likely to describe father as democratic or equalitarian. The prevalence of each mother-youth pattern does not vary meaningfully by sex.

The extreme patriarchal is more than three times as common as the extreme matriarchal family, of which there are approximately 200 in our sample. Of course, the most prevalent type is the equalitarian family reported by well over 1,000 youths. As is evident in Table 5, paternal dominance vis à vis the adolescent is equally probable whenever there is asymmetry of any kind in husband-wife relations. In wife-dominant and equalitarian families, on the other hand, lack of equality between parents in child-rearing authority is associated with relatively large percentages reporting autocratic mothers.

Perhaps the most interesting result in this regard is the low frequency of authoritarian mothers in middle-class homes in which father is seen as the head of the family and mother is perceived as the authority figure in child rearing. This type of family structure conforms most closely to the traditional American conception of the appropriate roles for man and wife; a man should be the head of the household, while a wife's primary domain is in child rearing. Less than 10 per cent of the older boys and girls from this type of middle-class family report that mother is autocratic in contrast to about 20 per cent among lower-class youth. Paternal autocratic or authoritarian control is substantially more common: an average for both sexes of 38 per cent among middle-class adolescents and 48 per cent among lower-class youth.

In conclusion, patterns of parental role differentiation do not accurately reflect role differentiation in parent-adolescent relations. Even when mother is seen as more powerful than father, she is just as likely to be described by her older children as permissive as she is to be described as autocratic. Among older youths from wife-dominant families, equality or democracy in parent-adolescent relations tends to be the modal pattern. Well over half of all adolescents in equalitarian families describe their parents as either democratic or equalitarian, and a similarly high degree of correspondence appears between husband-dominance and father-dominance in relations with adolescent children. In wife-dominated families, however, three fourths of the mothers are not described as autocratic.

Family Structure, Parental Warmth and Adolescent Behavior

1. PARENTAL SUPPORT. Are parents in wife-dominated families perceived as less affectionate and understanding than parents in other types of families? The data presented in Table 6 support our hypothesis that a high

Table 6   Perception of Parents as High on Emotional Support in Relation to Variations in Family Structure

Conjugal Power Structure	Authority in Child Rearing	Per Cent of Adolescents Reporting Parents as Supportive:[a]			
		MOTHER		FATHER	
		Middle Class	Lower Class	Middle Class	Lower Class
Wife Dominant	Mother	59.4 (315)	56.7 (488)	43.2 (315)	35.9 (492)
	Shared	70.1 (174)	61.1 (254)	52.9 (174)	41.3 (254)
	Father	53.4 (90)	57.6 (146)	40.7 (91)	39.5 (147)
Equali-tarian	Mother	72.2 (341)	69.1 (408)	51.8 (342)	43.5 (409)
	Shared	76.7 (841)	67.7 (1060)	67.2 (842)	56.0 (1062)
	Father	71.0 (303)	65.1 (324)	61.8 (302)	50.2 (325)
Husband Dominant	Mother	69.0 (232)	66.1 (224)	52.5 (232)	45.8 (225)
	Shared	66.0 (441)	56.9 (369)	62.4 (442)	52.7 (370)
	Father	63.9 (659)	58.4 (556)	57.4 (657)	48.6 (553)

[a] Supportiveness was measured by a two-item index for each parent. The percentage of youths indicating high support for mother and/or father includes those adolescents who felt they could "always depend on their mother/father for support and encouragement when they really needed it," and those who gave "sometimes" as a response to this question and also described mother/father as frequently praising and approving.

degree of supportiveness is not characteristic of the dominant mother and her husband in this type of family (see hypothesis 5). Approximately three fifths of these mothers are reported as highly supportive, encouraging and praising; about two fifths of the fathers are similarly described. In equalitarian families, the proportions of mothers and fathers who are considered highly supportive are larger than in any other type of family. This finding corroborates results obtained by Straus and by Bronfenbrenner and Devereux.

In per cent reported high on support, fathers who are described as dominant in family affairs and in child rearing are generally intermediate to fathers in the other two types of families. Thus, with the exception of mothers in father-dominated families, the data shown in Table 6 confirm the first part of hypothesis 5. Mothers are in all cases more likely than fathers to be reported as highly supportive. Though sex differences are not shown in Table 6, this difference is larger among girls than among boys. Middle-class parents are consistently more often described as encouraging and supportive than are lower-class parents, and middle-class mothers and lower-class fathers are at opposite ends of the supportive continuum. Social class differences are substantially larger for fathers than for mothers.

Variations in parental warmth and support are affected by parental authority patterns within each type of conjugal structure. In husband-dominated and equalitarian families, paternal support is most common when child-rearing authority is shared, and least common when mother dominates. Maternal support, however, tends to occur most often when mother is the child-rearing authority. In husband-dominant families, for example, mother is more likely to be high on support when she, not father, is seen as the authority figure in child rearing, and under these conditions, father is least apt to be described as supportive. When father is the principal authority in child-rearing, he is most likely to be perceived as encouraging and approving, while mother is least apt to be so described. Similar but smaller differences occur in the wife-dominated family.

These results indicate that the parental authority pattern does have a significant effect on perceptions of parents as sources of support and affection. They are also consistent with Devereux's description of the wife-dominated family; mother is perceived as assuming both the instrumental and expressive roles, while father is seen as contributing little to either task.[37] We cannot conclude, however, that father withdraws from child-rearing, for, as we have observed, as many as 50 per cent of fathers in wife-dominated families are perceived as democratic or equalitarian, and a disproportionate number are perceived by their children as exercising extreme forms of behavior control. Middle-class fathers in wife-dominated families are more apt to be reported as adopting the permissive approach, while lower-class fathers are more inclined to be autocratic or authoritarian. Previous research has indicated that permissive fathers (not including the laissez-faire and ignoring types) are much more likely to be perceived as supportive than autocratic fathers, with an average percentage difference of more than 25 per cent.[38]

2. ACADEMIC MOTIVATION AND ASPIRATIONS. In what type of family are we most likely to find boys with high academic motivation and educational goals? The research by Straus and Bronfenbrenner and Devereux mentioned earlier indicates that boys from mother-dominated homes tend to have high, if not the highest, grades and aspirations, while Strodtbeck's research suggests that a democratic type of family is the most favorable environment for high achievers. Father-dominated families have been pictured consistently as settings for incompetent, low-achieving, dependent boys. In a recently completed analysis of the achievement and mobility aspirations of the adolescents in the present study, both husband-wife structure and father-adolescent structure were related to a five-item scale of academic motivation.[39] An analysis of variance revealed that the effect of paternal power in child-rearing relations on the academic motivation of older adolescent boys was greater than the effect of paternal power in

[37] Devereux, "Children of Democracy," *op. cit.*, p. 4. See also Judson T. Landis, "A Re-examination of the Role of the Father as an Index of Family Integration," *Marriage and Family Living*, 24 (May, 1962), 122–128.

[38] Elder, "Structural Variations in the Child-Rearing Relationship," *op. cit.*

[39] Elder, *Adolescent Achievement and Mobility Aspirations, op. cit.*

conjugal relations. Variations in the structure of father-son relations explained two to three times as much of the variance in academic motivation as did variations in conjugal structure. (Social class was controlled throughout.) Boys with autocratic fathers in husband- and wife-dominated families generally had the lowest mean scores; of the three types of husband-wife structures, wife-dominance was associated with the lowest mean scores. Academic motivation appeared to be strongest among boys who saw their fathers both as head of the family and as democratic in relations with the boys. Roughly similar results were obtained with comparable data from girls of high school age.

Conceivably, boys who are motivated to do well in school may not have high educational goals. Since authority relations in school are in many respects similar to those in the family, boys from father-dominant families may do well in structured school situations, but have little desire to achieve beyond a high school education. They may view their environment as something to accept rather than master, to passively tolerate rather than change. But if results on educational goals should parallel those secured on academic motivation, our interpretation of structural effects would be strengthened. To examine these possibilities, we have presented in Table 7 the

Table 7   College Plans of High School Boys in Relation to Paternal Power in the Marital and Parent-Child Relationships

SOCIAL CLASS	CONJUGAL POWER STRUC- TURE	Per Cent Expecting to Go to College				
		TYPE OF FATHER-SON RELATIONS [a]				
		AUTO- CRATIC	AUTHORI- TARIAN	DEMO- CRATIC	EQUALI- TARIAN	PER- MISSIVE
Middle Class	Wife	24.9 (17)	38.8 (18)	63.1 (46)	58.6 (29)	54.1 (37)
	Equal	40.5 (42)	64.4 (45)	56.6 (90)	62.5 (56)	54.7 (64)
	Husband	47.7 (65)	62.4 (96)	69.9 (163)	54.0 (50)	55.1 (69)
Lower Class	Wife	18.4 (49)	34.8 (23)	33.3 (54)	12.0 (25)	16.2 (68)
	Equal	11.1 (63)	13.7 (51)	26.4 (121)	23.3 (60)	24.4 (90)
	Husband	18.1 (72)	25.0 (64)	36.4 (118)	18.6 (43)	22.0 (59)

[a] The percentages in each cell represent the proportion of older adolescent boys who, when asked what they thought about the chances that they would go on to college, gave "I expect to go" as a response. The other four responses to this question ranged from "I probably will go" to "I definitely will not go."

percentage of older boys who expect to go to college, in relation to variations in conjugal and father-adolescent relations.

These results are very similar to those obtained for academic motivation. In both social classes, democratically-reared youths from husband-dominated families are more likely to expect to go on to college. The largest differences in per cent planning to go to college are between autocratic and authoritarian structures and between the wife-dominated and equalitarian patterns. Percentage differences between wife-dominant and equalitarian structures are largest among boys with autocratic and authoritarian fathers.

Thus, either wife-dominance in the family or autocratic paternal control in child-rearing, or both in combination, are relatively unlikely to promote high educational aspirations among boys. (Educational goals of parents are also an important factor, however, since less than a third of these boys report that their parents want them to go to college.) These results and those reported on academic motivation, suggest that the effects of conjugal structure are mediated to a considerable degree by the structure of parent-child relations. The data consistently indicate that parental power in parent-adolescent relations explains more of the variation in motivation to achieve in school and in college plans than the conjugal structure.

Although some of these results may appear to conflict with findings reported by Bronfenbrenner and Devereux and Straus, the differences are probably more apparent than real. This is best appreciated by a more detailed look at the design and findings of Bronfenbrenner and Devereux's Ithaca study. We mentioned earlier that they developed five empirical types of family structure from adolescent responses to a series of questions on decision making in four areas, thus permitting division of the 10th graders in their sample into five groups. These groups were compared on teachers' ratings of personality and behavior and on a number of family variables. The relation they obtained between the conjugal structure and authority patterns in child-rearing is quite similar to the one we have reported.

On achievement and aspirations, the results of the Ithaca study do not correspond to ours. This may be due to the substantial variation we have observed in parent-child relations, even when *extreme* types of husband-wife structure are delineated, as in the Ithaca study. By working with categories derived from conjugal and parent-child relations, we may have controlled some of the variance in family structure that is uncontrolled in the Ithaca study.

We have found that the characteristics of parent-adolescent relations appear to affect adolescent attitudes and behavior more than do characteristics of other family relationships. Nevertheless these other relationships not only help to explain the nature of parent-child interaction but also have independent effects on the development of children. The complexity of personality seems to require investigation of the full range of variation in family structure and its effects if we are to comprehend the relation between personality and family structure. (*Perception* of family power structure is, of course, not the same as the *actual* power structure of the family.[40] Construction of valid measurement techniques for the study of family structure is an important task for future research on this problem.)

Approximately one fourth of the adolescents who report their mothers as dominant in conjugal and child-rearing decisions describe their mothers as either autocratic or authoritarian. This type of family structure is relatively rare in our sample, but in a recent study Kohn and Clausen found that the strong mother–weak father constellation was more common in the families

[40] Hess and Torney, "A Comparison of Methods Used to Measure Family Power Structure," *op. cit.*

of schizophrenics than it was in the families of controls.[41] Their research focused on authority and affection patterns in child-rearing relations; hence data on the balance of power between mother and father was not obtained. A more complete picture of the structure of the families of schizophrenic patients would require information as to whether this same sharply asymmetrical pattern was also reported for mother-father relations. Are fathers in these families submissive to their wives *and* to their children? Since several studies suggest that this pattern is common in families of mental patients, future research on family structure and mental illness should examine simultaneously the structure of marital and parent-child relations.[42]

SUMMARY

This research has examined structural variations in three basic family relationships: the conjugal, the parental, and the parent-adolescent. Drawing from a large number of studies of family structure, six hypotheses were proposed on variations in each relationship by age, sex and social class of the adolescent, on structural patterns in the family and on the effect of different family structural patterns on adolescent educational goals and parental support. Measures of family structure and adolescent motivation and goals were obtained from structured questionnaires administered in classrooms to a large sample of adolescents living in Ohio and in North Carolina. The analysis of the data largely confirmed the hypotheses.

A crude typology of parental power in decision making was developed for both marital and parental relations: wife or mother-dominance, equalitarian or shared, and husband or father-dominance. The largest proportion of adolescents reported that their parents had equal power in family decision making with husband-dominance and wife-dominance next in order of prevalence. Husband-dominance was most commonly reported by middle-class older boys, while lower-class older girls most often described their families as wife-dominant. The equalitarian structure was reported most often by younger adolescent girls.

The shared type of child-rearing structure was indicated by almost half of the adolescents in the sample; equal proportions reported mother- and father-dominant structures. Controls for age, sex and social class revealed marked variations by sex among older youths, the same-sex parent being reported as the principal authority figure more often than the parent of the opposite sex.

More often than not, adolescents who perceive a parent as more powerful in family matters tend also to see this parent as being the authority figure in

---

[41] Melvin L. Kohn and John A. Clausen, "Parental Authority Behavior and Schizophrenia," *American Journal of Orthopsychiatry*, 26 (April, 1956), 297–313.

[42] See, for instance, Theodore Lidz, Beulah Parker, and Alice Cornelison, "The Role of the Father in the Family Environment of the Schizophrenic Patient," *American Journal of Psychiatry*, 113 (1956), 126–132, and Murray Bowen, Robert H. Dysinger, and Betty Basamania, "The Role of the Father in Families with a Schizophrenic Patient," *American Journal of Psychiatry*, 115 (1959), 1017–1020.

child-rearing policy. Very little association was observed between dominance in conjugal relations and dominance in parent-child relations. While some variations in this pattern by age and sex were observed, no class differences were obtained. Fathers were most often described as autocratic or authoritarian if they *or* their wives were seen as most powerful in either family affairs or in child rearing, or in both. Mothers were most likely to be considered autocratic or authoritarian if they were seen as having more power than father in conjugal relations. The results of this analysis clearly indicated that parental power in child-rearing relations is not accurately pictured from knowledge of a child's perception of one parent's power over the other. This is most dramatically illustrated by the finding that less than a fourth of the older adolescents in mother-dominant homes report that their mothers are autocratic or authoritarian.

The effects of the structure of marital and parental relations on perceptions of parental support and warmth were most striking with respect to father's role in child rearing. Fathers who neither share nor individually assume leadership responsibilities in family affairs and child-rearing were relatively unlikely to be perceived as a major source of support and encouragement. High scholastic performance and goals among high school boys were most frequent when father was seen as most powerful in family decision making and democratic in parent-child relations.

Our analysis has several implications for study of the relation between family structure and personality development. First, the effects of family structure vary depending on the relationships involved. For instance, an adolescent's motivation and college plans are influenced more by the structure of his relations with his mother and father than by the balance of power between his parents. Secondly, the abbreviated model of structural differentiation in the family explored in this paper shows that family structure is extremely complex; research and theoretical development sensitive to this complexity are essential.

John Scanzoni

Inconclusiveness in
Family Sources of Achievement

When a citizen of contemporary America expresses an ambition "to do well" or "to get ahead," cultural approval is nearly unanimous. A certain amount of achievement motivation appears to be one of the prime requisites for successful citizenship in the twentieth century. Generally speaking, children develop achievement motivation when parents compel them to excel and to rely on their own resources. However, as Scanzoni suggests below, the myriad antecedents of achievement-oriented behavior have yet to be fully specified. He reviews several viewpoints, derived from both psychoanalytic and modeling or role theories, regarding family sources of achievement motivation. The notions emerge bipolarized, stressing on the one hand that achievement behavior may result from identification with the same-sex parent, and on the other, that it may issue from the opposite-sex parent. Also, what about father-rejection and father-absence? To remedy the impreciseness, Scanzoni investigates achievement orientation in relation to family power structure, parental child-rearing attitudes, and social class. The results are equivocal; thus, he calls for an expanded theoretical framework, encompassing peer relations, in order to develop a systematic explanation of this exceedingly important attribute of socialization.

THE literature on achievement values and motivation places great stress on the role that family socialization experiences play in the development of these orientations. Yet beyond this level of general agreement there exists what Goode calls "a mass of complex and sometimes conflicting evidence."[1] Specifically, the disparity often centers over the kinds of parent-child relationships that actually result in either high or low achievement. For example, Dynes, *et al.*, found that "feelings of not being wanted by parents," "low attachment to parents," only "average or less childhood happiness," i.e., "unsatisfactory interpersonal relationships in the family," are related to *high* levels of aspiration.[2] "Satisfactory" family relationships (feeling wanted,

FROM *Pacific Sociological Review*, IX (1966), 108–114. Reprinted by permission of the author and the publisher.

[1] William J. Goode, *The Family*, Englewood Cliffs, N.J.: Prentice-Hall, 1964, p. 77.
[2] Russell R. Dynes, Alfred C. Clarke, Simon Dinitz, "Levels of Occupational Aspiration: Some Aspects of Family Experience as a Variable," *American Sociological Review*, 21 (April, 1956), 212–215.

high parental attachment, high childhood happiness) are, they concluded related to low achievement. The authors suggest that their findings support the psychoanalytic theme that rejection of parents and lack of identification with them results in overcompensation through extrafamilial means such as occupational achievement.

Goode, unlike Dynes, *et al.*, does not treat parents as a parcel. He does, however, draw on Freud to stress the "importance of the mother-son tie," i.e., the "special grace of the boy who knew he was his mother's favorite." [3] The mother of the achieving boy, says Goode, is demanding, nurturant, trains for independence through permissiveness, and rewards achievement with affection. The role of the father is apparently unimportant so long as he does not attempt to dominate the boy. To do so would be to reduce his level of achievement. Thus, for Goode, it is not so much *rejection* of parents but *identification* with the mother that results in achievement.

McClelland also traces his arguments to "psychoanalysis," [4] and agrees that "dominating behavior does not interfere with development of n achievement if it comes from the mother, but only if it comes from the father." [5] He argues that it is important for the father to be present and active when the boy is young (through age 8) so as to prevent a matri-centric situation which is characteristic of low achievement, for example, among lower-class Negro males. But as the boy leaves his primary years McClelland asks, "What general conditions are likely to promote the *absence* of the father from the home so that he cannot *interfere* with the boy's development of high n achievement?" He cites evidence from the Abegglen study of highly mobile top executives which indicates that these men had "rejected" their fathers due to unsatisfactory childhood relationships.[6] Cross-cultural studies are also cited which seem to indicate that father-absence is related to high achievement. Therefore, while McClelland agrees with Goode about the import of mother-identification, he goes beyond him to stress strongly the significance of father-rejection, or at least father-absence in later childhood.

What makes Bronfenbrenner's report different from those above is that while he begins with the familiar "Freudian theory" which "implies that punitiveness by the father is particularly traumatic for boys," he concludes on a different note. "We are led from a psychological (Freudian) to a sociological or structural level of explanation." [7] What this means is that we have come full circle from the emphasis of Dynes, *et al.*, on rejection of *both* parents to a position in which identification with both parents—particularly the one of the same sex—is considered vital for achievement. Bron-

[3] *Op. cit.*

[4] David C. McClelland, *The Achieving Society*, New York: D. Van Nostrand, 1961, p. 340.

[5] *Ibid.*, pp. 344 ff.

[6] *Ibid.*, p. 404.

[7] Urie Bronfenbrenner, "Responsibility and Leadership in Adolescents," in Luigi Petrullo and Bernard M. Bass, *Leadership and Interpersonal Behavior*, New York: Holt, Rinehart and Winston, 1961, p. 266.

fenbrenner argues that responsibility and leadership (behavioral indicators) are maximized among *boys* when the *father* is the principal disciplinarian and source of emotional, affective support; and in *girls* when the *mother* is the principal source of instrumental and expressive interaction. "In short, boys thrive in a patriarchal context, girls in a matriarchal." [8] Thus, positive identification with the parent of the same sex—rather than rejection or low identification—is said to result in achievement behavior. His major departure from the other studies is his stress on the positive contribution that the father can make toward male achievement. It is this unique feature that distinguishes his findings from these others—particularly from those of McClelland. Due to limited space, no attempt has been made to conduct an exhaustive review of this type of literature. However, it is felt that these studies are representative of the differing sets of conclusions one might encounter within the child socialization literature.

It is not uncommon today in sociology and social psychology to discover conflicts and ambiguities among substantive research findings. To remedy this inconclusiveness, more research is needed. But what variables should be examined? The reports discussed above suggest that questions such as the following must be asked. What is the exact role of the *father* in male and in female achievement? Is it a question of power plus support (Bronfenbrenner) or is it one of permissiveness (McClelland)? Is it a question of high or low identification and perhaps even rejection? And what part does the *mother* actually play with regard to the boy—to the girl? To what extent do answers to these questions vary by social class? Careful examination of these kinds of questions reveals that they continue in the traditional pattern of examining achievement values solely within the intra-familial context, apart from external considerations. The data which follow are couched within this familiar pattern. Through them, a systematic attempt is made to answer the questions just posed. Can we discover what kinds of socialization experiences with which parent are most strongly linked to certain achievement orientations?

The data were collected as part of a larger study to investigate the consequences of achievement orientations on marital organization. Classrooms of juniors and seniors taking a required course were randomly selected from two predominantly white high schools, and questionnaires were administered to every student during the class period. To measure parent-child interaction, eighteen dimensions were borrowed from Bronfenbrenner,[9] and the student was asked to indicate how father and mother *separately* behaved toward him in terms of *each* dimension. The Likert-type responses were: extremely true, quite true, slightly true, not true. The dimensions with a sample item (from among three) are as follows:

1. Principled Discipline: "Reasoned with me when I misbehaved."
2. Material Reward: "Rewarded me for doing well by giving me money."

[8] *Ibid.*, p. 267.
[9] *Ibid.*, p. 243.

3. Instrumental Companionship: "Took part in activities and projects with me."
4. Authority and Power: "Insisted that they knew best and that I must accept their decisions."
5. Physical Punishment and Threat: "Spanked and whipped me."
6. Parental Absence: "Missed supper with children at least two nights a week."
7. Parental Neglect: "Was too busy or unconcerned to answer my questions."
8. Achievement Demands: "Pushed me to excel in everything I did."
9. Isolation-type Punishment: "Punished me by sending me out of the room or to bed."
10. Parental Rejection: "Let me know I wasn't wanted."
11. Affective Punishment: "Punished me by trying to make me feel ashamed."
12. Affiliative Companionship: "Spent a lot of time with me not doing anything special."
13. Nurture: "Made me feel wanted and needed."
14. Parental Intercession: "Tried to get the other parent to give in to me."

Table 1 Middle-Class Boys

	Father		*Mother*		*Parents Combined*	
	Multiple	*Partial*	*Multiple*	*Partial*	*Multiple*	*Partial*
Familism	.481	.246(3)	.413	.164(3)(8)	.648	.293(7F)
Activism	.465	.143(4)	.437	.169(4)	.590	.238(4M)
Trust	.333	.092(16)	.535	.319(16)	.627	.288(13M)
Individualism	.396	.125(12)	.434	.205(17)	.609	.286(10M)
Deferred Gratifications	.462	.175(16)	.480	.213(2)	.604	.199(2M)
Occupational Primacy	.374	.103(10)	.482	.260(3)	.572	.313(3M)
Anomy	.484	.203(12)	.462	.206(7)	.661	.266(8F)
N = 119						

Table 2 Middle-Class Girls

	Father		*Mother*		*Parents Combined*	
	Multiple	*Partial*	*Multiple*	*Partial*	*Multiple*	*Partial*
Familism	.411	.181(2)	.481	.182(18)	.591	.208(15M)
Activism	.472	.195(1)	.476	.198(5)	.607	.264(5M)
Trust	.389	.183(7)	.393	.131(13)(18)	.515	.208(7F)
Individualism	.394	.198(13)	.418	.192(13)	.598	.275(13M)
Deferred Gratifications	.355	.134(17)	.312	.153(6)	.497	.182(2M)
Occupational Primacy	.373	.210(1)	.434	.197(5)	.587	.247(5M)
Anomy	.395	.222(2)	.348	.175(2)	.535	.262(2F)
N = 138						

15. Indulgence: "Couldn't say 'no' to me."
16. Affective Reward: "Rewarded good behavior by praising me and saying nice things to me."
17. Support: "Was always ready to listen to my problems."
18. Protectiveness: "Wouldn't let me go places because something might happen to me."

Kahl, using factor analysis, has derived at least four different scales (based on the kinds of items used by McClelland, Strodtbeck, etc.) to measure the "component dimensions" of achievement: [10] *familism* (loyalty

Table 3   Lower-Class Boys

	Father		Mother		Parents Combined	
	Multiple	*Partial*	*Multiple*	*Partial*	*Multiple*	*Partial*
Familism	.312	.193(17)	.401	.275(2)	.499	.260(2M)
Activism	.334	.188(13)	.402	.102(12)	.587	.252(2F)
Trust	.454	.161(13)	.406	.112(9)	.561	.192(9M)
Individualism	.313	.175(8)	.318	.167(3)	.574	.278(8F)
Deferred Gratifications	.442	.399(17)	.546	.269(4)	.594	.239(9M)
Occupational Primacy	.441	.220(17)	.451	.215(17)	.598	.253(17M)
Anomy	.452	.238(11)	.472	.260(2)	.557	.246(7M)
N = 114						

Table 4   Lower-Class Girls

	Father		Mother		Parents Combined	
	Multiple	*Partial*	*Multiple*	*Partial*	*Multiple*	*Partial*
Familism	.286	.101(17)	.405	.169(13)	.575	.348(2F)
Activism	.358	.115(13)	.483	.354(16)	.613	.387(16M)
Trust	.395	.215(15)	.310	.131(11)	.500	.221(15F)
Individualism	.366	.132(18)	.273	.156(10)	.501	.237(18F)
Deferred Gratifications	.440	.238(8)	.517	.213(13)	.646	.262(13M)
Occupational Primacy	.410	.114(17)	.403	.185(6)	.574	.200(6M)
Anomy	.353	.197(8)	.398	.151(10)	.511	.167(10M)
N = 133						

[10] Joseph A. Kahl, "Some Measurements of Achievement Orientation," *American Journal of Sociology,* 70 (May, 1965), 669 ff. Sample items include: *familism,* "Nothing in life is worth the sacrifice of moving away from your parents"; *activism,* "It is important to make plans for one's life and not just accept what comes"; *trust,* "Most people are fair and do not try to get away with something"; *occupational primacy,* "The best way to judge a man is by his success in his occupation"; *individualism,* "A person should rely on himself rather than on others"; *deferred gratifications,* "A person shouldn't let his plans for the future keep him from having a good time now."

to parents instead of to self or to career), (row 1 in the tables); *activism* (emphasis on planning for a controllable future), (row 2); *trust* (mastery over life-chances depends on an ancillary belief in the stability of life and the trustworthiness of people . . . one must have faith in human relationships to plan carefully for his future through orderly commitment to successive steps in career advancement), (row 3); *occupational primacy* (occupational success comes ahead of alternative possibilities), (row 4). To these we have added *individualism* (willingness of the individual to rely on himself rather than on external sources), (row 5), and *deferred gratifications* (willingness to forgo current pleasures and enjoyment in lieu of long-range benefits), (row 6). We have also included the McClosky-Schaar scale of *anomy* which they define as a view of "society as normless, morally chaotic, and adrift—in a word, anomic." [11] As thus defined, "anomy" has been linked to low levels of achievement.[12] Furthermore, the authors claim that anomy is the result of "faulty socialization," which in turn is related to low levels of achievement. Therefore, a measure such as this becomes useful as a type of validity check on the kinds of relationship that might emerge between socialization and achievement.

RESULTS

The sample was divided into four categories on the basis of father's occupation. "Middle-class" includes business, professional, and white-collar workers, plus foremen and skilled workers.[13] "Lower-class" includes semi-skilled and unskilled workers. The multiple correlations under "father" in each table reflect the combined impact of all the 18 socialization variables listed above. (For example, "extremely true" that *father* "reasoned with me when I misbehaved.") The partials under "father" represent the one variable of the 18 which has the *highest* correlation with a particular dependent achievement variable, holding the remaining 17 constant. The identification number of the "socialization variable" is in parentheses. The same explanation applies to multiples and partials within the "mother" columns except that the 18 socialization variables represent how the *mother* behaved toward her children, and are distinct from the 18 father variables.

When we move to the "parents combined" columns, the multiples reflect

11 Herbert McClosky and John H. Schaar, "Psychological Dimensions of Anomy," *American Sociological Review*, 30 (February, 1965), 14–39.

12 Ephraim Mizruchi, *Success and Opportunity*, New York: The Free Press, 1964, p. 150.

13 It can be argued that when one is interested primarily in gross categorizations, these kinds of upper-manual workers are probably part of the broad "middle-class." Certainly, in terms of income and power they equal and sometimes surpass many low-level non-manual occupations. The same can be assumed in terms of their values, aspirations for children, life-style, and perhaps even prestige. For example, in a 1963 replication of the 1947 North-Hatt study, it was found that the national prestige rating score of blue-collar craftsmen went up 2.3 per cent, while the score of clerical and sales occupations went down 0.4 per cent. See Robert W. Hodge, Paul M. Siegel, and Peter H. Rossi, "Occupational Prestige in the United States, 1925–63," *American Journal of Sociology*, 69 (November, 1964), 299.

the relationship of the father's 18 plus the mother's 18 socialization variables. The partials show which one of the 36 has the highest correlation to the particular dependent variable, holding constant the remaining 35. The identification number of the socialization variable along with F or M (for father or mother) is in parentheses.

It will be recalled that our chief purpose is not to compare these four categories in terms of scores on either socialization experiences or achievement orientations. Instead, our objective is twofold: (1) to discover the *total impact* of intra-family (father-child and mother-child) experiences on achievement orientations; (2) to determine whether we can identify what particular kinds of parent-child relations are linked to certain achievement orientations. In terms of the first objective, we note that in all four tables most of the 56 multiple correlations for father or mother are on the order of .3 (21 relationships) or .4 (30 relationships). These relatively low-order correlations leave a great deal of the variance in these relationships unexplained. In other words, these correlations are sufficiently weak to suggest that there are other significant variables that may affect achievement orientations.

Even when we look at the 28 multiples for parents-combined, 18 are at the order of .5, 8 are at the .6 level, and 2 are at the order of .4. If the traditional approach to sources of achievement (i.e., emphasis on intra-familial relations) has validity, then we would have expected much stronger relationships between the joint affects of both parents and achievement values. The same inconclusiveness applies when we look at the partials. Of those 56 correlations dealing with one parent alone, 35 are at the order of .1, one at the .0 level, 17 at the .2 level, and 3 are at the .3 level. When the 28 partial relationships between parents combined and the dependent variables are examined, 21 are at the .2 level, four at the .1 level, and three are at the .3 level.

Therefore, whatever substantive patterns one might look for between, for example, nurture, control, support, rejection, etc., and various achievement orientations, such relationships would have to be considered highly tentative due to the low-order correlations. Furthermore, in terms of the *total* impact of intra-familial relations, it seems clear that these elements are not the necessary *and sufficient* phenomena, in terms of child-achievement, as sometimes has been implied. Necessary, to be sure, but whether sufficient *per se* is uncertain.

Even if one wished to make statements on the basis of these low-order relationships, his conclusions would not serve the stated objective of helping to resolve the inconclusiveness in this area. On the contrary, the patterns within these data seem to add to it. For example, the multiples show that *familism* is stronger among middle-class boys than among lower-class boys, a finding that one might expect if he agreed with Bronfenbrenner, but not if he agreed with McClelland. In looking at the parent-separate partials for middle-class boys, it would seem that familism is related to a supportive situation (companionship) (Bronfenbrenner). Yet, when we examine the parents-combined partial, we find a relationship with father-neglect, the meaning of which is uncertain. For the lower-class boy, familism is related to support from his father, and material reward from his mother. Both of these kinds of situations would tend to produce identification, yet since these partials do not deal with the same variables as those for middle-class boys, it is difficult to make comparisons. The question then arises as to why, among lower-class boys, where there appears to be evidence of more consistent support, there should be less overall familism.

As we would expect, *activism* is higher among middle-class than lower-class boys. For the former, it seems related to authority, especially from the mother. While this would not necessarily clash with the McClelland approach, it does not harmonize with Bronfenbrenner in that it is the mother, and not the father, who is the principal authority figure. However, the apparent significance of the mother would support Goode's conclusions. For the lower-class boy, activism is associated with nurture (father), and with companionship and material reward (mother). From this, one could argue that the lower-class boy is more dependent on his parents, and that this accounts for lower achievement in general. However, this does not jibe with the McClelland explanation for lack of lower-class activism, viz., the extreme authoritarianism of the father.

Trust is lower for middle- than for lower-class boys when we look at the multiples for father, yet just the reverse is true when we examine the other two multiples. Father-nurture is associated with trust for the lower-class boy, and with isolation punishment from his mother. For the middle-class boy, trust is associated with affective reward from father and mother, and also mother-nurture. None of these data suggests that negative relationships with either parent contribute to this particular achievement dimension, and thus lend some support to the Bronfenbrenner approach. Significantly, however, in terms of Goode's stress on the role of the mother, this is the first dimension in which the mother appears in the parent-combined partial for both strata.

Individualism is higher among middle-class boys and, in terms of father relations with them, is associated with affiliative companionship—a supportive relationship. Interestingly, for lower-class boys, it is related to father-achievement demands, both when fathers are examined alone, and when parents are combined. Therefore, one might argue that both categories of boys are "thriving in the patriarchal context" (in one form or other) described by Bronfenbrenner. On the other hand, when we examine the parents-combined partial for middle-class boys, we note *rejection by mother*, which while it is the highest of the six relevant partials, does not seem to fit perfectly any of the theories regarding male achievement. It comes closest, however, to Dynes *et al.* who suggest that negative parental relationships in general implement achievement.

Straus has argued that "deferred gratification patterns" do not vary by social class.[14] Nevertheless, when we compare middle and lower-class boys over the multiples, we observe some variation. Middle-class boys score higher vis-à-vis father relations and parents-combined, but lower for mother relations. Over the partials, lower-class boys score consistently higher in terms of a supportive relationship with fathers and authority and isolation type relations with mothers. For middle-class boys, this component of achievement is consistently related to a reward situation (either affective or material). Once again, the element of support seems to be more pervasive than that of rejection. More specifically, if we use the parents-combined partial as an indicator, the model which once again seems to fit these data best is the one suggested by Goode, viz., that positive identification with *mother* is the factor basic to achievement.

When it comes to *occupational primacy,* besides the variation between strata over multiples and partials, it is significant to note the consistent relationship for lower-class boys between this dimension and *support* (17). For middle-class boys, occupational primacy is related to father-rejection and mother-instrumental companionship. On the basis of what we know about the higher occupational attainments of middle-class boys, one could argue that the contrast between these strata is a verification for the McClelland approach. The lower-class boy is dependent on both parents, he apparently perceives the rewards in this situation as satisfactory, and consequently he finds it difficult to perceive the primacy of rewards in the occupational sphere. By way of contrast, the middle-class boy finds fewer rewards in the family due to unsatisfactory father relationships, and aided by the encouragement of his mother, perceives the occupational sphere as a prime realm for rewards important to his self-esteem.

For *anomy,* the picture is less clear. There is variation between strata, and for lower-class boys it seems to be related to affective punishment by the father and to material reward and neglect by the mother. For the middle-class boy, contrasting relations such as affiliative companionship and achievement demands from the father, plus maternal neglect, are associated with anomy. The problem of interpreting these data is that of suggesting how these kinds of relations contribute to a view of the world as disorderly, a view which presumably hinders achievement. One possible hint comes from the parents-combined partial for lower-class boys, and the mother-partial for middle-class boys, both of which reveal maternal neglect. Since this is the only consistent finding between strata, it could be argued that when the mother fails to interact "fully enough" with her son, the male finds it difficult to structure the world. It may be that in a complex society the father often is unable or unwilling to play this vital socializing role for his son. If the mother *also* fails to carry it out, the child finds himself with no familial resources on which he can draw to perform the task of imposing order on his world.

Since, as Turner points out, girls have, by and large, been neglected in

---

[14] Murray A. Straus, "Deferred Gratification, Social Class and Achievement Syndrome," *American Sociological Review,* 27 (June, 1962), 326–336.

achievement studies, it is even more difficult than with boys to interpret parent-daughter relations.[15] The one clear hypothesis is Bronfenbrenner's, viz., that girls tend to possess higher achievement level whenever the relative position of the mother is strong and, concomitantly, when the daughter is highly involved with her mother. Therefore, we may attempt to determine how valid this notion may be, as well as see what kinds of relations (negative or positive) contribute to particular achievement dimensions.

Over the parents-combined multiples, lower-class girls have a lower familism score, yet this is reversed for the partials. For lower-class girls this variable is associated with material reward from the father; for middle-class girls it is related to indulgence by the mother. Thus, it may be that indulgence by the mother serves to weaken familism, whereas material reward from the father may serve to maintain it. In a limited fashion this tends to give some support to the Bronfenbrenner theme of mother-daughter involvement and achievement. But the different kinds of socialization variables revealed in the single-parent partials must make such an interpretation only tentative.

In terms of *activism*, a father relationship is not found in either parents-combined partial. If affective reward (lower-class) can be taken as greater evidence for mother-daughter involvement than physical punishment (middle-class), this may explain the higher partial for lower-class girls. Exactly the same kinds of variables pertain in both categories when we consider mother relations as well as the parents-combined cells.

However, the mother identification pattern breaks down when we examine the dimension of *trust*. The partials (parents-combined and father alone) are consistent for both categories. For middle-class girls, trust is related to father-neglect, for lower-class girls it is related to paternal indulgence. Just how father neglect and indulgence might contribute to trust is uncertain. Even more puzzling is how father *protectiveness* can contribute to *individualism* for lower-class girls. For middle-class girls, the pattern reverses back to the mother, for nurture on her part is associated consistently with this dimension.

In contrast with the data for boys, we more frequently have found consistency between the parents-combined and single parent partial in terms of a particular socialization variable. This continues to hold for *deferred gratification* among lower-class girls where maternal nurture seems to be important. They have a higher score than middle-class girls where, however, we find an association with material reward and absence on the part of the mother. With regard to *occupational primacy,* the consistency returns for both categories of girls. However, for lower-class girls the variable is maternal absence; for the middle-class girls we find physical punishment and threat from the mother. Consistency of dimension, but not of parental figure, continues for *anomy*. Material reward from father is linked to this variable for middle-class girls, whereas it is associated with maternal rejection for lower-class girls.

15 Ralph Turner, *The Social Context of Ambition,* San Francisco: Chandler Press, 1964.

Whatever else is not clear from these data, what does seem to emerge is that they simply do not appear to resolve the inconclusiveness (what **Goode** labeled "conflicting evidence") regarding the relationships between socialization factors and achievement. Neither the data for boys nor for girls clearly supports any of the extant hypotheses. *Nevertheless, they do serve an important function in that they strongly suggest the need for an expanded theoretical purview.* It may be that to restrict the sources of achievement to family socialization alone, without considering the interactive affects of other kinds of variables, is too narrow. Therefore, the fact that some studies show one set of consequences as the result of certain parent-child interaction, and other studies report findings that are apparently opposite, may be the result of random affects due to the absence of certain crucial variables, perhaps extra-familial in nature.

To be sure, there have been important recent studies which have examined the impact of external variables (peer groups relations, school, and/or neighborhood relations, etc.) on aspirations and achievement.[16] However, the type of design used in these studies has tended to ignore the variables of parent-child interaction. The question has often been posed as "What is the relationship between external factor X and achievement aspirations, holding social class of the family constant?" While this is a highly useful procedure, it needs to be further refined to include the social psychological elements of parent-child interaction as well. In other words, it is not enough to elaborate the complexities inherent in various types of external relations, as some of these studies have done, without *also* elaborating the differing and complex patterns of family socialization and their consequences, which may exist in the same stratum.[17] This is particularly important if we are to begin to develop some systematic explanations of social mobility (upward and downward) as well as of position maintenance.

Therefore, we would expect that a comprehensive "theory of achievement" would include as independent variables, for instance, peer relations, as well as parent-child interaction and occupation of father. The dependent variable, of course, is achievement—aspirations and/or behavior. The following may serve as examples of ways in which a schema like this may help to resolve differences such as those which now exist between the several approaches discussed above. For example, it may be that rejection of the authoritarian father is related to high achievement if the son can then identify with the kind of peer group, adult significant-other, or external situation

16 For example, William H. Sewell and J. Michael Armer, "Neighborhood Context and College Plans," *American Sociological Review*, 31 (April, 1966), 159–168; Ernest Q. Campbell and C. Norman Alexander, "Structural Effects and Interpersonal Relations," *American Journal of Sociology*, 71 (November, 1965), 284–289; Richard L. Simpson, "Parental Influence, Anticipatory Socialization, and Social Mobility," *American Sociological Review*, 24 (December, 1959), 836–845; and C. Norman Alexander and Ernest Q. Cambell, "Peer Influences on Adolescent Aspirations and Attainments," *American Sociological Review*, 29 (August, 1964), 569–575.

17 See Albert K. Cohen, "The Sociology of the Deviant Act: Anomie Theory and Beyond," *American Sociological Review*, 30 (February, 1965), 5–14, for a discussion of the linkage between structural and social psychological variables.

which *fosters* achievement. That the son from a middle-class home is more likely to have access to this type of external relationship, may help to account for his observed maintenance and/or rise in class position. The absence of these particular types of relations for the boy who rejects his father may help to account for that slightly understood phenomenon, downward mobility. Almost equally unexplained is the phenomenon of upward mobility by the lower-class boy. One explanation for some of these boys may be that they reject their fathers and then identify with an external situation appropriate to foster social mobility. However, since lower-class boys have relatively less access to this kind of opportunity, they are more likely simply to maintain their class position.

If the middle-class boy does not reject an authoritarian father, and is dominated by him, the relatively high probability of being able to participate in appropriate peer group relations may still result in upward mobility, or at least position-maintenance. Caught in a dominant relationship, and lacking such relations, he may move downward. Likewise, if his father is supportive, the son's identification may be so strong, that, lacking external relations to pry him loose from this dependence, he may move downward. If, in a supportive context, the boy is able to make appropriate extra-familial identifications, mobility and/or maintenance should be fostered. The same kinds of notions would apply, in general, to the lower class boy both in terms of dominance and dependency. In other words, whether we take the McClelland approach of rejection and/or low identification, or the Bronfenbrenner emphasis on support and positive identification, theoretically we can come up with the same kinds of achievement behavior, depending on the varying types of external situations we introduce into the relationship. By these means, the seeming incongruities of these approaches can be reconciled.

Summary

An attempt was made to resolve what has been alleged to be conflicting evidence over the relationship between family socialization and achievement orientations. The data which were presented, however, only seemed to confirm this inconclusiveness. It therefore was suggested that the theoretical scope of the sources of achievement be expanded to include relationships between types of parent-child interaction and peer interaction, as well as occupation of father. In this way, it may be possible to reduce the seemingly conflicting results that now emerge from various socialization studies by introducing the kinds of extra-familial variables that may help to account for convergence or divergence between present approaches. Therefore, it seems reasonable to assume that under certain external conditions those who argue that rejection of father by son (or at least argue for a minimal father role) leads to achievement may be correct. Under other kinds of external conditions, however, a strong and/or positive role for the father may result in high achievement by the son.

Howard A. Moss

Jerome Kagan

Stability of Achievement and Recognition Seeking Behaviors from Early Childhood Through Adulthood[1]

In the following study, drawn from longitudinal data collected at the Fels Research Institute at Yellow Springs, Ohio, Moss and Kagan describe several achievement and recognition seeking behaviors that are characteristic of individuals at different ages. Concerned principally with the stability of achievement and recognition behaviors from early school years through young adulthood, the researchers show, in essence, that "achievement strivings during the first four years of school are a moderately good index of future achievement behavior during adolescence and adulthood." Their data also suggest that intellectual activities rather than athletic activities for the 10 to 14 age range are positively related to achievement behavior in adulthood.

THE supposition that selected adult response patterns are established at an early age is a primary assumption of developmental theory. Although literary documents and psychotherapy protocols have provided anecdotal support for this hypothesis, more objective validation has been difficult to obtain. The present paper is a second report that has emerged from a larger project on the stability of childhood behavior. The first paper indicated that dependent behavior in girls showed moderately high stability from the early school years through young adulthood.[2] The present report is concerned with the developmental consistency of two related behaviors: the

FROM the *Journal of Abnormal and Social Psychology*, LXII (1961), 504–513. Reprinted by permission of the authors and the American Psychological Association.

[1] This research was supported, in part, by Research Grant M-1260 from the National Institute of Mental Health, United States Public Health Service.
[2] J. Kagan and H. A. Moss, "The Stability of Passive and Dependent Behavior from Childhood Through Adulthood," *Child Development*, XXXI (1960), 577–591.

tendency to strive for (a) mastery of selected skills (achievement behavior), and (b) social recognition through acquisition of specific goals or behaviors (recognition behavior).

The achievement variable emphasizes mastery of intellectual, athletic, mechanical, and artistic skills as well as competence in specialized crafts. Social recognition is obtained through acquisition of most of the above behaviors. For intellectual competence, athletic ability, acquisition of money, and positions of power in social groups are the primary methods of obtaining social recognition in the cultural milieu of our middle-class population. Thus, the overt behaviors involved in achievement and recognition strivings overlap to some degree.

In an attempt to differentiate between these two variables, the investigators evaluated the degree to which the individual's mastery behavior was directed at satisfaction of an internal standard of excellence in order to gain self-approval (achievement motivation), in contrast to seeking approval from the social environment (recognition motivation). This is a difficult differentiation to make. The data to be presented reveal a high, positive correlation between ratings of these two behavioral variables. This interdependence suggests that it may be impossible to measure the "desire to improve at a skill" independent of the individual's "desire for social recognition" for this improvement.

METHOD

Subjects and General Procedure

The subjects were 36 males and 35 females from the Fels Research Institute's longitudinal population. They were enrolled in the project at birth, during the years 1929–1939. At the time of a recent adult assessment (1957–1959) they were between 20 and 29 years of age. The subjects came from predominantly middle class backgrounds, over half of the group were married; 70 per cent had college degrees or were enrolled in a college, and the majority were living within a 30-mile radius of the institute. The adult group included 5 Protestants, 15 Catholics, and 1 Jew.

The heart of this study consists of correlations between the childhood information on these subjects and their adult behavior. The childhood data included (a) longitudinal observations of the child's behavior during the first fourteen years of life in a variety of settings, (b) observations of the mother-child interaction during these years, (c) TAT protocols obtained in adolescence, and (d) annual Stanford-Binet intelligence test scores during the ages 5 to 11. Although the data collected during adulthood (age range 20–29) sampled a variety of techniques, this report utilizes only two sources of adult information, five hours of interview, and a TAT protocol.

Longitudinal Observations: Birth to Age 14

As a standard procedure of the Fels longitudinal program, psychologists or psychologically trained personnel summarized their observations of the child in the home, in the Fels nursery school and day camp, and in the subject's public school. The home reports were based on a visit to the home where mother and child were observed for half-day sessions. These home visits were generally made semiannually for the first 6 years of life and annually from age 6 to 12. Most of the mothers were interviewed each year for the first 14 years of the child's life. The nursery school summaries were based on semiannual, free-play sessions from age 2.5 to 5. The sessions usually consisted of 15 consecutive half-day periods in groups of 10 to 12 children. Day camp typically consisted of an annual two week session of half-day periods during age 6 to 10 in which free and structured group activities were observed. Public school visits, made semiannually, consisted of a half-day observation of the child in his routine classroom activities. Finally, the subjects of age 6 to 14 were interviewed each year at the institute and a summary of the interview was prepared. All of the longitudinal reports for each subject were collated in chronological order and placed in the subject's individual file.[3]

Scoring of longitudinal variables. A comprehensive list of rating scale variables (seven-point scale) was defined for the purpose of evaluating the narrative material just outlined. The material for each subject was divided into four age periods: 0 to 3, 3 to 6, 6 to 10, and 10 to 14. The senior author, who had no knowledge of the adult psychological status of the subjects, first read all the information for each subject for age 0 to 3 and made those ratings for which he had adequate information. Following a period of interpolated work, he studied each subject's material for age 3 to 6 and again made his ratings. This procedure was repeated for ages 6 to 10 and 10 to 14. A period of approximately 6 months intervened between the evaluation of the data for any one subject for each age period. This paper deals only with the stability of achievement and recognition behaviors and abridged definitions of these variables follow.

Childhood Variables

Achievement behavior: (Rated for ages 0 to 3, 3 to 6, and 6 to 10). This variable assessed the degree to which the subject tended to persist with challenging tasks, games, and problems, and his involvement in activities in which a standard of excellence was applicable. For 0 to 3, emphasis was given to persistence with perceptual-motor activities (e.g., making block towers, stringing beads, drawing, and coloring). For ages 3 to 6 and 6 to 10 the greatest weight was given to interest in and persistence with intellectual, mechanical, athletic, and fine motor activities.

For age 10 to 14 the general achievement variable defined above was differentiated into three variables dealing with different achievement areas (intellectual, mechanical, and athletic).

[3] The staff of the institute during the twenty-four years of data collection included Alfred L. Baldwin, Thomas W. Richards, Horace Champney, Virginia L. Nelson, assisted by Leah Levinger, Helen Marshall, Mary Frances Hartson, Joan Kalhorn Lasko, Faye Breese, Margaret Slutz, Marjorie Powell, Frances Best, and a group of assistants to whom the authors are indebted. Their efforts made this project possible.

Intellectual achievement: (Rated for age 10 to 14). This variable assessed the degree to which the subject attempted to master language and numerical skills and showed involvement in the acquisition of knowledge.

Mechanical achievement: (Rated for age 10 to 14). This variable assessed the degree to which the subject attempted to master mechanical skills and manifested involvement in activities such as carpentry, construction of model vehicles, engines and motors, and craft work.

Athletic achievement: (Rated for age 10 to 14). This variable assessed the degree to which the subject attempted to master and showed involvement in athletic activities. These behaviors included swimming, hiking, baseball, football, basketball, tennis, acrobatics, and track events.

Recognition seeking behavior: (Rated for ages 6 to 10 and 10 to 14). This variable assessed the subject's striving to obtain goals that led to recognition from parents, teachers, and peers. The behaviors emphasized in the rating were (*a*) grades in school and school honors, (*b*) stated desire for status-laden vocations or ostentatious material goods, (*c*) striving for leadership in teams or clubs, (*d*) attempts to get recognition from farm activities (e.g., raise the best calf, the highest corn, etc.).

Maternal Variables

Maternal acceleration of developmental skills in child: (Rated for ages 0 to 3, 3 to 6, and 6 to 10). The home visits and maternal interviews yielded information on the mother's behavior and attitudes toward her child. The maternal variable that is directly relevant to the subject's achievement behavior was called *maternal acceleration.* It was defined in terms of the degree to which the mother showed concern over the subject's cognitive and motor development, and the degree to which she exhibited desires for precocious achievement in her child. The rating reflected the degree to which the mother "pushed" the subject's development beyond his abilities and her concern with his general achievement level.

Adult Interview

The junior author, who had no knowledge of the subject's childhood information, interviewed each subject and rated him (seven-point scale) on a variety of variables. The definitions of the variables related to achievement and recognition seeking behaviors follow.

Achievement behavior. This variable evaluated the subject's behavioral attempts to master tasks for which "self-satisfaction" rather than social recognition was the *salient* goal. In achievement behavior, the subject was striving to attain a *self-imposed* standard of excellence. The rating was based on the subject's emphasis and concern with task mastery in his job and avocational pursuits.

Recognition seeking behavior. This variable evaluated the subject's behavioral attempt to obtain symbols of status and social recognition. The rating was based on evidences of strivings for (*a*) vocational recognition, (*b*) academic awards and honors, (*c*) positions of leadership or recognition in community or vocational groups, (d) concern with conspicuous material display, (e) striving for upward mobility in social class position.

Concern with intellectual competence. This variable assessed the value the subject placed upon intelligence, knowledge, academic achievement, and intellectual superiority regardless of whether the goal was to satisfy inner standards or to obtain social recognition.

Reliability of Longitudinal and Adult Interview Ratings

A random sample of 32 tape-recorded adult interviews were independently studied and rated by a second judge to assess the reliability of the junior author's adult ratings. The reliabilities of the longitudinal variables were also assessed through independent ratings, by a second judge, of samples of 50 to 60 cases at each of the four age periods. The reliabilities of the adult and child ratings were determined by product-moment correlation coefficients.[4] For the adult ratings of achievement behavior, recognition behavior, and intellectual concern the reliability coefficients were .84, .99, and .98, respectively. With the exception of one child behavior variable, the reliabilities of the longitudinal ratings ranged from .74 to .90 with a median coefficient of .81. The one low longitudinal reliability was for child's achievement for age 0 to 3 ($r = +.35$; $p < .01$; two-tailed).

TAT Achievement Fantasy: Adolescent and Adult Protocols

Early adolescent (median age of 14 to 16) protocols were available for 67 of the 71 subjects, and all 71 subjects were administered TAT stimuli following the adult interview. The adolescent protocol was based on seven cards from the Murray [5] series (Cards 1, 5, 14, 17BM, 3BM, 6BM, and 3GF). The male adult protocol was based on 13 cards (4, 8BM, 7BM, 6BM, 12M, 17BM, 13MF, 14, 3BM, 5, 1, 3GF, and 18GF). The adult females were also administered 13 cards (4, 6GF, 12F, 2, 8GF, 17BM, 13MF, 14, 3BM, 5, 1, 3GF, and 18GF). For both the adolescent and adult protocols achievement themes were scored according to the scheme described by McClelland, Atkinson, Clark, and Lowell.[6] Since incidence of the subcategories of the McClelland scoring system were infrequent, only stories in which achievement behavior was the major aspect of the plot were considered. These are scored Ach Th in the McClelland scheme. For the adolescent protocol, there was a lack of comparability among the examiners with respect to the inquiry questions and only the spontaneous verbalization of the subject was scored. Agreement between two independent coders was 95 per cent. The longitudinal and interview ratings of achievement and recognition behavior were made *without knowledge* of the subject's adolescent or adult TAT stories.

---

[4] All correlations were corrected for restricted range of scores using a procedure described by C. C. Peters and W. R. Van Voorhis, *Statistical Procedures and Their Mathematical Bases* (New York: McGraw-Hill Book Co., 1940), pp. 395–398.

[5] H. A. Murray, *Thematic Apperception Test Manual* (Cambridge: Harvard University Press, 1943).

[6] D. C. McClelland, J. W. Atkinson, R. A. Clark and E. L. Lowell, *The Achievement Motive* (New York: Appleton-Century-Crofts, 1953).

Thus, the behavior and interview ratings were independent of each other and of the TAT thematic scores.

IQ Change

Each child was given the Stanford-Binet, Forms L and M alternately, annually from ages 5 through 11 by the same psychologist.[7] The mean IQ for the entire Fels population is about 120 (*SD* of 15). For each subject, a smoothed plot of his IQ scores was obtained by averaging his three IQ scores around each age. For example, a child's smoothed or average IQ at age 6 was the result of averaging his IQ scores at ages 5, 6, and 7; his smoothed IQ at age 10 was the average of his IQs at ages 9, 10, and 11. This procedure tends to remove the chance variation associated with any one IQ score and has been used in other studies.[8] Each subject's smoothed IQ at age 6 was then subtracted from his smoothed IQ at age 10 and the resulting difference was used as a measure of IQ change. As with achievement themes, the child and adult achievement ratings were made without knowledge of the subject's IQ or his IQ change score.

In summary, four independent sources of data were analyzed: child and maternal behaviors for the first fourteen years of life, adult behavior, adolescent and adult achievement themes, and childhood IQ change scores.

Statistical Analysis

Relationships among the following variables were evaluated (*a*) childhood achievement and maternal acceleration ratings with the adult interview ratings, (*b*) adolescent achievement themes with adult achievement themes, (*c*) adolescent and adult achievement themes with the longitudinal and adult ratings, and (*d*) IQ change scores with the childhood and adult ratings. Product-moment correlations were used except when the TAT achievement score was involved. Since achievement themes were not normally distributed, contingency coefficients [9] were used for all tests of association using this variable. Mechanical achievement for age 10 to 14 was the only variable for which there was a significant sex difference; the boys having a higher mean rating than the girls ($p < .05$; two-tailed).

Results

Stability of Achievement and Recognition Behaviors

Table 1 presents the relationships between the child and adult ratings of achievement and recognition behavior, as well as the relation between ma-

[7] Virginia L. Nelson administered all of the IQ tests.

[8] J. Kagan, L. W. Sontag, C. T. Baker and V. L. Nelson, "Personality and IQ Change," *J. Abnorm. Soc. Psychol.*, LVIII (1958), 261–266; L. W. Sontag, C. T. Baker and V. L. Nelson, "Mental Growth and Personality Development," *Monogr. Soc. Res. Child Development*, XXIII, No. 68 (1958).

[9] The contingency coefficients were based on chi squares computed from Mood's likelihood ratio test for a 3 × 2 distribution (A. M. Mood, *Introduction to the Theory of Statistics* [New York: McGraw-Hill Book Co., 1950], p. 257).

Table 1   Relation between Longitudinal Ratings of Childhood Achievement and Early Maternal Acceleration with Adult Achievement Behavior (product-moment correlations)

| Childhood Variables | AGE | Adult Variables | | | | | |
| | | ACHIEVEMENT | | RECOGNITION | | INTELLECTUAL CONCERNS | |
		Males	Females	Males	Females	Males	Females
Recognition	6–10	.47‡	.40†	.42†	.48‡	.37†	.55**
	10–14	.25	.20	.36*	.39†	.24	.40†
Achievement	0–3	−.12	−.02	.01	−.22	−.08	−.02
	3–6	−.03	.45†	−.11	.49‡	.13	.44†
	6–10	.46‡	.38†	.57**	.51‡	.69**	.49‡
Achievement							
Intellectual	10–14	.40†	.42†	.60**	.56‡	.66**	.49‡
Mechanical	10–14	.20	.20	.46†	.02	.47†	.27
Athletic	10–14	−.18	.01	−.17	−.09	−.47†	.02
Maternal							
acceleration	0–3	.22	.36*	.44*	.41*	.09	.36*
	3–6	.31	.09	.24	.12	.42†	.12
	6–10	.14	.33*	.16	.23	.32*	.43†

* $p < .05$; one-tailed.
† $p < .02$; one-tailed.
‡ $p < .01$; one-tailed.
** $p < .001$; one-tailed.

ternal acceleration and the adult achievement variables. There are several important results in this table. The rating of achievement behavior for age 6 to 10 showed a significant, positive association with all three adult variables for both sexes. The rating of achievement for age 3 to 6 was predictive of adult behavior for the females but not for the males, a finding that suggests the earlier emergence of stable achievement strivings in girls' development than in boys'. Of the three achievement behaviors rated for age 10 to 14, only intellectual mastery was predictive of adult achievement for both sexes. Involvement in mechanical activities was predictive of adult achievement for boys but not for girls. Athletic achievement showed no relationship to the rating of general adult achievement, and was negatively associated with intellectual concern for adult males ($p < .02$).

Recognition seeking behavior for age 6 to 10 was also predictive of adult achievement behavior. A few of the child variables were moderately intercorrelated and the three adult variables were highly intercorrelated (Tables 4, 5, and 6). This lack of independence makes some of the stability correlations between childhood and adulthood somewhat redundant.

Maternal Acceleration and Adult Behavior

Maternal concern with the child's developmental progress during the first ten years of life showed low to moderate correlations with adult achievement behavior. The maternal rating for age 6 to 10 was not a better predictor of adult behavior than the maternal rating for the first three years of life. Moreover, the age 0 to 3 rating was associated with all three adult, achievement variables for girls, while it predicted only recognition behavior for adult males.

Stability of TAT Achievement Fantasy

Although different sets of TAT pictures were used in obtaining the adolescent and adult protocols, the three pictures that usually elicited achievement stories were presented at both administrations. Cards 1, 14, and 17BM, which elicited 77 per cent of all the achievement themes, were common to both protocols. The strong tendency for these particular cards to elicit achievement themes has been noted in another study.[10] A typical achievement theme to Card 1 concerned a boy who wanted to master the violin and/or become a famous violinist. A typical achievement story to Card 17BM involved a person who was in a rope climbing contest and wanted to do his best to win. A common achievement story to Card 14 concerned an artist or student who had been working hard and was looking forward to fame and success as a result of his accomplishments.

The stability of the TAT achievement score between the adolescent and adult protocols was determined through the use of contingency coefficients. The stability coefficients were .34, .36, and .31 for boys, girls, and total group ($p < .10$, $< .05$, $< .02$; one-tailed). Thus, achievement themes also showed some degree of stability over this ten-year period. These data extend the findings of an earlier investigation,[11] in which the authors reported a three year stability coefficient of .32 ($p < .01$) for achievement themes obtained at median ages of 8–9 and 11–16. The stability coefficients between the adolescent and adult protocols are of the same magnitude as those found for the earlier age period.

Validity of Achievement Themes: Relations with Child and Adult Behavior

Contingency coefficients were computed relating the occurrence of adolescent and adult achievement themes with the longitudinal and adult achievement ratings. These results are presented in Table 2. The highest and most consistent relations were between the adult achievement themes and adult interview ratings. The only significant relation between adult themes and the childhood ratings held for mechanical achievement ($C = +.63$; $p < .001$ for boys, and $-.50$; $p < .02$ for girls).

The adolescent TAT was also more predictive of adult behavior than it was of the childhood ratings. Adolescent achievement themes predicted adult achievement behavior for women ($C = +.44$; $p < .01$) and intellectual concerns for men ($C = +.44$; $p < .01$). Adolescent achievement themes showed minimal association with the child's achievement behavior.

[10] J. Kagan and H. A. Moss, "The Stability and Validity of Achievement Fantasy," *J. Abnorm. Soc. Psychol.*, LVIII (1959), 357–364.
[11] *Ibid.*

Table 2   Relation between TAT Achievement Themes and Child and Adult Achievement Behavior (contingency coefficients)

LONGITUDINAL VARIABLE	AGE	Adolescent TAT (Median Age 14–16)		Adult TAT (Median Age 25)	
		MALES	FEMALES	MALES	FEMALES
Recognition	6–10	.21	.17	.26	.22
	10–14	−.20	−.18	−.31	.39
Achievement	0–3	−.15	−.25	−.20	.16
	3–6	.42*	.19	.19	.36
	6–10	.24	.15	.13	.30
Achievement					
Intellectual	10–14	.30	−.25	.26	.16
Mechanical	10–14	.31	−.62‡	.63**	−.50†
Athletic	10–14	−.20	.12	.12	.17
Maternal acceleration	0–3	.11	.51†	.25	−.08
	3–6	.37	.23	.27	.28
	6–10	.51‡	.26	.24	.41*
Adult interview variables (median age 25)					
Recognition		.17	.25	.40†	.52**
Achievement		.19	.44‡	.37	.52**
Intellectual Concerns		.44‡	.25	.31	.59**

  * $p < .05$; one-tailed.
  † $p < .02$; one-tailed.
  ‡ $p < .01$; one-tailed.
  ** $p < .001$; one-tailed.

The only significant positive association was with age 3 to 6 achievement for boys. Once again the rating of mechanical achievement for girls was negatively associated with achievement themes. This negative correlation may be due to the fact that this is the only variable for which markedly different behavioral referents were used in rating the two sexes. For boys, involvement in carpentry, engines, motors, and model airplanes was emphasized in the rating. These activities are sex-typed and girls showed no interest in them. Participation in craft work (making jewelry, leather articles) and sewing was also used as evidence of involvement in mechanical activities and girls tended to choose these behaviors.

Maternal acceleration during the first ten years of life showed suggestive relationships with the adolescent achievement themes. For example, maternal acceleration for age 0 to 3 predicted achievement themes at adolescence for girls (C = +.51; $p < .02$), but not for boys. Maternal acceleration for age 6 to 10 predicted adolescent achievement themes for boys (C = +.51; $p < .01$) and adult achievement themes for girls (C = +.41; $p < .05$).

In summary, the adult and adolescent TAT stories showed moderate correlations with adult achievement but minimal association with the childhood achievement ratings. Maternal acceleration was associated, to some degree, with adolescent achievement themes.

IQ Increase and Achievement Behavior

The difference between the child's smoothed IQ at ages 6 and 10 was used as a measure of IQ change. Earlier studies [12] have demonstrated that the amount of increase in IQ correlated both with independent behavioral indices of achievement strivings for age 6 to 10, and with early adolescent (age 10 to 14) achievement stories. These latter relations remain significant when the influence of the child's IQ at age 6 is statistically controlled. The present data allowed for a partial validation of these results and an extension of the Sontag *et al.* findings for adolescence and adulthood.[13]

Table 3 presents the correlations between changes in IQ during age 6 to

Table 3   Relation between IQ Change and Childhood and Adult Achievement Variables (product-moment correlations)

Longitudinal Variables	Age	Males	Females
Recognition	6–10	.24	.21
Recognition	10–14	.41†	.09
Achievement	0–3	.13	.04
Achievement	3–6	−.02	.24
Achievement	6–10	.39‡	.47‡
Achievement-intellectual	10–14	.37*	.41‡
Achievement-mechanical	10–14	.15	.14
Achievement-athletic	10–14	−.16	−.46‡
Maternal acceleration	0–3	−.06	.20
Maternal acceleration	3–6	−.03	−.12
Maternal acceleration	6–10	.10	.54‡
Adult interview variables			
Recognition		.48‡	.25
Achievement		.38‡	.38†
Intellectual concern		.49‡	.42‡

* $p < .05$; one-tailed.
† $p < .02$; one-tailed.
‡ $p < .01$; one-tailed.

10 and the longitudinal and adult behaviors. The amount of IQ increase was a fairly sensitive predictor of both intellectual achievement for age 10 to 14 ($r = .37$ and .41 for boys and girls; $p < .01$), and concern with intellectual competence in adulthood ($r = .49$ and .42; $p < .01$). These results support and extend the earlier studies and indicate that amount of IQ

[12] Kagan *et al., op. cit.;* Sontag *et al., op. cit.*

[13] In the present sample of 71 subjects, 50 per cent of the males and 20 per cent of the females overlapped with the group of 70 subjects studied by Sontag, Baker, and Nelson (see Sontag *et al., op. cit.*). However, their data only dealt with the period from 3 to 10 years of age. The present behavioral material covered adolescence and early adulthood.

increase during the first four years of school is a moderately accurate index of the subject's motivation to master intellectual tasks during adolescence and early adulthood. It is important to note that IQ change showed no relation to mechanical or athletic strivings for boys, and was negatively associated with athletic achievement for girls ($r = -.46$; $p < .02$). Thus, IQ increase is not a general measure of achievement strivings for all areas of task mastery. The IQ change measure predicts all three adult achievement ratings because the three adult variables are heavily weighted with concern over intellectual competence. Finally, the maternal acceleration rating for age 6 to 10 showed a positive relation with IQ change for girls ($r = +.54$; $p < .01$) but not for boys.

Intercorrelations Among the Measures

There were, as might be anticipated, positive correlations among the achievement and recognition ratings. Tables 4, 5, and 6 present the inter-

Table 4   Intercorrelations Among Variables Rated for Age 6 to 10

	Recognition	Achievement	Maternal Acceleration
Recognition	—	.77‡	.57‡
Achievement	.60‡	—	.59‡
Maternal acceleration	.39*	.44‡	—

Note. Data for males are in upper right; for females, in lower left.
* $p < .05$; two-tailed.
‡ $p < .01$; two-tailed.

Table 5   Intercorrelations Among Variables Rated for Age 10 to 14

	Recognition	Intellectual Achievement	Mechanical Achievement	Athletic Achievement
Recognition	—	.74‡	.23	.04
Intellectual achievement	.60‡	—	.53‡	−.11
Mechanical achievement	.17	.32	—	−.23
Athletic achievement	.24	.12	.07	—

Note. Data for males are in upper right; for females, in lower left.
‡ $p < .01$; two-tailed.

correlations among the variables that were rated for ages 6 to 10, 10 to 14, and adulthood. The correlations for the males are above and to the right of the diagonal; the female data are to the left and below the diagonal.

For all three age periods there were high, positive correlations among the achievement and recognition variables. For age 10 to 14, recognition behavior was highly correlated with achievement strivings in the intellectual

Table 6 Intercorrelations Among Adult Interview Variables

	Achieve-ment	Recog-nition	Intellec-tual
Achievement	—	.72‡	.73‡
Recognition	.79‡	—	.72‡
Intellectual	.77‡	.84‡	—

Note. Data for males are in upper right; for females, in lower left.

‡ $p < .01$; two-tailed.

area, but only minimally related to mechanical or athletic achievement. This finding suggests that, for this middle class sample, mastery of intellectual skills is the primary method chosen to obtain social recognition. Perhaps for lower-class samples this generalization might be less valid. The high correlations between recognition behavior and intellectual concern in adulthood, together with the fact that maternal acceleration predicted both variables, suggests that it is difficult to separate "recognition seeking behavior" from "attempts to improve intellectual competence."

DISCUSSION

Stability of Achievement Strivings

The results indicate that strivings for intellectual mastery are moderately stable from the school years through early adulthood. This behavioral disposition emerges as a stable phenomenon at ages 3 to 6 for girls and 6 to 10 for boys. The stability of the behavior ratings is paralleled by the moderate stability of TAT achievement stories over a shorter age span. Moreover, achievement stories in adolescence and adulthood also predicted the adult behavior ratings. This consistent cluster of correlations adds construct validity to the TAT achievement variable and support to the conclusion that this class of behaviors is stable over time.

Involvement in athletics for age 10 to 14 showed no strong, positive relation to either IQ increase or adult achievement behavior and, in a few instances, negative relationships occurred. This was not because the interviewer failed to assess adult involvement in this particular activity. Rather, many of the adults who had been involved in athletics as early adolescents were not overly concerned with task mastery as adults and they tended to avoid intellectual activities.

The majority of the sample regarded positions of responsibility, intellectual challenge, and knowledge of the environment as highly desirable goals. If a subject had strong achievement motives he tended to gratify them through intellectually oriented endeavors. It is suggested that the mass media and social environment differentially emphasize the importance of different skills in accordance with the sex and age role characteristics of the individual. For adults, there tends to be an emphasis on intellectual competence and a de-emphasis on active mastery of athletic skills. Moreover, intellectual mastery is less involved in potential sex role conflict than mechanical or athletic behaviors. To excel at sports is one of the defining characteristics of masculinity. Some boys become involved in athletics in order to maintain their sex role identity and avoid peer rejection. An athletic girl will be subject to peer rejection for excessive participation in athletics. Thus, athletic mastery is under the control of motives and conflicts related to sex role identification in addition to needs for task mastery.

This latter point raises the question of the appropriate definition of achievement behavior and motivation. It is suggested that the concept of a general achievement motive is too broad a term, and it may be useful to replace this construct with a series of variables that relate to more specific behaviors. It seems more reasonable to talk about "desire to improve intellectual skills," or "desire to improve athletic skills" than to use the more global concept of need achievement. Individuals strive to perfect skills in different areas, and the motivations for these strivings are multiple. Prediction and comprehension of these phenomena might be facilitated if there was some differentiation among the behaviors and motives that are involved in task mastery.

The lack of predictive power of age 0 to 3 mastery behavior might have been due to the greater difficulty in rating this variable (the interrater reliability was .35). On the other hand, the behavioral referents for this rating differed from those used to assess mastery for the older age periods. Since 2-year-olds do not initiate intellectual or athletic mastery behavior, persistence with simple, perceptual-motor tasks (stringing beads, building towers) was the basis for this early rating. A high rating for 0 to 3 reflected a high threshold for satiation with simple, sensori-motor activities. At the older ages, the achievement rating was based on involvement with problem solving behaviors that were more similar in form to adult achievement behavior. The age 0 to 3 rating is dynamically different from the symbolic behaviors that characterize achievement during the preschool and school years.[14] This statement is supported by the fact that achievement for age 0 to 3 was negatively correlated with achievement for age 3 to 6 ($r = -.20$) and age 6 to 10 ($r = -.03$), and showed no relationship to achievement themes or IQ change. Persistence with simple sensori-motor tasks during the first 2 or 3 years of life is not an index of future intellectual, achievement strivings. The 2-year-old who will sit for twenty minutes trying to put a peg in a hole is not necessarily the ambitious scholar of the fifth grade.

[14] The differences in the content of mastery behaviors for ages 0 to 3 and 3 to 6 are analogous to Piaget's (J. Piaget, *The Origins of Intelligence in Children.* [New York: International University Press, 1952]) description of intellectual development. Piaget suggests that during the first two years the child is in the sensori-motor stage of intelligence in which simple perceptual-motor activity is salient. During the subsequent preschool years the child's intellectual activity becomes more symbolic and more comparable to adult problem solving behavior.

Maternal Acceleration and Achievement

The ratings of maternal concern with the child's developmental skills were heavily weighted with encouragement of intellectual progress. The most consistent correlates of maternal acceleration were found with the ratings of adult concern with intellectual competence. Maternal acceleration for age 0 to 3 was slightly more predictive of adult behavior for girls than for boys. Similarly, maternal acceleration for age 6 to 10 was more predictive of IQ increase for daughters than for sons. The sex difference between these latter two correlations was significant at the .05 level. It is suggested that since the girl was more likely than the boy to identify with the mother, maternal encouragement of intellectual mastery should have had a greater effect on the development of the girl than on the boy.[15]

TAT Achievement Stories

Achievement themes on the TAT were moderately stable and were correlated with adult achievement behavior. The fact that the correlations were as high for females as for males, although the three critical cards illustrated male heroes, raises some question concerning the validity of the hero hypothesis. Since Cards 1, 14, and 17BM all picture a male in a potential achievement situation, one might expect that achievement themes for women would not be highly correlated with their achievement behavior. The present results indicate that the production of achievement themes may be more influenced by the subject's conception of what behaviors are appropriate for the hero, than by the degree of identification of storyteller with hero. Perhaps high achievement girls conceptualize the male role as being more associated with task mastery than do low achievement girls.

Atkinson [16] has suggested that achievement themes have differential validity depending on whether or not the criterion task engages the subject's motivation. The achievement variables used in this study (ratings of overt behavior, IQ increase scores) measured "real life" behaviors that would be expected to engage the subject's motivation. The positive correlations obtained indicate that achievement themes are valid indices of intellective mastery when the conditions under which the behavioral samples are obtained are motive arousing.

Limitations on Generalizability

Although the stability correlations for achievement behavior are fairly high, the nature of this particular sample favored stability. The social milieu of these subjects remained constant throughout the first 17 years of their lives, and the parents and peers of these subjects retained their same values. The degree of stability obtained with this sample might not hold for populations

---

[15] Research in progress at the institute, under the direction of Vaughn J. Crandall and Walter Katkovsky is assessing the role of both mother and father in the adoption of achievement motives and behaviors.

[16] J. W. Atkinson, "Motivational Determinants of Risk Taking Behavior," *Psychol. Rev.,* LXIV (1957), 359–372.

that were more mobile, for different ethnic or social class groups, or for children subjected to major developmental traumata.

Social Reinforcement and Stability

The stability of achievement behavior is congruent with general reinforcement theory. Each time achievement strivings are rewarded through social approval or internal feelings of satisfaction, the strength of this behavioral tendency should be increased. If achievement strivings lead to failure, these behaviors should extinguish. The child who attains scholastic honors through effort is rewarded by the social environment, and this experience frequently leads to an expectancy of future success for similar behavior. This rewarding experience, coupled with the strong cultural approval for intellectual competence, increases the probability that the child will continue to engage in intellectual tasks. On the other hand, persistent failures in intellectually challenging situations are likely to lead to an expectancy of failure, and these expectancies can result in avoidance and/or withdrawal from involvement in intellectual behavior.

SUMMARY

This paper summarized results from a larger investigation on the stability of behavior from childhood through adulthood. This investigation dealt specifically with the long term stability of achievement and recognition seeking behaviors in subjects who were part of the Fels Research Institute's longitudinal population.

The subjects were 36 males and 35 females for whom extensive longitudinal information was available from birth through 14 years of age. One psychologist, who had no knowledge of the adult behavior of these subjects, studied narrative reports based on observations of the child in a variety of settings, and rated each child on achievement and recognition seeking behaviors for four age periods: 0 to 3, 3 to 6, 6 to 10, and 10 to 14. In addition, ratings were made for maternal acceleration of developmental skills for the first three age periods. A second psychologist, who had no knowledge of the childhood information, interviewed each subject in adulthood (age range 20 to 29) and rated him on three variables related to achievement and recognition seeking behavior in adulthood.

In addition, the following information was available for most subjects: (a) a 7 card TAT protocol administered during early adolescence (median age 14 to 6) and a 13 card TAT protocol following the adult interview, and (b) annual Stanford-Binet IQ tests from ages 5 through 11 which furnished an IQ change score over the years 6 to 10.

The major results were as follows:

1. Both achievement and recognition striving behaviors for age 6 to 10 showed significant positive correlations with similar behaviors during adulthood, the correlations ranged from .38 to .68 and all were significant at the .05 level or better.

2. Involvement in intellectual activities for age 10 to 14 showed high positive correlations with achievement behavior in adulthood while involvement in athletics during these years showed no positive relationship with adult achievement behavior. Involvement in mechanical tasks for age 10 to 14 showed positive correlations with adult achievement behavior for boys but not for girls.

3. Maternal acceleration of the child's developmental skills during the first three years of life predicted adult achievement behavior for women but not for men. Maternal acceleration of developmental skills during age 6 to 10 showed moderate correlations with adult concern with intellectual competence in both sexes.

4. Achievement stories told during adolescence and adulthood showed high positive correlations with adult achievement behavior. Maternal acceleration of developmental skills showed suggestive correlations with the occurrence of achievement stories in both adolescence and adulthood.

5. The amount of increase in IQ score during the years 6 to 10 showed high positive correlations with the ratings of achievement behavior during adulthood. In addition, increase in IQ showed positive correlations with age 6 to 10 achievement behavior, and with strivings for intellectual competence during age 10 to 14. Amount of IQ increase showed negative correlations with athletic achievement for age 10 to 14.

The results suggested that achievement strivings during the first four years of school are a moderately good index of future achievement behavior during adolescence and adulthood. There were high correlations between strivings for social recognition and intellectual achievement and it was suggested that these variables are intimately related in a middle class population.

Robert Shellow
Juliana R. Schamp
Elliot Liebow
Elizabeth Unger

Suburban Runaways of the 1960's

The seven papers already presented in this section reveal clearly that, as a consequence of child-rearing experiences, children and adolescents inevitably become, both emotionally and attitudinally, "images" or "replicas" of their parents. An individual cannot escape the psychological pressures exerted by family influence. He may, however, try on occasion to remove himself physically from them, repudiating parental solace and support. As Shellow and his colleagues explain below, the "runaway" is frequently diagnosed as possessing impulsive, disorganized, and delinquent personality disturbances. However, in an elaborate investigation of 776 youths from 10 to 17-years-old who had left home voluntarily, aware that they would be missed, the researchers find that only a small minority are "disturbed." Instead, the data show that for the majority, running away from home is largely a matter of avoiding unpleasant situational pressures. Assuming that this represents a response to common problems, the researchers in the concluding section of the report of their investigation, which is presented here, suggest ways for making school experiences more meaningful, creating youth boards and recreational programs, and improving relations among peers and families.

RESEARCH on children who run away from home has a history of some forty years or more. This past research does not present a single sharp image of the runaway child but rather a blurred and shifting configuration. Why children run away from home and the meaning of running away to the child, to his family, and to society seem not to be constants but ever-changing functions of time and place.

Because our study was carried out during a period of unprecedented national affluence, it is not surprising that our runaway children bear only slight resemblance to the children set to wandering during periods of social and economic upheaval. Nor do most children in our study look much

FROM *Monographs of the Society for Research in Child Development*, XXXII (1967), 28–33. Reprinted by permission of the authors and the Society for Research in Child Development.

like the clinic-captured runaways of, say, the Worcester Center, although both groups were drawn from comparable suburban metropolitan areas.

It was only when we looked at the relatively small minority who ran away repeatedly that we were able to identify runaways who more nearly conformed both to the picture so consistently drawn by clinic investigations and to the popular stereotype of the runaway. Here, among the repeaters, and especially the frequent repeaters, we did run across evidence of personal and family disorganization, serious difficulties in school, and consistent involvement with law-enforcement agencies. However, it is not so much the repeated running away which attracts the concern of controlling and helping agencies but the fact that it is coupled with more threatening and destructive behavior. It is as if the frequent repeater appears in the runaway population by accident; perhaps he would more appropriately be located in the clinic population with those in need of special and professional help with many aspects of their lives. For the most part, however, the majority of runaways we encountered showed little evidence of severe personal or family disorganization. In many respects, they looked very much like their nonrunaway counterparts.

We found, then, two analytically separable groups of children who knowingly and purposefully removed themselves from the effective control and surveillance of their parents. One was a relatively small group for whom running away was intimately bound up with individual or family pathology. This group appeared almost exclusively among frequent runaways. The second and much larger group consisted mainly of those who ran away only once, but included many repeaters as well. This second group, though distinguishable from nonrunaways in many respects, resemble more closely the nonrunaways than they do the seriously disturbed minority.

Attempts to understand and deal with the problem of running away from home must take these two distinct populations into account. Though the overt act may be the same for both groups, what lies behind it, the social and psychological meaning of it, is different for the two groups, and each group must be considered separately.

Had we considered only the seriously disturbed minority, we would have arrived at essentially the same conclusion as those previous studies which attacked the problem through clinical and agency populations—that is, runaways are damaged children badly in need of individual and expert care. Such a conclusion would be entirely inappropriate for children in the other, larger group, however. These, too, are troubled children, but they are troubled in much the same way that other adolescents are troubled. Unlike the pathologically driven frequent repeater, the others need no custodial care and have no special need for individualized professional services.

In part, their difficulties lie outside themselves, in the different social systems in which they move, in their relations with their parents, with the school system, and with their peers. For them, running away may be a calculated maneuver in their dealings with parents, ultimately designed to change the relationship rather than to deny it. It may be a way to break free from a long-standing conflict with an unyielding and profitless educational system. Or it may be simply a desire to step back, take stock, and rest before engaging again with parents, teachers, or friends. Running away may be any one of a number of things ranging from a cry of despair to a victory yell. Most frequently, perhaps, it is something in the middle: a plain, forthright expression of dissatisfaction at home or school. The problems facing most runaway adolescents are the same as those facing many other young people; in this sense, running away from home can be seen as one way of dealing with these problems. Other adolescents deal with these problems differently but not necessarily in ways that are better either for themselves or for the community.

From the very beginning of this study, our collaboration with the juvenile court, the county commissioners, the police, the schools, and other county agencies oriented us toward community action. Since we believe that the vast majority of runaways are adolescents responding in a particular way to problems common to adolescents generally, the remainder of this section will be devoted to recommendations centered on those problem areas which confront all adolescents and which we believe to be susceptible to community action.

School, for example, is a problem for a major part of the general adolescent population. Our own data show clearly the connection between school as a problem area and running away. Runaways tended to perform poorly at school. Not only was this poor performance frequently a direct source of trouble for the child, but it was also an important indirect one, causing conflict between him and his parents. Parental dissatisfaction with the child's school performance often led to nagging and disciplinary measures that, over a period of time, became conflicts in their own right. Although school problems appeared more marked among the runaways, the school questionnaire and our knowledge of other nonrunaway adolescents suggested a widespread dissatisfaction with school.

There were indications, never tested, in our data that children, whether runaway or not, generally appeared to meet increasing difficulty as they moved through the secondary school system. The diminishing holding power of schools throughout the entire country, as seen in the high rates of absenteeism, truancy, and dropouts, may well be symptomatic of this progressive difficulty encountered by students. Not so easily observed are the psychological dropouts, those who are present in body but whose thoughts are regularly elsewhere. Truancy and dropping out psychologically, which appear on the surface to be a child's rejection of school, might, in many instances, better be seen as the school's rejection of the child, especially the one who does not accept academic values.

The major problem appears to lie with those students—and they are in the majority—who will *not* go on to college. A way must be found to increase the ability of the school system to tolerate students who are not academically oriented. The prevailing sink-or-swim philosophy is a wasteful one. There is a need to make the daily six hours of school more meaningful to more students. For many students, the school experience might be improved by broader, better vocational programs. Work-study programs which allow for a split schedule of employment and studies are promising on several counts: they offer students firsthand acquaintance with skills and attitudes necessary for employment, and they draw representatives of industry, business, professions, and labor directly into the development of vocational training, which serves to keep the planners of school curricula abreast of the actual job market. It may be that much of the responsibility for vocational training can be assumed by industry and business, where equipment and methods of training are more likely to be up to date than they are in the schools. The investment of public funds in expensive, quickly obsolete equipment often has limited the utility of vocational programs in the past. In a world which has seen in a ten-year period the creation and elimination of actual job skills—for example, the clerical phase in preparing data for computers—such a shift of responsibility would help avoid the costly mistake of training students for nonexistent jobs. Vocational programs of this scope might go a long way toward helping these students make sense of school for their present lives as well as their future goals.

The present lives of adolescents require that schools provide other kinds of education as well. Our interviews with adolescents and our post-questionnaire discussions led us to recognize once again the imperative need of adolescents to make a place for themselves among those of their own age. Neither parents nor schools seem to be able to answer basic questions that adolescents sometimes hesitate or fear to ask adults. We therefore suggest the establishment of *peer-relations education* programs on a voluntary basis to discuss dating, associations and pressures in peer groups, sex facts and practices, early marriage, and the responsibilities of parenthood. Though peer-relations education would be the responsibility of the school and would be offered during school hours, this program could succeed only if the discussions were led by group leaders and professionals not in a formal evaluative relation to the students.

Another recommendation has to do directly with runaways and their families. The disruption of family life occasioned by running away may leave both parents and child in need of first aid. Police officers can provide sound advice and offer comfort to parents whose children have run off, but they do not have the time nor are they equipped to provide family counseling. Our interviews with parents pointed up the need for such counseling. Families frequently asked for help, and even those who did not explicitly do so welcomed the opportunity to talk about their recent troubles. Since most people are more willing to seek help when they are worried, a lot can be accomplished during the runaway crisis. Once the child has returned, however, the crisis is considered to be over, and the families comfort themselves with the belief that everything is all right. In many cases, however, it is not. The runaway crisis offers an opportunity to give assistance to families when they most want it, and to wait at all may be to wait too long. We recommend that communities set up an around-the-clock, on-the-spot *emer-*

gency aid service. This emergency service of aid and referral would be a unit of professionally trained counselors supervised by a member of the mental health professions. It could operate as a special group of consultants attached to the juvenile bureau of the police department.

There is evidence from interviews with parents and intensive interviews with children that adolescents encounter constant criticism from impatient adults. Parents consistently complain about misbehavior and school performance, and teachers register their disapproval through the medium of grades. Adolescents sometimes respond to this disapproval by fighting it, ignoring it, or running away from it, any one of which may alienate them further from the adult world.

As long as an adolescent is able to obtain satisfaction in peer relations, he may be able to compensate for loss of self-esteem in his relations with teachers and parents. Perhaps the adolescent who runs away only once does so because of a momentary breakdown of satisfactions in all spheres at once. In the school questionnaire, many of those who seriously considered running away but did not do so reported that their change of mind occurred after reflecting on what they might lose in being away from their friends. It is likely that the repeater's peer-group ties are not so strong, and he is therefore less restrained by such considerations. With virtually nothing to lose, of all adolescents he is most prone to act on the fantasy that life can be better outside his home territory.

Though public policy cannot easily and directly improve the quality of family life, it can greatly influence the way other institutions meet the needs of adolescents. In most communities, for example, there is no single agency that concerns itself with all areas in the lives of adolescents. There is a fragmentation of concern among existing agencies—secondary schools, juvenile court, police department, recreation board, and a host of voluntary organizations. Most communities could benefit from the establishment of a central *youth board* to develop an overall picture of the needs of youth, to plan programs beyond those already under way, and to coordinate and balance efforts in the community. The youth board would not only survey and study but would be empowered to take positive action through a permanent staff working with a budget of its own. The primary function of the youth board would be to assess and respond to the needs of youth—to have its staff constantly working with youth and to use young people themselves as advisors and program staff.

One such need is in the area of recreation, which we define as going beyond team sports. In the helter-skelter suburbias with their minimal or nonexistent systems of public transportation, recreational facilities typically are lacking, and what few exist are inaccessible to large numbers of adolescents. Recreational facilities need to be distributed throughout the community for ready access. The youth board would develop and operate a network of youth centers staffed by full-time professionals, each youth center offering a wide range of activities from performing arts to automotive repair. Since school property has always been used as a site for recreational activities, schools offer a ready-made base on which to build such a program. School plants could be kept open afternoons, evenings, weekends, and all summer, too.[1]

The range of these recommendations—only one of which deals directly with running away—reflects the shift in our concerns as the study progressed. Our initial concern with runaway adolescents steadily pressed us toward a concern with adolescents generally. More and more, running away came to appear as a reaction to the ambiguities and problems associated with the social role of the adolescent in the modern world. Runaways are frequently among those adolescents who are too shrewd, too questioning to accept comfortably the mere promise of adulthood in the indefinite future while pacified with privilege in the present.

Increasingly, school has become the only agent of meaningful initiation into full and valued participation in the community. The academic, career-oriented young person finds its relatively easy to accept his dependency status because he knows it leads directly to such participation. At the peak of his physical and sexual energy, he expends this energy in ways that support his goals. He sees his teachers and other adults as trainers whose task it is to assist him in reaching these goals. He submits more easily to their discipline and is eager for their approval.

But for many others, school is not a means to an end. For the adolescent unprepared or unwilling to pursue the career curriculum prescribed by the school system, school is a sort of deep freeze designed to preserve him in childhood or child status. Nor does society offer him any real alternatives. Child labor laws, compulsory school attendance, and the growing indiscriminate demand for formal educational credentials conspire to shut off the possibility of direct entrance into the full participation of earning a living and raising a family. Socially approved and self-promoting outlets for his energy typically are unavailable to him. He must contain this energy or get rid of it in ways that are socially unacceptable; he must spend it in the meaningless exercises of academic life or dissipate it in self-defeating irritation, impatience, and hostility with the system. For him, teachers and parents are not trainers preparing and leading him to his goals, but keepers who stand between him and a valued place in society.

Clearly, current methods of preparing adolescents for adult life are simply not suitable for all young people. In a recent year, there were several thousand who ran away in a fairly typical suburban county, and there were many times more who considered doing so. In a sense, these runaways have taken the initiative; their usually inept attempts to escape from the nowhere of adolescence into the somewhere of adult status are a comment on our lack of inventiveness when it comes to youth. Whether we respond with our usual reflex of worry and criticism or whether we act to provide for the real needs of the adolescent generation will be a measure of our society.

---

[1] To do this, additional paid help would have to be provided, and in suburban areas the school bus system would need to be revised and perhaps expanded to provide adolescents with easy access to activities.

Socialization: Youth-Culture Involvement

Clay V. Brittain

Adolescent Choices and
Parent-Peer Cross-Pressures

Parents and adults often believe that adolescents, while seeking stature and status among peers, will reject nearly every sphere of parental values. In the following study, in which adolescent girls respond to real-life dilemmas involving conflicting parent-peer expectations, the data fail to support this assumption. Brittain reports instead that the girls incline toward the reference group that seemingly provides the more competent advice or imparts the greater status. Part-time jobs, more difficult choices, and ethical situations dispose the girls toward parent-conforming choices whereas matters of taste in attire and of separation from friends draw peer-conforming choices. He demonstrates that parent-peer cross-pressures are dependent on the nature of the alternatives confronting adolescents. Peer-conformity is apparently less comprehensive than generally believed. "Lack of parent-adolescent communication about certain types of choices contributes to this impression."

A s THEY are commonly portrayed, adolescents confronted with parent-peer cross-pressures tend to opt in favor of the peer-group. But to what extent and under what circumstances does this image square with reality? [1] Does the tendency toward peer-conformity vary as a function of the type of choice to be made by the adolescent?

The concept of reference group is useful in attacking this problem. Following Shibutani's [2] formulation that a reference group is one whose perspective constitutes the frame of reference of the actor, both peers and parents might be thought of as reference groups; i.e., as groups each provides perspectives in terms of which adolescents make choices. Does the extent to which adolescents tend to adopt these different perspectives vary systematically across situations? We hypothesized that in making certain

FROM *American Sociological Review*, XXVIII (1963), 385–391. Reprinted by permission of the author and the American Sociological Association.

[1] There is controversy about the legitimacy of this image. For contrasting views see Frederick Elkin and William A. Westley, "The Myth of the Adolescent Peer Culture," *American Sociological Review*, 20 (December, 1955), 680–684; and James S. Coleman, *The Adolescent Society*, New York: The Free Press, 1961, Ch. 1.

[2] Tamotsu Shibutani, "Reference Groups as Perspectives," *American Journal of Sociology*, 60 (May, 1955), 562–569.

kinds of choices, adolescents are inclined to follow peers rather than parents; in making certain other types of choices, the opposite is true.

PROCEDURE

Situations involving conflict between parent-peer expectations were described to the subjects—girls in grades 9 through 11. Each situation was structured around an adolescent girl who was trying to choose between two alternatives, one of which was favored by her parents and the other by her friends. The following item illustrates the procedure:

> A large glass in the front door of the high school was broken. Jim broke the glass. But both he and Bill were seen at the school the afternoon the glass was broken and both are suspected. Bill and Jim are friends and they agree to deny that they know anything about the broken glass. As a result, the principal pins the blame on both of them. Nell is the only other person who knows who broke the glass. She was working in the typing room that afternoon. She didn't actually see the glass broken, but she heard the noise and saw Jim walking away from the door a few moments later. Nell is very much undecided what to do. The three girls she goes around with most of the time don't think Nell should tell the principal. These girls hate to see an innocent person punished. But they point out to Nell that this is a matter between Jim and Bill and between Jim and his conscience. Nell talks the matter over with her mother and father. They felt that Jim is unfairly using Bill in order to lighten his own punishment. Her parents think Nell should tell the principal who broke the glass. Can you guess what Nell did when the principal asked her if she saw who broke the glass?
> —— She told him that she didn't see it broken.
> —— She told him who broke the glass.[3]

Two versions of 12 items each were constructed to make up two forms (A and B) of the present instrument, which will be called the Cross-Pressures Test, or CPT. The two forms were identical in all respects except for the opinions and preferences attributed to parents and friends. These were reversed from one form to the other. The parent-favored alternatives on Form A were the peer-favored alternatives on Form B, and vice versa.[4] The instructions accompanying the CPT were:

> The following stories are about young people like your friends and the people you know. These people are in situations where they are not sure what to do.

[3] Item number 4 on the instrument used in the study.

[4] The alternate version of the item given above read as follows: "The three girls she goes around with most of the time feel that Jim is unfairly using Bill in order to lighten his own punishment. They think that Nell should tell the principal who broke the glass. Nell talks the matter over with her mother and father. They don't think Nell should tell the principal. Nell's parents hate to see an innocent person punished. But her father points out to Nell that this is a matter between Jim and Bill and between Jim and his conscience." There are obviously many situations for which this type of reversal would not be plausible.

We would like to have you read each story carefully and tell us which one of the two things the person in the story is more likely to do. Do *not* tell us what the person should do, but what she is *likely* to really do. We hope you will enjoy doing this.

The CPT was administered to an experimental group and a small control group. The experimental group responded to one form and then to the other; the control responded twice to the same form. Both were divided into subgroups and tested as follows:

Experimental Group	First Testing	Second Testing
Group AB	Form A	Form B
Group BA	Form B	Form A
Control Group		
Group A	Form A	Form A
Group B	Form B	Form B

One to two weeks intervened between the testing dates. The subjects were not told that they were to be tested a second time.

As can be seen from the specimen item, the dilemmas described on the CPT were double-barrelled (as well as double-horned). There is the dilemma embodied in the content of the alternatives (e.g., telling who broke the glass in the door of the high school versus not telling; or going steady with a boy having certain personal qualities versus going steady with a boy having other personal qualities), and, on top of this, the dilemma posed by the cross-pressures from parents and friends. The subjects could respond to either dilemma or to both. We anticipated that they would respond to both; i.e., the tendency to choose the parent-favored or the peer-favored alternative would depend upon what the dilemma was about. Hence, there would be marked inter-item variation in the frequency of parent-conforming and peer-conforming choices.

The experimental group data were analyzed for differential preferences for the parent-favored and peer-favored alternatives. In response to each item there were three possibilities: (1) The subject, responding to the content of the dilemma, chooses the same content alternative on both forms of the CPT. (2) The peer-favored alternative is selected on both forms. (3) The parent-favored alternative is selected on both forms. In event of 2 or 3, the choice of content alternative shifts from the first testing to the second. The data, then, were analyzed for shifts in choice of content alternatives from one form of the CPT to the other.[5] The control group was used to help establish that the shifts in the experimental group were due to

---

[5] Biases toward parent-favored or peer-favored alternatives showed up also as differences in first test responses between experimental subgroups AB and BA. A comparison of these groups, not reported here, reveals substantially the same trends as shown in the present analysis.

differences in the forms of the test and not simply to the tendency to respond randomly.

Items on which peer-conforming response shifts were more frequent and those on which parent-conforming shifts were more frequent were identified. From the content of these items inferences were drawn about the bases of preferences for peer-favored and parent-favored alternatives.

Following the second testing, 42 girls in grades 9 and 10 were individually interviewed.[6] The interview data help to clarify the above analysis of responses to the CPT.[7]

SUBJECTS

The subjects were girls [8] from high schools in Alabama and Georgia. The 280 girls in the experimental group came from an urban high school, a high school in a small city, and three small rural high schools. Analysis of the data did not reveal any rural-urban differences. The 58 control respondents were from a high school in a small town and a rural high school.

RESULTS

Comparison of the experimental and control groups indicates that the findings reported below were not due to the tendency to respond randomly, but that changes in form did elicit changes in choice of content alternatives. The data are given in Table 1. On item one, for example, 23 per cent of the control subjects, who responded twice to the same form, shifted content alternatives from the first testing to the second as compared to 52 per cent in the experimental group. On each of the 12 items, shifts in choice of content alternative occur more frequently in the experimental group. On 11 of the items the experimental-control differences were significant at the .01 level or better.

An analysis of the experimental group data is given in Table 2. The responses to each item were first broken down in terms of the following two categories: (1) The choice of content alternatives did not shift from one form to the other. (2) The content choice did shift; i.e., the peer-favored or parent-favored alternative was consistently chosen. (See columns NS and S.) The second category was then broken down into peer-conforming and parent-conforming choices. (See columns P and F.) As can be seen from this break-down, items 1, 6, and 8 tended more strongly to elicit peer-conforming choices; items 3, 4, 5, 7, 9, 11, and 12 tended to elicit parent-

---

[6] Both the interviewing and the testing were done by the writer.

[7] Sociometric data were collected in one of the schools included in the study, but only brief reference is made to them in this paper.

[8] This imposes an important qualification in generalizing the findings. If a sample of adolescent boys were studied in similar manner, the findings would undoubtedly diverge at some points from those presented here.

Table 1 *Proportion of Control Group and Experimental Group Shifting Responses*

Item	Experimental Group $N = 280$	Control Group $N = 58$	Difference $P_E - P_C$	Chi Square [1]
1. Which course to take in school	.52	.23	.29	15.60**
2. Which boy to go steady with	.50	.28	.22	12.71**
3. How to get selected for a school honor	.33	.28	.05	.94
4. Whether to report boy who damaged school property	.35	.14	.21	13.57**
5. Whether to enter beauty contest or be cheerleader	.44	.16	.28	22.52**
6. How to dress for football game and party	.51	.19	.32	26.42**
7. Whether to be beauty contestant or appear on TV program	.39	.14	.25	18.56**
8. Which dress to buy	.58	.19	.39	39.39**
9. Which one of two boys to date	.49	.16	.33	29.00**
10. Which part-time job to take	.34	.16	.18	10.66*
11. Whether to report adult who damaged public property	.38	.19	.19	10.23*
12. How to let boy know she is willing to date him	.36	.21	.15	6.66*

[1] Chi square computed from frequencies. df=1, * p<.1 ** p<.001.

conforming choices. All of these differences except that for item 4 are significant at the .05 level or better. Parent-conforming and peer-conforming choices were distributed equally on item 2.

Before interpreting these findings, note the following observations. They suggest the results were not dictated simply by the method.

1. The subjects responded naively. Of the 42 girls individually interviewed soon after the second testing, only two were able to tell how the two forms of the CPT differed.

2. Responding to the CPT seemed to be accompanied by anxiety. In informal group discussions immediately following the second testing there were expressions of irritability at having to make the choices called for. This suggests that the subjects did tend to become emotionally involved in the hypothetical situations themselves.

3. Groups of subjects differentiated on the basis of their responses to the CPT were also differentiated on the basis of sociometric data. For example, subjects who most frequently chose peer-favored alternatives tended not to be well accepted by their peers.

4. At least some of the response trends were consistent with what in-

formal observation of adolescent behavior would lead one to expect. For example, choices relating to dress were especially likely to be peer-conforming.

Discussion

The findings, as reported in Table 2, are consistent with the hypothesis that responses of adolescents to parent-peer cross-pressures are a function of the content of the alternatives and that peer-conformity in adolescence, rather than being diffuse, tends to vary systematically across situations. The response variation across items supports the hypothesis.

More specific interpretations of the response trends are now in order.

Table 2   Frequency of Shifts in Choice of Content Alternatives From One Form to the Other

Item	Not Shifting Content Alternatives (NS)	Shifting Content Alternatives			Chi Square [1]
		TOTAL (s)	ALTERNATIVE SELECTED PARENT(P)	PEER(F)	
1. Which course to take in school	135	145	48	97	16.56***
2. Which boy to go steady with	141	139	70	69	.01
3. How to get selected for a school honor	187	93	63	30	11.70***
4. Whether to report boy who damaged school property	182	98	58	40	3.30
5. Whether to enter beauty contest or be cheerleader	156	124	93	31	28.26***
6. How to dress for football game and party	138	142	47	95	16.22***
7. Whether to be beauty contestant or appear on TV program	170	110	83	27	31.00***
8. Which dress to buy	118	162	59	103	11.92***
9. Which one of two boys to date	143	137	81	56	4.56*
10. Which part-time job to take	184	96	69	27	18.37***
11. Whether to report adult who damaged public property	174	106	73	33	15.09***
12. How to let boy know she is willing to date him	180	100	64	36	(7.84)**
Column totals	1908	1452	808	644	—

[1] Chi square for differences between columns P and F computed on the basis of 50/50 assumption. df=1, *p<.05; **p<.01; ***p<.001.

Why were the peer-favored alternatives more commonly selected in response to some of the hypothetical situations and parent-favored alternatives in response to others? This question relates to the more general problem of understanding the processes involved in coming to terms with conflicting pressures, which, as Merton [9] has pointed out, is salient for reference group theory.

From the content of the hypothetical dilemmas, viewed against the response trends shown in Table 2, the following hypotheses are offered:

1. The responses reflect the adolescent's perception of peers and parents as competent guides in different areas of judgment.

The general social orientation of adolescents is of a dual character. Choices tend to derive meaning from either of two general reference groups, or both: the peer society in which many status and identity needs are gratified, and the larger society in which the status positions which one can aspire to as an adult are found. When choices pertain to the latter, parents are perceived as the more competent guides. In response to the hypothetical situation involving choice of part-time jobs (item 10), for example, preferences commonly were for the parent-favored rather than the peer-favored alternatives.

2. The responses reflect concern to avoid being noticeably different from peers. Two of the items to which responses showed clearcut peer-conforming trends involved a choice of dress; i.e., item 6—how to dress for a football game and party, and item 8—which one of two dresses to buy.

3. The responses reflect concern about separation from friends. Peer-conforming choices were predominant in response to item 1—which one of two courses to take in school, where the consequence of a peer-defying choice would have been some degree of separation from friends.[10]

4. A fourth hypothesis overlapping but different from those above is that the choices reflect perceived similarities and differences between self and peers and self and parents. Adolescents, for example, perceiving themselves to be more like peers in regard to tastes in clothes and in regard to feelings about school, find peer-favored alternatives in these areas psychologically closer and more acceptable. But in other areas the greater perceived similarity is between self and parents. For example, with respect to values involved in the difficult choice whether to report a person who has destroyed property (items 4 and 11), the parent-favored alternatives are closer and more acceptable.[11]

The interviews referred to above provided a source for further inferences. According to one hypothesis derived from the interview data, responses to

9 Robert K. Merton, *Social Theory and Social Structure.* Revised and Enlarged Edition (New York: The Free Press, 1957), p. 244.

10 An example identical on both forms concerned which one of two high schools to attend. Responses to it were predominantly peer-conforming.

11 This hypothesis holds, in effect, that there is a close interrelationship between what Merton refers to as normative type and comparison type reference groups. Merton, *op. cit.,* p. 283.

the CPT were a function of the perceived difficulty of the content choices. Parent-conformity was more prevalent in response to dilemmas posing what were perceived to be the more difficult choices. The forty-two subjects interviewed soon after the second testing were asked to rank the content choices according to difficulty. The items from the CPT, with the parent-versus-peer aspect deleted, were typed on small cards; the subjects were asked to select from among them, first the situation in which the girl would have the greatest difficulty making up her mind, then the situation in which she would have the least difficulty. This was repeated until the choices were ordered from most to least difficult. Median ranks were computed. The items eliciting predominantly peer-conforming trends fell at the least difficult end of the resulting rank order. Hence, the tendency toward parent-conformity was directly related to the perceived difficulty of the choice.

A second inference was suggested by a discrepancy between the interview data and CPT responses. Interviewees were asked to select from among the content dilemmas, as presented on the cards, the two about which a girl would most likely talk to her friends rather than her parents. Neither of the two items most frequently selected had elicited predominantly peer-conforming CPT response shifts. Choices in response to one of them (item 9—which one of two boys to date) were more frequently parent-conforming; while in response to the other (item 2—which one of two boys to go steady with) parent-conforming and peer-conforming choices were equally frequent. No such discrepancy was found when the girls were asked to select the two dilemmas about which a girl was most likely to talk to her parents rather than her friends. The three items most commonly selected (i.e., 4, 10, and 11) had all elicited predominantly parent-conforming response shifts.

This divergence of interview and test data may indicate that the latter lead to an overestimate of parent-conformity. But it also suggests a device used by adolescents in coping with parent-peer cross-pressures, namely, avoiding communication with parents. This would be likely to occur in areas in which parent-peer conflict is most acute. If this is the case, such discrepancies as those reported here could be used to identify points at which adolescents tend to be most disturbed by cross-pressures from parents and peers.

Let me note one other aspect of the data. Despite the greater overall incidence of parent-conformity, there was greater convergence relative to peer-conformity choices. As shown in Table 2, a majority of the items elicited a preponderance of parent-conforming over peer-conforming choices. On each of the items where there was a reversal of this trend (i.e., items 1, 6, and 8) there were, however, more peer-conforming choices than parent-conforming choices on any single item. This suggests the following possibility: Analogous trends in the social behavior of adolescents create the impression that peer-conformity in adolescence is more diffuse than actually is the case. Lack of parent-adolescent communication about certain types of choices contributes to this impression.

Summary and Further Applications

The study explored the hypothesis, suggested by reference-group theory, that adolescent choices in response to parent-peer cross-pressures are dependent upon the character of the content alternatives presented. Hypothetical dilemmas were described to adolescent girls. In each dilemma a girl was confronted with a complex choice where one course of action was favored by parents and another by peers. The respondents were asked in each case to indicate what the girl would probably do. With the situations remaining otherwise unchanged, peer-favored and parent-favored alternatives were interchanged and the hypothetical dilemmas again presented to the respondents. Comparison of responses to the two forms of the test revealed that peer-conforming choices were more prevalent in response to certain of the dilemmas and parent-conforming choices in response to others. These results were taken to support the hypothesis.

The content of the items suggested additional specific hypotheses as partial explanations of the trends toward peer-conforming and parent-conforming responses: (1) The responses reflect the adolescent's perception of peer and parents as competent guides in different areas of judgment. (2) The responses reflect a concern to avoid being noticeably different from peers. (3) The responses reflect concern about separation from peers. (4) The choices reflect perceived similarities and differences between self and peers and self and parents.

Additional data were collected by interviewing a number of the respondents. From the interview data and from discrepancies between test and interview it was hypothesized that: (1) The tendency toward parent-conformity is directly related to the perceived difficulty of the choices. (2) Adolescents attempt to come to terms with parent-peer cross-pressures by simply not communicating with parents.

The present study argues the value of the approach exemplified here in exploring an important facet of adolescence. What considerations predispose adolescents toward peer-conformity in situations where they are confronted with parent-peer cross-pressures? What are the persisting cognitive schemata against which choices in such situations are made? We believe that through applications of the present method or adaptations of it, hypotheses relating to these questions could be investigated. For example:

1. Stability of social values: Adolescents are more strongly given to peer-conformity in making choices in areas in which social values are changing rapidly, than in making choices in areas in which social values are relatively stable.

2. Time perspective: Adolescents are more strongly disposed toward peer-conformity in making choices where immediate consequences are anticipated than in making choices where the emphasis is on long term effects.

In addition, the present procedure might be used to assess individual differences in predispositions toward peer- versus parent-conformity. Although the study did not deal with the problem, the subjects were found to differ from one another in their tendencies to make parent-conforming or peer-conforming choices. At the extremes four groups were identified: (1) subjects manifesting relatively strong tendencies toward parent-conformity; (2) subjects manifesting relatively strong tendencies toward peer-conformity; (3) a mixed-conformity group composed of subjects making parent-conforming choices and peer-conforming choices with relatively great and about equal frequency; and (4) subjects making very few responses of either type; i.e., subjects whose responses were mostly consistent by content. The stability of these response biases and their possible correlates remain a problem for further study.

Henry Kaczkowski

Sex and Age Differences in
the Life Problems of Adolescents

Psychologists are perennially intrigued by adolescents' perceptions of such concerns as health, marriage, recreation, and philosophy of life. The measurement of interests like these offers formidable problems. It is impossible to assess the degree of absolute concern; hence, rankings of relative involvement are usually employed. Although investigations of adolescent interests began before the turn-of-the-century, the basis for a series of studies was first instigated in 1936 by Percival Symonds. After extended discussions with youth, he selected fifteen issues for study, and then asked several hundred adolescents to rank them. Dale B. Harris replicated Symonds' investigation in 1957, finding considerable similarity across the years. In the discussion below, Kaczkowski extends the study to yet another period, and in the process points to a possible defect in the earlier investigations. On the whole, however, the consistency of the three studies is striking. Such concerns as money, love, and marriage seem always salient.

THIS study is a replication of studies on life problems of adolescents carried out by Symonds and Harris.[1] The hypothesis common to these studies is: "Change the social and economic structure of society and you immediately change the relative emphasis of these problems and interests."[2] The following modifications have been made from the original survey design: (1) subjects came from grades 9 to 12 rather than grades 7 to 13; (2) the sample was drawn from a rural rather than urban area; (3) problems rather than both problems and interests were considered.

The survey consisted of ranking 15 issues considered problems by adolescents in order of importance to the individual. Two samples, one of 400 students and the other 200 students were selected from the student body of

FROM *Journal of Psychological Studies*, XIII (1962), 165–169. Reprinted by permission of the author and the publisher.

[1] P. M. Symonds, "Life Interests and Problems of Adolescents," *Sch. Rev.*, XLIII (1936), 506–518; P. M. Symonds, "Sex Differences in the Life Problems and Interests of Adolescents," *Sch. and Soc.*, XLIII (1936), 751–752; D. B. Harris, "Sex Differences in the Life Problems and Interests of Adolescents," *Child Developm.*, XXX (1959), 453–459.

[2] Symonds, "Life Interests . . .," *op. cit.*, pp. 506–518.

Table 1 Ranks Accorded Issues Considered as Problems by High School Boys and Girls in 1935, 1957, and 1961

Issue	Boys				Girls			
	1935 RANK	1957 RANK	1961 RANK	1961 REVERSE ORDER	1935 RANK	1957 RANK	1961 RANK	1961 REVERSE ORDER
Health	2	12	5.5	10	2	12.5	1	13
Love, marriage	15	13.5	7.5	6	15	10	6.5	8
Safety	8.5	13.5	11	14	12	14.5	15	15
Money	1	2	1	4	3	2	2	6
Mental hygiene	13	8	3.5	7	9.5	3.5	3	4
Study habits	3	1	2	2	6	1	4	1
Recreation	8.5	15	14	15	11	14.5	13.5	14
Personal and moral qualities	4	3	3.5	1	4	5	6.5	2
Home and family relationships	7	10	5.5	3	9.5	6	8	9
Manners	11.5	5	13	13	6	11	11	12
Personal attractiveness	6	6	9	8	1	3.5	13.5	5
Daily schedule	14	9	15	12	14	12.5	13.5	10
Civic interest	11.5	7	10	9	13	9	12	7
Getting along with other people	10	11	12	11	8	8	10	11
Philosophy of life	5	4	7.5	5	6	7	9	3

a high school located in rural Wisconsin. The larger sample consisted of 50 students of each sex drawn from each grade of the high school. The smaller sample consisted of 25 students of each sex drawn from each high school grade. The problems and instructions were taken verbatim from the original study.[3] The smaller sample was given the 15 issues in reverse order from the larger sample. The survey was administered in regular classroom sessions and took approximately ten minutes to complete.

Table 1 shows a comparison of the various issues considered as problems by boys and girls of secondary school age. Issues involving love and mental health have become more problematic in 1961, while recreation and courtesy have decreased. The coefficients of concordance (Kendall's W), which indicate high agreement among the rankings of the three studies, range from .65 to .72 (Table 2). It should be noted that presenting the problems in

Table 2   Coefficient of Concordance (Kendall's W) in Respect to Ranking of Issues as Problems by Various Groups of High School Students in Various Years

Group	Kendall's W
Boys—regular order	.49
Boys—reverse order	.59
Boys—combined	.47
Girls—regular order	.68
Girls—reverse order	.58
Girls—combined	.55
Boys and Girls—regular order	.52
Boys and Girls—reverse order	.57
Boys—1935, 1957, 1961 (regular order)	.70
Boys—1935, 1957, 1961 (reverse order)	.65
Girls—1935, 1957, 1961 (regular order)	.75
Girls—1935, 1957, 1961 (reverse order)	.72

reverse order does have some effect in their rank standing (e.g., health and philosophy of life).

Tables 2 and 3 show a comparison of ranks accorded issues by high school boys and girls at various grade levels. The coefficients of concordance are given in Table 4. They range from .47 to .68 and are all significant at the 1 per cent level. Some variation, however, does exist among the grade levels. For example, home and family relations are of little significance to 9th graders, but of great importance to 10th graders, while philosophy of life ranks high with 12th graders but is of median or less importance to all other grades.

The variation among the sexes by grade is greater in 1961 than in 1957. Personal attractiveness remains high as a problem to girls but is generally of less interest to boys. Love and marriage is high in rank for all girls. It

[3] *Ibid.*

Table 3   Ranks Accorded Issues Considered as Problems by Various Grades of High School Girls in 1961

Issue	Regular Order				Reverse Order			
	9	10	11	12	9	10	11	12
Health	5	2	12	7	11	5	13	14
Love, marriage	4	8	4.5	6	9	2	10.5	3.5
Safety	13	13	15	15	12	13	14.5	13
Money	2	3	2	1	3	8	6	3.5
Mental hygiene	1	9	1	5	5.5	11	8	1
Study habits	7	10	4.5	2	1	3.5	3	8
Recreation	14.5	12	13.5	13	14	14	14.5	12
Personal and moral qualities	6	4	7	4	2	6	4	2
Home and family relationships	11	1	6	11.5	13	9	5	7
Manners	8	11	10	14	10	10	10.5	15
Personal attractiveness	3	6	3	8	7.5	1	9	9
Daily schedule	14.5	15	13.5	9	5.5	15	12	10
Civic interest	12	14	11	10	4	12	1.5	6
Getting along with other people	9	5	8	11.5	15	7	7	11
Philosophy of life	10	7	9	3	7.5	3.5	1.5	5

Table 4   Ranks Accorded Issues Considered as Problems by Various Grades of High School Boys in 1961

Issue	Regular Order				Reverse Order			
	9	10	11	12	9	10	11	12
Health	8	3	9	5.5	10	7	8	13
Love, marriage	15	12	2.5	7	13	5.5	4	5.5
Safety	4	5.5	14	13	15	15	11	11
Money	3	5.5	1	1	12	4	1	4
Mental hygiene	9	1	4	3	8	8	6.5	7
Study habits	1	4	2.5	4	2	3	5	1
Recreation	12	7	13	15	14	14	15	14.5
Personal and moral qualities	2	8	5	10.5	1	1	2	2
Home and family relationships	14	2	6	5.5	6.5	2	3	9.5
Manners	5	9	12	14	6.5	9.5	10	14.5
Personal attractiveness	6.5	13	7	8	9	11.5	6.5	9.5
Daily schedule	11	15	15	10.5	11	11.5	14	5.5
Civic interest	6.5	11	10	12	3	9.5	13	8
Getting along with other people	13	14	8	9	5	13	9	12
Philosophy of life	10	10	11	2	4	5.5	12	3

assumes less importance for freshmen and sophomore boys, but grows in importance for junior and senior boys. Safety appears of higher interest to boys than to girls in the 9th and 10th grades but drops off sharply to the last ranks for juniors and seniors.

There is little doubt that reversal of the order of presentation of the issues has a bearing on selection by students. Items toward the beginning of the list assumed a greater importance. Civic interest shows a sharp gain in importance when presented at the top of the list. Daily schedule moved up several ranks although there is fluctuation from grade to grade. Among the issues which ranked high as problems regardless of order of presentation were money, personal and moral qualities, and study habits.

There is greater agreement among the three studies than reported by Harris for the years 1937 and 1957. Money is still a problem in 1961 as it was in 1937. The reason for its high ranking may not necessarily be the same. No doubt the student of 1961 has more money but the higher cost of items plus the concept of easy spending necessitates having more of it. Perhaps the importance of mental health in the 1957 and 1961 studies is partly due to increased publicity on this area. Concern with love and marriage again is reflected in the increase in early marriage of individuals.

The data do not completely support or reject the original hypothesis. They point out that certain problems are common to all periods (e.g., money) while others (e.g., recreation) are variable. However, the consistency of findings, considering the differences between this replication and the prior studies, is striking.

Raymond G. Kuhlen

Nancy Bryant Houlihan

Adolescent Heterosexual Interest
in 1942 and 1963

Kuhlen and Houlihan compare two identical sociometric studies conducted twenty-one years apart. Employing the first study as a basis for comparison, the researchers investigate the assumption that contemporary youths are more actively involved in heterosexual social behavior than those of a generation ago. The data affirm that youths do make more cross-sex friendship choices today. The researchers point out that the changes in heterosexual interest are in the direction of choosing rather than being chosen. "About the same proportion of boys and girls have the qualities that attract choices of the opposite sex today as was true in the early 1940's." It is noteworthy that these data also indicate that adolescents "show a greater heterosexual interest throughout the age range"; the data "do not necessarily suggest an earlier onset of interest."

A NUMBER of writers [1] have suggested that children today become interested in the opposite sex at an earlier age than was true a generation ago. Thus far evidence presented on this issue is somewhat less than direct, there being no comparisons between actual data obtained by identical procedures at different points in time in the same places. The present note reports a comparison of the frequency of cross-sex choices in grades 6 through 12 in the spring of 1963 compared to frequency of such choices in the same schools in the spring of 1942, as reflected in responses to the same questionnaire. In view of a seemingly greater current emphasis in the culture of the United States upon social interaction, and particularly interactions between sexes, it was predicted that a larger proportion of today's youngsters would make cross-sex choices than was true at the earlier testing.

FROM *Child Development*, XXXVI (1965), 1049–1052. Reprinted by permission of the second author and the Society for Research in Child Development.

[1] C. B. Broderick and S. E. Fowler, "New Patterns of Relationships between the Sexes among Preadolescents," *Marriage Fam. Lvg.*, XXIII (1961), 27–30; G. M. Lewis, *Educating Children in Grades Four, Five, and Six* (Washington, D.C.: U.S. Office of Education, U.S. Department of Health, Education, and Welfare, 1958).

SUBJECTS AND METHOD

In 1942, a sociometric questionnaire was administered to slightly more than 100 boys and 100 girls in each of grades 6, 9, and 12 in six central high-school systems in central New York.[2] In the spring of 1963, in connection with another study, the same questionnaire was readministered in four of these six schools, but, because of population increases, the number of subjects was much larger. Also, at the latter testing, data were obtained for each of grades 6 through 12. The number of subjects at the time of testing is recorded in Table 1.

Table 1   Number of Subjects

	Grades						
	6	7	8	9	10	11	12
1942:							
Boys	109	—	—	120	—	—	108
Girls	120	—	—	124	—	—	119
1963:							
Boys	167	120	182	194	148	119	104
Girls	159	135	147	180	159	137	110

The questionnaire employed was a sociometric instrument in which each subject was asked to indicate a first and second choice of companions for nine activities: (1) occupying the next seat in the classroom, (2) attending the movies, (3) going for a walk, (4) going skating, (5) making things (as model boats, dresses, etc.), (6) playing outdoor games, (7) playing indoor games, (8) studying schoolwork, (9) reading for fun. The only restriction placed upon an individual's choice was that he must choose from his own grade. As earlier noted, the questionnaire used in 1963 (including instructions) was identical to the one used in 1942.

It was, of course, necessary to utilize the same procedure for analyzing the data as was employed in the 1942 study, and, accordingly, results are presented in terms of the proportion of children of each sex and grade level who made at least one choice involving a member of the opposite sex, or was chosen at least once by a member of the opposite sex.

RESULTS

The results for all seven grades obtained in 1963 and for grades 6, 9, and 12 obtained in 1942 are shown in Table 2. Since a directional prediction

---

[2] R. G. Kuhlen and B. J. Lee, "Personality Characteristics and Social Acceptability in Adolescence," *J. Educ. Psychol.*, XXXIV (1943), 321–340.

Table 2   Percentages of Boys and Girls at Various School Grades in 1942 and 1963 Who Chose the Opposite Sex, Were Chosen by the Opposite Sex, and Were Chosen by No One

	Grades						
	6	7	8	9	10	11	12
Boys choosing girls:							
1942	45.0	—	—	72.5	—	—	75.0
1963	48.8	68.9	69.2	79.9°	81.6	83.3	91.0°°
Girls choosing boys:							
1942	39.2	—	—	59.7	—	—	63.0
1963	52.8°	46.7	69.6	72.9°	68.3	72.7	82.7°°
Boys chosen by girls:							
1942	31.2	—	—	49.1	—	—	65.8
1963	46.7°°	40.0	40.7	47.4	54.7	69.4	74.0
Girls chosen by boys:							
1942	30.8	—	—	52.4	—	—	59.7
1963	39.6	46.7	51.7	52.2	59.1	43.7	61.8
Boys chosen by no one:							
1942	5.5	—	—	5.0	—	—	1.9
1963	5.9	5.8	7.1	8.2	4.7	9.2	5.7
Girls chosen by no one:							
1942	2.5	—	—	3.2	—	—	4.2
1963	2.5	2.2	2.7	3.8	3.7	4.3	5.4

° Difference between 1942 and 1963 percentages significant at the .05 level.
°° Difference significant at the .01 level.

was made, the .01 and .05 levels of significance relating to reliabilities of differences were determined for one-tailed tests.

It will be noted that all of the six comparisons involving the *choosing* of the opposite sex are in the predicted direction, and that five of those six differences are statistically significant. Thus, the hypothesis of greater heterosexual interest today (1963) compared to twenty-one years ago is supported. In contrast, only one of the six comparisons involving proportions *chosen by* the opposite sex is reliable. Apparently, about the same proportion of boys and girls have the qualities that attract choices of the opposite sex today as was true in the early 1940's, the greater interest in heterosexuality being evident in the *choosing* rather than in the being chosen. Although the more recent data contained a number of minor irregularities, the substantial drop in percentage of girls *chosen by* boys at the 11th grade level is notable. Since no particular explanation presents itself, it is assumed tentatively that this decrease is due to sampling error.

Two minor findings may be mentioned. The first involves the number of social isolates, those chosen by no one. About the same proportion fell in this category at all grades in 1963 as in 1942, none of the differences being significant. The second finding (also in agreement with the results of the 1942 study) relates to the greater frequency of cross-sex choices by boys as compared to girls, a difference that is fairly consistent in direction, though only two of the five differences favoring boys are significant at the .05 level or beyond. Since girls generally appear to evidence earlier social and heterosexual interest than do boys, it seems reasonable to interpret the present finding as reflecting less reticence on the part of boys in expressing overtly an interest in particular girls, rather than as implying earlier and greater interest in the opposite sex on their part.

DISCUSSION

Although the present writers have no information as to whether the population of these communities has changed over the twenty-one years in ways that would result in more frequent cross-sex choices (Kanous, Daugherty, and Cohn[3] suggest that there are more such choices in lower socio-economic groups), the facts do seem to lend support to the view that adolescents evidence greater heterosexual interest now than a near generation ago. However, the data show a greater heterosexual interest throughout the age range and do not necessarily suggest an earlier *onset* of interest. Earlier studies [4] suggest a V-shaped curve during the school years, with cross-sex choices being more frequent in the very early grades and in the high-school years. An *earlier* emergence of heterosexuality could be shown only by data that indicated that the age of greatest unisexual choice (i.e., the trough of the V) occurred at an earlier age now than was true a generation ago. The present study does not encompass a broad enough age range to answer this question. However, there is no evidence that this V-shaped curve has been "flattened" with passage of time.

[3] L. E. Kanous, R. A. Daugherty, and T. S. Cohn, "Relation between Heterosexual Friendship Choices and Socioeconomic Level," *Child Developm.*, XXX (1962), 251–255.
[4] E. H. Campbell, "The Social-Sex Development of Children," *Genet. Psychol. Monogr.*, XXI (1939), 461–552; J. L. Moreno, *Who Shall Survive? A New Approach to the Problems of Human Interrelations* (Washington, D.C.: Nervous and Mental Disease Publishing Co., 1934).

Dexter C. Dunphy

The Social Structure of
Urban Adolescent Peer Groups

The influence of peer groups in the transition from playgroup innocence to heterosexual prowess is considerable. But how is the influence exerted? To explore the issue, Dunphy embarked upon a field investigation of adolescent peer groups. He identifies five hierarchies of groups, involving crowds, cliques, and networks of reciprocal role relationships. Dunphy shows that crowd and clique leaders are important models for heterosexual behavior. Two distinct, mutually-supportive central roles were differentiated in the crowd—crowd leader and sociocenter—the former setting the pace of social development, and the latter relieving the tension created by the pressures toward achieving heterosexuality. The methods by which this researcher obtained data are especially impressive. Whereas most investigators are restricted by limited resources to survey-type studies, Dunphy consumed hours upon end at street corners, hang-outs, homes, and beach parties until he gained the confidence of the adolescents and, thereby, doubtlessly learned more about the participants than they knew about themselves. His careful and painstaking attention to the intricacies of peer-group interaction surely lends credence to his conclusion that "the social structure of urban adolescent peer groups has the effect of maintaining a high level of achievement which ensures that most adolescents progressively acquire an increasingly mature heterosexual role."

M OST writers on adolescence emphasize the influence of peer groups on the course of adolescent social maturation. Indeed some regard the peer group as of comparable significance to the family and the school in the socialization of urban adolescents. Parsons, for example, states: "The family offers a wide enough range of role participations only for the young child. He must learn, by actual participation, progressively more roles than his family of orientation can offer him. It is at this point that the peer group and school assume paramount importance." [1] Existing research has estab-

FROM *Sociometry*, XXVI (1963), 230–246. Reprinted by permission of the author and the American Sociological Association.

[1] Talcott Parsons and Robert F. Bales, *Family, Socialization and Interaction Process* (London: Routledge and Kegan Paul, 1956), p. 38.

lished that a major difference in sex composition exists between typical preadolescent and adolescent groups. Preadolescent groups are almost universally unisexual in composition, with play centering around sex-categorized activities and role models.[2] The "gang age" thus appears to consolidate the oedipal crisis by reinforcing the child's learning of his basic sex role, such learning taking place mainly at this stage through identification with the parent of the child's own sex. Adolescence by contrast is marked by an increasing volume of heterosexual choices of preferred associates. During adolescence most persons achieve membership in a heterosexual group and acquire a heterosexual role.[3]

With some notable exceptions, field studies of adolescent peer groups have been few and inadequate and most studies of adolescent groups have aimed to assess the importance of isolated factors rather than to study groups as functioning entities. With the exception of studies of delinquent gangs, the literature is practically devoid of thorough analyses of particular groups and their dynamics. Consequently documented information on the forms and functions of adolescent peer groups is limited. Many writers distinguish two types of adolescent groups, usually referred to as "cliques" and "crowds." The most obvious difference between these two groups is their size. Hurlock, for instance, refers to the crowd as "the largest of the social units formed by adolescents." [4] The clique is usually regarded as smaller, more clearly defined and more cohesive than the crowd. Hollingshead states: "When there is a lack of homogeneity the peer group may be a clique, which is smaller and more purposefully organized than is the crowd. Exclusion of those who do not belong is the express purpose of the clique." [5] A wide survey of the use of these two terms in the literature on adolescence reveals no clear indication of the relative size limits of the two types of group nor agreement on what different functions, if any, these two groups perform for their members. While Hurlock suggests that cliques are the basic elements in a crowd,[6] Cole states that the clique "prevents many social contacts from taking place and reduces the effectiveness of

---

[2] David P. Ausubel, *Theory and Problems of Adolescent Development* (New York: Grune and Stratton), 1954; James H. Bossard, *The Sociology of Child Development* (New York: Rinehart, 1948); Paul H. Furfey, *The Gang Age: A Study of the Preadolescent Boy and His Recreational Needs* (New York: The Macmillan Co., 1926); Jacob L. Moreno, *Who Shall Survive?* (Washington, D.C.: Nervous and Mental Disease Publishing Company, 1934); Frederic M. Thrasher, *The Gang* (Chicago: Chicago University Press, 1936); William F. Whyte, *Street Corner Society* (Chicago: Chicago University Press, 1943).

[3] Luella Cole, *Psychology of Adolescence* (New York: Rinehart, 1948); William F. Connell, Elizabeth P. Francis, and Elizabeth E. Skilbeck, *Growing up in an Australian City* (Melbourne: Australian Council for Educational Research, 1957); Paul H. Furfey, "The Group Life of the Adolescent," *Journal of Educational Sociology*, 14 (Dec., 1940), 195–204; August B. Hollingshead, *Elmtown's Youth* (New York: McGraw-Hill Book Co., 1949); Elizabeth B. Hurlock, *Adolescent Development* (New York: McGraw-Hill Book Co., 1949); Jacob L. Moreno, *op. cit.*

[4] *Op. cit.*, p. 173.

[5] *Op. cit.*, p. 448.

[6] *Op. cit.*, p. 173.

those that do occur." [7] Similarly no clear picture exists of the internal structural properties of adolescent peer groups (e.g., leadership) nor of the dynamics by which groups function to induce the learning of a mature heterosexual role. The study reported here was therefore undertaken to provide some detailed information on the types, sizes, structure, and dynamics of adolescent peer groups in non-institutionalized urban settings.

THE RESEARCH DESIGN

This article summarizes some of the results of a field study undertaken in Sydney, Australia, between February, 1958, and December, 1960. Informal peer associations of adolescents were located in the community and studied in their natural settings. The research methods were developed in a pilot project with 60 adolescents. The subjects of the investigation itself were 303 adolescents among whom boys and girls were included in approximately equal numbers.[8] Ages ranged from 13 to 21 years. The groups were scattered throughout the Sydney Metropolitan area, were from differing socio-economic backgrounds (although predominantly middle class) and were in most cases connected in some way with sponsored youth organizations. These clubs were used as points of departure for an exploration of the natural groups to which their members belonged, each group being studied for a period of from four to six months. Two natural associations of "unattached" youth were included to check a possible bias arising from the method of choosing subjects; no important differences were found between the structure and dynamics of these groups and the other groups in the study.[9]

The main problem in investigating the structural properties of adolescent groups is to find an appropriate method of research. Because of their informal nature, the most satisfactory method is participant observation. However, since these are adolescent peer groups, the adult observer is denied membership and full participation in them. A modified version of the participant observer approach was developed in a pilot study. This consisted in making initial contacts with youth through institutional settings, establishing rapport, and subsequently moving out into non-institutional settings. The author spent many hours on streetcorners, in milkbars and homes, at parties and on Sydney beaches with the groups being studied. All groups were informed of the nature of the study and agreed to cooperate. Other more formal methods were used in conjunction with informal observation and participation. Questionnaires were administered to all subjects, diaries were kept concurrently by the members of each group in which

[7] *Op. cit.,* p. 264.

[8] In natural groups such as these, there are some membership changes over time. The numbers refer to the total membership of the groups at the time the sociometric questionnaire was administered.

[9] However, the extent to which this sample of Sydney youth is "typical" is not known. Of the "natural associations," one was a hierarchy consisting of two crowds, the other, a lower-class gang at Stage 1 (see Figure 1).

interaction with peers for a period of a week was recorded in detail; the majority of the subjects were interviewed at length, their answers to questions being recorded on tape. The result was a flexible method of observation designed to gather a large amount of detailed information with as little interference as possible to the normal functioning of the groups under study.

RESULTS

Group Types

An initial attempt to locate group boundaries through sociometric means proved confusing because of a considerable lack of correspondence between individual subjects' responses when asked to list those who belonged to their "crowd." However, observation of interaction, and interviewing, revealed a high level of consensus on the boundaries of membership groups. Groups were clearly recognized as definite entities, and high status members of these groups could give accurate (i.e., verifiable by observation of interaction) descriptions of group boundaries and could also list members in status terms. In fact, while many members could not accurately describe their own positions in the group structure, they could usually describe the positions of others with some precision.

Two kinds of groups were located by participant observation, by interview, and by analysis of the diaries. These corresponded fairly closely with those referred to as cliques and crowds in the literature, and this terminology will be applied to them here. Both types of groups are true peer groups since group members are of similar age and regard each other as acceptable associates.

The first and most obvious basis of differentiation between the group types was size, the clique being smaller than the crowd. Forty-four cliques were located varying in size from three to nine members and having an average membership of 6.2. Crowds were considerably larger. Twelve crowds were located having a range of membership from 15 to 30 and an average size of 20.2. On the average then, the clique is only about one third the size of a crowd. No group was observed with a membership in the range ten to 14. Therefore, if these groups are typical, cliques and crowds are not two ends on a continuum of size but two distinct groups on a numerical basis alone. An examination of the two types of groups shows why this is so. *The crowd is essentially an association of cliques.* There was little variation in the number of cliques within the twelve crowds. No crowd had more than four or less than two component cliques. The average number of cliques forming a crowd was 3.1.

The distinct upper limit of nine members for the clique suggests the intimacy of the relationships between members. The limited membership makes possible the strong cohesion which is a marked characteristic of these groups. Their similarity in size to the family possibly facilitates the transference of the individual's allegiance to them and allows them to provide an alternative center of security. The larger number in the crowd obviously precludes such close relationships between members. Interviews showed that from the point of view of a member within one clique within a crowd, members of other cliques are acceptable asssociates but not "real buddies" like the members of his own clique.

While the cliques are the basic units in crowd structure, not all cliques were associated in crowds. This held for five of the forty-four cliques in the study whose members either were not accorded or did not seek, status in a crowd. They were outside the crowd structure as some individuals (isolates) were outside the clique structure. Clique membership appears to be a prerequisite of crowd membership, since no case was found of an individual possessing crowd membership without at the same time being a member of a clique. On the other hand, one could be a clique member without being a crowd member. The members of cliques normally lived in close residential proximity and this appeared to be the main ascriptive requirement for clique membership. The cliques associated in a crowd were from adjacent residential localities and their members were of similar age and level of social development. Contrary to Cole's view, quoted above, cliques do not limit social contacts, but, on the contrary, the acquirement of clique membership is virtually the only way in which such contacts can be established and expanded.

Within localities, crowds were differentiated on an age basis, with two or three crowds associated in a status hierarchy. Five of these hierarchies, each in a different suburb, were objects of investigation in the study. Invariably the mean age of members of a crowd higher in the hierarchy was higher than the mean age of members of a crowd lower in the hierarchy. All but one of the crowds in the study formed part of a hierarchy of two or three crowds, and in some hierarchies, upper status members of one crowd occupied low status positions in the crowd above. The difference between age means of crowds adjacent in such hierarchies varied from seven months to three years and seven months, but averaged about two years.

Since age was a major factor underlying crowd differentiation, it is not surprising that where two crowds were adjacent in a crowd hierarchy, the social distance between them (as measured by relative frequency of interaction) varied with the difference between the mean ages of their members. When there was a large gap between the mean ages of adjacent crowds, interaction between the members of the two crowds was extremely limited. Where the gap was small, interaction was far more frequent and the upper status members of the lower crowd tended to hold low status positions in the crowd above.

All crowds were heterosexual, and within crowds there was a consistent difference between the ages of boys and girls. In all crowds boys were older on the average than the girls with whom they associated. Differences between the mean ages of boys and girls in the same crowd ranged from three months to one year and ten months but averaged ten months. Many of the cliques of later adolescents were heterosexual and in all these the same age relationship between the sexes was apparent. The differentiation of the sexes along age lines parallels the typical age relationship between spouses in marriage.

Cliques and crowds perform different functions for their members. The clique centers mainly around talking. The members of one hierarchy, for example, recorded 69 clique settings and 25 crowd settings in their diaries. Of the 69 clique settings, the predominant activity in 56 of them was talking, while it was the main activity in only five of the 25 crowd settings. A similar trend was found in all groups. Analysis of the content of conversation in the clique shows that it performs an important instrumental function in that it is the center for the preparation of crowd activities, for dissemination of information about them, and for their evaluation after they are over. The crowd, on the other hand, is the center of larger and more organized social activities, such as parties and dances, which provide for interaction between the sexes. It acts as a reservoir of acceptable associates who can be drawn on to the extent required by any social activity. Thus cliques and crowds are not only different in size; they are also different in function.

There is a tendency for clique and crowd settings to be distributed differently throughout the week. In the hierarchy mentioned above, 16 of the 25 crowd settings took place at the weekend and only nine during the week. Of the clique settings, however, 47 occurred during the week and only 22 at the weekend. In all hierarchies the majority of crowd settings occurred at weekends, while the majority of clique settings occurred on weekdays.

Structural Change

In considering the hierarchial arrangement of crowds, certain general trends in the structural development of peer groups through the adolescent period become apparent. Some structural characteristics consistently appear before others in all hierarchies. An abstract ideal-typical outline of structural development is portrayed in Figure 1.

The initial stage of adolescent group development appears to be that of the isolated unisexual clique: i.e., isolated in terms of any relationship with corresponding groups of the opposite sex. This primary stage represents the persistence of the preadolescent "gang" into the adolescent period. Stage 2 introduces the first movement towards heterosexuality in group structure.[10] Unisexual cliques previously unrelated to cliques of the opposite sex now participate in heterosexual interaction. At this stage however, interaction is

10 I have deliberately not specified modal ages for the onset of the stages outlined in Figure 1. The variation in the ages at which these phases of group development are encountered is so great that measures of central tendency, by themselves, would be misleading; and any useful estimate of standard deviations would require a much more comprehensive study than that described here. The average age of members in one isolated clique of girls (Stage 1), for example, was 16 years 0 months. On the other hand, Stage 3 had been reached by another clique of girls with an average age of only 13 years 10 months, and the average age of the interacting clique of boys was 14 years 6 months. The figure suggests the order of structural changes in the adolescent peer group but the differing rates, and conditions affecting these rates, need further, more extensive investigations.

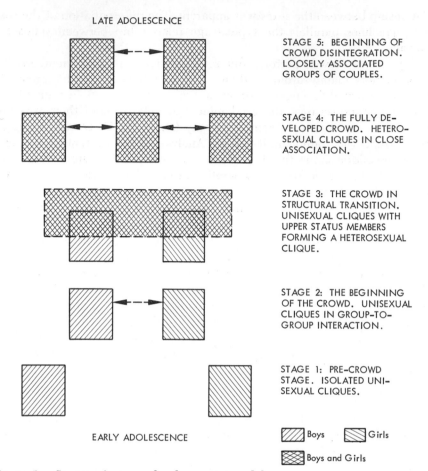

Figure 1. *Stages of group development in adolescence.*

considered daring and is only undertaken in the security of a group setting where the individual is supported by the presence of his own sex associates. Interaction at this stage is often superficially antagonistic. Stage 3 sees the formation of the heterosexual clique for the first time. Upper status members of unisexual cliques initiate individual-to-individual heterosexual interaction and the first dating occurs. Those adolescents who belong to these emergent heterosexual groups still maintain a membership role in their unisexual clique, so that they possess dual membership in two intersecting cliques. This initiates an extensive transformation of group structure by which there takes place a reorganization of unisexual cliques and the reformation of their membership into heterosexual cliques (Stage 4). While the cliques persist as small intimate groups, their membership now comprises both sexes. Stage 5 sees the slow disintegration of the crowd and the formation of cliques consisting of couples who are going steady or engaged. Thus there is a progressive development of group structure from predominantly unisexual to heterosexual groups. In this transition, the crowd—an extended heterosexual peer group—occupies a strategic position. Membership in a crowd offers opportunities for establishing a heterosexual role. The crowd is therefore the most significant group for the individual, but crowd membership is dependent upon prior membership in a clique. In fact, the crowd is basically an interrelationship of cliques, and appears to consolidate the heterosexual learning appropriate to each stage of development. The majority of clique members, therefore, possess a determinate position in an extended hierarchical arrangement of cliques and crowds, in which high status is accorded to groups most developed in heterosexual structure. The course of the individual's social development appears to be strongly influenced by his position within this structure.

Internal Properties

Boundaries of peer groups were clearly defined and boundary definition operated as a form of social control. Crowd boundaries were most rigidly defined. When peer group members were asked to choose associates to join them in a number of situations, only 4 to 8 per cent of choices were directed outside the crowd. On the other hand 37 to 47 per cent of choices were directed outside the members' own cliques to members of cliques within the same crowd. The majority of choices were made within the respondent's own clique. Clique boundaries were less sharply defined than crowd boundaries since some individuals were willing to choose members of other cliques in the same crowd. Very few were prepared to choose outside their own crowd.

Boundary definition was a constant process which could be observed in recurring decisions such as who would be invited to parties or on swimming excursions. The meaning of boundary definition in practice can be illustrated by describing a party in which members of two crowds from the same hierarchy were involved. The hierarchy consisted of three crowds, the upper and middle crowds being fairly narrowly differentiated by age and therefore having two "marginal" members in common. At the instigation of the author, members of these two crowds were invited to a party held by one of the members of the upper crowd. Clique boundaries were most obvious at the beginning and the end of the evening. Members arrived and left in cliques. At the party itself, however, the cliques within each crowd showed a tendency to merge and members interacted across clique boundaries. The crowds were strongly differentiated. Although everyone was initially in the lounge room, the younger crowd gradually relegated itself to the kitchen, leaving the upper crowd in possession of the lounge room. This arrangement persisted throughout the rest of the evening. The two marginal members were clique leaders in the middle crowd, low status followers in the upper. Their behavior reflected their position in the hierarchy, for they oscillated from one room to the other throughout the evening. Two isolates, whom the author had arranged to be invited, showed contrasting ways of adjusting to the situation. The girl made no attempt to relate herself to either group, remained seated in one corner of the lounge room all evening, rarely spoke, and was left to make her own way home, unaccompanied. The boy attempted to relate himself to the upper crowd leader, was ignored, and remained on the fringe of those who gathered around this status figure. Thus both cliques and crowds are boundary-maintaining systems in certain situations. When together, cliques in the same crowd tend to merge. However, only boundaries between cliques are relaxed. Those who did not possess membership in a component clique were not accepted into the crowd, whether or not they attempted to relate themselves to it.

In order to acquire a membership role, an individual has to pass from outside through the boundary into the group. This is definitely a matter of achievement. Members of groups reported that they had to "push themselves forward" to enter a group. A typical statement was: "Someone who gets in and pushes, gets into a group easiest. You just have to get in and push. People who stand back just don't make the grade." Acceptance into a group was not just a matter of achievement but also of conformity. It was reported by those who had achieved membership that a new member had to "fit in," "be the same to us." Or, as one boy put it: "All groups have a certain temperament of their own. Anyone new has to fit in; he must have similar aspects and outlooks and like similar things." By demanding initial conformity to peer group standards, members ensured that the group would be a cohesive entity capable of controlling the behavior of those in it in the interests of the dominant majority. The basic consensus of values which results is a major factor in the strong *esprit de corps* of most adolescent peer groups.

It is possible to lose a membership role and to pass through the group boundary out of the group. This was due to one of two causes, as was shown by an examination of a number of concrete cases. Firstly, ostracism was sometimes the result of a member's rejection of the authority of the group. A member who regarded himself as superior to others in the group, or his judgment as superior to the judgment of the group, was quickly cut down to size. Persistence in such an attitude involved exclusion from the group and the redefinition of the boundary to exclude the offender. Loss of a membership role could also occur where an individual failed to maintain achievement, especially heterosexual achievement, at the level of his peers. This involved at first a loss of status. Continued failure to achieve meant that the member was simply dropped from the group with a consequent readjustment of the group boundary.

Entrance to a peer group depends on conformity, and failure to continue to conform at any stage means exclusion from the group. Thus the definition of the group boundary is an important means of social control which ensures the maintenance of a high level of achievement in social development.

Role differentiation: Leader and Sociocenter

Most adolescents claimed that their groups did not possess leaders. ("We don't like to think that there's a boss over us.") However, cliques were normally referred to by the name of one person in the group, e.g., "John Palmer's group." Other statements showed that while adolescents strongly denied that they had leaders, they did in fact implicitly recognize one person in the group as the incumbent of a leadership position. The following statement is typical of many made when adolescents discussed the groups they knew. "Rod has a group at Waverton, Joanne down there at North Sydney, and Julia up at Crows Nest. The groups revolve around them." In each peer group in the study there was one individual who occupied the major leadership position and who played an important and distinctive role in relating the group to its environment.

The structure of the external system of the cliques was basically composed of the relationship of the clique leaders' positions to each other, and these positions were integrated primarily through a common relationship with a crowd leader. In fact, the clique leaders assumed group representative roles in the external system of the clique. They were better known outside their group than any of their followers—a finding consistent with Whyte's account [11] of gang structures. Thus there were two types of leadership position differentiated, corresponding with the two main types of adolescent groups. There were both clique and crowd leaders. Clique leaders were more socially mobile than their followers and were in more frequent contact with others outside the clique. The communication structure of the crowd consisted in the interrelationship of the clique and crowd leadership positions. Consequently clique leaders were better informed than their followers about what was going on in the crowd, and played a decisive part in decision making. The high status accorded the crowd leader's position is reflected in verbal and written comments about those who occupied these positions. The crowd leader appeared to be a coordinating and integrating figure in the social structure of the crowd whose presence set the seal of success on a crowd event. The incumbent of this position was always a male, and usually the leader of the largest and most heterosexually advanced clique in the crowd. Thus he had already shown his organizational capacity in a clique setting. Each clique leader was also the focus of intra-clique interaction. He was thus not only the best informed person in his clique about events and people in the crowd but also the best informed person about what was going on in his own clique. As such, he occupied a strategic position between the external and the internal systems of his own group. His followers realized this and relied on the leader for information about others in the clique and in the crowd and about clique and crowd activities. While the clique leader's position is subordinate to that of the crowd leader, it is also invested with power and high status.

The clique leader's role in the coordination of his clique with others in the crowd exposes him to two sources of role expectations. In his position as leader of the clique he is expected by members of the clique to perform essential leadership functions. As a key figure in the crowd structure, he is subject to the expectations of the other clique leaders in the crowd. His sub-

[11] *Op. cit.*

ordinate position in relation to the crowd leader means that he is particularly susceptible to influence from that source. He is thus in a position where he relays the general wishes and attitudes of his followers to others in the crowd and the influence of others, particularly status superiors, to his followers. The leader role consists of organizational skills required for the coordination of clique activities with the activities of other cliques in the crowd. It also consists of personality traits allowing the leader to mix freely with others outside his clique and maintain friendly relations within the clique. *Most importantly he has to play an advanced heterosexual role since the crowd is essentially a heterosexual association.* Leaders dated more often, were more likely to be going steady, and had achieved this relationship earlier than other members of their cliques. Where a follower attained a superior level of heterosexual achievement than the leader, there was a change of leadership or a splitting of the group structure. The admired form of heterosexual role varies with the stage of structural development of the group. For instance, an aggressive role towards the opposite sex is admired at Stage 2 (see Figure 1), but results in loss of a leadership position if maintained by the leader at Stage 3.

Leaders were not only superior in heterosexual development but were responsible for maintaining the general level of heterosexual development in their cliques. They acted as confidants and advisors in matters of heterosexual behavior and even organized "partners" for "slow learners." They thus brought about a progressive development in heterosexual relationships on the part of those in their groups. The clique leaders, one of whom is also the crowd leader, form an elite within the extended peer group or crowd. An elite is a small proportion of the population who together exercise a degree of control over persons and resources disproportionate to their number. The leaders are an elite in this sense in that, together, they strongly influence the behavior of those in their cliques by consistently maintaining the pressure to achieve higher levels of social development. They do this through their centrality in the communication structure and their possession of the most valued "resources" of their groups: organizational skills, desired personality traits, and the ability to play an advanced sex role.

Within the crowd, role differentiation occurred also along the expressive dimension. Just as there was a central instrumental role in the crowd (the crowd leader), so there was a major expressive role referred to here as a "sociocenter." The sociocenter was a specialist in humor. While the status accorded this position varied from one crowd to another, the position was well established in all crowds. The incumbent was always popular, well-liked and the most extroverted member of the crowd. When the crowd gathered he usually dominated the center of the group's attention with a continual flow of witticisms and practical jokes. Because of the attention paid him in crowd settings, adults frequently regarded the sociocenter as the leader and inferred that the group was therefore essentially frivolous in character.

The degree to which the sociocenter role was differentiated varied considerably from one crowd to another, and the extent of the differentiation appeared to be influenced by the character of the crowd leader's role. In crowds where the crowd leader was seen by the members as playing an authoritarian, directive role, the sociocenter was highly differentiated. Where the crowd leader was seen as non-directive, as leading simply by virtue of superior social skills, the role was less differentiated. The more the crowd leader directly or indirectly forced the pace of social achievement in the crowd, the more highly differentiated the role of the sociocenter appeared.

This bears a similarity to R. F. Bales' finding [12] that differentiation in small problem-solving laboratory groups occurred along two axes, instrumental and expressive, and resulted in the emergence of a "task specialist" and a "best-liked man." These types appear to correspond to the "crowd leader" and the "sociocenter" reported above. Bales suggested that [13]

> a certain amount of ambivalence tends to center on the task specialist. He tends to be liked because he is satisfying needs in relation to the task area. But he also tends to arouse a certain amount of hostility because his prestige is rising relative to the other members, because he talks a large proportion of the time, and because his suggestions constitute proposed new elements to be added to the common culture, to which all members will be committed if they agree. Whatever readjustments the members have to make in order to feel themselves committed will tend to produce minor frustrations, anxieties and hostilities. These are centered to some degree on the object most active in provoking the disturbance—the task specialist.

In the adolescent peer group, the leader is the person who plays the most advanced heterosexual role. He moves the group to participate in heterosexual activities and encourages members to develop more mature heterosexual roles. While the members are generally motivated to achievement, this still implies new levels of conformity and commitment. The crowd leader's role is therefore particularly analogous to that of the task specialist who is similarly concerned with increased performance and similarly induces culture change. Like the task specialist, also, the peer group leader is the center of the communication pattern and high in status relative to the other members. It seems likely that the sociocenter performs the system function of relieving the tension created in the group by the leader, tension which is at its highest in the heterosexual crowd situation. His specialization in humor, a form of tension release, supports this interpretation. The more the leader dominates, the more tension is created and the more differentiated the sociocenter role becomes. If this did not occur, the tension would tend to destroy the cohesion of the group and thus impede progress towards higher goals. Bales has noted the interdependence of these two roles in his groups and this was apparent in the peer groups. They are by nature high consensus groups since only members who conform to the culture of the group are admitted. The crowd leader and the sociocenter play mutually

[12] Parsons and Bales, *op. cit.*
[13] *Ibid.,* p. 297.

supportive roles in the crowd structure, the complementarity of the two roles preserving the equilibrium of the crowd.

Socialization Process in the Adolescent Peer Group

The primary stage of socialization, which occurs in the family, is largely achieved through the identification of the child with his parents and his consequent incorporation of their norms. This stage has a strong effect on the acquisition of a basic sex role. The peer group at adolescence assumes many of the functions previously performed for the individual by the family and is thus of considerable significance in promoting his increasing independence from the family. If there is an internal consistency in the whole process of socialization through childhood and adolescence, we would expect socialization to take place through an identification with the peer group leaders similar to that with the parents. At the beginning of this article it was mentioned that discrepancies were observed when subjects were asked to name those in their crowd. The list given by an individual usually did not match very well the group others named as his associates and which could actually be observed in concrete situations. However, in the social structure of these membership groups as identified by participant observation, through interviews, and through analysis of diary records, these discrepancies showed up as a highly consistent and meaningful trend. When clique members were asked to name those in their crowd, they tended to name those in their own clique and the leadership elite of their crowd. The leadership elite was in fact highly "overchosen" in the sense that they received many more choices than they themselves made. There was a consistent discrepancy in the direction of high status between the groups in which the individuals actually participated and the groups to which they referred themselves.

By using a chi square technique, the probability of this trend occurring by chance could be tested. However, the test could be applied only to hierarchies where there were proportionately few intercrowd choices so that the crowds could be treated as if they were independent entities. Four of the five hierarchies met this criterion. Two hypotheses were tested. (1) Leaders, when choosing outside their own clique and within the same crowd, choose other clique leaders significantly more than they choose followers, when allowance is made for the relative proportion of leaders to followers. (2) Followers, when choosing outside their own clique and within the same crowd, choose clique leaders significantly more than they choose followers, when allowance is made for the relative proportion of leaders to followers. Hypothesis 1 was supported in three of the four hierarchies at the 0.1 per cent, 1 per cent, and 2 per cent levels respectively, but the chi square was not significant in the fourth. Inspection of the fifth hierarchy shows that those choices made within the crowd boundaries show the same trend. Hypothesis 2 was supported in all four hierarchies at the .1 per cent, .1 per cent, .01 per cent, and 5 per cent levels respectively. Inspection of those choices made within crowd boundaries in the fifth hierarchy shows the same trend.

In some cases, choices were made of members of other crowds in the same hierarchy. These were usually choices between high status members of one crowd and low status members of another older crowd. Fifty-three choices of this kind were made in all the hierarchies. Forty-nine of these were directed upwards to members of crowds higher in status than the ones to which the choosers belonged. The remaining four were directed downwards to members of crowds lower in status. Thus an examination of all extra-clique choices reveals a strong and highly significant tendency to list clique leaders in the same crowd and members of a crowd higher in the status hierarchy when naming associates. In particular, those lower in status than the chooser tend to be omitted. Members of the leadership elite within crowds were particularly overchosen. These results can be interpreted as showing a general upward trend in status terms in the pattern of identification in these groups. In naming those who belong to their "crowd," therefore, these adolescents apparently listed their *reference* rather than their *membership* groups, suggesting that the social structure is stabilized by the ego-involvement of clique members with the clique and crowd leaders.

These data lend support to Freud's notion, advanced particularly in his *Group Psychology and the Analysis of the Ego*,[14] that a primary group is a number of individuals who have taken the same person, the leader, as their ego-ideal. "We already begin to divine that the mutual tie between members of a group is in the nature of an identification of this kind, based upon an important emotional common quality; and we suspect that this common quality lies in the nature of the tie with the leader." [15] Thus Freud's view emphasizes that the bond with the leader is of more importance to group stability than are the ties between the members and that, in fact, it is the former which confers significance on the latter. "A primary group of this kind is a number of individuals who have put one and the same object in the place of their ego ideal and have consequently identified themselves with each other in their ego." [16] Freud regarded the family as the prototype of every human group and the leader as a parent substitute. Certainly the position of the leader in the peer group is analogous in some ways with that of the parent and a similar identification appears to occur. However, the evidence above does suggest that there is identification not only with the leader of one's clique, but beyond that an identification with a number of status figures in the wider peer group—the crowd. The interviews suggested that there is a progressive differentiation of this object system. Generally speaking, the lower a member's status in the social structure, the less differentiated the mental picture he possessed of the positions of others and their relationships with each other. It seems reasonable to deduce from this that the first stage of socialization into a group of peers, the clique, is dependent on the differentiation by the initiate of the leader, and his identification with him. From this stage the pattern of identification suggests that there is a progressive differentiation of the whole object system and a single reference idol (the clique leader) is replaced by a system of social objects which consists

14, 15, 16 Sigmund Freud, *Group Psychology and the Analysis of the Ego* (New York: Liveright, 1922), pp. 108, 120.

basically in the pattern of crowd leadership positions and roles in their interrelationships.

DISCUSSION

In the socialization of the individual his transition from the nuclear family to wider adult society can take place in many ways. In western urban society, the peer group is one important avenue through which this can occur. In Sydney, for instance, where this study was undertaken, it appears that about 70 per cent of boys and 80 per cent of girls at ages 14 and 15 belong to peer groups similar to those dealt with here.[17] If the groups reported are typical, socialization within the peer group system is an extension of socialization within the family system and shows important resemblances in pattern. There is, for instance, a similar differentiation of structure along instrumental and expressive lines with both high status instrumental and expressive roles functioning to preserve the equilibrium of the peer group system. As in the family, the individual proceeds through a series of successively more complex systems of relationships and in the process identifies with status figures, internalizing their roles. Thus his personality continues to expand through the progressive differentiation of his object system.

It appears of some significance that socialization within the adolescent peer group system begins as the stable state the individual enjoyed as latency child in the family is upset by new social expectations at puberty, leading him to establish an increased dependence on the peer group. Initially this group is the unisexual clique, which represents the continuation of the preadolescent "gang" and at this stage is a group comparable in size to the family. In order to achieve and maintain membership in this group, the individual must show his readiness to conform to the group's authority. This is made easier through his identification with the clique leader who embodies many of the social skills and personality traits admired in the group. The clique establishes and reinforces the individual's drive to achieve heterosexuality, since it is, or becomes, a subsystem of the crowd: the crowd in its turn is only a subsystem of a hierarchy of crowds. Thus through clique membership the individual is inducted into an extended peer group system markedly different from the family in size. About middle adolescence there is a major transformation of the clique system which has persisted in a relatively stable form. A new clique system evolves from this structurally unstable stage. Groups become heterosexual, members having established a significant relationship with a member of the opposite sex. The crowd persists long enough to ensure that the basic role characteristics underlying this relationship are thoroughly acquired. It then breaks up into cliques of loosely associated couples as members move towards marriage. The social structure of urban adolescent peer groups has the effect of maintaining a high level of achievement which ensures that most adolescents progressively acquire an increasingly mature heterosexual role.

17 Connell *et al.*, *op. cit.*

Barry Sugarman

Involvement in Youth Culture, Academic Achievement and Conformity in School

Are there values and norms that operate among youth which set them apart as a subculture from the adult society? Sugarman assumes that indeed there are, and in a study of 540 secondary school boys in London, provides valuable perspective on the issue. He starts from the assumption that adult insistence that youth delay gratification and maintain subordinate status leads them to emphasize "spontaneous gratification or hedonism," a contrasting and rival view of life. In the context of this reasoning, he shows that high commitment to the youth culture is associated with under-achievement in school and poor conduct ratings. In a provocative discussion, he suggests that low-quality home environment may lead to both "teenage commitment" and school under-achievement. Moreover, he contends that school norms may affect youth-culture participation. He notes, for example, that "it is no accident that the heroes of youth culture, the pop singers, song writers, clothes designers and others, have mostly achieved their positions without long years of study, work or sacrifice." Finally, Sugarman distinguishes between youth cultures in the United States and Great Britain, suggesting that the former encompasses a strong teenage social system within the school whereas the latter fosters a proportionately strong out-of-school system.

A DOLESCENCE is a point of great structural vulnerability for the modernized society. As its members go through this phase in their lives, the survival of the society requires that most of them should gain a certain basis of knowledge and social values, as well as certain intellectual and social skills. Yet at this phase of their lives, it seems that the young are undergoing considerable psychic strains (partly determined by the structure of their society) and are exposed to the temptations of a youth culture that encourages at the least a considerable diversion of time and energy from these educational pursuits and at the most an inversion of the related values of deferred gratification, academic achievement and conformity to rules.

From the perspective of the young themselves the same basic facts have a different significance. Their futures are in the balance during the years of

FROM *The British Journal of Sociology*, XVIII (1967), 151–164. Reprinted by permission of the author and the publisher.

youth. It can be a future holding career success, prosperity and high status or the opposite; it can be a future of rebellious rule-breaking, conventional conformity or many alternatives inbetween. In modernized society the advantages or handicaps of social background are not automatically translated into certain kinds of career and adult life. Career success depends to an ever-increasing extent on educational certificates.[1] To acquire these even children from the most privileged homes must make some effort of their own. Though success in school is unquestionably easier for those from such homes than it is for others, even they cannot afford to be as totally indolent as they could have done in times when inherited capital or a position in the family business were more important avenues of advancement. The increasing importance of diplomas and hence of behavior in school means that downward social mobility is a more real possibility for them. It also means that, in some circumstances, those from homes that are socially and economically under-privileged have improved chances.

This being so, we turn to consider the main problem of this article: the features of youth culture and how it is related to young people's adjustment to school.

The view that a youth culture exists, embodying values in conflict with those of the adult world was stated by Parsons[2] as early as 1942. He regarded it as a special feature of the U.S.A. and characterized it as being "more or less specifically irresponsible," with a heavy emphasis on "having a good time," much cross-sex socializing and "a certain recalcitrance to the pressure of adult expectations and discipline." Ernest A. Smith also argues for a generational conflict of norms but sees it as applying mainly to the area of sex.[3] In addition he calls attention to the differentiated appearance, dress and language of the American teenagers, the pressure for conformity among them and the secrecy vis à vis adults. Smith also makes the point, demonstrated by Hollingshead over ten years previously, that there is a significant class cleavage in American youth culture.[4]

Coleman[5] examined another aspect of youth culture, showing how the student social system rewarded values other than intellectualism and forms of achievement other than the academic. He also found that this youth culture centered on the high school reinforced the desire to attend college. Coleman has no direct evidence, however, connecting differential *achievement* as distinct from academic values. Even so far as his evidence goes, though, it would be wrong to interpret it in terms of conflict between the values of adults and youth. Rather the conflict seems to be between teachers

---

[1] S. M. Lipset and R. Bendix, *Social Mobility in Industrial Society* (Berkeley, Calif.: University of California Press, 1960).

[2] T. Parsons, "Age and Sex in the Social Structure of the United States," in *Essays in Sociological Theory* (Glencoe, Ill.: The Free Press, 1954), pp. 89–103.

[3] Ernest A. Smith, *American Youth Culture* (Glencoe, Ill.: The Free Press, 1962).

[4] August B. Hollingshead, *Elmtown's Youth* (New York: John Wiley and Sons, 1949), p. 441.

[5] James S. Coleman, *The Adolescent Society* (Glencoe, Ill.: The Free Press, 1961).

on one side and most pupils and their parents on the other. Coleman's "youth culture" seems to be a rather close reflection of some adult American values, such as sociability, athleticism, glamour and status, as Bennett Berger has noted.[6]

Two propositions are being put forward by the writers mentioned so far. One asserts the existence of distinct values and norms among youth which conflict with some of those held in adult society; the other asserts that there are strong social pressures among the young enforcing conformity to the norms of youth culture in preference to those of the adults.

The study which will be reported here is mainly concerned with the first of these propositions, that is, with the values and norms that operate among the young. This proposition has not gone unchallenged: perhaps the most convincing challenge coming from Remmers and Radler.[7] They claim on the basis of many surveys that the American teenager recognizes the sovereignty of peer group standards in some matters (such as dress and grooming) and that of parental standards in others (such as how to spend his money, what to think about political issues).

It seems that a youth culture has emerged in Britain, some twenty years after it was noted in the U.S.A. The symbols of youth culture manifestly differ over time and space, although whatever the current local teenage fashion may be in dress and adornment, music and dancing, slang and other mannerisms, usually it will contrast quite clearly with the fashion accepted by most adult members of the same community. Indeed this may well be the real function that youth culture serves for its adherents, to assert their independence from adult dominance and authority. By dressing and adorning themselves in styles not shared by their parents and perhaps abhorred by them, they are saying in effect that they are not dependent on parental approval. There are two different attitudes that young people may show in their choice of styles: one is to strive for real individuality in dress and manner, the other is to express solidarity with fellow teenagers by wearing what serves as their uniform. Both involve the repudiation of parental and adult standards.

This repudiation, so I hypothesize, extends beyond matters of taste and fashion to a repudiation of other adult standards, so affecting the behavior of the young over a wide area. In order to test this hypothesis we shall obviously need a method of estimating degrees of involvement in youth culture. Before doing this, however, we must state some assumptions that underlie this and related hypotheses.

We may picture the teenager as being placed between the rival appeals of two cultures or sets of assumptions and standards: the youth culture and the "official," middle-class, adult culture represented by the schools and, for

---

[6] Bennett Berger, "Adolescence and Beyond," *Social Problems*, 10 (Spring, 1963), 394–408.

[7] H. H. Remmers and D. H. Radler, *The American Teenager* (Indianapolis: Bobbs Merrill Co., 1957), pp. 222–223.

some, by their parents too. Below a certain age the young are obliged by law to attend school. There they find that teachers and others have constructed a complex set of rules and unstated expectations for them to conform to, with rewards and punishments of very limited kinds to back them up. These schools only work really successfully to the extent that they can elicit from their pupils a commitment to their role as pupil; to the extent that pupils *care* about doing well and being well thought of by their teachers.

Out of all the expectations attached to the "pupil" role as defined by teachers, two seem especially significant. One is that his indulgence in various things that give instant pleasure should be restricted in favor of other things that are less agreeable at present but supposedly rewarded in the future: less T.V., fewer comics, less play and more homework. This is the deferred gratification value. The other expectation is that he should accept a subordinate status compared to all adults in the same or higher *general* social status categories. (That is, all middle-class youths are subordinate to all middle-class adults.) In school he is also expected to accept subordination to all teachers regardless of their general social status relative to his own.

Of course, there have always been pupils who would not accept these expectations. What has happened in the last few years in Britain, it seems, is not just that the number of such pupils has increased but that a new "contra-role" has emerged within the context of the emergent youth culture. This is the role of a "teenager" which is, roughly, an inversion of the official "pupil" role. In place of the officially-expected deferred gratification it puts an emphasis on spontaneous gratification or hedonism. Similarly it repudiates the idea of youth being subordinate to adults and asserts, in effect, that teenagers are "grown up" in the sense that they are equal in status to adults though different in kind. What I am suggesting is that, on any given social level, the amount of support a schoolboy can get from his fellows for rejecting the values that the school is trying to put over is now greater than ever. In conflict with the school is a rival view of life which is held fairly self-consciously though not very explicitly by a fair number of pupils in common.

Data to test these notions were obtained from a survey of 540 4th-year boys in four London secondary schools. All four sample schools (one grammar, two secondary modern and one comprehensive) had a distinctly larger proportion of their pupils from non-manual homes than the national average (especially the grammar school). All four were boys-only schools and in all of them the entire fourth year was surveyed by questionnaire which the investigator administered in person.

Commitment to the role of teenager was defined in terms of behavioral indicators, with pupils reporting on their own habits. Their concept of "making the teen scene" seemed to correspond quite well to the spontaneous hedonism to which we referred earlier. Under this rubric pupils reported whether they considered themselves regular listeners to pop music radio stations, wearers of teenage fashions, keen dancers or frequenters of coffee bars. Two further items in youth culture were taken to reflect the assertion of adult status: smoking and going out with girls.

The three component indicators of teenage commitment (making the teen scene, dating and smoking) are quite highly and significantly inter-correlated [8] and therefore are combined together to give a more powerful measure of the degree of teenage commitment or involvement in British youth culture.

On the assumption that youth culture involves a repudiation of the values and norms of the school, we hypothesize that high teenage commitment tends to go along with unfavorable attitudes to school. This is indeed so (see Table 1). One of the key value conflicts hypothesized here concerns the value of

Table 1   Attitude to School and Teenage Commitment

Teenage Commitment	Attitude to School		
	UNFAVORABLE	MIDDLE	FAVORABLE
Low	.21 (43)	.28 (44)	.43 (77)
Middle	.46 (94)	.49 (77)	.48 (85)
High	.31 (65)	.22 (34)	.08 (14)
	(202)	(155)	(176)

$x^2 = 42$ (df 4) $p < .001$ $C = .27$

deferred gratification or future orientation. We are hypothesizing that high teenage commitment goes along with low scores on future orientation. This value orientation was assessed by a series of agree-disagree statements. To score highly one would have to *disagree* with items such as "There is no sense in worrying about the future so long as you are doing all right now" and to agree to items such as "You have to give up having a good time now to do well later on." In fact those pupils with high teenage commitment do tend to have low scores on future orientation, as predicted (see Table 2).

Table 2   Future Orientation and Teenage Commitment

Teenage Commitment	Future Orientation		
	LOW	MIDDLE	HIGH
Low	.23 (46)	.32 (60)	.39 (58)
Middle	.47 (96)	.48 (90)	.47 (70)
High	.29 (59)	.19 (35)	.13 (19)
	(201)	(185)	(147)

$x^2 = 19$ (df 4) $p < .001$ $C = .19$

[8] The contingency coefficients (based on 3 × 3 tables) are:
　　　　　　making teen scene and smoking   .39
　　　　　　making teen scene and dating   .43
　　　　　　dating and smoking   .35
(All are significant at .001 level by chi squared.)

Commitment to the "pupil" role was defined and measured separately on the basis of respondents' answers to the question:

Which of these would you most like to be?:
  One of the school's best scholars.
  One of the school's best sportsmen or athletes.
  One of the school's best prefects.
  One of the school's most popular pupils.
  None of these appeals to me.

They were allowed three choices in order of preference. A first choice for "best scholar" was taken to represent the highest level of commitment to the "pupil role," a second choice the next highest, a third choice the third level and no choice for "best scholar" as the lowest level of pupil commitment. Rather than just assuming that the strength of a boy's commitment to the pupil role tends to be inversely related to the strength of his commitment to the role of teenager, this was put to the test, and in fact the hypothesis is confirmed. While respondents giving their first choice to "best athlete" fell slightly more often into the high teenage commitment category than the low one, respondents choosing "best scholar" fell into the low teenage category three times as often as into the high one.

To measure *differential achievement* it was first necessary to stratify the boys of each school by I.Q. as measured at the age of eleven and then to divide each stratum of boys with matched I.Q.s into roughly equal thirds on the basis of attainment. The top third will be called "over-achievers," the middle third "middle-achievers" and the lower third "under-achievers." These terms are intended to carry no implication other than these. Unfortunately we were forced to rely on each school's own assessments of attainment which were not uniformly satisfactory. In view of the varying quality of these attainment measures all data pertaining to achievement were examined for each school separately as well as for the aggregate.

On the assumption that involvement in youth culture, with its rejection of school values, will tend to correlate with a low level of effort in relation to the goals of the school, we hypothesized that under-achievement tends to be associated with high commitment to the teenage role and low commitment to the pupil role. This is indeed what we find (see Tables 3 and 4).

Table 3   Pupil Commitment and Academic Achievement

	Achievement		
	OVER	MIDDLE	UNDER
(Proportion in each achievement category who gave first choice to "Best Scholar")	.37 (138)*	.22 (170)	.21 (144)

$x^2 = 19$ (df 6) $p < .01$ $C = .20$
* Figures in parentheses give the base number on which the proportion is calculated.

Table 4   Teenage Commitment and Academic Achievement

Teenage Commitment	Achievement		
	OVER	MIDDLE	UNDER
High	.14 (21)	.22 (37)	.28 (41)
Middle	.45 (67)	.47 (80)	.52 (76)
Low	.40 (59)	.29 (52)	.18 (27)
	(147)	(169)	(144)
$x^2 = 18$ (df 4)	p < .001	C = .19	

And it is true not only for the aggregate of four schools but for each one individually, in spite of the uneven quality of our attainment data in the different schools.

The conduct of pupils or their conformity to school norms was assessed by teachers specifically for this study, in three of the schools by the form-teachers and in the comprehensive school by the housemasters. All were provided with an identical rating scheme and asked to base their rating on what they knew of pupils' conduct from other teachers as well as their observations. Still it proved impossible to get ratings that were comparable across schools and so we examined results for each school separately as before.

On the assumption that youth culture involves a rejection of the teenager's subordination to adults, we hypothesized that poor conduct ratings would go along with high commitment to the teenage role. This is what we find (see Table 5). As before it applies to each of the schools individually

Table 5   Teenage Commitment and Conduct Rating

Teenage Commitment	Conduct Rating		
	GOOD	MIDDLE	POOR
High	.06 (9)	.17 (27)	.36 (76)
Middle	.42 (63)	.55 (88)	.48 (101)
Low	.52 (79)	.28 (46)	.16 (33)
	(151)	(161)	(210)
$x^2 = 82$ (df 4)	p < .001	C = .36	

despite the uneven rigor of conduct ratings. It is noteworthy that the relationship between conduct and teenage commitment is the strongest one found in this study.

It might be contended that this relationship was partly spurious to the extent that boys who were high on teenage commitment and demonstrated this in dress and hair-styles of which their teachers disapproved were given undeservedly bad ratings. On the other hand two points must be made. Firstly, not all the boys high on teenage commitment wore long hair or extravagant clothes, not even the majority. Some wore short but delicately coiffured hair-styles; some expressed themselves in variations of costume within the bounds of school uniform. Secondly, the boys who did appear at school in extravagant styles probably were less conforming and really earned their bad conduct ratings. These two points *may* both apply. That is, it may be true that not all boys with bad conduct have long hair. At the same time it may also be true that all boys with long hair do have bad conduct. However, it could also be that some boys who started as non-conformers in appearance alone became more general rebels as a result of being persecuted by teachers for their appearance. All in all, though, I do not think the conduct ratings were seriously biased.

Of course, it is hard to know what is cause and what is effect in this interesting pattern of relationships. Boys who are strongly committed to the teenage role tend to be under-achievers and to have poor conduct ratings. But which came first? For some it may be that a fortuitous flirtation with the teenager role came first and led to lower achievement and poorer conduct in school, as the influence of new associates and self-fulfilling prophesies by teachers began to operate. For some, low achievement may have come first and led to increasing teenage identification as a means of restoring damaged self-esteem. For most, I suggest, there is some common factor or set of factors that leads to *both* teenage commitment and these other aspects of behavior at school.

In this study teenage commitment, achievement and conduct were all found to be related to a common and prior factor, namely the intellectual quality of the pupil's home background. This was assessed from their reports on how many books their homes contained, what newspapers their parents read and whether they ever take or send them to museums, plays or concerts. Even on the basis of so simple a measure the associations are clear [9] (see Table 6).

Table 6   Intellectual   Quality   of   Home   Background   and Teenage Commitment

Teenage Commitment	*Intellectual Quality of Home Background*		
	HIGH	MIDDLE	LOW
High	.16 (29)	.18 (40)	.32 (44)
Middle	.45 (83)	.52 (112)	.44 (61)
Low	.39 (73)	.29 (62)	.21 (29)
	(185)	(214)	(134)
$x^2 = 22$ (df 4)	p < .001	C = .20	

[9] The coefficients of contingency and significance levels by chi squared (for 3 × 3 tables) are:

home background and teenage commitment	C = .20 p < .01
home background and achievement	C = .17 p < .01
home background and conduct rating	C = .25 p < .001

Speculatively we may account for these findings in terms of two patterns. The dominant pattern is for differences in the intellectual quality of home background to lead to differences in the degree of commitment to the teenage role. Both of these factors then operate to affect the level of achievement (relative to I.Q.) and conformity to school norms. Thus a high quality home tends to go with low teenage commitment, being an over-achiever and having a good conduct rating. The secondary but very important pattern is that boys deviating from the behavior which is modal for their kind of background tend to reflect their deviance also in their degree of teenage commitment. Thus pupils from high quality homes who are under-achievers or have bad conduct ratings are much more likely to be high on teenage commitment than other pupils from such a background. Similarly those from low quality homes who are over-achievers or have good conduct ratings are very much more likely to be low on teenage commitment than others from such backgrounds.

Let us now return to our model of the schoolboy standing between two cultures or alternative roles, the pupil role as defined by teachers and the teenager role as defined within youth culture. Firstly, we have seen that the teenager role does not have an equal appeal to all. It appeals most strongly to boys from homes of lower intellectual quality, thus tending to reflect and perhaps reinforce rather than to eliminate differences based on background. Secondly, we have seen that the level of teenage commitment is intimately involved in the process of deviating from the modal behavior associated with one's background. Although in some special conditions teenage commitment may operate as an independent casual factor, its main function seems to lie elsewhere. Pupils who are already becoming alienated from school are likely to turn to teenage commitment as a symbolic expression of this attitude and pupils who are ambitious in the conventional terms of the school are likely to avoid teenage commitment for the same reasons. Once set on this course of deviance from their background, though, their orientation to the youth culture and the teenage role is likely to strengthen them in their course.

One important facet of this process, I suggest, is that a schoolboy's level of involvement in youth culture marks him as eligible for membership in certain cliques or peer groups and ineligible for others. The ambitious boy from a home of low intellectual quality who adopts a low degree of teenage commitment simultaneously disqualifies himself from membership in the clique of typical boys from this kind of background and fulfills one of the minimum conditions of eligibility for membership in a clique of boys from homes of high intellectual quality (mainly high achievers with good conduct records). Both his exclusion from the one kind of group and his membership in the other increase his chances of reaching the level of achievement in school and the kind of conduct rating that he seeks. From his clique-mates he is likely to get two important kinds of assistance that he cannot get from his home: the example of conscientious effort and social reinforcement for his aspirations and goals. In this way, friends and clique-mates of the "right kind" can help to compensate a pupil for what his home lacks.

This is just one side of the youth culture coin though. The other side is represented by the boys who are strongly committed to the teenager role and to the youth culture. We have seen that these boys are on the whole rebelling against the norms imposed by the school and performing academically below expectations; they have unfavorable attitudes towards school and score low on deferred gratification. To the extent that performance in school and the recommendations of teachers count in later life, either in getting jobs or places in further education, these young people have very poor chances of career success. Youth culture, defined and measured this way, is in this sense the culture of the non-mobile working-class, the downwardly-mobile and those who cherish hopes of mobility along channels where the criteria of school do not apply.[10]

It is no accident that the heroes of youth culture, the pop singers, song writers, clothes designers and others, have mostly achieved their positions without long years of study, work or sacrifice. This is probably one of the qualities that is important for their appeal. Youth culture is the new opium of the (teenage) masses. What they want to forget is not any material hardship but the futility and failure of school-days, the frustrations of being a sub-adult with one's life restricted by unsympathetic and square teachers, and the dullness of adult life lying ahead.

In conclusion there is one point of comparison with some of the American studies that should be considered. Whereas this study found youth culture to be linked to a thoroughgoing alienation from school, the studies of Coleman [11] and Gordon [12] in the U.S.A. have found something different. They found that although the basic values of youth culture conflict with those of the academic world, the institutional focus of youth culture is, nevertheless, at the high school. Hollingshead is one of the few sociologists who give due recognition to the existence of two youth cultures, one at the high school being mainly supported by middle-class pupils bound for college and the other outside the school supported mainly by lower class youths who either have dropped out of school early or will do so. The youth culture we have analysed in this article is more like the lower class one.

The problem that we must consider, however briefly, is why the most visible youth culture in Britain should be the one kind and the most visible one in the U.S.A. the other. Perhaps in each country a different youth culture really is more important, in which case we shall want to ask what specific social and cultural differences between the two countries account for this difference. Perhaps, however, there are "secondary" factors obscuring the basic similarity between the two societies and their youth cultures.

[10] An alternative but not incompatible interpretation may be found in Orlando Patterson, "The Dance Invasion," *New Society*, 15 (September, 1966), 401–403.

[11] Coleman, *op. cit.*

[12] C. Wayne Gordon, *The Social System of the High School* (Glencoe, Ill.: The Free Press, 1957).

For instance, Britain may be going through a developmental phase that the U.S.A. passed through earlier, or both kinds of youth culture may be important in both countries but differences in researchers' orientations and methods may have produced an illusory difference.

It may be helpful to distinguish between youth *culture* as a set of symbols, assumptions and standards on the one hand, and a teenage *social system* as a group or groups of interacting teenagers who orient their behavior by reference to the standards, assumptions and symbols of youth culture.[13] Presumably youth culture developed out of a teenage social system (perhaps helped by commercial interests) but now that it is in existence a teenager may be oriented to the symbols, assumptions and standards of youth culture (committed to the teenage role, as we have put it) without necessarily participating in any group of teenagers which is so oriented. One implication that follows from this is that involvement in youth culture may be a solitary, asocial phenomenon. Thus an individual's degree of involvement in youth culture can be a fairly direct reflection of his attitudes whereas his involvement in the social system of his age-mates is a function both of his personal characteristics and of the reaction of his age-mates to him.

Let us now apply this distinction to the problem of reconciling the findings of this study with those of Coleman. In the present study we have tried to measure involvement in youth *culture,* whereas Coleman was concerned with involvement and status in the teenage *social system* at high school, specifically that of the "leading crowd" of the high school.

There are also differences in the structure and functioning of the secondary school in Britain and the U.S.A. which would account for different patterns of teenage life even when these discrepancies in methodology were ironed out. Although these differences in youth patterns may cover a wide ground, here we are only concerned with the degree to which in-school and out-of-school teenage social systems have developed in the two societies.

The U.S. high school supports a very strong teenage social system, to a large extent through the wide range of extra-curricular activities in which pupils not only play the star roles but also handle the administration. These are not the quiet activities of a small coterie of stamp-collectors or nature-lovers as in the British secondary school, but highly public activities which are felt to be extremely important by most of the pupils. The debating society in the British grammar school comes closest to providing a focus for a teenage social system in school. This operates only in a minority of schools, though, and even there represents a far less institutionalized extra-curricular social system compared to the U.S. high school, where activities include organizing the school dances, editing the commemorative yearbook, being a cheerleader, competing for the title of one of the seasonal beauty queens, serving as president of the class. In most of these activities moreover the pupils themselves elect the leaders so increasing their own sense of involvement, not to mention actual support. Sports are important in both Britain

---

[13] This distinction is based on that made by Talcott Parsons in *The Social System* (Glencoe, Ill.: The Free Press, 1951), Ch. I.

and the U.S. schools but, whereas in the U.S.A. games are watched by large crowds from the community (U.S. schools being neighborhood institutions) in Britain these games have no interest to the outside world and are not even watched by many of the pupils.

It should be clear, even from so brief an account, that the extra-curricular life of the U.S. high school is far more elaborate than that of the British secondary school and is far more oriented to the interests and tastes of the average teenager. It is very significant that the broad extra-curricular life of the U.S. high school embraces many items of youth culture that in Britain are rigidly excluded from school and hence strengthen the out-of-school teenage social system. For example, the British secondary school usually has a choir but not a glee club; it imposes a school uniform that often severely violates teenage concepts of fashion; it may offer a term dance but it is likely to seem very square to the average pupil in the way it is run. The average pupil in Britain is therefore more attracted to youth clubs, discothèques, coffee bars (the out-of-school teenage social system) to find opportunities to "be himself" with his age-mates. This is one reason why in Britain the focus of the teenage social system lies outside the school far more so than it does in the U.S.A. Whether this is desirable or not is no concern of ours here.

Two other factors contribute to the strength of the teenage social system outside school. One is the fact that in Britain (compared to the U.S.A.) a far larger proportion of fifteen- to twenty-year-olds are no longer in school and that generally all connection with school ceases at the end of one's full-time education. The support of these young people strengthens the teenage social system of the youth club, coffee bar and discothèque. So also does the fact that the efflorescence of youth culture in this country has been so recent, so exciting (for most of the young) and so highly publicized.

We may perhaps clarify some points in this interpretation by considering what changes in teenage social systems would be expected, in this view, if the British secondary school were to become more like the American. Suppose, then, that we have a secondary school system that is comprehensive, a large proportion of pupils staying on to age eighteen and a fairly large proportion proceeding to further education, and pupils organizing an extensive social life for themselves at school after hours.

If we may speculate, some crucial features of teenage life in such a new Britain would include the following. The average teenager (being still at school in his 16th year) would find a large part of his social life and enjoyment of youth culture focusing at school. The leaders of this teenage society would be more middle-class and more pro-school in orientation than in the days when school was more square and youth society focused exclusively on youth clubs and coffee bars. These leaders would not be intellectual in orientation, however, and over-achievers would be relatively uninvolved in either youth culture or youth society, in or out of school. A proportion of teenagers would still be highly alienated from school. Under-achievers with poor conduct, they would shun the teenage social system at school and probably participate in the one outside. The out-of-school youth society has meanwhile become more emphatically rebellious and probably delinquent as the more conforming teenagers transferred their loyalty to the new, in-school youth society.

These comparisons between youth in contemporary Britain and the U.S.A. should serve to throw some light on our theoretical problem of how the relationship between young people's involvement in youth culture and their behavior and attitudes is affected by the structure of the teenage social system. One relationship alone seems to be unaffected by the factor. In a comprehensive school over-achievers are always likely to be withdrawn from the general youth culture, though they may be highly involved in an intellectually oriented youth culture of their own. The greater their degree of segregation from lower achievers, the more likely does this seem to be. Thus the likelihood that there will be an intellectual youth culture is greater in a streamed comprehensive school than in an unstreamed one and greater still in a grammar school.

We can see the importance of this factor most clearly perhaps in the case of Newsom's children,[14] those whose academic performance puts them into the middle (say) 60 per cent. When the teenage social system is located outside of school, involvement in both youth culture and in the teenage social system will tend to be correlated inversely with achievement and conduct. This is what we found in the present study of four London schools. When, however, there is a teenage social system centered on the school, relationships are more complex. Pupils who are highly involved both in youth culture and the in-school teenage social system are most likely to be middling in achievement and conduct. Pupils who are highly involved in youth culture but *not* the in-school teenage society may be quiet, unsocial individuals who under-achieve but give their teachers no trouble, or, if they are highly involved in the outside teenage society, they will have bad conduct ratings as well as being under-achievers. Pupils who are involved neither in youth culture nor in in-school teenage society are most likely to be over-achievers. As for their degree of conformity we cannot be so sure. Those of them with very high ambitions relative to their social origins are likely to be highly conforming to teachers' expectations but those with highly intellectual orientations may be extremely non-conforming, though in different ways to the pupils who are involved in the out-of-school teenage social system.

Here we have an abundance of speculative hypotheses that call for critical examination and careful testing. The study of youth culture and teenage social systems is just beginning.

---

[14] Central Advisory Council on Education (England), *Half Our Future* (London: H.M.S.O., 1963).

Gary Schwartz

Don Merten

The Language of Adolescence:
An Anthropological Approach
to the Youth Culture[1]

Schwartz and Merten view youth culture as a unique cultural system. To them it is less a rivalrous contraculture than a genuinely independent subculture. Youths, the researchers point out, possess a status terminology or argot that contributes meaning to their world view, life-style, and personal standards. Their analyses, predicated on David Reisman's observation that adolescent social life is partially hidden from adults by linguistic devices, show the youth culture as consisting of norms, standards, and values communicated by a language system essentially unintelligible to adults. Nonetheless, they argue that youth reference groups are also dependent on adult orientations. For example, youth status systems, described by such terms as "hoody," "socie," "snob," "stuck-up," "greaser," and "scragg," reflect the different social-class segments of the adult society. The researchers illustrate how youth-culture norms for dating may be interpreted to explain inconsistencies inherent in such cultural categories as "cool," "cute," and "elite." In brief, "cuteness" and "coolness" are shown on the one hand to be complementary social categories from the boys' perspective, but relatively contradictory from the viewpoint of girls' standards, where "coolness" is more highly idealized.

FROM *The American Journal of Sociology,* LXXII (1967), 453–468, slightly abridged. Reprinted by permission of the authors and the University of Chicago Press.

[1] This paper reports on the first part of an on-going anthropological study of the youth culture in an urban community which is supported by the National Institute of Mental Health grant MH 12172-01. Our data are derived from field observation of peer groups operating in their natural habitats and from intensive, free-flowing interviews with selected informants. Initial contacts were made with this youth population through an established youth-serving agency, and subsequent relationships were established by following out friendship networks, i.e., meeting and talking with friends of our initial contacts. We found that these networks seldom bridged the several strata of the status system; thus, it was necessary to establish new contacts and follow out friendship networks in each of the strata. Thus far, most of our informants have come from the higher reaches of the adolescent status system (24), rather than its lower levels (10). There are more girls (23) than boys (11) at present in our formal interview sample. Much of our data on the boys came from less structured contexts such as conversations in cars. Although the number of interviews with each informant varies, we find that some of our more articulate informants have remained with the study for a year on the basis of two or three hour-and-a-half tape-recorded interviews per month. The interviews were usually with individual informants, although occasionally small groups of 2–4 students were interviewed. A considerable portion of our data was gathered in talks with students at dances, parties, hangouts, card games, etc.

THE PROBLEM

The question of whether there is a relatively self-contained adolescent sub-culture in this society stimulates recurrent, inconclusive sociological controversy. Contrary to the model of the youth culture as a contraculture, we hold that its reality as a subculture does not rest upon its power to repudiate or undermine basic adult values. We shall argue that peer-group interaction is guided by expectations which do not govern the behavior of other members of the community. And we claim that the understandings which transform what might otherwise be transitory encounters into stable peer-group relationships are not fully comprehensible to the rest of the community. More simply, adolescent social relationships are predicated upon premises not completely accessible or intelligible to adults.[2]

From our point of view, the specifically subcultural aspects of adolescent social life reside in those symbolic elements (values, beliefs, and standards) which integrate various concrete norms [3] into a coherent system of action. Later in this paper we will examine some of the symbolic resolutions of adolescent role dilemmas and ambiguities, for example, adolescent beliefs about their own social world which reduce logical and moral inconsistencies between incongruous orientations to various social situations.

As Reisman suggests, the significance of much of adolescent social life is partially hidden from adults by linguistic devices. Consequently, the data which can best reveal the character of the youth culture are linguistic, and the relevant aspect of adolescent language is obviously semantic.

LANGUAGE AND ACTION

In this paper, we will show that adolescent perceptions and assessments of their own social universe are embodied in a distinctive argot, their status terminology. These status terms refer to moral attributes (those qualities which make some persons admirable, others reprehensible, etc.) and moral dispositions (the kinds of things these people are likely to do and say). The members of a status category are thought to possess common social virtues and defects. Status terms, then, are not affectively neutral labels for structural positions in the youthful social system. They bestow either negative or positive esteem on those who manifest or exemplify these personal characteristics. Consequently, an individual's rank in the local prestige hierarchy is partly a function of the meanings inherent in those terms his peers use to describe his character and his group affiliations. . . .

The linguistically conditioned ways in which the members of a group per-

[2] In a comparatively recent view of the "adolescent society," Bennett Berger, "Adolescence and Beyond," *Social Problems*, Vol. X (1963), asserts that "there is absolutely no good body of data on adolescents, Coleman's included, which indicates the existence of a really deviant system of norms which govern adolescent life" (p. 395).

[3] By concrete norms we mean specific prescriptions and proscriptions which refer to particular types of social contexts (e.g., dating) and which govern or which actors feel ought to govern behavior (e.g., sexual) in these kinds of social settings.

ceive and evaluate their social environment have determinant consequences for their behavior. Here we follow Clyde Kluckhohn, who says that "the *vocabularies* of different languages both reflect and perpetuate habitual and distinctive ways of categorizing experience or modes of thought." [4] He goes on to say that "how people behave toward one another is, in part, a function of what they call each other and of *how* they conceive objects, themselves, other people and types of events which enter into their relations." [5] Elucidation of the meanings implicit in the adolescent status terminology will illuminate the complex relationships between the norms of this subculture and the behavior of its members in various social settings.

Stated in functional terms, cultural categories contained in language do not usually determine the particulars (i.e., the who, how much, and when) of any behavioral sequence but, rather, provide the cognitive and evaluative parameters of social interaction in any social setting.[6] These categories identify the appropriate motives, values, roles, and rules which transform the actor's external physical world into what Hallowell calls the behavioral environment of the self. "A *second* function of all cultures is the orientation of the self to a diversified world of objects in its behavioral environment, discriminated, classified, and conceptualized with respect to attributes which are culturally constituted and symbolically mediated through language. The role of language in object-orientation is as vital as in self-orientation." [7] As we shall see in the case of the meaning of the term "cool," these categories tie both the actor's moral orientations and cognitive definitions of social situations to the critical motivational dimensions of the self, that is, his judgments about his own worth—"Any kind of self-depreciation, loss of self-esteem, or threat to the self impairs the complex motivational systems that focus upon the self and its needs. At the same time, self-evaluation through culturally recognized norms is inescapable." [8]

THE STRUCTURAL ORIGINS OF THE YOUTH CULTURE

Considered as a phenomenon indigenous to modern societies, the youth culture can be traced to the problem of socialization in industrial societies.[9]

---

[4] "Culture and Behavior," *Handbook of Social Psychology,* Vol. XX, ed. Gardner Lindsey (Reading, Mass.: Addison-Wesley Publishing, 1954), p. 938, italics in original.
   [5] *Ibid.*
   [6] For a persuasive statement of a somewhat different point of view, see Frake, "A Structural Description of Subanum 'Religious Behavior,'" *Explorations in Cultural Anthropology,* ed. Ward Goodenough (New York: McGraw-Hill Book Co., 1964).
   [7] A. I. Hallowell, "The Self and Its Behavioral Environment," *Culture and Experience* (Philadelphia: University of Pennsylvania Press, 1955), p. 91, italics in original.
   [8] *Ibid.,* p. 106.
   [9] S. N. Eisenstadt's classic study, *From Generation to Generation* (Glencoe, Ill.: The Free Press, 1956), points out that there is a radical social-psychological transition between childhood and adulthood in industrial societies. Thus, every child in our society must eventually leave his family circle where he is appreciated for *who* rather than *what* he is. According to this theory, the youth culture serves as a "halfway house" between a young person's particularistic and universalistic associations. While youth groups are based upon ascriptive ties, the youth culture enables adolescents to try out roles and form relation-

Certainly adolescent norms refer to these structural problems at various levels of meaning. But this does not exhaust the cultural connotations and the behavioral implications of distinctively adolescent modes of communication. For there is great latitude in the selection of the cultural forms which provide adequate solutions to these structural exigencies and concomitant developmental crises—witness the differences in the content of the peer-group norms in various communities and classes.[10] Therefore, it is not possible to account for the substance and imagery of the youth culture solely in terms of the difficult passage from childhood to adulthood in a highly differentiated society.

The Youth Culture Defined

Part of our society's ideology about the nature of human growth asserts that youth must not prematurely assume adult roles. Thus, it is often said that adolescents need an exemption from the pressures of adult responsibilities in order to discover their individual talents. These ideological sanctions encourage adolescents to transform developmental necessities into aesthetically satisfying as well as socially adaptive modes of behavior. In other words, the efflorescence of adolescent styles results from this license to experiment with the possibilities inherent in adult roles. In turn, the youth culture symbolically affirms and celebrates its freedom from conventional restraints on social behavior which have little or no immediate practical significance. For example, many of our informants lavishly praise what they call "idiot"[11] behavior: actions and attitudes which are childish or foolish from an adult point of view and which sometimes treat situations from seemingly incompatible perspectives, for example, dealing with a love relationship in a manner that is at once flippant and romantic. According to some of our most articulate informants, the ability to engage in any sort of silly collective action requires a certain amount of inner freedom and *joie de vivre*. In general, these informants tend to associate these sorts of peer-group activities with independence from adult supervision and with actions which demonstrate this autonomy.[12]

---

ships which involve more universalistic considerations: An adolescent must *earn* his status in the peer group. The youth culture, then, allows the adolescent to experiment with objective, universalistic standards without sacrificing the psychological security of highly solidary primary groups.

[10] For a very detailed account of the attitudes and activities of various types of adolescent peer groups, see Muzafer and Carolyn Sherif, *Reference Groups: Exploration into Conformity and Deviation of Adolescents* (New York: Harper & Row, 1964).

[11] Words enclosed by quotation marks (e.g., "cool") are terms used with considerable frequency by our informants. This is not to say, however, that the notions contained in these words are not also expressed by circumlocution. These terms are ordinarily used in reference and rarely in address.

[12] According to some of our informants, "idiot" should not be equated with childish behavior. We have been told that those persons who are able to act this way are often the same people who appear most sophisticated (i.e., adult-like) in other social contexts. Perhaps, this connection between silly and sophisticated personal styles is a symbolic

Stated more formally, the youth culture consists of those adolescent norms, standards, and values which are discussed in a language particularly intelligible to members of this age-grade. At this point, we should note that members of the youth culture do not deal with or even "talk" about all the concerns which vitally interest or agitate adolescents, and they may even ignore or overlook those concerns which are of enduring significance to the members of this society.[13] Yet the youth culture contains a distinctive vision of social reality. It is embodied in a normative order predicated upon conceptions of those personal qualities which its members believe make a male admirable and a female desirable.

THE YOUTH CULTURE AS A CONTRACULTURE

The sociological conception of the youth culture as a contraculture assumes that the cultural and structural aspects of the youth culture are inextricably linked. Thus, evidence which reveals serious structural discontinuities between the generations is also supposed to show a set of youth norms which are opposed to adult values.[14] According to the contraculture model, if adolescents substantially accept core adult roles and values, then the youth culture is essentially epiphenomenal.[15] But if they doubt the legitimacy of societal values, then the youth culture is the appropriate label for this truly rebellious posture. In contrast, our approach to the youth culture holds that the symbolic components of adolescent social life form a relatively coherent subculture *irrespective* of whether its norms eventually subvert, reinforce, or have no lasting effect upon adult values. Our position rests upon a basic theoretical assumption: that the cultural categories which shape adolescent orientations to their own social milieu are largely auton-

---

means of demonstrating what Erving Goffman (*Encounters* [Indianapolis: Bobbs-Merrill Co., 1961]), calls role distance. They seem to say that we now have mastered the developmental tasks of childhood, and hence these sorts of performances (playing games which have no extrinsic social significance) can now be slightly ridiculed because it no longer constitutes a vital part of our social identities.

[13] This idea was stimulated by James F. Short's remarks on delinquent gangs in "Social Structure and Group Processes in Gang Delinquency," *Problems of Youth: Transition to Adulthood in a Changing World*, ed. Sherif and Sherif (Chicago: Aldine Publishing, 1965), esp. p. 173.

[14] Cf. James Coleman, *The Adolescent Society* (New York: The Free Press, 1961), and F. Elkin and W. Westley, "The Myth of Adolescent Culture," *American Sociological Review*, Vol. XX (1955), who have tried to determine whether the norms of the youth culture impede or inhibit the socialization of adolescents into adult occupational roles.

[15] As subordinate and quite powerless members of our society, youth are said to experience social and psychological deprivation because of the conflicting demands which are placed upon them. Viewed as a contraculture, the youth culture evolves out of a normative "reaction-formation" to these pressures. According to Milton Yinger, "Contra-Culture and Subculture," *American Sociological Review*, Vol. XXV (1960), it involves "the creation of a series of inverse or counter values (opposed to those of the surrounding society) in the face of serious frustration or conflict" (p. 627).

omous inasmuch as they are embodied in systems of meanings whose implications are not immediately apparent to adults.[16]

The structure of advanced societies generates a certain amount of adolescent rebelliousness against adult authority.[17] But this does not mean that opposition to the goals of the older generation is the only, or even the most important, disjunction between adolescent and adult views of social reality. Nor is it true that the norms of the youth culture derive their subcultural attributes from intergenerational conflict.

In fact, the traditional cycle of intense intergenerational conflict followed by reconciliation when the younger generation takes its place in society seems less common today than in the past. Instead of direct confrontations over the moral validity, the relevance, and the appropriateness of the other generations' goals and aspirations,[18] both the older and younger members of this society subscribe to a laissez-faire ideology. This encourages generational segregation, rather than opposition. Keniston notes that "another salient fact about young people today is a relative lack of *rebelliousness* against their parents or their parents' generation. . . . The result is frequently an unstated 'gentleman's agreement' between the generations that neither will interfere with the other." [19] According to one of our informants, a senior girl:

(Q) Do you know what adults in this community think about various issues?
(A) I'd say there is a very small amount of contact between the teen-agers and the adults because we're self-centered, I think, and the adults are too. We think "I'll leave them alone," and they do too.

Our informants almost instinctively measured their own worth against the standards of the youth culture. And the cardinal concerns of the youth culture are in those domains over which they exercise direct control: friendships, relations with the opposite sex, and various types of expressive activities. This sort of partial cultural isolation is reinforced by the paucity of enduring intergenerational contacts outside of formal socializing agencies, such as the school and family.[20] Thus most of the adolescents we have

[16] For example, most adults in this community are aware of, and many approve of, the fraternity and sorority system which operates despite an official school ban on such activity. However, if our adolescent informants are correct, very few adults know why one person is "rushed" and another is not. Though many parents seem to want their children to succeed in this social world, most adults are ignorant of the specific social criteria fraternity and sorority youth use to select certain kinds of persons for their exclusive social circles.

[17] See K. Davis, "The Sociology of Parent-Youth Conflict," *Social Perspectives on Behavior,* ed. H. D. Stein and R. A. Cloward (Glencoe, Ill.: The Free Press, 1958).

[18] See Walter Laquer, *Young Germany* (New York: Basic Books, 1962), for a description of youth movements which opposed the prevailing ethos of their society in their early stages of development.

[19] K. Keniston, "Social Change and Youth in America," *Daedalus,* XCI (1962), 151–156, italics in original.

[20] See F. Musgrove, *Youth and the Social Order* (Bloomington: University of Indiana Press, 1965), for an interesting historical perspective on the present separation of the generations.

observed accept a socially imposed hiatus in their life cycle, regardless of whether they are eager, reluctant, or uninterested in becoming an adult; and most of them assume that only their peers can truly understand those kinds of interpersonal accomplishments and failures which make their lives in the adolescent world either gratifying or mortifying.

Open intergenerational conflict in this community revolves around the question of how much control adults rightfully can exercise over adolescents.[21] Both sides in these disputes agree that intrusion into private generational matters is generally unwarranted, for example, adults usually allow adolescents to arrange their own social affairs. The issue, then, concerns the definition of those aspects of adolescent behavior which are legitimately public and hence subject to adult control.

THE RELATIONSHIP BETWEEN ADULT VALUES AND YOUTH NORMS

In our study of this upper-middle-class urban community,[22] we found that these adolescents successfully internalized adult occupational goals. None of our informants questioned the notion that a high school diploma was a minimal requirement for even a half-decent job, and comparatively few students in the local high school dropped out before graduation. Most of these adolescents intended to go to college, and many of them worked reasonably hard to get good grades. They wanted a college degree because they felt it would help them get the professional job or husband which insures a middle-class way of life. However, very few of these adolescents, even the best students, had marked intellectual or scholarly interests. In short, we discovered that adolescent conceptions of the validity of adult roles and values are, at least, largely independent of the standards they use to estimate the relative excellence of their peers.[23]

[21] According to the data collected by Henry McKay for the Institute for Juvenile Research, this area, in the 35-year period from 1927 to 1962, had the lowest mean delinquency rate in the city (these rates are based upon official Juvenile Court cases). However, this low rate of delinquency should not be interpreted as evidence of a complete lack of intergenerational conflict. We have observed that behavior which slightly violates adult norms, such as surreptitiously playing poker for high stakes or putting a fraternity picture in the school annual (fraternities and sororities are forbidden), is often sufficient to demonstrate one's autonomy vis-à-vis adult controls. Since the tolerance of deviant youth behavior in the community is small, one can establish one's autonomy through relatively minor acts of defiance of adult authority.

[22] The community we studied is located in a large midwestern city and has a population of approximately 25,000. It has most of the socio-economic characteristics commonly associated with upper-middle-class residential areas. Since it may be useful to compare this community to the city as a whole, the figures for the latter will be given in parentheses; and the figures for both will be given in approximate percentages. According to data from the 1960 Census, the median family income in this community was $11,000 ($6,700). Only 5 per cent (14 per cent) of the families earned less than $3,000 a year, and 58 per cent (21 per cent) had an income of $10,000 a year or more. Eighty-six per cent (24 per cent) of the families lived in single-dwelling units, and of these 82 per cent (33 per cent) were owned by the occupants. For this population the median number of years of education was almost 13 (10), and 21 per cent (6 per cent) had four years of college or more. Seventy-two per cent (37 per cent) of this population held white-collar jobs.

[23] In "Values and Gang Delinquency: A Study of Street-Corner Groups," *American*

The youth culture in this area is not completely oblivious to an individual's potential capacity to assume his adult roles. But, as far as his peers are concerned, his success or failure in the academic system of the high school (i.e., his grades) is a relatively minor component of his social identity, although very negative connotations are associated with the status of a "brain"—a person who devotes all his energies to getting high marks. Our informants usually call such a person "twinky," which implies that his demeanor manifests an underlying effeminacy. The choice of a term which connotes less-than-manly behavior follows a peculiarly subcultural logic. The standards of the youth culture are focused on those sorts of behaviors which its members think reflect one's sex-role identity. Their judgments of personal worth are closely linked to general conceptions of those attributes and performances which are thought to reveal a person's masculinity or femininity. For boys, the crucial external signs of inner manhood are physical strength, athletic talent, courage in the face of aggression, a willingness to defend one's honor at all costs, and sexual and drinking prowess. According to girls, the most admirable feminine traits are physical attractiveness, personal vivacity, and the ability to delicately manipulate various sorts of interpersonal relationships.

As a cultural system, the youth culture in this area consists of those norms, life styles, and ideals which are intimately associated with a *variant*, age-graded system of cultural meanings. Of course, the youth culture does not emerge out of a cultural vacuum. Adolescent social patterns obviously are based upon adult conceptions of the desirable types of social relationships and upon adult images of personal virtue. Adolescents, however, do not slavishly copy these general cultural norms. The youth culture experiments with and elaborates on some of the partially unrealized or alternative possibilities in the adult moral order. This is particularly true in the interpersonal realm: Adolescents distinguish various kinds and degrees of trust among friends. Our informants habitually discriminate among "good," "best," and "casual" friends. One informant distinguished among these types of friends in the following terms:

(Q) What are some of the things you expect of a friend?
(A) When you leave [a group], when you walk out, they don't all of a sudden start stabbing knives in your back. It all depends upon the degree of friendship you want [in response to the question].
(Q) What are the various degrees of friendship?

Journal of Sociology, Vol. LXIX (1963), R. A. Gordon, J. F. Short, D. S. Cartwright, and F. L. Strodtbeck report that even the most socially disadvantaged, delinquent youth not only evaluate a middle-class way of life very highly but that they also see the conventional path to this end—saving, working at a steady job, and education—as a legitimate, although not always realistic, way to attain a respectable adult status. Yet, as Short, *op. cit.,* points out, these adolescents do not use these values to regulate peer-group life. Similarly, it is wrong to infer that, just because middle-class adolescents are even less ambivalent about adult values, these standards determine the norms of their peer groups.

(A) With some girls you just have a casual friendship, and she's got her friends and I've got mine, but we'll sit down and talk. Then like the girls in my club, we are pretty good friends. We know who we are going out with. With the casual friend you don't sit and talk about your boyfriend to them. I have one best friend.

(Q) Are there certain things you share with a best friend that you don't share with a fellow club member [i.e., a "pretty good friend"]?

(A) You talk about your boyfriends if you had an argument, but you wouldn't tell them personal things [i.e., to a "pretty good friend"]. I could tell my best friend anything, and she wouldn't think badly of you. You don't have to worry that, will she tell anybody else? While the members of my club, I expect them not to stab knives in my back when I leave, *but my best friend, if someone else does, I expect her to stand up for me. My club members, I wouldn't expect them to stand up for me.*

From a comparative point of view, then, the differences among the cultural categories which shape adult and adolescent orientations to some social situations are admittedly slight. Nevertheless, and this is the important point, the differences between adult standards of personal worth and the meaning of adolescent status terms are great enough to sustain an independent adolescent status system. The multitude of discrete norms which regulate a person's relations with his peers are integrated into a meaningful system of action by distinctively adolescent conceptions of personal worth. The cultural core of the adolescent social system is formed by the meanings of adolescent status terms and prestige categories. An adolescent's estimation of his own interpersonal competence depends, to a great extent, upon whether the particular terms his peers use to describe his status have laudatory or pejorative connotations. These terms indicate whether he is able convincingly to present a "cool" self-image in highly competitive social contexts.

THE MEANING OF KEY STATUS TERMS

The adolescents in this community do not see their status system as a perfectly linear, clearly defined series of hierarchically arranged status positions. Rather, they perceive it as a set of ranked, slightly ambiguous prestige categories which are internally differentiated. This status system is structured along two dimensions. First, there are horizontal social strata defined by differentially evaluated life styles, that is, modes of dress, speech, and interpersonal demeanor. In general, our informants perceive two salient life styles which they refer to as "hoody" and "socie." However, we see another way of life which lacks an explicit folk designation, though most of our informants distinguish it from "socie" and "hoody" styles. For the lack of a better term, we call this the conventional way of life. It is an essentially residual category which includes all those patterns which are neither clearly "socie" nor "hoody."

The dominant values institutionalized in the status system of the local

high school are those held by the majority of the upper-middle-class segment of this youthful population (the high school draws students from a
stable working- and lower-middle-class community as well as from our
upper-middle-class area).[24] Consequently, most adolescents in this area
perceive the "socies" as the top stratum of this prestige system. Since
"hoody" and "socie" youth do not agree about who has the most valuable
way of life (e.g., our "hoody" informants tell us that "socies" are hypocrites,
etc.), an individual's estimation of his own status depends, in part, upon his
particular adolescent reference group. From an observer's point of view,
the "hoody" adolescents have evolved a truly independent style of life.
Nevertheless, our "hoody" informants see their own life style as at least a
partly antagonistic response to "socie" values and material advantages.
"Hoody" adolescents, by and large, refuse to and often cannot financially
afford to compete with "socies" on the latter's terms, and they feel that
their mode of life is not accorded general esteem in this system. Those who
adopt what we have called a conventional way of life gain some social recognition only to the extent to which they can imitate "socie" patterns.

The vertical component of this status system locates an individual's rank
within one of these horizontal strata. As far as we can ascertain, a person's
rank is a function of how well he is known by the other members of his
stratum, and this, in turn, seems closely related to his ability to conspicuously live up to its standards of excellence. This vertical dimension, then,
is quantitative rather than qualitative and refers to what our informants
mean when they say someone is more or less "popular." Since public renown
is a basic value in the "socie" world, those who achieve fame are called
"elites." This, however, says nothing about their commitment to one of the
various substyles available to the members of this stratum. Although all our
informants subscribe to a highly egalitarian social ideology (no one is
inherently better than anyone else), "hoody" adolescents take it very seriously. Though many of our "hoody" informants admitted that certain persons in their social circle are more "popular" than others, they have no term
which designates high position.

An adolescent's socioeconomic status certainly affects his ability to assim-
ilate "socie" styles. Nevertheless, the decisive factor is his ability to act in
terms of these standards whatever his family background. In other words,
an adolescent's status identity is created by his overt commitment to an
adolescent life style.[25] Some of our lower-middle- and stable working-class

[24] In numerical terms, this upper-middle-class group does not constitute a majority
of this school population. Yet, through the fraternity and sorority system which it dominates and through less overtly stratified, adult-sponsored youth groups which it co-opts
as a recruiting ground, these adolescents control both the formal (e.g., the cheerleaders
at this high school are not only restricted to sorority girls but to the members of one
sorority) and informal activity systems which emerge out of school associations but which
are definitely not confined to this location.

[25] Most of the adolescents who fall into the conventional category seem more oriented
to "socie" than "hoody" dress styles, and some have attempted and failed to join "socie"
groups. In contrast to "socies" and "hoods," conventionals have a life style which does
not appear to involve a code of honor vis-à-vis other groups. Conventionals, however,

informants are among the most influential "socies," while a few of our informants from upper-middle-class homes are labeled "hoods" by their peers. "Socies" tend to associate "hoody" life styles with very stereotyped conceptions of the attitudes and aspirations which distinguish the lower and middle classes. For instance, even those "socie" informants from stable working- and lower-middle-class families, repeatedly tell us that "hoods" are the sort of people who do not care about their grades, about school activities, about their personal appearance, about morals, etc. In essence, they believe that the "hoods" incorporate what they think is the critical lower-class social-psychological attribute—a complete lack of interest in "bettering oneself."

At this point, we should note that there are alternate terms for these status categories; for example, the words "socie" and "socialite" are used interchangeably. Also, certain status terms change over time. For instance, many of our informants feel that it is more "in" to use the term "mellow" in those contexts where they formerly used the term "cool," but they also agree that these terms have the same meanings. Status terms also take on special meanings according to the structural position of the speaker. Thus, a "socie" speaker will use the term "hoods" interchangeably with "greasers," "scraggs," etc.; all of these terms have very derogatory implications. Similarly, "hoods" use the terms "snob" and "stuck-up" as synonyms for "socie."

"Hoods" and "socies" very rarely use these terms to describe themselves but almost obsessively use them to describe each other. It is difficult for adults to appreciate the discrepancy between the adolescent meaning of a term like "hoody" and its conventional referents, that is, to delinquents. For example, one of our most articulate informants belongs to the "hoody" stratum, and she accepts this designation insofar as she defines her own personal style as one which consistently opposes "socie" styles. Yet adults would not ordinarily call her "hoody" because she takes a college mathematics course in her spare time and participates in a tutoring project for culturally deprived children.

These status terms do not refer directly to bounded social units which have a clearly demarcated membership. Yet membership in certain cliques, clubs, fraternities, and sororities makes it very likely that a person will be considered a "socie" by his peers. The precise meaning of these terms, however, cannot be understood apart from the nature of the youth culture in an upper-middle-class community. Here adolescents have a dual orientation to the standards of the youth culture and to the values of the adult world.[26]

---

tend to define the local social system in terms of what all its members perceive as polar, antagonistic social categories, i.e., "socie" and "hoody." Hence conventionals are difficult to place unambiguously in the status system and lack the definite social identities ascribed to "socies" and "hoods."

[26] N. Riley, J. Riley, and M. More, "Adolescent Values and the Riesman Typology: An Empirical Analysis," *Culture and Social Character*, ed. Seymour M. Lipset and Leo Lowenthal (Glencoe, Ill.: The Free Press, 1962), found this same dual orientation to parental and peer-group standards. Also see C. V. Brittain, "Adolescent Choices and

The adult world is represented by the achievement orientation of the high school. Our "socie" informants claim that this stratum is divided into the "clean-cut" or "all-around" and the "hoody-socie" segments. The "clean-cut socies" stress role performances which are explicitly linked to the school's activity system. They usually do well in team sports, get fairly good but not necessarily high grades, and most importantly, know how to get along with their teachers and classmates—they are very "sociable." [27] In fact, it seems that part of a non-"socie" social identity involves the belief that one does not have enough social skill and organizational ability to give a "swinging" or "cool" affair, and non-"socie" social gatherings generally reinforce this self-fulfilling prophecy.

"Clean-cut socies" must also realize the "cool" patterns of adolescent social life. They must succeed in the intense competition for dates with high-status persons; the social circle from which a person selects his dating partners partially establishes his or her standing in the larger social system. After the second year of high school, "socie" boys must be "conditioned" drinkers, which means not getting prematurely or obnoxiously inebriated in social situations. Sexually, "socie" boys must "make out" and thereby provide some concrete evidence for their frequent and exaggerated boasts about their sexual prowess.

For these boys, drinking and dating are the definitive areas in which one's manhood is tested and proven. They talk a great deal about and admire toughness but studiously avoid situations where they might have to fight. Buying liquor or beer in a store is viewed as a potential threat to their image as autonomous "men," and, conversely, it is seen as a challenge which, if handled properly, can add greatly to one's stature in the group. As our informants perceive it, buying beer in a bar or package store is a battle-ground reserved only for the courageous: the risks to one's self-esteem are great. If a boy reveals that he is afraid to show a false identification card or otherwise bluff his way through demands that he prove his age, then he loses considerable face within his peer group. But if he stands his ground

---

Parent-Peer Cross Pressures," *American Sociological Review,* Vol. XXIII (June, 1963), and in Part Three of this book.

[27] Being "sociable" often means that a person is able to articulate previously unconnected persons or cliques into larger and sometimes bounded social networks. This trait, in turn, is closely related to a person's standing in the "socie" world. For example, one of our informants who actively aspired to this stratum told us that part of her lack of success was due to her inability to bring her various, disparate friendship groups together. She sat in the middle of the lunch table between these two groups but could not promote social intercourse between them and felt marginal to both. However, another informant, who lacked the usual physical attributes of a "socie" girl, was an "elite" largely because she could not only integrate separate dyads into larger friendship networks, but could then combine these networks into a named group whose membership was drawn from both the sorority world and from those girls who were by and large sorority "material" but who were excluded by the "blackball" system—one vote against a prospective member was enough to reject her. This girl provided the rationale, the occasions (e.g., "hen parties"), and most importantly, the contacts which enabled some girls to validate their status in the larger social system through membership in this group.

when accused of being under age and does not give in to his desire to flee the situation, then he proves that he has "guts" regardless of whether the store ultimately sells him the beer. Our informants tell us that it is crucial not to "lose your cool" in these situations, and anyone who fails to rise to the occasion has his claims to "coolness" ruthlessly deflated by his peers.

Girls prove their worth in a more contracted arena. They must attract many high-status boys as dates, and to do so they must occasionally engage in rather intense petting without endangering their "reputations." While their prestige depends partly on the status their presence bestows upon their dating partners, it can be compromised if they give sexual favors to all who request them.

The "socies" (our informants usually employ the term "socie" and qualify it when they want to refer to those who adhere to the "clean-cut" or "hoody" variant) fully realize the adolescent dimensions of this social system. Though a member of the "clean-cut socies" adopts many "cool" patterns, he never relinquishes his commitment to adult standards of accomplishment. On the other hand, the "hoody-socies" devote themselves wholeheartedly to adolescent conceptions of excellence. They are the most enthusiastic fraternity and sorority members and are not usually very interested in academic pursuits. Instead they spend a good deal of time and energy systematically refining their dating and drinking techniques. And they are the avant-garde leaders in musical tastes, dress styles, etc.

The "hoods" and the "hoody-socies" should not be confused. The latter represent the furthest an adolescent in the "socie" stratum can move away from adult values without openly rejecting them, that is, they rarely openly defy adult authority in acts of serious delinquency, and, unlike some of the "hoods," they rarely drop out of high school before graduation.

"Socies" have developed a special set of status terms which distinguish various social segments among those who occupy the lower orders of the status system. These terms have depreciatory connotations because they imply that these social types are represented by persons with morally defective or socially underdeveloped personalities. From the "socie" perspective, the "hoods" belong to the more encompassing social category of "out-of-its." One informant described the "out-of-its" as follows: "They're misfits; they're insecure, they don't think they're cute enough, or they're awkward, or they have a lisp or something." This is a heterogeneous category; here one finds the rebels, the retarded or slow learners, the intellectuals, and anyone else who is deviant from the point of view of the prestige criteria which define this status system.

"Socies" also perceive another category of persons who are not attached to or even loosely associated with "socie" cliques and yet who do not fit into the "out-of-its." Some of our "socie" informants call them the "others," and they are just ordinary students who are not distinguished by some success or blatant failure in the adolescent social system. One student described the "others" in this way: "Some of them may not come out of their shell until they get to college, and they may find a group whether it's intellectual or social. These kids will usually gravitate toward getting the higher grades—some don't concentrate on anything at all. They just go along and get by in school and don't join activities, but just sit home and watch television all the time." The derogatory implications associated with the term "others" do not simply derive from exclusion from "socie" social circles: It means that a person has no definite social identity in this social system. As far as "socies" are concerned, these people are faceless because they are not demonstrably attached to a discernible adolescent style. As one of our informants put it, "others" are people you do not notice or know anything about unless you happened to go to elementary school with them.

As we have seen, the process of status attribution is quite complex and does not result simply from objective talents and characteristics, for example, a boy's athletic ability, a girl's physical attractiveness, etc. Thus, an individual must take the esteem he has gained in a variety of contexts and transform this diffuse prestige into a subculturally validated image of the successful adolescent. He must present himself as "cool," and our informants tell us that if a person truly believes he is "cool" he generally acts "cool." In other words, concrete achievement buttresses the crucial mode of presentation of self in the adolescent subculture, and *it is this self-image and not the concrete role performance which ultimately interests adolescents. Confidence about one's essential masculinity or femininity and the ability to manifest this in smooth performances in many spheres is the essence of high status in this social system.*

One might expect a normative shift toward adult success standards over time in a youthful population largely oriented to college. But as an adolescent progresses through high school he discovers that the tension between adult and adolescent patterns increases rather than decreases. By the final year of high school the social category of the "clean-cut socies" has very few members. Those who cling to "clean-cut" patterns and hence are not trying to be "cool" no longer dominate the status system. In fact, those "clean-cut socies" who do not perceive this shift toward "cool" patterns are called "milk and cookies boys" and rapidly descend in the status system. One informant described what happened to a fraternity which did not make the shift to the "socie" patterns: "The Lambdas aren't well liked now because the Lambdas don't drink, and the other kids are all getting to drink, and they [the Lambdas] are not that well liked anymore because they look down upon it [drinking]. So now if you want social prestige with the kids, you wouldn't dare mention the Lambdas." The former members of the "clean-cut socies" who retain their social supremacy do so by appearing to adhere to responsible adult standards while, at the same time, actively participating in covert adolescent patterns.

CULTURAL SOURCES OF INTEGRATION IN THE YOUTH CULTURE

Every cultural system has internal normative inconsistencies. In this section, we will show how certain cultural categories partially resolve some of the paradoxical or contradictory behavioral implications of the norms which govern dating. "Cute" and "cool" are prestigeful terms in this system, and an "elite" girl should be both. Girls see these as consistent personal attributes when they refer to the norms which regulate the ways in which a person achieves pre-eminence in the prestige system. But when girls talk about the ideal norms which should control relationships between members of the opposite sex, these two terms assume partly antagonistic meanings.

Both our male and female informants define a "cute" girl as a person who exudes a certain kind of sexual attractiveness but who does not demonstrate her sexual superiority in intercourse. In fact, if it is widely known that a high-status girl has had sexual intercourse, she very likely will be dropped from the "elite" circles even if she did not get pregnant. Yet, if she is "cool," a girl must be quite adept in the dating system. This means that she must "make out" with a comparatively large number of boys without, on the other hand, being "made." She must allow herself to reach a relatively high level of sexual excitement and intimacy without giving in to what are described as persistent demands for greater sexual favors. Consequently, if a girl is considered both "cool" and "cute" by her age mates, she must not only be physically attractive but also confidently manage the sexual self-aggrandizement which marks these temporary unions.

So far, "cuteness" and "coolness" are somewhat different but essentially complementary social categories. But girls have their own moral standards which form part of the meaning of these terms. When the social context is restricted to feminine interests and when the norms of proper behavior vis-à-vis males are at issue, "cool" and "cute" become partly contradictory categories.

Adolescent girls in this community discuss the motives and the norms which should govern dating in terms of "good clean fun." A good dating partner should be companionable, have similar interests, and should be a sympathetic and lively person. In this context, the "cute" girl is viewed as the friendly, "all-American girl" whom everyone likes and admires. She is vivacious, attractive, and, above all, not overly interested in the leverage one can obtain over boys through the judicious allocation of her affections. In short, she is a very wholesome girl. However, this category of the "all-American girl" quickly drops out of the picture when the girls talk about the realities of the power struggle which almost invariably accompanies dating. Incidentally, "going steady" is an institutionalized way of emphasizing the solidarity rather than the individualism of dating oriented to the status system. But among "elites" the dominant concern of who is going to control the relationship—all of our informants were convinced that long-term dating was an intrinsically asymmetrical relationship and were afraid that their peers would see them as the subordinate partner [28]—almost in-

---

[28] Many of our male informants expressed what seemed to us an almost pathological fear of being "pussy whipped," but we shall let psychoanalysts reveal the psychological implications of this term.

evitably leads to its dissolution in a relatively short time. One girl viewed dating as follows:

(Q) You see this [dating] as pretty much of a game of strategy?

(A) Definitely! It's one of the most fun games around too. Because you never know what's going to happen. . . . It's up to you. There are no rules really. There might be a couple of rules that you take for granted, but basically. . . .

(Q) Like what [rules]?

(A) Well, not to do anything really nasty. Like go out with his best friend— break a date with him and go out with his best friend or something like that. Nothing really drastic, but aside from that there aren't too many rules, and you've just always got to make sure that you're on top, that you're winning because otherwise if you're not winning you're losing and there's no tie. So you always make sure you're winning.

According to ideal feminine norms, real sex, as distinguished from the "good-night kiss," is out of place, undesirable, and, in some sense, morally wrong on a good date. The feminine vision of a romantic relationship holds that a date should come from mutual concern with the other partner's true or inner qualities. As even a cursory glance at love comics and true romance magazines will attest female ideology maintains that it is possible to appreciate the true worth of another person only if one is willing to rise above the ordinary trivial absorption in the competitive aspects of cross-sex relations, that is, with the other person's physical appearance, with his or her superficial manners (usually with their sophistication or lack of it), with the other person's prestige value (whether one's peers think he or she is "cool"), etc.

In light of these norms, "coolness," which is manifest in an attachment to "making out," is apparently incompatible with purely feminine conceptions of "cuteness." Thus when girls talk solely in terms of their own moral standards, the "cute" girl is defined less by reference to her physical attractiveness than by her attractive "personality." Nevertheless, if a "cute" girl is to retain or achieve a position among the "elite" of the adolescent social system, she must attract high-status boys. How, then, does she retain her image of "cuteness" and the esteem that goes with it in the eyes of her girlfriends if she must also engage in a wide range of petting activities with many boys? Or, to phrase this in motivational terms, how does she keep her "cool" orientation toward sex within the moral boundaries of the feminine universe? That is, how can she participate in a rather promiscuous pattern of sexual intimacy with many boys and, at the same time, exercise considerable control over her sexual encounters?

This somewhat contradictory pattern of normatively encouraged sexual promiscuity and restraint is resolved by a higher-order cultural category. This category defines the sexual nature of boys in both cognitive and evaluative terms. Our girl informants tell us that boys "naturally" try to "get all

they can" sexually because boys are born with uncontrollable sexual urges.[29]
One girl discussed the issue in the following terms:

(Q) Whose responsibility is it [regarding how far things go sexually on a date]?

(A) The girl's. I mean because guys can't help it. I mean they are born that way, but then girls get carried away because guys can't help themselves and girls can. To a point, but once past that point there's no hope.

(Q) Are all guys like this or just particular guys?

(A) Some guys would get as far as they could get, just for kicks, but there are other boys who are just as nice as they can be, but any boy who likes a girl enough . . . I don't think he would do it intentionally to hurt her, but just can't help to get as far as he can get. I don't think even the nicest guy can help being that way.

In terms of dating norms, girls say that it is their responsibility both to satisfy part of this inborn male desire for continual sexual satisfaction and to keep the situation from getting out of hand. Though girls admit that they also have strong sexual feelings, they agree that they and not the boys are capable of rational control, of setting limits.[30] Thus, girls claim that nature has burdened them with the responsibility of keeping petting relationships within the prescribed moral limits. In a basic sense, girls see boys as morally defective—or, if not as morally defective, at least as morally immature. Boys are said to be simply incapable of realistically assessing the negative consequences of giving free rein to sexual impulses in a dating situation. And, from what we have been able to observe, boys often fulfil these cultural expectations which have been phrased in such biological terms.

Although success in dating seems superficially completely tied to ascriptive criteria, there are important performance aspects to dating. Female competence is culturally defined as the ability to manipulate the sexual component of dating relationships to one's own advantage. Some girls have told us about a technique of "dumping" which they use to entice boys and yet keep them in a dependent position, never certain of whether they will be abandoned for a more attractive partner. One girl described her dating relationship in the following way:

Like when Jim and I first started dating, we got along just fine. Then I started to dump on him, being a little snotty once in a while and stuff like this. Then I decided to be nice because it would be nice to be nice for a while, just as a change. Then I figured if he was so nice to me when I was dumping on him,

[29] The Ngulu, by way of contrast, are convinced that women are born sexually unsatisfiable (see T. Beidelman, "Pig [Gulwe]: An Essay on Ngulu Sexual Symbolism and Ceremony," *Southwestern Journal of Anthropology*, Vol. XX [1964]).

[30] For a long time we were puzzled about the reasons why one of our informants was systematically excluded from the girls' group mentioned above. Our other informants in this group told us, at first, that her clinical attitudes toward sex repulsed them, but upon reflection they admitted that they too collectively discussed sex in a similar manner. Upon further investigation, we found that this girl revealed her desire for sex, she "needed it," and hence she violated these norms.

just think if I was nice to him, he would really be nice to me. Well then he decided that wasn't such a hot idea [and] that he would start dumping on me which I didn't think was such a good idea either. So when he started dumping on me, I just decided to give him the shaft.

One of the latent and unintended consequences of this dating system is the widespread fear among "popular" girls that they are being exploited by the boys. A "popular" girl often feels that if she becomes too attached to a boy he may, in reality, be dating her only for the prestige which comes from being in the company of a "cool" and "cute" girl or, what is worse, he may play upon her romantic proclivities to seduce her.

Incidentally, we have found that many of the girls who "fall in love with" a popular entertainer, such as one of the Beatles, are often marginal in a very special way. They may have all the prerequisites for success in the dating system; they are often physically attractive and personable. But these girls reject the hostility and exploitation inherent in the dating system and prefer an imaginary but romantically perfect relationship with these remote figures.

Conclusion

In conclusion, we do not hold that the youth subculture is a closed normative system. The normative integrity, coherence, and identity of a subculture is not always based upon estrangement from the larger culture nor does it always reside in social organizations which resist integration into the larger society. On the other hand, in a discussion of the reality of the youth culture, Berger declares that subcultures must not only have "relatively distinctive styles of life, but styles of life which are to a great extent self-generated, autonomous, having institutional and territorial resources capable of sustaining it in crisis and insulating it from pressures from without." [31] In our opinion, this limits the concept of a subculture to very special, and possibly almost non-existent, cases of cultural differentiation in this society. The high degree of interdependence of functionally differentiated sub-systems in this society makes it unlikely that many subcultures will fulfil all of Berger's stringent prerequisites.

In contrast to Berger's strictures, we propose a more catholic and perhaps more fruitful view of a subculture. Rather, we suggest that the core of the youth culture resides in its distinctive evaluative standards. They endow the adolescent status terminology (and thus the social categories through which the members of this age-grade orient themselves to their peers) with qualities and attributes which do not dominate adult status judgments. Here we follow Anselm Strauss' view of the connection between social categories linked to a person's position in age and other societal structures and the ways in which people perceive social reality:

[31] Berger, *op. cit.*, p. 396.

These changes in conceptual level involve, of course, changes in behavior, since behavior is not separate from classifying. Shifts in concept connote shifts in perceiving, remembering and valuing—in short, radical changes in action and person. . . . Terminological shifts necessitate, but also signalize new evaluations: of self and others, of events, acts and objects; and the transformation of perception is irreversible; once having changed, there is no going back. One can look back, but he can evaluate only from his new status.[32]

From our point of view, then, the members of a subculture can be integrated into basic societal institutions even though their definitions of ordinary social situations are predicated upon a special set of cultural meanings. Consequently, the crucial criterion for the identification of a youth subculture is whether its norms provide its members with a distinctive world view, a style of life, and the standards against which they can measure their own worth. Here again it is worthwhile to quote Strauss on age-graded perceptions of the world: "But the world is different for persons of different age and generation even if they share in common sex, class, and nationality, and occupation." [33]

Finally, our approach emphasizes the element of free cultural play in the genesis of the youth culture. Of course, we do not deny that the typical psychological and role problems of this age-grade provide the raw materials out of which youth culture is built. But we do point to the ways in which the meanings inherent in this adolescent normative order transcend the requirements of simple adjustment to these exigencies. In other words, these adolescent cultural inventions and innovations impose a discernible order upon the crises and dilemmas of adolescence.

[32] Strauss, *Mirrors and Masks: The Search for Identity* (Glencoe, Ill.: The Free Press, 1959), p. 92.
[33] *Ibid.*, p. 138.

Socialization: Value Commitments

Lawrence Kohlberg

Moral Education in the Schools:
A Developmental View

A generation or two ago, descriptions of character education programs appeared often in pedagogical literature. Optimism ran high, for the anticipation of effecting meaningful change in children's moral characters seemingly conveyed deep social significance. Kohlberg observes below, however, that traditional, formal moral educational programs have been largely ineffective, and in view of the long-standing failures, suggests that a new approach is in order. He rejects the two common interpretations "that moral behavior is purely a matter of immediate situational forces and rewards" and "that moral character is a matter of deep emotions fixed in earliest childhood in the home." As an alternative, he offers the outlook that, while a specific act of cheating may be determined by situational factors, predisposition to acts of misconduct is related to children's capacity for judgment and to children's "ego strength," including such traits as ability to predict consequences, delay gratification, and focus attention. He describes six, age-related sequential stages through which children and adolescents presumably proceed step by step, and he argues persuasively that the concept of "moral character" is meaningful if moral character is conceived of as developmental rather than as a set of fixed conventional traits of honesty. This stimulating analysis of problems of moral education is complemented with pointers on how teachers might facilitate children's and adolescents' moral development.

For many contemporary educators and social scientists, the term "moral education" has an archaic ring, the ring of the last vestiges of the Puritan tradition in the modern school. This archaic ring, however, does not arise from any intrinsic opposition between the statement of educational aims and methods in moral terms and their statement in psychological terms. In fact, it was just this opposition which the great pioneers of the social psychology of education denied in such works as John Dewey's *Moral Principles in Education*[1] and Emile Durkheim's *Moral Education.*[2] Both of

FROM *The School Review*, LXXIV (1966), 1–29. Modified and updated for this volume by the author. Reprinted by permission of the author and the University of Chicago Press.

[1] J. Dewey, *Moral Principles in Education* (Boston: Houghton Mifflin Co., 1911).
[2] E. Durkheim, *Moral Education* (Glencoe, Ill.: The Free Press, 1961; originally published in 1925).

these works attempted to define moral education in terms of a broader consideration of social development and social functions than was implied by conventional opinion on the topic, but both recognized that an ultimate statement of the social aims and processes of education must be a statement couched in moral terms.

Unfortunately, the educational psychologists and philosophers who followed Dewey's trail retained his concern about a broad phrasing of the goals of education in terms of the child's social traits and values (e.g., co-operation, social adjustment, "democraticness," mental health) without retaining Dewey's awareness that intelligent thought about these traits and values required the concepts dealt with by moral philosophers and psychologists. More recently, however, thoughtful educators and psychologists have become acutely aware of the inadequacies of dealing with moral issues under cover of mental-health or group-adjustment labels. We have become aware, on the one hand, that these mental-health labels are not really scientific and value-neutral terms; they are ways of making value judgments about children in terms of social norms and acting accordingly. On the other hand, we have come to recognize that mental-health and social-adjustment terms do not really allow us to define the norms and values that are most basic as ideals for our children. The barbarities of the socially conforming members of the Nazi system and the other-directed hollow men growing up in our own affluent society have made us acutely aware of the fact that adjustment to the group is no substitute for moral maturity.

It is apparent, then, that the problems of moral education cannot be successfully considered in the "value-neutral" terms of personality development and adjustment. In this paper, I shall attempt to deal with some of the value issues involved in moral education but will approach these issues from the standpoint of research findings. I believe that a number of recent research facts offer some guide through the problems of moral education when these facts are considered from Dewey's general perspective as to the relationship between fact and value in education.

RESEARCH FINDINGS ON THE DEVELOPMENT OF MORAL CHARACTER RELEVANT TO MORAL EDUCATION IN THE SCHOOLS

One of the major reasons why the social functions of the school have not been phrased in moral-education terms has been the fact that conventional didactic ethical instruction in the school has little influence upon moral character as usually conceived. This conclusion seemed clearly indicated by Hartshorne and May's findings that character-education classes and religious-instruction programs had no influence on moral conduct, as the latter was objectively measured by experimental tests of "honesty" (cheating, lying, stealing) and "service" (giving up objects for others' welfare).[3] The small amount of recent research on conventional didactic moral edu-

[3] H. Hartshorne and M. A. May, *Studies in the Nature of Character* (3 vols.; New York: Macmillan Co., 1928–30).

cation provides us with no reason to question these earlier findings. Almost every year a professional religious educator or community-service educator takes a course with me and attempts to evaluate the effect of his program upon moral character. While each starts by thinking his program is different from those evaluated by Hartshorne and May, none comes away with any more positive evidence than did these earlier workers.

While recent research does not lead us to question Hartshorne and May's findings as to the ineffectiveness of conventional, formal moral education, it does lead us to a more positive view as to the possibility of effective school moral education of some new sort. In particular, recent research leads us to question the two most common interpretations of the Hartshorne and May findings: the interpretation that moral behavior is purely a matter of immediate situational forces and rewards and the interpretation that moral character is a matter of deep emotions fixed in earliest childhood in the home. Instead, recent research suggests that the major consistencies of moral character represent the slowly developing formation of more or less cognitive principles of moral judgment and decision and of related ego abilities.

The first interpretation of the Hartshorne and May findings mentioned was essentially that of these authors themselves. Their conclusions were much more nihilistic than the mere conclusion that conventional moral-education classes were ineffective and essentially implied that there was no such thing as "moral character" or "conscience" to be educated anyway. Hartshorne and May found that the most influential factors determining resistance to temptation to cheat or disobey were situational factors rather than a fixed, individual moral-character trait of honesty. The first finding leading to this conclusion was that of the low predictability of cheating in one situation for cheating in another. A second finding was that children were not divisible into two groups, "cheaters" and "honest children." Children's cheating scores were distributed in bell-curve fashion around an average score of moderate cheating. A third finding was the importance of the expediency aspect of the decision to cheat, that is, the tendency to cheat depends upon the degree of risk of detection and the effort required to cheat. Children who cheated in more risky situations also cheated in less risky situations. Thus, non-cheaters appeared to be primarily more cautious rather than more honest than cheaters. A fourth finding was that even when honest behavior was not dictated by concern about punishment or detection, it was largely determined by immediate situational factors of group approval and example (as opposed to being determined by internal moral values). Some classrooms showed a high tendency to cheat, while other seemingly identically composed classrooms in the same school showed little tendency to cheat. A fifth finding was that moral knowledge had little apparent influence on moral conduct, since the correlations between verbal tests of moral knowledge and experimental tests of moral conduct were low ($r = 34$). A sixth apparent finding was that where moral values did seem to be related to conduct, these values were somewhat specific to the child's social class or group. Rather than being a universal ideal, honesty was more characteristic of the middle class and seemed less relevant to the lower-class child.

Taken at their face value, these findings suggested that moral education inside or outside the school could have no lasting effect. The moral educator, whether in the home or in the school, could create a situation in which the child would not cheat, but this would not lead to the formation of a general tendency not to cheat when the child entered a new situation. Carried to its logical conclusion, this interpretation of the findings suggested that "honesty" was just an external value judgment of the child's act which leads to no understanding or prediction of his character. It suggested that concepts of good or bad conduct were psychologically irrelevant and that moral conduct must be understood, like other conduct, in terms of the child's needs, his group's values, and the demands of the situation. "While from the standpoint of society, behavior is either 'good' or 'bad,' from the standpoint of the individual it always has some positive value. It represents the best solution for his conflicting drives that he has been able to formulate." [4] This line of thought was extended to the view that moral terms are sociologically as well as psychologically irrelevant. From the standpoint of society, behavior is not clearly good or bad either, since there are a multiplicity of standards that can be used in judging the morality of an action. As sociologists have pointed out, delinquent actions may be motivated by the need to "do right" or conform to standards, to both the standards of the delinquent gang and the great American standard of success.[5]

A second interpretation of the Hartshorne and May findings was somewhat less nihilistic. This interpretation was that suggested by psychoanalytic and neopsychoanalytic theories of personality.[6] In this interpretation, moral instruction in the school was ineffective because moral character is formed in the home by early parental influences. Moral character, so conceived, is not a matter of fixed moral virtues, like honesty, but of deep emotional tendencies and defenses—of love as opposed to hate for others, of guilt as opposed to fear, of self-esteem and trust as opposed to feelings of inadequacy and distrust. Because these tendencies are basically affective, they

[4] I. M. Josselyn, *Psychosocial Development of Children* (New York: Family Service Association, 1948).

[5] It is evident that the cheating behavior so extensively studied by Hartshorne and May does not represent a conflict between unsocialized base instinctual impulses and moral norms. The motive to cheat is the motive to succeed and do well. The motive to resist cheating is also the motive to achieve and be approved of, but defined in more long-range or "internal" terms. Moral character, then, is not a matter of "good" and "bad" motives or a "good" or "bad" personality as such. These facts, found by Hartshorne and May, have not yet been fully absorbed by some clinical approaches to children's moral character. If a child deviates a little he is normal; if he deviates conspicuously, he is believed to be "emotionally disturbed," i.e., to have mixed good and bad motives; if he deviates regularly or wildly, he is all bad (a "psychopathic" or "sadistic" personality).

[6] E.g., S. Freud, *Civilization and Its Discontents* (London: Hogarth Press, 1955; originally published in 1930); E. Fromm, *Man for Himself* (New York: Rinehart, 1949); and K. Horney, *The Neurotic Personality of Our Time* (New York: W. W. Norton & Co., 1937).

are not consistently displayed in verbal or behavioral test situations, but they do define personality types. These types, and their characteristic affective responses, can be defined at the deeper levels tapped by personality projective tests, but they are also related to other people's judgments of the child's moral character. This point of view toward moral character was mostly clearly developed and empirically supported in the writing and research of Robert Havighurst and his colleagues.[7]

While both the "situational" and the "psychoanalytic" interpretations of moral-character research have some validity, recent research findings support a different and more developmental conception of moral character with more positive implications for moral education.[8] While a specific act of "misconduct," such as cheating, is largely determined by situational factors, acts of misconduct are also clearly related to two general aspects of the child's personality development. The first general aspect of the child's development is often termed "ego strength" and represents a set of interrelated ego abilities, including the intelligent prediction of consequences, the tendency to choose the greater remote reward over the lesser immediate reward, the ability to maintain stable focused attention, and a number of other traits. All these abilities are found to predict (or correlate with) the child's behavior on experimental tests of honesty, teacher's ratings of moral character, and children's resistance to delinquent behavior.[9]

The second general aspect of personality that determines moral conduct is the level of development of the child's moral judgments or moral concepts. Level of moral judgment is quite a different matter from the knowledge of, and assent to, conventional moral clichés studied by Hartshorne and May. If one asks a child, "Is it very bad to cheat?" or "Would you ever cheat?" a child who cheats a lot in reality is somewhat more likely to give the conforming answer than is the child who does not cheat in reality.[10] This is because the same desire to "look good" on a spelling test by cheating impels him to "look good" on the moral-attitude test by lying. If, instead, one probes the reasons for the moral choices of the child, as Piaget and I have done,[11] one finds something quite different. As an example, we present the child with a series of moral dilemmas, such as whether a boy

[7] R. J. Havighurst and H. Taba, *Adolescent Character and Personality* (New York: John Wiley & Sons, 1949); and R. F. Peck and R. J. Havighurst, *The Psychology of Character Development* (New York: John Wiley & Sons, 1960).

[8] L. Kohlberg, "Moral Development and Identification," in H. Stevenson, ed., *Child Psychology* (Chicago: University of Chicago Press, 1963): "The Development of Children's Orientations Toward a Moral Order: I. Sequence in the Development of Moral Thought," *Vita Humana*, VI (1963), 11–33; and "The Development of Moral Character and Ideology," in M. Hoffman and L. Hoffman, eds., *Review of Child Development Research* (New York: Russell Sage Foundation, 1964).

[9] Kohlberg, "The Development of Moral Character and Ideology," *op. cit.* These factors are also stressed in the works of Peck and Havighurst, *op. cit.*, who found extremely high correlations between ratings of moral character and ratings of ego strength.

[10] L. Kohlberg, *Stages in the Development of Moral Thought and Action* (New York: Holt, Rinehart and Winston, 1969 [in preparation]).

[11] J. Piaget, *The Moral Judgment of the Child* (Glencoe, Ill.: The Free Press, 1948; originally published in 1932); Kohlberg, "The Development of Children's Orientations Toward a Moral Order: I," *op. cit.*

should tell his father a confidence about a brother's misdeed. In reply, Danny, age ten, said: "In one way, it would be right to tell on his brother or his father might get mad at him and spank him. In another way, it would be right to keep quiet or his brother might beat him up." Obviously, whether Danny decides it is right to maintain authority or right to maintain peer "loyalty" is of little interest compared to the fact that his decision will be based on his anticipation of who can hit harder. It seems likely that Danny will not cheat if he anticipates punishment but that he has no particular moral reasons for not cheating if he can get away with it. When asked, the only reason he gave for not cheating was that "you might get caught," and his teacher rated him high on a dishonesty rating form.

Danny's response, however, is not a unique aspect of a unique personality. It represents a major aspect of a consistent stage of development of moral judgment, a stage in which moral judgments are based on considerations of punishment and obedience. It is the first of the following six stages found in the development of moral judgment: [12]

Level I—Premoral

Stage 1. Obedience and punishment orientation. Egocentric deference to superior power or prestige, or a trouble-avoiding set. Objective responsibility.

Stage 2. Naïvely egoistic orientation. Right action is that instrumentally satisfying the self's needs and occasionally others. Awareness of relativism of value to each actor's needs and perspective. Naïve egalitarianism and orientation to exchange and reciprocity.

Level II—Conventional Role Conformity

Stage 3. Good-boy orientation. Orientation to approval and to pleasing and helping others. Conformity to stereotypical images of majority or natural role behavior, and judgment of intentions.

Stage 4. Authority and social-order-maintaining orientation. Orientation to "doing duty" and to showing respect for authority and maintaining the given social order for its own sake. Regard for earned expectations of others.

Level III—Self-accepted Moral Principles

Stage 5. Contractual legalistic orientation. Recognition of an arbitrary element or starting point in rules or expectations for the sake of agreement. Duty defined in terms of contract, general avoidance of violation of the will or rights of others, and majority will and welfare.

Stage 6. Conscience or principle orientation. Orientation not only to actually ordained social rules but to principles of choice involving appeal to logical universality and consistency. Orientation to conscience as a directing agent and to mutual respect and trust.

Each of these stages is defined by twenty-five basic aspects of moral values. Danny's responses primarily illustrated the motivation aspect of Stage 1, the fact that moral motives are defined in terms of punishment. The motivation for moral action at each stage, and examples illustrating them, are as follows:

[12] Kohlberg, "The Development of Children's Orientations Toward a Moral Order: I," *op. cit.*

Stage 1. Obey rules to avoid punishment. Danny, age ten: (Should Joe tell on his older brother to his father?) "In one way it would be right to tell on his brother or his father might get mad at him and spank him. In another way it would be right to keep quiet or his brother might beat him up."

Stage 2. Conform to obtain rewards, have favors returned, and so on. Jimmy, age thirteen: (Should Joe tell on his older brother to his father?) "I think he should keep quiet. He might want to go someplace like that, and if he squeals on Alex, Alex might squeal on him."

Stage 3. Conform to avoid disapproval, dislike by others. Andy, age sixteen: (Should Joe keep quiet about what his brother did?) "If my father finds out later, he won't trust me. My brother wouldn't either, but I wouldn't have a *conscience* that he (my brother) didn't." "I try to do things for my parents; they've always done things for me. I try to do everything my mother says; I try to please her. Like she wants me to be a doctor, and I want to, too, and she's helping me to get up there."

Stage 4. Conform to avoid censure by legitimate authorities and resultant guilt. Previous example also indicative of this.

Stage 5. Conform to maintain the respect of the impartial spectator judging in terms of community welfare or to maintain a relation of mutual respect. Bob, age sixteen: "His brother thought he could trust him. His brother wouldn't think much of him if he told like that."

Stage 6. Conform to avoid self-condemnation. Bill, age sixteen: (Should the husband steal the expensive black-market drug needed to save his wife's life?) "Lawfully no, but morally speaking I think I would have done it. It would be awfully hard to live with myself afterward, knowing that I could have done something which would have saved her life and yet didn't for fear of punishment to myself."

While motivation is one of the twenty-five aspects of morality defining the stages, many of the aspects are more cognitive. An example is the aspect of "The Basis of Moral Worth of Human Life," which is defined for each stage as follows:

Stage 1. The value of a human life is confused with the value of physical objects and is based on the social status or physical attributes of its possessor. Tommy, age ten: (Why should the druggist give the drug to the dying woman when her husband couldn't pay for it?) "If someone important is in a plane and is allergic to heights and the stewardess won't give him medicine because she's only got enough for one and she's got a sick one, a friend in back, they'd probably put the stewardess in a lady's jail because she didn't help the important one."

(Is it better to save the life of one important person or a lot of unimportant people?) "All the people that aren't important because one man just has one house, maybe a lot of furniture, but a whole bunch of people have an awful lot of furniture and some of these poor people might have a lot of money and it doesn't look it."

Stage 2. The value of a human life is seen as instrumental to the satisfaction of the needs of its possessor or of other persons. Tommy, age thirteen: (Should the doctor "mercy kill" a fatally ill woman requesting death because of her pain?) "Maybe it would be good to put her out of her pain, she'd be better off that way. But the husband wouldn't want it, it's not like an animal. If a pet dies you can get along without it—it isn't something you really need. Well, you can get a new wife, but it's not really the same."

Stage 3. The value of a human life is based on the empathy and affection of family members and others toward its possessor. Andy, age sixteen: (Should the doctor "mercy kill" a fatally ill woman requesting death because of her pain?) "No, he shouldn't. The husband loves her and wants to see her. He wouldn't want her to die sooner, he loves her too much."

Stage 4. Life is conceived as sacred in terms of its place in a categorical moral or religious order of rights and duties. John, age sixteen: (Should the doctor "mercy kill" the woman?) "The doctor wouldn't have the right to take a life, no human has the right. He can't create life, he shouldn't destroy it."

Stage 5. Life is valued both in terms of its relation to community welfare and in terms of life being a universal human right.

Stage 6. Belief in the sacredness of human life as representing a universal human value of respect for the individual. Steve, age sixteen: (Should the husband steal the expensive drug to save his wife?) "By the law of society he was wrong but by the law of nature or of God the druggist was wrong and the husband was justified. Human life is above financial gain. Regardless of who was dying, if it was a total stranger, man has a duty to save him from dying."

We have spoken of our six types of moral judgment as stages. By this we mean more than the fact that they are age-related. First, a stage concept implies sequence, it implies that each child must go step by step through each of the kinds of moral judgment outlined. It is, of course, possible for a child to stop (become "fixated") at any level of development, but if he continues to move upward he must move in this stepwise fashion. While the findings are not completely analyzed on this issue, a longitudinal study of the same boys studied at ages ten, thirteen, sixteen, and nineteen suggests that this is the case. Second, a stage concept implies universality of sequence under varying cultural conditions. It implies that moral development is not merely a matter of learning the verbal values or rules of the child's culture but reflects something more universal in development which would occur in any culture. In order to examine this assumption, the same moral-judgment method was used with boys aged ten, thirteen, and sixteen in a Taiwanese city, in a Malaysian (Atayal) aboriginal tribal village, and in a Turkish village, as well as in America. The results for Taiwan and for America are presented in Figure 2.

Figure 2 indicates much the same age trends in both the Taiwanese and the American boys. It is evident that in both groups the first two types decrease with age, the next two increase until age thirteen and then stabilize, and the last two continue to increase from age thirteen to age sixteen. In general, the cross-cultural studies suggest a similar sequence of development in all cultures, although they suggest that the last two stages of moral thought do not develop clearly in preliterate village or tribal communities.

In the third place, the stage concept implies personality consistency. We said that there was little consistency to honest behavior as such. There is,

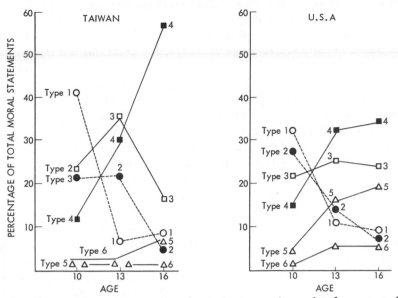

Figure 2. Mean per cent of use of each of six stages of moral judgment at three ages in Taiwan and the United States.

however, a high degree of consistency, a "g-factor" of moral stage, from one verbal moral situation to the next.[13]

In order to consider the relevance of these moral-judgment stages for our conceptions of moral character, we must consider a little further their relationship to moral conduct. We have already noted that verbal agreement to moral conventions does not generally predict to moral behavior. We noted that when Hartshorne and May measured the child's "knowledge" of the society's moral conventions (as opposed to his response to moral-attitude tests, assessing strength of verbal assent to these convictions), slightly better predictions were obtained; tests of moral knowledge correlated with experimental tests of cheating in the low 30's, about as well as a single cheating test correlates with another. These tests of moral knowledge require somewhat more cognitive understanding of cultural moral prescriptions than do verbal moral-attitude tests, and they are somewhat more age developmental. Our tests of moral judgment, which are more genuinely developmental and reflective of basic cognitive structuring of values than moral-knowledge tests, are still better predictors of moral conduct, however, if moral conduct is conceived in developmental terms.

In referring to a definition of moral conduct, in developmental terms, we refer to the implications of the fact found by Hartshorne and May and corroborated by more recent investigations [14]—the fact that such behaviors as

[13] L. Kohlberg, "Stage and Sequence: The Developmental Approach to Moralization," in M. Hoffman, ed., *Moral Processes* (Chicago: Aldine Press, 1966).

[14] Kohlberg, "The Development of Moral Character and Ideology," *op. cit.*

honesty (resistance to cheating) do not increase with age during the elementary school years.[15] In contrast, we saw that moral judgment and values were developing in sequential fashion during these years. For the majority of these elementary school years, however, the child has not developed any clear or internal moral values or principles that condemn cheating, so it is not surprising that cheating behavior does not decline in these years. While most elementary school children are aware of, and concerned about, the harm done others by acts of aggression or theft,[16] their only reason for not cheating is their fear of being caught and punished. Even at older ages, teachers give children few moral or mature reasons to think cheating is bad. Sixth-grade children tell us their teachers tell them not to cheat because they will get punished (Stage 1) "or because the person you copied from might have it wrong and so it won't do you any good" (Stage 2, expediency). In these years, then, resistance to cheating is not so much a matter of internal moral principles as of the situational and expediency factors stressed by Hartshorne and May. With regard to the type of cheating test situation used by Hartshorne and May, the critical issue for the subject's moral judgment is that of trust, what the experimenter or the teacher expects and what he has the right to expect. The experimenter explicitly leaves the subject unsupervised in a situation where he ordinarily expects supervision. This abandonment of control or authority is interpreted in varying ways. A very high degree of cheating in such a situation seems to primarily reflect a naïve abandon to the surface impression that the experimenter doesn't care. A lesser degree of cheating seems to reflect the child's belief that the experimenter doesn't care very much about his not cheating or he wouldn't leave him unsupervised and that a little cheating isn't too bad anyhow, so long as it is not too obvious and excessive or more than the others do.

In one study of sixth graders [17] almost all (80 per cent) of the children cheated somewhat. The majority of children at the premoral level of moral judgment (Stages 1 and 2) cheated a great deal, and the majority of the children at the conventional level of moral judgment (Stages 3 and 4) cheated a slight or moderate amount.[18] In contrast, adolescents at the level of moral principle (Stages 5 and 6) do interpret the opportunity to cheat as involving issues of maintaining trust, contract, social agreement, and equality

[15] This has sometimes been viewed as consistent with the psychoanalytic view that character is fixed at an early age in the home. In fact, this does not seem to be true, as there is little predictability from early moral conduct to later adolescent moral conduct (*ibid.*).

[16] R. Krebs, "The Development of Moral Judgment in Young Children" (Master's thesis, Committee on Human Development, University of Chicago, 1965).

[17] R. Krebs, "Relations between Attention, Moral Judgment and Conduct" (Unpublished Ph.D. dissertation, University of Chicago, 1966).

[18] The attitude of this latter group is probably well expressed by the following anonymous student article in a British school paper written after a siege of experimental studies of honesty: "The next test reminded me of the eleven plus exam. I had great fun doing these but they are sure to think I am barmy. But then they made a fatal mistake; they actually gave us our own papers to mark. We saw our mistakes in time and saved the day by changing the answers."

of reward for equal effort and ability. The one sixth grader in the Kohlberg study at this level did not cheat at all.[19] Among a group of college students also studied, only one of nine principled-level subjects cheated on an experimental test while about one half of the twenty-six conventional-level subjects did so. (There were no premoral-level subjects in this group.)

Cheating, then, is not a good indicator of moral character until the child has developed in adolescence a set of inner moral principles that prohibit it. By that time, cheating behavior may reflect a lack of full development of moral values (i.e., a failure to reach the level of moral principles) or a discrepancy between action and moral values (a discrepancy due to a variety of possible deficits in ego strength or ego abilities).

More generally, then, there is some meaning to "moral character" as an aim of moral education if moral character is conceived of in developmental terms rather than as a set of fixed conventional traits of honesty, responsibility, etc.

Hartshorne and May's critique is justified insofar as it is a critique of a tendency of teachers to respond to isolated acts of deviance as indicating the child's bad or dishonest character. Specific acts of conformity or deviance in themselves reflect primarily situational wishes and fears rather than the presence or absence of conscience or moral character. Nevertheless, there is evidence that repeated misconduct tends to indicate general deficits or retardation of general moral-judgment capacities, or related guilt capacities, and the lack of internal ego control rather than simply situational values or emotional conflicts. While everyday judgments of moral character and worth are often psychologically erroneous, they do correlate with important consistencies in personality and development, which are positive from almost any viewpoint.

In addition to giving new meaning to notions of moral character, recent research also suggests that it may be possible to stimulate the development of moral character in the school. We said that there has been no recent research evidence to suggest revision of Hartshorne and May's finding that convention moral- and religious-education classes had no direct influence on moral conduct as usually conceived. (More recently, ongoing research by Jacob Kounin also suggests that the teacher's use of various techniques of punishment and reward for misconduct has no relationship to the amount and type of misconduct that occurs in the classroom.) These negative results have usually been interpreted as indicating that only the home can have any real effect in moral teaching, because only the home teaching involves the intense and continuing emotional relationships necessary for moral teaching or for induction of potential guilt feelings for wrongdoing. In fact, the failure of conventional moral education in the school is probably not the result of the powerlessness of the school to influence the child's character but the result of the inadequacy of prevalent American conceptions of character education. These conceptions usually center on the training of good "habits" of honesty, responsibility, etc., through preaching, example, punishment,

[19] Kohlberg, *Stages in the Development of Moral Thought and Action, op. cit.*

and reward. This conception of character education appears to be just as ineffective in the home as it is in the school. Extensive research on parental practices has found no positive or consistent relationships between earliness and amount of parental demands or training in good habits (obedience, caring for property, performing chores, neatness, or avoidance of cheating) and their children's actual obedience, responsibility and honesty. Amount of use of praise, of deprivation of physical rewards, or of physical punishment is also not found to relate consistently or positively to measures of moral character.[20]

There are, of course, a number of unique influences of the home on the development of character which the school cannot reproduce. These are not matters of specific moral training, however, but of the emotional climate in which the child develops. The only parent-attitude variables consistently found to relate to children's moral character are not "moral training" variables but variables of parental warmth.[21] These emotional-climate variables, however, only account for a very small percentage of the differences between children in moral development or moral character. Many of the environmental influences important in moral development are more cognitive in nature than either the "good habits" or the "early emotions" views have suggested. In part, this cognitive influence is meant in a relatively conventional mental-age or I.Q. sense. Intelligence quotient correlates well with maturity of moral judgment (31 to 53 at varying ages) and almost equally well with behavioral measures of honesty. At the kindergarten level, the capacity to make judgments of good or bad in terms of standards rather than in terms of punishment and egoistic interests is a capacity almost completely determined by cognitive development on Piaget tests of cognition.[22]

We have discussed the influence of general intellectual advance upon the development of moral judgment. In addition, advances in a number of aspects of social concepts customarily thought of as part of the social-studies curriculum are correlated with advance in moral judgment. Children in the original Kohlberg study were asked to say how much and why various occupations (such as judge, policeman, soldier, artist, senator) were respected by most people, an apparent question of comprehension of social fact and function. Responses to this task could be scored in a fashion similar to the moral-judgment questions, and individual children's levels were similar on the two tasks.

This task pointed up the fact that some of the difficulties in moral development of lower-class children are largely cognitive in nature. Sociologists and social critics like Paul Goodman and Edgar Friedenberg have stressed the notion that the school not only transmits middle-class moral values at the expense of lower-class moral values but that there is a certain funda-

---

[20] Findings reviewed in Kohlberg, "Moral Development and Identification," *op. cit.,* and "The Development of Moral Character and Ideology," *op. cit.*

[21] See footnote 20.

[22] Krebs, *op. cit.*

mental "immorality" or "inauthenticity" about these middle-class values to the lower-class child in comparison with lower-class values. While sociologists are correct in stressing class-linked value systems, they are not correct in postulating class-based differences in *basic moral* values. The lower-class parent and the middle-class parent show little difference in the rank order of moral values desired for their children; for example, both put honesty at the top of the list.[23] In the Kohlberg studies of moral ideology middle-class and working-class children (matched for I.Q.) differed considerably. These differences, however, were developmental in nature. At one age, middle-class and working-class children differed in one way, at another in a different way. At all ages, however, the middle-class children tended to be somewhat in advance of the working-class children. The differences, then, were not due to the fact that the middle-class children heavily favored some one type of thought, which could be seen as corresponding to the prevailing middle-class pattern. Instead, middle-class and working-class children seemed to move faster and farther.

This finding becomes intelligible when it is recalled that the institutions with moral authority (law, government, family, the work order) and the basic moral rules are the same regardless of the individual's particular position in society. The child's position in society does to a large extent, however, determine his interpretation of these institutions and rules. Law and the government are perceived quite differently by the child if he feels a sense of understanding and potential participation in the social order than if he does not.[24]

The slower development of moral judgment of the working-class boys seemed largely accountable for by two factors, lesser understanding of the broader social order and lesser sense of participation in it. Both factors showed up especially in the social-concept task conceiving occupations but were apparent in their moral judgments as well. It seems likely that social-studies programs in the school could have considerably more positive effect

---

[23] M. Kohn, "Social Class and Parental Values," *American Journal of Sociology*, LXIV (1959), 337–51.

[24] The effect of such a sense of participation upon development of moral judgments related to the law is suggested by the following responses of sixteen-year-olds to the question, "Should someone obey a law if he doesn't think it is a good law?" A lower-class boy replies, "Yes, a law is a law and you can't do nothing about it. You have to obey it, you should. That's what it's there for." For him the law is simply a constraining thing that is there. The very fact that he has no hand in it, that "you can't do nothing about it," means that it should be obeyed (Stage 1).

A lower-middle-class boy replies, "Laws are made for people to obey and if everyone would start breaking them. . . . Well, if you owned a store and there were no laws, everybody would just come in and not have to pay." Here laws are seen not as arbitrary commands but as a unitary system, as the basis of the social order. The role or perspective taken is that of a storekeeper, of someone with a stake in the order (Stage 4).

An upper-middle-class boy replies, "The law's the law but I think people themselves can tell what's right or wrong. I suppose the laws are made by many different groups of people with different ideas. But if you don't believe in a law, you should try to get it changed, you shouldn't disobey it." Here the laws are seen as the product of various legitimate ideological and interest groups varying in their beliefs as to the best decision in policy matters. The role of law-obeyer is seen from the perspective of the democratic policy-maker (Stage 5).

upon these class-differentiating aspects of moral development than is true at present.

Our discussion of social class stressed opportunities for social participation and role-taking as factors stimulating moral development. Perhaps a clearer example of the importance of social participation in moral development is the finding that children with extensive peer-group participation advance considerably more quickly through the Kohlberg stages of moral judgment than children who are isolated from such participation (with both groups equated for social class and I.Q.). This clearly suggests the relevance and potential of the classroom peer group for moral education. In pointing to the effects of extra-familial determinants upon moral development, we have focused primarily on their influence upon development of moral judgment. However, these same determinants lead to more mature moral behavior as well, as indicated by teachers' ratings and experimental measures of honesty and of moral autonomy.[25]

A Developmental Conception of the Aims and Nature of Moral Education

The facts, then, suggest the possibilities of useful planning of the moral-education component of schooling. Such planning raises more fundamental value issues, however, the issues as to the legitimate aims and methods of moral education in the American public schools. The writer would start by arguing that there are no basic value problems raised by the assertion that the school *should* be consciously concerned about moral education, since all schools necessarily are constantly involved in moral education. The teacher is constantly and unavoidably moralizing to children, about rules and values and about his students' behavior toward each other. Since such moralizing is unavoidable, it seems logical that it be done in terms of conscious formulated goals of moral development. As it stands, liberal teachers do not want to indoctrinate children with their own private moral values. Since the classroom social situation requires moralizing by the teacher, he ordinarily tends to limit and focus his moralizing toward the necessities of classroom management, that is, upon the immediate and relatively trivial behaviors that are disrupting to him or to the other children. Exposure to the diversity of moral views of teachers is undoubtedly one of the enlightening experiences of growing up, but the present system of thoughtlessness as to which of the teacher's moral attitudes or views he communicates to children and which he does not leaves much to be desired. Many teachers would be most mortified and surprised to know what their students perceive to be their moral values and concerns. My seven-year-old son told me one day that he was one of the good boys in school, but he didn't know whether he really wanted to be. I asked him what the differences between the good and bad boys were, and he said the bad boys talked in class and didn't put

[25] Kohlberg, "The Development of Children's Orientation toward a Moral Order: II," *op. cit.*

books away neatly, so they got yelled at. Not only is it highly dubious that his teacher's moralizing was stimulating his or any of the children's moral development, but it is almost inevitable that this be the case in an educational system in which teachers have no explicit or thought-out conception of the aims and methods of moral education and simply focus upon immediate classroom-management concerns in their moralizing.

The value problems of moral education, then, do not arise concerning the necessity of engaging in moral education in the school, since this is already being done every day. The value problems arise, however, concerning the formulation of the aims and content of such education. At its extreme, such a formulation of aims suggests a conception of moral education as the imposition of a state-determined set of values, first by the bureaucrats upon the teachers, and then by the teachers upon the children. This is the system of "character education" employed in Russia, as described by U. Bronfenbrenner.[26] In Russia, the entire classroom process is explicitly defined as "character education," that is, as making good socialist citizens, and the teacher appears to have an extremely strong influence upon children's moral standards. This influence rests in part upon the fact that the teacher is perceived as "the priest of society," as the agent of the all-powerful state, and can readily enlist the parents as agents of discipline to enforce school values and demands. In part, however, it rests upon the fact that the teacher systematically uses the peer group as an agent of moral indoctrination and moral sanction. The classroom is divided into co-operating groups in competition with one another. If a member of one of the groups is guilty of misconduct, the teacher downgrades or sanctions the whole group, and the group in turn punishes the individual miscreant. This is, of course, an extremely effective form of social control if not of moral development.

In our view, there is a third alternative to a state moral-indoctrination system and to the current American system of moralizing by individual teachers and principals when children deviate from minor administrative regulations or engage in behavior personally annoying to the teacher. This alternative is to take the stimulation of the development of the individual child's moral judgment and character as a goal of moral education, rather than taking as its goal either administrative convenience or state-defined values. The attractiveness of defining the goal of moral education as the stimulation of development rather than as teaching fixed virtues is that it means aiding the child to take the next step in a direction toward which he is already tending, rather than imposing an alien pattern upon him. An example of the difference may be given in terms of the use of the peer group. In Russia the peer-group structure is created by the teacher (i.e., he divides the classroom into groups), and the peer group is then manipulated by punishments and rewards so as to impose the teacher's or the school's values upon its deviant members. If one took the stimulation of

26 "Soviet Methods of Character Education: Some Implications for Research," *American Psychologist*, XVII (1962), 550–565.

the moral development of the individual child as a goal, one would consider the role of the peer group in quite a different way. In the previous section we discussed the fact that classroom isolates were slower in development of moral judgment than were integrates. This suggests that inclusion of the social isolates in the classroom peer group might have considerable influence on their moral development, though not necessarily an influence of immediate conformity to teacher or school demands.

The implementation of this goal would involve various methods to encourage inclusion of isolates such as are under investigation in a research project at the University of Michigan conducted by Ronald Lippett. Some of these methods involve creating a classroom atmosphere encouraging participation rather than attempting to directly influence sociometric integrates to include isolates. Some of these methods involve more direct appeal to integrated members of sociometric groups, but an appeal to the implementation of already existing social and moral values held by these children rather than an effort to impose the teacher's values upon them by reward or punishment. The process raises many valuable issues potentially stimulating the moral development of the integrates as well, since they must cope with the fact that, "Well, we were finally nice to him and look what he did." These issues involve the opportunity for the teacher to play a different and perhaps more stimulating and open role as a "moral guide" than that involved in supporting conformity to school rules and teacher demands.

A definition of the aims of moral education as the stimulation of natural development is most clear-cut in the area of moral judgment, where there appears to be considerable regularity of sequence and direction in development in various cultures. Because of this regularity, it is possible to define the maturity of a child's moral judgment without considering its content (the particular action judged) and without considering whether it agrees with our own particular moral judgments or values or those of the American middle-class culture as a whole. In fact, the sign of the child's moral maturity is his ability to make moral judgments and formulate moral principles of his own, rather than his ability to conform to moral judgments of the adults around him.[27]

How in general, then, may moral maturity as an aim of education be defined? One general answer starts from the conception of maturity in moral judgment and then considers conduct in terms of its correspondence

[27] A research indication of this comes from the Kohlberg study. After individual moral-judgment interviews, the children in the study were subjected to pressure from an adult and from disagreeing peers to change their views on the questions. While maturity of moral judgment predicted to moral behaviors involving conformity to authority (e.g., cheating), it predicted better to behaviors involving maintaining one's own moral views in the face of pressure from authorities ($r = .44$). Among college students, not only were principled subjects much less likely to cheat, but they were much more likely to engage in an act of moral courage or resistance when an authoritative experimenter ordered them to inflict pain upon another subject (Kohlberg, *Stages in the Development of Moral Thought and Action, op. cit.*).

to such judgment. Maturity levels are most clearly apparent in moral judgment. Furthermore, the general direction of maturity of moral judgment is a direction of greater morality. Each of the Kohlberg stages of moral judgment represents a step toward a more genuinely or distinctly moral judgment. We do not mean by this that a more mature judgment is more moral in the sense of showing closer conformity to the conventional standards of a given community. We mean that a more mature judgment more closely corresponds to genuine moral judgments as these have been defined by philosophers. While philosophers have been unable to agree upon any ultimate principle of the good that would define "correct" moral judgments, most philosophers agree upon the characteristics that make a judgment a genuine moral judgment.[28] Moral judgments are judgments about the good and the right of action. Not all judgments of "good" or "right" are moral judgments, however; many are judgments of esthetic, technological, or prudential goodness or rightness. Unlike judgments of prudence or esthetics, moral judgments tend to be universal, inclusive, consistent, and to be grounded on objective, impersonal, or ideal grounds.[29] "She's really great, she's beautiful and a good dancer"; "the right way to make a Martini is five to one"—these are statements about the good and right that are not moral judgments since they lack these characteristics: If we say, "Martinis should be made five to one," we are making an esthetic judgment, and we are not prepared to say that we want everyone to make them that way, that they are good in terms of some impersonal ideal standard shared by others, and that we and others should make five-to-one Martinis whether they wish to or not. In a similar fashion, when Danny answered our "moral should" question, "Should Joe tell on his older brother?" in Stage 1 terms of the probabilities of getting beaten up by his father and by his brother, he did not answer with a moral judgment that is universal (applies to all brothers in that situation and ought to be agreed upon by all people thinking about the situation) or that has any impersonal or ideal grounds. In contrast, the Stage 6 statements quoted earlier not only specifically use moral words, such as "morally right" and "duty," but use them in a moral way; for example, "regardless of who it was" and "by the law of nature or of God" imply universality; "morally, I would do it in spite of fear of punishment" implies impersonality and ideality of obligation, etc. Thus the value of judgments of lower-level subjects about moral matters are not moral responses in the same sense in which the value judgments of high-level subjects about esthetic or morally neutral matters are not moral. The genuinely moral judgment just discussed is what we mean by "judgments of principle" and "to become morally adult is to learn to make decisions of

28 R. M. Hare, *The Language of Morals* (New York: Oxford University Press, 1952); I. Kant, *Fundamental Principles of the Metaphysics of Morals,* trans. T. K. Abbott (New York: Liberal Arts Press, 1949); and H. Sidgwick, *Methods of Ethics* (London: The Macmillan Co., 1901).

29 L. Kohlberg, "The Development of Modes of Moral Thinking and Choice in the Years Ten to Sixteen" (Ph.D. dissertation, University of Chicago, 1958).

principle; it is to learn to use 'ought' sentences verified by reference to a standard or set of principles which we have by our own decision accepted and made our own." [30]

How can the teacher go about stimulating the development of moral judgment? We have already rejected the notion of a set curriculum of instruction and exhortation in the conventional moral virtues, a conception killed by Hartshorne and May's demonstration of ineffectiveness. Dewey [31] pointed to the inadequacy of such a conception long ago and traced it to the fact that it assumed a divorce between moral education and intellectual education on the one side, and a divorce between education and real life on the other. To put Dewey's critique more bluntly, both conventional character-education classes or preaching and conventional moralizing by teachers about petty school routines are essentially "Mickey Mouse" stuff in relationship to the real need for moral stimulation of the child. To be more than "Mickey Mouse," a teacher's moralizings must be cognitively novel and challenging to the child, and they must be related to matters of obvious, real importance and seriousness.

It is not always necessary that these matters be ones of the immediate and real-life issues of the classroom. I have found that my hypothetical and remote but obviously morally real and challenging conflict situations are of intense interest to almost all adolescents and lead to lengthy debate among them. They are involving because the adult right answer is not obviously at hand to discourage the child's own moral thought, as so often is the case. The child will listen to what the teacher says about moral matters only if the child first feels a genuine sense of uncertainty as to the right answer to the situation in question. The pat little stories in school readers in which virtue always triumphs or in which everyone is really nice are unlikely to have any value in the stimulation of moral development. Only the presentation of genuine and difficult moral conflicts can have this effect.

We have mentioned that the stimulation of moral communication by the teacher should involve issues of genuine moral conflict to the child and represent new cognitive elements. There is also an important problem of match between the teacher's level and the child's involved in effective moral communication. Conventional moral education never has had much influence on children's moral judgment because it has disregarded this problem of developmental match. It has usually involved a set of adult moral clichés that are meaningless to the child because they are too abstract, mixed up with a patronizing "talking down" to the child in concrete terms beneath his level. In fact, the developmental level of moral-education verbalizations must be matched to the developmental level of the child if they are to have an effect. Ideally, such education should aim at communicating primarily at a level one stage above the child's own and secondarily at the child's own level. Experimental demonstration of this principle is

[30] Hare, *op. cit.*
[31] *Op. cit.*

provided in a study by E. Turiel.[32] Turiel ascertained the moral level of sixth graders on the Kohlberg stages, matched them for I.Q., and divided them into three experimental groups (and a fourth control group). All the groups (except the controls) were then exposed to short role-playing and discussion sessions with the experimenter centered on hypothetical conflict situations similar to those used in the Kohlberg tests. For one experimental group, the experimenter presented a discussion using moral judgments and reasons *one level above* the child's own. For a second group, the experimenter used moral judgments *two levels above* the child's own. For the third group, the experimenter used moral judgments *one level below* the child's own. All the children were then retested on the original test situations as well as on the situations discussed with the experimenter. Only the children who were exposed to moral judgments one level above their own showed any appreciable absorption of the experimenter's moral judgments. The children exposed to judgments one level below their own showed some absorption (more than those exposed to judgments two levels above) but not nearly as much as those exposed to one level above. Thus, while children are able to understand moralizing that is talking down beneath their level, they do not seem to accept it nearly as much as if it is comprehensible but somewhat above their level. It is obvious that the teacher's implementation of this principle must start by his careful listening to the moral judgments and ideas actually expressed by individual children.

The two principles just mentioned were used by Blatt [33] to develop a four month program of once-weekly moral discussions for a class of twelve children aged 11 to 12. Children discussed and argued hypothetical dilemmas. The teacher supported and clarified the arguments of the children which were at an average (Stage 3) level as against those one step below that level (Stage 2). When these arguments seemed understood, using new situations, the teacher would challenge the level (Stage 3) previously supported, and support and clarify the arguments of those one stage above (Stage 4) the previous consensus. The children were given a pre- and post-test, using different stories than those involved in the classroom discussions (with some new stories given only for the post-test). Fifty per cent of the children moved up one stage, 10 per cent moved up two stages, the remainder staying the same. In contrast, 10 per cent of a control group moved up one stage during this period, the remainder staying the same. Blatt and others are continuing this experimental work in varying settings (e.g., ghetto schools) and at varying ages.[34] The potential value of such educational efforts appears in terms of some recent longitudinal findings (on a small sample of middle class males), which indicate that moral maturity at age 13 is an extremely good (r = 78 to 92) predictor of adult

[32] "An Experimental Analysis of Developmental Stages in the Child's Moral Judgment," *Journal of Personality and Social Psychology,* 3 (1966), 611–618.

[33] M. Blatt, and L. Kohlberg, "The Effects of Classroom Moral Discussion upon Children's Level of Moral Judgment," submitted to *Merrill Palmer Quarterly,* 1968.

[34] M. Blatt, "Experimental Studies in Moral Education Using a Developmental Approach" (Unpublished Ph.D. dissertation, University of Chicago, 1959).

moral maturity (at age 24 to 27).[35] This is not because moral judgment development stops at age 13, it continues past college in most of this group. (As an example, while none of the 13-year-olds were primarily at the principled level, 36 per cent of the 24-year-olds in this sample were at the principled level (Stage 5 and 6).) Those who did not develop some (over 15 per cent) thinking by later high school, however, did not develop into the principled stage in young adulthood. In general, then, while moral development continues into adulthood, mature 13-year-olds retain their edge in development, presumably because development is stepwise and the advanced boys have less further steps to go through. Blatt is now conducting longitudinal follow-ups to see if those whose moral judgment was raised in his group retain this developmental advantage in subsequent years.

So far, we have talked about the development of moral judgment as an aim of moral education. The sheer ability to make genuinely moral judgments is only one portion of moral character, however. The remainder is the ability to apply these judgmental capacities to the actual guidance and criticism of action. We have pointed out that advance in moral judgment seems to produce more mature moral action. Principled subjects both cheat much less and resist pressures by authorities to inflict pain on others much more than do less mature subjects. We do not yet know whether educational stimulation of moral judgment advance would actually produce more mature conduct in conflict situations. In any case, in addition to stimulating the development of general moral judgment capacities, a developmental moral education would stimulate the child's application of his own moral judgments (not the teacher's) to his actions. The effort to force a child to agree that an act of cheating was very bad when he does not really believe it (as in the case of the author of the school-newspaper article) will only be effective in encouraging morally immature tendencies toward expedient outward compliance. In contrast, a more difficult but more valid approach involves getting the child to examine the pros and cons of his conduct in his own terms (as well as introducing more developmentally advanced considerations).[36]

In general, however, the problem of insuring correspondence between developing moral judgments and the child's action is not primarily a problem of eliciting moral self-criticism from the child. One aspect of the problem is the development of the ego abilities involved in the non-moral or cognitive tasks upon which the classroom centers. As an example, an experimental measure of high stability of attention (low reaction-time vari-

---

[35] L. Kohlberg, *Stages in the Development of Moral Thought and Action, op. cit.*

[36] This is actually more valuable for acts of good conduct than for acts of bad conduct. We expect children to justify defensively acts of misconduct. If we take the trouble to find out, however, we will often be surprised that the acts of good conduct we praise are valued by the child himself for immature reasons and that we are really rewarding "selfish" rather than moral values. In such cases it is relatively easy to foster the application of developmentally more advanced values in the child's repertoire to his own behavior.

ability) in a simple monotonous task has been found to clearly predict to resistance to cheating in Hartshorne and May's tests (r = .68).[37] The encouragement of these attentional ego capacities is not a task of moral education as such but of general programming of classroom learning activities.

Another aspect of the encouragement of correspondence between the child's moral values and his behavior is more difficult and fundamental. In order to encourage the application of his values to his behavior, we need to make sure that the kinds of behavior demands we make have some match to his already existing moral values. Two major types of mismatch occur. One type, which we have already mentioned, occurs when teachers concentrate on trivial classroom routines, thus moralizing issues that have no moral meaning outside the classroom. If the teacher insists on behavioral conformity to these demands and shows no moral concerns for matters of greater relevance to the child's (and the society's) basic moral values, the child will simply assume that his moral values have no relevance to his conduct in the classroom. It is obvious that the teacher must exert some influence toward conformity to trivial classroom rules, but there are two things he can do to minimize this sort of mismatch. The first is to insure that he does communicate some of his values with regard to broader and more genuinely moral issues. The second is to treat administrative demands as such and to distinguish them from basic moral demands involving moral judgment of the child's worth and moral sanctions. This does not imply that no demands should be treated as moral demands but that the teacher should clearly distinguish his own attitudes and reactions toward moral demands from his more general conformity demands.

The most serious and vital value issues represented by school life are not moral values per se but are intellectual in nature. As Dewey points out in discussing moral education, the serious business of the school is, and should be, intellectual. The principal values and virtues the teacher attends to are intellectual. However, the teacher may attend to these values and virtues either with awareness of their broader place in moral development or without such awareness. If such awareness is not present, the teacher will simply transmit the competitive-achievement values that dominate our society. He will train the child to think that getting a good mark is an absolute good and then suddenly shift gears and denounce cheating without wondering why the child should think cheating is bad when getting a good mark is the most important value. If the teacher has a greater awareness of the moral dimensions of education, his teaching of the intellectual aspects of the curriculum will illustrate the values of truth integrity, and trust in intellectual affairs and intellectual learning in such a way as to carry over to behaviors like cheating.

The second form of mismatch between the teacher's moral demands and the child's moral values arises from the fact that the teacher feels that

[37] P. Grim, L. Kohlberg, and S. White, "Some Relationships between Conscience and Attentional Processes," *J. Pers. Soc. Psychol.*, 8 (1968), 239–253.

certain behavioral demands are genuine moral demands, but the child has not yet developed any moral values that require these behaviors. We gave as an example the fact that resistance to cheating on tests does not derive from anything like moral values in young children aged five to seven, whereas resistance to theft and aggression do correspond to more spontaneous and internal moral values at this age. Given this fact, it does not seem wise to treat cheating as a genuine moral issue among young children, while it may be with older children. In general, the teacher should encourage the child to develop moral values relevant to such behavior as cheating but should not treat the behavior as a moral demand in the absence of such values.

It is clear, then, that a developmental conception of moral education does not imply the imposition of a curriculum upon the teacher. It does demand that the individual teacher achieve some clarity in his general conceptions of the aims and nature of moral development. In addition, it implies that he achieve clarity as to the aspects of moral development he should encourage in children of a given developmental level and as to appropriate methods of moral communication with these children. Most important, it implies that the teacher starts to listen carefully to the child in moral communications. It implies that he becomes concerned about the child's moral judgments (and the relation of the child's behavior to these judgments) rather than about the conformity of the child's behavior or judgments to the teacher's own.

Derek Wright
Edwin Cox

Religious Belief and Co-education in a Sample of Sixth-Form Boys and Girls

In the following study, based on a questionnaire about religious beliefs and practices which was administered to 2,276 boys and girls who ranged from 16 to 18 years of age, Wright and Cox show that frequency of church-going is higher among adolescents than adults but that incidence of belief is lower. Boys less than girls emerge as religious and benevolent in their concepts of God. Interestingly and inexplicably, girls in co-ed schools are less religious than girls in single-sex schools; the same findings hold for boys only in science programs. In general, religiosity is exceedingly difficult to evaluate with presently available research techniques. Moreover, evidence bearing on religious behavior of adolescents other than that provided by anecdotal or case material is not plentiful. Only modest precedence exists for Wright and Cox, whose study contributes valuable information about a rarely examined aspect of adolescent development and raises useful questions for those interested in the religious behavior of youth.

THE main purposes of the present study are as follows:

1. To provide evidence of the incidence of certain indices of religious belief and practice in a socially-defined segment of the population. This is defined as all boys and girls in the second year of the sixth forms of maintained grammar-schools in England.

2. To examine how, for this population, the different indices are related to each other.

3. To discover some of the factors related to belief in God, and in particular to examine the relationship between experience of co-education and belief.

The data to be discussed form part of the results of a large-scale questionnaire survey concerned primarily with problems of religious education.

FROM *British Journal of Social and Clinical Psychology*, VI (1967), 23–31. Reprinted by permission of the authors and the publisher.

METHOD

The instrument used was a questionnaire. After a series of reformulations and a pilot study, a form was finally evolved which contained a number of closed, multiple-choice items, and a number of open, essay-type questions. The topics covered, apart from factual questions of age, parental occupation and subject studied, were: religious belief and practice, the Bible, the Church, religious education in schools, and certain moral issues. Only the first of these will be discussed here. On the average, the questionnaire took a little over one hour to complete. In addition, a short questionnaire was sent to the parents of pupils, dealing with their own religious beliefs and practices, and their views on religious education. The questionnaires were distributed and completed during the school year 1963–64.

Sampling

A list of 100 schools, drawn at random from the total number of maintained grammar-schools in England, excluding Scotland and Wales, was obtained from the Ministry of Education, and the headmasters and headmistresses invited to co-operate. Sixteen schools declined. Of these, twelve gave fairly full reasons for refusing, all of which were of a practical nature and none of which suggested a relevant, systemmatic bias. However, the only two Roman Catholic schools declined to co-operate. A further random sample of sixteen schools was approached. All were prepared to co-operate, but the scripts from four arrived too late or were lost in the post.

Within each of the ninety-six schools used, twenty-five Ss were selected from the second year of the sixth form according to a pre-arranged scheme.

The Ss totalled 2,276, of whom 49.6 per cent were boys, and 50.4 per cent girls. Some 43.9 per cent of the boys and 29.2 per cent of the girls were in co-educational schools. Ages varied from sixteen to over eighteen years, with the majority falling between seventeen and eighteen.

The Relevant Questionnaire Items

A. Place a tick against the ONE sentence that MOST NEARLY expresses your own feelings:
   1. I am completely confident that God exists.
   2. I am fairly sure that God exists.
   3. I am uncertain whether God exists or not.
   4. I am fairly sure that God does not exist.
   5. I am completely confident that God does not exist.

Ss were then given plenty of space and urged to express in their own words those ideas about God which they found both acceptable and unacceptable.

B. Place a tick against the ONE sentence which MOST NEARLY expresses your own feelings:
   1. I am completely confident that Jesus was the Son of God who became Man.

2. I am fairly sure that Jesus was the Son of God who became Man.
3. I am uncertain whether Jesus was the Son of God who became Man.
4. I am fairly sure that Jesus was not the Son of God who became Man.
5. I am completely confident that Jesus was not the Son of God who became Man.

C. Is the question of life after death an important issue for you?
   1. Yes   2. No

   What are your ideas about life after death?

D. Do you attend a place of public worship:
   1. Weekly.
   2. Monthly.
   3. Occasionally (apart from christenings, weddings, and funerals).
   4. Never?

E. If you attend, what is the denomination of your church?

F. What is your main reason for going, or for not going?

G. Do you pray on your own:
   1. Daily.
   2. Sometimes.
   3. Never?

Administration of the Questionnaire

The questionnaires were completed in school time under the supervision of the staff of the school. Ss were given a code number, and Heads were required to give them a guarantee that anonymity would be preserved, and that their responses would be treated as confidential. To give proof of this, the supervisor was expected to seal the completed forms in a stamped addressed envelope in front of the subjects, and to assure them beforehand that this would be done.

The Parental Questionnaire

Parents were also asked to complete item A above, and this is the only item on the parents' questionnaire to which reference will be made in this report.

In all, 76.5 per cent of the parents responded. Of these, 21.1 per cent were fathers, 38.5 per cent mothers, and 34.9 per cent fathers and mothers in agreement. The remainder were guardians or parents in disagreement. Since the type of parental response was not related to sex-difference of pupil, nor to type of school, all parental responses to item A have been combined.

RESULTS AND DISCUSSION

1. General

The frequencies of responses to the multiple choice items are given in Table 1 in the form of percentages of the total number of boys and girls answering each question.

Table 1   Distributions of Responses to Religious Indices, Given as Percentages of Total Number of Boys and Girls

	Boys					Girls				
	1	2	3	4	5	1	2	3	4	5
A. Belief in God	19.6	28.7	27.8	15.5	8.4	39.1	34.9	18.3	5.8	1.9
	1	2	3	4	5	1	2	3	4	5
B. Belief in Christ	20.9	23.1	16.8	19.6	19.6	39.4	28.1	16.9	8.9	6.7

	Yes	No				Yes	No			
C. Importance of Life after death	50.0	50.0				65.0	35.0			

	Weekly	Monthly	Occa-sionally	Never		Weekly	Monthly	Occa-sionally	Never	
D. Churchgoing	30.1	6.6	29.2	34.1		49.7	8.6	29.5	12.2	

E. Denomination

	Boys	Girls
Roman Catholic	3.1	1.8
Church of England	45.2	54.8
Methodist	8.5	15.2
Presbyterian and Congregational	4.3	5.9
Baptist	2.8	4.4
Other Christian	2.5	3.3
American sects	0.4	0.8
Non-Christian	0.1	0.7
None	33.1	13.1

	Daily	Sometimes	Never	Daily	Sometimes	Never
G. Private Prayer	20.4	40.3	39.3	37.7	47.7	14.6

Note: On a chi-squared analysis, the distributions for the two sexes differ significantly ($p < 0.001$) on every index except denomination, where the result approaches but does not reach the conventional levels.

There are certain features of these distributions which deserve comment.

1. First it is necessary to make the obvious caution that, though the distributions for the various indices are skewed in the positive direction, it needs to be remembered that in interpreting these percentages, the steps on the various scales were logically, not empirically determined; it cannot be said that the interval between, for example, A3 and A2 is psychologically the same as the interval between A2 and A1, and in the case of the behavioral items, the data is based on self report and must be evaluated accordingly.

2. Though comparison with other studies cannot be other than tentative because the phrasing of questions differs between studies, the suggestion is plain that for this population, and especially for the boys, belief in God is weaker than in the general adult population. In this population 48.3 per cent of the boys and 74.0 per cent of the girls are at least fairly sure of the existence of God. These values can be compared with 66 per cent of men and 80 per cent of women who believe in God,[1] and 67.5 per cent men and 88.7 per cent women who replied "Yes, certainly" to the question "Do you

[1] M. Argyle, *Religious Behavior* (London: Routledge and Kegan Paul, 1958), p. 73.

believe that there is a God?"[2] Comparison with parental responses to the same question yields a similar result.

If we consider those parents who replied, in comparison with their own children, the percentages who fall into categories A1 and A2 become: for boys 52.7, and for their parents 81.7; for girls 75.5, and for their parents 82.6. It is noteworthy, too, that though for this population belief in the existence of God is probably weaker than in the general adult population, reported attendance at church is much higher.

3. Thouless[3] has reported evidence of a general tendency towards certainty in religious belief. When he asked Ss to indicate the degree of certainty with which they agreed or disagreed with various religious beliefs, he found a U-shaped distribution. This contrasted sharply with the same Ss' responses to items of a factual kind, where the distribution indicated a much greater endorsement of the uncertain category. Brown[4] confirmed these findings, but found that the tendency to certainty was most evident when "the beliefs belong to a formally prescribed religious or theological system," and when the Ss already adhere strongly to other parts of the system and think of themselves as members of the institutions which sanction the beliefs. Brown found no difference in certainty between belief in God and belief in Christ. However, his belief in God item explicitly referred to a "personal God," and therefore takes its place within a particular system of beliefs. In the present study, the item on belief in God was intended to be as free as possible from beliefs about God, and therefore from particular metaphysical systems. The results suggest the possibility that, at least for many Ss, belief in the reality of God, or of "metaphysical referring," is functionally distinct from belief in particular metaphysical statements. For both sexes there is a significant difference ($p < 0.001$ on a chi-squared test) between the distributions for belief in God and belief in Christ, and the difference is in the direction of greater certainty for the belief in Christ item. In so far as the boys are concerned, the U-shaped distribution is discernible for belief in Christ, but is plainly not present for belief in God, where the distribution is more that of an inverted U.

4. In addition to answering item A, Ss wrote at some length about the ideas of God they found acceptable and unacceptable. Nearly all Ss made some comment. The comments were analysed and the frequency of particular themes tabulated. A result worth mentioning in this context is that, though both sexes, in describing the God they believed in, used the idea of fatherhood with equal frequency, the proportion of girls who thought of God as loving, merciful, comforting and forgiving was more than twice that of boys. Boys were rather more likely to characterize God as a planner or controller, or as responsible for life and evolution, or as a supreme power

[2] National Opinion Polls Ltd. (Survey conducted on behalf of the British Humanist Association, 1964).

[3] R. H. Thouless, "The Tendency to Certainty in Religious Belief," *British J. Psychol.*, XXVI (1935), 16–31.

[4] L. B. Brown, "A Study of Religious Belief," *British J. Psychol.*, LIII (1962), 259–272.

or driving force. They were much more likely than the girls to reject explicitly the notion that God intervenes in, or modifies, the physical world. In short, there was a tendency for boys to stress the explanatory function of the concept of God, and for girls to emphasize the idea of a being who is the object of a close and loving personal relationship.

The tendency for females to stress more than males the benignly personal aspects of God has also been found by Larson and Knapp.[5] These authors point out that the finding is consistent with the psychoanalytic theory of religion. Essentially, the relevant aspects of this theory are as follows: where the cultural image of God is that of a father, the individual's selective emphasis among the culturally available attributes of God will be influenced by his experience of his own father; under normal conditions in our culture, the boy's relationship with his father is more conflictful and less erotic than the girl's; therefore boys tend to conceive of God as less benevolent and more power-orientated than do girls. Some support for the view that experience of socialization is related to the concept of deity comes from a cross-cultural study by Lambert and Triandis,[6] who found that societies which emphasized punishment rather than reward, and which stressed training for self-reliance and independence, also tended to have more aggressive and less benevolent conceptions of their gods. However, there is evidence which may be thought to conflict with this account and with the results of the present study. Nelson and Jones, Strunk and Godin and Gallez [7] asked subjects to do a Q-sort on items stating feelings of protection, acceptance, etc. for the concepts of God, Father and Mother. Broadly, three results emerged: (a) the correlations between God and Mother tended to be slightly higher than those between God and Father when the results for all Ss were averaged, and the difference was greater when the correlation between Father and Mother was low; (b) for males, the God–Mother correlations were on average markedly higher than the God–Father correlations, and the reverse was true for females, though the difference was smaller; (c) preference for one parent led to higher correlation between that parent and God, and especially if the preferred parent was of the other sex.

This suggests that the male's conception of God is more influenced by his relationship to mother than to father. However, it seems likely that the Christian religion encourages feelings towards God that are more often spontaneously evoked by the mother than by the father, even though God is defined in terms of paternity. Since the Ss in these experiments were

[5] L. Larson and R. H. Knapp, "Sex Differences in Symbolic Conceptions of the Deity," *J. Project. Tech.*, XXVIII (1964), 303–306.

[6] W. W. Lambert, L. M. Triandis, and M. Wolf, "Some Correlates of Beliefs in the Malevolence and Benevolence of Supernatural Beings: a Cross Cultural Study," *J. Abnorm. Soc. Psychol.*, LVIII (1959), 162–169.

[7] M. Nelson and E. Jones, "An Application of the Q-Technique to the Study of Religious Concepts," *Psychol. Reps.*, III (1957), 293–297; O. Strunk, "Perceived Relationships between Parental and Deity Concepts," *Psychological Newsletter*, X (1959), 222–226; A. Godin and H. Gallez, *Lumen Vitae: Studies in Religious Psychology*, III (1964).

older and more firmly identified with religious organizations than those in the present sample, the discrepancy between the results is not surprising.

II. Belief in God in Relation to Other Indices

As is to be expected, there is a strong association between belief in God and the other indices of religiosity. The main points emerging from an examination of the relevant contingency tables are as follows:

BELIEF IN CHRIST.   If some degree of positive belief in God and in the incarnation, as formulated here, is taken as a definition of a Christian, then 36.8 per cent of the boys and 62.9 per cent of the girls fall into this category. Although a majority of both sexes endorsed the same degree of belief in both God and Christ, 31.4 per cent of the boys and 24.2 per cent of the girls expressed a less positive or more negative belief in Christ than in God, and 8.9 per cent of the boys and 13.7 per cent of the girls expressed a more positive or less negative belief in Christ than in God. (See Section I (c) above.)

LIFE AFTER DEATH.   This item was strongly related to belief in God, and the relationship was linear. From the comments added, it was plain that concern about life after death was related to belief in it.

CHURCH-GOING.   In all, 7.2 per cent of the boys and 2.7 per cent of the girls reject the existence of God in some degree yet report that they attend church at least occasionally. These percentages are not large, but they constitute approximately one in four of those who disbelieve. The explanation probably lies in the reasons that subjects gave for going. Some 26.8 per cent of the boys and 47.2 per cent of the girls gave what might be called religious reasons for going, such as worship, communion, moral and spiritual help, and fellowship with other Christians. On the other hand, 25.7 per cent of the boys and 25.8 per cent of the girls gave nonreligious reasons, such as family pressure, the desire to belong to a Youth Club, or the fact of being in the choir. Almost without exception, the disbelievers gave nonreligious reasons for going.

PRIVATE PRAYER.   Some 4.6 per cent of the boys and 2.3 per cent of the girls reveal some degree of belief in God but report that they never pray. On the other hand, 2.6 per cent of the boys and 1.2 per cent of the girls disbelieve in God yet report that they engage in private prayer at least sometimes. These percentages are smaller than the corresponding ones for churchgoing, though for girls the differences are slight.

III. Co-education and Belief in God

On every index of religious belief and behavior, boys and girls in co-educational schools were less religious than boys and girls in single-sex schools, though the differences were not always statistically significant. The probabilities for the relevant chi-squared tests are given in Table 2.

Whatever the factors responsible for these differences between type of school, the pattern of the results suggests that their influence varies with

Table 2   Significance Levels for Chi-squared Tests Between Single-sex and Co-educational Schools

	Boys	Girls
A. Belief in God	0.10	0.001
B. Belief in Christ	N.S	0.10
C. Life after death	0.01	0.05
D. Churchgoing	0.01	0.05
E. Denomination	N.S.	N.S.
G. Private Prayer	0.05	N.S. (0.20)

index and sex. For girls, co-education is most strongly related to belief in God, much less strongly to belief in Christ, concern about life after death, and church-going, and not at all related to denomination and private prayer. For boys, co-education is most strongly related to concern about life after death and church-going, less strongly to belief in God and private prayer, and not at all related to belief in Christ and denomination. When the results for boys were analysed in terms of subject studied, it became plain that the differences between types of school among boys were mainly due to those studying science. When male scientists alone were considered, the associations with type of school were found to be much stronger than for the total sample of boys (belief in God, $p < 0.01$; belief in Christ, p nearly 0.10; church-going, $p < 0.01$; and private prayer, $p < 0.02$). For nonscientists, the associations virtually disappear. No such interaction between subject studied and type of school could be found for girls. This strongly suggests that the factors responsible for these associations are not the same for the two sexes.

From the data available, several possible explanations for these differences could be checked by seeing what factors were associated with both type of school and the belief of subjects. In doing this, belief in God was taken as the pivotal index of religiousness, and all tests were based upon the distributions for this item. The results indicate that such factors as age, area served by the school, size of population of nearest town, parental occupation, and parental belief cannot account for the differences between types of school, for, though some of these were related to either type of school or belief of pupils, none was related to both. It seems probable that of all these background factors, the most important is parental belief, for whatever factors associated with home affect the child's belief, they are most likely to operate through the mediation of parental belief. Of course, parental belief was strongly associated with that of the Ss, but it was not in any way associated with type of school.

Survey data of the kind presented here do not permit conclusive inferences about the presence and direction of particular effects. But such evidence can serve to make some speculations more plausible than others. It is impossible to rule out background influences which the present survey has not touched, but the results discussed establish an initial likelihood that the differences between types of school, for girls and for boy scientists, are due to differences in school situation rather than differences in home background. In considering the factors which operate in the school situation, it is convenient to deal with the sexes separately.

GIRLS. Plainly, the most obvious difference between the types of school is that in co-educational schools, girls experience a great deal more social interaction with members of the other sex, and are influenced by them. It is possible to distinguish three related aspects of this influence: (a) there is the factor of sex difference, (b) there is the fact that girls are in a minority among a majority in whom religious belief is characteristically less strong, and it may be that it is majority group pressure rather than sex difference which is decisive, and (c) since in co-educational schools the sexes are taught together, it may be that girls receive a different sort of religious education from the one they would receive in single-sex schools.

It was possible to test (b) in two ways. Firstly, on the assumption that the proportion of girls from co-educational schools in the sample reflected the true proportion in the sixth forms of the schools sampled, the girls from co-educational schools were divided into two groups, those from schools where they were in a small minority, and those from schools where they were in a large minority, or even in the majority. These two groups were tested for differences in frequency of belief in God. No sign of any significant difference could be found. Secondly, there was a significant association between sex difference and subject studied in co-educational schools. Girls tended to predominate in the arts subjects and to be a very small minority in the sciences. There was no sign of any tendency for girls studying science to believe in God less than girls studying the arts. These tests are not conclusive, but they suggest that majority group pressure is not the decisive factor.

It was not possible to test (c), but it does seem likely that girls in single-sex schools receive a more intensive religious education than girls in co-educational schools. However, there are two comments which can be made. Firstly, from the evidence of this survey, it does not appear that the aims and syllabuses of religious education courses differ between the two types of school. It is likely, therefore, that such differences as do exist are a function of the fact that in one type of school there are boys present. There is evidence from several sources, including the present survey, that boys tend to be more critical of the religious education they receive than are girls. They are more inclined to argue. In short, it is the presence of boys which makes religious education different for girls in co-educational schools. Secondly, there is not enough evidence yet for us to know whether religious education in schools is a major factor in influencing belief, though there is some evidence which suggests that it is not.[8]

The last two explanations cannot be wholly ruled out, and there may be other possibilities. But until further evidence is forthcoming, we may

[8] D. S. Wright, "A Study of Religious Belief in the Sixth-Form Boys," *Researches and Studies,* XXIV (1962), 19–27.

draw the tentative conclusion that there are grounds for thinking that, for this population of girls, interaction with the other sex, both as teachers and fellow pupils, is a factor which influences negatively belief in God. This factor has much less influence when the girls are also committed to such doctrinal formulations as that of the incarnation, and when they report that they engage in private prayer.

BOYS.   It would seem that interaction with the other sex does not have an influence upon belief comparable with that found among girls. Scientists and non-scientists at single-sex schools, and non-scientists in co-educational schools form a homogenous group with regard to belief in God. It is the scientists in co-educational schools who are significantly less often believers. It cannot be that interaction with girls makes boys less religious, for in co-educational schools, scientists have less contact with them than non-scientists. Nor can it be said that interaction with girls disposes boys to greater belief, for it is the non-scientists in co-educational schools who have most contact with them, and they do not differ in belief from boys at single-sex schools.

We are left, then, with the problem of explaining why boys studying science in co-educational schools are less religious than boys studying the arts, or than boys in single-sex schools, when the difference cannot be easily attributed to home background or the content of the subject. It would seem that there must be some other factor which determines both the disinclination to believe in God and the choice of subject, and which is intrinsic to the co-educational school situation. We do not know what this factor is, but we can suggest that it may be related to the fact that to choose science in a co-educational school is to choose a subject in which teachers and fellow pupils will be predominantly male, in contrast to other subjects which are more the province of females. It may be, therefore, that science in co-educational schools has a "masculine" connotation to a degree absent in single-sex schools, and this leads to its more frequent selection by boys who are also less likely to be religious. We may speculate that, once the "masculine" role in the co-educational setting has been chosen, there is a tendency to emphasize its other aspects, which include disbelief in God.

Paul Lerman

Argot, Symbolic Deviance and
Subcultural Delinquency

Several researchers have investigated youth culture from the perspective of values and behavior, but few have also focused on the youth language system. The selection included below is one such unusual study which discusses slum youth's knowledge of deviant words or argot and shows how these words may be used as predictors of participation in a deviant subculture. Lerman reveals that adolescent boys know more non-standard language than girls and that its usage peaks in late adolescence. Contrary to expectation, the argot indices suggest that the symbolic elements reflect a common deviant subculture regardless of the youth's ethnicity. The study clarifies further the relationship between the value and the symbolic dimensions of youth culture. Finally, for those interested in predicting youth's behavior, the "combined index of argot and peer values" offers a promising procedure "of classifying youth according to the likelihood of participation in an illegal youth culture."

FOR more than a generation, since the publication of Shaw's famous studies,[1] many American sociologists have insisted that the most serious forms of officially known male juvenile delinquency can be described as distinctively subcultural phenomena, manifestations of a deviant peer-group tradition, or way of life. Recent examples are the statements by Cohen, Cloward and Ohlin, Bloch and Niederhoffer, Toby, Miller, Kobrin, and Eisenstadt.[2] A reading of the literature, however, indicates that the "sub-

FROM *American Sociological Review,* XXXII (1967), 209–224. Reprinted by permission of the author and the American Sociological Association.

[1] Clifford R. Shaw, "Juvenile Delinquency—A Case History," *Bulletin of the State University of Iowa,* No. 24, N.S. No. 701 (1933); Clifford R. Shaw and Henry D. McKay, *Juvenile Delinquency and Urban Areas* (Chicago: University of Chicago Press, 1942).

[2] Albert K. Cohen, *Delinquent Boys* (Glencoe, Ill.: Free Press, 1955); Richard A. Cloward and Lloyd E. Ohlin, *Delinquency and Opportunity* (Glencoe, Ill.: Free Press, 1960); Herbert Bloch and Arthur Niederhoffer, *The Gang: A Study in Adolescent Behavior* (New York: Philosophical Library, 1958); Jackson Toby, "Hoodlum or Businessman: An American Dilemma," in Marshall Sklare, ed., *The Jews: Social Patterns of an American Group* (Glencoe, Ill.: Free Press, 1958), pp. 542–550; Walter B. Miller, "Lower Class Culture as a Generating Milieu of Gang Delinquency," *Journal of Social Issues,* 14 (1958), 5–9; Solomon Kobrin, "The Conflict of Values in Delinquency Areas," *American Sociological Review,* 16 (October, 1951), 653–661; S. N. Eisenstadt, *From Generation to Generation* (Glencoe, Ill.: The Free Press, 1957).

culture" part of the concept "subculture delinquency" has yet to be systematically examined by quantifiable research methods. Following Thrasher,[3] Cohen, Miller, and Cloward and Ohlin, among others, tend to describe and "prove" the existence of a distinct way of life among delinquents on the basis of intensive case studies of street gangs. Whatever the merits of this method of collecting evidence, the data it yields are neither precise nor replicable and cannot provide adequate evidence for testing competing descriptions and theories regarding subcultural delinquency.

In the past few years, several empirically oriented investigations have attempted to relate behavioral measures of deviance to a subcultural context. The studies by Reiss and Rhodes, Jackson and Marcia Toby, and Dentler and Monroe are useful for supplying evidence that delinquency is most likely to occur among boys who have distinctive interaction patterns. However, they fail to define and measure "culture" but, rather, make inferences on the basis of the interaction dimension of presumed delinquent subcultures.[4]

These studies also focus on official and non-official measures of deviance—i.e., indices of police observation and self-reports of deviant action. Both of these measures refer to *behavioral* action only. In the study reported here, we attempt to move beyond legally proscribed actions to other indicators of deviance.

It is the contention of this study that a delinquent youth subculture refers to symbolic as well as behavioral deviance, and that both types of deviance are distinguishable from patterns of interaction. The study posits that if the subculture approach to delinquency has merit, it should be possible, by observing a randomly selected youth population, to obtain empirical evidence that describes a subculture in terms of the relationship between behavioral and symbolic dimensions. A subculture is hypothesized to exist if the behavior is consonant with shared symbols. As indicators of deviant behavior we use the self-reports of youth. As indicators of the shared symbols comprising the "culture" of deviant youth we use deviant *values* and deviant *words* (argot) shared with peers. All three indicators are viewed as necessary elements for asserting the existence of a subculture. The types of interaction patterns utilized by youths who share deviant symbols are regarded as problematic and open to empirical investigation.

The reasoning underlying this approach to the delineation of a subculture is applicable to fields other than delinquency. The stock-market subculture, for example, ought to yield a disproportionately large number of

---

[3] Frederick M. Thrasher, *The Gang* (Chicago: University of Chicago Press, 1927).

[4] Albert J. Reiss, Jr., and Albert L. Rhodes, "Delinquency and Social Class Structure," *American Sociological Review*, 26 (October, 1961), 720–733; Jackson Toby and Marcia L. Toby, *Low School Status as a Predisposing Factor in Subcultural Delinquency* (New Brunswick, N.J.: Rutgers University) n.d., mimeo.; and Robert A. Dentler and Lawrence J. Monroe, "Early Adolescent Theft," *American Sociological Review*, 26 (October, 1961), 733–744. Reiss and Rhodes use as a criterion association with delinquent peers or adult criminals. The Tobys use sociometric choices that are found to have police records. Dentler and Monroe refer to a "peer orientation," measured by whether youths spend most of their evenings at hangouts or are frequently at home with their parents.

people who know about "odd lots" and "buying on margin," prefer the actions of business executives to those of labor-union officials, and buy stocks. The avid fans who are part of the baseball world ought to be disproportionately knowledgeable about "squeeze plays" and "stretching hits," to regard the outcomes of games as significant, and to enjoy watching games. Any subculture can be conceived in terms of a combination of language, values, and behavior.

Argot is itself a mode of deviance and hence worthy of study in its own right. In this paper, however, we are concerned primarily with argot knowledge as an indicator of participation in a deviant subculture. We shall first discuss the sociological characteristics of deviant word usage and then present empirical evidence that argot is related to deviant peer values as well as to official and unofficial indicators of behavioral deviance.

SOCIOLOGICAL ASPECTS OF NON-STANDARD SPEECH

The problem of establishing criteria for standard and non-standard word usage is analogous to the problem of selecting criteria for conforming and non-conforming behavior. In each case, actions are subject to arbitrary evaluations as defined by interest groups that claim legitimacy for this discretionary power. In the case of unconventional language, the guideposts are usually dictionaries compiled by lexicographers and other language experts. The "word judges" of America and England have had their task confounded by the problem of distinguishing "correct" English from "correct" Americanisms without implying that either is inferior.[5]

Standard-setters must also bear in mind that yesterday's deviant speech is today's "standard" vocabulary; as new words and expressions appear, they are labelled "slang." Traditionally, word judges have distinguished three modes of deviant speech: colloquialisms, jargon, and argot (or cant). *Colloquialisms* constitute the informal language used in conversation by a cross-section of a population, "educated" as well as not. *Jargon* is the specialized language of conventional groupings—e.g., occupational, professional, military, religious, or scientific. *Argot* (or cant) words and expressions are part of the language of deviant groupings that are often legally proscribed—e.g., thieves, beggars, addicts, racketeers, and prostitutes. Earlier writers stressed the secret nature of cant as a distinguishing characteristic, but present-day authorities—Partridge[6] and Maurer,[7] for example—minimize this attribute.

[5] Sophisticated neutrality is a relatively recent accomplishment for the standard-setters of English and American word usage. See, for example, the defense of "Americanisms" by J. Brander Matthews, "The Function of Slang," *Harper's Magazine* (July, 1893); and by H. L. Mencken, *The American Language,* 4th ed. (New York: Alfred A. Knopf, 1934), pp. 555–589, 643–786.

[6] Eric Partridge, *Slang: Today and Yesterday,* 3rd ed. (New York: Crown Publishers), n.d., pp. 1–36. (The original edition was published in London by Macmillan in 1933.)

[7] David W. Maurer is the recognized linguistic authority on American argot. The following writings are important sources of his point of view and original work on types of argot:

a. "The Argot of the Racetrack," *American Dialect Society,* No. 16 (November, 1951);

Only within the last century have slang authorities taken cognizance of the relation of the origins, uses, and function of slang to the social or occupational circumstances of the speaker.[8] Historically, this viewpoint emerged when the compilers of slang dictionaries began to challenge the convention that the language of the deviant and lowest strata of society was the only type of non-standard speech worthy of special attention.[9] Once the social ubiquity of slang was recognized, the social determinants of language innovation and usage could be explored. Argot could be accepted as a type of slang, subject to the same kinds of social influence as jargon or colloquial speech.

M. M. Lewis, an English linguist, summarized the modern view of the social character of all slang as follows:

> . . . slang begins as the language of a gang. On the one hand there are the terms needed to make organized actions speedy and effective; on the other, the need to sustain unity of emotion and social experience. Slang, then is partly an instrument of effective common action and partly the means and symbol of group loyalty; in the end it is zealously fostered as the outward expression of the unity of thought, feeling, and action in the group.[10]

David Maurer, probably the outstanding authority on American underworld slang, has applied the same reasoning to the argots of criminal groups:

> The argots are more than specialized forms of language; they reflect the way of life in each of the numerous criminal cultures and subcultures: they are keys to attitudes, to evaluation of men and society, to modes of thinking, to social organization and to technology.[11]

The position that people who share modes of verbal communication are likely to share participation in a social and cultural community as well implies that groups that fail to provide evidence of special language usage, however distinctive they may appear, cannot be considered subcultures. A

---

b. "The Argot of the Dice Gambler," *Annals of the American Academy of Political and Social Science*, No. 269 (May, 1950), 114–133;

c. "Prostitutes and Criminal Argot," *American Journal of Sociology*, 44 (January, 1939), 546–550;

d. "Whiz Mob: A Correlation of the Technical Argot of Pickpockets with Their Behavior Patterns," *American Dialect Society*, No. 24 (November, 1955).

[8] Partridge, *op. cit.*, p. 3.

[9] As recently as 1873, for example, the author of an English dictionary of slang complained about the restriction of the term to "those lowest words only which are used by the dangerous classes and the lowest grades of society." (John C. Hotten, *The Slang Dictionary: Etymological, Historical and Anecdotal* [London: Chatto and Windus, 1873]. Cited by Partridge, *ibid.*).

[10] M. M. Lewis, *Language in Society* (New York: Social Science Publishers, 1948), p. 49. See also Frank K. Sechrist, "The Psychology of Unconventional Language," *Pedagogical Seminary*, 20 (December, 1913).

[11] Maurer, "The Argot of the Dice Gambler," *op. cit.*, p. 119.

test of language knowledge also provides a useful way of distinguishing individuals who are likely or unlikely to be participants in a subculture.[12]

PAST STUDIES OF SLANG AND ARGOT

The use of non-standard speech as important evidence of the existence of a deviant subculture should not be surprising to sociologists. However, few social scientists, and scarcely more linguists and anthropologists, have made attempts to investigate slang empirically and systematically. There are even fewer examples of empirical studies of argot. Further, on the rare occasions when it has been studied, slang has been investigated without relation to the general linguistic literature, much less to previous research in non-standard speech. As a result, the empirical study of slang is episodic in occurrence and non-cumulative in results.

This characterization does not apply to purely linguistic studies of slang, which emanate from traditions that are quite different and which were not deemed useful for the purposes of this review.[13] The works of Maurer and Sykes also fall outside the classification of empirical studies, even though they are not strictly linguistic in focus.[14]

The earliest report of an empirical study of youthful slang was published in 1903 by Conradi.[15] Melville's study,[16] the next to be reported, was published in 1912. Both of these early investigators were interested in slang as a means of expression at different ages. The Melville study is the more important, both methodologically and substantively, since to this day there is no other reported study that empirically relates general slang use to indicators of sex, age, class, and verbal skills.

[12] Church reports the positive results of such an experiment using avid bridge players and nonplayers as subjects. See Joseph Church, *Language and the Discovery of Reality* (New York: Random House, 1961), p. 110.

[13] For recent examples see: George C. Barker, "Pachuco: An American-Spanish Argot and its Social Functions in Tucson, Arizona," *University of Arizona Bulletin Series,* 21 (December, 1958); William C. DeLannoy and Elizabeth Masterson, "Teen-Age Hophead Jargon," *American Speech,* 28 (February, 1952), 23–31; Haldeen Braddy, "Narcotic Argot Along the Mexican Border," *American Speech,* 30 (May, 1955), 84–90; "The Pachucos and Their Argot," *Southern Folklore Quarterly,* 24 (December, 1960), 225–271; and "Smugglers' Argot in the Southwest," *American Speech,* 31 (May, 1956), 96–101; Lurline Coltharp, *The Tongue of the Tirilones—A Linguistic Study of a Criminal Argot* (University, Ala.: University of Alabama Press, Linguistic and Philological Series, No. 7, 1965).

[14] Using informants, Maurer (*op. cit.,* see note 7) compiled the distinctive argot of various adult criminal groupings and described their social and cultural life-styles. Gresham Sykes' work, *The Society of Captives* (Princeton, N.J.: Princeton University), is an attempt by a sociologist to describe prison "society" by means of the classification used by inmates. Neither author offers evidence that bears directly on the language usage of youth, although their efforts support the relationship between language and subculture.

[15] Edward Conradi, "Children's Interests in Words, Slang, Stories, etc," *Pedagogical Seminary,* 10 (1903), 349–404.

[16] A. H. Melville, "An Investigation of the Function and Use of Slang," *Pedagogical Seminary,* 19 (March, 1912), 94–100.

The first study of *argot* was reported in 1926 by Schwesinger; [17] her purpose was to construct a test that would differentiate incarcerated delinquents from non-delinquents. She obtained positive results with her first set of experimental and control subjects but failed to obtain similar results on a retest with younger groups in a different locale. Unwittingly, she set a series of precedents that many later researchers have followed: [18] (1) There are no references to the linguistic literature or to previous empirical studies. (2) The test was administered in written form with multiple-choice answers. (3) The list of words included both colloquial and argot terms. (4) Only boys were tested. The few studies reported since Schwesinger's are not only non-cumulative but also biased, as will become clear in the next section.

SPECIAL PROBLEMS IN THE STUDY OF ARGOT

The use of a *spoken* test of *argot* knowledge with a *random* youth population for the purpose of determining the likelihood of their participation in a deviant subculture is a new departure and poses a number of special issues for empirical research.

The Choice of Words

Social scientists are very sensitive about the "reification" of concepts—i.e., the danger of confusing the "name" of a conceptual category with the referents of that category. Adherence to this distinction is important in studying language, since slang words can be non-standard (deviant) in the naming or in the referents or both.[19] When the word "busted," for example, is used as a non-standard name for "broken," the referent category is not deviant. However, when "busted" is used to mean "being picked up by the police," not only is the name non-standard, but the referent category is related to proscribed activities.

This distinction is basic to the construction of a vocabulary test of argot, since, by definition, argot refers to non-standard activities. Schwesinger's initial attempt to mix colloquialisms and argot is instructive; she found that it was mainly "crook terms" (words with deviant referents) that discriminated between delinquents and non-delinquents.

"Crook terms" indicates the appropriate category of words, but it is also important to be aware that the activities which are part of youthful misconduct are not the same as those of adult criminals. A test measuring

[17] Gladys C. Schwesinger, "Slang as an Indication of Character," *Journal of Applied Psychology*, 10 (June, 1926), 247.

[18] See, for example, Harold E. Russell and A. W. Bendig, "The Development of a Test of Criminal Cant," *Journal of General Psychology*, 56 (January, 1957), 21–25; Delbert S. Elliott, "Delinquency, Opportunity, and Patterns of Orientations," unpublished Ph.D. dissertation, University of Washington, 1961, pp. 164–168; H. B. Gibson, "A Slang Vocabulary Test as an Indicator of Delinquent Association," *British Journal of Social and Clinical Psychology*, 3 (February, 1964), 50–55; and Lowell S. Selling and Seymour P. Stein, "Vocabulary and Argot of Delinquent Boys," *American Journal of Sociology*, 39 (March, 1934), 674–677.

[19] Roger Brown, *Words and Things* (Glencoe, Ill.: The Free Press, 1958).

knowledge of items associated with adult deviance would be inappropriate for eliciting knowledge of deviant actions of interest to juveniles.[20] From this perspective, the words included in a test of argot can be chosen only *after* the activities of interest to deviant youth have been delineated.

Oral Presentation of the Word List

Most of the empirical studies of slang have employed paper-and-pencil tests, symbols of a written language, and have offered multiple-choice answers, again relying on a written language. But argot, like other slang, is primarily a type of *spoken* language, the speech of intimate and expressive conversation. The ability to name slang words or to give definitions for slang words presented orally is quite distinct from the ability to write words or read definitions. This difference in abilities is not just a function of differences in respondents' level of formal education but is also due to the distinctions between spoken and written language. "What particularly characterizes spoken language," according to Vendryes, is that:

> . . . it contents itself with emphasizing the main lines of thought. These alone emerge and dominate the sentence, while the logical relations of words and component parts of a sentence are either imperfectly indicated, with the help, if necessary, of intonation and gesture, or are not indicated at all and have to be supplied by intuition. This spoken language thus approximates to spontaneous language . . . in definite contrast to grammatical language.[21]

Concerning written language, he notes:

> Contrary to the opinion of many people, we never write as we speak; we write (or attempt to write) as others write. The least cultured people have the feeling directly they take hold of a pen that they are making use of some special language, different from the spoken tongue, which has its rules and customs as well as its own purpose and significance, and this feeling has its justification.[22]

These observations, written almost a half century ago, are still pertinent.[23] It is not surprising that investigators utilizing the medium of *written* language have found a strong association between measures of slang and measures of "verbal skill" or "English proficiency." [24] Until tests are conducted with *both* a spoken and a written form and the results correlated, it is a mistake to assume that those who have completed the most schooling or are high in intelligence are also superior in their knowledge of the spoken language and its special vocabularies of colloquialisms, jargon, and argot.

[20] See, for example, Russell and Bendig, *op. cit.*

[21] J. Vendryes, *Language* (New York: Alfred Knopf, 1925), p. 148.

[22] *Ibid.*, p. 332.

[23] Basil Bernstein, "A Public Language," *British Journal of Sociology,* 10 (December, 1959), 311–326; and "Language and Social Class," *British Journal of Sociology,* 11 (September, 1960), 271–276.

[24] See Russell and Bendig, *op. cit.*, and Gibson, *op. cit.*

A second reason for presenting words orally is that written tests place a premium on the ability to use and respond to standard language. Written language, as Vendryes notes, is the "ideal norm" and represents "the concrete expression of the standard language normalized by grammarians. . . ." [25] Language tests couched in standard language are normalized by those who are skilled in its use and thus complicate the important empirical question: can non-standard words be recognized and responses communicated without burdening the respondent with rules of "correct" usage? Testing non-standard usage with the *rules* of standard language hardly seems "cricket."

The third reason is quite pragmatic, although it is related to the previous reasons. Slang words are rarely used in writing and therefore may seem quite foreign to the respondent in this form—particularly if the spelling and the pronunciation are at variance, as is frequently the case for all written languages. "In the history of the English language," Brown notes, "spelling has changed less rapidly than speech. Many of the spellings of Middle and Old English are preserved in the living language although the pronunciations of the words have drastically changed." [26]

In summary, prudence, as well as neutrality, dictates that the formal pencil-and-paper test not be used to measure the informal traditions of deviant youth. Logic aside, who wants to "flunk" another test?

Replication Problems

The general instability of slang words has been noted by many observers. In youthful circles, cigarettes, for example, have at one time or another been called "reefers," "fags," "weeds," "butts," "smokes," and "coffin nails." Only the most current information could assure that the modern term would appear on a word list, if cigarette smoking were the object of inquiry. This faddism or impermanence poses an important problem in the creation of replicable instruments. If the words change, how is it possible to test the reliability of an instrument by attempting to obtain the same results with other samples at other times?

It may be that this problem is intrinsically insoluble. One approach might be to focus on the *referent category* rather than the name. If a consistency that is related to the referent categories can be demonstrated, then the equivalence of name usage can perhaps be assumed. Longitudinal research, as well as analysis of age cohorts, could serve to demonstrate the efficacy of this approach, since at some point in time there will be age groupings that know similar "names" of the referent categories.

Since the study reported here is the first to use argot with a random sample of youth, a baseline for testing equivalence over time does not exist. Unfortunately, item intercorrelations producing significant results will have to be supported by the logical assumption discussed in the previous para-

[25] Vendryes, *op. cit.*, p. 335.
[26] Brown, *op. cit.*, p. 64; also see Vendryes, *op. cit.*, pp. 335–343.

graph. Further research will indicate the extent to which this assumption is supported by evidence.

Multiplicity of Meanings

There are few words in the English language that have one and only one unrestricted meaning. Furthermore, many slang words are actually old words with new meanings.[27]

If words can have more than one correct meaning, then scoring must take this into account. In a written test, the problem is easily addressed by providing multiple choices, with the implicit rule that only *one* answer is correct. But this study is concerned not just with correct definitions but with specific referent categories. The test of words is actually designed to determine the "availability" of these cognitive categories; thus we can treat answers referring to other cognitions as irrelevant. This *projective* use of the word test is based on Brown's proposition concerning the relative frequency of word use: "A perceptual category that is frequently utilized is more available than one less frequently utilized."[28]

It is hypothesized that relationships in accord with this proposition will be found between "correct" knowledge of argot and the variables of shared values, illegal behavior, and police contact.

EMPIRICAL FINDINGS

The findings reported here are based on information derived from a survey of youth residing in randomly selected household units of a portion of New York City's Lower East Side.[29] The original target group consisted of 706 boys and girls aged 10 to 19 years; interviews were completed with 555 youth, a rate of 79 per cent. Processing of the entire sample through the official police files disclosed that interviewed boys, even with age controlled, were as likely to be "delinquent" as their non-cooperative peers.

The argot words used were chosen after consultation with ex-gang members, experienced gang workers, and the unpublished field notes of Irving Spergel.[30] The list contained five terms referring to each of four hypothesized subcultures presumed to be relevant to youth,[31] plus the word "square," which was used as a dummy, warm-up word, and the word "busted," which

[27] M. M. Lewis (*op. cit.*, p. 49) reports a study of slang in the British Armed Forces in which about 72 per cent of the expressions were found to be of this variety; only 28 per cent were really new words.

[28] Brown, *op. cit.*, p. 236.

[29] For further details about the sample and a copy of the questionnaire used, see *A Proposal for the Prevention and Control of Delinquency by Expanding Opportunities* (New York: Mobilization for Youth, December 9, 1961), Appendix R4, R5.

[30] Dr. Spergel's field notes, on file at the Research Center of the Columbia University School of Social Work, were gathered as part of the research for his recently published work, *Racketville, Slumtown, and Haulburg* (Chicago: University of Chicago Press, 1964).

[31] Cloward and Ohlin (*op. cit.*) assert that there are three distinct types of delinquent subculture—bopping, criminal, and drugs. The fourth—unorganized crime—was suggested by Spergel (*op. cit.*).

was designed to cross-cut all four subcultures. Within each subcultural category an attempt was made to rank the words or phrases in terms of recognizability. Using this criterion, the list was modified as a result of three pretests, with a state reformatory sample, with members of five male gangs, and with settlement-house members. The final list presented to the sample used in this study included the following words (but not in this order), classified here by hypothesized subcultural referent:

Argot:	*Current Definition:*
Bopping	
A piece	A gun
Burn	Shoot with gun
Got heart	Has guts, bravery
Our turf	Territory of gang
Game of knock-knock	Rival opens door and is shot
Unorganized Crime	
Lifted something	Stole
Heist	Robbery
A hustle	Any illegal means of making money
Pull a score	Succeed in a theft
A booster	A shoplifter
Drugs	
Some pot	Marijuana
A bag	A package of pot or drugs
A spike	A needle for drug injection
To turn on	To start somebody on drugs
To pull a bomb	To substitute inferior drugs for drugs of good quality
Organized Rackets	
The syndicate	An organization of racketeers
A fence	A buyer of stolen goods
A runner	A numbers salesman
A banker	A numbers pay-off man
Single action	A bet on one number
All Subcultures	
Got busted	Was stopped or picked up by police

The answers were coded independently by two research assistants who had little previous knowledge of this type of argot. Fewer than 10 per cent of the meaningful replies evoked disagreement between the coders. In general, coding of the list of words presented far fewer problems than coding of the usual open-ended questions.

MALE DOMINANCE

Throughout the literature on delinquency and criminology, there is one fact so demonstrably evident that it is often assumed, rather than made explicit. This fact refers to the greater behavioral deviance of males, in all cultures and during all historical periods investigated, which is one of the basic facts in criminology.[32]

If subcultural ideas have any merit, there ought to be wide discrepancies between the sexes in verbal action also. Common experience indicates that men are the swearers and the oath-givers, and more likely than women to experiment with new words. Argot, even more than slang, ought to reveal sizable sex differences.[33] Confirmation of the hypothesis that males will surpass females in argot knowledge by a wide margin will support the use of argot as a measure of verbal deviance and will further suggest that deviant subcultures tend to be dominated by the slang vocabularies of males.

The differences between the sexes in general ability to recognize argot can be portrayed by using a summary measure and controlling for age. Table 1 presents the results of such a comparison on the basis of general

Table 1 Comparison of Boys and Girls by Number of Words Defined Correctly, by Age

	Age and Sex					
	10–12		13–15		16–19	
Correct Definitions	BOYS	GIRLS	BOYS	GIRLS	BOYS	GIRLS
None	66%	89%	29%	46%	39%	43%
1–2	19	8	24	28	14	25
3–5	10	4	33	21	13	20
6 or more	4	0	14	4	44	12
N =	(113)	(106)	(100)	(89)	(63)	(84)

argot knowledge, ignoring subcultural referents. At each age-range, boys are far more knowledgeable than girls.

These findings have relevance to theories of child development as well as to subcultural delinquency. When argot words are presented orally, refer to non-standard meanings, and evoke spoken responses, then *boys* exhibit a marked superiority in ability to identify them correctly. This contradicts the literature of standard language development.[34] When words are pre-

---

[32] For a convenient summary of this basic fact in criminology, see Edwin H. Sutherland and Donald Cressey, eds., *Principles of Criminology*, 6th ed. (Philadelphia: J. B. Lippincott Co., 1960), esp. pp. 111–115.

[33] It is possible that the sex differences would be less pronounced if terms referring to sexual delinquency were included in the word list. However, precocious sexual activities have not figured in the writings of the major subcultural theorists; therefore, this type of argot was excluded. Although much has been written about female sexual delinquency, based largely on official evidence, it is unlikely that a distinctive female delinquent subculture exists. Even at the adult level, the argot production of the female prostitute seems quite minimal. Maurer's study of prostitution argot ("Prostitutes and Criminal Argot," *op. cit.*) suggests that this is the case, even though he does not explicitly use the sex variable to account for the low argot invention of this female "hustle."

[34] See Dorthea McCarthy, "Language Development in Children," in Leonard Carmichael, ed., *Manual of Child Psychology*, 2nd ed. (New York: John Wiley and Sons, 1954).

sented in writing, refer to standard meanings, and are responded to by means of reading and choosing one of several given answers, then *girls* exhibit superiority.

The key issue concerning sex differences in verbal comprehension may be *not* which sex is superior but, rather, under what conditions different *types* of linguistic references are more likely to be known by boys or by girls. Further exploration of this issue would aid greatly in understanding the differential socialization of boys and girls and its impact on cognitive functioning.

The findings concerning age do not contradict the child-development literature but challenge earlier slang studies. Argot, as a type of language indicator, appears to behave as if growth in symbol usage is an accompaniment of adolescent maturation. Since the child-development literature also makes reference to this growth in symbolic ability,[35] the findings indicate that likely participants in a deviant youth subculture are not dissimilar in this regard to conforming populations. The differences lie in the types of interest and activity that guide the acquisition of new symbols. Understanding this fact permits observers of youthful delinquency to utilize child-development findings in tracing the dynamics of participation in a deviant subculture.

Schools frequently judge symbolic ability on the basis of responses to standard written tests. But awareness of the arbitrary distinctions between standard and non-standard language, as well as between written and spoken forms of speech (i.e., "formal" and "informal"), should qualify judgments concerning the difference between delinquents and non-delinquents in symbolic growth. This point of view will be supported by evidence that boys who are knowledgeable about specific word patterns that are related to shared values and measures of illegal behavior are also likely to exhibit developmental growth in the use of these symbols.

INDICES OF ARGOT KNOWLEDGE

Of the three subcultural variables used in this study (values, argot, and self-reports of deviant behavior), the argot items revealed the greatest potential for discerning tendencies toward delinquent specialization. This was because an equal number of words referred to the activities of all four hypothesized subcultures.

Only 154 of the 276 boys in the sample knew one or more argot words in addition to "square," which did not count. This means that if the total sample was used as the basis for calculations, 122 boys would be classified as "no-no" for all inter-item correlations. Computing coefficients on this basis would inflate the intercorrelations in the "no-no" cell. Utilizing only the knowledgeable boys, however, would risk the possibility of missing

---

[35] See David Ausubel, *Theory and Problems of Adolescent Development* (New York: Grune and Stratton, 1954), p. 285; and Raymond G. Kuhlen, *The Psychology of Adolescent Development* (New York: Harper and Bros., 1952), p. 426.

significant intercorrelations that were relevant for the whole sample. In order to deal with this problem, the following lines of analysis were followed:

1. Only the 154 boys who were knowledgeable concerning the argot items were used in the analysis of *item* intercorrelations (for each presumed subcultural area that referred to bopping, drugs, organized rackets, and unorganized crime).

2. Indices of subcultural knowledge were then intercorrelated, both including and excluding the 122 "no-no" boys, and all indices were cross-tabulated simultaneously using the entire sample.

3. All major indices were cross-tabulated with a peer-value index for the whole sample to test whether the argot indices were relevant for subcultural analysis and conformed to the model of this study.

4. All major indices were cross-tabulated with a self-report behavior summary, as well as with measures of police contact.

Four indices of argot word knowledge were identified that approximated the subcultural entities hypothesized by Cloward and Ohlin and by Spergel. This was accomplished by using significance levels based on *phi* coefficients for the reduced sample of 154 boys, according to each of the four subcultural areas. (When N = 154, then P = 0.001 if *phi* is .27 or greater; P < 0.01 if *phi* is .21 or greater.) The indices identified by this approach were bopping, drugs, organized crime, and unorganized crime. The bopping index included all of the words listed earlier; the drug index included all except "pull a bomb"; the organized-crime index included two racket items ("syndicate" and "fence"), plus one hypothesized unorganized-crime word ("heist"). The unorganized-crime index included only two words ("hustle" and "score").

The unorganized-crime index was treated as a minor one, however, since fewer than 12 per cent of the most knowledgeable boys could correctly identify at least one of the words referring to this subcultural area.

Regarding the unorganized-crime words, "hustle" and "score" are related to the bopping and drug indices but *not* to the organized-crime pattern. "Hustle" and "score" are also related to the cross-cutting term "busted," which is also related to the bopping and drug words but *not* to the organized-crime words.

Intercorrelations of the three major indices are presented in Table 2, with the 122 "no-no" boys both included and excluded. The bopping and drug indices are clearly interrelated. This relationship holds whether the 122 "no-no" boys are included or excluded. The basis for accepting the pattern of a combined knowledge of bopping and drug terms is clear whether the reference is to knowledgeable boys only or to the total sample.

If only the knowledgeable boys are considered, the organized-crime index is *not* related to either the bopping or the drug index. If the total sample is utilized, the organized-crime index *is* significantly related to the other two indices.

Before turning to the relationship between these argot patterns and

Table 2 Phi Intercorrelations of Three Major Argot Indices, for Knowledgeable Boys and Total Sample

Subculture	Knowledgeable Boys Only (N = 154)			Total Sample of Boys (N = 276)		
	BOP.	DRUGS	ORG. CRIME	BOP.	DRUGS	ORG. CRIME
Bopping	×	.47	.02	×	.63	.34
Drugs	—	×	.07	—	×	.25
Organized crime	—	—	×	—	—	×

shared peer values, it will be useful to determine whether the indices conform to the model of argot acquisition described in Table 1. Table 3 presents four age-groupings of boys classified by the percentage knowing no words,

Table 3 Indices of Argot Knowledge, by Age and Pattern (N = 276)

Argot Knowledge	Age			
	10–11 (N = 67)	12–13 (N = 84)	14–15 (N = 62)	16–19 (N = 63)
Bopping Index				
0 terms	88%	77%	56%	45%
1 term	6	12	11	11
2+ terms	6	11	31	44
Drug Index				
0 terms	97	86	63	52
1 term	3	13	32	24
2+ terms	0	1	5	24
Organized-Crime Index				
0 terms	81	71	45	52
1 term	10	18	19	22
2+ terms	9	11	35	25
Combined Bopping-Drug Index				
0 bopping and 0 drug terms ($\bar{B}$-$\bar{D}$)	88	57	47	41
1+ bopping *or* 1+ drug term (B or D)	9	13	27	14
1+ bopping *and* 1+ drug term (BD)	3	12	26	44

one word, and two or more words for the three major indices considered separately and for the combined bopping-drug index.

The bopping, drug, and combined indices behave in conformity with the findings concerning general argot development. The younger ages (10–13) are the time of onset and entry, middle adolescence (14–15) is the period of full participation, and older adolescence (16–19) is characterized by elaboration and expansion. This is particularly true in the case of the drug index; knowledge of two or more terms tends to be monopolized by boys over 16.

The organized-crime index, however, does not behave in this fashion. The middle age-range is the cohort exhibiting both the fewest "0" boys and the greatest percentage of "2+" boys. This index appears to conform to early slang studies reported in the literature, which depicted slang development as reaching its zenith in middle adolescence and tapering off thereafter.

It may be that the words forming the organized-crime index have become colloquial items as a result of their general diffusion. The various types of slang words (colloquial, jargon, and argot) *may* be acquired at different age levels.

ARGOT, SHARED VALUES, AND ETHNICITY

In order to explore argot knowledge as a subcultural element, Table 4 presents a cross-tabulation of a peer-value index and the combined bopping-drug index for two age-ranges of boys. The peer-value index is treated as the independent variable, since shared values begin much earlier than full

Table 4   Relationship of Peer-Value Index and Combined Bopping-Drug Index, by Age (N = 276)

Combined Bopping-Drug Index	Age and Peer-Value Index					
	10–13			14–19		
	LOW	MEDIUM	HIGH	LOW	MEDIUM	HIGH
B-D̄	88%	82%	70%	54%	43%	28%
B or D	10	12	11	25	20	16
BD	2	6	19	21	37	56
	—	—	—	—	—	—
N =	(48)	(67)	(36)	(52)	(41)	(32)

argot knowledge. This index was constructed by scoring responses to items referring to friends' admiration of toughness, outsmarting others, keeping one's mouth shut to the cops, kicks, making a fast buck, and connections with a racket. At ages 14–19 all of the items are significantly intercorrelated; for younger boys only toughness, kicks, and keeping one's mouth shut form a significant pattern.

The relationship between these two indicators of subculture is quite similar to findings concerning shared values and illegal behavior: it exists at the younger age but is strongest at the older age-range. At ages 14–19, when the value patterns are more consistently shared, the accompanying growth of symbolization is apparent for all peer-value categories. At this age-range, however, the argot profile of boys with a low peer-value index is almost the exact opposite of the profile of boys who score high on peer values. Peer values and argot, the symbolic referents of a deviant subculture, are definitely associated.

The organized-crime index and the peer-value index, however, are *not* associated (table not shown). This finding tends to account for the finding that the organized-crime index is not related to the combined bop-drug index when only probable subcultural participants are considered.

According to the Cloward-Ohlin model, non-minority ethnic groups that have been members of the lower class in this country for a relatively long time are likely to have forged links with adult forms of organized crime. As a result, they are hypothetically able to offer their young access to organized criminal activities. Given this opportunity, youth of these ethnic backgrounds should not be attracted to a subculture with "conflict" components.

The evidence of this study suggests that *all* youth in this slum area, with the exception of Jewish youth (whose names are not to be found in the police files), form a sub-cultural pattern that includes the elements of peer values and combined bopping-drug argot knowledge. The non-Jewish youth in our sample include ethnic categories that can test the Cloward-Ohlin model. These boys, of Italian, Irish, East European, and other European extraction, are generally the offspring of second-generation Americans. They can all be called "other European." Negro youth in the sample also tend to be third-generation Americans. It is only the Puerto Rican boys who are the children of recent immigrants, and a majority of these were born in Puerto Rico.

Table 5 presents the relationship between shared values and knowledge

Table 5   Relationship of Peer-Value Index and Organized-Crime Index, "Other European" Boys Only

Organized-Crime Index	Peer-Value Index		
	LOW	MEDIUM	HIGH
No words	41%	35%	50%
1 word	18	39	17
2+ words	41	26	33
	—	—	—
N =	(27)	(31)	(18)

of organized-crime words for the "other European" boys only. Age is not controlled in order to maximize the number for each category; if age were controlled, the result would not be affected.

Table 5 reveals that compared to high-value boys, slightly *fewer* low-value boys know no words and slightly more know 2+ words. These differences tend to be small, but the important finding is that they run in an *opposite* direction from the bopping-drug pattern. The absence of relationship between organized-crime and peer-value indices for this ethnic category sustains the earlier finding for the total sample.

Evidence exists, however, that these same "other European" youth, as well as the Puerto Rican and Negro youth in the sample, do provide a subcultural pattern if the combined bopping-drug index is used. Table 6 shows that this

Table 6 Relationship of Peer-Value Index and Combined Bopping-Drug Index, "Other European" Boys Only

Combined Bopping-Drug Index	Peer-Value Index		
	LOW	MEDIUM	HIGH
$\overline{\text{B}}$-$\overline{\text{D}}$	78%	68%	50%
B or D	7	16	11
BD	15	16	39
	—	—	—
N =	(27)	(31)	(18)

group, which according to the Cloward-Ohlin position should *not* be attracted to a subcultural orientation having a strong aggressive component, in fact provides a relationship similar to that of the Puerto Rican and Negro boys. Again, boys of all ages are combined in the table.

The relationship is clear-cut and similar to the findings for the total sample. "Other European" boys who are low on peer values also tend to be low on the combined argot pattern; the high peer-value boys are most likely to know these argot items. The fact that a similar relationship was found for Negro and Puerto Rican boys suggests that *all* illegal youth cultures in this slum area include elements measured by these two indices. Since we know that the combined bopping-drug index also is related to "hustling," "scoring," and "getting busted," it appears that these symbolic elements denote a versatile subculture that is common to all youth whose names appear in the police files, regardless of ethnicity. The subculture is an *area-wide* one, not specific to any ethnic group.

Argot and Illegal Behavior

Since relationships between shared values and argot, and between shared values and illegal behavior, have already been reported, evidence of a relationship between argot and illegal behavior would indicate that all three subcultural elements are interrelated.

Self-Reports

To test this relationship, the index of combined bopping-drug argot will again be utilized. Table 7 presents the relationship between this index and the life-history behavior summary of self-reported deviant acts for two age-ranges of boys. When comparisons are made within as well as between

Table 7   Relationship of Combined Bopping-Drug Index and Behavior Summary, by Age (N = 276)

| Life-History Behavior Summary | Combined Bopping-Drug Index | | | | | |
| | 10–13 | | | 14–19 | | |
	B-D̄	B OR D	BD	B-D̄	B OR D	BD
0–1 act	68%	76%	25%	73%	46%	18%
2–3 acts	24	6	42	20	31	25
4+ acts	8	18	33	7	23	57
N =	(122)	(17)	(12)	(55)	(26)	(44)

age-ranges, these variables give evidence of a very strong relationship. Within both age-ranges, the profiles of the boys who know both bopping drug words (BD) are strikingly dissimilar from those of the boys who know no argot (B̄-D̄). At the younger age-range, the category of "B or D" departs from this relationship by being slightly overrepresented in the group reporting 0–1 acts and underrepresented in the group reporting two or three. As expected, the relationship within the older age-range is clearest, and unambiguous for all argot categories.

Looking at the relationship *between* age-ranges discloses that the most knowledgeable of the 10–13 year olds (BD) tend to report more deviant acts than older boys in the other two argot categories. This is a striking finding, since age already has been found to have an impact on the increase in self-reported acts. Younger boys are most likely to have entered the sub-culture and have already engaged in more illegal behavior than older boys. This line of analysis appears to suggest that there is an early age of onset not only for illegal behavior but also for subcultural entry and participation.

Measures of Police Contact

The findings concerning illegal behavior as measured by self-reports are confirmed by the use of police contact as an indicator.

In Table 8, boys are classified both by their knowledge of organized crime

Table 8   Comparison of Two Argot Indices and Measures of Police Contact (N = 276)

| Measures of Police Contact | Organized-Crime Index | | | Combined Bopping-Drug Index | | |
	NONE	1	2+	B-D̄	B OR D	24
In police files	12%	10%	11%	6%	11%	30%
Stopped by police	10	16	13	5	14	30
N =	(175)	(48)	(53)	(177)	(43)	(56)

and by their knowledge of combined bopping-drug argot. Both argot indices are then cross-tabulated with appearance in police files (recorded) and self-reports of having been stopped by the police (recorded or unrecorded). Comparison of the two argot indices clearly suggests that the combined bopping-drug index is related to measures of police contact whereas the organized-crime index is not.

The absence of relationship between the organized-crime index and police-contact measures is not affected by age; therefore, it appears that this argot indicator does not increase our understanding of the relationship between elements of a subculture and official police behavior. This finding, coupled with previously reported findings, appears to rule out the existence of a youthful subculture organized around systematic crime for *any* of the ethnic groups. Adult-oriented argot is not a relevant variable in subcultural analyses focusing on youthful illegal behavior and shared symbols.

Argot and Shared Values Combined As an Index of Subculture

Until now all analyses have used one of the symbolic elements as an indicator of subculture. However, both elements must be present to demonstrate that *probable* subcultural participation is being measured. The empirical evidence for this is provided by Table 9, in which boys are classified by

Table 9   Boys Reporting Four or More Illegal Acts by Peer-Value and Argot Indices, 14–19 Year Old Boys (N = 125)

Peer-Value Index	Combined Bopping-Drug Index		
	B-D	B OR D	BD
Low	0%	15%	36%
	—	—	—
	N = (28)	(13)	(11)
Medium	17	25	60
	—	—	—
	N = (18)	(8)	(15)
High	11	40	67
	—	—	—
	N = (9)	(5)	(18)

both their peer-value scores and their combined bopping-drug scores; this combined symbolic indicator of subculture is then cross-tabulated with the life-history measure of illegal behavior. For clarity of presentation, only 14–19 year olds reporting four or more illegal acts are presented.

Table 9 shows that even when we consider only the low peer-value boys, the rates of high illegal behavior are influenced by knowledge of argot. The same is true of medium peer-value boys. At this medium level of peer values there are some high illegal actors with *no* knowledge of argot. Yet the difference between the low and medium peer-value levels at the highest argot level is quite large (36 per cent *vs.* 60 per cent).

Examination of the high peer-value boys expands the analysis in the expected direction, except for the slight reversal for those with no argot knowledge. The two categories of argot knowledge continue to record increases in the percentage of boys reporting four or more illegal acts as shared peer values increase.

The use of *both* symbolic variables produces results ranging from 0 per cent to 67 per cent. This is a notable accomplishment that neither variable is able to produce alone. This combined usage can also help to clarify the extent of argot elaboration at older ages and the relative distribution of organized-crime argot. To simplify the analysis, the twin symbolic variables of peer values and bopping-drug argot can be combined into a subcultural typology, as shown in Table 10.

Table 10   The Components of a Subcultural Typology

COMBINED BOPPING-DRUG INDEX		Deviant-Value Index		
		(LOW) WT. 0	(ME-DIUM) WT. 1	(HIGH) WT. 2
$(\bar{B}\text{-}\bar{D})$	Wt. 0	0	1	2
(B or D)	Wt. 1	1	2	3
(BD)	Wt. 2	2	3	4

Each of the indices has been placed in its usual tripartite classification and given simple weights of 0, 1, and 2. Adding the weights produces the results shown in the cells, which refer to the possible combinations that can be obtained. These classifications range from very low (0) to very high (4).

Table 11 shows the relationship of the subcultural typology to knowledge of the terms "busted," "hustle," and "score" and the organized-crime index for 14–19 year old boys. (No 10–13 year old boys knew "score" and only one knew "hustle.")

For the words "busted" and "hustle," it is clear that the typology discriminates well and consistently the youth most likely to be fully participating in the argot world and elaborating their knowledge. Although relatively few respondents defined "score," five of the six boys who did are high subcultural types. Evidently knowing about getting "busted," "hustling," and even how to "score" tends to be part of the subcultural world for older boys. This older-boy knowledge is consonant with the shared values of

Table 11   Relationship of Subcultural Typology and Knowledge of Other Argot, 14–19 Year Old Boys Only (N = 125)

	Subcultural Typology			
	VERY LOW	LOW	MEDIUM	HIGH–VERY HIGH
Other Argot	(0)	(1)	(2)	(3–4)
Busted	0%	13%	25%	58%
Hustle	0	6	21	34
Score	0	3	0	13
Organized-crime word	32	58	50	61
	N = (28)	(31)	(28)	(38)

keeping one's mouth shut to the cops, outsmarting others, and making a fast buck. Younger boys, who are likely to be interested in being hard and tough and enjoying kicks, evidently begin their argot knowledge with words referring to aggression ("piece," "heart") and to oral enjoyment ("pot"). Younger boys who are high subcultural types are also more likely to know "busted," since they comprise five of the nine younger boys who know this word; this is consonant with an interest in keeping one's mouth shut to the cops.

Making connections with a racket, the only deviant peer value not accounted for in terms of argot knowledge, may be an ideal value rather than an operational one. Knowledge of organized-crime argot does not distinguish enough subcultural types of youth. This is striking in comparison to the effect of the other argot terms. Only the very low subcultural boys (type 0) are distinctive in their lack of knowledge of the words "fence," "syndicate," or "heist." The relative uniformity of knowledge for the other subcultural types again suggests that these terms are colloquial, known to a majority of all likely candidates for subcultural participation by ages 14–19. Even the "other European" boys, who tend to know more of this argot than any other ethnic group, follow this pattern of equal knowledge. (See Table 5, for example.)

COMPARATIVE MEASURES OF DEVIANCE: SYMBOLIC VS. BEHAVIOR INDICES

A central thesis of this study has been confirmed: youth who share deviant symbols with peers tend also to engage in more illegal activities. In the process of testing this thesis and exploring related issues, new measures of deviance have been constructed. A major question emerges, broader in scope than subcultural problems: How well does the combined symbolic measure of deviance compare with self-reports of deviant behavior in distinguishing boys who are actually noticed by the police?

Since older boys are the most likely to be noticed by the police, comparison of the two indices will deal only with 14–19 year old males. In Table 12 such boys are simultaneously classified according to the subcul-

Table 12 Relationship of Subcultural Typology and Behavior Summary to Two Measures of Police Contact, 14–19 Year Old Boys Only (N = 125)

Police Contact	Subcultural Typology				Life-History Behavior Summary			
	LOW			HIGH	LOW			HIGH
	0	1	2	3–4	0	1	2–3	4+
In police files	4%	3%	21%	40%	11%	9%	17%	31%
Total contact	4	13	21	61	15	9	23	60
N =	(28)	(31)	(28)	(38)	(27)	(33)	(30)	(35)

tural typology portrayed in Table 10; they are then classified by their summary scores on a self-report instrument. Both classifications are cross-tabulated with presence in police files and an index of police contact which combines presence in police files and admission to having been stopped, with duplications eliminated.

There tends to be a continuous progression in the rate of police contact for each classification of the subcultural typology, particularly for the total-contact measure. The behavior summary performs well at the high end, where the rates are similar to those for the high subcultural boys. The other categories of the behavior summary, however, yield small differences and inconsistency in the rates. For both measures of police contact there is only a slight difference in rates between the boys who report no illegal acts and those who report two or three. In the total-contact measure, boys reporting one act are lower than those who report none.

At the high end, it appears that the subcultural typology does as well as the behavior summary for both police-contact measures. For the other three categories, it performs more evenly, as a result of its ability to differentiate boys admitting to nothing and boys admitting to lying only—two categories which are combined in the behavior summary. The measure of symbolic deviance is therefore a potent indicator of measures of illegal behavior.

The findings of Table 12 can be extended even further, for a serious oversight that theorists of youthful deviance can make is to assume that the police react only to specific behavioral actions. A way of demonstrating that shared symbolic deviance also contributes to the likelihood of being noticed by the police is to classify boys by both their life-history reports of deviance and their subcultural involvement. If police contact is as likely to occur for "high subculture—low self-reports" as for "low-medium subculture—high self-reports," shared symbolic deviance can be defined as providing an *independent* cue for police actions.

The results of Table 13 provide strong evidence that both deviant be-

Table 13 *Boys in Contact with Police, by Subcultural Typology and Behavior Summary, 14–19 Year Olds Only (N = 125)*

BEHAVIOR SUMMARY	Subcultural Typology	
	LOW-MEDIUM	HIGH
0–3 acts	(75) 9%	(15) 40%
4+ acts	(12) 33	(23) 74

havioral actions and shared symbolic involvements, taken separately, are capable of providing cues for police action (33 per cent and 40 per cent). Interaction of high subcultural participation and high deviant actions is the best condition for being noticed by the police (74 per cent). Not only is high subcultural involvement prevalent *per se,* but it appears that shared symbolic deviance is another operating criterion utilized by police in their everyday activities.

SUMMARY AND CONCLUSIONS

Argot is a type of non-standard language that is deviant in the naming and referent categories. It was expected that boys would exhibit a greater ability than girls to respond correctly to a list of twenty-one spoken words referring to four hypothesized subcultures. The finding that boys were in fact more knowledgeable was in conformity with the literature on slang but at variance with the language studies based on standard written speech reported in the child-development literature. Sex differences held for all age groups, indicating that males are probably dominant in linguistic deviance.

From a developmental perspective, the learning of argot appears to begin slowly at 10 or 11 years of age, increases in the years immediately preceding adolescence, and shows the greatest growth spurt during middle adolescence (14–15), the years of full participation. Late adolescence (16–19), contrary to earlier slang studies, is not a time of decline in learning argot but, rather, a period of consolidating and expanding particular types of argot knowledge.

Together with the data on values and behavior, the argot data suggest that there are age differences in general knowledge rather than in specialization. The period of greatest knowledge is adolescence, years that are also characterized by general growth in symbol usage and in cognitive consistency. This cognitive maturation serves as the developmental foundation for the sharing and communication of values and language among peers. Symbol growth and cognitive consistency are necessary conditions for any subculture; the deviant direction of these symbolizations appears to follow fundamental developmental processes. Subcultural boys, then, differ from conformists in the *content* of their symbolizations, not in the processes.

After extensive analysis, the ideal types of subculture proposed by some theorists proved to be illusory. Terms referring to aggression (bopping), kicks (drugs), and illegal gains (crime) were found to cohere as a pattern with the cross-cutting term "busted." This coherence increases with age and appears to conform to the three developmental stages of argot learning.

The relationship between the peer-value index and the indicator of argot knowledge was found to hold for all of the diverse ethnic groups that were in contact with the police. This finding undermines the Cloward-Ohlin thesis that illegal youth cultures tend to be specialized according to the relationship of adults to organized crime. Non-Jewish, "other European" youth are co-participants with Negroes and Puerto Ricans in a versatile subculture that is oriented toward *youthful* concerns. Organized crime appears to play little part in determining the active concerns of these youth, since all youth except the most extreme conformists are likely to be aware of this type of argot. Interest in the rackets may be an ideal rather than an operational concern.

The combined index of argot and peer values provides a means of classifying youth according to the likelihood of participation in an illegal youth culture. This index of shared symbolic deviance compares favorably to a measure based on self-reports of behavioral deviance in selecting youth who are most likely to be noticed by the police. Although argot, peer-values, self-reports, and police contacts measure different referents, they are highly intercorrelated. This intercorrelation is due to the likelihood that argot, values, and self-reports are consonant elements comprising a subculture, and to the fact that police tend to pay more attention to deviant youth who are involved in a subculture than to "loners."

LaMar T. Empey

Delinquency Theory and
Recent Research

In comparing sophisticated present-day analyses of delinquency with those made earlier in the century, one is reminded of the venerable adage, The more one learns the less one knows. Research on delinquency has been proceeding apace, but in the following comprehensive examination of evidence relating to contemporary delinquency theory, Empey stops to question three of its basic assumptions: (1) the universality of a relationship between social-class status and delinquency involvement, (2) the characterization of delinquent groups as having high "internal cohesion—esprit de corps, solidarity, cooperative action, shared tradition, and a strong group awareness," and (3) the idea of a "singularly-focused," oppositional and autonomous delinquent subculture. He convincingly argues that researchers need (a) perspective on the differences that exist in rates of apprehension and kinds of violations across social classes, (b) baselines for evaluating the cohesiveness of delinquent groups, and (c) understanding of the extent to which the delinquent subculture is part of "a more amorphous and widespread tradition of deviance." Empey hopes that through a study of these issues a better insight may be gained into "the total mosaic composed of delinquent values, actual behavior, and official reaction."

A TTEMPTS to explain delinquency traditionally have been concerned with two fundamental sets of data: (1) evidence from official sources that delinquency is concentrated most heavily among lower-class juveniles [1] and (2) evidence that the delinquent act is typically a group phenomenon, not

FROM *Journal of Research in Crime and Delinquency*, IV (1967), 28–42. Reprinted by permission of the author and the publisher.

[1] For examples see Ernest W. Burgess, "The Economic Factor in Juvenile Delinquency," *Journal of Criminal Law, Criminology and Police Science* (May–June, 1952), pp. 29–42; Joseph W. Eaton and Kenneth Polk, *Measuring Delinquency: A Study of Probation Department Referrals* (Pittsburgh: University of Pittsburgh Press, 1961), p. 4; Clifford R. Shaw and Henry D. McKay, *Juvenile Delinquency in Urban Areas* (Chicago: University of Chicago Press, 1942); Albert K. Cohen's analysis of several studies in *Delinquent Boys: The Culture of the Gang* (Glencoe, Ill.: The Free Press, 1955), pp. 37–44.

a solitary enterprise.[2] The result has been a number of influential theories which, despite many differences, have a common theme,[3] viz., that delinquency is primarily the product of provincial, lower-class gangs whose members share a common subculture. The factors which set delinquents apart from nondelinquents are thought to be their face-to-face interactions within gangs, the deviant norms and beliefs which the gangs engender, and the group rewards and publicity which the gangs provide.

Comparatively little attention has been paid to middle-class delinquency, principally because middle-class delinquency has not been considered serious, either in frequency or in form.[4] However, a growing number of empirical studies question both the basic facts which the theories must encompass and the theoretical constructs themselves. This paper reviews some of the questions that have been raised.

SOCIAL CLASS AND DELINQUENCY

The accuracy of official statistics regarding the relationship of social class to delinquency has long been a bone of contention. Many people have argued that official records are biased.[5] The reason, they say, that lower-class juveniles are overrepresented in delinquency statistics is simply that official agencies are more inclined to record the offenses of lower-class offenders. But can this conclusion be substantiated by fact or is it, as Cohen asks, the product of "egalitarian proclivities and sentimental humanitarianism"? [6]

[2] For examples see William Healy and Augusta F. Bronner, *New Light on Delinquency and Its Treatment* (New Haven: Yale University Press, 1936), p. 52; Sheldon and Eleanor Glueck, *Delinquents in the Making* (New York: Harper, 1952), p. 89; Clifford R. Shaw and Henry D. McKay, "Social Factors in Juvenile Delinquency," *Report on the Causes of Crime* (Washington, D.C.: National Commission on Law Observance and Enforcement, 1931), pp. 195–196; Joseph D. Lohman, *Juvenile Delinquency* (Cook County: Office of the Sheriff, 1957), p. 8; Norman Fenton, *The Delinquent Boy and the Correctional School* (Claremont: Claremont Colleges Guidance Center, 1935), as quoted by Karl G. Garrison, *Psychology of Adolescence* (Englewood Cliffs, N.J.: Prentice-Hall, 1956), p. 350; Peter Scott, "Gangs and Delinquent Groups in London," *British Journal of Delinquency* (July, 1956), pp. 4–26.

[3] Cohen, *op. cit. supra* note 1; Richard A. Cloward and Lloyd E. Ohlin, *Delinquency and Opportunity: A Theory of Delinquent Gangs* (Glencoe, Ill.: The Free Press, 1960); Walter B. Miller, "Lower-Class Culture as a Generating Milieu of Gang Delinquency," *Journal of Social Issues* (Summer, 1958), pp. 5–19. See also Frederic M. Thrasher, *The Gang: A Study of 1,313 Gangs in Chicago*, abridged and with a new introduction by James F. Short, Jr. (Chicago: University of Chicago Press, 1963); Lewis Yablonsky, *The Violent Gang* (New York: The Macmillan Co., 1962).

[4] For some discussions of the subject see Ralph W. England, Jr., "A Theory of Middle-Class Delinquency," *Journal of Criminal Law, Criminology and Police Science* (April, 1960), pp. 535–540; Herbert A. Bloch and Arthur Niederhoffer, *The Gang: A Study of Adolescent Behavior* (New York: Philosophical Library, 1958); Cohen, *op. cit.*, pp. 88–91; William C. Kvaraceus and Walter B. Miller, *Delinquent Behavior, Culture and the Individual* (Washington, D.C.: National Education Association, 1959), pp. 77–84.

[5] Austin L. Porterfield, *Youth in Trouble* (Fort Worth: Leo Potishman Foundation, 1946), *passim*; Milton A. Barron, *The Juvenile in Delinquent Society* (New York: Alfred A. Knopf, 1956), p. 32; Lloyd Warner and Paul S. Lunt, *The Social Life of a Modern Community* (New Haven: Yale University Press, 1941), p. 427; William C. Kvaraceus, *What Research Says to the Teacher: Juvenile Delinquency* (Washington, D.C.: National Education Association, 1958), pp. 331–332.

[6] Cohen, *op. cit.*, p. 42.

Universality of Inverse Relation between Class and Delinquency

The first issue that reflects on Cohen's question has to do with the universality of the supposed inverse relation between social class and delinquency. On one hand, the Short and Strodtbeck studies of delinquent gangs in Chicago tended to support official findings. Lower-class gang boys *were* the most delinquent. They were followed, in turn, by lower-class non-gang boys and then by middle-class boys. These differences held up for both Negro and white respondents, although Negro gang members were not so different from their Negro middle-class peers as were white gang boys from white middle-class peers.[7]

On the other hand, most studies of undetected delinquency in smaller cities and towns have not found significant differences among adolescents from different classes,[8] and those which have, have reported differences which are not nearly so strong as those indicated by official data.[9] For example, Gold, in a Michigan study, found a statistically significant, inverse relation between class and delinquency, but the strength of the relationship was extremely slight, a coefficient of —.12.[10] The degree of variance which could be explained by this relationship would be small indeed.

Empey and Erickson report similar findings from Utah.[11] The degrees of association between social class and three different delinquency scales were: for *general* theft, —.20; for *serious* theft, —.17; and for *common* delinquency, —.17. They discovered further that the inverse relationship was due more to a small amount of delinquency among upper-class respondents than it was to an excessive amount of delinquency among lower-class respondents. The lower- and middle-class groups did not differ significantly from each other while the degree of difference between each of them and the upper-class group was considerable.

Actual Violation v. Apprehension

Empirical studies have indicated that the amount of undetected delinquency is great.[12] The degree of apprehension is extremely low, somewhere

[7] James F. Short, Jr., and Fred L. Strodtbeck, *Group Process and Delinquency* (Chicago: University of Chicago Press, 1965), pp. 164–171.

[8] F. Ivan Nye, James F. Short, Jr., and V. J. Olsen, "Socio-Economic Status and Delinquent Behavior," *American Journal of Sociology* (January, 1958), pp. 318–329; John P. Clark and Eugene P. Wenninger, "Socio-Economic Class and Area as Correlates of Illegal Behavior Among Juveniles," *American Sociological Review* (December, 1962), pp. 826–834; Robert Dentler and Lawrence J. Monroe, "Early Adolescent Theft," *American Sociological Review* (October, 1961), pp. 733–743; Porterfield, *op. cit.* An exception is Albert J. Reiss, Jr. and Albert L. Rhodes, "The Distribution of Juvenile Delinquency in the Social Class Structure," *American Sociological Review* (October, 1961), pp. 730–732.

[9] LaMar T. Empey and Maynard L. Erickson, "Hidden Delinquency and Social Status," *Social Forces* (June, 1966), pp. 546–554; Martin Gold, "Undetected Delinquent Behavior," *Journal of Research in Crime and Delinquency* (January, 1966), pp. 27–46.

[10] Gold, *op. cit.*, pp. 40–43.

[11] Empey and Erickson, *op. cit.*, pp. 549–550. See also Maynard L. Erickson and LaMar T. Empey, "Class Position, Peers and Delinquency," *Sociology and Social Research* (April, 1965), pp. 271–272.

[12] Maynard L. Erickson and LaMar T. Empey, "Court Records, Undetected Delin-

between 3 and 5 per cent of all self-reported offenses. Yet, when apprehension does occur, officials are more likely to record and process lower-class youngsters.[13]

The picture is further confused by the fact that the police and other officials are charged by juvenile court law to respond to poor home and family conditions, neglect, truancy, and other factors which may come to light when some "predatory" act is detected. Their interest is often solicitous rather than punitive, but since these factors are more often associated with lower-class than middle-class juveniles, the former are more inclined to be processed legally. These two conditions distort the idea of the epidemiological character of delinquency and probably lend credence to the notion of an inverse relation between class and delinquency.

Seriousness

There are many who feel that the offenses of lower-class youngsters are more likely to be serious. Ohlin, for example, maintains that middle-class delinquency is "petty" in comparison with lower-class delinquency.[14] The inclination to violate the law, he believes, is more deeply ingrained in the lower-class youngster who therefore possesses a greater potential for the development of a criminal career. The evidence pertinent to this question is limited but that which is available is not entirely supportive of Ohlin's position.

The Myerhoffs, in their observations of middle-class "gangs" in Los Angeles, reported that the violations of these "gangs" were often more "mischievous" than violent.[15] However, violence is not the only dimension of seriousness. Included in these "mischievous" acts was the frequent and regular theft of articles that were by no means small nor inexpensive: radios, phonographs, car accessories, television sets, all usually taken from employers or personal acquaintances.

Such findings were corroborated by Empey and Erickson in a more systematic enumeration of offenses in a *nonmetropolitan* center.[16] They found that, while the more serious forms of delinquency were less common among

---

quency and Decision-Making," *Journal of Criminal Law, Criminology and Police Science* (December, 1963), pp. 456–469; Fred J. Murphy, M. Shirley, and Helen L. Witmer, "The Incidence of Hidden Delinquency," *American Journal of Orthopsychiatry* (October, 1946), pp. 686–696; Gold, *op. cit.;* Porterfield, *op. cit.*

[13] Gold found that the police were more likely to record lower-class offenders; see Gold, *op. cit.,* p. 38. Empey and Erickson found that low-class adolescents were over-represented in a training school in proportion to the offenses they reported having committed; see Empey and Erickson, *op. cit.*

[14] Lloyd E. Ohlin, *The Development of Opportunities for Youth* (New York: Youth Development Center, Syracuse University, 1960), pp. 8–9; and Cloward and Ohlin, *op. cit.,* p. 12.

[15] Howard L. and Barbara G. Myerhoff, "Field Observations of Middle-Class Gangs," *Social Forces* (March, 1964), pp. 328–336. See also Andrew Greely and James Casey, "An Upper-Middle-Class Deviant Gang," *American Catholic Sociological Review* (Spring, 1963), pp. 33–41.

[16] Empey and Erickson, *op. cit.,* pp. 551–554.

all class groups, such violations as grand theft, forgery, breaking and entering, destroying property, and even arson, when they did occur, were more often committed by middle- than lower-class juveniles. This rather surprising finding held true whether the self-reported data came from boys with no official record or boys who were incarcerated in a training school.[17] Middle-class groups in both populations were the ones who rated disproportionately high on these kinds of offenses.

Even with respect to violence, Karacki and Toby found fighting gangs that did not come from economically deprived homes.[18] These gangs placed emphasis on many of the characteristics traditionally associated with lower-class delinquent groups: physical aggression, loyalty to peers, and immediate gratification. Shanley located a similar group of middle- and upper-class boys in the suburbs of Los Angeles who had patterns of police contact which were as extensive and serious as samples of adjudicated delinquents from lower-class neighborhoods.[19] Finally, other analyses suggest that particular patterns of delinquency may be associated as much with differences in place of residence—rural, urban, or type of neighborhood—as with social class position.[20]

In summary, these findings suggest that the inverse relationship between social class and delinquency may be less potent than has been traditionally assumed and that we should search for other determinants;[21] social class by itself may be a poor clue. The behavior of some middle-class groups suggests that we might discover as many differences *within* classes regarding delinquency as we now discover between them. In other words, instead of using a two- or three-celled table to compare lower-, middle-, and upper-class groups across the board, we should use four- or six-celled tables to compare the delinquent acts of various groups within, as well as between, classes.[22] More precise distinctions of this type might provide better clues to the nature of delinquency than do gross comparisons between classes.

[17] Albert H. Herskovitz, Murray Levene, and George Spivak, "Anti-Social Behavior of Adolescents from Higher Socio-Economic Groups," *Journal of Nervous and Mental Diseases* (November, 1959), pp. 1–9. They found no sharply different patterns between middle- and low-class incarcerated offenders and little variation in the seriousness of their offenses.

[18] Larry Karacki and Jackson Toby, "The Uncommitted Adolescent: Candidates for Gang Socialization," *Sociological Inquiry* (Spring, 1962), pp. 203–215.

[19] Fred J. Shanley, "Middle-Class Delinquency as a Social Problem," paper presented at the Annual Meetings of the Pacific Sociological Association, Salt Lake City, April 1965, p. 2. A recent article in *Life* magazine was also devoted to the extensive drug use and other delinquent patterns of middle-class groups on Sunset Strip in Hollywood. The Strip is also the locale of the heaviest concentration of "gay" (homosexual) hangouts in the city; see *Life* (August 26, 1966), pp. 75–83.

[20] Irving Spergel, *Racketville, Slumtown, Haulburg: An Exploratory Study of Delinquent Subcultures* (Chicago: University of Chicago Press, 1964); and Clark and Wenninger, *op. cit.*

[21] Identification with particular sets of peers is one that has appeared. See Erickson and Empey, *op. cit.*, pp. 272–281.

[22] Miller, for example, noted differences in theft behavior among three different groups, all *within* the lower class. See Walter B. Miller, "Theft Behavior in City Gangs," *Juvenile Gangs in Context: Theory, Research and Action*, Malcolm W. Klein and Barbara G. Myerhoff, eds. (Englewood Cliffs, N.J.: Prentice-Hall, 1967).

DIMENSIONS OF GROUP DELINQUENCY

What about the second set of facts which theory must fit—the proposition that delinquency is typically a group phenomenon? The available evidence has a paradoxical quality which illustrates both the complexity of the subject and the meagerness of our information.

There are few findings which question seriously the basic proposition that delinquency is typically a group phenomenon. Most studies, including some which use self-reported data, place the incidence of group delinquency somewhere between 60 and 90 per cent of the total.[23] It may be that with more systematic data this range will be extended, since some offenses—defying parents or running away—are by nature less likely to be group-related than others. However, the group aspects of delinquency seem to be well established with a modal figure of about 75 per cent.

What is not well established is a consensus regarding the nature of delinquent groups—their cohesiveness, their structural qualities, their subcultural characteristics. The most commonly used term to refer to delinquent groups has been the word "gang." The term has been so overworked and is so imprecise that its use in scientific discourse may well be questioned. An examination of evidence relative to the cohesiveness and structural qualities of delinquent groups illustrates the elusiveness of the "gang" and other group concepts.

Group Cohesiveness

Conflicting themes run through the literature regarding cohesiveness. The first theme, exemplified most clearly by Thrasher and the Chicago school, emphasizes the idea that delinquent groups are characterized by *internal cohesion*—*esprit de corps,* solidarity, cooperative action, shared tradition, and a strong group awareness.[24] Despite the qualifications which Thrasher placed on this theme—and he did qualify it—there is no denying that a traditional perspective has developed emphasizing the romantic quality of delinquent gangs, the free and easy life, the joint commitments of members to one another. The key to this theme is its emphasis upon the culture-generating qualities and attractiveness of the peer group.

The second theme, as Bordua notes, is irrationalistic and deterministic in its emphasis. "Gang boys are driven," he notes, "not attracted. Their lives are characterized by desperation rather than fun." [25] Such theories as those of Cohen,[26] Cloward and Ohlin,[27] and Miller [28] emphasize the idea that

[23] See footnote 2, page 294 for relevant studies. Unpublished data in our possession on self-reported delinquency, both from Utah and California, confirm this figure.

[24] Thrasher, *op. cit.,* pp. 40–46. See also Short's discussion of this theme in his introduction to the abridged edition, *passim.*

[25] David J. Bordua, "Some Comments on Theories of Group Delinquency," *Sociological Inquiry* (Spring, 1962), pp. 245–246; see also David J. Bordua, "A Critique of Sociological Interpretations of Gang Delinquency," *Annals of the American Academy of Political and Social Science* (November, 1961), pp. 120–136.

[26] Cohen, *op. cit.*

[27] Cloward and Ohlin, *op. cit.*

[28] Miller, *op. cit.*

lower-class children are downgraded in both the child and the adult status hierarchies of our middle-class institutions. They are ill-prepared by family background and cultural heritage to achieve successfully and, as a consequence, their lives are characterized by frustration, negativistic retaliation, alienation, and radical separation from conventional successes and satisfactions. This theme is much less romantic in its emphasis than the first and implies, not internal attraction, but external pressure as the source of gang cohesion.

It is the role of the individual youngster in the social structure, not his role in the street group, that is of primary significance. He is alienated before he enters the group, not because of it. The group is simply the instrument that translates his individual discontent into a collective solution.[29] By implication, the group can do little to remedy his sensitivity to the middle-class measuring rod, to provide him with the material and social satisfactions to which he aspires.

The fundamental question, then, asks what the forces are that hold delinquent groups together. Are they the group rules and loyalties which emerge from gratifying relationships within the group, as the first theme suggests, or are they due to the position of gang boys in the class structure as suggested by the second theme?

First of all, we are confronted with the apparent fact that, if the delinquent group were not rewarding to the individual, it would cease to exist. In this vein, Short and Strodtbeck have observed that when it comes to assuming adult roles—occupation and marriage—". . . the lure of the gang may spell disaster." [30] Even when challenging jobs are obtained for them, when the pay is good or when gang members are married and have children, the lure of the street is not easily forgotten and any inclination to return to it is supported by the gang. The implication, of course, is one of *internal* cohesiveness and attraction: gang membership has much to offer. However, as might be expected, there are other interpretations. . . .

Klein and Crawford argue that *internal* sources of lower-class gang cohesion are weak.[31] Group goals which might be unifying are minimal, membership stability is low, loyalty is questionable, and even the names of gangs— Gladiators, Vice Lords, Egyptian Kings—are unifying only when external threat is present. When the threat is diminished, cohesion is diminished. It is their feeling that were it not for the external pressures of police and other officials, the threats of rival groups, or the lack of acceptance by parents and employers, many delinquent gangs would have nothing to unify them. By themselves, such gangs do not develop the kinds of group goals and instrumentally oriented activities which are indicative of much organization and cohesion.

---

[29] Bordua, *op. cit.*, pp. 252–257.

[30] Short and Strodtbeck, *op. cit.*, pp. 221–234.

[31] Malcolm W. Klein and Lois Y. Crawford, "Groups, Gangs and Cohesiveness," *Journal of Research in Crime and Delinquency* (January, 1967), p. 63.

Group Cohesion and Delinquent Acts

The commission of delinquent acts seems to illustrate this lack of organization. One of the most striking things about them is not their planned and patterned characteristics but their episodic and highly situational character.[32] One would think that if delinquent groups were highly cohesive or highly structured this would not be the case. Yet, most delinquent acts are more·spontaneous than planned and, even though they involve groups, they rarely involve all members of a gang acting together.

Even complex crimes reveal considerable spontaneity and what Matza calls "shared misunderstanding." [33] Thrasher describes three college students who began to phantasize about robbing a post-office.[34] Subsequent interviews with them revealed that none of them wanted to be involved in the actual robbery but the more they talked the deeper they became involved, each hoping, actually believing, that the others would call a halt to this crazy phantasy but each reluctant, on his own, to "chicken out." The result was that, in a state of almost total individual disbelief, they robbed the post-office and found themselves in legal custody.

Careful observation of delinquents reveals countless repetitions of this phenomenon—the wandering kinds of interaction that lead to delinquent acts and the mixed motivations that accompany them. Even in regard to fighting, as Miller points out, "A major objective of gang members is to put themselves in the posture of fighting without actually having to fight." [35]

Group Cohesion and Member Interaction

Observations of delinquent gangs led Short and Strodtbeck, like Klein and Crawford, to depreciate nostalgic references to "that old gang of mine" and to deny the image of the delinquent gang as a carefree and solidary group. They report that such an interpretation may derive more from the projections of middle-class observers than from the realities that dominate street life.[36] They document this interpretation with a considerable amount of data.

They found that, compared with others, gang boys were characterized by a long list of "social disabilities": unsuccessful school adjustment, limited social and technical skills, a low capacity for self-assertion, lower intelligence scores, and also a tendency to hold other gang members in low esteem.[37] Interaction within the gang seemed to be characterized by an omnipresent tone of aggression as a result of these disabilities and the insecurities they engendered.

[32] Many works allude to this phenomenon. For examples see Thrasher, *op. cit.;* Short and Strodtbeck, *op. cit.;* Yablonsky, *op. cit.*

[33] David Matza, *Delinquency and Drift* (New York: John Wiley and Sons, 1964), pp. 35–59.

[34] Thrasher, *op. cit.,* pp. 300–303.

[35] Walter B. Miller, "Violent Crimes in City Gangs," *Annals of the American Academy of Political and Social Science* (March, 1965), p. 110.

[36] Short and Strodtbeck, *op. cit.,* p. 231.

[37] *Ibid.,* Ch. 10 and 12.

This account is complemented by Matza's use of the term "sounding," which refers to the incessant plumbing and testing through insult by delinquent boys of one another's status and commitment to delinquency.[38] Miller speaks of the "focal concerns" of lower-class gang culture as toughness, smartness, and excitement.[39] Whatever the terms, it appears that delinquent boys are under constant pressure to protect status and assert masculinity.

While this pressure to project a particular image may not be qualitatively different from many of the highly stylized kinds of interaction found in a host of other status-conscious groups, the point is that such interaction is not characteristic, at least hypothetically, of *primary* groups. Primary groups, ideally, are supposed to provide warmth and support. With the constant "sounding" that goes on in delinquent groups it is questionable whether lower-class gangs are conducive to close friendships.[40]

The picture that is painted suggests that gang members, like inmates in a prison, are held together, not by feelings of loyalty and solidarity, but by forces much less attractive. It is not that structure is lacking but that it is defensive and highly stylized, not supportive. Group members stay together simply because they feel they have more to lose than to gain by any breach in their solidarity. While they may appear to the outsider to be dogmatic, rigid, and unyielding in their loyalty to each other, the sources of this loyalty are not internal but external. Remove the pressure and you remove the cohesion.

Seeming to comment on this very point, Short and Strodtbeck report that they "find the capacity of lower-class gangs to elaborate and enforce norms of reciprocity is very much below what might be required to sustain the group if alternative forms of gratification were available."[41] Similarly, Matza argues that the majority of delinquents are not strongly committed either to delinquent groups or to a criminal career but are "drifters" who are held together by a kind of pluralistic ignorance.[42] When in the company of others, the boy is inclined to attribute to them a greater commitment to delinquent relationships and values than he has himself.

These points of view indicate the need for more direct investigation of delinquent group cohesiveness *per se* and for the study of middle-class as well as lower-class groups. Our lack of information is so great that we do not have even an adequate baseline from which to begin; that is, we know very little about the cohesiveness and inherent gratifications of adolescent groups in general. Therefore, until we can establish a baseline, it will be difficult either to generalize about delinquent groups or to compare them with other groups. Furthermore, the possible lack of cohesiveness in delinquent groups raises questions regarding the nature of delinquent subculture. If delinquent groups are not cohesive and internally gratifying, can it be expected that

[38] Matza, *op. cit.*, pp. 53–55.
[39] Miller, *op. cit.*, p. 519.
[40] Short and Strodtbeck, *op. cit.*, p. 233. See also Lewis Yablonsky, "The Delinquent Gang as a Near-Group," *Social Problems* (Fall, 1959), pp. 108–117.
[41] Short and Strodtbeck, *op. cit.*, p. 280.
[42] Matza, *op. cit.*, pp. 27–30, 56.

delinquents, especially those in the lower class, have either the personal motivation or the organizational skills to promote and maintain a deviant subculture which is in total opposition to prevailing values?

DELINQUENT SUBCULTURE

Such theorists as Cloward and Ohlin have defined the subcultural concept in narrow terms.[43] They see a delinquent subculture as unique and as autonomous. Organization around a specific delinquent activity, they say, distinguishes a delinquent subculture from other subcultures. Such behaviors as truancy, drunkenness, property destruction, or theft are legally delinquent activities but these they would not include as characteristic of a delinquent subculture unless they were the focal activities around which the dominant beliefs and roles of a group were organized.

The narrowness and rigor of their postulates regarding criminal, retreatist, and conflict-oriented subcultures characterize the logical structure of their theory but do these postulates accurately characterize delinquent groups and subculture? Are they this focused? Are they this unique and autonomous?

When Short and his associates set about trying to study these kinds of subcultures, they had extreme difficulty in locating them.[44] They found a number of gangs in which marijuana smoking was rather common and in which there was experimentation with heroin and pills, but it took more than a year of extensive inquiries among police and local adults to locate a clearly drug-oriented group. They never did find a full-blown criminal group. Consequently, they concluded that their failure casts doubt on the generality of the Cloward-Ohlin postulates.[45]

Short, *et al.*, had no difficulty in locating a number of gangs who were well-known for their conflict, toughness, and fighting but one still must question what it means to say that the "focal" concern of gangs is conflict. The bulk of even the most delinquent boys' time is spent in nondelinquent activity and their delinquent acts make up a long list of different offenses.[46] How precise can we be, then, in referring to the characteristics of a "conflict" subculture or gang?

In observing "typical," "tough" city gangs over a two-year period, Miller found that assault was *not* the most dominant form of activity.[47] In fact, two thirds of the male gang members who were observed were not known to have engaged in *any* assaultive crimes over the two-year period and 88 per cent did not appear in court on such a charge. Similarly, Klein and his colleagues in Los Angeles have found that less than 10 per cent of the recorded

---

[43] Cloward and Ohlin, *op. cit.*, p. 7.
[44] Short and Strodtbeck, *op. cit.*, pp. 10–13.
[45] *Ibid.*, p. 13.
[46] Short, Introduction in Thrasher, *op. cit.*, pp. xlvii–xlviii.
[47] Miller, *op. cit.*, pp. 105, 111.

offenses for gang members are assaultive.[48] Instead, the *frequency* with which adolescents commit a long list of different offenses seems to better characterize their commitments to delinquency than their persistent adherence to a particular offense pattern.[49] There seems to be limited empirical support for the idea of autonomous and highly focused delinquent subcultures and somewhat more support for the notion of a ubiquitous, "parent" subculture of delinquency in which there is a "garden-variety" of delinquent acts.[50]

A ubiquitous, but amorphous, subculture would be more consistent with the notion of weak internal bonds in delinquent groups and highly situational delinquent acts than with the idea of internally cohesive groups who participate in planned and highly patterned delinquent activities. Furthermore, if delinquent subculture is not highly focused and autonomous, question is raised regarding its relation to the larger culture.

Subculture: Contraculture or Infraculture?

Most contemporary theory has suggested that lower-class delinquent subculture is *contra*culture [51] in which status is gained by demonstrating opposition to prevailing middle-class standards.[52] Theories of middle-class delinquency suggest that the delinquent group is a collective response to adolescent efforts to establish sexual identity and to deal with frustrations attendant on the transition from childhood to adulthood.[53] But does this mean that a middle-class delinquent group is, like a lower-class gang, the instrument that translates individual discontent into a delinquent *contraculture?*

Matza takes issue with the notion of *contra*culture on any class level and emphasizes a subtle but important distinction. He argues that "there is a subculture of delinquency but it is not a delinquent subculture." [54] American culture, he believes, is not a simple puritanism exemplified by the middle-class. Instead, it is a complex and pluralistic culture in which, among other cultural traditions, there is a "subterranean" tradition—an *infra*culture of delinquency.[55]

This *infra*culture does not represent ignorance of the law nor even general

---

[48] Malcolm W. Klein, Youth Studies Center, University of Southern California, Personal Communication, September 1966.

[49] Erickson and Empey, *op. cit.*, pp. 465–469; Gold, *op. cit.*, pp. 27–46.

[50] Albert K. Cohen and James F. Short, Jr., "Research in Delinquent Subcultures," *Journal of Social Issues* (Summer, 1958), pp. 20–36.

[51] J. Milton Yinger, "Contraculture and Subculture," *American Sociological Review* (October, 1960), pp. 625–635.

[52] Cohen, *op. cit.*; Cloward and Ohlin, *op. cit.*; Miller, *op. cit.*

[53] England, *op. cit.*; Bloch and Niederhoffer, *op. cit.*

[54] Matza, *op. cit.*, p. 33; David Matza and Gresham M. Sykes, "Juvenile Delinquency and Subterranean Values," *American Sociological Review* (October, 1961), pp. 712–719.

[55] The idea of *infra*culture was suggested by J. A. Pitt-Rivers, *The People of the Sierra* (Chicago: University of Chicago Press, 1961), who referred to "infrastructure" rather than "infraculture."

negation of it; instead, it is a complex relationship to law in a symbiotic rather than an oppositional way. It is not a separate set of beliefs which distinguish delinquents from other youth, or youth from adults; it is that part of the overall culture which consists of the personal, more deviant, and less-publicized version of officially endorsed values. The two sets of traditions—conventional and deviant—are held simultaneously by almost everyone in the social system and, while certain groups may be influenced more by one than the other, both determine behavior to a considerable degree.

Daniel Bell's analysis of crime as an American way of life is probably a good illustration of Matza's point.[56] Bell notes that Americans are characterized by an "extremism" in morality, yet they also have an "extraordinary" talent for compromise in politics and a "brawling" economic and social history. These contradictory features form the basis for an intimate and symbiotic relationship between crime and politics, crime and economic growth, and crime and social change, not an oppositional relationship. The tradition of wanting to "get ahead" is no less an ethic than wanting to observe the law.

Crime has been a major means by which a variety of people have achieved the American success ideal and obtained respectability, if not for themselves, for their children. The basic question, therefore, is whether this deviant tradition contributes more than we realize to the behavior of younger as well as older people. Rather than delinquent subculture being uniquely the property of young people, it may have roots in the broader culture.

Empirical investigation of the matter would seem to involve two questions: (1) the extent to which adolescents legitimate official, conventional patterns and (2) the extent to which they simultaneously participate in, or espouse in some way, deviant patterns. With reference to the first question both Kobrin [57] and Gordon *et al.*[58] suggest that adolescents from all strata are inclined to legitimate official patterns. The gang members they studied did not seem to be alienated from the goals of the larger society and ". . . even the gang ethic, is not one of 'reaction formation' *against* widely shared conceptions of the 'good' life." Gang, low-class and middle-class boys, Negro and white ". . . *evaluated images representing salient features of the middle-class styles of life equally high.*" [59] This finding confirmed that of Gold in Michigan with a much different population [60] and led to the conclusion that ". . . if the finding is valid, three separate theoretical formulations [Cohen, Miller, and Cloward-Ohlin] fail to make sufficient allowance for the meaningfulness of middle-class values to members of gangs." [61] In fact, given the

[56] Daniel Bell, *The End of Ideology* (Glencoe, Ill.: The Free Press, 1959), pp. 115–136.

[57] Solomon Kobrin, "The Conflict of Values in Delinquency Areas," *American Sociological Review* (October, 1951), pp. 642–661.

[58] Robert A. Gordon, James F. Short, Jr., Desmond F. Cartwright, and Fred L. Strodtbeck, "Values and Gang Delinquency," *American Journal of Sociology* (September, 1963), pp. 109–128, as reproduced in Short and Strodtbeck, *op. cit.*, Ch. 3.

[59] Short and Strodtbeck, *op. cit.*, pp. 271, 59. Italics theirs.

[60] Martin Gold, *Status Forces in Delinquent Boys* (Ann Arbor: University of Michigan, Institute for Social Research, 1963).

[61] Short and Strodtbeck, *op. cit.*, p. 74.

strength of the findings, one wonders whether we are correct in referring to official values as "middle-class" values or whether we should be using some more inclusive term.

The second question, regarding the simultaneous possession of deviant patterns, presents a more confused picture. A curious omission in our conjectures and research has been our failure to examine the extent to which deviant values are widely transmitted to young people. Several elaborate theories hypothesize that all children, including those in the lower class, are conditioned by official, "middle-class" stimuli. They watch television, listen to the radio, go to the movies, read the ads, and attend middle-class dominated schools; as a consequence, they acquire common desires for status, recognition, and achievement. Despite these conjectures, we have not had similar conjectures regarding the possible transmission of deviant patterns.

Kvaraceus and Miller have suggested that middle-class delinquency represents an upward diffusion of lower-class attitudes and practices; [62] but are lower-class patterns all that are diffused? To what extent are children on all class levels conditioned not just by lower-class values but by mass stimuli which emphasize violence, toughness, protest, kicks, and expedience? These are certainly important aspects of our "brawling" American history, a part of our cultural tradition. If we pay too little heed to them then we may be inclined to overemphasize the narrowness and autonomy of delinquent subculture, especially as the sole possession of the lower class. It is seductively easy to overemphasize the uniqueness of problem people and thereby to obscure their similarities to non-problem people. For example, studies of self-reported delinquency reveal that the extent of hidden law violation is widespread,[63] so widespread, indeed, that Murphy, Shirley, and Witmer were led to remark that "even a moderate increase in the amount of attention paid to it by law enforcement authorities could create the semblance of a 'delinquency wave' without there being the slightest change in adolescent behavior." [64] This finding, coupled with the questionable strength of the theory of an inverse relationship between social class and delinquency, suggests that, unless we are to assume that deviant traditions actually predominate, they must occupy a symbiotic tie of some kind with conformist traditions.

Conventional Values and Deviance

In order to investigate the matter further, several factors should be considered. One important factor is the nature of adult-youth relationships. What perspectives, for example, are transmitted from adults to youth? Is the youthful search for "kicks" or the irresponsible acquisition of wealth and leisure profoundly different from adult desires for the same things or, rather, a projection of them? A double standard for judging adult and youthful behavior is certainly not uncommon and could be far more influential than

[62] Kvaraceus and Miller, *op. cit.*, pp. 77–79.
[63] Erickson and Empey, *op. cit.*; Gold, *op. cit.*
[64] Murphy, Shirley, and Witmer, *op. cit.*

a double standard distinguishing between the sexes. Personal access to various adult role models, as contrasted to a vague and abstract relationship with them, would likely affect the selection of deviant or conformist behavior. The absence of a strong personal relationship would make the juvenile more dependent upon the images projected by such secondary sources as the movies or television.

A second important factor has to do with the relative valences of delinquent and conformist values for different populations of adolescents. How do they balance? Short and Strodtbeck found that, while conventional prescriptions were generally accepted, subterranean, deviant values were accepted differentially. While gang boys were as willing as lower- and middle-class nongang boys to legitimate official *prescriptions*, they were not as inclined to support official *proscriptions*.[65] This particular research failed to explore other important aspects of the issue.

Besides obtaining some indication of the general valences of both deviant and conventional values, we need to explore their valences in various specific contexts. We know, for example, that if changes in group context or social situation occur, both behavior and the espousal of particular values are likely to change also. The citizen who is in favor of racial equality in a general way is often one of the first to sell his home when integration occurs in his neighborhood. Specific considerations alter his behavior. Similarly, the delinquent boy, when placed in the context of having to exercise leadership over his peers in a conventional setting, will often act remarkably like a conventional adult. His actions are surprisingly stereotyped, a response not to norms in general but to norms as they apply in a specific context.

In studying the relative valences of conventional and deviant *proscriptions* we also need to compare not only lower-class gang boys with others, as Short and Strodtbeck did, but excessively delinquent boys from other classes with their peers as well. We need a better indication of the extent to which deviant values are diffused either throughout the entire class structure or through subgroups on all class levels.

Finally, we need more careful study of the way official and societal responses to juvenile behavior contribute to definitions of delinquency and delinquent subcultures, either by overemphasizing their uniqueness or by contributing to their development. Becker argues that the process by which some juveniles but not others are labeled may be as crucial in defining the problem as the behavior of the juveniles themselves.[66] For example, as mentioned earlier, there are those who think that the coalescence and persistence of delinquent gangs may be due as much to external pressure from official and other sources as to the internal gratifications and supposedly unique standards of those groups.

The contribution which could be made by a study of official systems—the police, the courts, the correctional agencies—would be clarification of the

[65] Short and Strodtbeck, *op. cit.*, pp. 59–76.

[66] Howard S. Becker, *Outsiders: Studies in the Sociology of Deviance* (Glencoe, Ill.: The Free Press, 1963), Ch. 1.

total *gestalt* to which officials respond: how legal statutes, official policies, and perceptual cues affect the administration of juvenile justice.[67] It seems apparent that official and societal reactions to juveniles are due not entirely to criminalistic behavior but also (1) to acts which, if committed by adults, would not warrant legal action and (2) to a number of "social disabilities" that are popularly associated with deviance: unkempt appearance, inappropriate responses due to lack of interpersonal skills, and educational deficiencies.[68]

These are characteristics which traditionally have been more closely associated with lower- than middle-class juveniles and are characterized in legal terms by truancy, dependency, or incorrigibility. It would be important to learn the extent to which these identifying characteristics, as contrasted to demonstrably delinquent *values*, contribute to the definition of some groups, but not others, as seriously delinquent. Since only a small fraction of their time and attention is devoted to law violation, even among the most seriously delinquent, the meanings which these juveniles assign to themselves are usually far less sinister than the meanings which officials assign to them.

CONCLUSION

It seems apparent that, in order to complete the picture of the total phenomenon, we need a series of related studies which would, first, identify a representative population of adolescents, their class positions, their value-beliefs and commitments, various measures of delinquent acts (self-reported and official), their symptoms of disability, and their group affiliations; and, second, follow these adolescents through the institutional paths—educational, economic, or correctional—along which they are routed by officials. Which juveniles are processed legally and on what criteria? In what ways are they the same or different from nonprocessed juveniles in terms of values, class position, group affiliations, actual delinquent acts, and so on.

Given such research we might then be in a better position to know not only what the consequences are for those who are apprehended and processed by legal and correctional institutions but also what the consequences are for those who are *not* processed. This would most certainly apply to middle-class as well as lower-class juveniles. Hopefully, we might gain better insight into the total mosaic composed of delinquent values, actual behavior, and official reaction. Are delinquent values widely shared and is delinquent behavior common? Does legal or semilegal processing contribute

[67] See Irving Piliavin and Scott Brian, "Police Encounters with Juveniles," *American Journal of Sociology* (September, 1964), pp. 206–215; Joseph D. Lohman, James T. Carey, Joel Goldfarb, and Michael J. Rowe, *The Handling of Juveniles From Offense to Disposition* (Berkeley: University of California, 1965); Nathan Goldman, *The Differential Selection of Juvenile Offenders for Court Appearance* (National Research and Information Center, National Council on Crime and Delinquency, 1963).

[68] For conflicting evidence, see A. W. McEachern and Riva Bouzer, "Factors Related to Disposition in Juvenile Police Contacts," *Juvenile Gangs in Context*, Klein and Myerhoff, eds., *op. cit.*

to the solidification of delinquent groups? Is there differential treatment of juveniles based not on actual behavioral or value differences but on other identifying characteristics? Information of this type would help to indicate whether delinquent subculture is *contra*culture or *infra*culture.

We are only recently becoming aware of the extent of the symbiotic and mutually supporting characteristics of official and client roles in a long list of social systems; for example, policeman-offender, captor-captive, teacher-pupil, therapist-patient, caseworker-client. These are inextricably tied together by a host of traditional expectations and definitions. Change one and you are likely to change the other. We need to know more clearly the extent to which these definitions and the systems of which they are a part make delinquency and delinquents appear to be what they are, as well as the standards, beliefs, and behavior which may be unique to delinquents. Interactive relations between and among juveniles and official agencies may be as important as the behavior exhibited by juveniles in delimiting delinquency for purposes of both etiological inquiry and social control.

Norman E. Zinberg

Facts and Fancies About Drug Addiction

Students of adolescence generally are hard-pressed when asked to dis-
tinguish between heroin, marijuana, and hallucinogenic drugs. They are
usually befuddled when confronted with the problems of drug abuse and
drug addiction. Zinberg, below, places the effects of the common drugs
in proper perspective; he shows that drug-taking is more a group than
a solitary activity and, in the process, explodes the myth that there is
only one kind of drug problem. He contends, further, that drug addicts,
rather than being reprobate criminals, are often intelligent, maternally
dependent, and low in homosexual activities and psychotic illnesses. He
questions strongly the "punitive rigidity" of law enforcement officials, and
in his provocative discussion, holds that U. S. Government authorities
have provided young people "who always like to puncture balloons of
pompous self-righteousness, with a gratuitous sense of purpose in drug
taking."

MISUNDERSTANDING of the problems of drug abuse in this country is the greatest current obstacle to attempts at their solution. It is my purpose in this essay to sort out what is actually known from what passes as fact; to show something of how these misconceptions have come to be accepted as truths; to point out what we do not know but urgently need to; and, finally, to indicate what lines of investigation seem at the moment to promise the most fruitful results.

How, first, is the problem of drug addiction commonly conceived? In most people's minds, drug addicts are a group of reprobate criminals who "mainline" heroin. This concept is not confined to the general lay public, but pervades even relatively sophisticated discussions of the drug problem. Unhappily, it also dominates professional attitudes toward legislation, law enforcement, and clinical treatment. But in its crudity it simply does not correspond with the true picture, even in so far as it is known; and, worse, it subtly undermines attempts to learn more. Given this distortion, the drug problem is rarely looked at for what it is—an endemic disease about which we need more information and less ideology. As a matter of fact, the very notion of the drug problem is wildly misleading. There is more than one drug problem, just as there is more than one kind of drug taker and more than one kind of pernicious drug.

FROM *The Public Interest*, VI (1967), 75–90. Reprinted by permission of the author and the publisher. © 1967 by National Affairs, Inc.

Two Varieties of Drug Experience

At least two separate types of drug abusers can be clearly distinguished even in our present state of limited knowledge. They differ in terms of their places in our society, the kinds of drugs they use, and what they hope to get out of drugs. The first group comes mainly from the lower socio-economic strata of the population; they use drugs to escape from lives that seem unbearable and hopeless. Whatever their individual psychological problems, the general profile of members of this group reflects a direct relationship between social deprivation and specific personality types. I call them *the oblivion-seekers*.

Most public discussion of narcotics "addicts" recognizes only this first group. But there is a second, much larger, group who come from the middle and upper socio-economic strata. They use drugs not to get away from life but to embrace it. Drugs give them a sense of liberation from convention, a feeling that a level of genuine experience which is closed to them by their culture is opened for them by the drug. If they are thought of as presenting a social problem, it is their rebellion, not their addiction, which is viewed with alarm. Because of their class origins and their youth, they are commonly identified not as addicts but simply as participants in the rebellion our culture has come to expect from every rising generation. I call them *the experience-seekers*.

Members of these two groups typically use different drugs—the oblivion-seekers use heroin, the experience-seekers a considerable variety of other drugs. This difference is important, because heroin is illegal in this country for any purpose, medicinal or otherwise, and is reputed among the knowing to have both a greater kick and a greater pull toward dependency than any other drug. Before the typical heroin-taker became addicted, therefore, he probably knew he was committing himself to constant law-breaking and to drug dependency. Experience-seekers, who try other dependency-inducing drugs, rarely think of themselves in this way. Indeed, many of them—though they know the drug they are using does often induce dependency—think they are exceptions, and insist that they are not "hooked" long after this is manifestly untrue.

It would not be unreasonable to expect these differences to have been noticed long ago. Yet the situation as it stands now is so muddled that even so elementary a distinction as that which divides the oblivion-seekers from the experience-seekers has not been made by the medical profession. Lacking this or any other meaningful sort of distinction, and in the absence of any accepted clinical procedure, doctors respond to their drug patients emotionally, each according to his own bent. They fill in what they do not know with unexamined notions and feelings. The sentimentalists, the "soft" school, tend to see a curiously attractive innocence in the drug takers. The punishers, the "hard" school, refuse to see drug abuse as a physical and social disease, but insist it is rooted in moral turpitude.

ROMANTIC ILLUSIONS

The "soft" school looks upon the oblivion-seekers as new incarnations of the noble savage. For it, members of the lower class have a special "earthy" knowledge about Life.

The moral support given to the drug taker by sentimentalists is sufficiently pernicious and persistent to warrant a closer look. In a recent *New Yorker* article, Dr. Marie Nyswander, well-known for her work with drug addicts, discussed her sad, tortured charges with a reporter. After describing a young, confirmed opiate dependent who *wanted* to be committed to a state hospital for three years, she was reported as having said: "Man may be able to experience freedom in a degree we can't yet imagine. . . . That's why drug addicts . . . strike me as being among the few comparatively free people I've met. . . . The addict's relationships, except when he's scrounging for drugs, are honest and direct. Deceit is not a basic part of his personality."

Here is a clear instance of the sentimental mystique at work. The nature of the drug addict is assimilated to the supposedly unspoiled nature of the child—he is someone who rejects our hard, competitive adult world and returns to the simple world of children, where truth and beauty are self-evident. He experiences life freely, he is untouched by fraud, oppression, pettiness, and despair. What matter if his arms are somewhat scarred?

In an odd way, it is true that the absence of responsibility for one's self or for the welfare of others does permit an engaging directness and lack of guile. Many oblivion-seekers lie and cheat to get drugs, but they can do so with disarming openness, because, like children, they want nothing but the immediate satisfaction of specific, pleasurable desires. The indirection and ambiguity necessary to manage adult responsibilities, the need to slight one wish or responsibility in order to give fuller expression to another, militate against simplicity. Many of those who admire drug users seem unaware that the charm which enchants is nothing more than simple single-mindedness—the conviction that few things other than drugs are worth the complexity and strain of striving for.

An earlier member of the sentimental school, Mabel Dodge Luhan, once decried the dismal accretion of cars, stoves, and sinks in white American homes, and proclaimed the superiority of the American Indian because he did not want this paraphernalia of progress. Indeed, as D. H. Lawrence said of Mrs. Luhan, "She hates the white world and loves the Indian out of hate." And, like Mrs. Luhan, many of those who sentimentalize the drug taker are dissatisfied with their lives and are moved by a hatred of their own worlds. But what is more important to note is that Lawrence's statement applies even more accurately to the drug user. To view the drug taker as an adventurer into brave new worlds of experience in contrast to whom the ordinary member of society is a conformist or a coward, is seriously to miss the point. Our society has ills in plenty, but to regard the frightened runner into oblivion or the equally panicky fleer from inner emptiness as in some way superior to this society is perverse in the extreme.

"HARD-HEADED" ILLUSIONS

The hard school, on the other hand, the punishers who see drug abuse almost entirely as crime, find their rationale in the legal history of the drug problem in this country. After many false starts, the medical profession in 1902 did accept as a serious medical problem Dr. Charles Towns' now classical description of the dependency triad—the compulsive need for the drug, the development of tolerance, and the emergence of a withdrawal syndrome if the drug is withheld. But it was already too late; the lawmakers had taken over. At the turn of the century, before the Flexner Report, there was good reason to mistrust the calibre of doctors produced by our medical schools. Partly for this reason, the 1904 Boylan New York State Law—and the 1914 Harrison Federal Narcotic Act which was patterned on it—gave no discretion to physicians in dispensing drugs to addicts. The Harrison Act, a Federal taxing law, was passed in the same atmosphere which a bit later resulted in the prohibition of alcoholic beverages being written into law. The right of the physician to prescribe narcotics in the course of his professional practice became an issue of law enforcement, and it was on this battleground that the "hard" school was able to win a decisive victory for their punitive point of view. Beginning in 1919, in a series of highly moralistic rulings ("a physician who prescribed narcotics" was stigmatized as intending "to cater to the appetite or satisfy the craving of one addicted to the use of the drug"), the Supreme Court decided that physicans could not prescribe narcotics to habitual users to keep them comfortable even if they were en route to a hospital. In this state of the law, drug abuse could only be seen as a criminal matter. Led by the American Medical Association, the medical profession simply abandoned the field. After the formation of the Federal Bureau of Narcotics in 1930, public discussion of drug abuse was confined to a discussion of criminality. Harry Anslinger, who was head of the Federal Bureau of Narcotics from its inception until four years ago, fabricated reports for public dissemination out of adroit compounds of fact and fiction. As a result, an automatic association between narcotics and criminal activity has been set up in both the public's and the professional's minds. Until recently, this atmosphere made research and experimentation virtually impossible.

Probably no more moralistic government agency than the Federal Bureau of Narcotics has ever existed. Reflecting as it does the nineteenth-century attitude of the temperance societies (i.e., one drink makes a confirmed drunkard) or of the nineteenth-century public attitude toward sex (i.e., one illicit experience makes a prostitute), the Federal Bureau of Narcotics has pointed out over and over again that, after even one single dose of any of the drugs on their list, dreadful moral deterioration sets in. For example, Mr. Anslinger, writing about "a few of many cases which illustrate the homicidal tendencies and the generally debasing effects arising from the use of marijuana," cites the case of a cotton-picker, 25 years old, who smoked a "reefer," picked up a 17-month-old baby girl who had been left in her family car, violated and suffocated her. Ignoring the complexity of the motives in so heinous a crime, Anslinger concludes that "the real criminal in this case is marijuana."

The young people who try drugs probably don't read these publications, but their pronouncements do effectively help shape the general public view. By first enormously oversimplifying and then overstating their case, government authorities have thus provided young people, who always like to puncture balloons of pompous self-righteousness, with a gratuitous sense of purpose in drug taking.

The punitive rigidity of law enforcement officials changed not at all until the 1962 White House Conference on Narcotic and Drug Abuse; since, they have changed their attitude only minimally. In spite of the enlightened proceedings of this Conference, the old simplistic thinking persists. Recently, when a Justice Department official was asked off the record about his views on the drug problem, he said it was very simple. "Now, about $5 million a year is spent enforcing the Harrison Act; to keep an addict comfortable costs about $25,000 per year, most of which comes from crime. If only 50,000 addicts are involved, by simple arithmetic you arrive at a figure of $125 million yearly that the public, in a sense, pays for the narcotics habit. Put that much money in the hands of the proper [enforcement] agency and we will eliminate the drug traffic." Both his thinking and his arithmetic fail to take into account such obviously germane facts as previous criminality among drug users, the lesson of prohibition, the constantly increasing difficulty any one country has in sealing its borders and acting unilaterally. Most importantly, however, he fails entirely to consider the drug problem as it is related to the experience-seekers.

DRUGS AND PSYCHOSIS

Nor is this punitive point of view confined to law enforcement agents. Evidence that even professionals working directly with addicts are affected by it crops up in surprising places. Two well-known studies of schizophrenia among drug takers, one by Donald L. Gerard and Conan Kornetsky and the other by Isadore Chein, contend that approximately 20 per cent of adolescent drug takers suffer from schizophrenia or some form of thought disorder. Even the government clinic at Lexington reports that among the bizarre symptoms manifested during withdrawal are occasional acute psychotic breaks. If these studies are correct, at least 10 to 20 per cent of drug takers could be expected to end up as psychotics. As it turns out, however, only a small number of drug takers develop psychoses. In a study which followed those cited above, George Vaillant showed that, after a search of the remarkably complete files of the New York State Department of Mental Hygiene, "not one addict was currently hospitalized [in a mental hospital] in New York and only eight had ever been hospitalized for mental disorder. . . . Only one addict appeared to fulfill the diagnostic criteria for schizophrenia." (There are other surveys which support Vaillant's findings and place the incidence of schizophrenia among addicts at less than 1 per cent.) Further Vaillant states that even when addiction is experimentally induced in chronic schizophrenics, if the drug is suddenly withheld, these patients do not ask for it.

Vaillant's convincing study thus concludes that the rate of overt psychosis in drug addicts is very low. How, then, can the other studies be explained? The point here is that those diagnoses which confuse addiction with schizophrenia tell us something further about the attitudes of many who are professionally concerned with drug takers. The emotional reactions of many professionals to drug takers' curiously anti-social personalities skew their diagnoses in a way that may be the converse of the sentimentalization we discussed earlier. The addict's obvious disdain for social conventions, his willingness to abuse his body, and his underlying fury at any effort to intervene, no matter how helpfully it is meant—all this offends the professional observer. Where the sentimentally-inclined doctor tends to see the addict's responses as a measure of his closeness to the deepest well-springs of life, the doctor who is offended by the addict's scorn for society, and for society's doctors, sees him as bizarre, sick, outside reality, and therefore psychotic.

FACTS AND QUERIES

These, then, are the sort of errors the ideologies of both the "hard" and the "soft" schools have led to. To show how fundamentally the substitution of fiction for fact has impeded research, let us look at what seems at first to be a relatively simple question. How many heroin users are there in the United States? Surprisingly, estimates differ widely. If the Federal Bureau of Narcotics' figure of 60,000 is correct, then the number of hard-core drug abusers in this country has hardly changed at all in the last four decades. (Indeed, relative to the rise in population, it has declined.) But the World Health Organization estimates the number of drug dependents as closer to one million!

How can we explain this fantastic disparity? Does the second figure actually include not only heroin users, but other kinds of drug addicts? Does it include persons who have been drug abusers only temporarily? How many times are chronic recidivists counted? The correct figure seems to be difficult to come at, but clearly this is the sort of question that cannot be answered meaningfully without the sort of typological distinctions we have been making.

To ask an even more fundamental question: are we sure that the oblivion-seekers present as dangerous a social problem as they have long been held to do—or is it rather the experience-seekers, hitherto hardly recognized as a problem at all, who present the real threat?

In 1965, John O'Donnell presented a careful analysis of figures about relapse rates. He states that, after a time, many heroin users dose themselves less frequently rather than more; and, further, he suggests that all heroin addiction may be time-limited, since his data point to a precipitous drop-off of drug abuse after the age of 35. This study supports an earlier one by Charles Winick, who concluded from the Federal Bureau of Narcotics' files that "addiction may be a self-limiting process for perhaps two thirds of the addicts." If this is true, then despite the important social, economic, legal, and criminal problems which the oblivion-seekers present, they may not in fact be the fundamental problem they are thought to be. In the present state of our knowledge, however, we do not know enough, even about the much-studied oblivion-seekers, to answer this question.

Some things about the oblivion-seekers are, of course, well-known. Their personal histories have been shown to follow a distinct pattern: cigarettes at age 6 or 7, liquor and sex by 13, marijuana soon after. Promiscuity and petty thievery merge almost automatically, in late adolescence, into prostitution and organized crime. Drug abusers of this type show a definitely ascending use of drugs, typically moving toward the one with the big kick, H. But other things we know about this type are puzzling—in particular, the ways in which their pattern differs from that of the non-addicted delinquent. To begin with, Billy E. Jones finds that the Lexington drug users are surprisingly intelligent: their average verbal I.Q. is 105. Contrast this with the Gluecks' study of penitentiary prisoners; there, 67 per cent have a verbal I.Q. of less than 90. Nor are the family histories of criminals and addicts identical. Fifty-two per cent of addicts come from homes broken by death before age 16. (Indeed, 28 per cent of these occurred before age 6.) These figures do not refer simply to the loss of fathers, so common to the lower socio-economic class strata; more than 20 per cent lost their mothers very early. But non-addicted delinquents are even more deprived of a stable family situation, with 71 per cent of homes broken by all means and 28 per cent having lost their mothers by age 6. So while broken families seem to have something to do with addiction, it is not clear how much they have to do with it.

It also turns out that the drug takers are only or youngest children to a statistically significant degree. Yet birth order has never been proven to be a significant factor among delinquents, alcoholics, or the mentally ill.

But the most striking single correlation to have been established between parental history and drug dependency was parent-child cultural disparity. Among Negroes, for example, Northern-born drug takers had Southern-born parents twice as often as would be expected from the census figures. This statistical incidence is shown to the same degree by children of immigrant parents. By contrast, the incidence of drug dependency in a Northern urban sample who were themselves immigrants or Southern-born Negroes was only 12 per cent, which is less than half of the percentage an average projection from census figures would lead one to expect.

Most surprising of all, however, is the fact that 72 per cent of the patients studied by Vaillant still lived with their mothers at age 22; indeed, after age 30, 47 per cent continued to live with a female relative. Approximately 70 per cent were either married or maintained a relatively stable, common-law relationship. These marriages tended to continue in spite of hospitalization. This is holding on to people to a striking extent—an extent markedly greater than similar studies show for alcoholics or other delinquent groups. Glueck's study of criminal delinquents, for instance, shows only 22 per cent continuing to live with their family of origin after 30, while about the same proportion maintained some form of married life.

An incidental finding of the same study supports the contention that the drug taker strives for closeness with a maternal figure. When hospitalized or imprisoned, drug takers, like other institutionalized persons, frequently engage in homosexual activity. But in only 3 per cent of the cases studied by Vaillant do the patients report that homosexual activity is a source of significant gratification to them in their outside adult life. This is a surprisingly low figure, particularly in view of the popular notion that drug addiction and homosexuality go together.

DRUGS AND CRIME

One of the most damning arguments used by the punitive school is the relationship of drug-taking to crime. They quote statistics showing that drug takers commit a high percentage of the crimes in the United States and strongly imply that crime results from drug taking. Now, it is true that oblivion-seekers get a lot of the money they need to buy drugs from criminal acts; but, nevertheless, drugs do not make criminals. It is the other way around: criminals take drugs. Hill, Gerard and Kornetsky, among others, indicate that over 70 per cent of known drug abusers had criminal records *before* turning to drugs.

What seems to happen is that once a criminal is caught up in drug taking, a vicious circle commences. Drugs are illegal and expensive, large sums of money are needed to maintain a habit, and it takes a lot of time to make sure a connection is available. Moreover, once a habit is established, despite growing tolerance, drugs are debilitating in a way that makes regular work almost impossible. These conditions reinforce previous criminal activities.

This undeniable link between drugs and crime does not, however, invalidate the distinction between the oblivion-seekers and other types of delinquents. The oblivion-seekers' pattern—an intensity of attachment to family of origin and later to a significant female, the preponderance of youngest children, the low rate of psychotic illness, the high rate of intelligence—meaningfully marks addicts off from the others. Certainly, with their high intelligence, the oblivion-seekers know that the drug dependency they court demands antisocial activity of them, and it is inevitably asked how significantly aggression against society is involved as a motive for drug taking. From what we know now, such aggression is not very important. The oblivion-seeker seems, rather, to be a surprisingly dependent person.

His drug dependency is a measure of his childishness, immaturity, and inability to cope with adult responsibility. The incidence of schizophrenia, as Vaillant shows, is low; rather, the oblivion-seekers have a high suicide rate. The search for oblivion is above all a flight from the pain of rejection and the fear of loneliness.

This proposition is reinforced by the fact that solitary drug users are an infinitesimal minority. Drug addicts depend on each other; drug taking is a group activity. Drug use spreads by contagion, that is, one drug user encourages, teaches, and recruits so that he can share his activity with others. Once the epidemiology of drug abuse is understood in the context of the character of the oblivion-seekers, the punishers will no longer be able to justify treating the drug abusers as simple moral delinquents. Some steps have already been taken in this direction. For example, the 1962 White House Conference on Narcotic and Drug Abuse specifically labeled as false the widely-held notion that drug abuse in the young was primarily initiated by narcotic salesmen hanging around public schools, coaxing juveniles into trying free shots, and thus working up an insatiable market for their trade.

From all that we know, the basic truth seems to be that drug abuse is simply another way to express fear, deprivation, and aimlessness. For the oblivion-seekers, drug taking in the end is self-defeating; for, in time, drugs reproduce the very situations from which users had hoped to escape. Even at this dead end, however, drug-taking is hard to stop. The impulse to escape survives the failure to escape.

THE OTHER KIND OF ADDICT

To turn now to the experience-seekers, the one trait that characterizes them as a group is a terrible fear of lifelessness, of missing something important, of not really living. Beyond this, no such pattern as typifies the oblivion-seekers has as yet been discerned. Here, more than with the oblivion-seekers, the question of what part physiology plays in their drug dependency, and what part psychology,[1] confuses every attempt to analyze

[1] We know that all of the pernicious drugs mentioned produce dependency in varying degrees. In no case do we know the degree to which this dependency is physiological or psychological. We can set up a rough continuum of physiological response, putting heroin, which produces maximum physiological response to withdrawal, at one end, and perhaps marijuana or nicotine at the other. However, we find that these reactions are not nearly as clearcut as had been thought. Many users of narcotic drugs seem not to develop a direct physiological dependency. Some people continue on unvaried doses of morphine or heroin without demanding more, and show a minimum withdrawal reaction when taken off the drug (cf. Norman E. Zinberg, M.D., and David C. Lewis, M.D., "Narcotic Usage. I. A Spectrum of a Difficult Medical Problem," *New England Journal of Medicine,* CCLXX (May 7, 1964), 989–993). In fact, they may periodically remove themselves from any source of supply so as to maintain their semi-independence. On the other hand, many smokers, when they quit, suffer from the twitching, automatic movements of a hand used to a cigarette, a feeling of restlessness and increased appetite which chewing gum does not satisfy, a change in pulse rate, a decidedly unpleasant skin sensation, and a dryness of the mouth. Which of these symptoms are secondary to the psychological trauma of no smoking, and which are primarily physiological?

experience-seeking addiction. The drugs of choice are often varied; there is no such clear pattern as the oblivion-seekers' relentless preoccupation with heroin. The one characteristic common to them all, one which they share with the oblivion-seekers, is the need for others to share drug-taking with them. Indeed, they outdo the heroin takers in their proselytizing efforts.

Because the effects of most of the drugs used by this group vary so widely, all that we know about what individual drug users experience comes from the subjective responses they themselves report. Controlled experiments are simply not feasible; drug users insist that in a clinical setting—such as a hospital or a laboratory—the effect, probably the group effect, is largely cut off, the drug does not convey the real kick. It is hard not to conclude that, at least some of the time, the experience-seekers want so desperately to have drug-induced experiences that they have them psychologically even if not physiologically. What is more, like the Emperor in his new clothes, they want to be sure everyone around them has the same experience, sees the same cloth of gold. If others who have been persuaded to join the group testify that they, too, have had an experience and, more to the point, an "exciting" or "beautiful" experience, the original members of the group feel their drug-taking takes on enhanced validity. They can put aside their doubts and fears about drugs at least for a little while. From the point of view of contagion, the desire of the experience-seekers to proselytize presents a real and present danger to our society.

MARIJUANA

Most experience-seekers begin by smoking "pot"; these are the youngsters who stage demonstrations against the classification of marijuana as a narcotic by Federal Drug legislation. They contend that marijuana is probably less and certainly no more harmful than alcohol; they deny the Federal Bureau of Narcotics' claims that people under the influence of "pot" are socially destructive. Above all, they insist that the notion that "pot" leads inevitably down the road to H is nonsense. The delight they take in exploding these official misconceptions, and their sense of pursuing an idealistic cause certainly stimulates their age-specific, culturally-expected rebellion and helps to attract adherents.

Although the experience-seekers are probably right in their contention that the above-mentioned ideas about "pot" are silly, they are not as right as they think. Each of the conventional ideas they pooh-pooh deserves more careful investigation. Thus, it is true that, for the great majority of the experience-seekers and for the much greater number of the young who try smoking "pot" once or twice, marijuana has little connection with heroin. Still, one small segment of those who begin with marijuana, and who, in addition, are seriously neurotic, finds the nonconformist support they need in such a drug-experimenting, "pot"-smoking group. Because everyone in adolescence seems in turmoil, these neurotics don't look much different from the rest. But after two or three years pass, the regular bunch—even if they are still a little "beat"—have gone ahead and made necessary life decisions. Yes, they take a year off, but they still manage to be graduated from college or to acquire an interest that leads somewhere. The neurotic, however, who may have thought he was just like the rest of the bunch, fails to take these steps when they should be taken. Suddenly he is no longer really part of the bunch. What can he do but reach out for another group who will accept him? This group is likely to be closer to the hard-core drug abusers; it may even be a heroin-taking, oblivion-seeking group where big money is needed to stay "in."

While there are not many who follow this path—indeed, most users of this type seek out a psychiatrist rather than a pusher—they deserve attention because they show dramatically what marijuana can mean to troubled youngsters. Marijuana is a disorganizing agent; it offers no help to people who are already more than sufficiently disorganized. Perhaps it is no worse than alcohol—there are 5 million disabled alcoholics in the United States— but that does not mean that we need yet one more relatively potent intoxicant to be made readily available to all. Undoubtedly, many people can handle marijuana, use it, and perhaps enjoy it without ill effects. Allentuck and Bowman, Murphy, and the LaGuardia Report, among others, agree that physiological dependency is not induced by marijuana. But the World Health Organization reports that marijuana-hashish-hemp-bange is the most abused drug in the world. Long-term excessive use results psychologically in a stultifying condition of lethargy, dissociation, and general withdrawal from human contact, a reaction not very different from that of chronic alcoholism. Physiologically, furthermore, marijuana can cause hyperglycemia, hyperthermia, and depression of respiration.

The most pernicious property of marijuana is not its potency but its relative weakness. Many experience-seekers want to extend themselves in inner and outer time and space; they strain against personal boundaries, they want *all* knowledge and feeling to be available to them. It is precisely for this reason that the languid release of the opiate does not interest them. Their intolerance for the strictures of reality, for the limitations imposed by both the outside and the inside worlds, makes the brief and easily terminable "high" of marijuana insufficient. Therefore, a sizable, but currently indeterminable, group of fairly regular "pot" smokers goes on to experiment with the hallucinogens—LSD, mescaline, psylosibin, peyote, dimethyl triptan, or some other variety of the magic mushroom.

THE HALLUCINOGENS

We may really have opened up a Pandora's box with these drugs. For we understand very little about the action of the hallucinogens. A "high" on a 200 microgram dose of LSD usually lasts from eight to twelve hours, that is, the time during which there is a high degree of concentration in the cerebral system. As soon as almost any other known drug is excreted from the system, so are its effects. But many experiments indicate that this is not true of LSD. A possible return of effect long after no demonstrable blood level remains has been proven to exist. Is this return physiological or psychological? We do not know.

We do, however, know enough to suggest that, for several months after even a single hallucinogenic experience, no one should make an important life decision. Most young people, of course, wrestle with potential changes in their lives all the time. The nature of that struggle often may be characterized as a pull between a more structured or a less structured way of life: serious music or folk music, attending school or taking a year off, and so on. Clearly, each of these ways of life can have validity; that is not the point at issue here. What does concern us is that under drug influence— which means for months after taking the drug—he invariably chooses the looser or less structured alternative; he seems to be deprived of free choice, to be unduly influenced by his drug experience.

The scientific fascination with hallucinogens is easy to understand; these kinds of drugs mimic schizophrenia, a disease that is one of the scourges of mankind. By studying the drug effect we may learn about the disease in much the same way as Jenner evoked cow pox to study smallpox. Without great chemical know-how, we have rapidly learned to synthesize the drug. The process is technically so simple that our marvelously facile mass media immediately make it known that any student who knows freshman chemistry can do it in his kitchen. The drug is odorless and tasteless and effective in very high dilutions. Strange rumors are heard, rumors from usually creditable sources. One hears even in academic circles that government agencies have, with great cost, arrived at projections of what would happen to a large city if quantities of LSD were dumped in its water.

It comes as no surprise, considering the nature of LSD's effect, to learn that primitive tribes used it in religious rituals. In no time, modern priests spring up who proselytize for the new faith of "expanded experience." They do collect followers. And, as is usual, many are those very people who are least capable of tolerating "expanded" experience. Adolescents or young adults, whose time of life demands the ability to cope with the diffusion of their aims and the contradictions of their decisions, are most easily persuaded to try LSD. The socially and psychologically disturbed are frequent recruits. *The New England Journal of Medicine* reports that a new, consistent, and discernible fraction (6 to 8 per cent) of the admissions to mental hospitals in our large cities come from a trip that failed.

Unfortunately, the hue and cry about the hallucinogens has reduced the amount of valid research being done, and made it unpopular. Few researchers want to take responsibility for having the drug around or risk its accidental dissemination. We come full circle back to the beginning of the history of narcotic usage. Again, public alarm strengthens the hand of those who see drugs primarily as a problem of law enforcement and punishment, and has little patience for essential social and psychological considerations.

ARE WE DRUG HAPPY?

Our discussion of the little understood, indirect, but potent psychological roots of the experience-seekers' drug abuse must not fail to consider the extent to which this country maintains a drug culture. Our culture's rapidly increasing medical dependency on drugs, both for survival and for longevity, makes drug taking a sacred cow indeed. The extent to which we as a nation have become drug eaters was given shocking, but short-lived, publicity during the Kefauver hearings in 1951 and again during the thalidomide scandal. At the 1966 American Medical Association's convention, a great deal of perhaps belated attention was given to this growing phenomenon. Dr. Don Francke sounded the keynote by saying, "The American public is drug happy. Our culture is flooded with remedies of all kinds." In 1963, American consumers spent 4.2 billion dollars on drugs. This figure does *not* include drugs charged to hospital or clinic bills or money spent on drugs by public or government agencies of any kind. The latter figures are hard to obtain, but would unquestionably swell the total tremendously. When the 4.2 billion figure of 1963 is compared with the 5.2 billions spent in 1965, it becomes clear that the amount spent on drugs is rising faster than either general consumer spending or population growth. As a nation our doctors are prescribing, and we are taking, a rapidly increasing amount of drugs. Measured in doctor visits and hospital days, adverse drug reaction—that is, the noxious side effects—has become one of our largest disease entities.

Along with these alarming effects are the heartening facts of constantly increasing longevity, better national health, and a falling death rate for many diseases. However, the overall efficacy of many of the drugs (e.g., the tranquilizers and energizers) is as yet unproved. Doctors argue that they must prescribe new and unproven drugs because their patients demand them and need them. Not everyone who needs a tranquilizer, they contend, can or should go to a psychiatrist. This argument has considerable validity, but, in many respects, it oddly resembles the rationale of the experience-seekers themselves.

The young drug experimenter is, in fact, imitating his elders when he uses drugs; at the same time, he establishes his independence and rebellion by using those illegal drugs his elders officially decry. To those of his peers whom he wishes to enlist in the drug taking army, he points out the hyperbole of the Federal Bureau of Narcotics and the hypocrisy of his elders as reasons *for* taking drugs. Untenable as this argument is, a lot of college students in the United States have been persuaded by it.

The oblivion-seekers are a relatively clearcut group: they can be studied as a problem. But, in order to study the experience-seekers, we find ourselves studying our society. All too often, they are only exaggerations or caricatures of so much we see everywhere. Indeed, it is the closeness and at the same time the vastness of the problem presented by the experience-seekers that prevents any study of them. We simply do not know what the extent and quality of experience-seeking drug abuse is, nor what are its implications for the future. For instance, we see many users of LSD becoming patients in mental hospitals. Does their number represent only a small proportion of those who take trips, or is there a high ratio between those who take LSD and eventual psychosis?

The medical profession has now, at long last, taken a stand against the crime-oriented Federal Bureau of Narcotics; it is trying to reassert the right it once abdicated, to diagnose and treat drug abusers as sufferers from a disease. But its well-meant effort may be defeated before it begins. In its call for increased research and treatment, organized medicine has placed first importance on sick individual patients, rather than on the broad social problem which drug dependents present to medical practice. The profession may well find itself in a camp as narrow in its own way as that of the Federal Bureau of Narcotics. The emphasis on individual patients limits interest to the oblivion-seekers who, as I have indicated, may be much less of a problem than the experience-seekers. By putting the greatest priority on the search for a nondependency-producing analgesic, and on local treatment rather than specialized regional public health hospitals far from their patients' homes, the profession is undoubtedly supporting worthy causes. But it is not facing the enormity of the problem and it is not searching for truly fresh approaches. Indeed, all too often, it repeats past mistakes. For example, Vaillant shows that involuntary parole is the most effective means of keeping the drug taker abstinent and employed. The experiments with methadone require the patient to report to someone at the hospital who gives him his drug regularly. Consequently, we do not know as yet whether the methadone itself is essential in the results obtained or whether the effective agent is merely the replication of an involuntary parole situation, stringently enforced by methadone's very severe withdrawal reaction. Yet claims for methadone as a cure-all appear constantly in the press, claims that sound very much like those that were made for heroin as a cure for opium addiction in 1898 when heroin was first synthesized.

Obviously, there is no one solution to "the" drug problem. Before any research effort can begin, there must be a basic shift in public attitudes. Neither hard-school prejudices nor soft-school sentimentalizing can be allowed to continue to distort the public vision. Many approaches and real social flexibility will be necessary to diagnose, prevent, and treat this multifaceted, economic, psychological, physiological, and social problem. The known possibilities give some sense of the scope that is needed. Some drugs might be legalized; the British system of a license for certain users of certain drugs might be tried; opiate antagonists might be developed; nondoctrinaire, nonritualized, psychiatric approaches might be effective; Synanon-like, cohesive group-living units show some promise; institutional settings could be made available for those who can find tolerable stability only as institutional workers, attendants, or patients. The study of the peculiar nature of this disease, its incidence in groups more than in individuals, its spread by contagion and subsequent infection of those who want warmth, closeness, and social support for some anti-social or dependent propensities, will teach us about a great deal more than just drug taking. But we must begin by knowing that much of what we think we know about this problem is mistaken.

Louis Stewart
Norman Livson

Smoking and Rebelliousness: A Longitudinal Study from Childhood to Maturity

Stewart and Livson investigate the hypothesis that rebelliousness contributes to the etiology of cigarette smoking. The rebelliousness of smokers and nonsmokers, who were distinguished on the basis of their smoking behavior at age 30, was traced from kindergarten through high school. The evidence suggests that persons who later were smokers were likely to have been rebellious during elementary and junior-high school years. Moreover, the relationship between smoking and rebelliousness persisted into adulthood, for even then the smokers held more rebellious attitudes than the nonsmokers. The findings imply that if smoking is viewed as an addiction having its origin "in some underlying resentment to authority," then efforts to prevent smoking "based upon authoritative pronouncements have little chance of success."

SMOKING and adolescent rebellion against authority have long been linked in popular thought. The validity of such a hypothesis is obviously of considerable importance for the design of programs aimed at deterring young people from smoking. If resistance to authority *is* a motivating factor in the initiation of smoking, and perhaps also in its continuance, it will be no simple matter (for even the kindliest of authorities) to persuade some adolescents not to take up smoking. Nor, for that matter (as recent experience has already established), will it be easy through authoritative statements, to persuade adults to give up the habit. Clearly, a more subtle strategy would then be required.

Despite the aura of plausibility which surrounds this hypothesis, there is practically no evidence available with which to determine its validity. This state of affairs is exemplified by the recently published report to the United States Surgeon General, entitled *Smoking and Health*,[1] in which the conclusion is reached that

FROM *Journal of Consulting Psychology*, XXX (1966), 225–229. Reprinted by permission of the authors and the American Psychological Association.

[1] United States Public Health Service, *Smoking and Health*, Report of the Advisory Committee to the Surgeon General, PHS Publ. No. 1103 (Washington, D.C.: USPHS, 1964).

While rebellion may play a role in the initiation of smoking, perhaps an important one, there is not much evidence for it. Claims in the literature are at best based on circumstantial suggestive evidence, linked to conclusions by a chain of questionable assumptions [p. 313].

At the present time, reliable knowledge about the personality characteristics of smokers is limited as may be seen from recent reviews.[2] Moreover, the relatively few studies so far conducted have all dealt either with the current personality of adult smokers or with retrospective reconstructions of their earlier attitudes and traits. There are as yet no prospective studies of the *presmoking* personality characteristics of smokers. Such studies are essential for an adequate test of hypotheses which view personality as a determinant of smoking behavior. Such a study has become possible as a result of recent follow-ups with the subjects of the Oakland Growth Study (OGS) and the Guidance Study (GS), two longitudinal research programs of the Institute of Human Development (University of California, Berkeley) in which information on smoking habits was obtained.

METHOD

Sample

A detailed discussion of the nature of the original longitudinal samples and of the procedures of the OGS and the GS may be found in earlier publications.[3] However, in brief, the two samples were composed of the subjects born in the 1920's and residing in two neighboring urban communities of the San Francisco Bay area. The OGS subjects were originally studied intensively between the ages of 11.5 and 17.5 years. They were seen for medical and psychological follow-up study at about 33 years of age. The GS subjects were studied from birth to age 18 and were seen again for follow-up at the average age of 31 years. In both follow-up studies, the smoking habits of the subjects were ascertained during a medical interview with a physician.

The subsample for this study was defined by two criteria: (a) Information on smoking habits which permitted assigning a person to either of two categories: nonsmokers or regular smokers (smoking a half pack of cigarettes or more per day). Mixed cigarette, pipe, or cigar smokers were not included in these groups. (b) Availability of early personality data as described below. The sample as finally constituted varied somewhat in size at different ages during childhood and adolescence: for males, from 86 to 103; for females, from 86 to 93. In this sample, on the average, 57 per cent of men and 55 per cent of women were smokers. Smokers and nonsmokers

[2] *Ibid.*, p. 359; J. Matarazzo and G. Saslow, "Psychological and Related Characteristics of Smokers and Nonsmokers," *Psychological Bulletin*, LVII (1960), 493–513.

[3] H. E. Jones, "Procedures of the Adolescent Growth Study," *Journal of Consulting Psychology*, III (1939), 177–180; J. W. McFarlane, "Studies in Child Guidance. I. Methodology of Data Collection and Organization," *Monographs of the Society for Research in Child Development*, VI (1938), 1–254.

of either sex did not differ significantly in socio-economic status as assessed by the Warner Occupational Scale.[4]

Data

Several indexes of what may be considered as rebelliousness were available extending from childhood to adulthood. The earliest, for the GS, were teacher ratings on two scales: (a) behavior in school and (b) attitude toward school and, for the OGS, regular report cards with grades of conduct in school. These measures were available from kindergarten through the ninth grade. In order to increase reliability of the GS data, the two ratings (attitude and behavior) were combined at each grade level and then adjacent ages were composited, that is, kindergarten with first grade, second grade with third grade, etc. For the OGS, the school conduct grades were grade-composited in the same fashion.

Another measure of rebelliousness covering the adolescent period was available for the OGS subjects in the form of a behavior rating of "resistance to authority." The scores used were the average of independent ratings made each school year, from the eighth through the eleventh grades, by three staff members who had observed the subjects in a variety of social situations. For these measures, the sample varies from 51 to 55 boys and from 48 to 51 girls.

Although the focus of this report is primarily upon the presmoking period of childhood and early adolescence, the groups have also been compared on an adult measure of rebelliousness, the Socialization scale of the California Psychological Inventory (CPI), which was available for both OGS and GS subjects (83 men, 82 women). This empirically derived 54-item scale has been found to differentiate with considerable efficiency between groups differing in their degree of conformity to the mores of our society.[5] For example, group means provided in the CPI manual[6] range from a high point of socialization for bankers, through such groups as medical students and social workers, to a low point for juvenile delinquents and criminals.

RESULTS

Table 1 presents the evidence for the hypothesis that children who later become smokers are more rebellious in their elementary and junior high school years. (Since the scores entering into these comparisons are composites of standard score transformations of single age raw values, means and standard deviations would be uninformative and are not reported.) All mean differences are in the predicted direction so that, whether assessed

---

[4] W. L. Warner, M. Meeker, and K. Eells, *Social Class in America* (Chicago: Science Research Associates, 1949).

[5] H. G. Gough and D. R. Peterson, "The Identification and Measurement of the Predispositional Factors in Crime and Delinquency," *Journal of Consulting Psychology*, XVI (1952), 207–212.

[6] H. G. Gough, *Manual of the California Psychological Inventory* (Palo Alto, California: Consulting Psychologists Press, 1957).

Table 1 *Significance Levels from Comparisons of Smokers and Nonsmokers on Presmoking School Measures of Rebelliousness*

		Males			Females		
		NON-SMOKERS	SMOKERS		NON-SMOKERS	SMOKERS	
School Grades		N	N	P	N	N	P
Kindergarten/first grades	OGS	19	21	+	15	28	.10
	GS	16	31	.01	24	19	+
Second/third grades	OGS	20	22	.10	16	29	.10
	GS	17	33	.10	25	20	.10
Fourth/fifth grades	OGS	23	27	.05	17	29	+
	GS	17	33	+	23	17	+
Sixth/seventh grades	OGS	25	28	.05	16	32	.05
	GS	16	33	.05	22	18	.05
Eighth/ninth grades	OGS	25	28	.05	16	30	.05
	GS	16	32	+	22	18	.10

Note.—OGS measures were teachers' ratings of "conduct"; GS measures were composites of teachers' ratings of positiveness of attitude and behavior in the school situation. Comparisons made by Mann-Whitney U test. All differences were in the predicted directions; a plus sign indicates $p > .10$.

by teacher ratings (as in GS) or by "conduct" grades (as in OGS), potential smokers show more evidence of rebellious attitudes over the approximate age range 5 to 15 years. The fact that differentiation is most clear at Grades 6 and 7 possibly reflects more overt expression of underlying rebellious attitudes resulting from the stresses experienced by these children for whom the transition from elementary to junior-high school occurred at that point.

This personality difference is maintained through high school, as evaluated by the "resistance to authority" rating which was available for OGS Ss. Tested separately at Grades 8, 9, 10, and 11, this rating is significantly higher ($p < .05$) on each occasion for smokers of both sexes.

The greater rebelliousness of smokers is equally apparent in adulthood. The Socialization scale (So) of the CPI discriminated smokers from nonsmokers for both sexes in the GS and OGS samples considered separately; the results of the combined analysis are presented in Table 2. The stability of these adult findings is attested to by results obtained at about age 36 in a later OGS follow-up when the Minnesota Multiphasic Personality Inventory (MMPI) was administered. At that time the smokers of both sexes had significantly higher elevations of the Psychopathic Deviate (Pd) scale than did nonsmokers. (The Pd scale is in many respects similar in conception and construction to the So Scale of the CPI and moreover includes a number of items which also appear on the So scale.)

Discussion

The results of this study consistently support the hypothesis that cigarette smokers are more rebellious than nonsmokers and that this rebelliousness

Table 2   Comparison of Smokers and Nonsmokers on the Socialization Scale of CPI

	Males			Females		
	N	MEAN [a]	SD	N	MEAN	SD
Nonsmokers	31	38.9	4.3	37	40.2	4.4
		(54.0)			(51.0)	
Smokers	52	34.7	5.6	45	36.8	5.4
		(46.0)			(43.0)	
Difference Nonsmokers		+4.2**			+3.4*	
		(+8.0)			(+8.0)	
minus smokers						

[a] Raw scores with *T* scores in parentheses.
* $p < .01$.
** $p < .001$.

antedates smoking. This has been demonstrated in school behavior from the earliest elementary school grades through adolescence. Furthermore, adult smokers continue to hold more rebellious attitudes than do non-smokers. In discussing the significance of these findings, it is important to consider them in relation both to the initiation of smoking and its continuance and habituation.

Initiation of Smoking

If recent surveys [7] had not indicated the extent to which smoking represents for teen-agers the attainment of adult status and of peer acceptance, sufficient evidence for the currency of this attitude in American thought is provided by the literature of boyhood and adolescence. Descriptions of the first experience with smoking in all its clandestine mystery and initial misery have been stock aspects of the novel of boyhood from the time of Mark Twain's Tom Sawyer and Huck Finn. (To be sure, the more sophisticated adolescents of modern novels may have turned to stronger stimulants, for example, alcohol and drugs, yet it is clear that the symbolic value of the experience is the same.) At the simplest level of explanation, then, it seems reasonable that the teen-agers who are most rebellious will take up more openly and more vigorously, and at earlier ages, all those activities which adults seem to find so pleasurable and which have been reserved as prerogatives of maturity, for example, smoking, drinking, and sexual intercourse.

The view that in modern-day society smoking is no longer forbidden to young people would contradict this analysis. We question this view. There still persists a sharp line of demarcation in terms of chronological age for the beginning of smoking, indicating the presence of some age-contingent taboo. A summary of the available data indicates that few children smoke

[7] D. Horn, "Modifying Smoking Habits in High School Students," *Children,* VII (1960), 63–65.

regularly before age 12, probably less than 5 per cent of boys and 1 per cent of girls; however, by 17 years of age, 40 per cent to 55 per cent are smoking.[8]

Also overlooked in this view is the tendency of many adult cigarette smokers still to consider smoking an undesirable practice and to wish that they could discontinue it. The attitude "it's a dirty habit" is not uncommon. In the past many religious groups condemned smoking as sinful; today there are still a number of sects which maintain a ban on smoking. Furthermore, smokers often experience their inability to stop smoking as a sign of lack of will power and of moral weakness. Such self-inflicted retribution would suggest that smoking has not entirely lost its taboo quality in modern-day society.

Continuance and Habituation of Smoking

It might be postulated that, in part, the continuance of smoking is motivated by the same needs and attitudes which led to its initiation, since in some measure smoking continues to serve as a symbol of rebellion. However, in addition, we must not forget that smoking is pleasurable and that tobacco contains nicotine, a substance akin to all the other stimulating and intoxicating materials which man has so avidly sought out. As Sigmund Freud,[9] himself a tobacco "addict," has so eloquently stated it:

> The services rendered by intoxicating substances in the struggle for happiness and in warding off misery rank so highly as a benefit that both individuals and races have given them an established position within their libido-economy. It is not merely the immediate gain in pleasure which one owes to them, but also a measure of that independence of the outer world which is so sorely craved. Men know that with the help they can get from "drowning their cares" they can at any time slip away from the oppression of reality and find a refuge in a world of their own where painful feelings do not enter. We are aware that it is just this property which constitutes the danger and injuriousness of intoxicating substances.

In the foregoing quotation from his *Civilization and its Discontents,* Freud was undoubtedly speaking of the potent addictive substances, such as alcohol and narcotics, yet his words are appropriate to a consideration of smoking. The close kinship of smoking with other addictions is borne out by recent research. For example, on the physiological side, Knapp, Bliss, and Wells [10] have demonstrated that in reaction to the cessation of smoking or even to a decrease in the nicotine content of cigarettes, smokers show a kind of "withdrawal syndrome" involving cardiac slowing and a decrease in blood pressure. Psychological similarities among the addictive groups have also been reported along the dimension of social deviancy. Several studies

[8] United States Public Health Service, *op. cit.,* p. 361.

[9] S. Freud, *Civilization and its Discontents* (Garden City, N.Y.: Doubleday Anchor Books, 1958), p. 19.

[10] P. H. Knapp, C. M. Bliss, and H. Wells, "Addictive Aspects in Heavy Cigarette Smoking," *American Journal of Psychiatry,* CXIX (1963), 966–972.

of alcoholics and narcotics addicts, utilizing the MMPI, have found a significant elevation of the Psychopathic Deviate (*Pd*) scale.[11] In a recent investigation, Stewart and Cartwright [12] have found a similar elevation of the *Pd* scale for smokers of both sexes in a psychiatric outpatient population. The same difference has been reported in two samples of college males.[13] These latter findings, of course, strongly support the CPI results and directly replicate the OGS MMPI findings we reported above.

In view of these similarities, it may well prove heuristic to think of smoking as an addiction. If, as the evidence suggests, the addictions share a common origin in some underlying resentment of authority, then, as we noted at the outset, efforts to prevent smoking (as well as the other addictions) based upon authoritative pronouncements have little chance of success. Of this there would already seem to be sufficient evidence from the long history of unsuccessful efforts to discourage alcoholism and the use of narcotics through legislative prohibitions and punitive measures. The consensus of experience has by now clearly shown that addictions are not isolated habits but expressions of pervasive personality tendencies. To delineate further the nature of these tendencies promises deeper understanding of the etiology of smoking and should provide clues to guide society's response to this problem. Along these lines, more intensive investigations of aspects of this problem, such as the influence of family background and the factors associated with variations in smoking habits, including the ability to discontinue smoking, are currently in progress with the longitudinal data of the Institute of Human Development.

[11] H. E. Hill, "The Social Deviant and Initial Addiction to Narcotics and Alcohol," *Quarterly Journal of Studies on Alcohol*, XXIII (1962), 562–582.

[12] L. H. Stewart and D. S. Cartwright, "Smoking and Addiction: Personality Similarities of Smokers, Alcoholics and Narcotic Addicts" (unpublished manuscript, Presbyterian Medical Center Library, 1964).

[13] D. S. P. Schubert, "Personality Implications of Cigarette Smoking Among College Students," *Journal of Consulting Psychology*, XXIII (1959), 376; B. C. Straits and L. Sechrest, "Further Support of Some Findings about the Characteristics of Smokers and Non-Smokers," *Journal of Consulting Psychology*, XXVII (1963), 282.

Stanley H. Schuman

Donald C. Pelz

Nathaniel J. Ehrlich

Melvin L. Selzer

Young Male Drivers: Impulse Expression, Accidents, and Violations

The following analysis of young male drivers indicates that weak orientation toward mature responsibilities may be ultimately related to reckless driving. Young male drivers from ages 16 to 24, as one might expect, are shown to be a distinct high-risk group for both accidents and violations. In this study, 288 unmarried males were interviewed concerning their driving habits, attitudes, accidents, and violations. The results show that whereas accidents begin to decline during the 21 to 55 age range, violations persist at a high level until 23 or 24. Further, younger rather than older drivers seemingly have more frequent but less serious accidents. The data suggest that the younger drivers involve themselves in more daredevil and blow-off-steam type activities. It is after reaching age 21, however, that the drivers report an increase in their driving self-confidence.

Deaths and injuries due to motor vehicle accidents have reached epidemic proportions here and abroad.[1] A major concern is the young male driver, whose death rate between ages 20 and 25 is more than twice that of drivers between 30 and 50 (Fig. 1).[2] Although drivers less than age 25 represent only 20 per cent of the registered drivers in the United States, they were involved in one third of the fatal accidents last year.[3] In a 15-month Michigan study of nearly 100,000 problem drivers (whose oper-

FROM *The Journal of the American Medical Association*, CC (1967), 1026–1030. Reprinted by permission of the authors and the American Medical Association.

[1] Automotive Safety, *JAMA*, editorial, CXCVII (July 4, 1966), 50; L. G. Norman, *Road Traffic Accidents: Epidemiology, Control, and Prevention*, XII (Public Health Papers, World Health Organization; Geneva, 1962); R. A. McFarland, "Epidemiology of Motor Vehicle Accidents," *JAMA*, CLXXX (April 28, 1962), 289–300.

[2] *Vital Statistics of the U.S. 1963*, II, Part A, Tables 1–23, 24, and 26 (Public Health Service: U.S. Department of Health, Education, and Welfare).

[3] *Accident Facts 1966 Edition* (Chicago: National Safety Council), p. 54.

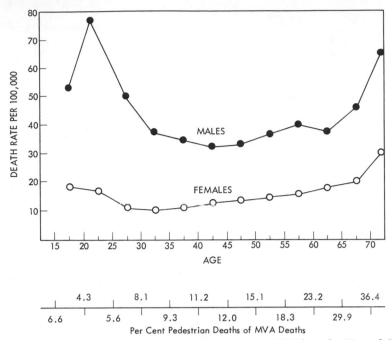

Figure 1. *Death rates due to motor vehicle accidents (MVA) in the United States in 1963 by age and sex. Proportion of pedestrians among motor vehicle deaths rises steadily after age 40.*

THIS and Figures 2–6 are from U.S. Public Health Service, *Vital Statistics of the US, 1963*, vol. 2, pt. A., U.S. Department of Health, Education, and Welfare.

ators' licenses are in jeopardy) more than half were between 18 and 24 years of age.[4]

Why does the young male driver have such a poor driving record? His assets are evidently outweighed by his liabilities.[5] It has been suggested that his sharp senses, keen reflexes, automotive knowledge, and recent driver training are countered by such factors as inexperience, bravado, chance-taking, experimentation with drinking, lack of judgment, and peer group pressure toward irresponsible behavior.

To provide factual data for testing such speculations, a pilot survey was undertaken with unmarried male drivers aged 16 to 24 years in Washtenaw County, Michigan, during the summer of 1966. The purpose was to obtain data on "normal" drivers in this category, rather than sampling from accident lists. A 30-minute interview covered a variety of topics: driving experi-

---

[4] Press release by J. M. Hare, Secretary of State (Lansing, Michigan, September 28, 1966).

[5] J. E. Barmack and D. E. Payne, "Injury-Producing Private Motor Vehicles Among Airmen: Psychological Models of Accident Generating Processes," *J. Psychol.* LII (January, 1961), 3–24.

ence, financial responsibility, risky driving practices, frustrations in daily life, drinking, anger in traffic situations, awareness of danger, and demographic information, in addition to self-reports on accidents and tickets for moving violations. Because a component of suicide has appeared in psychiatric studies of male drivers responsible for fatal accidents,[6] a question about suicidal thoughts was asked. Questions about driving behavior emphasized recent recall, i.e., experience within the past month.

For this pilot study, limited time and funds did not permit a strict probability sample of all drivers in the county (a fuller but slower survey is now being undertaken with such a sample). Instead, nine locations were arbitrarily selected at which large numbers of young drivers congregated: four drive-in restaurants and one bar-restaurant in the largest city, two drive-in restaurants in the next largest city, and two popular beaches.

At each location during specified afternoon and evening hours, respondents were selected by a systematic random process to eliminate interviewer judgment. Beginning with a preselected number between 1 and 5, the interviewer took every fifth male thereafter who appeared to be in the desired age range and requested an interview, provided he met the specifications (16 to 24 years of age, single, with driver's license).

After a brief explanation of the survey and assurance of confidentiality, most respondents complied willingly (83 per cent of those eligible). Those who did not typically were in a hurry and could not spare the time. In some cases the driver's companions remained in the car during the interview; this fact did not appear to inhibit responses.

FACTUAL CHARACTERISTICS

An even distribution between 16 and 24 was obtained, with an average age of 21. One should remember that each town contains a university; more than half of the respondents were attending college part-time or more, and 13 per cent were in high school. Relative to national averages the sample seemed high on reported income of parents (median about $13,000) and reported miles driven during the past year (median about 14,000 miles).

Among these 288 respondents, 35 per cent reported one or more accidents during the past year. (An "accident" was defined as involving $50 or more in damage or injury, while respondent was driving a car, whether or not responsible.) Another 30 per cent reported accidents previously but not in the past year (Table 1). Somewhat less than half (44 per cent) reported one or more tickets for moving violations during the past year.

There was some association between these two facts. Among those with no moving violations, the proportion with an accident last year was about 1:3, while among persons with one or more moving violations it was almost 1:1. Nevertheless, each did occur without the other; 24 per cent of the

[6] M. L. Selzer and S. Weiss, "Alcoholism and Traffic Fatalities: Study in Futility," *American J. Psychiat.*, CXXII (January, 1966), 762–767.

Table 1   Percentages of Self-Reported Accidents and Violations in Sample of 288 Young Drivers

Accidents	Violations Last Year, %		
	None	One or More	Total
Before last year	18 ⎱ 41	12 ⎱ 24	30 ⎱ 65
None	23 ⎰	12 ⎰	35 ⎰
One or more last year	15	20	35
Total	56	44	100

sample had a moving violation but no accident during the past year, and 15 per cent had an accident without a violation.

From the time they started to drive, 187 of these 288 drivers (almost two thirds) reported one or more accidents, with an average of 1.6 per involved driver. Features of 303 accidents are tabulated in Table 2. Almost half of all first accidents occurred before the legal driving age of 18, and the median age of all accidents was 19. One resulted in a fatality. Crashes involving death or injury were in the minority (14 per cent); the large majority resulted in property damage only. The picture for this group of

Table 2   Features of 303 Accidents Involving 187 Young Male Drivers

Features	First Accident, % (N = 187)	2nd–4th Accidents, % (N = 116)	Total Accidents, % (N = 303)
Severity			
Fatality	0	1 ⎱ 17	14
Injury	12	16 ⎰	
Damage only	85	78	82
Not ascertained	3	5	4
	100	100	100
Age at time of accident			
14–15	2	0	1
16–17	43	20	34
18–19	31	34	32
20–24	24	46	33
	100	100	100

Other features	First, %	2nd–4th, %		First, %	2nd–4th, %
Reported to police	80	79	1 car, lost control	25	22
Alcohol mentioned	5	12	2 cars, same direction	40	35
Respondent felt responsible	53	45	2 cars, intersection	18	30
			2 cars, head-on	5	2

"normal" drivers was thus one of accidents of relatively mild character occurring well before adulthood.

Among these crashes, one quarter were of the one-car, loss-of-control type, and respondents felt responsible for half of them. Alcohol was reported less frequently in first accidents (5 per cent) than in subsequent accidents (12 per cent).

FACTUAL CHARACTERISTICS BY AGE

When only those crashes occurring within the past year were examined, a similar age trend appeared. Accidents were more frequent at ages 16 to 20 and declined during ages 21 to 24 (Fig. 2). Moving violations, however,

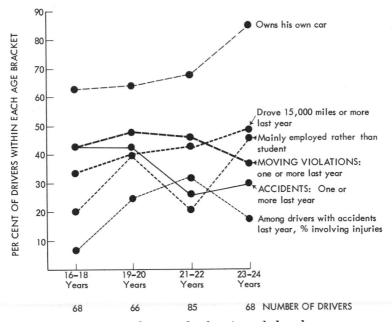

Figure 2. *Accidents and other factual data by age.*

did not decline until ages 23 to 24. (Violation point schedule in Michigan includes 6 points for driving under influence of alcohol, manslaughter, leaving scene of accident, reckless driving, etc.; 4 points for speeding 16 mph or more above limit; 3 points for speeding 11 to 15 mph above limit and disobeying stop sign or traffic signal; 2 points for speeding 10 mph or less above limits and other minor violations.)

A discrepancy between Figs. 1 and 2 was puzzling: although national fatalities peaked between ages 20 and 25, our accident rate dropped during that span. Was our sampling unrepresentative? An alternate hypothesis was that younger drivers (less than age 21) have more accidents of a mild character; older drivers between ages 21 and 25 perhaps have fewer crashes, but those that occur are more serious.

This interpretation is consistent with the bottom curve in Fig. 2: among drivers with accidents in the past year only (numbers varied from 29 to 21 in the four age brackets), the proportion involving injury rose steadily up to ages 21 to 22 and then dropped.

As one might expect, Fig. 2 indicates that with increasing age these young men drove greater distances, were more likely to own their own car, and more likely to hold a job (although because of the universities, most of those in the 21- to 22-year-old age bracket were college students rather than wage earners).

EMOTIONAL FACTORS IN DRIVING

Several questions designed to measure emotional factors in driving showed definite changes with age, usually a decline (Fig. 3). Among drivers aged

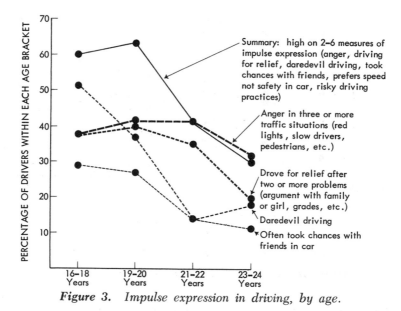

Figure 3.   *Impulse expression in driving, by age.*

16 to 18, half reported that in the past month they had engaged in "daredevil" practices such as racing or taking dares, whereas fewer than one in five reported such practices after age 21. Twice as many in the 16 to 18 bracket said that they had "often taken chances" with one or more friends in their car during the past month compared with those aged 23 to 24.

Asked about driving to "blow off steam" after arguments with family or girl friend, financial problems, etc., 40 per cent in the 16- to 20-year-old age range reported such reactions to two or more problems during the past year, whereas only half of this number did so in the 23- to 24-year-old age group.

To tap feelings of aggression, respondents were asked how angry they felt at obstacles such as red lights in a row, slow traffic, pedestrians crossing illegally, etc. Such feelings were common throughout much of the span observed, but like other measures they subsided by age 24.

A summary score of "impulse expression in driving" was obtained from six such measures. Twice as many respondents aged 16 to 20 scored high on this scale compared with those aged 23 to 24.

Other data on emotional factors are given in Fig. 4. Self-reports of

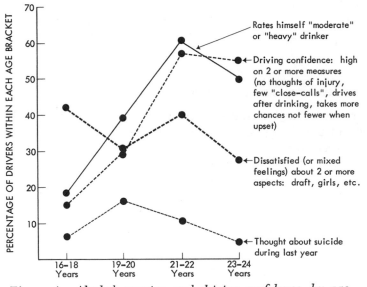

Figure 4. *Alcohol, worries, and driving confidence, by age.*

"moderate" or "heavy" drinking peaked at ages 21 to 22. On questions about satisfaction or dissatisfaction with several aspects of daily living, some problems were found dominant for the 16- to 18-year-old group (e.g., grades and the draft); others emerged at ages 21 to 22 (e.g., problems with girls). A resulting summary score of dissatisfaction with current aspects hence peaked twice—in the first and third age brackets. Thoughts about suicide occurred most often at ages 19 to 20.

In many ways, then, the period between ages 16 and 22 had its frustrations and anxieties, and the automobile was viewed as an outlet for expressing impulses. It is also clear, however, that the eight-year span from ages 16 to 24 was more heterogeneous in emotional character than is customarily assumed.

With increase in age, one observes not only a decline in impulse expression through the automobile, but concomitantly a drop in anxiety about driving, i.e., an increase in driving confidence. This was evident in several ways. Older drivers thought less often about possible injury or death to themselves, to passengers, or other drivers. The number reporting "close calls" decreased with age, indicating a lessened awareness of danger. Older drivers admitted that when angry or upset they took "more" instead of "fewer" chances, i.e., they were less afraid of driving when under tension. Among those who drank, an increasing proportion said that they often drove after drinking, again indicating confidence in ability to handle their liquor. These trends are represented in Fig. 4 by a summary scale; the proportion of confident drivers doubled after age 21.

One wonders whether the lack of confidence before age 21 restrains the impulsiveness of the younger group, such that when accidents occur they are minor. Perhaps the increased confidence after 21—combined with stronger anxieties about job or girls—leads the young adult to risk more serious accidents.

Factors Related to Accidents

Do such age-related characteristics help account for the accidents and moving violations reported by respondents? Fig. 5 shows certain measures as related to accidents.

It is clear that both situational and motivational factors play a part. A strong relationship appeared for a situational factor of exposure, i.e., the number of miles driven last year. Among those drivers with two or more accidents during the year, the proportion who said they drove 15,000 miles or more was triple that of drivers with no accidents.

Motivational factors, however, were also important. Among those with no crashes last year, fewer than half scored high on the summary measure of impulse expression, compared with two thirds of those with two or more accidents.

Thoughts about suicide were slightly higher among those with several accidents. Moderate or heavy drinking was lower among those who had never had an accident. (It was highest, oddly, among those with accidents prior to last year who were, on the whole, an older group.)

No clear connection was observed between accidents and the measures of driving confidence or general dissatisfaction plotted in Fig. 4.

In addition to exposure and emotions, Fig. 5 demonstrates the importance of socio-economic characteristics. Drivers with a high accident rate were more likely to own their own car, to be employed rather than attending school, and (by a factor of 2 or 3) to have only a high-school education (including those who had completed high school only or had dropped out).

Almost by definition persons going to college, and those who are primarily studying rather than working, are preparing for the future in addition to living in the present. Future orientation may thus be linked with a more cautious use of the automobile.

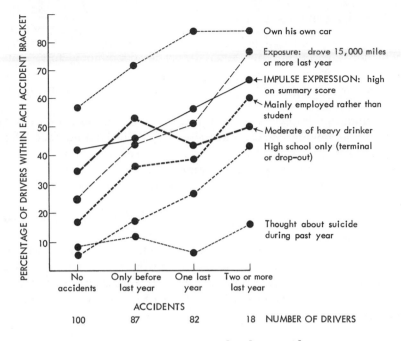

Figure 5. *Selected factors related to accidents.*

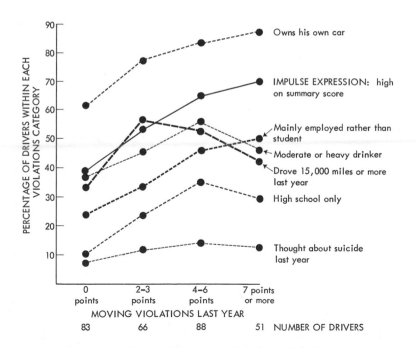

Figure 6. *Selected factors related to violations.*

FACTORS RELATED TO VIOLATIONS

As shown in Fig. 6, emotional impulses were perhaps even more important in violations than were situational or socio-economic factors. Note that young drivers who received tickets by no means drove a great deal; those with a single conviction (2 to 3 violation points) drove more than those with several convictions.

The summary measure of impulse expression distinguished clearly among those with no violation points and those with increasing numbers of points. The component measure of racing or daring with automobiles (curve not shown) was three times as common among those with high violation records as among those with no violations. Alcohol showed a moderate association, with a maximum at 4 to 6 violation points (approximately two convictions during the year). Thoughts of suicide, although not common, doubled with increasing violations.

Socio-economic factors were again involved, although less sharply than for accidents. Drivers with several violations were more likely to be working than studying and more likely to have stopped their education at high school. Both accidents and violations—especially the former—were "working class" phenomena.

COMMENT

Recent literature on human aspects of highway safety has emphasized factors of age, alcohol, and attitudes in the accident process.[7] This report emphasizes an epidemiologic and multifactor approach to a distinct high-risk group, the unmarried male driver less than age 25. Survey research methods were applied to a "normal" population to measure driving characteristics and to test insights gained from recent clinical studies.

The results indicate, as suggested by others, that multiple and complex factors operate in the young driver, even across a relatively narrow age span.[8] For example, drivers with a high accident rate in this category did not necessarily receive tickets for violating traffic laws. Contrary to expectation, fiscal responsibility for one's car accompanied greater risk rather than less. Emotional factors involving use of the automobile as an expressive instrument were important in accidents and particularly in moving violations. Both phenomena were more characteristic of those who stopped their education at high school than of those who went to college.

The suggestion is made—with tentative support from our limited data—that the driver less than 21 years old uses the automobile as an emotional

[7] L. G. Goldstein, "Human Variables in Traffic Accidents: A Digest of Research," *Traffic Safety Res. Rev.*, VIII (March, 1964), 26–31.

[8] Barmack and Payne, *op. cit.;* J. J. Conger, W. C. Miller and R. V. Rainey, "Effects of Driver Education: The Role of Motivation, Intelligence, Social Class and Exposure," *Traffic Safety Res. Rev.*, X (September, 1966), 67–71; W. A. Kemper, *A Teenage Pattern: A Study of 20,000 High School Students and the Interrelationship of their Grades, Cars, and Jobs* (Skokie, Ill.: Accident Prevention Division, Allstate Insurance Companies, 1966).

outlet, but his greater caution (as well as lower mileage) keeps his accidents mild in character. A greater danger may arise after age 21; his increased skill enables the driver to avoid minor accidents, but with growing confidence and exposure he risks more serious accidents that can maim or kill.

The need to validate self-reported accidents and violations against official files is recognized and is under study in a larger probability sample of young licensed drivers throughout the county. It is expected, however, that more traffic offenses may be reported in a confidential interview than are verifiable in the files. Also, the survey approach may yield information on attitudes and habits which are impossible to obtain from official inquiries.

As better roads and automobiles are built, human error becomes more critical. The issue of driver fitness will increasingly involve the physician, not only to certify the physical and psychological limitations of a given patient,[9] but to provide leadership in the community to meet the problem of the young male driver who presents a risk to himself and a hazard to others.

[9] J. A. Waller, "Chronic Medical Conditions and Traffic Safety: Review of the California Experience," *New Eng. J. Med.,* CCLXXIII (December 23, 1965), 1413–1420.

Socialization: High-School Achievement and Vocational Orientation

Daniel A. Gawronski

Claude Mathis

Differences Between Over-Achieving, Normal-Achieving, and Under-Achieving High-School Students

Academic performance falls into one of three categories, above, at, or below capacity. Persons thus classified are known as over-, normal-, and under-achievers. Achievement standards are relative, but nonetheless, teachers for the most part are deeply committed to improving the academic success of both normal- and under-achieving students. In an effort to distinguish among the three groups of achievers, and thereby highlight the behavioral patterns that enhance academic productivity, Gawronski and Mathis here describe the achievement categories in terms of study habits, task persistence, grade consciousness, and personality traits. The discussion clearly indicates that the majority of high-school teachers and administrators would find working with over-achievers a fairly effortless endeavor, but that both parents and school personnel have yet to learn to respond effectively to under-achievers.

THE phenomenon of over-achievement and under-achievement among school populations and the probable correlates of these two achievement patterns has been the subject of a number of studies reported in the literature.[1] The study reported here was designed to determine what differences, if any, exist between high-school seniors classified as over-achievers, normal-achievers, and under-achievers on the basis of a relationship between IQ

FROM *Psychology in the Schools*, II (1965), 152–155. Reprinted by permission of the authors and the publisher.

[1] W. D. Altus, "A College Achiever and Non-Achiever Scale for the Minnesota Multiphasic Personality Inventory," *Journal of Applied Psychology*, XXXII (1948), 385–397; E. Burgess, "Personality Factors of Over- and Under-Achievers in Engineering," *Journal of Educational Psychology*, XLII (1956), 89–99; J. C. Gowan, "The Underachieving Gifted Child: A Problem for Everyone," *Exceptional Children*, XXI (1955), 247–249; M. Krugman and I. H. Impellizzeri, "Identification and Guidance of Under-Achieving Gifted Students in New York City," *Exceptional Children*, XXI (1960), 283–286; W. A. Owens and W. C. Johnson, "Some Measured Personality Traits of Collegiate Underachievers," *Journal of Educational Psychology*, XL (1949), 41–46; M. C. Shaw and J. T. McCuen, "The Onset of Academic Achievement in Bright Children," *Journal of Educational Psychology*, LI (1960), 103–108; C. A. Wedemeyer, "Gifted Achievers and Non-Achievers," *Journal of Higher Education*, XXIV (1953), 25–30.

scores and grade point average, and measures of their attitudes toward study, certain personality traits, and problems which they manifest.

PROCEDURE

A sample of 475 seniors in two urban Indiana high schools was used as the subject. For the total sample of 475 an IQ score was obtained from performance on the Otis Quick Scoring Mental Abilities Test (Gamma Test, Form C). In addition, a grade point average representing grades earned in three years of high-school study in the four course areas of English, science, mathematics, and social science was computed for each student. After the selection of the three subsamples (over-achievers, normal-achievers, and under-achievers), these three groups were given the Brown-Holtzman Survey of Study Habits and Attitudes, the California Psychological Inventory, and the High School Form of the Mooney Problem Check List.

The three groups of under-achievers, over-achievers, and normal achievers were selected by first constructing a scattergram based on the Otis IQ and the collective grade point averages for all 475 senior students. Grade point average was computed by assigning a weight of 100 to "A," 75 to "B," 50 to "C," 25 to "D," and 0 to "F." The mean IQ for the total sample was 99.2 with a standard deviation of 12.1. The mean grade point average for the three year sequence of English, mathematics, science, and social science was 49.8 with a standard deviation of 17.4. On the basis of these means, the scattergram was divided into four sections. Although, on inspection, the scattergram indicated a positive correlation, patterns of atypical groupings were identified. One group was labeled under-achieving on the basis of grade point averages below the mean for the total sample with IQ scores above the total sample mean for IQ. Another group was identified by inspection and labeled over-achieving on the basis of grade point averages above the mean and IQ below the mean. The normal-achieving group was made up of students whose IQ and grade point average most nearly conformed to the regression line indicating high positive correlation.

A ratio of mean grade point average to mean IQ was calculated for each subject in the three groups. The differences between all groups compared on the basis of these ratios were significant at the .01 level of confidence.

From the method described above, 18 over-achievers, 27 normal-achievers, and 25 under-achievers were identified. Responses on the Brown-Holtzman Survey of Study Habits, the California Psychological Inventory, and the Mooney Problem Check List were obtained from these groups.

The Brown-Holtzman Survey of Study Habits and Attitudes was designed to show the relationship between students who do well in academic work and those who do not do as well in such work.[2] The seventy-five items used in the survey are aimed at anxiety before and during examinations and at general personality characteristics. The survey is heavily pointed in the

[2] W. F. Brown and W. H. Holtzman, "A Study-Attitudes Questionnaire for Predicting Academic Success," *Journal of Educational Psychology*, XLVI (1955), 75–84.

direction of assessing motivation for study and attitudes toward academic work.[3]

The California Psychological Inventory was considered an appropriate measure for subjects in high school because it was originally designed for use with normal rather than psychiatrically disturbed subjects. Its use as a research tool has been varied and extensive.[4]

Personal problems were assessed by means of the Mooney Problem Check List. The high school form of this instrument was developed for the purpose of providing students, teachers and counselors with an objective indication of the problems which confront high school students.

Differences between the groups with respect to the measures of study habits, personality traits, and problems were tested by means of *t* ratios.

RESULTS

In comparing under-achievers, normal-achievers, and over-achievers on the basis of responses to the Brown-Holtzman Survey of Study Habits, no significant differences were found between the under-achievers and the normal-achievers. Over-achievers, however, showed significant differences, at or near the .01 level of confidence, in study habits when compared to the normal achievers. Significant differences, at the .01 level, were also obtained between the over-achievers and under-achievers. These significant differences were in the direction of a higher mean score for the over-achieving group indicating better study habits for the over-achievers.

On the basis of these findings and evidence from an analysis of responses to individual items on the testing instrument, the following conclusions seem justified:

1. Over-achievers indicated more effective study habits than either normal-achievers or under-achievers in this study.

2. The study habits of these normal-achievers and under-achievers may not be the same, but testing did not reveal that either group had study habits which were consistently more effective than the other.

3. The differences which existed between over-achievers and normal achievers as well as those between over-achievers and under-achievers, in this study, appeared to be differences directly related to persistence and interest. Over-achievers were relatively more interested in school work and seemed to be more persistent in doing assignments.

4. Over-achievers appeared to be more grade-conscious than either the normal-achievers or under-achievers. Over-achievers in this study seemed to have the desire to work for higher grades.

[3] W. H. Holtzman, W. F. Brown, and W. W. Farquhar, "The Survey of Study Habits and Attitudes: A New Instrument for the Prediction of Academic Success," *Educational and Psychological Measurement*, XIV (1954), 726–732.

[4] L. M. Lessinger and R. A. Martinson, "The Use of the California Psychological Inventory with Gifted Pupils," *Personnel and Guidance Journal*, XXXIX (1961), 572–575; G. Liddle, "The California Psychological Inventory and Certain Personal and Social Factors," *Journal of Educational Psychology*, XLIX (1958), 144–149.

5. These over-achievers planned their study periods and appeared more likely to be systematic in their study procedures than the normal-achievers and under-achievers.

6. Although the findings of this investigation were not considered sufficiently significant to conclude that the problem of under-achievement can be attributed directly to a lack of effective study habits, the evidence does suggest that study habits, both attitudes and methods, play an important role in academic success. Developing effective study habits may well be considered one way to increase the academic success of both normal- and under-achievers.

A comparison of scores on the California Test of Personality indicated a number of statistically significant differences. Over-achievers differed significantly from normal-achievers (.02 level of confidence) on one scale, that of Responsibility (Re), with over-achievers tending toward a higher score. Normal-achievers differed significantly from under-achievers on six scales of the CPI. As a group, the under-achievers had significantly lower mean scores than normal-achievers on Socialization (So), Self-control (Sc), Good Impression (Gi), Achievement via Conformance (Ac), Responsibility (Re), and Flexibility (Fx). So, Sc, and Gi represent differences significant at the .01 level of confidence, Ac at the .02 level, and Re and Fx at the .05 level. A comparison of under-achievers and over-achievers produced significant differences on Responsibility (Re), Socialization (So), Good Impression (Gi), Achievement via Conformance (Ac), Self-control (Sc), Flexibility (F), and Dominance (Do). Re, So, Gi, and Ac represent differences significant at the .01 level, Sc and Fx at the .02 level, and Do at the .05 level. All group means for these differences were higher for the over-achievers than for the under-achievers with the exception of Flexibility (Fx), on which the under-achievers tended to score higher.

An examination of individual items and trait descriptions for the CPI scales suggest the following observations concerning differences between over-achievers, normal-achievers, and under-achievers as defined in this study:

1. Over-achievers in this study seemed more responsible than normal-achievers. They appeared to be more conscientious in pursuit of high standards. They tended to plan their activities more carefully and appeared more efficient and resourceful in carrying out their plans than did the normal-achievers.

2. Under-achievers in this study seemed to have more difficulty than normal-achievers with self-regulation. Under-achievers appeared more impulsive and uninhibited. They tended to overemphasize personal pleasure and self-gain.

3. The interpersonal relationships of these under-achievers tended to be less satisfying than those of normal-achievers. Under-achievers in this study seemed less capable of creating a good impression. They appeared generally less cooperative, less sociable, and less diligent in their efforts to attain socially acceptable goals.

4. The CPI responses of normal-achievers in this study suggested that they were more socially mature than the under-achievers. Under-achievers seemed less capable of relating to others in an unselfish way. They enjoyed both home and school less than the normal-achievers. Under-achievers seemed from their CPI responses to be more defensive and resentful. They appeared less dependable than the normal-achievers.

5. Under-achievers, in this study, tended to be characterized by a pattern of disorganization under pressure, especially pressure to conform.

6. These under-achievers were somewhat less structured in their mode of living. They appeared to be more adventurous, and more rejecting of authority, custom, and tradition, when these interfered with their pursuit of personal pleasure.

7. Over-achievers in this study were more accepting of authority than under-achievers. These over-achievers seemed more socially mature, and unlike under-achievers, indicated that they received satisfaction in their interpersonal relationships. Responses of the over-achievers suggested that they tended to cooperate more effectively with others and had a higher regard for the rights and feelings of others than did the under-achievers. Under-achievers seemed to be motivated more by personal bias and the desire for personal gain.

8. The responses of these over-achievers to the CPI indicated that they had a much higher regard for intellectual achievement than did the under-achievers.

9. The under-achievers tended to be pessimistic about their future.

10. The over-achievers in this study seemed to have a greater capacity for self-regulation than did under-achievers. These over-achievers tended to be better adjusted to externally oriented regulations, and they seemed to find greater satisfaction in following planned procedures.

11. Under-achievers in this study showed less desire to create a good impression. Over-achievers, on the other hand, seemed more sensitive to the mutual benefits of cooperative action.

12. The over-achievers indicated a greater capacity for leadership than did the under-achievers.

Although this study produced no evidence to directly answer this question, the relationship between the CPI traits which describe the under-achiever in this study and the divergent intellect appear, on the surface, to be well pronounced.

The comparison of responses on the Mooney Problem Check List produced no statistically significant results. Several trends in responses were noted, however, although they were not supported statistically in terms of significance in differences between groups. Normal-achievers indicated more frequently that they did not have enough time for their studies and that they had trouble keeping their mind on their studies. Under-achievers reported fewer problems than over-achievers or normal-achievers on this test.

SUMMARY

IQ scores and grade point averages were obtained from 475 senior students in two urban high schools. On the basis of relationships between these two indices, 18 over-achievers, 27 normal-achievers, and 25 under-achievers were identified. The Brown-Holtzman Survey of Study Habits and Attitudes, the California Psychological Inventory, and the Mooney Problem Check List were administered to these three groups. Over-achievers differed significantly from normal-achievers and under-achievers in expressing a pattern of better study habits. Over-achievers differed significantly from normal-achievers in Responsibility, with over-achievers having a higher score. Over-achievers and normal-achievers differed significantly from under-achievers in Socialization, Self-control, Good Impression, Achievement via Conformance, Responsibility, and Flexibility. The direction of the difference was toward lower scores for the under-achieving group, with the exception of Flexibility, with under-achievers scoring higher. In addition, over-achievers scored significantly higher in Dominance than under-achievers. No significant differences in problems stated on the check list were obtained.

David A. Kolb

Achievement Motivation Training for Under-Achieving High-School Boys

To assume adult responsibilities, adolescent boys must possess strong achievement needs and abilities to sustain themselves while working toward remote goals. Youths acquire these attributes routinely during socialization, but a sizeable proportion of American youth, especially those whose socializing experiences are haphazard, fail to acquire sufficient achievement drive. An adequate solution to the problem is still unavailable; however, in the selection below, Kolb describes a promising training program. Under-achieving boys were counseled in achievement "constructs" or "symbols" by being taught the scoring system of a widely-used projective test, devised earlier to measure magnitude of achievement motivation. The trainees negotiated contracts, played racing-car games, indulged in group discussions, and offered analyses of "Insight Stories." Kolb reasons that once boys understand how to think achievement-wise they may be motivated to act accordingly. The results, after a one and one-half year follow-up, were equivocal, but Kolb's basic approach is hopeful, for it specifies operationally which cues are to be discerned and learned in developing achievement motivation. The program is particularly novel in that it attempts to bring about affective as well as conceptual modifications in personality structure.

A SUBSTANTIAL body of research using widely differing measurement techniques has indicated that under-achieving students are low in their motivation and/or concern for achievement.[1] In addition, a number of studies have demonstrated a small but positive significant relationship between achievement motivation and academic performance in high school.[2]

FROM *Journal of Personality and Social Psychology*, II (1965), 783–792. Reprinted by permission of the author and the American Psychological Association.

[1] E. Burgess, "Personality Factors of Over- and Under-Achievers in Engineering," *Journal of Educational Psychology*, XLVII (1956), 89–99; H. F. Garrett, "A Review and Interpretation of Investigations of Factors Related to Scholastic Success in Colleges of Arts and Sciences and Teachers Colleges," *Journal of Experimental Education*, XVIII (1949), 91–158; G. G. Gebhart and D. P. Hoyt, "Personality Needs of Under- and Over-Achieving Freshman," *Journal of Applied Psychology*, XLII (1958), 125–128.

[2] J. W. Atkinson (ed.), *Motives in Fantasy, Action, and Society* (Princeton, N.J.: Van Nostrand, 1958); D. C. McClelland, J. W. Atkinson, R. A. Clark, and E. L. Lowell, *The Achievement Motive* (New York: Appleton-Century-Crofts, 1953); C. A. Uhlinger and M. W. Stephens, "Relation of Achievement Motivation to Academic Achievement in Students of Superior Ability," *Journal of Educational Psychology*, LI (1960), 259–266.

The present study tests the effect of a training program designed to increase concern for academic achievement in a group of under-achieving high-school boys. The content of the training program derives from the research on achievement motivation carried on by McClelland and his associates.[3] A study by Burris [4] suggests that counseling centered around a student's n Achievement score can produce significant changes in his academic performance. Burris found that the grades of college under-achievers who received n Achievement counseling improved significantly more than those of similar students who received nondirective counseling.

The training techniques used in this program stem from four different experimental backgrounds.

1. Identification: The identification models of Kagan and Hill [5] maintain that learning takes place through emulation of effective role models, this learning being reinforced through vicarious affective experience. Goldberg [6] has found that identification with a positive role model seems to be associated with academic improvement in under-achieving boys.

2. Expectation: There is a growing body of research which indicates that the expectations held by the experimenter and subject [7] or the therapist and patient [8] can measurably affect the outcome of the experiment or therapy. In this study the research team model developed by Schwitzgebel and Slack [9] was adapted. Schwitzgebel [10] has found the research team model useful in reducing juvenile delinquency.

3. Ideomotor response: The hypothesis that thought determines action has a long history in psychology. Braid maintained that an idea firmly implanted in the mind during hypnosis later issues into behavior. Through the influence of Herbart, nineteenth century educational psychology promoted the copybook to implant in children's minds the "right ideas" which would lead to "right action." [11] William James formulated a think-talk-act

---

[3] Atkinson, *op. cit.;* D. C. McClelland, *The Achieving Society* (Princeton, N.J.: Van Nostrand, 1961); McClelland *et al., op. cit.*

[4] R. Burris, "The Effect of Counseling on Achievement Motivation" (Unpublished Ph.D. dissertation, Indiana University, 1958).

[5] J. Kagan, "The Concept of Identification," *Psychological Review,* LXV (1958), 296–305; W. F. Hill, "Learning Theory and the Acquisition of Values," *Psychological Review,* LXVII (1960), 317–331.

[6] M. Goldberg, "A Three-Year Experimental Program at Dewitt Clinton High School to Help Bright Under-Achievers," *High Points* (January, 1959), 5–35.

[7] M. T. Orne, "On the Social Psychology of the Psychological Experiment: With Particular Reference to Demand Characteristics and Their Implications," *American Psychologist,* XVII (1962), 776–783; R. Rosenthal, "On the Social Psychology of the Psychological Experiment: The Experimenter's Hypothesis as the Unintended Determinant of Experimental Results," *American Scientist,* LI (1963), 268–283.

[8] A. Goldstein, *Therapist-Patient Expectancies in Psychotherapy* (New York: Pergamon Press, 1962).

[9] R. Schwitzgebel and C. Slack, *A Handbook: Reducing Adolescent Crime in Your Community* (Cambridge, Mass.: Authors, 1960).

[10] R. Schwitzgebel, "Analysis and Evaluation of the Experimenter-Subject Role Relationship in the Reduction of Known Male Adolescent Crime" (Unpublished Ph.D. dissertation, Harvard University, 1962).

[11] G. W. Allport, "The Historical Background of Modern Social Psychology," *The Handbook of Social Psychology,* ed. G. Murphy (I; Reading, Mass.: Addison-Wesley,

model recently elaborated by Leary.[12] Perhaps the most sophisticated modern statement of this theory is George Kelly's [13] role construct theory. He maintains that behavior is determined in large measure by the way a person construes the world. The Burris [14] study suggests that teaching under-achievers achievement constructs and encouraging them to think in achievement terms can lead to better performance in school. In the current study the technique is to implant the idea of achievement by teaching the students the n Achievement scoring system and to observe the results in action, that is, academic performance.

4. Games: The use of games to simulate life situations is becoming more and more prevalent in the training of managers and administrators, military leaders, diplomats, and others requiring complex skills.[15] These games provide a well-defined psychologically safe situation where men can try out new ways of thinking and behaving. In this study the game concept was used in two ways: in actual games designed to teach achievement skills [16] and as an analytic device in counseling to aid in understanding real-life problems.[17]

METHOD

Setting

The Achievement Motivation Training Program (AMTP) was carried out as part of a summer school for under-achieving high-school boys held at Brown University. The summer school was designed to give stimulating instruction using outstanding teachers and exciting subject matter. In addition, the planners of the program hoped that exposure to college living and positive college role models (counselors were chosen to be outstanding in both scholarship and athletics) would increase the under-achievers' desire to go to college.

The project was 6 weeks long, beginning in late June and ending in the first week of August. The schedule was a 5-day week of classes in history,

---

1954), pp. 3–56.

[12] T. Leary, "Thinking, Talking, and Doing" (Unpublished Manuscript, Harvard University Press, 1961).

[13] G. Kelly, *The Psychology of Personal Constructs* (I; New York: W. W. Norton Co., 1955).

[14] Burris, *op. cit.*

[15] O. Benson, "Simulation of International Relations and Diplomacy," *Computer Applications in the Behavioral Sciences*, ed. H. Borko (Englewood Cliffs, N.J.: Prentice-Hall, 1962), 574–575; M. Kibbe, C. Croft, and B. Nanus, *Management Games: A New Technique for Executive Development* (New York: Reinhold Publishing Corp., 1961); R. C. Sprowls, "Business Simulation," *Computer Applications in the Behavioral Sciences*, ed. H. Borko (Englewood Cliffs, N.J.: Prentice-Hall, 1962), pp. 556–573.

[16] G. H. Litwin and J. A. Ciarlo, *Achievement Motivation and Risk-Taking in a Business Setting, Technical Report* (Ossining, N.Y.: General Electric Company, Behavioral Research Service, 1961).

[17] T. Leary, "How to Change Behavior" (Paper read at the XIVth International Congress of Applied Psychology, Copenhagen, 1961).

English, and mathematics, with weekend recreation at various parks and beaches in the area. The boys lived together on three floors of a college dormitory on the campus and ate in the college dining hall.

Subjects

Fifty-seven boys drawn mainly from public and private schools in New England were enrolled in the project. These were selected from 95 applicants on the basis of IQ (120 or higher) and school grade average (C or lower). Boys with serious reading defects were generally not admitted. Attempts were made to screen out applicants with serious psychiatric problems. Two general classes of students were recruited: boys from homes where sufficient interest, parental background, and finances favored college entrance and boys from homes where these were lacking. Parents of the first type were requested to pay tuition, room, and board. Lower-class boys were granted scholarships to cover their expenses. About half of the participants received scholarships.

A breakdown by social class based on occupation [18] shows 14 boys in Class 1, 11 in Class 2, 11 in Class 3, 5 in Class 4, 6 in Class 5, 2 in Class 6, and 1 in Class 7. The mean IQ score (WISC) of the boys was 126 (range: 109–149) and their mean school grade average was D to D+ (range: F–C+). The average year in school was 9.0 (range: 7–11) and their average age was 14 years (range: 12–16). Stanford Achievement Test scores showed them to be at an average grade level of 10.9 (range: 8.8–12.7).

Experimental Design

Twenty of the 57 students were randomly assigned to the fourth floor of the dormitory. This group received the AMTP in addition to their regular summer school schedule. The remaining 37 students received only the regular summer school program.

Subjects were tested in the following manner.

PRETESTING. On the second day of the summer school, 57 subjects were given the following tests: the Test of Insight, Form A (this test was an adaptation of the form used by French,[19] and was scored for n Achievement according to the published scoring manuals—Atkinson); [20] the Stanford Achievement Test; the Taylor Manifest Anxiety (MA) scale; and the Mandler-Sarason Test Anxiety Scale (TAS). In addition the following data were collected for each subject: age, year in school, IQ (WISC), 1961 school grade average, and parents' socio-economic status based on father's occupation.[21]

[18] W. L. Warner, M. Meeker, and K. Eells, *Social Class in America* (Chicago: Science Research Associates, 1949).

[19] E. G. French, "Development of a Measure of Complex Motivation," *Motives in Fantasy, Action, and Society*, ed. J. W. Atkinson (Princeton, N.J.: D. Van Nostrand, 1958), pp. 242–248.

[20] Atkinson, *op. cit.*

[21] Warner *et al., op. cit.*

AUGUST 1961 POST-TEST. On the next-to-last day of the project, subjects were given the following tests: the Test of Insight, Form B, a parallel form; the Stanford Achievement Test; the MA scale; and the TAS. In addition all subjects received grades in each of the three subjects taught in the summer school. AMTP members were ranked on their participation in the AMTP and assessed in moderate risk-taking ability using the Litwin-Ciarlo [22] Business Game.

JANUARY 1962 FOLLOW-UP. The midyear school grades were collected for all boys who completed the project.

APRIL 1962 FOLLOW-UP. At this time 33 of the summer-school participants were selected on the basis of proximity to Brown University to return for a testing session. Twenty-seven boys returned (experimentals = 10, controls = 17) and were given the Test of Insight, Form A.

JANUARY 1963 FOLLOW-UP. School grades were collected for the Spring 1962 semester. Unfortunately these were available for only 37 boys (experimentals = 12, controls = 25).

The initial, post-test, and follow-up Insight Tests scored for n Achievement were included to determine whether experimental subjects would learn and retain the achievement scoring categories better than controls. School grades and Stanford Achievement Test scores were chosen as indicators of achievement-oriented performance. WISC scores, social class, MA scale, and TAS scores were included as potential predictors of change, for example, high MA scale subjects might change more than low MA scale subjects, though no specific hypotheses were made.

To check for n Achievement scoring reliability, a sample of 30 Tests of Insight (10 from each testing period) was scored by a trained scorer not connected with the training program. Scores thusly obtained correlated (rho) .85 with the experimenter's scores.

School grades were all converted to a numerical scale: A = 95, B = 85, C = 75, D = 65, E or F = 55.

Experimental Condition: The Achievement Motivation Training Program

The experimenter lived in the dormitory with the AMTP boys and served as their counselor. The experimenter behaved in a manner consistent with the behavior of a person with high n Achievement, so that the subjects would have a visible high n Achievement role model to imitate.

The procedure changed from the use of external rules and discipline to internal control and personal responsibility: Structured classes and required meetings gradually gave way to individual appointments made at a subject's request and optional group meetings. Responsibility for running the fourth floor and the AMTP was gradually given to the boys themselves. After a few initial required meetings the boys were free to choose how much they wanted to participate in the program. This policy reflected the research team contract (see below) and was further encouraged by the time limitations of the experimenter. It was felt that time would be more profitably

---

[22] Litwin and Ciarlo, *op. cit.*

spent working with interested students than trying to involve those who were not interested.

Initially the boys met with the experimenter in a classroom twice a week for one hour. As the weeks progressed this meeting time was changed to better fit the summer-school schedule and meet the needs of the boys. The program is described below in detail.

FIRST SESSION. The first session was concerned with negotiating a contract. The role relationship emulated was that of a team doing collaborative research on the problem of under-achieving. The aim was to involve the students in the hypothesis that the course would improve academic performance and achievement motivation thereby creating in them the expectation that the course would work. The essence of the contract was this:

> We at Harvard have some ideas about how to help the under-achiever play the school game better. Our goal is to try out these ideas to see if they work, and to discover new ways to prevent the problems associated with under-achievement. If you will work with us we think that we can in return, introduce you to some strategies which will help you in school and, more generally, in life. Whether you want to do this or not is entirely your decision. Your involvement with this program is not required; you can participate to the extent to which you feel it is useful to you.

After negotiating the contract, the characteristics of a person with high achievement motivation were described. Subjects were told that the person with high n Achievement has three major characteristics: he likes and chooses to take personal responsibility for his actions, he takes moderate risks, and he likes and attempts to obtain knowledge of the results of his actions.[23] The remainder of the session was spent describing the racing car game the subjects would play in the next session and suggesting how the characteristics of the person with high achievement motivation would be valuable to a racing driver.

SECOND SESSION. The entire second session was spent playing the race game. The game consisted of a miniature race track around which small electric cars could be driven. The "racers" each had a transformer which controlled the speed of his car. The boys raced against the clock two at a time. The boy in each pair with the fastest time was declared the winner. If by going too fast the boy left the track three times he was disqualified. As they raced the boys were asked to keep in mind the characteristics of the achieving personality in relation to the race, for example, (a) personal responsibility— How involved am I in the race? Do I care if I win or not? (b) moderate risk taking—How much of the time did I take too much of a risk? How often was I too cautious? (c) using knowledge of results—How well did I use my practice trials to judge my ability?

THIRD SESSION. This session began with an introduction to the process of assessing motivation by analysis of thought.[24] The boys were then shown

[23] Atkinson, *op. cit.;* McClelland, *op. cit.;* McClelland *et al., op. cit.*
[24] Atkinson, *op. cit.*

how their n Achievement scores related to their performance in the racing game (boys with low n Achievement tended to be disqualified).

The discussion then turned to time orientation. During the previous evening the boys had estimated a 30-second interval on a stopwatch. Subjects with high n Achievement tended to see time as passing more quickly than subjects with low n Achievement. Further discussion centered around future orientation, delay of gratification, and ability to control impulses.

FOURTH SESSION. This session marked the beginning of the shift from structured lecture meetings to a program oriented more toward the individual. In essence the session was a renegotiation of the contract. The group's commitment to the "research team" model was reaffirmed, emphasizing the boy's role in determining the nature of the course. The follow-up and the experimenter's interest in knowing the boys' future grades were discussed.

The last half of the session was spent discussing how thought influences action. The think-talk-act model was explained: If you think and talk in a certain way you will act that way. In particular the direct relationship of achievement thinking to achievement behaviors was discussed. At the end of this session the boys were given n Achievement scoring manuals.

FIFTH SESSION. This session was devoted to a group discussion on the analysis of Test of Insight stories. Example stories from the protocols of control students were read to the class and discussed. Following this discussion the students were given their own Insight test protocols. They were offered help in scoring their protocols for n Achievement. The expert scoring was given to them upon request. The remainder of the hour was spent in teaching the n Achievement scoring system.

SIXTH SESSION. A major theme that occurs over and over in the Insight Tests is a conflict between achievement and affiliation goals.[25] One of these stories is quoted below. (Written to Test of Insight, Form A, Story 4, "Bill may not be the best student in his class, but he is the friendliest and the best-liked.")

> He fools around a lot to make friends and doesn't do his school work the best he can. He didn't take school seriously and just had a lot of fun. He thinks more about making friends than about getting his homework done. He probably wants to be a mechanic. His marks will keep slipping down and he won't get a good job when he gets out of school.

The session was focused on this conflict and on learning to take realistic risks. An article on how to assess risks was given to the class members. The group discussed risk taking in terms of planning goals and strategies in life situations, making conscious decisions, taking action to attain desired goals, and knowing one's own ability. The Litwin-Ciarlo Business Game (discussed below) which they would all play later that week was described.

INFORMAL SESSIONS. Beginning on Thursday of the fifth week, the group

---

[25] T. Parsons, "The School Class as a Social System—Some of Its Functions in American Society," *Harvard Educational Review*, XXIX (1959), 297–316.

began meeting every evening on the lawn on an informal basis. Attendance at these sessions was not required and subjects could come and go as they pleased. The boys wanted this arrangement so they could discuss how the techniques they had learned could be applied to specific problems in their lives. These discussions were intense and seemed to be of considerable benefit to those who attended. Approximately 12 out of the 20 boys attended regularly. The remainder had more or less dropped by the wayside.

INDIVIDUAL COUNSELING SESSIONS.   Counseling on an individual basis was done informally. The problems discussed in individual sessions were usually concerned with the application of principles talked about in class to the life of the boy. These ranged from using the principles of moderate risk taking to playing a better tennis game, to setting realistic goals in study tasks, to staying out of arguments at home.

LITWIN-CIARLO BUSINESS GAME.   This training device was perhaps the most popular aspect of the whole project. It is designed to train a person to take moderate risks and use knowledge of results, and to assess his capacity to do so. The subject in this game plays the role of a manufacturer and actually builds the products he contracts for with tinkertoys. He is told that he is the head of a company just starting to manufacture three new products— a missile, an atomic cannon, and an airplane. He must order sufficient parts to build each of these products and actually try to assemble them in three separate 5-minute production periods. Only completed units are purchased, so if he orders too many he loses what is invested in the leftover parts, and if he orders too few his profit is lower than it should have been. The subject makes his decisions and assesses risks using two types of information: printed statistics giving prices, profits, and average construction times for each product and his own timed practice construction trials for each product. The game takes an hour to play and gives scores on risk taking and use of past performance as an indicator of future performance. A couple of boys learned to run the game and did a large part of the administration for the other boys.

RESULTS

Eight of the original 57 boys were not included in the final data analysis. Five of these boys (4 controls and 1 experimental) were dropped from the summer school for either disciplinary or emotional problems. The other 3 boys (2 experimentals and 1 control) completed the school but were so withdrawn or rebellious that they were rated unsatisfactory in all three of their courses.

Initial Comparisons of Experimental and Control Groups

To determine the success of random assignments, the experimental and control groups were compared on all variables in the study. Using the Mann-Whitney U test, p values were greater than .20 (two-tailed) on the following variables: year in school, age, IQ (WISC), n Achievement, 1961 school grade average, average Stanford Achievement Test score, *MA* scale, and TAS. A chi-square comparison of the two groups by social class (Classes 1 and 2 versus Classes 3–7) yielded a *p* value of .50.

Comparison of Experimental and Control Group Changes

In Table 1 the n Achievement change scores are reported for experimental

Table 1 *Change in n Achievement*

	M *Change*		
Testing Intervals	EXPERI-MENTAL GROUP	CONTROL GROUP	*p*[a]
Pretest to August 1961 post-test	6.72 (n = 18)	−.34 (n = 32)	< .005
Pretest to April 1962 follow-up	4.4 (n = 10)	−3.8 (n = 17)	< .025

[a] Mann-Whitney *U* test, one-tailed probability.

and control subjects, pretest to August post-test and pretest to April post-test for the 27 subjects who attended that follow-up. It is assumed that this latter group represents an unbiased sampling of the total summer-school population since they were selected on nonacademic criteria—proximity of their home to the testing site. Note that the experimental group shows significantly greater increases in n Achievement score in both periods, indicating that experimentals both learned and retained the n Achievement scoring system better than the untrained controls.

Comparison of experimental and control changes on the Stanford Achievement Test from the pretest to August post-test indicated no significant differences either for total score or any subtest score although in most cases experimentals tended to improve more than controls. The two anxiety scales (TAS and *MA*) also showed no significant differential changes. An analysis of the final grades that the boys received in the summer school showed no significant differences.

In comparing changes in school grades, each boy received, whenever possible, a change score for five subject areas: English, science, foreign language, mathematics, and history/civics, plus a change score for his total semester grade average. Change scores for the subject areas were the average grade that the boy received in the courses he took in that area. Many times these subject change scores were not available because the boy would not have taken a given course in both the pretest and the follow-up periods. In Table 2, change scores for experimental and control groups are compared for the January 1962 follow-up and the January 1963 follow-up. Note that while in the January 1962 follow-up experimental boys had not improved significantly more in grade average than the control boys, by

Table 2   Change in School Grades: All Boys

| School Subjects | M Change | | p [a] |
	EXPERI-MENTAL GROUP	CONTROL GROUP	
Pretest to January 1962 follow-up			
Total grade average	6.3 (n = 18)	4.1 (n = 31)	
English	8.3 (n = 18)	3.1 (n = 30)	< .03
Science	−4.0 (n = 10)	7.0 (n = 21)	< .02 [b]
Foreign language	8.1 (n = 12)	5.1 (n = 14)	
Mathematics	6.1 (n = 17)	4.8 (n = 28)	
History/civics	6.3 (n = 7)	2.9 (n = 20)	
Pretest to January 1963 follow-up			
Total grade average	7.1 (n = 12)	2.6 (n = 24)	< .05
English	8.7 (n = 12)	4.7 (n = 23)	
Science	3.5 (n = 6)	9.2 (n = 15)	
Foreign language	7.8 (n = 7)	−0.9 (n = 10)	
Mathematics	1.7 (n = 12)	3.8 (n = 20)	
History/civics	9 (n = 8)	4.9 (n = 15)	

[a] Mann-Whitney U test, one-tailed probability.
[b] Contrary to prediction; two-tailed probability.

the January 1963 follow-up the experimental group's improvements in grade average were significantly greater than the control group's improvements. In addition, the mean experimental improvement increased from 1962 to 1963 while the mean control group improvement decreased in this period. In the subject areas, experimentals improved significantly more than controls in English while controls improved significantly more than experimentals in science in the January 1962 follow-up (contrary to prediction). None of these differences held in the January 1963 follow-up.

In the 1963 follow-up, grades were available for only 73 per cent of the subjects in the 1962 follow-up. One might question the validity of the 1963 change scores since ordinarily one would expect students who improved least to drop out in later follow-ups. An analysis of the 13 dropouts' change scores in the 1962 follow-up showed a nonsignificant trend in this direction—8 were below the 1962 total mean change and 5 were above. These boys, however, were evenly divided between the experimental and control groups (experimental = 2/4, control = 3/4). Thus we would suspect that any artificial increase in average change scores would not affect the experimental and control groups differentially.

Effect of Social Class

·As described in the section on method, the boys in the project were of two types—boys from homes where interest, parental background, and finances favored college entrance (i.e., high SES boys) and boys from homes where these were lacking (low SES boys). Because of these differences, all of the change comparisons were made by social class (high SES = Classes 1 and 2, low SES = classes 3–7). In Table 3 are reported the changes in n Achieve-

Table 3   Change in n Achievement by Social Class

| Testing Interval | M Change | | p [a] |
	EXPERI-MENTAL GROUP	CONTROL GROUP	
High social class (1 and 2)			
Pretest to August post-test	8.4 ($n = 9$)	−0.3 ($n = 9$)	< .05
Pretest to April follow-up	5.7 ($n = 7$)	−5.8 ($n = 5$)	< .025
Low social class (3 through 7)			
Pretest to August post-test	5.0 ($n = 9$)	−.6 ($n = 20$)	< .01
Pretest to April follow-up	0.3 ($n = 3$)	−3.2 ($n = 12$)	< .10

[a] Mann-Whitney U test, one-tailed probability.

ment score divided by social classes. In lower- and upper-class groups, experimental subjects increase significantly more than control subjects.

While Mann-Whitney U tests indicated no significant differential changes in Stanford Achievement Test scores, MA scale, TAS, or summer-school grades, there were differential changes in school grades in both the January 1962 and January 1963 follow-up periods. These effects are reported in Tables 4 and 5 for the high SES and low SES groups, respectively.

The total grade average of high SES experimentals improved significantly more than controls in the January 1962 follow-up and in the January 1963 follow-up. In addition, high SES experimentals improved significantly more than controls in English and mathematics in 1962. No subject areas were significant in the 1963 follow-up.

Table 4 Change in School Grades: High Social Class Boys

	M Change		
School Subjects	EXPERI-MENTAL GROUP	CONTROL GROUP	p [a]
Pretest to January 1962 follow-up			
Total grade	9.5	1.8	< .005
average	($n = 10$)	($n = 13$)	
English	9.4	0.7	< .01
	($n = 10$)	($n = 13$)	
Science	0.5	4.4	
	($n = 3$)	($n = 8$)	
Foreign language	10.5	10.0	
	($n = 8$)	($n = 3$)	
Mathematics	13.0	−12.0	< .01
	($n = 10$)	($n = 11$)	
History/civics	7.2	4.6	
	($n = 4$)	($n = 7$)	
Pretest to January 1963 follow-up			
Total grade	11.9	1.9	< .05
average	($n = 6$)	($n = 11$)	
English	9.5	3.7	
	($n = 6$)	($n = 11$)	
Science	8.8	7.1	
	($n = 5$)	($n = 8$)	
Foreign language	9.8	−2.0	
	($n = 5$)	($n = 8$)	
Mathematics	11.2	3.0	
	($n = 6$)	($n = 10$)	
History/civics	6.0	5.2	
	($n = 4$)	($n = 6$)	

[a] Mann-Whitney U test, one-tailed probability.

The trend reported for high SES experimentals was reversed for low SES experimentals. In most cases they improved less than control subjects although these improvements only approached significance in science and mathematics in the 1963 follow-up. Low SES subjects showed no significant differential changes in total grade average in either follow-up period.

In Figure 1 the total grade averages are plotted for high SES and low SES experimentals and controls for the initial pretest and the two follow-up periods. The data reported in Figure 1 do not correspond exactly with that presented in Tables 4 and 5 since the tables use only subjects for whom change scores were available whereas the figure uses all subjects in each testing period to obtain the mean score. The high SES experimental group is the only group to show an improvement in grade average in the 1963

Table 5 Change in School Grades: Low Social Class Boys

	M *Change*		
School Subjects	EXPERI-MENTAL GROUP	CONTROL GROUP	p[a]
Pretest to January 1962 follow-up			
Total grade	2.4	5.7	
average	($n = 8$)	($n = 18$)	
English	7.0	4.8	
		($n = 17$)	
Science	−10.7	15.8	$< .10$
	($n = 4$)	($n = 14$)	
Foreign language	−3.2	3.7	
		($n = 11$)	
Mathematics		8.6	$< .10$
	($n = 7$)	($n = 17$)	
History/civics	5.0	3.4	
	($n = 3$)	($n = 11$)	
Pretest to January 1963 follow-up			
Total grade	2.3	3.2	
average	($n = 6$)	($n = 13$)	
English	7.8	6.5	
	($n = 6$)	($n = 13$)	
Science [b]			
Foreign language [b]			
Mathematics	−7.6	4.4	$< .05$
	($n = 6$)	($n = 10$)	
History/civics	12.0	4.7	
	($n = 4$)	($n = 9$)	

[a] Mann-Whitney U test, two-tailed probability (contrary to prediction).

[b] Not enough cases for comparison.

follow-up. This group shows a 12-point increase in grade average in the 1963 follow-up, moving from a D− to a C average.

Similar change comparisons were made with the data divided into high MA and low MA, high TAS and low TAS, high IQ and low IQ, but no significant differences were found.

Analysis of Change within the Experimental Group

To analyze patterns of change within the experimental group, seven variables were intercorrelated: three predictor variables—social class, initial n Achievement score, and WISC IQ score; three participation variables—ranking on course participation by the counselor, a moderate risk-taking score from the Business Game, and the change in n Achievement score from

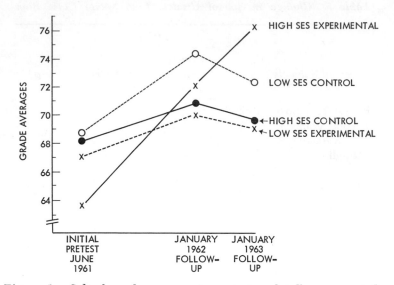

Figure 1. *School grade average in pretest and follow-up periods.*

the pretest to the August post-test; and the criterion variable—change in school grades. Changes in grades in the January 1962 follow-up were used since using 1963 changes would too much reduce the already small sample. These correlations are reported in Table 6.

None of the three predictor variables showed significant correlations with

Table 6   Experimental Group Intercorrelations (n = 18)

	Social Class	Initial n Achieve- ment	IQ	Par- ticipa- tion	Busi- ness Game	n Achieve- ment Change	Change in Grades
Predictor variables							
Social class [a]	22	—					
Initial n Achievement							
WISC IQ	−32	−31	—				
Participation variables							
Course participation [b]	−03	−02	−01	—			
Business Game score	−15	06	34	15	—		
Change in n Achieve- ment [c]	11	02	35	58°°	25	—	
Criterion variable							
Change in grades [d]	32	−30	20	27	63°°°	42°	—

[a] Scores inverted for ease of interpretation: 7 = high SES, 1 = low SES.
[b] All rank-order correlations.
[c] Change to August post-test.
[d] Change to January 1962 follow-up.
° $p < .10$, one-tailed.
°° $p < .02$, one-tailed.
°°° $p < .01$, one-tailed.

change in school grades although when SES was divided into high and low groups as was done for control group comparisons, a median test showed that high SES boys tended to improve more than low SES boys ($x^2 = 7.29$, $p < .01$). None of the predictor variables were significantly related to participation variables, although there was a weak relationship between IQ and Business Game and IQ and n Achievement change.

Two of the participation variables can be seen as measures of how well the boys learned major themes of the course. The Business Game score gives an indication of the boy's ability to take moderate risks and use the results of his previous experience (i.e., feedback) at the end of the course. This score correlated .63 with change in school grades. The change in n Achievement score gives an indication of how well the boy learned to think like a person with high need for achievement. This score correlated .42 with change in grades. The multiple correlation coefficient of Business Game score and change in n Achievement with change in school grades was .68 ($p < .025$, one-tailed). The third participation variable, the participation ranking by the counselor, did not correlate significantly with the criterion, although it did with change in n Achievement.

Discussion

The fact that improvement in experimental group grades differs significantly from control group improvement in the 1963 but not the 1962 follow-up seems to be based mainly on a decrease in the control group improvement score in 1963. This would suggest that while the summer school alone gave some boost to the grades, there is a tendency for this effect to decay over time, while the addition of the AMTP to the summer program seems to promote a more permanent and perhaps increasing improvement in school grade average. This effect is seen most strikingly when the data are analyzed by social class (see Figure 1).

The significant differences in subject areas, especially when controls improve more than experimentals, are difficult to explain with the data available.

The strong differential effect that social class had on change in grades requires some examination. The fact that only high social class experimental boys seemed to benefit significantly from the AMTP might be explained in two ways.

One might reason that the course was designed to appeal more to boys from the upper classes where education is valued more than to lower-class boys.[26] The course was, in fact, pitched at a rather intellectual level and expounded high educational values—Harvard, research, and good grades. But if this argument were so, one would expect social class to be positively correlated with the participation variables—course participation ranking, Business Game score, and change in n Achievement. As is indicated in Table

[26] J. A. Kahl, "Adolescent Ambition" (Unpublished Ph.D. dissertation, Harvard University, 1952).

6, this is not the case. In addition, *both* high and low SES experimentals increased significantly more than controls in n Achievement score.

The alternative explanation is not based on the differential reaction of high and low SES boys to the AMTP but on the different environments to which they returned. An under-achieving upper-class boy finds himself in sharp dissonance with his subculture. There is constant pressure for him to achieve and do well in school. The underachiever from the lower classes is not pushed by such strong values on achievement and hence he is more likely to be in harmony with his subculture. Hence when the boys returned home after learning new techniques for achieving, the high SES boys used these techniques to alleviate the tensions their failure to achieve had created. Although we would have to assume that the low SES boy also felt some of these tensions (his parents did care enough to send him to the summer school), the aspirations that the subculture holds for the boy are not so high,[27] and thus he need not improve his performance as much to bring himself in harmony with his subculture.

The experimental group's improvement over controls in school grades lends encouraging support to the hypothesis that teaching under-achieving boys the characteristics of the person with high achievement motivation can lead to better academic performance. The hypothesis is further supported by the high correlation of change in n Achievement and Business Game score with improvement in school grades in the experimental group.

This experiment, however, does not allow any conclusions about what techniques produced the experimental group's improved academic performance. The improvements could theoretically be a result of any or all of the following: the experimenter's particular personality (identification theory), learning n Achievement thought categories (ideo-motor response theory and n Achievement theory), learning to take moderate risks and use feedback (n Achievement theory), learning to take personal responsibility for actions (n Achievement theory), and expectations of improvement created by participation in a research project and by the research team contract (expectation theory). Further research should attempt to measure and/or isolate the differential effects of these factors.

[27] *Ibid.*

Richard P. Boyle

The Effect of the High School
on Students' Aspirations

In the following paper, Boyle reviews four highly regarded investigations which demonstrate that adolescents' scholastic aspirations are influenced by the nature of the high schools which they attend. In general, there appears to be a tendency for aspirations to incline toward those held by the majority social class. The four studies are consistent in reporting the major finding, but because they are inconsistent in methodological details, yield explanations difficult to summarize. Boyle suggests that the differences may be resolved by considering the impact of the size of the community in which the high schools are located. He hypothesizes that the larger centralized educational systems will impose restraints upon variability in educational standards on the one hand, and that, on the other, patterns of social-class segregation will exert informal pressures toward divergence. His research with 1,700 Canadian girls in seventy high schools confirms his expectations. The population composition of high schools is shown to have an important effect on aspirations, and the effect appears to be greater in large cities than in smaller communities. Boyle suggests that the basic answer may lie in the differential success that high schools have in developing scholastic ability and in the effect of peers in influencing adolescent values.

R̲ECENT research strongly suggests that the experiences that adolescents encounter in the high school have an important influence on their aspirations for further education. Studies by Wilson, Ramsøy, Coleman, and Turner have found that, when high schools are classified according to the *average* socio-economic status of the student body, the aspirations of the *individual* students are influenced in the direction of the majority.[1] Working-class

FROM *The American Journal of Sociology,* LXXI (1966), 628–639. Reprinted by permission of the author and the University of Chicago Press.

[1] Alan B. Wilson, "Residential Segregation of Social Classes and Aspirations of High School Boys" (hereinafter cited as "Residential Segregation"), *American Sociological Review,* XXIV (December, 1959), 836–845; Natalie Rogoff Ramsøy, "American High Schools at Mid-Century" (New York: Bureau of Applied Social Research, Columbia University, 1961); James S. Coleman, *The Adolescent Society* (New York: The Free Press, 1962); Ralph H. Turner, *The Social Context of Ambition* (San Francisco: Chandler Publishing Co., 1964). As they pertain to this paper, these studies have all been concerned with differences *between* high schools. For research into differences

students attending predominately *middle-class* high schools plan to attend college much more frequently than those attending more working-class high schools. The reverse process is evident among middle-class students attending predominately working-class high schools.

On this central finding there is agreement. But on the answers to more specific questions the separate studies often disagree. In particular: (1) Given that the population composition of a high school is important, *how* important is it? What, for example, is the effect of the high school relative to the effect of family background? Some studies found the high school equal in importance to the family, while other studies found it much less important. (2) *Why* should population composition show this effect? Some writers emphasize the importance of peer-group culture, while others give greater priority to pedagogical characteristics of the high school. (3) How is this effect expressed in terms of the individual student? Again, there is disagreement over whether explanation should be in terms of values and attitudes or in terms of scholastic abilities.

Each of the four studies cited above has inherent limitations which preclude final answers to these questions. However, each study provides clues which, taken together, suggest a consistent underlying pattern. This paper will examine closely the available evidence as it pertains to each question, add to this new evidence from a recently completed Canadian study, and finally attempt, as tightly as possible, to draw together these separate fragments into a consistent, unified statement about the consequences of variation in population composition among high schools.

FAMILY AND HIGH SCHOOL: RELATIVE IMPORTANCE

The sample for Alan Wilson's study consisted of boys from eight high schools in the San Francisco metropolitan area.[2] When these high schools were classified according to population composition, and individual students were classified according to their fathers' occupations, cross-classification allowed evaluation of the independent effects of family and high school on the students' plan about attending college.[3] In order to have a measure of these effects, which will allow comparison with other studies, Coleman's unweighted estimate of effect for polytomous ordinal variables has been cal-

---

within high schools, as these differences influence aspirations, see especially Edward L. McDill and James Coleman, "High School Social Status, College Plans, and Interest in Academic Achievement: A Panel Analysis" (hereinafter cited as "High School Social Status"), *American Sociological Review*, XXVIII (December, 1963), 905–918, and "Family and Peer Influences in College Plans of High School Students," *Sociology of Education*, XXXVIII (Winter, 1965), 112–126.

  [2] *Op. cit.*

  [3] Wilson first classified his high schools on the basis of census data describing the neighborhoods in which the schools were located. He then examined other indexes, such as population composition of the student bodies, and concluded that the same ranked categories would result from any classification strategy. He used three categories for high schools and four for father's occupation.

culated and standardized to the dichotomous form.[4] In terms of this statistic, the effect of the high school in Wilson's study was 0.22, and the effect of family background was 0.19.[5] The effect of the high school, in other words, was slightly greater than the effect of the family. Closer inspection of Wilson's data also indicates that this pattern of effect was fairly consistent over all the various categories.

Comparable data from a much larger, nationwide survey of high-school students were available to Natalie Rogoff Ramsøy.[6] Applying the same statistical analysis to these data, the effect of the high school on college plans was 0.07, while the effect of family background was 0.24.[7] The population composition of the high school was thus a much less important influence on the aspirations of the students studied by Ramsøy.

Apart from slight differences in operationalization, two major differences in the studies stand out. First, Wilson studied only boys, while Ramsøy's sample included both sexes. Perhaps the effect of the high school is much stronger for boys than for girls. Second, all of Wilson's high schools were located in a single metropolitan area, while Ramsøy used a national, and hence geographically heterogeneous, sample. This could imply either that San Francisco schools are a special case or that metropolitan high schools in general have characteristics that make them distinctive. Indirect support for this last possibility is offered by a further finding of Ramsøy's, that the effect of the high school was almost entirely concentrated in the much higher aspirations of students attending the most predominately middle-class schools.[8] Since middle-class occupations comprise a much larger proportion of the total occupational structure in large cities than in smaller communities, and since residential segregation on a large enough scale to be reflected in the high school is also most likely in large cities, it seems quite probable that the predominately middle-class high schools in Ramsøy's sample were disproportionately those located in large metropolitan areas. There is at least a hint, in other words, that controlling for community size would resolve some of the conflict between the findings of Ramsøy and Wilson.

The two remaining studies help to evaluate the possibility that sex and community size are underlying factors which could reconcile this disagreement. Ralph Turner's study was closely similar to Wilson's in that all ten of his high schools were located in the Los Angeles metropolitan area.[9] Using

[4] This statistic may be interpreted as the average difference between proportions of students planning on college within each level of father's occupation, corrected to be comparable to the proportion-difference that would obtain if high schools had been classified into two categories instead of three (see James S. Coleman, *Introduction to Mathematical Sociology* [New York: The Free Press, 1964], Chap. VI).

[5] Calculated from Wilson, *op. cit.*, Table 3, p. 839.

[6] Ramsøy, *op. cit.* Students were first classified according to five "family background" categories on the basis of father's occupation and education. The proportion of students in the top two of these categories was then used to classify high schools into five ranked categories.

[7] Calculated from *ibid.*, Table 8-2, p. 318.

[8] *Ibid.*

[9] Turner, *op. cit.* Students were first assigned a "background-index" value on the basis of the family breadwinner's occupation, education, and independent-employee status.

an "ambition index" that combined educational, occupational, and material aspirations, Turner carried out a partial correlation analysis which showed the high school to be only slightly less important than the family in determining ambition.[10] His findings thus agree more closely with Wilson's than with Ramsøy's. Furthermore, Turner carried out his analysis separately for boys and for girls and found that there were only slight differences.[11] Population composition of the high school did show a slightly higher correlation with ambition for boys than for girls, but this sex difference does not appear great enough to account for the divergence between the findings of Wilson and Ramsøy. Turner's work therefore provides further evidence that, at least in metropolitan areas, the high school is an important influence on aspiration.

James Coleman's sample for *The Adolescent Society* included ten high schools in northern Illinois, but only two of these were located in a large metropolitan area.[12] These two schools also recruited students from distinctly different family backgrounds. When father's education was controlled, students attending the more middle-class schools were much more likely to plan on college. [13] Among the *nonmetropolitan* high schools, however, differences in college planning associated with population composition were minimal. At the same time, Coleman's work indicates little difference in the effect of the high school on boys and on girls.

When these four studies are considered as a whole, their implication is therefore clear, although tentative. The effect of population composition on the aspirations of high-school students is considerable, but it varies according to the size of the community in which the high school is located. In large cities, the effect of the high school is roughly the same as the effect of the family, but in smaller communities this effect is much weaker. Finally, the influence of the high school appears to be fairly similar for both sexes, although slightly less important for girls.

EXPLANATORY FACTORS

While this pattern is clearly indicated, reasons for its existence are not obvious. The various explanations that have been proposed fall into two roughly distinct categories and suggest the operation of two mechanisms which account for the differences in aspirations under consideration. First, the manifest function of the high school is to impart knowledge and develop

---

The mean background-index value for all students in each high school was computed and used to index high schools.

[10] The partial correlation between school and ambition with background controlled was .21 for boys and .18 for girls. The partial correlation between background and ambition with school controlled was .29 for boys and .31 for girls (*ibid.*, Table 11a, p. 58).

[11] See n. 10, above.

[12] Coleman, *op. cit.,* "Executive Heights" and "Newlawn" were both located in suburbs of Chicago.

[13] *Ibid.,* figs. 9.9 and 9.10, pp. 270–271. The remainder of this paragraph also refers to these figures.

skills. The possibility that schools vary in their success at doing this could therefore be one important explanation. Second, a latent function of the high school may be to influence the values and attitudes of the student, thus affecting his motivation to attend college or otherwise aim high in life. These two explanations will be considered in turn.

Divergent Educational Standards and Scholastic Development

If some high schools provide their students with a better education than other high schools, this might explain the variation in the aspirations of these students. Several authors have pointed in this direction, but they have advanced different arguments. Ramsøy suggests that it is important to consider the *structural* characteristics of the formal educational system. She argues that the decentralized nature of American education, which delegates autonomy to the local school district and does not require students to compete with one another on any sort of standardized examination, allows and encourages divergence in the educational standards of individual high schools.[14]

On the other hand, later work by Wilson emphasizes the *informal social pressures* toward divergence which arise from residential segregation along social class lines.[15] He found that within a single elementary school district, teachers in predominately working-class schools came to expect less of their students than teachers in more middle-class schools and to key their teaching to these expectations. The result was that by sixth grade the level of the subject matter taught in class varied widely between the two kinds of schools.

A hint that this process of divergence operates in high schools as well as in elementary schools is offered by Coleman's finding that, "The amount of homework done depends largely on two things: upon the amount of homework assigned by the teachers, and upon family background." [16] Students at predominately middle-class high schools spent more time studying than those at predominately working-class schools, even when father's education was controlled.

The major consequences of this divergence, therefore, should be found in the level of knowledge and the scholastic abilities of the students in different kinds of high schools. However, the suggested interplay of structural restraints and informal social pressures in determining divergence has some interesting implications. Residential segregation on a large enough scale to be reflected in the high school should be most frequent in metropolitan areas. Informal social pressures should therefore be strongest among these schools. At the same time, metropolitan high schools will most typically be single units in large school districts containing several high schools. Since the local school district is the functional administrative unit in American education,

14 Ramsøy, *op. cit.*, p. 126 and *passim.*
15 Alan B. Wilson, "Social Stratification and Academic Achievement," in A. Harry Passow, ed., *Education in Depressed Areas* (New York: Bureau of Publications, Teachers College, Columbia University, 1963), pp. 217–235.
16 *Op. cit.*, pp. 266–268.

it might be expected that these metropolitan high schools *would* be subject to restraints against divergence, stemming from the central school-district administration. Insofar as divergence *does* occur among these schools, therefore, it seems better explained on the basis of strong *informal* social pressures. These ideas will be important when the Canadian data are presented, because in Canada administrative centralization at the *provincial* level provides formal restraints against divergence.

While no one has actually determined exactly what the different high schools were teaching in their courses, there is empirical support for the general notion that students from similar families show greater scholastic aptitude when they attend "higher status" high schools. Wilson, Ramsøy, and Turner all report this pattern. In order to really *evaluate* the importance of this pattern as an explanation for differences in aspirations, however, a direct statistical analysis is appropriate. Control scholastic ability and then see by how much the relation between high school and aspiration has been reduced (with family background controlled in both cases).

This kind of analysis is reported for two of the studies. With Ramsøy's data, this control eliminated almost all of the effect attributable to the high school.[17] The only exception occurred among the most middle-class high schools, which continued to send a higher proportion of students to college than other schools. On the other hand, Turner's partial correlation analysis showed a decrease, but not a drastic one, in the correlation between high school and ambition when scholastic ability was controlled.[18] The reduction was from .21 to .16 for boys and from .18 to .12 for girls.

The disagreement between these two sets of findings might be attributable to differences in measurement and analysis. However, it appears more reasonable to call attention to the probability that Ramsøy's *middle-class* schools were typically located in metropolitan areas. In this light, the two sets of findings are consistent in suggesting that (1) Differential scholastic development is an important explanation for the effect of the high school, but (2) while this may be the total explanation in smaller communities, it is only a partial explanation in metropolitan areas.

Peer-group Influence and Motivation

A second, sociologically appealing explanation would hold that student bodies in high schools of different population composition develop different subcultures, which in turn affect the motivation of the student to plan on college. Obviously, if scholastic development provides only a partial explanation for the effect of metropolitan high schools, there is a need for additional explanation. There is even some indication that peer-group influence may account for the dissimilar patterns discovered for metropolitan and nonmetropolitan schools. Coleman found rural and small-town youth to

[17] This analysis is reported in John A. Michael, "High School Climates and Plans for Entering College," *Public Opinion Quarterly*, XXV (Winter, 1961), 585–595. See especially his discussion on p. 593.

[18] Turner, *op. cit.*, Table 11b, p. 59.

be more parent-conforming and less peer-conforming than students living in metropolitan areas.[19] Again, however, adequate evaluation of the explanatory power of this factor requires a more direct analysis. The only report of such an analysis is provided by Turner.

Turner collected extensive data on those values "which can be translated into goals for the individual's behavior and those which the researches of others have suggested are linked to socio-economic status." [20] From these he constructed a "class-value index" which showed a fairly high correlation with ambition when family background was controlled.[21] The essential point is this: If the high school is the important remaining influence on these values, then the partial correlation between values and ambition should be reduced considerably when high school is controlled. But this did not occur. When the high school was added as a second control variable, this correlation was reduced only from .25 to .22 (for boys), and from .33 to .31 (for girls).[22] Apparently a major source of these values lies in factors indexed by neither the socio-economic status of the student's father nor by the population composition of his high school.

This finding, of course, does not prove that the peer group is not an important source of influence on the student's motivation to go to college or to achieve high social position. It indicates only that this influence is not expressed through values of a certain kind, having to do with long-range, lifetime goals. It is quite possible that the high school, through the peer group, exerts an influence on other motivational factors. A likely candidate here may be the student's perception of what college life is like, of how enjoyable the experience is likely to be. As McDill and Coleman note, "For a teenager in a generally middle-class environment, college holds promise of such activities (as) campus social life, freedom from parental control, a shift to new friends, and all other social attributes of college." [23] In a generally working-class environment, on the other hand, these values and the expectations that college will fulfil them may not become a part of the student culture. It may be that influence by the peer group is expressed in terms of *short-range* values such as these.

Summary of Explanatory Mechanisms

Quite an array of ideas and findings has been examined here, but the effort has been to show that these all fit together in suggesting an underlying pattern. At the risk of over-simplification, the suggested interplay of these different factors is represented diagrammatically in Figure 1. To interpret this diagram, it may be best to start at the bottom. Whether or not students plan on college is seen as an immediate consequence of two "psychological" factors: their level of scholastic ability and certain "moti-

[19] *Op. cit.*, pp. 138–140.
[20] Turner, *op. cit.*, p. 66.
[21] *Ibid.*, p. 91.
[22] *Ibid.*, Table 17, p. 94.
[23] McDill and Coleman, "High School Social Status," *op. cit.*, p. 918.

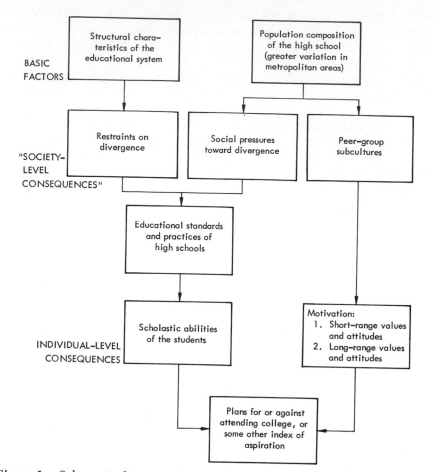

Figure 1. Schematic diagram of factors leading to a variation in the aspirations of students attending different high schools.

vational" factors, as yet unknown. While both of these general factors are probably determined in part by experiences in other social contexts, important sources lying within the high school can be identified.

Much of the variation in scholastic ability occurs because the educational standards of high schools vary. Because educational standards vary, students in some schools develop their abilities to a higher level than students in other schools. But the extent to which standards are divergent is, in turn, a consequence of the interplay of two other factors. First, structural characteristics of the educational system (e.g., centralized or decentralized) can impose more or less severe *restraints* on this divergence. In the United States these restraints will be strongest in large metropolitan school districts, weak among isolated rural high schools. Second, variation in the population composition of high schools creates informal social pressures *toward* divergence. It is easier for teachers to teach when the bulk of their students bring with them better preparation for learning and greater willing-ness to cooperate with school assignments. But the important point here is that those students in generally middle-class schools who lack this back-ground appear to be carried along by the majority.

In more specific terms, existing research suggests that variation in scholas-tic development is an important explanation, that it is a *sufficient* explana-tion in smaller communities, but that among high schools located in large metropolitan areas it provides only a partial explanation. It is in large metro-politan areas, furthermore, that *both* structural restraints and informal social pressures should be strongest, at least in the United States.

Turning to the second explanatory mechanism, it seems likely that the adolescent subcultures which are typical of different kinds of high schools may have an important influence on the student's *motivation* to attend col-lege. Available evidence indicates that this factor, if it operates at all, operates most strongly in metropolitan areas. There are at least two reasons why this might be so. First, since population composition should vary more widely in these areas, differences between adolescent subcultures should also be greater. Second, there is some suggestion, from Coleman, that stu-dents living in larger communities are more peer-conforming than students living in smaller communities.

However this may be, direct research into motivational factors and peer-group influences is quite limited. An attempt by Turner to locate these motivational factors with a set of values keyed to social class and long-range goals did not prove successful, but the hypothesis itself remains open.

A Study of Canadian Girls

During the late spring of 1962, questionnaires were administered to 1,701 girls in their final year at seventy high schools in western Canada.[24] Data were obtained that provided measures of family background and college aspirations.[25] In addition, high schools were classified according to popula-

[24] The girls were in their junior matriculation year in predominately coeducational high schools. Completion of this year qualifies the student to enter college, although further high-school work leading to senior matriculation and college credit is possible. The year at which junior matriculation is granted varies from province to province. In Ontario and British Columbia it is granted at grade 12; in all other western provinces it is granted on completion of grade 11. The proportion of youth completing high school, and the proportion going on to college, is more similar to the United States in western Canada than in eastern Canada. For further discussion of the comparability of this sample with American students see my "Social Context and Educational Aspiration: In-fluence of High School and Community on College Plans" (Ph.D. dissertation, Univer-sity of Washington, 1964), pp. 58–64.

[25] Father's occupation and education were used to classify students into four cate-gories of family background, in the following way: (I) all fathers with at least some college education, whatever their occupation; (II) all other fathers with professional or managerial occupations, and all other fathers with clerical or sales occupations except those with only grade-school educations; (III) all other clerical and sales workers, and all other blue-collar workers and farmers with at least some high-school education; (IV) all other blue-collar workers and farmers (i.e., those with only grade-school education).

tion composition and the size of the community in which they were located.[26] While the Canadian educational system is quite similar to the American in most respects, there is one important difference. Administrative authority in Canadian education is much more centralized. This is particularly evident in the system of province-wide standardized examinations which determine the student's grades in all provinces except Ontario. This should result in less divergence in the standards and practices of individual high schools and a lower correlation between population composition and the scholastic abilities of the students.

The statistical procedure employed in this analysis is similar to the one used earlier to compare the findings of Wilson and Ramsøy, with one major exception. Instead of basing effect estimates on subsample proportions, the present procedure is derived in such a way as to give equal weight to each case.[27] This means that analysis is not so directly limited by the number of cases failing in each cell of the partial tables and also allows the addition of numerous control variables. As before, however, the resulting effect estimates can be interpreted as weighted averages of differences between proportions.

The effect of the high school on college aspirations, with family background controlled, is shown in Table 1. Attending a "high-status" school in comparison with one of "medium status" has a fairly strong effect on the student's aspirations (0.21), but there is almost no difference between "medium status" and "low status" schools (0.01). The effect of family background, standardized to be comparable to the dichotomous case,[28] is 0.24, or slightly more than the effect of the high school when the medium- and low-status categories are combined.

This pattern of influence is somewhat different from that predicted on the basis of earlier work. The findings fit the predictions much better, however, when community size is taken into account. In Table 2 the effect of the high school is shown separately for metropolitan and nonmetropolitan areas.[29] The relationship between community size and population composition is so pronounced that *all* of the high-status schools, but *none* of the low-status

[26] In each high school the percentage of girls completing questionnaires who were in the upper two family-background categories (see n. 25, above) defined three categories of high schools as follows: over 65 per cent; 33–64 per cent; less than 33 per cent. A community population of 200,000 was used to distinguish between "metropolitan" and "non-metropolitan" high schools.

[27] Coleman derives his procedure from a model of continuous time, discrete space stochastic processes. His strategy is to estimate effect parameters in such a way as to most accurately describe the observed subsample *proportions*. If, instead, one sets out to describe the distribution of individual *cases*, it turns out that effect parameters are best estimated by a weighted average of the separate proportion-differences $(p_i - p_j)$, where the weighting function is $(n_i n_j / n_i + n_j)$. For further discussion of this procedure see my "Multivariate Effect Analysis: Some Modifications and Extensions of Coleman's Work" (unpublished manuscript).

[28] See Coleman, *Introduction to Mathematical Sociology*, pp. 218–219.

[29] For a discussion of the effects of community size evident in this table, see my "Community Influence on College Aspirations: An Empirical Evaluation of Explanatory Factors" (unpublished manuscript).

Table 1 *Proportion Planning on College by High-School Status and Family Background*

Family Background°	High-School Status†			Effect Estimates	
	HIGH	MEDIUM	LOW		
High:					
I	0.71 (211)	0.45 (71)	0.48 (25)	High school: high vs. medium status	0.21
II	.47 (214)	.31 (134)	.32 (62)	Medium vs. low status	.01
IIII	.49 (59)	.19 (124)	.26 (184)	Family background (standardized to dichotomous form)	
Low:					
IV	0.36 (42)	0.20 (143)	0.11 (227)		0.24
Total	(526)	(472)	(498)		

° Measured by father's occupation and education.
† Proportion of students in family-background categories I and II.

Table 2 *Proportion Planning on College by High-School Status and Family Background for Metropolitan and Non-metropolitan Areas Separately*

Family Background	Metropolitan High Schools°		Non-metropolitan High Schools†	
	HIGH STATUS	MEDIUM STATUS	MEDIUM STATUS	LOW STATUS
High				
I	0.71 (211)	0.36 (28)	0.51 (43)	0.48 (25)
II	.47 (214)	.19 (31)	.35 (103)	.32 (62)
III	.49 (59)	.29 (38)	.14 (86)	.26 (184)
Low:				
IV	0.36 (42)	0.20 (25)	0.20 (118)	0.11 (227)
Total	(526)	(122)	(350)	(498)

° Effect estimate for high-school status, 0.25.
† Effect estimate for high-school status, 0.01.

schools, were located in metropolitan areas. As a consequence, the only comparison possible among metropolitan schools is between high- and medium-status categories, while the only comparison possible among non-metropolitan schools is between medium- and low-status categories. Among the former, the effect of population composition is quite strong ($a_1 = 0.25$), while among the latter the effect is minimal ($a_1 = 0.01$). This finding is consistent with the interpretation that more centralized administration in Canada will discourage divergence among nonmetropolitan high schools but that residential segregation in metropolitan areas will create even stronger pressures toward divergence.

The problem of further analysis is simplified somewhat by this finding. The only relationship that needs to be explained occurs among the metropolitan high schools. The two explanatory variables that can be investigated in this regard are scholastic ability and occupational values. Scholastic ability is defined in terms of the student's grade average, as determined by her performance on province-wide examinations.[30] As such, the present measure of ability should be more directly influenced by the educational program of the high school than the measures employed by Ramsøy and Turner. The occupational values used here represent a preference for "creativity" or "security." [31] This is very roughly similar to the "class-values" index Turner used. No measure was available of short-range values which, according to earlier discussion, are more likely to be a result of peer-group influence.

Since the partial tables on which this analysis is based are rather cumbersome, the effect estimates are summarized in Tables 3 and 4.[32] In Table 3,

Table 3   Summary of the Effect of Scholastic Ability and Values on College Plans

Independent Variable	Dependent Variable	Control Variables	Effect Estimate
Scholastic ability	College plans	Values and family background	0.27
Values	College plans	Scholastic ability and family background	.19
Family background	College plans	Values and scholastic ability	0.26

with family background controlled, ability and values both show fairly strong relationships with college plans. The effect of ability is about as

[30] There is, obviously, no universally agreed on definition of "scholastic ability." If performance in college is taken as the criterion with which to evaluate various instruments for "measuring" scholastic ability, then tests that depend strongly on scholastic achievement and prior learning have been shown to be better predictors than tests that are more "culture-free" (Lee J. Cronbach, *Essentials of Psychological Testing* [New York: Harper & Row, 1960]). The Canadian system of province-wide examinations should therefore provide a good measure of this kind of ability. In Ontario, province-wide examinations were used until recently but are no longer employed. It can only be assumed, therefore, that grade averages are still meaningful when comparing schools. Students were classified as high or low in scholastic ability, depending on whether or not their grades were 70 or above. This criterion gives roughly equal distributions in all provinces and is similar to distinguishing between A's and B's and all lower grades in the United States.

[31] The statements were "a job which will permit me to be creative and original" and "a job which will enable me to look forward to a stable, secure future." Girls choosing "creativity" more frequently planned on college. Several studies of high-school students support this finding. See, e.g., Harry Beilin, "The Pattern of Postponability and Its Relation to Social Class Mobility," *Journal of Social Psychology*, XLIV (August, 1956), 33–48; Harry K. Schwarzweller, "Value-Orientations in Educational and Occupational Choices," *Rural Sociology*, XXIV (September, 1959), 246–256, and "Values and Occupational Choice," *Social Forces*, XXIX (December, 1960), 126–135.

[32] The partial tables from which these summaries are taken are similar in appearance to Tables 1 and 2. Copies of the full tables will be supplied by the author to anyone interested. Inspection of the partial tables indicates no evidence of interaction effects. At the same time, the relatively small number of girls attending the two medium-status metropolitan schools in the sample dictate caution in basing conclusions on these results. Analysis of each metropolitan school separately, however, shows consistent similarities *within* each category (high status and medium status) and consistent differences between each category. See my "Social Context and Educational Aspiration," *op. cit.*, pp. 87–89.

Table 4 **Summary of Explanatory Power of Scholastic Ability and Values for Effect of High-School Status on College Plans (Metropolitan High Schools Only)**

Independent Variable	Dependent Variable	Control Variables	Effect Estimate
High-school status	Scholastic ability	Family background	0.30
High-school status	College plans	Family background	.22°
High-school status	College plans	Family background and scholastic ability	.15
High-school status	Values	Family background	.10
High-school status	College plans	Family background	.25
High-school status	College plans	Family background and values	0.24

° Grade averages were not available for all girls, so the effect of high-school status on college plans was calculated separately for the full sample and for the smaller sample of girls for whom grade averages *were* available.

great as the effect of background, while the effect of values is somewhat less than this. There is good reason for suspecting, in other words, that either of these "psychological" factors could provide an explanation for the higher aspirations of the students attending the high-status metropolitan schools.

With family background controlled, the high school has a pronounced effect on scholastic ability (0.30) (see Table 4). With ability *controlled*, the effect of the high school on college plans is reduced, from $a_1 = 0.22$ to $a_1 = 0.15$, a reduction of about one third.[33] Or, in other words, the greater scholastic ability of students attending the high-status metropolitan schools is a *partial* explanation for their higher aspirations.

Whatever the explanation may be for the remaining effect of the high school, the present findings concur with Turner's in indicating that occupational values do not tap the important factors. The effect of the high school on these values is slight (0.10), and controlling for values does not appreciably reduce the effect of high-school status on college plans (the reduction is from 0.25 to 0.24).[34]

Concluding Remarks

The findings from the Canadian study accord very well with the predictions advanced on the basis of interpretation of other research. This is not altogether surprising—the framework of ideas presented here was developed after the fact, on the basis of all available information. What is not *ad hoc*, as a matter of fact, is the facility with which Turner's findings fit into this

[33] Grade averages were not available for all girls, so the effect of high school on college plans was recalculated for this smaller sample. This figure is slightly lower than the effect estimate for the full sample.

[34] These estimates are for the full sample.

framework, since his work did not become known to the author until the framework presented here was fully developed. However, what is important is that the somewhat diverse findings of five independent pieces of research do fit together in a consistent pattern. The present framework thus provides an explicit target for future research.

There are serious weaknesses in the design of all the research examined here. The problems of inferring causality from survey data are especially severe with studies of social context. Where it is necessary to infer contextual characteristics on the basis of individual characteristics, it is essential that the measure of individual characteristics employed be precise and that this measure have the same meaning in different groups. In terms of the research discussed here, this means that, first, there must be enough categories of socio-economic status to reduce intra-category variation to an effective minimum. For example, "middle class" might include both doctors and sales clerks; if the middle-class students at one school were mostly children of doctors, while at another school they were mostly children of sales clerks, the magnitude of the bias is obvious. There is some evidence that use of four categories provides satisfactory precision. Wilson carried out his analysis first with four categories of father's occupation, then with nine, then with various detailed combinations of father's and mother's education, without appreciably changing his findings.[35]

The second requirement, that the measure mean the same thing in the different groups, points to potentially more serious weaknesses. Socio-economic status has been used in this research to "control" for family background. But there is considerable evidence that other aspects of the family, such as mobility orientation, values, and child-rearing practices, are also related to the aspirations of the children.[36] It is quite plausible to argue, for example, that working-class families living in neighborhoods where their children go to predominately middle-class schools are not the same as other working-class families. These families may be especially concerned that their children "get ahead." At the same time, it has been shown that middle-class students attending working-class schools have *lower* aspirations than other middle-class students and that this "downward" pull is as strong as the above mentioned "upward" pull. To argue that middle-class families move to working-class neighborhoods in order to inhibit the opportunities of their children is much less plausible. The fact remains, however, that

[35] Wilson, "Residential Segregation," *op. cit.*, pp. 839–844.

[36] See, e.g., David J. Bordua, "Educational Aspirations and Parental Stress on College," *Social Forces*, XXXVIII (March, 1960), 262–269; Elizabeth D. Cohen, "Parental Factors in Educational Mobility" (Ph.D. dissertation, Harvard University, 1958); Glen H. Elder, Jr., *Adolescent Achievement and Mobility Aspirations* (Chapel Hill, N.C.: Institute for Research in Social Science, 1963), and "Parental Power Legitimation and Its Effect on the Adolescent," *Sociometry*, XXVI (March, 1963), 50–65; Joseph A. Kahl, "Educational and Occupational Aspirations of 'Common Man' Boys," *Harvard Educational Review*, XXIII (Summer, 1953), 186–203; Wilbur L. Layton, "Socioeconomic Status and After-High School Plans," in Ralph F. Berdie, *After High School, What?* (Minneapolis: University of Minnesota Press, 1954), pp. 178–192.

family characteristics other than socio-economic status can and should be controlled in future research.

The best conclusion possible given the existing information, therefore, is that the framework of ideas developed in the first two sections is quite reasonable. To summarize the main findings: (1) The population composition of a high school does have an important effect on the aspirations of its students, but a much stronger effect in large cities than in smaller communities. (2) One important, but (at least in metropolitan areas) partial explanation for this effect is the differential success of high schools in developing the scholastic abilities of their students. (3) The failure of scholastic ability to explain all of the effects of metropolitan high schools points to the existence of other explanations, such as the influence of the peer group, but occupational or social-class values do not provide this explanation.

Harwin L. Voss

Aubrey Wendling

Delbert S. Elliott

Some Types of High-School Dropouts

If youth is to be rehabilitated through the educational system, programs for arresting attritions must be devised. This task is complicated by the fact that adolescents leave high school for diverse reasons. Voss, Wendling, and Elliott observe below that while the majority of high-school dropouts earn poor grades and are poor readers, the saliency of such dropout correlates masks differences among the youths. The researchers, for example, differentiate three categories of dropouts: (a) the "involuntary," encompassing those who leave school for reasons of personal crises, often dropping out as soon as the law permits, (b) the "retarded," including those who leave for reasons of limitation in ability, under-achievement, and failure, or (c) the "capable," encompassing those who are under-achievers because of conflict or frustration and who may drop out even when graduation is within grasp. The latter category represents persons who seemingly possess the necessary attributes and skills required for graduation, and, hence, represent examples of social waste. To reduce the high proportion of persons in the third category, Voss, Wendling, and Elliott insist that subsequent analyses of dropouts must be in terms of the sociological, psychological, and philosophical values by which youths relate to high school and contemporary society.

THERE has been a growing concern in recent years over the number of students who leave high school prior to graduation. Many writers have decried the potential waste of human resources occurring as a consequence of school dropout; the mass of under-educated, unemployed, and frustrated youth in the United States is said to constitute "social dynamite."

Many studies have been conducted, and these have led to the accumulation of many conclusions about dropouts. Frequently, the conclusions about dropouts are contradictory, and thus are confusing. Such contradictory results stem from a basic limitation of much of this research; namely, the conception, either explicit or implicit, that those who drop out of high school are a homogeneous group. This perception gave rise to the widespread stereotype of dropouts as "dummies," or persons lacking the ability to complete

FROM *The Journal of Educational Research*, LIX (1966), 363–368. Reprinted by permission of the authors and the publisher.

high school. Variations on this theme stress the dropouts' difficulties with reading, poor grades, and grade retardation. If an exception is noted, it is that problems of health or economic pressures might lead a student to drop out.

CHARACTERISTICS OF DROPOUTS

An effective response to the problem of high-school dropouts will only be possible after order is imposed on the heterogeneous data available. This requires specification of *types* of dropouts. In this paper, the apparently contradictory findings concerning the dropouts' level of intelligence, difficulties with reading, grade retardation, and poor grades are analyzed, and a typology of dropouts is presented as a means of integrating the available evidence.

Intelligence Scores

Many Americans are convinced that dropouts are drawn from the bottom of the intelligence distribution. This view is supported by studies which have found that limited intellectual capacity is a definitive characteristic of dropouts.[1] For example, the U.S. Department of Labor recently conducted a survey of dropouts in seven communities scattered throughout the United States, and the results which are presented in the accompanying table are fairly typical of the studies which emphasize the association between low intelligence test scores and school dropouts.[2] The Otis Mental Ability Group Test was the most widely used in the areas studied, and "a quotient of 85 is the point below which successful completion of most high-school subjects is regarded by educational authorities as generally difficult."[3] Students with IQ's between 85 and 89 are usually slow learners; 90 to 109 represents the normal range and 110 or above is the level of ability required for college work.

Clearly, the most obvious difference between the dropouts and graduates lies in the proportion whose IQ's are under 85, and hence lack the requisite ability to complete high school. Not to be overlooked in this comparison of dropouts and graduates is the overlap in IQ scores. Many of the dropouts have higher IQ's than some of the high school graduates, and some dropouts have the intellectual equipment necessary to do college work. Nevertheless,

[1] E. S. Cook, Jr., "An Analysis of Factors Related to Withdrawal from High School Prior to Graduation," *Journal of Educational Research,* L (November, 1956), 191–196; E. S. Cook, Jr., "How IQ Figures in the Drop-Out Problem," *School Executive,* LXXIV (September, 1954), 56–57; J. F. Delaney, "That Vacant High School Seat," *American School Board Journal,* CXXI (November, 1950), 22–23; R. H. Dresher, "Factors in Voluntary Dropouts," *Personnel and Guidance Journal,* XXXII (January, 1954), 287–289; U.S. Department of Labor, *School and Early Employment Experience of Youth: A Report on Seven Communities, 1952–57,* Bulletin No. 1277 (Washington, D.C.: U.S. Government Printing Office, 1960).

[2] U.S. Department of Labor, *op. cit.,* p. 14.

[3] *Ibid.,* p. 13.

this investigation offers evidence that low intelligence is related to dropout, and further support for this view has been reported by Delaney, who has observed that only 46 per cent of the dropouts he surveyed have average or above average intellectual ability.[4]

Table 1   Measured Intelligence of Dropouts and High-School Graduates

	IQ			
	85 AND UNDER	85–89	90–109	110 AND OVER
High-School Graduates	10%	11%	63%	16%
Dropouts	31	15	48	6

On the other hand, studies conducted in California and New York City conclude that dropouts do not differ significantly in intelligence from those who remain in school. A comparison of 72 dropouts who were in continuation school and 72 students from regular high schools in Stockton and Fresno, California, in which the two groups were matched on age, sex, grade, scholastic aptitude and paternal occupation, revealed no significant difference with regard to IQ.[5] However, the group of regular students is not representative of the student population, since these students were matched with the continuation students, in part, in terms of scholastic aptitude. Among the studies reported by McCreary and Kitch is one conducted by Sando in California's Contra Costa County. The investigator studied 100 consecutive sophomore withdrawals from eight high schools and matched each of them as nearly as possible with 100 sophomores who remained in school on the basis of school attended, sex, socio-economic status, and rate of promotion. The groups were not matched in intelligence, but they showed no significant difference when their IQ's were compared.[6] Again, in New York City, the Board of Education found little difference in the average IQ scores of graduates and non-graduates; further, all of the IQ scores were within the normal range.[7]

Somewhat different results were obtained in a study conducted in Detroit, in which Layton compared dropouts with the norms of standard tests of "native learning ability." According to the test norms for the total student population, 20 per cent are rated above average, 60 per cent average, and 20 per cent below average. In comparison, only 9 per cent of the dropouts

---

[4] Delaney, *op. cit.*

[5] W. Euraiff, "How 'Different' Are Our Drop-Outs?" *Bulletin of the National Association of Secondary-School Principals,* XLI (February, 1957), 212–218.

[6] W. H. McCreary and D. E. Kitch, "Now Hear Youth," *Bulletin of the California State Department of Education,* XXII (October, 1953), 37.

[7] Board of Education, "Experiment in Guidance of Potential Early School Leavers" (New York: May, 1956), p. 26.

were rated above average, while 67 per cent were rated average, and 24 per cent were rated below average.[8] Similar results have been obtained by other investigators.[9]

These contradictory findings may stem partially from the use of different definitions of school dropouts. In addition, some of the discrepancies between these investigations presumably result from the use of different, though often unspecified, intelligence tests which have different norms.

The results differ primarily, however, as a consequence of the failure to differentiate between *early and late school dropouts*. Those who drop out prior to entering high school may be considered early dropouts. There appears to be as much difference between students who leave school early and those who leave later, that is, after entering high school, as there is between all dropouts and high-school graduates. In statistical language, this is the notion of within-group or intraclass variation in contrast to between-group or interclass variation. Consequently, when dropouts at all levels are studied as a single, homogeneous group, significant differences may be obscured and the analysis confounded. Examination of the literature indicates that this possibility has rarely been recognized, though there are notable exceptions.[10]

Analysis of those who drop out early shows a high proportion of students with limited ability, as in the Labor Department survey. On the other hand, when the intelligence scores of late school dropouts are analyzed, little or no difference is found in comparison with high-school graduates, as was the case in the New York City Board of Education study of students who left school after entering high school. Findings intermediate between these extremes may well result from investigation of varying, but unspecified, proportions of early and late dropouts.

Evidence for this interpretation—that the students with limited ability are the first to leave school—is provided by Dillon. He found that 36 per cent of 1,018 dropouts in grades seven through twelve had IQ scores below 85; in contrast, 75 per cent of the dropouts who left school in the seventh grade scored below this level.[11]

One additional point deserves mention here. It is important to recognize that IQ test scores correlate highly with reading ability. Those who have learned to read well will do better on this kind of test than children who are poor readers.[12] Using the California Test of Mental Maturity, Cook and Lanier found that the language IQ of dropouts was considerably below that

[8] W. K. Layton, *Special Services for the Drop-out and the Potential Drop-out,* Publication No. 408 (National Child Labor Committee, October, 1952), p. 7.

[9] McCreary and Kitch, *op. cit.,* p. 31.

[10] H. Dillon, *Early School Leavers: A Major Educational Problem,* Publication No. 401 (National Child Labor Committee, October, 1949); A. Livingston, "Key to the Dropout Problem: The Elementary School," *Elementary School Journal,* LIX (February, 1959), 267–270; U.S. Department of Labor, *op. cit.*

[11] Dillon, *op. cit.,* p. 34.

[12] J. B. Conant, *Slums and Suburbs* (New York: McGraw-Hill Book Co., 1961), p. 13.

of those who remained in school.[13] In addition, the nonlanguage IQ scores of dropouts were higher than their language IQ scores. This suggests that difficulties with reading may also be an important factor related to leaving school.

Reading Achievement

The Rochester study of dropouts from the ninth through the twelfth grades offers a clue to the nature of this problem by presenting a cross-tabulation of the dropouts' measured IQ and reading test scores. These scores were obtained from the American College Entrance Test and the Nelson Silent Reading Examination; the scores of students in Rochester schools were used to establish norms. The dropouts measured lower on the reading tests; the median IQ score for boys was at the forty-first percentile, whereas their reading score was at the thirty-first percentile. This difference was significant at the .01 level.[14]

This suggests that reading achievement is significantly related to the dropouts' academic difficulties. Using the California Reading Achievement Test (Advanced), Bledsoe found that dropouts from the ninth and tenth grades had a mean reading comprehension score of 7.9, while the rest of the ninth graders had a mean score of 8.9.[15] Penty also found a relationship between reading ability, as measured by the Iowa Silent Reading Test, and withdrawal from high school: more than three times as many poor readers as good readers dropped out of school.[16] Nachman and his co-workers found that 75.4 per cent of the dropouts scored below the median of their level on a reading test, and 53.4 per cent were in the lowest quarter.[17]

Disabilities in reading may have serious repercussions. Pupils who are poor readers have difficulty in doing the work required. One of the consequences of poor reading is failure and grade retardation.

Grade Retardation

In the literature on dropouts, one finds literally dozens of studies which point to grade retardation as one of the outstanding characteristics of dropouts.[18] Livingston, for example, reported that of all dropouts who with-

[13] E. S. Cook, Jr., "How IQ Figures in the Dropout Problem," op. cit.; J. A. Lanier, "A Guidance-Faculty Study of Student Withdrawals," Journal of Educational Research, XLIII (November, 1949), 205–212.

[14] Division for Youth, The School Dropout Problem: Rochester, Part I (State of New York, May, 1962), pp. 14–16.

[15] J. C. Bledsoe, "An Investigation of Six Correlates of Student Withdrawal from High School," Journal of Educational Research, LIII (September, 1959), 3–6.

[16] R. C. Penty, Reading Ability and High School Drop-Outs (New York: Teachers College, Columbia University, 1956), p. 51.

[17] L. R. Nachman, R. F. Getson, and J. C. Odgers, Pilot Study of Ohio High School Dropouts, 1961–1962 (Columbus, Ohio: State Department of Education, February, 1963).

[18] C. M. Allen, Combatting the Dropout Problem (Chicago: Science Research Associates, Inc., 1956); Dillon, op. cit.; Division for Youth, op. cit.; Dresher, op. cit.; A. Livingston, "High School Graduates and Dropouts—A New Look at a Persistent Problem," The School Review, LXVI (Summer, 1958), 195–203; R. A. Tesseneer and L. M.

drew prior to entering ninth grade, every one was retarded at least one grade and 84 per cent were retarded two grades. Of those who graduated from high school, only 1 per cent were retarded one grade and none were retarded more than a single grade.[19] In its survey of seven communities, the U.S. Department of Labor included grades eight through twelve in four areas and grades nine through twelve in the remaining three; it was found that 84 per cent of the dropouts were retarded at least one year, and 53 per cent were retarded two or more years. Specifically, 87 per cent of the boys and 80 per cent of the girls were retarded one or more years, and 59 per cent of the boys were retarded two or more years as were 44 per cent of the girls.[20]

Retardation is considered one of the most reliable indicators of future dropout.[21] Any pupil retarded two years by the time he reaches the seventh grade is unlikely to finish the tenth grade and has only a negligible chance of finishing high school. If the pupil is retarded three years, he is not likely to enter the ninth grade.[22]

The crucial importance of differentiating between early and late school dropouts also is apparent in the reports which consider grade retardation. Some studies have failed to make this distinction, and, as a consequence, the relationship between dropout and grade retardation has been confounded. The studies in which this distinction has been made, such as the ones conducted by Livingston and by the Department of Labor, suggest that those who leave school early, that is, before the ninth grade, are most likely to be retarded, whereas those who drop out later are much less likely to be retarded. Closely related to the area of grade retardation is the question pertaining to the grades of dropouts.

Grades

A number of studies have reported the grades of dropouts but, with the exception of Dillon's investigation, these are of limited utility because early and late dropouts are not distinguished. Dillon found that 180 in a sample of 1,018 dropouts earned A's or B's in elementary school, and 65 per cent of these students maintained a comparable level of performance in junior high school. However, only 17 per cent (31 of the 180) maintained this level of

---

Tesseneer, "Review of the Literature on School Dropouts," *Bulletin of the National Association of Secondary-School Principals*, XLII (May, 1958), 141–153; U.S. Department of Labor, *op. cit.*

[19] Livingston, *op. cit.*

[20] U.S. Department of Labor, *op. cit.*, p. 17.

[21] In the interpretation of data on grade retardation, it is important to recognize that some school districts limit the number of grades that a child may be retained. Consequently, data on grade retardation as an indicator of future dropout may apply only to those school districts that do not impose these limitations. It may also be necessary to take into account those students who have not been retained more than one year but are enrolled in remedial classes.

[22] National Education Association, Research Division, "School Dropouts" (April, 1963), p. 8.

performance in high school.[23] On the basis of this evidence, Dillon suggests that a clear trend is evident—the grades of dropouts are not always poor, but become worse as they progress through the several educational levels.

The inference that students leave school because they cannot, or do not, maintain high grades does not necessarily follow. Dropouts show a general decline in scholarship from the elementary to the senior high school, but information concerning the grades of a control group of graduates is required before one can be certain that such a general decline is not the result of more rigorous grading policies. In short, a similar decline might also characterize those who remain in school.

The data provided by Dillon suggest that many dropouts do not earn more than average or "C" grades. These are, of course, early dropouts, and many of them have limited intelligence. Dillon's study also revealed that, of the dropouts who reached the eleventh or twelfth grade, approximately 45 per cent were doing passing work.

Poor or even failing grades do not necessarily imply a lack of ability. A capable student may perform poorly either through lack of motivation or prolonged absence from school. Consequently, grades alone cannot be used as an index of ability—measured intelligence and reading skill may be of equal or greater importance as indices of intellectual capacity.

Summary

In summary, a review of the available literature suggests the critical importance of distinguishing between early and late school dropouts. Students with limited ability generally leave school early—often before entering senior high school. Among the late school dropouts, one finds few who lack the requisite ability to complete high school. Since the U.S. Department of Labor survey of seven communities found that 10 per cent of high school graduates score below 85, the lower limit of the normal range of intelligence test scores, it is reasonable to expect a comparable percentage of retarded students to be found among late school dropouts. Thus, while many early dropouts are youngsters with limited ability, the evidence suggests that there is little difference in ability between late school dropouts and high school graduates.

Implicit in this examination of the findings of previous research are several distinct types of dropouts. The remainder of this paper is devoted to the presentation of this typology.

Types of Dropouts

Analysis of the findings on dropouts suggests that three major types of dropouts may be distinguished. These types are: 1) the involuntary dropouts, 2) the retarded dropouts, and 3) the intellectually capable dropouts.

---

[23] Dillon, *op. cit.*

The Involuntary Dropouts

Those individuals who leave school as a result of some personal crisis constitute involuntary dropouts. Each year as a result of illness or accident, a small number of students are physically disabled and forced to withdraw from school. For others, the death of a parent, particularly the father, requires an immediate entry into the world of work. Regardless of the specific reason, the involuntary dropouts leave school because of external circumstances over which they have no control. A student may use physical health or economic problems as his reason for dropout when, in fact, he is retarded. For typological clarity, one may require that only intellectually capable students may be considered for inclusion as involuntary dropouts. The number of dropouts who would fit into this category presumably is quite limited, and the nature of the relationship between these cases of personal crisis and dropout is readily apparent. Nevertheless, it is important to distinguish this type of dropout, for their academic and social characteristics might confound the analysis, if included with the other types.

To identify and explain involuntary dropouts is a relatively easy task. Since these cases occur as a result of physical health or economic problems, it does not, however, appear feasible to predict potential dropouts of this type.

The Retarded Dropout

The retarded dropouts are those who are not capable of doing the necessary work required for promotion to higher grades and eventual graduation.[24] Two types of students contribute to the category of retarded dropouts. In general, retarded dropouts may be identified by their low scores on achievement and intelligence tests, poor grades, grade retardation, and reading disability. In some cases of school retardation, however, the adolescents have average or high intelligence, if tested with a nonverbal IQ test. For such students, their low reading ability results in low achievement scores, low grades, and possibly even grade retardation. Some writers have recognized such cases, and they have suggested that reading disability is the cause of a wide range of school problems, including dropout and delinquency.[25] While this is a particularistic fallacy, the existence of school retardation among students whose IQ scores are within the normal range must be recognized. Thus, within the category of retarded dropouts one finds students who lack the innate ability to do the required work, and also students who may have the potential ability to do adequate work, but lack the requisite skills to perform satisfactorily.

Like the involuntary dropouts, the retarded dropouts can be identified and explained with relatively little difficulty; retarded dropouts lack the

---

[24] In some districts, a policy of "passing" such students from grade to grade and finally awarding a certificate of attendance has come into vogue.

[25] R. Flesch, *Why Johnny Can't Read* (New York: Harper and Bros., 1955); S. Terman and C. C. Walcutt, *Reading: Chaos and Cure* (New York: McGraw-Hill Book Co., 1958), pp. 85–88.

skills or abilities necessary for academic pursuits. Many dropouts of this type are officially labeled "uneducable," and are dropped from school by administrative authority because of their inability to succeed academically. The available evidence suggests that retarded dropouts leave school early, whereas capable dropouts tend to remain in school longer.

The Capable Dropouts

The term capable dropout is used in reference to those students who have the requisite ability to do passing or even superior work in high school, but who may or may not be making satisfactory academic progress. These students leave school for reasons other than low ability.

This type has two identifying characteristics. The capable dropouts are students who have average or high IQ's and adequate or high reading ability. In general, they have adequate academic standing in terms of grades and achievement scores and the absence of grade retardation, though these are not definitive characteristics. A word of caution is in order. A student who is a capable dropout might be incorrectly designated a retarded dropout on the basis of his low grades and achievement scores. The key to identifying the capable dropout is his adequate reading ability and IQ. His grades may, in fact, be primarily D's and F's. In such cases, the capable dropout is "flunking" for reasons connected with citizenship, lack of attendance or truancy, or the fact that he is a behavioral problem in school. His response to the school situation may indicate a lack of motivation, but he is not failing because he lacks ability for academic pursuits. When he does his work, it is not F work; his major difficulty is that he does not do his required work.

Of the various types of dropouts, it is the capable dropout that is considered a contemporary social problem, because his abilities and potentialities are not realized, and thus constitute a societal waste. The available data indicate that at least half and perhaps as many as three fourths of all dropouts have the necessary ability to graduate from high school.[26] Involuntary dropouts, who have adequate ability, comprise a relatively small percentage of these dropouts. This implies that many dropouts are intellectually capable, but the evidence is by no means clear. This poses an important research question: What is the proportion of dropouts in each of the types identified?

Analysis of intelligence scores, reading achievement scores, grades and other information readily available in school records will be of limited utility in attempting to identify which students, among those who are intellectually capable, are potential dropouts. To determine why capable students drop out will require investigation of sociological and psychological variables and examination of the educational philosophy governing the schools. In another paper it is proposed that the explanation of why capable students drop out must be sought in an analysis of the social milieu of the

[26] Layton, *op. cit.*; McCreary and Kitch, *op. cit.*; U.S. Department of Labor, *op. cit.*

school, peer and parental attitudes toward education, and the student's position in the web of peer group interaction.[27]

CONCLUSION

The prevalent stereotype of dropouts depicts them as persons lacking in intellectual ability; but the evidence indicates that many dropouts are capable of doing satisfactory work in high school. Further, the available data demonstrate that while some dropouts earn poor grades, are retarded in their grade placement, and are poor readers, many other dropouts do not face these particular problems.

Many of the apparent contradictions in the findings concerning dropouts can be resolved by distinguishing between early and late dropouts. Students with limited ability generally leave school early, whereas capable dropouts tend to remain in school longer. Hence, the stereotype of the dropout emphasizes the characteristics of early dropouts, of whom a significant proportion are of limited intellectual capability, receive poor grades, are poor readers, and are retarded in their grade placement.

Comprehension of the diverse data concerning dropouts requires the specification of three types: 1) involuntary dropouts, those who leave school as a consequence of some personal crisis such as the death of a parent; 2) retarded dropouts, those who lack sufficient ability to handle academic pursuits and who tend to drop prior to entering high school; and 3) capable dropouts, those who terminate their education prior to high school graduation, despite the fact that they have the ability to do the required academic work.

[27] D. S. Elliott, H. L. Voss, and A. Wendling, "Capable Dropouts and the Social Milieu of the School" (Unpublished manuscript).

Janet Combs
William W. Cooley

Dropouts: In High School
and After School

The difficulty of distinguishing between high-school dropouts and non-dropouts is illustrated clearly in the elaborate, empirical study presented below. Drawing their subjects from the original Project TALENT survey of 440,000 pupils, Combs and Cooley employed 7,494 boys and girls, including both dropouts and those who graduated from high school but entered neither a four-year college nor a junior college. Differences between the dropout and control groups, for each sex, were compared on the three following bases: (a) Project TALENT tests of academic ability, interests, self-perceptions, high-school activities, and socio-economic environment, which were administered in the ninth grade, (b) measures of reasons for leaving high-school and post-high-school activities, the data of which were obtained through mailed questionnaires in an after-leaving-school follow-up study, and (c) comparison of the results of the ninth-grade and post-high-school studies in respect to high-school curriculum and career plans. The carefully executed study reveals that major differences between dropouts and nondropouts are elusive, at least before age 20, and that expressed reasons for leaving school may be unrelated to actual reasons. The data, nonetheless, underscore the importance of acquiring during the high-school years relatively adult-oriented interests and mature self-perceptions.

I N 1960 Project TALENT tested approximately 440,000 students attending over 1,300 public and private high schools in all parts of the country. The second phase of this large-scale longitudinal study of American youth was the collection of follow-up data from the same young people tested in 1960. Using data collected from one of the grades participating in the original testing, the ninth grade, Project TALENT has identified students who did not complete high school. These boys and girls who dropped out of school after grade nine are the topic of this study.

Although numerous studies of dropouts have already been reported in the education literature, the particular combination of characteristics of this study make it somewhat unique in comparison with other efforts. First of

FROM *American Educational Research Journal*, V (1968), 343–363. Reprinted by permission of the authors and the American Educational Research Association.

all, it is longitudinal in nature; the initial measurements were made when the subjects were in ninth grade in 1960, with a follow-up in 1964. Secondly, the sample of subjects is a probability sample of the entire national ninth-grade population. Therefore, it is possible to estimate parameters of the dropout population which could not be estimated previously. Also, the TALENT test battery covers a broad spectrum of attributes. Thus, not only "IQ," but differential aptitudes and abilities, interests, self-perceptions, socio-economic environment, school curriculum, career plans, and a variety of post-high-school activities can be considered. Another important aspect of this study is that the sample consists of both males and females. Too often only male dropouts are considered, even though females drop out just as frequently as males. Finally, comparisons can be made between dropouts and their former classmates who remained in school until graduation.

In most of the analyses reported in this article, all of the known dropouts in the original TALENT ninth-grade sample are contrasted with random subsamples of high-school graduates from the same grade sample who did not enter a four-year or junior college. These subsamples, designated the "controls," consist of 23 per cent of the male and 20 per cent of the female graduates on the TALENT data file who did not continue their education beyond high school. Comparing dropouts with these control groups seemed more meaningful than comparing them with high-school graduates in general. The number of subjects constituting each of the four samples used in this study is as follows:

Dropout Males	1,864
Control Males	1,757
Dropout Females	1,817
Control Females	2,056

(Missing data reduced these *N*'s for some of the analyses. As indicated in the several tables which follow, the losses were only slight.)

Information about the post-high-school activities of dropouts and controls was obtained through a follow-up survey conducted in 1964. For most of the members of the ninth-grade class of 1960, this was one year after high-school graduation. For the dropouts, it could have been as many as four years after leaving high school. The first phase of the follow-up survey consisted of four waves of mailed questionnaires. Thirty-seven per cent of the sample responded to one of these four mailings. To correct the nonrespondent bias, field surveys of a stratified sample of approximately four per cent of the nonrespondents were conducted. Then, by combining and weighting data from these two groups, respondents and the sample of nonrespondents, unbiased estimates of national subpopulations such as dropouts after grade nine, can be made. Analyses using these weighted data are so indicated. (See Flanagan and Cooley,[1] 1966, for a description of the Project TALENT follow-up surveys.)

[1] J. C. Flanagan and W. W. Cooley, *Project TALENT One-Year Follow-Up Studies* (Pittsburgh: Project TALENT Office, 1966).

Although dropouts tended not to respond to the mailed questionnaires, a comparison of dropout respondents with those dropouts found in the non-respondent follow-up revealed that the dropout respondents do not differ significantly from the dropout nonrespondents. It was also found that the nonrespondents located in field surveys do not differ significantly on traits previously measured in high school from those nonrespondents who were not located. Therefore, even though all possible dropouts were not located, the evidence indicates that the descriptions of the dropouts reported here are not significantly biased by incomplete data. The bias is that our sample of dropouts is smaller than would be expected, but this, of course, is adjusted by the weighting system.

THE BOYS WHO DROPPED OUT

Abilities

The first measure which will be discussed is the General Academic Ability Composite in the TALENT battery. (See Flanagan,[2] 1962 and 1964 for descriptions of the Project TALENT tests.) The percentages of dropouts and controls in each of four ability levels are shown in Table 1.

Table 1   Academic Ability of Dropouts, Graduates, and All Grade 9 Males (Percentages Based on Weighted Frequencies)

Level	Dropouts (N = 1,686)	Controls (N = 1,655)	All Grade 9 Males (N = 48,734)
1 (Bottom Quarter)	55	28	25
2	25	39	25
3	15	22	25
4 (Top Quarter)	5	11	25
	100	100	100

These levels represent quarters in the 1960 grade nine population. Quartiles are estimated from the total national Project TALENT norms, which include individuals who enter college.[3]

As this table indicates, more than one half of the dropouts were in the bottom quarter (1), compared to 28 per cent of the controls. In the middle levels (2 and 3) were 40 per cent of the dropouts and 61 per cent of the graduates. Only 5 per cent of the dropouts ranked in the highest level, compared to 11 per cent of the controls.

[2] J. C. Flanagan, J. T. Daily, M. F. Shaycoft, D. B. Orr, I. F. Goldberg, and C. A. Neyman, *Design for a Study of American Youth* (Boston: Houghton Mifflin Co., 1962); J. C. Flanagan, F. B. Davis, J. T. Daily, M. F. Shaycoft, D. B. Orr, I. F. Goldberg, and C. A. Neyman, *The American High-School Student* (Pittsburgh: Project TALENT Office, 1964).

[3] J. C. Flanagan, *et al., The American High-School Student, op. cit.*

As Table 1 reveals, not all dropouts are below average in ability, as many people think. Other studies are in line with this finding. A report by Warner [4] presented the results of three statewide studies, one U.S. Department of Labor study involving seven communities, and five studies conducted by city schools. There were 21,497 dropouts involved. Approximately 19 per cent of this sample were reported to have IQ's between 90 and 109 and 11 per cent with 110 or above IQ's. French [5] summarizes additional studies revealing that not all dropouts are below average in ability.

Table 2 shows the mean scores of dropouts and controls on 19 Project

Table 2   Mean Scores of Male Dropouts and Controls on TALENT Ability Tests

	Dropout Mean (N = 1,494)	Control Mean (N = 1,533)	Pooled Standard Deviation	F Ratio*
English Total	63.9	71.5	13.5	255
Information I Total	100.7	117.8	32.1	232
Information II Total	49.4	57.8	17.6	181
Reading Comprehension	19.0	23.5	9.9	167
Introductory High-School Math	7.0	8.5	3.4	156
Arithmetic Reasoning	5.9	7.0	3.0	114
Arithmetic Computation	9.0	19.8	28.9	110
Abstract Reasoning	6.8	8.0	3.1	109
Word Functions in Sentences	5.8	7.0	3.3	105
Table Reading	1.9	5.5	12.3	67
Disguised Words	9.8	11.4	5.6	63
Memory for Words	8.1	9.3	4.2	62
Creativity	6.4	7.3	3.5	52
Memory for Sentences	7.9	8.7	3.1	51
Clerical Checking	8.8	14.7	23.2	50
Visualization in Three Dimensions	7.4	8.1	3.2	47
Mechanical Reasoning	10.2	11.1	4.0	39
Visualization in Two Dimensions	11.4	12.6	5.6	37
Object Inspection	17.5	18.7	9.0	13

* All are significant at the .01 level (*nfd*'s are 1 and 3025).

TALENT ability tests. Controls scored significantly higher than dropouts on all these tests. The variables are ordered according to their *F* ratios, indicating the extent of the differences between the two groups. As can be seen in this list, the groups tended to exhibit smaller differences on the nonverbal tests than on the verbal ones.

[4] O. R. Warner, "The Scholastic Ability of School Dropouts," *Selected Reports and Statistics on School Dropouts* (U.S. Office of Education, 1964).

[5] J. French, "High School Dropouts of High Ability," *Vocational Guidance Quarterly* (Winter, 1965–1966), 123–127.

Interests

In the TALENT Interest Inventory the student was given a list of 205 occupational titles and names of vocationally-related activities and instructed to state his degree of liking for each. Seventeen scales were derived from this inventory. Table 3 reports the mean scores of dropouts and con-

Table 3   Mean Scores of Male Dropouts and Controls on TALENT Interest Inventory Scales

	Dropout Mean (N = 1,494)	Control Mean (N = 1,533)	Pooled Standard Deviation	F Ratio[*]
Controls Higher than Dropouts				
Sports	24.0	26.0	9.7	31
Physical Science, Engineering, Math	18.1	19.4	8.3	16
Dropouts Higher than Controls				
Labor	14.4	12.7	6.8	43
Skilled Trades	15.2	14.0	7.2	18
Musical	12.9	11.6	10.0	13

[*] Significant at the .01 level.

trols on each of the scales showing significant differences. The variables are organized according to the degree and nature of the observed differences.

Dropouts and controls differed significantly (.01 level) on only five of the seventeen scales. Dropouts had significantly higher scores on the Labor, Skilled Trades, and Musical scales. Although the musical interest result is puzzling, it is clear that the dropouts tended to be more willing to engage in manual labor. It is also interesting to note that boys expressing an interest in sports were less likely to drop out.

Self-Perceptions

To give the participants an opportunity to describe their concepts of themselves, the TALENT battery included a Student Activities Inventory. This inventory presented 150 statements, such as "I am sensitive," "I am usually at ease," and "I'd rather be with a group of friends than at home by myself." One set of distractors applied to all of the statements:

Regarding the things I do and the way I do them, this statement describes me:
A. extremely well
B. quite well
C. fairly well
D. slightly
E. not very well.

Each scored item contributed to the scaling of one of the ten scales.

The mean scores of dropouts and controls on each of these scales are presented in Table 4. Controls scored significantly higher than dropouts on seven

Table 4 *Mean Scores of Male Dropouts and Controls on TALENT Student Activities Inventory Scales*

	Dropout Mean (N = 1,494)	Control Mean (N = 1,533)	Pooled Standard Deviation	F Ratio
Controls Higher than Dropouts				
Tidiness	4.0	4.5	2.5	25
Calmness	3.0	3.3	2.1	20
Vigor	3.0	3.3	1.9	20
Self-Confidence	4.2	4.5	2.1	15
Culture	3.8	4.1	2.1	14
Mature Personality	8.6	9.2	4.5	12
Sociability	5.3	5.6	2.7	7
Dropouts Higher than Controls				
Impulsiveness	2.0	1.7	1.6	18
Leadership	1.1	1.0	1.2	7

of the scales: Tidiness, Calmness, Vigor, Self-Confidence, Culture, Mature Personality, and Sociability. Dropouts had higher mean scores on only two: Leadership and Impulsiveness. Lichter [6] has also indicated that dropouts have difficulty in controlling their impulses. And the results of a study by Kelly, Veldman, and McGuire [7] showed that an impulsivity measure significantly separated dropouts, delinquents, and normals.

High-School Activities

Part of the Student Information Blank consists of items on student activities, Lohnes [8] generated 11 scales based upon selected SIB items:

1. Memberships: 10 items on participation in school clubs.
2. Leadership: 3 items on frequency of elected office in various school activities.
3. Hobbies: 20 items indicating extent of participation in hobbies or extra-curricular activities.
4. Work: 17 items summarizing extent of paid work experience.
5. Social: 5 items on nature and extent of dating.
6. Reading: 9 items on extent of spare time reading.
7. Studying: 26 items based on study habits.

[6] S. O. Lichter, E. B. Rapien, F. Siebert, and M. A. Sklansky, *The Dropouts* (New York: The Free Press, 1962).
[7] F. J. Kelly, D. J. Veldman, C. McGuire, "Multiple Discriminant Prediction of Delinquency and School Dropouts," *Educational and Psychological Measurement*, XIV (Fall, 1964), 535–543.
[8] P. R. Lohnes and W. W. Cooley, *Predicting Development of Young Adults* (Palo Alto: Project TALENT Office, American Institutes for Research, 1968).

8. Curriculum: 1 item indicating difficulty level of school program in which student is enrolled.
9. Courses: 4 items on amount of college-preparatory work taken.
10. Grades: 7 items indicating school grades.
11. Guidance: 16 items on frequency with which school and work plans were discussed with counselors and other school personnel.

The differences between dropouts and controls on these 11 activities scales are summarized in Table 5. The two largest differences were the greater

Table 5   Mean Scores of Male Dropouts and Controls on TALENT Student Information Blank Scales

	Dropout Mean (N = 1,494)	Control Mean (N = 1,533)	Pooled Standard Deviation	F Ratio
Controls Higher than Dropouts				
Studying	49.8	56.2	17.1	108
Curriculum	2.5	2.8	1.7	23
Grades	11.5	12.5	7.3	14
Dropouts Higher than Controls				
Social	11.7	9.7	5.3	112
Work	21.8	19.2	8.6	68
Courses	3.8	3.0	3.2	58
Guidance	22.0	18.7	14.1	42
Memberships	11.5	9.6	9.7	28
Reading	14.7	13.4	9.3	15

frequency of dating among the dropouts (Social scale) and their reporting much more difficulty in studying and concentrating on their classwork than the graduates (Studying scale).

A very interesting difference is that the dropouts reported (as ninth-graders) having had many more guidance contacts with counselors and other school personnel than did the controls.

Socio-economic Environment

A socio-economic index was computed for each student on the basis of nine 1960 Student Information Blank questions. This index gives a measure of the general socio-economic level of the family environment. The items in the index are summarized as follows:

1. If your family has bought (or is buying) your home, what is its present value?
2. Please make the best estimate you can of your family's total income for last year (1959). Include money earned by both parents or anyone else in the household who worked.
3. How many books are in your home?

4. How many of the following articles are in your home: automatic washer, automatic clothes dryer, electric dishwasher, electric or gas refrigerator, vacuum cleaner, home food freezer (separate from refrigerator)?
5. How many of the following articles are in your home: telephone, television set, radio, phonograph?
6. How many of the following articles are in your home: a room of my own, my own study desk, a typewriter?
7. Which of the following comes closest to describing the work of your father (or the male head of your household)?
8. Mark the one answer indicating the highest level of education your father reached.
9. Mark the one answer indicating the highest level of education your mother reached.

Table 6 presents the percentages of dropouts and controls in each of the

Table 6   Socio-economic Level of Dropouts, Controls, and All Grade 9 Males (Percentages Based on Weighted Frequencies)

Level	Dropouts (N = 1,715)	Controls (N = 1,660)	All Grade 9 Males (N = 48,734)
1 (Bottom quarter)	51	48	25
2	27	30	25
3	16	19	25
4 (Top quarter)	6	3	25
	100	100	100

four socio-economic levels, the levels being determined by national norm quartiles. The percentages of dropouts and controls in each level were quite similar. Fifty-one per cent of the dropouts and 48 per cent of the graduates were in the lowest level. In the middle levels (2 and 3) ranked 43 per cent of the dropouts and 49 per cent of the controls. Six per cent of the dropouts were in the highest level, compared to 3 per cent of the young men who completed high school.

It is important to note that there was *no* significant difference between the dropouts and controls on this socio-economic environment variable, indicating that the economic conditions of the home do not appear to be forcing students out of school.

Reasons for Leaving

Before talking about what dropouts did after high school, their stated reasons for leaving school should be mentioned. Although the young men reported many reasons for dropping out (for example, needed at home, didn't like school, failing, got married, felt too old to stay in school), it is unwise to say that so many dropped out because of reason 1, so many because of reason 2, etc. A dropout may say that he left school because he was failing. The reason for his failure, however, may have been that he was working every night to help support his family. Another reason given was "felt too old to stay in school." The cause of his being older than his classmates was probably an early failure, which may have been due to physical or emotional problems or lack of ability. Therefore, this reason, "felt too old," really tells us little, as do most of the other reported explanations.

Other investigators share this feeling. For example, after reviewing data collected from 12,608 dropouts in Ohio in 1962–63, Nachman, Getson, and Odgers [9] concluded that the reason for leaving school given by the dropout was usually not supported by his school record or the opinion of his counselor. In a survey of dropouts in Maryland,[10] "lack of interest" was found to be above a dozen other reasons for leaving school, such as cost, marriage, pregnancy, institutionalization, and military service. In second place was "lack of scholastic success." But "lack of interest" or "lack of scholastic success" are only symptoms, not the problems.

As far as being sorry about their decision to leave school, 57 per cent of the young men reported that they regretted dropping out.

Post-High-School Activities

In 1964, the employment rates of dropouts and controls were quite similar. Ninety per cent of the dropouts who did not continue their education after leaving high school were employed, 87 per cent full-time, 3 per cent part-time. Of the controls with no further training, 89 per cent had full-time jobs and 2 per cent part-time. The greatest percentages of dropouts were unskilled workers (driver, laborer, miner, and so forth), skilled workers (electrician, machinist, mechanic, and so forth), or service workers (waiter, hairdresser, barber, and so forth). The greatest percentages of controls were unskilled, skilled, or clerical and sales workers.

Although the difference between the percentages on active military duty was not striking (30 per cent, dropouts; 33 per cent, controls), there was a difference between the percentages serving in each branch. The greatest numbers of dropouts were in the Army or Navy, while the controls were most likely to serve in the Navy or the Air Force.

For the dropouts who were employed, the mean yearly salary was $3650; for controls, it was $3500. The probable reason for this difference is that dropouts had been working longer than controls, in some cases four years longer.

In the analysis of employment rates and salaries reported above, dropouts and controls *who had had some additional training after high school* were excluded, i.e., 36 per cent of the dropouts and 38 per cent of the controls. The greatest percentages from both of these groups who furthered their

[9] L. R. Nachman, R. F. Getson, J. G. Odgers, *Ohio Study of High School Dropouts 1962–1963* (State Department of Education, 1964).

[10] P. W. Huffington, *Pupil Dropout Study: Maryland Public Schools* (State Department of Education, 1962).

education attended an Armed Forces enlisted man's school. Seven per cent of the dropouts and four per cent of the controls went to trade schools. Technical schools were attended by 5 per cent of the controls, compared to only 0.7 per cent of the dropouts.

Another comparison between male dropouts and controls concerns marriage. In 1964, 37 per cent of the dropouts were married, compared to only 15 per cent of the controls.

Comparisons between 1960 and 1964 Data

Because the 1960 Project TALENT testing and the one-year follow-up survey did not, in general, gather the same kinds of information, it is not possible to make many comparisons between dropouts and controls in 1960 and in 1964. However, two comparisons can be made. The first concerns high-school curriculum; the second, career plans.

HIGH-SCHOOL CURRICULUM. The percentages of dropouts and controls who, in ninth grade, were either enrolled in or expecting to follow one of six curricula are shown in the left-hand columns of Table 7. The percentages

Table 7   High-School Curriculum of Male Dropouts and Controls (Percentages Based on Weighted Frequencies)

	Curriculum Expected at Grade 9		Curriculum Membership at Time of Leaving High School	
	DROPOUTS (N = 1,655)	CONTROLS (N = 1,590)	DROPOUTS (N = 1,801)	CONTROLS (N = 1,734)
General	25.2	33.8	73.2	59.3
College Prep	21.9	22.8	5.0	14.9
Commercial-Business	15.8	9.2	2.3	7.8
Vocational	18.1	15.9	6.8	6.7
Agricultural	9.8	8.9	5.5	2.6
Other	9.2	9.4	7.2	8.7
	100.0	100.0	100.0	100.0

who answered on the one-year follow-up questionnaire that they *had* taken one of six curricula are shown in the right-hand columns of the same table. As indicated, the percentages in all curricula, except *general*, decreased from grade 9 to grade 12. For dropouts, the percentage in the general curriculum rose from 25 to 73 per cent; for controls, from 34 to 59 per cent. A question arises here: Did enrollment in this general curriculum, which generally offers neither the intellectual stimulation of the academic curriculum nor the practical instruction of the vocational courses, influence the dropouts' decision to leave school? An answer cannot be given here, but educators should give some thought to the matter.

CAREER PLANS. The second comparison which can be made from 1960 to

1964 concerns career plans. In ninth grade (1960), 36 per cent of both drop-outs and controls planned careers requiring a college degree. The greatest percentages of dropouts wanted careers as engineers (15 per cent), farmers (10 per cent) or skilled workers (6 per cent). As ninth-graders, controls were most likely to plan careers in engineering (15 per cent), the Armed Forces (10 per cent), or farming (8 per cent).

In 1964 only 2 per cent of the young men who dropped out and 7 per cent of the controls planned careers for which a college education was re-quired. The greatest percentages of dropouts wanted to be structural (13 per cent) or skilled workers (12 per cent). The most common choices of the controls were skilled worker (12 per cent), structural worker (7 per cent), and engineering or scientific aide (7 per cent).

THE GIRLS WHO DROPPED OUT

Abilities

In Table 8 are the percentages of female dropouts and controls who ranked in each of four General Academic Ability Composite levels. These levels represent quarters in the 1960 grade 9 female population.

Table 8   Ability Levels of Dropouts, Controls, and All Grade 9 Females (Percentages Based on Weighted Frequencies)

Level	Dropouts (N = 1,670)	Controls (N = 1,954)	All Grade 9 Females (N = 50,442)
1 (Bottom quarter)	40	17	25
2	34	36	25
3	19	32	25
4 (Top quarter)	7	15	25
	100	100	100

As this table indicates, 40 per cent of the dropouts were in the bottom quarter, compared to only 17 per cent of the controls. Fifty-three per cent of the dropouts and 68 per cent of the controls ranked in the middle quarters. In the top ability quarter were 7 per cent of the girls who left high school and 15 per cent of the controls.

Table 9 reports the mean scores of dropouts and controls on the TALENT ability tests. As in the males' analysis the graduates had significantly higher scores than the controls on all the tests. Also, the ordering of the variables by discriminating power (F ratios) is very similar to the male order in Table 2.

Table 9   Mean Scores of Female Dropouts and Controls on TALENT Ability Tests

	Dropout Mean (N = 1,537)	Control Mean (N = 1,847)	Pooled Standard Deviation	F Ratio°
Information I Total	92.8	107.4	27.3	260
Information II Total	49.8	58.3	16.0	257
Introductory High-School Math	7.3	9.1	3.5	241
English Total	72.9	79.3	12.9	220
Reading Comprehenison	21.5	25.8	9.6	176
Arithmetic Computation	18.2	27.6	23.2	144
Abstract Reasoning	6.8	8.0	3.1	143
Word Functions in Sentences	7.0	8.7	4.4	136
Arithmetic Reasoning	5.7	6.9	3.0	134
Disguised Words	11.0	13.3	6.2	111
Memory for Words	9.4	10.9	4.7	84
Creativity	6.2	7.2	3.3	82
Table Reading	6.0	8.3	8.8	60
Mechanical Reasoning	7.0	7.8	3.2	57
Memory for Sentences	8.6	9.4	3.0	55
Clerical Checking	18.6	22.8	20.4	34
Visualization in Two Dimensions	9.8	10.9	5.3	34
Visualization in Three Dimensions	6.7	7.2	2.7	27
Object Inspection	18.9	20.0	8.0	17

° All significant at .01 level.

Interests

Table 10 presents the mean scores of dropouts and controls on the significant Interest Inventory scales. Notice that the female dropouts tended to have higher scores on the more masculine interest scales, while the two most important scales on which the controls were higher were social service and biomedical interests. Interests seem to be more highly related to dropping out for the females than for the males, where only five scales produced significant differences (Table 3).

Self-Perceptions

The mean scores of dropouts and controls on the Student Activities Inventory are shown in Table 11. Controls were significantly higher than dropouts on eight of the scales: Tidiness, Mature Personality, Vigor, Culture, Calmness, Sociability, Social Sensitivity, and Self-Confidence. There was no significant difference between the groups on Impulsiveness or Leadership as was the case for the male dropouts (Table 4).

Table 10   Mean Scores of Female Dropouts and Controls on TALENT Interest
Inventory Scales

	Dropout Mean (N = 1,537)	Control Mean (N = 1,847)	Pooled Standard Deviation	F Ratio*
Controls Higher than Dropouts				
Social Service	22.3	23.4	7.3	17
Biological Science-Medicine	13.2	14.5	9.8	16
Computation	14.6	15.5	7.6	13
Sports	17.4	18.5	9.5	10
Physical Science, Engineering, Math	10.3	11.0	7.1	8
Public Service	10.0	10.9	10.6	6
Dropouts Higher than Controls				
Labor	8.9	7.9	6.3	21
Skilled Trades	9.0	8.2	5.4	20
Mechanical-Technical	7.8	7.2	6.3	8
Hunting-Fishing	13.8	12.8	11.6	6

* All significant at .01 level.

Table 11   Mean Scores of Female Dropouts and Controls on TALENT Student
Activities Inventory Scales

	Dropout Mean (N = 1,537)	Control Mean (N = 1,847)	Pooled Standard Deviation	F Ratio*
Controls Higher than Dropouts				
Tidiness	5.2	5.8	2.7	45
Mature Personality	9.1	10.2	4.8	44
Vigor	3.1	3.4	2.1	29
Culture	4.8	5.2	2.2	23
Calmness	3.5	3.8	2.3	22
Sociability	6.4	6.9	2.9	21
Social Sensitivity	4.4	4.7	2.3	15
Self-Confidence	4.5	4.8	2.3	10

* All significant at the .01 level.

Socio-economic Level

In Table 12 are the percentages of dropouts and controls in each of four
socio-economic levels. These levels represent quarters in the 1960 grade-
nine population. Sixty-one per cent of the dropouts were in the lowest level,
compared to only 41 per cent of the controls. In the middle levels ranked
36 per cent of the dropouts and 51 per cent of the controls, and in the top
socio-economic quarter were 3 per cent of the girls who dropped out and

Table 12 *Socio-economic Levels of Dropouts, Controls, and All Grade 9 Females (Percentages Based on Weighted Frequencies)*

Level	Dropouts (N = 1,711)	Controls (N = 1,958)	All Grade 9 Females (N = 50,442)
1 (Bottom quarter)	61	41	25
2	22	28	25
3	14	23	25
4 (Top quarter)	3	8	25
	100	100	100

8 per cent of the controls. Socio-economic factors appear to be more related to dropping out among the females than among the males (compare Table 12 with Table 6).

Reason for Leaving

Approximately three quarters of the girl dropouts reported, "Got married," as their reason for leaving high school. Of all the female dropouts, 56 per cent reported that they were sorry they did not graduate.

Post-High-School Activities

Although the employment rates were quite similar for male dropouts and controls, they were quite different for girls from these two groups, primarily because of the higher percentage of early marriages among the dropouts. About 26 per cent of the female dropouts had full-time jobs in 1964, 18 per cent of those who were married, and 58 per cent of those still single. Of the girls who graduated from high school, but who did not go on to college, 53 per cent were employed full-time. Two per cent of the dropouts had part-time jobs, compared to 6 per cent of the girl graduates. Three per cent of the dropouts and 5 per cent of the graduates reported that they held jobs, but did not indicate whether these jobs were full-time or part-time.

There were differences, too, in the kinds of jobs held. Dropouts were most likely to work as miscellaneous service workers (food preparation, catering, and other food services; masseuse and other personal services; domestic; boardinghouse keeper) or laborers (miscellaneous skilled occupations, machine operator, and so forth). Female controls, on the other hand, worked mainly as stenographers, secretaries, or clerical workers.

As previously reported, male dropouts earned more than controls. With the girls, however, this was not the case. The mean yearly salary for dropouts was $2,570; for graduates, $2,790. Remember here, too, that the dropouts had, in many cases been working longer than the controls.

Another interesting comparison is schools attended after high school. Only

16 per cent of the girls who dropped out had some further training, compared to 38 per cent of the controls. Of the dropouts, the greatest percentages went to trade or business school. These two schools were also the most common choices of the girl controls, although the percentages attending were higher than those for dropouts.

As would be expected, the percentage of girl dropouts married was quite a bit higher than that for boys. By August, 1964, 81 per cent of the female dropouts were married or had been married at one time. Of the controls, only 44 per cent were married or had been.

Comparisons between 1960 and 1964 Data

HIGH-SCHOOL CURRICULUM. Table 13 compares the expected curricula of future dropouts and controls at grade 9 with their curriculum membership at the time they left high schol. The percentages in each curriculum, except

Table 13 High-School Curriculum of Female Dropouts and Controls (Percentages Based on Weighted Frequencies)

	Curriculum Expected at Grade 9		Curriculum Membership at Time of Leaving High School	
	FUTURE DROPOUTS (N = 1,642)	FUTURE CONTROL (N = 1,885)	DROPOUTS (N = 1,722)	CONTROL (N = 2,036)
General	25.3	22.1	66.9	35.5
College Prep	16.1	22.0	4.0	14.0
Commercial-Business	38.6	41.8	20.8	41.5
Vocational	12.1	5.4	2.9	1.2
Agricultural	.4	.4	—	—
Other	7.5	8.3	5.4	7.7
	100.0	100.0	100.0	100.0

general, decreased between the time these young people were in grade 9 and the time they either dropped out or graduated. The percentage of dropouts in the general curriculum increased from 25 to 67 per cent; the percentage of controls, from 22 to only 36 per cent.

CAREER PLANS. Comparing the career plans of dropouts and controls in 1960 (grade 9) and in 1964 we find that in grade 9 the greatest percentages of future dropouts chose careers as housewives (24 per cent), office workers (21 per cent), or nurses (12 per cent). Of the graduates-to-be, 34 per cent planned to be office workers; 14 per cent, nurses, and 11 per cent, housewives. In 1964 over one-half of the dropouts planned to be housewives. The percentage previously planning to be office workers decreased to 4 per cent, the percentage planning nursing careers to 2 per cent. In the same year, 34 per cent of the controls reported that they expected to be housewives; 23 per cent, office workers; 7 per cent, service workers.

SUMMARY

Using data from the 1960 TALENT testing and the one-year follow-up study, comparisons were made between dropouts and high-school graduates not going to a four-year or junior college (the controls). In the 1960 testing, male controls scored significantly higher than dropouts on all the TALENT ability tests. The differences for verbal tests were greater than those for the nonverbal. The ability findings were similar for girls. On the Interest Inventory scales, male controls had significantly higher mean scores on Sports and Physical Science, Engineering, Math; dropouts, on Labor, Skilled Trades, and Music. The girl controls indicated greater interest than the dropouts in seven areas: Physical Science, Engineering, Math; Biological Science-Medicine; Public Service; Social Service; Sports; and Computation. Female dropouts scored higher than controls on Hunting-Fishing, Mechanical-Technical, Skilled Trades, and Labor. On the Student Activities Inventory scales, male controls perceived themselves to be more sociable, vigorous, calm, tidy, cultured, self-confident, and mature than did the boys who dropped out; dropouts had higher mean scores on two SAI scales: Leadership and Impulsiveness. As for the girls, controls scored significantly higher than dropouts on all the scales except Leadership and Impulsiveness, on which the two groups did not differ significantly. A comparison of the socio-economic levels of dropouts and controls revealed that the female controls were more likely to rank in the upper socio-economic levels than were dropouts. For boys, however, the differences were not significant.

Data from the one-year follow-up study also revealed differences between young people who graduated from high school and those who did not. The male dropouts reported many reasons for leaving school; for girls, the most common explanation was marriage. As far as employment was concerned, the percentages of male dropouts and controls with jobs in 1964 were similar. However, there was a slight tendency for controls to hold higher level jobs than dropouts. The difference between the percentages from the two groups on active military duty was not striking. A comparison of salaries revealed that the male dropouts earned slightly more than controls. The young men who completed high school were more likely to further their education after high school; they were less likely to be married by 1964.

As might be expected, female controls were much more likely than dropouts to be employed in 1964. Controls were also more likely to hold higher level jobs than dropouts and to earn more. Comparing the percentages continuing their education after high school reveals that more than twice as many controls as dropouts had some further training. The percentage married was also quite different for the two groups, the percentage of dropouts being almost twice that of the controls.

Two comparisons were made between 1960 and 1964 data. The first concerned high-school curriculum. For boys and girls, dropouts and controls, the percentage in each curriculum except *general,* decreased from 1960 to 1964. However, the percentages of dropouts, male and female, in the general curriculum at the time of leaving high school were higher than the percentage of controls in that curriculum. The second 1960–1964 comparison dealt with career plans. For all groups, male and female dropouts and controls, career plans were more realistic in 1964 than in 1960, with the percentages planning professional careers decreasing. For both males and females, there was a tendency for controls to plan higher level jobs than dropouts.

Of course, it is one thing to show a long list of significant differences between dropouts and controls and quite another to predict which ninth-graders will subsequently drop out of high school. Attempts to do the latter with multivariate prediction techniques are summarized in a Project TALENT monograph.[11]

One of the reasons for undertaking this dropout investigation was to try to develop data about dropouts for use in high-school guidance. It was hoped that the results would reveal that the noncollege high-school graduate (the control) was much better off than the high-school dropout as far as future employment and earnings are concerned. Large differences in this area might help to dissuade some students from leaving high school before graduation. Although there are other cultural advantages in continued education, such practical data would probably have a more direct impact on potential dropouts.

Unfortunately, the results were not consistent with these expectations. Not only were the male dropouts earning as much as the controls, but they had been earning it longer. Thus, economically, the dropout was certainly at an advantage over the student who stayed to graduate. Of course, it must be remembered that when the follow-up data were collected, the dropouts were only about 19 years old. Many of the consequences of leaving high school prior to graduation may not become apparent until later in life. Project TALENT is continuing to collect follow-up data on these people and perhaps subsequent criteria will show more precisely the disadvantages of dropping out of high school.

[11] P. R. Lohnes and W. W. Cooley, *op. cit.*

Brian Sutton-Smith

John M. Roberts

B. G. Rosenberg

Sibling Associations and Role Involvement

Social scientists have long been intrigued by the proposition that family experiences associated with brothers' and sisters' birth order and ordinal position influence personality development. In this paper, Sutton-Smith, Roberts, and Rosenberg review earlier studies that have shown "the higher achievement and responsibility training of first-borns" and "the greater amount of attention to them and preference for them." The researchers take the position that the effects of sibling associations result from social learning. They explore the likelihood that birth order parameters will be systematically related to adult role differentiation generally and to occupational preferences specifically. Although the variables they use are difficult to define operationally and the present state of science precludes analyses by birth order on individual bases, the results do indicate that birth order is associated with predispositions toward certain occupational styles. The researchers thus conclude that "the differences in ordinal position and sibling status may well have a bearing on the staffing, involvement, and recruiting of the members for the complex role system in our society."

THIS paper proposes that a person's experience of particular sibling associations may have a lasting effect upon his involvement in adult roles. It reviews the evidence from several earlier investigations dealing with the effects of ordinal position and sibling sex status on role involvement. A first monograph studied the responses of preadolescent children in the eight, two-child ordinal positions and the twenty-four, three-child ordinal positions to anxiety, impulsivity and masculine-feminine inventories.[1] A second article compared the effects of ordinal position at age 20 years with its effects at ages 10 and 6. In this study use was made of the Minnesota Multiphasic Inventory (MMPI), a device for clinical diagnosis.[2] A third article demon-

FROM *Merrill-Palmer Quarterly of Behavior and Development*, X (1964), 25–38. Reprinted by permission of the authors and the publisher.

[1] B. G. Rosenberg and B. Sutton-Smith, "Ordinal Position and Sex-Role Identification," *Psychological Monographs*, LXX (1964), 297–328.

[2] B. Sutton-Smith and B. G. Rosenberg, "Age Changes in the Effects of Ordinal Position on Sex-Role Identification," *The Journal of Genetic Psychology*, CVII (1965), 61–73.

strated that ordinal position affects responses not only on self-report inventories but also on cognitive variables.[3] The present paper adds data from the responses of 20-year-olds in the eight, two-child ordinal positions on the Strong Vocational Interest Inventory, the most widely used test for predicting vocational preferences.

In general, it can be said that the studies so far completed indicate that the effects of ordinal position and sibling sex status vary with age and with the nature of the variables being considered. Sex of sibling has stronger effects on adjustment, anxiety and interest inventories, and ordinal position has stronger effects upon mental abilities—with boys affecting girls more than vice versa, and first-borns affecting non-first-borns more than vice versa. In explaining the effects of different ordinal positions and sibling sex status on masculine-feminine role differences, the view has been taken that these positions and statuses are arbitrary phenomena, so that if systematic relationships are found, the problem is to locate the different types of learning experience involved.[4] In the recent literature there has been, perhaps, an overstress on primary socialization as the critical learning experience and the reason for the differences which occur between the different ordinal positions.[5] Less attention has been paid to the role of secondary socialization factors. Yet it was assumed traditionally that first-born males, as in the case of cultures stressing primogeniture, received special acculturative pressures throughout their development.

In the explanations that follow it will be assumed similarly that the effects of ordinal position are not due simply to infant patterns of reinforcement, but also to the fact that these continue to be supported by later socialization procedures on the part of adults. A number of investigators have suggested the nature of such procedures.[6] Mention has been made, for example, of the higher achievement and responsibility training of first-borns, the greater amount of attention to them and preference for them, and the like. Continuous and changing influences of these sorts on the part of parents are perhaps most appropriately termed *position-typing* influences, to distinguish them from *sex-typing* influences about which relatively more seems to be known.[7]

[3] B. G. Rosenberg and B. Sutton-Smith, "Relation of Birth Order, Sex-Role Identification and Mental Ability," Paper Presented at the Biennial Meeting of Society for Research in Child Development (Berkeley, California, April 3, 1963).

[4] R. R. Sears, "Ordinal Position in the Family as a Psychological Variable," *American Sociological Review*, XV (1950), 397–401.

[5] S. Schacter, *The Psychology of Affiliation* (Stanford, Calif.: Stanford University Press, 1959).

[6] J. H. S. Bossard, "Personality Roles in the Large Family," *Child Development*, XXVI (1955), 71–78; M. H. Krout, "Typical Behavior Patterns in Twenty-Six Ordinal Positions," *Journal of Genetic Psychology*, LV (1939), 3–30; J. K. Lasko, "Parental Behavior toward First and Second Born Children," *Genetic Psychology Monograph*, XLIX (1954), 97–137; B. C. Rosen, "Family Structure and Achievement Motivation," *American Sociological Review*, XXVI (1961), 574–578; E. E. Sampson, "Birth Order, Need Achievement and Conformity," *Journal of Abnormal and Social Psychology*, LXIV (1962), 155–159.

[7] B. R. McCandless, *Children and Adolescents: Behavior and Development* (New York: Holt, Rinehart and Winston, 1961), p. 329.

The learning experiences which a child gets in nuclear families as a result of his ordinal position and sibling sex status, however, do not derive solely from the position and sex-typing influence of his parents. The child is, in fact, involved in at least two broad classes of dyadic relationships. The first is with his parents. The second is with his siblings and may be conceptualized partly, at least, in terms of the sex and power of those siblings. In our previous work for example, the all-male dyad of two boys (M1M and MM2)[8] has been found to be more masculine than the other two-boy ordinal positions (M1F and FM2) at all age levels. The least well adjusted dyad has been the older girl with a younger brother (F1M and FM2). The evidence from these and other studies[9] seems to support the view that girls are more influenced by both their siblings and their parents than are boys. There may even be some respects and some relationships in which the influence of the siblings is more important than that of the parents. While it is impossible to say at this point how strong the respective influences are, it is clear that the matter is now open for debate, and the preponderant attention usually given to parents, called in question.

CULTURAL INTERPRETATION

At this juncture in the present program of research it is possible to go in either of two directions. The specific learning experiences that lead to the ordinal position and sibling sex status effects can be directly examined. Or, the general function of such positions and statuses in culture can be studied. This particular paper takes the latter alternative, and subsumes the previous interpretations of the data which were defined narrowly in social learning terms, within a broader cultural paradigm. The system presented is admittedly speculative, but if it serves to force our attention beyond its present theoretical encapsulation within the parent-child interaction, it may serve a useful purpose. The stance taken is that sibling association effects, because they are matters of social learning and not simple facets of nature, will demonstrate systematic relationships to cultural functions on the adult level. And that this occurs because the role differentiations that are learned in childhood lead to the development of interests and competencies which are functional both for the individual and the culture. (The notion of an implicit process of cultural selection and survival of adaptive social characteristics is implied by the statement.)

At the cultural level of analysis the relationships between role differentiation and the informational storage, retrieval, and decision-making processes found in simple and complex cultures has been discussed elsewhere.[10]

---

[8] The letters M or F denote the sex of the subject or the sibling. The number follows the letter designating the subject and refers to the subject's ordinal position (1=first-born; 2=second-born). Thus, "M1M"=first-born boy with younger brother; "FM2" =second-born boy with older sister.

[9] R. F. Winch, *Identification and its Familial Determinants* (Indianapolis: Bobbs-Merrill Co., 1962).

[10] J. M. Roberts, "The Self-Management of Cultures," *Exploration in Cultural Anthropology*, ed. Ward Goodenough (in press).

In simple cultures where the average adult controls a substantial portion of the total cultural content, role differentiation is minimal. But in complex cultures where the average adult cannot control more than the smallest fraction of the total cultural content, role differentiation or specialization is extreme. In any complex culture, therefore, role recruitment constitutes a cultural problem. In earlier research it has been suggested that in the case of the Zuni pueblo, differences in child socialization between and within families, variations in adult personalities, differences in value orientations, and a complex array of social roles are functionally related; further, that this totality constitutes a solution to the Zuni problem of using a small number of people to staff a moderately complex role system.[11] Thus, in general, it follows that if a culture is complex and there is considerable role variation in childhood, then the greater the predisposition the child is given by his childhood experience to play a specialized type of role, the more effective will be his subsequent performance in the adult culture.

Since a complex role system taps diverse interests and talents, it is to the advantage of society to socialize its members in such a way that they display diverse interests and talents, favorable to satisfying the diverse recruitment needs of the role system as a whole. At a general level this circumstance is dramatically achieved in the differential socialization of boys and girls and their recruitment into different sex roles. In more complex societies the same sex differentiation obtains but it is further varied by the different socialization patterns occurring in distinctive class, occupational, rural, urban, religious, military and other settings. It is our present contention that still another mechanism providing for the differential socialization of children is that provided by the social learning experiences associated with different ordinal positions and sibling sex statuses.

The current literature on ordinal position may be read to contain support for this type of position. Take, for example, the various writings that appear to imply greater affiliation needs in first borns.[12] Hypothetically we may generalize that in the nuclear family of modern industrial society it has been advantageous to have first-born children (on the farm, the eldest son), who were high in affiliation needs so that they would be responsible for the care of their parents and other aged and weak dependents, and younger children low in such needs so that they could easily set up independent lives in distant places. If the position-typing of the parents favored such differences in affiliation needs it would be culturally adaptive.

In order to take the discussion off this more speculative plane, however, we have currently been investigating relationships between different ordinal positions, sibling sex statuses, and occupational preferences. If the position-typing, sex-typing, and sibling association influences follow the lines we

---

[11] J. M. Roberts, "The Zuni," *Variations in Value Orientations*, eds. F. R. Kluckhohn and F. L. Strodtbeck (Evanston, Ill.: Row, Peterson, 1961), pp. 284–316.

[12] Schacter, *op. cit.*; Sears, *op. cit.*; P. C. Capia and J. E. Dittes, "Birth Order as a Selective Factor Among Volunteer Subjects," *Journal of Abnormal and Social Psychology*, LXIV (1962), 302; I. Sarnoff and P. Zimbardo, "Anxiety, Fear, and Social Affiliation," *Journal of Abnormal and Social Psychology*, LXII (1961), 356–363.

have suggested there should be a relationship between these positions and occupational preferences. It is unlikely, of course, that such variation in socialization as occurs regularly among different positions is enough to permit the prediction of specific occupational choices. Nevertheless, if it can be argued that life in a specific position predisposes a person to certain classes of occupation, some cogency will have been added to the general line of argumentation presented above.

METHOD

As a pilot study the Strong Interest Inventory was administered to 137 college sophomores in an elementary psychology class at Bowling Green State University. There were 72 women and 65 men, divided up amongst the eight ordinal positions as follows: F1F = 19; FF2 = 19; F1M = 18; MF2 = 16; M1M = 17; MM2 = 17; M1F = 16; FM2 = 15. The men were administered the 48-item male scale and the women the 29-item female scale. As 80 per cent of this group were sophomores in education and, therefore, already of homogeneous occupational grouping, it was not expected that many differences would be found between the varying ordinal positions, though it was felt that the directional findings might be of some value. There was no significant difference between groups on a manual/non-manual socio-economic comparison. The classification of occupations that follows was made on a variety of bases deriving from previous research. The classifications used made sense to these investigators, but must await further research if their reliability and validity is to be maintained, though as will be seen, most of them follow self-evident criteria.

RESULTS

The female groups showed a predominantly premarital career profile with higher scores in the occupations of elementary school teacher, office worker and stenographer secretary. For males the predominant profile in all groups included social science teacher, math and physics teacher, aviator, printer, and music performer. As Tables 1 and 2 indicate, the few differences found do not exceed chance expectation for the many possible comparisons involved. As this was an exploratory investigation, however, it was decided to compare the direction of the various scores across the ordinal position categories. In the following analysis, therefore, we will compare the frequencies with which particular ordinal groups have the highest average scores on the occupational categories. As each sex contains four ordinal groups (in a two-child family) it is possible for each group to have either the 1st, 2nd, 3rd or 4th highest score on a particular occupation. Further, it is possible to compare actual occupancy of the highest two positions (1st and 2nd) with the chance expectancy that high scores will be randomly distributed for each and all occupations across all ordinal groups. No levels of significance are given for this exercise as most of the group differences

Table 1   Group Differences on the Strong Interest Inventory: Males

Occupational Category	Sibling Positions			t	P
Psychologist	M1F	>	FM2	2.28	.05
	M1F ⎫ M1M ⎭	>	⎧ MM2 ⎩ FM2 ⎫⎭	2.43	.02
Architect	M1F ⎫ M1M ⎭	>	⎧ MM2 ⎩ FM2 ⎫⎭	1.91	.10
Public Administrator	M1M ⎫ M1F ⎭	>	⎧ MM2 ⎩ FM2 ⎫⎭	1.89	.10
CPA	M1M ⎫ M1F ⎭	>	⎧ MM2 ⎩ FM2 ⎫⎭	1.81	.10
Pharmacist	MM2	>	FM2	1.94	.10
Specialization Level	M1F	>	FM2	1.71	.10
	M1M ⎫ M1F ⎭	>	⎧ MM2 ⎩ FM2 ⎫⎭	2.19	.05

are not themselves significant, though many of the directional departures from chance distribution would be.

DISCUSSION

In the following discussion it will be assumed that high interest in an occupation disposes a person to ultimately find gratification in that occupation and to persist in it.[13] Which is to say that we are here assuming that occupation preference may be used as an index of role involvement, and that such role involvement may in turn be regarded as an index of suitability for recruitment to the role in question. The findings should be considered in that light.

1. It has been noted that first-borns appear to be higher on need achievement, academic achievement, and affiliation needs. There is research also suggesting that they have higher general responsibility training.[14] They are more often put in charge of other children and of household chores and in general get more extensive experience of playing an adult surrogate role than do non-first-borns. It might be predicted, therefore, that this would predispose them to take up parent surrogate occupational roles, in particular, teaching. On the male and female forms of the Strong Vocational Interest Inventory there are nine teaching occupations (English teacher,

[13] L. E. Tyler, *The Work of the Counselor* (New York: Appleton-Century, 1962).
[14] Bossard, *op. cit.*; Sampson, *op. cit.*

Table 2 **Group Differences on the Strong Interest Inventory: Females**

Occupational Category	Sibling Positions			t	P°
Artist	MF2	>	FF2	1.95	.10
Author	MF2	>	FF2	1.93	.10
Librarian	MF2	>	FF2	1.82	.10
	F1M	>	FF2	1.97	.10
English Teacher	F1F ⎱ F1M ⎰	>	⎰FF2 ⎱ ⎱MF2 ⎰	1.74	.10
Psychologist	FF2	>	MF2	1.83	.10
Lawyer	FF2	>	F1F	2.07	.05
Social Science Teacher	F1M	>	MF2	2.69	.02
YWCA Secretary	F1M ⎱ FF2 ⎰	>	⎰MF2⎱ ⎱MF2⎰	1.88 / 1.85	.10 / .10
Life Insurance Sales	MF2	>	F1F	1.94	.10
	FF2	>	F1F	1.86	.10
	MF2⎱ FF2 ⎰	>	⎰F1F ⎱ ⎱F1M⎰	2.25	.05
Nurse	F1F	>	FF2	2.18	.05
	F1F ⎱ F1M ⎰	>	⎰FF2 ⎱ ⎱MF2⎰	1.89	.10
Math-Science Teacher	F1F	>	MF2	2.40	.05
	F1M	>	MF2	1.71	.10
	F1F ⎱ F1M ⎰	>	⎰FF2 ⎱ ⎱MF2⎰	2.18	.05
Lab Technician	F1F	>	FF2	2.03	.05
	F1F	>	MF2	1.79	.10
	F1F ⎱ F1M ⎰	>	⎰MF2⎱ ⎱FF2 ⎰	1.83	.10
Engineer	F1F	>	MF2	2.29	.05

° All tests are two-tailed.

social science teacher, elementary school teacher, home economics teacher, math and science teacher, physical education teacher, business education teacher, industrial arts teacher, vocational agricultural teacher), which because of the overlap between the scales present 22 possibilities for scoring in the 1st or 2nd highest positions. While we might expect by chance a distribution of 11:11 first- and second-borns in these two highest scoring positions, we find in fact that 18 of the two highest scoring positions are occupied by first-borns. It will be noted that the relevant results in Table 2 are consistent with this direction. First-born girls have higher scores ($p = < .10$) on English teacher, social science teacher, and math and science teacher. Perhaps the surrogate training provided in the family has cultural advantages in predisposing first-borns, in particular first-born girls, to show greater interest in these roles.

2. The foregoing finding suggested the possibility that first-borns would, in general, prefer culturally conservative roles. There was support for this view in earlier work showing first-borns to be more conforming,[15] and to have stronger identification with parents.[16] Hypothetically it may have been culturally adaptive to have at least one segment of the population more or less committed to the preservation of the traditional social roles. Our definition of conservative occupation was derived rather tenuously from Getzels' and Jackson's work on creativity.[17] They demonstrated that less creative persons were more likely to prefer professional occupations. It has already been demonstrated that first-borns have a higher preference for the academic professions. Results for other professions, were not, however, so striking. There were 32 possible 1st or 2nd highest scoring positions and 21 of these were occupied by first-borns. This is not a sufficiently striking departure from chance expectation to suggest that this particular generalization merits much further consideration—though there is some support for the idea in Table 1, where first-born males show higher scores on Psychology, Public Administration and CPA. Results for females are inconclusive.

3. In addition to contrasts between ordinal positions, the present investigators were interested in the effects of particular sibling dyads [18] on occupational choices. It has already been mentioned that the all-boy dyad (M1M and MM2) was the most masculine in all previous studies, using the MMPI at age 20, the Rosenberg-Sutton-Smith masculinity-femininity play scale at preadolescence,[19] and scores derived from Koch's studies at age 6.[20] This dyad had the most masculine scores on the Strong Interest Inventory. Examination of the occupations for which this dyad shares the highest preferences (1st or 2nd) indicates that they include the activities of producing, buying, and selling—all of which may be ultimately related to standard economic transactions within this culture. These occupations are: life insurance salesman, buyer, real estate salesman, banker, purchasing agent, production manager, farmer, accountant, sales manager, president of manufacturing company. First or second highest positions are occupied by this dyad in 18/20 cases. If masculinity is interpreted in its traditional

[15] S. W. Becker and J. Carroll, "Ordinal Position and Conformity," *Journal of Abnormal and Social Psychology*, LXV (1962), 129–131.

[16] R. R. Sears, E. E. Maccoby, and H. Levin, *Patterns of Child Rearing* (Evanston: Row, Peterson, 1957); N. Storer, "Ordinal Position and the Oedipal Complex," Lab. of Soc. Relat., *Harvard University Bulletin*, X (1961), 18–21.

[17] J. W. Getzels and P. W. Jackson, *Creativity and Intelligence* (New York: John Wiley and Sons, 1962), p. 56.

[18] These are inferred dyads. The complementary ordinal positions were *not* from the same families.

[19] B. G. Rosenberg and B. Sutton-Smith, "The Measurement of Masculinity and Femininity in Children," *Child Development*, XXX (1959), 373–378.

[20] O. G. Brim, Jr., "Family Structure and Sex-Role Learning by Children: a Further Analysis of Helen Koch's Data," *Sociometry*, XXI (1958), 1–16.

sense for this culture it may mean that boys who are higher in masculinity show a higher interest in conventional economic types of achievement.[21]

Throughout previous research the girl with the older brother (MF2) has, in general, been the most masculine girl, even to the extent of having a male cognitive profile with, in general, higher quantitative than verbal scores. On the present female inventory this girl shows the highest interest in the two economic items on that list, life insurance and buyer.

We have been considering the characteristics which the members of the male dyad hold in common. It is also possible to consider the ways in which the members of this dyad are distinct. In a previous series of researches these investigators have been concerned with the development of two styles of achieving, or two success styles as they have been called. One of these is achievement by strategy; another is achievement by physical power. It has been contended that these styles are modelled by games of strategy and physical skill, and various sociometric and ludic correlates have been advanced in support of this position.[22] If particular ordinal positions predispose a person to one or other of these success styles and if it is possible to classify occupations in terms of the dominant success style involved, then it may be possible to discover a relationship between ordinal position and occupational choice.

Illustrations of physical power as a success style may be found in the application of physical power to persons, animals, and other living things. A case can be made for the presence of this style in eight of the occupations on the male scale: physician, osteopath, dentist, veterinarian, farmer, policeman, mortician (by extension), and YMCA physical director. In the present data for males, first place for all these roles is occupied by second-born males (MM2), except for physician, where the second-born holds 2nd place. In only one instance do the first-born males occupy either of the first two positions on any of these occupations, and that is 2nd place on mortician.

In sum, the second-born boy is always found in either a 1st or 2nd highest scoring position for power occupations; whereas with one exception, the first-born boy (M1M) is always found in a 3rd or 4th position. (8:0-1:7)

A second success style is that of the strategist where outcomes are determined through rational decisions. Several of the studies cited above have shown a relationship between games of strategy and aspects of managing social systems. One can argue that in all the following roles, management of a social system is involved: production manager, personnel director, public administrator, YMCA secretary, city school superintendent, social

21 D. R. Miller and G. E. Swanson, *The Changing American Parent* (New York: John Wiley and Sons, 1958); D. C. McClelland, *The Achieving Society* (Princeton: D. Van Nostrand, 1961).

22 J. M. Roberts, M. J. Arth, and R. R. Bush, "Games in Culture," *American Anthropologist*, LXI (1959), 597–605; J. M. Roberts and B. Sutton-Smith, "Game Involvement in Children," *Ethnology*, X (1962), 166–185; B. Sutton-Smith and J. M. Roberts, "Game Involvement in Adults," *Journal of Social Psychology*, LX (1963), 15–30; B. Sutton-Smith and J. M. Roberts, "Rubrics of Competitive Behavior," *Journal of Genetic Psychology*, LX (1963), 15–30.

worker, CPA, senior CPA, accountant, office man, purchasing agent, banker, sales manager, lawyer, president manufacturing concern. In all cases 1st or 2nd position is occupied by an M1M. The second-born boys are distributed randomly across all scoring positions, so that while it is true to say that first-borns are to be found exclusively in strategic occupations, it is not true to say that non-first-born boys are never found in strategic positions. There is slight support in Table 1 for this difference between older and younger boys. First-borns show a greater interest in the strategic occupations of CPA and Public Administrator. Early research [23] has suggested that differences in child training may help to account for these differences, though the second-born boy's preference for power style may perhaps result from a reaction to dominance by the elder brother.[24]

The male dyad then is distinguished by its masculinity and by its interest in conventional economic activities. The older brother shows a consistent preference for a strategic success style and the younger brother shows a preference for a power success style.

4. In general, we would expect the all-girl dyad to have high feminine scores on most inventories (F1F and FF2). But their scores have not been consistently the most feminine across all age levels and all scales, though there is a tendency for that to be the case. This feminine dyad does not, however, differ from other girl's groups in this inconsistency of scoring pattern on masculine-feminine scales. The two girls do have the highest feminine scores on the present inventory. They share additionally the two highest scoring positions on the occupations of office work and stenographer-secretary. There is a suggestion here, perhaps of some variable of routine-responsibility as a central kernel to the female role. This same dyad is not as clearly differentiated on the success styles as was the case with the male dyad, but such differences as there are, occur in the reverse direction from those found with the boys.

There are three occupations that fit within the definition of the strategic success style (social worker, lawyer and YWCA secretary) and the second-born girl (FF2) is always in one of the two highest scoring positions and the first-born girl (F1F) is never in one of those positions. There are six occupations on the female scale which appear to fit the definition of the power success style. These are: nurse, dentist, laboratory technician, physician, dietitian, and physical therapist. With one exception the highest score is always obtained by F1F. Without exception the second highest score is obtained by F1M. In sum, the power style is quite clearly a first-born girl's monopoly on this scale (11:1). First-born girls appear to prefer a power style, which together with their preference for surrogate parent roles, strongly suggests the importance of nurturance and the physical management of resources to the first-born girl. It is not difficult to conjecture that the position typing effect of rewarding older girls for carrying out nurturance and responsibility would lead to the learning of high need nurturance and

[23] Roberts and Sutton-Smith, "Game . . .," *op. cit.,* 166–185.
[24] Krout, *op. cit.*

would be reflected in an occupational interest in roles allowing the continuance of surrogation and physical care. (We might hazard that this first-born girl, backed up by her mother, needs exercise little deception in the management of her younger siblings. The cultural and adaptive value of having a segment of the population with such an interest is self-evident. We may conjecture similarly, that the second-born girls' development of a strategic style may be reactive to the overpowering pressure of two mothers —the real mother and the older sister.)

5. In earlier work, it has been found that the opposite sex siblings affect the masculinity-femininity scores of the subject in the direction of the sibling's sex. In the present study it was found that the most expressively creative occupations of artist, music performer, author, and architect were preferred most by subjects with opposite sex siblings. All possible 1st and 2nd highest scoring positions were occupied by subjects with opposite sex siblings (14:0). The highest scoring positions (1st) are always occupied by the boy with the younger sister (M1F) on the male scale, and the girl with an older brother (MF2) on the female scale. This older brother, younger sister dyad is apparently the most creative. The next most creative dyad is the older sister (M1F) with the younger brother (FM2). The success style of these two dyads (M1F and MF2; F1M and FM2) is presumably that of creating new solutions and new culture. In earlier research with the MMPI it has been shown that the second and less creative of these dyads (F1M and MF2) has also the highest scores on emotional conflict. It is apparently the cross-sex affect, rather than the emotional conflict which contributes to the interest of these two dyads in the expressive arts. Table 2 offers some partial corroboration of the present directional findings by showing that MF2 has higher scores ($p = < .10$) than FF2 on the occupations of artist and author. It is interesting to note that the girl who is highest on expressive creativity (MF2) is also the girl highest on the earlier conventional economic items.

If the technically creative professions are considered—psychologist, physicist, mathematician, engineer, and chemist on the male scale; psychologist and engineer on the female scale—we find again that all the highest scoring positions are held by boys with a younger sister (M1F) (6:0). There is not, however, any consistent finding with regard to the younger sister (MF2). That is, M1F shows high interest in both the expressively and technically creative occupations, while MF2 shows consistent interest in only the expressively creative occupations. Similarly though not so markedly for the girls, the older sister with the younger brother (F1M) is always in the two highest positions for both expressive and technical creativity (lawyer and psychologist) but her younger brother (MF2) is not. Thus, both older brother (M1F) and older sister (F1M) are high on expressive and technical creativity, but their younger sister (MF2) and brother (FM2) respectively are high only on expressive items.

Highest scores for the girls on the technically creative items are taken by FF2 and F1M, and for the boys by the M1F just mentioned and MM2.

These particular two girl groups also get highest scores on the items mentioned above as involving a strategic success style. Putting the technically creative female items (2) together with the strategy female items (3), these two girl groups occupy all 1st and 2nd positions (10:0). There are no similar consistent relationships for these two groups of boys between technical creativity and strategy.

In conclusion, it seems evident that the differences in ordinal position and sibling status may well have a bearing on the staffing, involvement, and recruiting of the members for the complex role system in our society. The precise nature of the interrelationships must await further research. The importance of the study of sibling associations in other than the nuclear and the two-child family is certainly established.

CONCLUSION

Although the present classification of occupations is arbitrary and most of the present data only directional, considerable support has been given to the worthwhileness of a more extensive investigation of the following propositions:

A. That ordinal position and sibling sex status involve distinctive social learnings, deriving from the position-typing and sex-typing influences of the parents and other adults and from the interactive influence of the siblings.

B. That these distinctive social learnings have survived in modern complex culture because they in turn lead to the development of dispositions which are individually and socially of functional value.

C-1. That social learning amongst first-borns includes high surrogate training and strong identification with the parents (conscience, conformity, affiliation, dependency, volunteering, internalization) and leads both to academic success and a readiness to take parent-surrogate roles as exampled by a preference for teaching.

C-2. That the social learning in the male dyad (M1M and MM2), leads to high sex-role masculinity and high interest in conventional economic activities. That within this dyad the first-born male is differentiated from the second-born male by his interest in a strategic success style, and the latter is differentiated by his interest in a power success style.

C-3. That social learning in the female dyad leads to high femininity and an interest in routine occupations. That within this dyad the first-born is distinguished by an interest in a power success style (F1F) and the second-born (FF2) by an interest in a strategic success style. The girl dyad thus reverses the male dyad in its success style interests.

C-4. That the social learning in the opposite sex sibling dyads (M1F and MF2) (F1M and FM2) contributes to an interest in expressive creativity. The older brother and the younger sister comprise the most creative dyads. For both dyads the older members (M1F and F1M) also show interest in technical forms of creativity.

J. Kenneth Little

The Occupations of Non-College Youth

In this selection, Little compares male high-school seniors' occupational aspirations, social class, and school experiences with their vocational attainment seven or eight years after high school. The results show that college-bound seniors accurately predicted their future plans, that over half of the college dropouts had not planned to enter college in the first place, and that prestige of occupational attainment increased with level of educational attainment. The data clearly demonstrate that low success in high school compounds with limited economic and cultural resources to make moving up the status ladder exceedingly difficult. Little reports that occupational attainments of non-college youth nearly approximate their earlier aspirations. The basic problem, however, is that "the profile of human characteristics most valued by the occupational world is not identical with the profile of characteristics most rewarded by the educational world." Little thus sees the need for changes in traditional educational programs in the period "between mid-high school and mid-college—during which three fourths of American youth end their formal schooling."

THE world of work is placing increasing premium upon advanced levels of education and specialized types of training. Yet, 75–80 per cent of American youths are not completing college. What is the occupational destiny of youths with differing levels of education? For what part of the occupational world is attainment dependent upon education beyond high school? What are the characteristics of youth who reach differing levels of occupational attainment?

In the spring of 1957, a state-wide inquiry gathered information from over 35,000 graduating seniors of Wisconsin's public and private high schools. About 95 per cent of all graduates from about 95 per cent of Wisconsin's high schools participated. This information included statements about educational plans beyond high school, statements of occupational aspirations, and much background data about the graduates, their parents, and their school experiences.[1]

FROM *American Educational Research Journal*, IV (1967), 147–153. Reprinted by permission of the author and the American Educational Research Association.

[1] J. K. Little, *A State-Wide Inquiry Into Decisions of Youth About Education Beyond High School* (School of Education; University of Wisconsin, September, 1958).

During the calendar years 1964 and early 1965, follow-up inquiries were directed to the parents of a probability sample of about one third of the male youths of this 1957 crop of graduates. Usable returns were received from 85 per cent of the sample.

Of the 4,186 graduates about whom information was received, 378 were attending a vocational school or college; 447 were in military service; and 58 were unemployed. The total number for whom occupational attainment scores were available was then 3,378.

RELATION BETWEEN PLANS AND ACTION

The plans of the youths as stated by them at their high school graduation considerably underestimated their further schooling. Of 511 boys who did not plan further education, 303 actually attended a vocational or trade school, and 208 attended a four-year degree granting college. On the other hand, 365 boys who had planned some further education failed to continue their schooling. The net result was that 40 per cent of the total group had no further schooling; 16 per cent attended a vocational or trade school; and 43 per cent attended college (Table 1). Of those who attended college,

Table 1   Educational Plans and Their Fulfillment

	Plan	Action	Difference
To Attend College	1584 (37.8%)	1792 (42.9%)	+208
To Attend Vocational School	363 (8.7%)	666 (15.9%)	+303
To Get No Further Schooling	2239 (53.5%)	1728 (41.2%)	−511
Total	N = 4186 (100.0%)	4186 (100.0%)	0

however, more than a third (35 per cent) did not complete baccalaureate degrees.

The relative stability of the stated plans varied considerably among the three groups of youth. For example, 82 per cent of those planning to attend college did enroll in college; 67 per cent of those who planned no further schooling did not enroll in a post-high school institution; and 39 per cent of those who intended to enroll in a vocational or trade school did so enroll.

Thus, while forces prompting youth to acquire education beyond high school are clearly visible, the formal education of almost 60 per cent of the graduates ended with high school graduation, and for almost three fourths of them (73 per cent) education stopped short of completing a baccalaureate degree.

OCCUPATIONAL ATTAINMENT

Attention now turns to the occupations attained by the three groups of graduates. On the scale used in this study, occupations that require professional, scientific, or technical training, or high level executive or managerial abilities, typically have prestige scores above 75. Occupations that require little or no specialized training, including service workers, operatives and laborers, have prestige scores below 55. The large body of middle level occupations which include clerical and sales workers, craftsmen, foremen, sub-professional technicians, farmers and farm managers, and many others, have prestige scores that range from 55 to 75. For convenience, these three groups of occupations are called high-prestige, low-prestige, and middle-level occupations.

About a fourth of the graduates attained high-prestige occupations; another fourth were in low-prestige occupations; and one half in middle-level occupations (Table 2).

Table 2   Occupational Prestige Scores by Level of Education

Occupational Prestige Scores	None (N = 1529)	Vocational (N = 576)	College (N = 1156)	All Graduates (N = 3261)
90–99	—	—	4	4
80–89	14	17	266	297
70–79	293	200	558	1051
60–69	442	211	205	858
50–59	636	132	107	875
40–49	132	14	16	162
30–39	8	1	—	9
20–29	4	1	—	5
10–19	—	—	—	—
0–9	—	—	—	—
75th percentile	68.3	73.7	79.6	75.0
50th percentile	59.8	66.7	74.3	64.4
25th percentile	53.8	59.7	67.3	57.7

As expected, the prestige level of occupations increased with the type and level of education attained, but the differences in occupational attainment within each group were as noteworthy as the differences between the groups. For example, more than half of the youths who attended college did not attain high-prestige occupations, and only two out of five graduates who had no further education were in low-prestige occupations. About half of each of the three groups were in middle-level occupations.

The major difference between the three groups was the extent to which their members were able to reach high-prestige occupations or to escape low-prestige occupations. In this respect the non-college going group were clearly at a disadvantage. The vocational school group was an approximate cross-section of the total group and attained occupations in all prestige levels somewhat proportionately.

To summarize, occupations at any of the prestige levels were attained by persons with any of the three levels of schooling. The overlapping was particularly large in the middle-level occupations where college degrees are not a stated prerequisite. However, the occupational advantage of most persons who had attended college is definite; the occupational handicap of most persons who had no education or training beyond high school is serious. This is not to imply, however, that the differences in occupational attainment were attributable to differences in educational opportunity. Variations in human aptitude and aspiration growing out of a complex of psycho-cultural factors were definitely at work.

BACKGROUND FACTORS IN OCCUPATIONAL ATTAINMENT

The attainment of high-prestige occupations was found to be associated with the following background factors: attendance at college, above average scholastic aptitude and achievement; family in upper third in socio-economic status; father in a white-collar occupation, and attended college; attended high school in a metropolitan community (Table 3).

Background characteristics associated with low-prestige occupations were: no education or training beyond high school; below average scholastic aptitude and achievement; father in a farming or unskilled occupation, and had not attended high school; attended high school in a rural community; and family in lower third in socio-economic status (Table 3).

Background characteristics associated with middle-level occupations showed no major difference from the background characteristics of the total group of graduates, except that slightly higher proportions were above average in scholastic ability and high school achievement, and had attended college. More than two thirds of the middle-level occupations were held by persons who did not attend colleges; one third, by college-going students. This two to one ratio is practically the same as the ratio of non-college-going to college-going youths in the total group.

The plight of those in the low-prestige occupations is sad. Meager economic and cultural circumstances plus lack of much success in school combine to depress both aspiration and achievement, whether educational or occupational. Such circumstances are especially prevalent although not limited to small, rural communities. In metropolitan areas, however, the handicap seems to be less frequent, probably because of a greater number and variety of occupational possibilities.

OCCUPATIONAL ASPIRATION

At the time of their high school graduation, the seniors had stated the occupations which they hoped eventually to enter. The prestige scores of these occupations were compared with those eventually attained. Two observations resulted from this comparison.

First, the occupational aspirations of the graduates were consistent with their educational plans. Non-college youth aspired to lower-level occupations than did either the vocational school or college-bound youth. The

Table 3   Characteristics of Graduates in High- and Low-Prestige Occupations

	High-Prestige			Low-Prestige		
	(1)	*(2)*	*(3)*	*(1)*	*(2)*	*(3)*
Characteristics	%	%	*diff.*	%	%	*diff.*
1. *Size of Community*						
Counties with cities:						
Not over 10,000	38	30	−8	38	48	+10
10,000–24,999	7	7	0	7	8	+1
25,000–49,999	22	22	0	22	22	0
Metropolitan areas	33	41	+8	33	22	−11
2. *Socio-economic Status*						
Low ⅓	33	20	−13	33	40	+7
Middle ⅓	34	33	+11	34	40	+6
High ⅓	33	47	+14	33	20	−13
3. *Father's Occupation*						
Farming	22	15	−7	22	35	+13
Unskilled	39	35	−4	39	42	+3
Skilled	10	10	0	10	9	−1
White collar	20	25	+5	20	11	−9
Professional	9	15	+6	9	3	−6
4. *Father's Education*						
No high school	46	34	−12	46	58	+12
Some high school	16	13	−3	16	17	+1
High-school graduate	26	32	+6	26	19	−7
Some college	12	21	+9	12	6	−6
5. *Scholastic Aptitude*						
Low ½	52	32	−20	52	67	+15
High ½	48	68	+20	48	33	−15
6. *High-School Achievement*						
Low ½	62	41	−21	62	77	+15
High ½	38	59	+21	38	23	−15
7. *Level of Education*						
High school only	43	18	−25	43	76	+33
Vocational school	16	14	−2	16	13	−3
Some college	41	68	+27	41	11	−30

Columns (1) Per cent of all graduates in sample
Columns (2) Per cent of all graduates who attained high- or low-prestige occupations
Columns (3) Difference and direction of difference

aspirations of the vocational school group were predominantly in the middle range.

Second, the occupational attainments of non-college-going youth were close to their expectations. In fact, the correspondence between the occupational aspiration and occupational attainment scores of all three groups suggests that the graduates had sorted and sized themselves with considerable accuracy and realism. Individual instances of unrealistic optimism and unnecessary pessimism occur among all three groups. College-going students were the only group that had not attained occupations equal to their aspirations. Many of the college group, however, aspired to occupations which require prolonged professional or advanced training; and some have been at work a comparatively short time. Others did not complete degrees and may have changed their occupational goals.

It is an interesting sidelight that college-going youths who did not complete degrees had definitely lower occupational aspirations than those who obtained degrees. Over half (53 per cent) of the college-dropouts had not planned to attend college.

RELATION OF OCCUPATIONAL ATTAINMENT TO HIGH SCHOOL ACHIEVEMENT

To test the relationship of scholastic performance in high school to level of occupational attainment, the graduates were ranked by deciles in total high school achievement and median occupational prestige scores were calculated for the graduates in each decile. The interesting fact emerged that although differences in level of education produced important differences in level of occupations, differences in high school performance had very little effect on the level of occupations attained in any of the three groups (Table 4).

Table 4   High-School Achievement and Occupational Attainment

High-School Percentile Rank	Median Occupational Prestige Scores		
	(1)	*(2)*	*(3)*
90–9	59	67	79
80–9	66	71	72
70–9	62	71	73
60–9	57	66	75
50–9	64	67	73
40–9	62	66	72
30–9	59	67	73
20–9	59	67	73
10–9	56	65	74
0–9	58	65	73

Column (1) No further schooling
Column (2) Attended vocational school
Column (3) Attended College

The median percentile rank of graduates who were in occupations that had prestige scores below 70 was the rank of the average male graduate—38th percentile. Graduates in occupations with a prestige score above 70, however, had a much higher median level of scholastic performance, ranking at the 55th percentile. Because girls receive a much larger proportion of the better marks in high school, a boy ranking at the 55th percentile in his total class would excel 80–85 per cent of his male classmates.

These facts are consonant with the knowledge that high-prestige occupations typically are open only to those who complete college degrees, and that those who complete college degrees are typically drawn from graduates who rank in the top fourth of their high school classes. High-achieving students who did not continue their schooling not only failed to attain occupations at a level equal to high-achieving students who did continue; they failed to attain occupations that were substantially better than the occupations of their lower-ranking classmates. Even more remarkable is the fact that low-achieving students who attended college attained occupations equivalent to their much higher-ranking college classmates. Only the college-going students in the top decile showed a sizeable difference in occupational attainment from college-going students in other deciles.

It is possible that within occupations, or within occupational levels, differences in occupational attainment may be associated with differences in scholastic achievement. The findings of this study, however, agree with the common sense observation that rank in high school class is a statistic seldom used outside educational institutions, except possibly for initial job entry of a new high school graduate. The profile of human characteristics most valued by the occupational world is not identical with the profile of characteristics most rewarded by the educational system.

Today's high school youth is subjected to a barrage of publicity by newspapers, magazines, television, and radio telling him that the road to occupational success is through advanced education. It is interesting that a very large part of youth either does not hear or does not heed this counsel.

The fact that only 16 per cent of the graduates enrolled in vocational and trade schools does not match either the increasing need for technicians and sub-professional workers, or the number of high school graduates who have aptitudes for such occupations. In fact, it might be expected that the largest part of the graduates would be preparing for middle-level occupations. As more than a third of the graduates who attended college did not graduate, a question occurs whether it would have been better for them to attend a two-year vocational or technical program and succeed than to begin a four-year college degree program and then drop out. Certainly also a sizeable part of the youth who did not continue their schooling had the abilities needed to complete a two-year program of vocational-technical training.

But the educational system and the society which supports it have much to do if they are to meet their responsibilities for non-college youth. Given the wide range of human aptitudes and aspirations, it is natural and right for youths to leave the educational system at different ages and stages. The tragedy is not leave-taking from school. The tragedy occurs when they leave school for the wrong reasons, whether because of economic barriers, racial discrimination, artificial or illusory incentives or unsuitable school programs. Our society must find work for the kinds of youths we have. And our schools must prepare youths for effective performance in the kinds of work that need to be done.

The purpose of the educational system, of course, is not merely to match people to jobs. This study emphasizes occupational objectives, however, because man's occupation is one of his chief characteristics. His occupation, and his achievements in it, lie close to the center of both his self-respect and the nature of his contribution to society.

An important item of unfinished educational business, then, is conceiving and developing realistic and practical programs of "middle education"—the level between mid-high school and mid-college—during which three fourths of American youth end their formal schooling. These are the youths who as adult workers occupy the great range of middle-level occupations and who as citizens are the bedrock of a democratic society.

Physical and Cognitive Growth During Adolescence: Relationships Between Maturational and Societal Factors

J. M. Tanner

The Course of Children's Growth

The spurt in physical growth that occurs during adolescence is one of the more reliable phenomena of this period. Although its magnitude and duration varies from one youth to another, every adolescent experiences a degree of suddenness in his growth. In the paper included here, Tanner describes the nature of the adolescent growth spurt, the order in which parts of the body develop, the changes in body size, shape, and athletic ability that occur, and the development of the reproductive system. As the next three papers in this volume profess, the relations between changes in physical growth and personality dynamics are intimate and pervasive.

THE GROWTH CURVE OF HEIGHT

In Fig. 1 is shown the growth curve in height of a single boy, measured every six months from birth to 18 years. Above is plotted the height attained at successive ages; below, the increments in height from one age to the next. If we think of growth as a form of motion, and the passage of a child along his growth curve as similar to the passage of a train between stations, then the upper curve is one of distance achieved, and the lower curve one of velocity. The velocity, or rate of growth, naturally reflects the child's situation at any given time better than does the distance achieved, which depends largely on how much the child has grown in all the preceding years. Accordingly it is usually more important to concentrate on the velocity rather than on the distance curve. In some circumstances the acceleration may reflect physiological events even better than the velocity; thus at adolescence it seems likely that the great increase in secretions from the endocrine glands is manifested most clearly in an acceleration of growth. In general, however, nothing more complex than velocity curves will be considered here.

The record of Fig. 1 is the oldest published study of the growth of a child; it was made during the years 1759 to 1777 by Count Philibert de Montbeillard upon his son, and published by Buffon in a supplement to the *Histoire Naturelle*. It shows as well as any more modern data that in general the velocity of growth in height decreases from birth (and actually from as early as the fourth intrauterine month) onwards, but that this

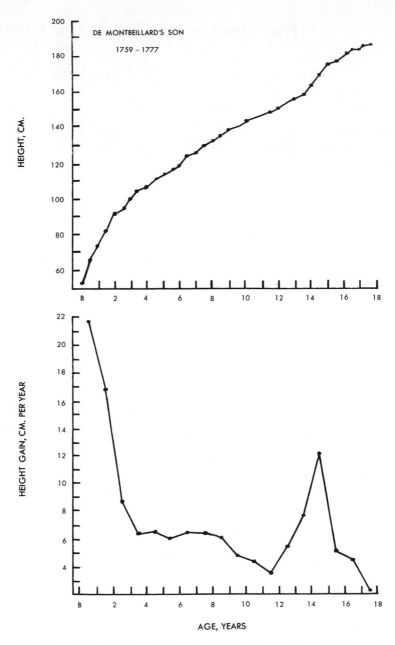

Figure 1. *Growth in height of de Montbeillard's son from birth to 18 years, 1759–77. Above, distance curve, height attained at each age; below, velocity curve, increments in height from year to year.*

DATA *from Scammon, 1927,* Amer. J. Phys. Anthrop. *(From J. M. Tanner,* Growth at Adolescence. *Oxford: Blackwell Sci. Publ.)*

decrease is interrupted shortly before the end of the growth period. At this time, from 13 to 15 in this particular boy, there is a marked acceleration of growth, called the *adolescent growth spurt*. From birth up to 4 or 5 the rate of growth declines rapidly, but the decline, or deceleration, gets gradually less, so that in some children the velocity is practically constant from 5 or 6 up to the beginning of the adolescent spurt.[1]

As the points of Fig. 1 show, growth is an exceedingly regular process. Contrary to opinions still sometimes met, it does *not* proceed in fits and starts. The more carefully the measurements are taken, with, for example, precautions to minimize the decrease in height that occurs during the working day for postural reasons, the more regular does the succession of points on the graph become. In a series of children each measured for seven years or more by the same measurer, my colleagues and I have found that at least over the age range 3 to 10 the deviations of the actual points from a very simple mathematical curve

$$\text{Height} = a + bt + c \, \log t, \qquad (\text{where } t \text{ is age})$$

were seldom more than 6 mm., or ¼ in., and were on average equally above and below the curve at all ages (see Fig. 2). There is no evidence for "stages" in height growth except for the spurt associated with adolescence. Perhaps the increments of growth at the cellular level are discontinuous, and proceed by starts and stops; but at the level of bodily measurements, even of single bones measured by X-rays, one can only discern complete continuity, with a velocity that gradually varies from one age to another.

[1] A slight increase in velocity of height growth from about 6 to 8 years, providing a second wave on the general velocity curve, has been sometimes thought to occur and has been called the juvenile or mid-growth spurt. I can find no satisfactory evidence of its presence in the individual records covering the period 3 to 13 that are known to me.

Some teachers have acquired the quite erroneous notion that growth occurs in a series of alternating periods of "stretching up" (increased velocity in height) and "filling out" (increased velocity in breadth). The idea seems to have originated in 1896 in a paper by Winfield Hall, an American school doctor, who measured, very carefully, some 2,400 boys aged 9 to 23. The study was cross-sectional, with between 100 and 300 in each yearly age group. Medians were calculated but no standard deviations. The 13-year-old value for height was rather higher than might have been expected. Though to the modern eye its deviation is well within the limits of sampling error, Hall took it at face value and thus obtained a large 12–13 increment, small 13–14 increment and large 14–15 increment, this last being the adolescent spurt proper. In circumferences of the joints this did not occur, the curves being fairly regular. Hence, when the values were expressed as percentages of the 9-year-old value, the distance curves for height and for circumferences crossed at 12–13, 13–14 and 14–15. Hall thereupon formulated (in italics) a Law of Growth: "When the vertical dimension of the human body is undergoing an acceleration in its rate of growth the horizontal dimensions undergo a retardation and vice versa." The idea was taken up and generalized to the whole period of growth by the German anthropologist C. H. Stratz, who in many articles wrote of a first *Streckung* at 5 to 7 and a second at 8 to 10. The data on which these opinions were based were quite insufficient to support them, but somehow they got into textbooks, where in some instances they have remained safely cocooned till the present day, despite the severest attempts to dislodge them by people such as Schiotz (see C. Schiotz, "Physical Development of Children and Young People during the Age of 7 to 18–20 Years. An investigation of 28,700 Pupils of Public [Elementary] and Higher [Secondary] Schools in Christiana," *Videnskapsselskapets Skr. I. Mat.-Naturv. Klasse*, No. 4 [1923]), whose measurements of children were adequate in number, taken longitudinally, and interpreted with statistical sense.

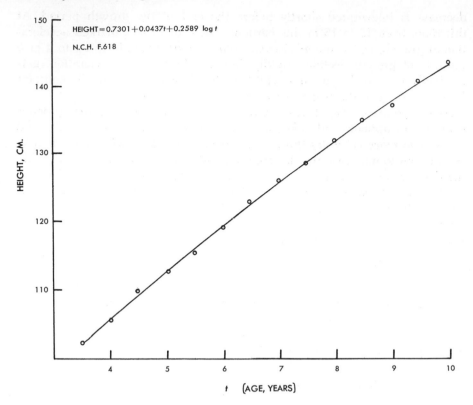

Figure 2.   *Curve of form y = a + bt + c log t fitted to stature measurements taken on a girl by R. H. Whitehouse every six months from age 3½ to 10.*

DATA from Harpenden Growth Study. (From W. J. Israelsohn, "Description and Modes of Analysis of Human Growth," *Human Growth*, J. M. Tanner, ed., Sym. Soc. Hum. Biol. [London: Pergamon, 1960], vol. 3.)

   The adolescent spurt is a constant phenomenon, and occurs in all children, though it varies in intensity and duration from one child to another. In boys it takes place, on the average, from 12½ to 15, and in girls about two years earlier, from 10½ to approximately 13. The peak height velocity reached averages about 4 inches per year in boys and a little less in girls; this is the rate at which the child was growing at about 2 years old. The sex difference can be seen in Fig. 3, which shows the velocity curves for a group of boys who have their peak between 14 and 15 and a group of girls with their peak between 12 and 13. The earlier occurrence of the spurt in girls is the reason why girls are bigger than boys from about 10½ to 13 years. Boys are larger than girls by only 1–3 per cent in most body measurements before puberty, so that the girls' adolescent spurt soon carries them ahead of the boys. The boys catch up and pass the girls when their greater and probably more sustained adolescent spurt begins to take effect, and they finish some 10 per cent larger in most dimensions. Thus the adult

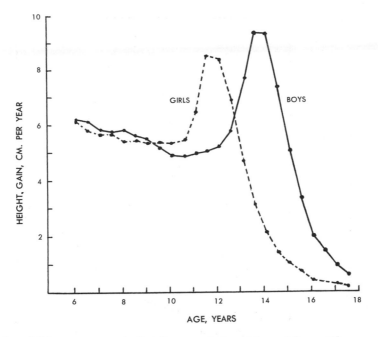

Figure 3. Adolescent spurt in height growth for girls and boys. The curves are from subjects who have their peak velocities during the modal years 12–13 for girls, and 14–15 for boys. Actual mean increments, each plotted at centre of its half-year period.

DATA from Shuttleworth, 1939, Tables 23 and 32. (From J. M. Tanner, *Growth at Adolescence*. Oxford: Blackwell Sci. Publ.)

difference in size between men and women is to a large extent the result of the difference in timing and magnitude of the adolescent spurt.

GROWTH CURVES OF DIFFERENT TISSUES AND DIFFERENT PARTS OF THE BODY

Most measurements of the body show a growth curve generally similar to the curve of height given in Fig. 1. The great majority of skeletal and muscular dimensions, whether of length or breadth, grow in this manner. But some exceptions exist, most notably the brain and skull, the reproductive organs, the lymphoid tissue of the tonsils, adenoids and intestines, and the subcutaneous fat. Fig. 4 shows these differences in diagram form, using size attained, or distance curves. Height follows the "general" curve. The reproductive organs, internal and external, follow a curve which is not, perhaps, very different in principle, but strikingly so in effect. Their pre-pubescent growth is very slow, and their growth at adolescence very rapid; they are less sensitive than the skeleton to one set of hormones and more sensitive to another.

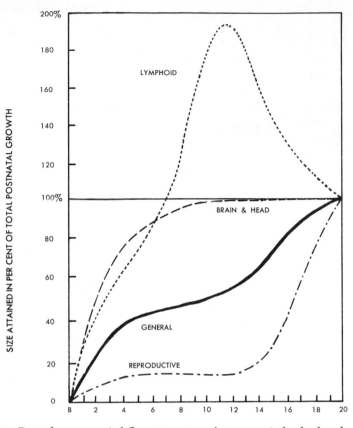

Figure 4. *Growth curves of different parts and tissues of the body, showing the four chief types. All the curves are of size attained (in per cent of the total gain from birth to maturity) and plotted so that size at age 20 is 100 on the vertical scale.*

Lymphoid type: thymus, lymph nodes, intestinal lymph masses.

Brain and head type: brain and its parts, dura, spinal cord, optic apparatus, head dimensions.

General type: body as a whole, external dimensions (except head), respiratory and digestive organs, kidneys, aortic and pulmonary trunks, musculature, blood volume.

Reproductive type: testis, ovary, epididymis, prostate, seminal vesicles, Fallopian tubes.

REDRAWN from Scammon, 1930, "The Measurement of Man," Univ. Minn. Press. (From J. M. Tanner, *Growth at Adolescence*. Oxford: Blackwell Sci. Publ.)

The brain and skull, together with the eyes and ears, develop earlier than any other part of the body and have thus a characteristic postnatal curve . . . by 1 year old the brain has attained about 60 per cent of its adult weight, and by 5 years about 90 per cent. Probably it has no adolescent spurt, although a slight spurt does occur in the measurements of head length and breadth due to thickening of the skull bones. The face, unlike the portion of the skull encasing the brain, follows a path closer to the general skeletal curve, with a considerable adolescent spurt in most measurements. The jawbone, for example, has only completed 75 per cent of its growth in length before adolescence in boys.

The eye seems probably to have a slight adolescent acceleration in growth, though no data are accurate enough to make the matter certain. Very likely it is this that is responsible for the increase in frequency of short-sightedness in children at the time of puberty. Though the degree of myopia increases continuously from at least age 6 to maturity, a particularly rapid rate of change occurs at about 11 to 12 in girls and 13 to 14 in boys, and this would be expected if there was a rather greater spurt in the axial dimension of the eye than in its vertical dimension.

The lymphoid tissue has quite a different curve from the rest: it reaches its maximum value by the beginning of adolescence and thereafter actually decreases in amount, largely under the influence of the sex hormones. Accordingly, children with troublesomely large, but otherwise normal, tonsils and adenoids, may generally be expected to lose their snuffles when adolescence starts.

The subcutaneous fat undergoes a slightly more complicated evolution. Its thickness can be measured either by X-rays, or more simply at certain sites by picking up a fold of skin and fat between the thumb and forefinger and measuring the thickness of the fold with a special, constant-pressure, caliper. In Fig. 5 the distance curves for two measurements of subcutaneous fat are shown, one taken at the back of the upper arm (triceps), the other at the back of the chest, just below the bottom of the shoulder blade (subscapular). The data come from different sources at each of the three age ranges, and this has been indicated by leaving the three sections separate. The thickness of subcutaneous fat increases from birth to reach a peak at nine months or a year, and thereafter decreases, rapidly at first and then more slowly, until about 6 to 8 years, depending on the individual child. At that time the width of fat begins to increase again. In the trunk fat (subscapular measurement) this increase continues up to maturity in both boys and girls. The limb fat (triceps measurement) follows this same pattern in girls, but in boys it thins out at the time of the adolescent spurt in height.

The curves for muscle and bone widths follow the general height curve. Because weight represents a mixture of these various components of the body its curve of growth is somewhat different from those discussed above, and often less informative. Though to some extent useful in following the health of a child, weight has severe limitations; an increase may be due to bone or muscle or merely to fat. A boy may cease growth in height and muscle and put on fat instead (as happens in certain clinical circumstances when large doses of cortisone are given) and his weight curve may continue to look perfectly normal. Even failure to gain weight or actual loss of weight in an older child may signify little except a better attention to

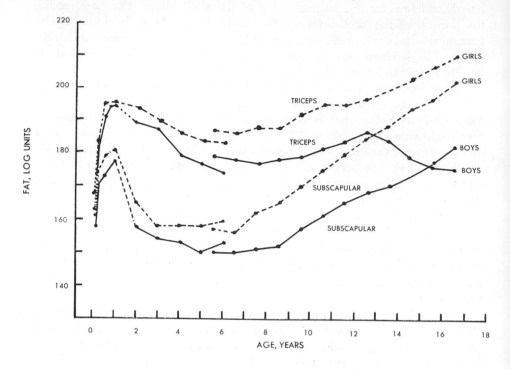

Figure 5. *Amount of subcutaneous fat on the back of the arm (triceps) and on the chest (subscapular) from birth to age 16. Distance curves; measurements by skin-fold calipers, reported as logs of readings less 1.8 mm.*

FROM J. M. Tanner, *Growth at Adolescence.* Oxford: Blackwell Sci. Publ.

diet and exercise, whereas failure to gain height or muscle would call for immediate investigation. For these reasons regular measurements of height and weight in the schools should be supplemented by measurements of subcutaneous fat by skinfolds, and muscular dimensions by circumference of upper arm and calf corrected for the covering subcutaneous fat.

GROWTH AND DEVELOPMENT AT ADOLESCENCE

Practically all skeletal and muscular dimensions take part in the adolescent spurt. There is a fairly regular order in which the dimensions accelerate; leg length as a rule reaches its peak first, followed a few months later by the body breadths and a year later by trunk length. Most of the spurt in height is due to trunk growth rather than growth of the legs. The muscles appear to have their spurt a little after the last skeletal peak.

At adolescence a marked increase in athletic ability occurs, particularly in boys. The heart, just like any other muscle, grows more rapidly, as can be seen from Fig. 6. The strength of the muscles also increases sharply,

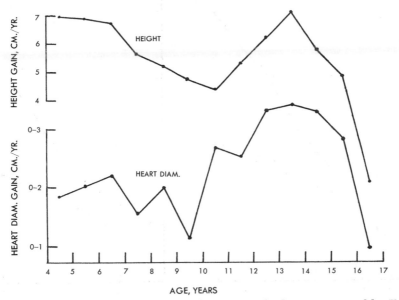

Figure 6. *Velocity curves of transverse diameter of the heart, measured by X-ray, for 71 boys. Mixed longitudinal data, reported cross-sectionally. Height curves of same boys given above for comparison.*

DATA from Maresh, 1948. (From Tanner, *Growth at Adolescence*. Oxford: Blackwell Sci. Publ.)

especially in boys. The results of two strength tests given to a group of girls and boys every six months throughout adolescence are plotted (as distance curves) in Fig. 7. Arm pull refers to the movement of pulling apart clasped hands held up in front of the chest, the hands each grasping a dynamometer handle; arm thrust refers to the reverse movement, of pushing the hands together. Each individual test represents the best of three trials made in competition against a classmate of similar ability, and against the individual's own figure of six months before. Only with such precautions can reliable maximal values be obtained. There is a considerable adolescent spurt visible in all four of the boys' curves from about age 13 to 16 (the curves turn more sharply upwards), and a less definite spurt from about 12 to 13½ in the girls' hand-grip curves. There is no sex difference before puberty in strength of arm thrust and little in arm pull (the same is true of calf and thigh muscle strength). The boys' later superiority arises partly from their greater adolescent growth in muscular bulk, and partly because the male sex hormone secreted then for the first time acts on muscle to produce more strength per cross-sectional area.

In hand-grip a more considerable sex difference appears to be present as early as age 11. This is a reflection of the greater development, even before puberty, of the male forearm. It is often forgotten that a number of sex differences, besides those of the reproductive organs, antedate pu-

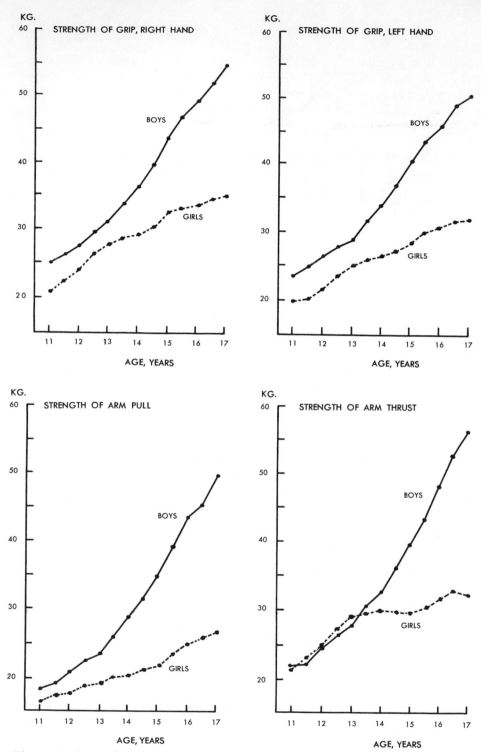

Figure 7. *Strength of hand grip, arm pull and arm thrust from age 11 to 17. Mixed longitudinal data, 65–93 boys and 66–93 girls in each age group.*

DATA from Jones, 1949, Tables 15–22. (From J. M. Tanner, *Growth at Adolescence*. Oxford: Blackwell Sci. Publ.)

berty, and are not the result of the endocrine gland secretions of adolescence. At birth boys have longer and thicker forearms, relative to upper arms, legs and other parts of the body, and the sex difference increases steadily throughout the whole growing period. (This is not peculiar to man, but occurs in several species of apes and monkeys as well.) Another difference which is already present at birth is the relatively greater length of the second finger in comparison to the fourth in girls. Whether any similar sex differences occur in the brain is not known, but the possibility of them clearly exists.

Not only the muscles increase in size and strength at adolescence; the vital capacity of the lungs, that is, the amount of air they will hold on maximum inspiration less the amount retained after maximal expiration, also shows a pronounced increase in boys. The number of red blood cells, and hence the amount of hemoglobin in the blood, also rises sharply in boys but not in girls, as shown in Fig. 8. Thus the amount of oxygen which can be carried from the lungs to the tissues increases.

It is as a direct result of these anatomical and physiological changes that athletic ability increases so much in boys at adolescence. The popular notion of a boy "outgrowing his strength" at this time has little scientific support. It is true that the peak velocity of strength increase occurs a year or so after the peak velocity of most of the skeletal measurements, so that a short period exists when the adolescent, having completed his skeletal, and probably also muscular, growth, still does not have the strength of a young adult of the same body size and shape. But this is a temporary phase; considered absolutely, power, athletic skill and physical endurance all increase progressively and rapidly throughout adolescence. It is certainly not true that the changes accompanying adolescence even temporarily enfeeble, through any mechanism except a psychological one.

Though the main change at puberty is in body size, there is also a considerable change in body shape. The shape change differs in the two sexes, so that boys acquire the wide shoulders and muscular neck of the man, and girls the relatively wide hips of the woman. Before puberty it is usually impossible to distinguish whether a particular child is a boy or girl from its body proportions or amounts of bone, muscle and fat alone (despite the few small but perhaps important differences mentioned above). After puberty it is easy to do so in the great majority of cases.

ENDOCRINOLOGY OF GROWTH

Thus at adolescence there is a great and sudden increase in body size and strength and a change in many physiological functions besides the reproductive ones. These changes all take place in a co-ordinated manner and a child who is early in respect of one feature is early in respect of all. The changes are mostly more marked in boys than girls, and take place approximately two years later in boys than in girls.

The immediate cause of all these changes is the secretion into the blood

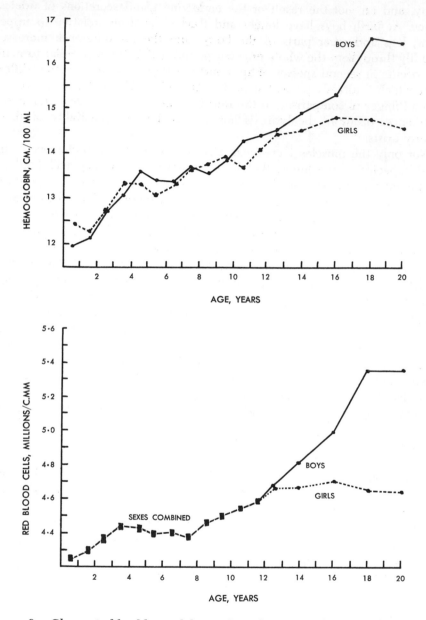

Figure 8.   *Change in blood hemoglobin and number of circulating red blood cells during childhood, showing the development of the sex difference at adolescence. Distance curves. Mixed longitudinal data reported cross-sectionally.*

REDRAWN from Mugrage and Andresen, 1936, 1938, "Amer. J. Dis. Child." (From J. M. Tanner, *Growth at Adolescence*. Oxford: Blackwell Sci. Publ.)

stream (and hence the contact with all tissues) of hormones from the ovaries, testes and adrenal glands. However, ovaries, testes and the particular functional part of the adrenal which secretes androgenic (i.e., male-determining) hormones have first to be stimulated to grow and function by other hormones. These come from the pituitary gland, which lies just underneath the base of the brain in approximately the geometrical center of the head. The pituitary itself, however, awaits the receipt of a chemical stimulus before manufacturing and releasing these trophic hormones, and this stimulus comes from a particular small area in the basal part of the brain known as the hypothalamus. What causes the hypothalamus to initiate all these events we do not know; it seems to be normally under some form of restraint emanating from its anterior portion. There is a hereditary disorder, manifested only in boys, in which this restraint is partially lacking and a precocious puberty occurs any time from 4 years onwards. When this happens all the events of puberty take place normally, including the production of sperm. In girls a similar, though not hereditary, condition occurs occasionally and the youngest known mother, who had a child by Cæsarian section at age 5, was an example of this. In these cases no other untoward effects take place; the children otherwise are quite healthy. In certain progressive diseases of the brain, however, the restraint on the hypothalamus may be destroyed and precocious puberty may also occur then.

Evidently certain maturational changes have to take place in the restraining anterior hypothalamus before it releases its grip and lets the mechanism begin; but we are totally ignorant of their nature. Starvation retards puberty, which simply waits for the body to reach its usual prepubertal size, irrespective of the passage of time. Maturation of the hypothalamus occurs at a certain sequence in a chain of events and not, fundamentally, at a certain chronological age.

The factors controlling growth before adolescence are imperfectly understood, but it is clear that another pituitary hormone, called growth hormone, controls to a great extent the speed of growth. Its absence causes the type of dwarf who has approximately normal body proportions. Thus the pre-adolescent phase of growth has been called the growth-hormone phase, and the adolescent the steroid-hormone phase (since the hormones concerned then belong to a class of compounds called by this name). Several other hormones, notably that secreted by the thyroid gland, have to be maintained within normal limits for growth to occur normally; but they do not act directly to regulate growth rate. Presumably because of the different hormonal control there is a considerable degree of independence between growth before, and growth at, adolescence.

DEVELOPMENT OF THE REPRODUCTIVE SYSTEM

The adolescent spurt in skeletal and muscular dimensions is closely related to the great development of the reproductive system which takes place at that time. The sequence of events for the average boy and girl is shown diagrammatically in Figs. 9 and 10. This sequence is not exactly the same

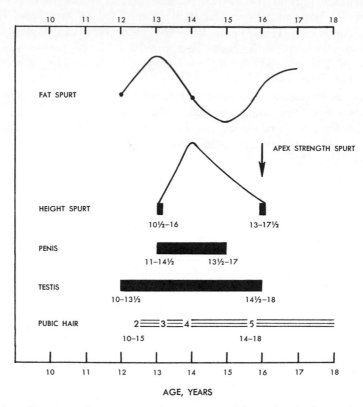

Figure 9. *Diagram of sequence of events at adolescence in boys. An average boy is represented: the range of ages within which each event charted may begin and end is given by the figure (appropriate to 1955) placed directly below its start and finish.*

FROM J. M. Tanner, *Growth at Adolescence.* Oxford: Blackwell Sci. Publ.

for every boy and girl, but it varies much less than the time at which the events occur.

The first sign of impending puberty in boys is usually an acceleration of the growth of testes and scrotum (beginning of bar marked "testis" in Fig. 9). Slight growth of the pubic hair may begin at about the same time, but proceeds slowly until the advent of the general spurt. The accelerations in height and in penis growth begin about a year after the testicular acceleration, when the cells of the testis have grown and begun to secrete male sex hormone. Axillary hair usually first appears about two years after the beginning of pubic hair growth, though the relationship is sufficiently variable so that very few children's axillary hair actually appears first. Facial hair in boys begins to grow at about the same time as axillary hair. There is first an increase in length and pigmentation of hairs at the corners of the upper lip, then a spread of this to complete the moustache, then the appearance of hair on the upper part of the checks and just below the lower lip, and

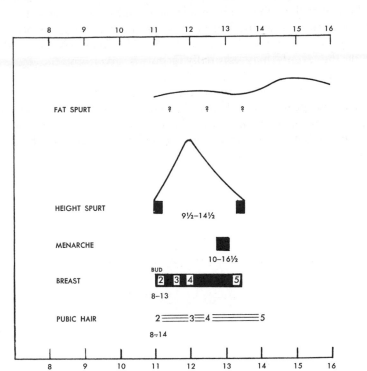

Figure 10. Diagram of sequence of events at adolescence in girls. An average girl is represented: the range of ages within which some of the events may occur is given by the figures (appropriate to 1955) placed directly below them.

FROM J. M. Tanner, *Growth at Adolescence.* Oxford: Blackwell Sci. Publ.

finally along the sides and border of the chin. This last development seldom occurs until genital and pubic hair development is far advanced. The enlargement of the larynx occurs a little after the spurt in height and the voice begins to deepen perceptibly during the period when the development of the penis is approaching completion. A few boys undergo a slight breast enlargement at puberty, which in the majority is temporary, and soon disappears; only a minority need medical treatment.

In girls the beginning of growth of the breast is usually the first sign of puberty, though the appearance of pubic hair sometimes precedes it. Menarche, the first menstrual period and a landmark much used by students of growth, almost invariably occurs after the peak of the height spurt is passed. It occurs currently in Great Britain at an average age of 13.1 years, with a normal range of 10 to 16. Though its occurrence marks a definitive and probably mature stage of uterine growth, it does not usually signify the attainment of full reproductive function. A period of infertility of a year or eighteen months follows in most, though not all, cases; and maximum fertility is probably not reached till the early or middle 20's.

In Figs. 9 and 10 the average age of occurrence of each event is given by the scale of age at the bottom on the diagram (e.g. menarche a little after 13 years, the figures being for 1955). The *range* of ages within which some of the events may normally occur is given by the figures placed directly below the event (e.g. for menarche 10–16½). A glance will suffice to show how very large these ranges are. One boy, for example, may complete his penis growth at 13½, while another has not even started at 14½. An early-maturing boy may have finished his entire adolescence before a late-maturing boy *of the same chronological* age has even begun his first enlargement of the testes.

Clellan S. Ford

Frank A. Beach

Development of Sexual Behavior in Human Beings

The sexual expressions of human beings extend in scope far beyond "genital and pelvic reflexes." To a large extent, the social sanctions within a society determine the forms and variations of sexual behavior that are allowable. In a world-wide survey of cultural practices, Ford and Beach classify societies whose adult attitudes toward sexual expression range from extremely restrictive to highly permissive. Their analyses suggest that "the social code pertaining to sexual behavior of children and unmarried adolescents in the United States is clearly a restrictive one." For students who desire a cross-cultural perspective of the development of sexual behavior in human beings, the next selection provides an excellent frame of reference.

IT has been explained that the attainment of sexual maturity is a gradual process and that the various organs and organ systems involved in reproduction become functional at different stages in the life of the individual. We have further noted that in many societies the individual's entrance into adolescence receives public recognition in the form of puberty ceremonials. But up to this point very little has been said about sexual behavior per se. The nervous and muscular mechanisms involved in sexual arousal and its overt expression can properly be classified as very important elements in the interrelated system of physiological factors that must become mature before reproduction can occur.

REFLEXIVE COMPONENTS

Some of these mechanisms for behavior are reflexive, whereas others develop only as a result of practice and learning. For example, the human male does not have to learn how to fill his penis with blood so that it becomes erect and rigid, but he may have to learn how to copulate; the conditions under which an adult man experiences erection undoubtedly are influenced

FROM C. S. Ford and F. A. Beach, *Patterns of Sexual Behavior* (New York: Harper and Brothers, 1951), pp. 178–192. Copyright, 1951, by C. S. Ford and F. A. Beach. Reprinted by permission of the authors and Harper and Brothers.

by his life experiences. There are decided differences between various animal species as regards the extent to which mating responses depend upon or are modified by learning and conditioning.

It is possible to analyze separately the several reflexes and more complex reactions that normally appear simultaneously or sequentially in the sexual act of adult males and females. When this is done it becomes obvious that different segments of the total response mature at different rates. In the human male, for example, complete genital erection is possible from the day of birth, and baby boys frequently show this reaction under the influence of bladder distention or in response to manipulation of the phallus. The power of ejaculation, in contrast, is not acquired until puberty, and the production of normal sperm is delayed until even later in life.

In grown men orgasm and ejaculation usually occur together, but they are not necessarily mutually dependent. As a matter of fact, it is reported that sexual climax or orgasm can be produced in very young human infants of either sex. Kinsey, Pomeroy, and Martin state that male infants less than one year of age respond to manipulation of the genitals by making thrusting movements with the pelvic muscle; and if the stimulation is continued the baby's movements become more rapid and vigorous and culminate in a general spasm quite similar to that which characterizes climax in most adults.

The evidence therefore suggests that the neuromuscular system of the human animal is capable at birth of mediating at least two of the basic reflexive patterns that will later be woven into the complete sexual act. But adult patterns of sexual behavior consist of a great deal more than genital and pelvic reflexes. What other mechanisms are involved, how do they develop, and when do they become mature? How are the simple, inherited reflexes elaborated into the much more complex and variable forms of sexual expression that characterize adults in different societies? A fully satisfactory answer to these questions could be obtained only by studying the sexual play of many children of varying ages in a large number of different cultural settings. Unfortunately, however, the amount of such activity that occurs and the ease with which the observer can obtain information concerning it are controlled to a large extent by the attitudes of adults. And these attitudes vary to a great extent from one society to the next.

RESTRICTIVE SOCIETIES

In a minority of the societies concerning which we have adequate information adults attempt to deny young children any form of sexual expression.[1] As will be explained later, this is the prevailing attitude in American society, although there is considerable variance between actual behavior and the idealized standards of the moral code.

The severity of restrictions and punishments associated with sexual trans-

---

[1] Abelam, Apinaye, Ashanti, Chagga, Chiricahua, Cuna, Dahomeans, Haitians, Kwoma, Manus, Murngin, Penobscot, Rengma, Trukese.

gressions in childhood varies from one restrictive society to another. Among the Apinaye, for example, boys and girls are warned from infancy not to masturbate and a severe thrashing awaits the child suspected of such behavior. In Africa, Ashanti boys are told by their fathers at an early age not to masturbate or engage in any sexual play. In New Guinea, Kwoma boys are constantly warned not to finger their genitals; if a woman sees a boy with an erection she will beat his penis with a stick, and boys soon learn to refrain from touching their genitals even while urinating. Kwoma girls also are told not to finger their genitals but are not punished for so doing. The Cuna specifically forbid their children to engage in either homosexual or heterosexual play; and youngsters among the Chiricahua are whipped if they are detected playing sex games.

Most of these restrictive societies maintain a public conspiracy against the acquisition of any sexual knowledge by children. Adults avoid mentioning matters of sexual significance in their presence, and make every attempt to keep them in total ignorance of the reproductive process. Among the natives of the western Carolines sex is never discussed before children, especially girls. Cuna children remain ignorant of sexual matters (as far as adult instruction is concerned) until the last stages of the marriage ceremony. They are not even allowed to watch animals give birth. Chagga children are told that babies come out of the forest.

In a number of these societies particular pains are taken to prevent young children from accidentally observing sexual behavior. In some instances, as among the Murngin of Australia, boys are removed from the dwelling to the boys' house or bachelors' hut when they are four or five years old, this is done for the specific purpose of preventing them from witnessing sexual behavior at home. The Kwoma husband and wife are always careful to wait until the children are asleep before indulging in sexual intercourse.

Such adult attitudes toward childhood sexuality may prevent youngsters from engaging in sexual practices in the presence of their elders, but whether they successfully suppress sexual activity in secret is another matter. There is evidence that in some of these societies children do engage in a certain amount of sexual behavior despite strong adult disapproval. In Haiti little boys and girls privately experiment in sexual activity from early childhood until puberty. Manus children masturbate, but always in solitude and surrounded by shame. When they are alone in the bush Kwoma boys scrape the penis with nettles. And on Truk, children play at intercourse at an early age, although their parents will beat them if they are caught. In Trukese society children do sometimes observe their elders engaging in sexual activities at night. Apinaye boys and girls masturbate frequently even though such play is punished whenever it happens to be observed, and despite the fact that at a ceremony which is conducted when they are half grown their genitalia are examined and the children are flogged if there appears to be evidence of masturbation. In the case of boys, this "evidence" is described "as retractibility of the prepuce." But the validity of such criteria is questionable. Actually, there are no known physical stigmata that constitute reliable evidence of habitual masturbation as far as the male is concerned. R. L. Dickinson has long held that prolonged habits of feminine masturbation involving vulvar traction and friction leave permanent signs in the form of lengthened and corrugated labia. However, Dickinson's thesis is not accepted by all authorities, and in any event it applies to mature women and not to "half-grown" girls.

Some peoples make a sharp distinction between socially immature and mature persons with respect to permissible sexual activity. These societies take the attitude that sexual intercourse before adulthood must be avoided; but once the person is mature by their standards, considerable freedom in sexual matters may be allowed.[2] For the most part these peoples seem particularly concerned with the prepubescent girl, believing that intercourse before the menarche may be injurious to her. Girls of the east central Carolines are strictly forbidden intercourse before puberty, but after that they enjoy almost complete sexual freedom. After menarche, Ao girls begin to sleep in dormitories where they indulge in intercourse with partners of their choice. Among the Siriono intercourse before puberty is forbidden, but premarital affairs are customary once the girl has menstruated. The Chukchee believe that intercourse will harm a girl until her breasts are fully developed or until she begins to menstruate. However, immature girls often engage in coitus despite this belief. In this society it is considered proper for a girl to carry on serious love affairs between the time of the first menstruation and marriage. The Ashanti are convinced that sexual intercourse with a girl who has not undergone the puberty ceremony is so harmful to the community that the offense is punishable by death for both partners. Premarital intercourse is also forbidden to the postpubescent Ashanti girl, but this rule is not nearly so strictly enforced.

In most of the African societies in our sample [3] boys are strictly forbidden to have intercourse before undergoing the puberty ceremony or initiation rite. The Chagga boy, for example, cannot have intercourse until he has been circumcised and properly initiated into adult status. If caught in the act the boy and his partner are laid one on the other and staked to the ground. After circumcision all Chagga boys have intercourse with a barren woman and subsequently they sally forth to seek other sex partners. Until marriage they are instructed to practice either interfemoral intercourse or coitus interruptus unless the girl places a pad in the vagina to avoid conception. A comparable attitude is taken by the Jivaro of Ecuador, who strictly forbid boys to engage in intimate relationships with girls until they have gone through an initiation ceremony at puberty.

In other societies the prohibitions against sexual intercourse continue unabated or, in some instances, are intensified after puberty and remain in force until marriage or at least until betrothal. The methods used to prevent

---

[2] Ao (girls), Ashanti (girls), Choroti (girls), Chukchee (girls), Haitians (boys), Jukun (girls), Lamba (girls), Mataco (girls), Seniang, Siriono (girls), Swazi, Toba (girls), Tupinamba (girls).

[3] Chagga, Masai, Pedi, Swazi, Thonga (inferred), Wolof.

premarital sexual activity during adolescence include segregation of the sexes, strict chaperonage of girls, and threats of severe disgrace or physical punishment. The extreme pains to which adults in these societies are forced to go in order to control the sexual behavior of young people is an eloquent expression of the strength of the tendency on the part of older children and adolescents to engage in such activity. There are indeed very few societies in which any method of control appears to be completely effective in preventing heterosexual intercourse among young unmarried couples.

Perhaps the most nearly successful method of controlling the sexual activity of young people is to separate the sexes and keep the girls under constant surveillance. Among the Abipone, for example, boys and girls were strictly segregated at all times and premarital chastity is said to have been universal. A similar situation exists among the Arapaho, Cheyenne, Papago, and Wapisiana, all of whom keep the sexes strictly apart from childhood. Boys and girls never play together, and until marriage young men and women never associate in the absence of chaperones. The only completely effective prevention of premarital relations has been devised by the Wapisiana. They define cohabitation as marriage, and thus rule out the possibility of intercourse between two unmarried people. At the same time, of course, they eliminate the problem of the unmarried mother.

In most of the societies that practice segregation and chaperonage to control the sexual behavior of adolescents, boys are less carefully watched than girls; and, in some cases at least, it appears that youths are able to circumvent the barriers, with the result that sexual intercourse before marriage not infrequently occurs. For example, among the Hopi a strong attempt is made to keep boys and girls apart from the age of ten until marriage; the girls are kept at home and are accompanied by an older woman whenever they go out. Girls are expected to be chaste until marriage. Boys, however, are not similarly restricted, and, whenever possible, they defeat the chaperonage system by crawling into the girl's house stealthily at night or by holding clandestine prearranged meetings. The Hopi place all the blame for illegitimate pregnancy squarely upon the girl who is involved. Her friends ignore her and her family scolds her, but the lover is not regarded as at fault and is neither forced nor expected to marry her.

A similar situation exists among the Kiwai Papuans of New Guinea. There, girls are carefully chaperoned by their parents and usually kept in ignorance of love-making for some time. The boy, however, is not similarly restricted and will take the initiative in attempting to get around the rules. The young pair have to be very clever to meet; they usually are able to do so only at night. The girl may slip out of the house after her parents are asleep or the boy may sneak into her house through the floor. And apparently, despite every effort on the part of adults, many couples find it possible to carry on love affairs in secret.

Threats of the most severe disgrace and punishment do not appear to be completely effective in preventing young people from engaging in sexual activity before marriage. In the Gilberts, for example, great emphasis is

placed on a girl's chastity before marriage. If a girl is seduced and it becomes public knowledge, both parties are put to death. Nevertheless, the
evidence indicates that many transgressions take place in secret. In only
a few societies—namely, the Vedda, Keraki, Chiricahua, and Sanpoil—is
the burden of guilt placed upon the boy. Among the Vedda, for example, if
a man were seen even talking to an unmarried girl her relatives would kill
him. In most of these restrictive societies, however, the threats of disgrace
and punishment are specifically directed toward misbehavior on the part
of the girl.

The attempts of adults to restrict the sexual behavior of adolescents seem,
in many of these societies, to be intended primarily as a means of insuring
the virginity of the unmarried girl. Some peoples attempt to determine
whether or not a girl has remained chaste by conducting a crude examination of her sexual organs. The hymen or "maidenhead" is a tab of tissue
which, in most virgins, partially obstructs the entrance of the vagina. Very
often this structure is nicked or stretched when the vagina is sufficiently
penetrated for the first time, and a certain amount of blood may be lost.
However, the size and thickness of the hymen vary from individual to individual. As a result, some fully virginal girls may bleed very little if at all during the first intercourse, whereas in other women a great deal of stretching
is necessary before the obstruction offered by this tissue is completely
removed.

Despite the actual unreliability of their tests, some societies use the
occurrence of bleeding in response to vaginal penetration as an important
index to chastity. Among the Kurds, for example, when the bridegroom has
intercourse with the bride the nuptial cloth is examined for blood. If a girl
is shown to have been a virgin, the cloth is paraded on a stick through the
village and the bride price is then paid. If, however, the bridegroom finds
himself disappointed, the girl is heaped with abuse, given back to her
parents, and in some instances subjected to further public disgrace. Yungar
girls are "deflowered" a week before marriage by two old women. If, at
this time, examination fails to indicate chastity severe penalties are meted
out to the girl, including starvation, mutilation, torture, and even death.

American Society

The social code pertaining to sexual behavior of children and unmarried
adolescents in the United States is clearly a restrictive one. In this country,
constant pressure is exerted, ideally at least, to prevent any form of sexual
behavior until it is legalized and can occur in the bonds of matrimony. In
this society, as in many others, there is a tendency toward a double standard
in respect to premarital sexual behavior. More pressure is brought to bear
upon unmarried girls than upon boys. In actual practice, furthermore, the
burden of protecting young persons from indulging in sexual activity falls
somewhat more heavily upon the parents of American girls than upon the
parents of boys. This tendency toward a double sex standard is also re-

flected in attitudes toward extramarital sexual activity. As has been shown, a double sex standard during late childhood and adolescence is characteristic of many societies, but not of human beings in general. There are societies in which there is little if any difference in the premarital sexual restrictions placed upon girls and boys, and in a few societies the more severe restrictions confine the male rather than the female.

Kinsey and his associates have shown in statistical fashion what has generally been recognized for many years, namely, that in spite of the attitudes of adults, children in our society frequently indulge in many forms of sexual activity. Although the strictness with which the moral code is enforced varies considerably from one social class to another, a more or less concerted attempt to prevent children from indulging in any form of sex play continues well into adolescence and up to the time of marriage. And, as we have noted, most other societies that discourage infantile and childhood sex play also attempt to control premarital experimentation in sexual matters on the part of adolescents or young adults.

Although this attitude is characteristic in America, the strength of condemnation varies somewhat from one social group to another. However, regardless of the prohibitions against it, premarital sexual behavior does occur in a fairly large proportion of the population. It does not necessarily involve actual copulation. Landis and his co-workers report that 59 per cent of the married women whom they questioned had indulged in extensive heterosexual play without coitus prior to marriage. Forty-two per cent of the unmarried women in this study admitted the occurrence of sex play.

According to Kinsey, Pomeroy, and Martin, more than 60 per cent of American males engage in petting before they are 20 years old. By the age of 25, approximately one third of the male population has achieved orgasm in this fashion. Men from the higher educational levels are likely to confine their adolescent activity to noncoital techniques, whereas individuals from the lower socio-educational strata tend to proceed more or less directly to coitus and indulge in a minimum of petting.

As far as actual copulation is concerned, Kinsey and his collaborators report that it was attempted during or before adolescence by 22 per cent of the American boys they interviewed. The first experiment usually takes place between the ages of 10 and 14. By the time he is 12 years old approximately one boy in every four or five has at least tried to copulate with a girl or woman. More than 10 per cent of these youths experience their first ejaculation in connection with heterosexual intercourse. Considering all the men interviewed in Kinsey's study, it becomes apparent that more than two thirds of them had at least one premarital experience involving copulation. The incidence of such behavior varies with the individual's socio-educational level, being least frequent in college-educated groups, and nearly universal among men who have no more than an eighth-grade education.

Terman found that approximately one half of 760 American husbands whom he studied admitted premarital intercourse with the women they later married. Seven per cent of this group said they had copulated with at least one other woman prior to marriage, and 26 per cent mentioned intercourse with five or more women before marriage. Only 13.3 per cent of the 777 wives represented in Terman's sample admitted premarital relations with the husband, and much smaller percentages listed intercourse with other males before marriage. The lack of agreement between accounts given by husbands and wives probably reflects chiefly a different degree of resistance to confessing premarital freedom. Terman was particularly impressed with differences between older and younger married couples as regards premarital behavior. He noted that the proportion of men and women who were virgins at marriage had steadily decreased between the approximate dates of 1910 and the early 1930's. *"If the drop should continue at the average rate shown for those born since 1890* virginity at marriage will be close to the vanishing point for males born after 1930 and for females born after 1940. It is more likely that the rate of change will become somewhat retarded as the zero point is approached and that an occasional virgin will come to the marriage bed for a few decades beyond the dates indicated by the curves. It will be of no small interest to see how long the cultural ideal of virgin marriage will survive as a moral code after its observance has passed into history." (L. M. Terman, *Psychological Factors in Marital Happiness* [New York: McGraw-Hill Book Co., 1938], p. 323).

Semirestrictive Societies

There is no clear-cut dividing line between restrictive and semirestrictive societies; and often, as we have pointed out, the sexual codes that adults attempt to enforce on immature members of the group differ according to the young person's sex or age. There are, however, many societies [4] in which the adult attitudes toward sex play in children or toward premarital affairs in adolescents are characterized by formal prohibitions that are apparently not very serious and in fact are not enforced. In such cases sexual experimentation may take place in secrecy without incurring punishment, even though the parents know perfectly well what is going on. The Alorese formally object to any form of sex play on the part of older children. But overt homosexual and heterosexual practices on the part of boys and girls occur, and children playing together in field houses imitate the sexual intercourse of their parents. Unless this is brought flagrantly to the attention of the adults they do nothing about it.

Among the Andamanese premarital promiscuity is common and the parents do not object as long as the love affairs are kept secret. Parents object

[4] Alorese (older children), Andamanese, Aranda (girls), Azande, Bena, Chagga (girls), Colorado (girls), Cree, Creek, Crow (girls), Dusun (girls), Flathead, Ganda (girls), Havasupai, Huichol, Kickapoo, Kiowa, Apache, Kiwai, Klamath, Kurtatchi (girls), Kutchin, Kutenai, Kwoma, Lango, Mailu, Mandan, Mangarevans (now), Manus, Mbundu, Menomini, Omaha, Orokaiva (girls), Papago, Pedi (girls), Purari (girls), Ramkokamekra, Reddi, Rengma (girls), Seminole, Sinkaietk (girls), Tinguian, Tokelauans, Venda, Wappo, Yagua, Yako, Zulu (older children).

to such activities in theory, but unless they are practiced openly no punishment is involved. Should a girl become pregnant, however, the parents of the couple usually arrange for them to be married. The Huichol uphold an ideal of premarital chastity for both sexes, but in practice this is rarely realized. If an adolescent couple is caught in sexual intimacy both individuals are beaten and they are forced to marry; but parents do not keep close surveillance over the activities of young people, and the latter have many opportunities to slip off into the bush in the evening during feasts and dances.

In some societies the only recognized sign of sexual transgression on the part of young people is premarital pregnancy. Among such peoples it appears that intercourse frequently takes place between unmarried couples, but numerous devices and techniques are employed either to prevent conception or to abort an unwanted fetus. In a number of African societies it is customary for adolescent boys to practice interfemoral intercourse or coitus interruptus to avoid impregnating the girl. Contraceptive measures used by young people in these societies include placing a pad of absorbent material in the vagina, washing the passage after intercourse, and orally ingesting certain medicines believed to insure temporary sterility. Should these fail to prevent conception the girl may resort to an abortion.

PERMISSIVE SOCIETIES

Adults in a large number of societies take a completely tolerant and permissive attitude toward sex expression in childhood.[5] Under such conditions youngsters engage in a certain amount of sexual play in public. The fingering of the child's own genitals follows exploratory movements of the hands which contact the various parts of the body. If adults do not attempt to discourage such behavior, fingering the genitals becomes an established habit of occasional occurrence. As the child grows old enough to walk about and play with others, he tends to extend the range and to increase the variety of sexual activities. Handling the genitals of others of the same or opposite sex occurs frequently under conditions of free sex play. Additional forms of sexual activity on the part of young children sometimes include oral-genital contacts and attempted copulation with a sex partner.

In a few permissive societies adults participate actively in the sexual stimulation of infants and young children. Hopi and Siriono parents masturbate their youngster frequently. And in these societies self-masturbation passes practically unnoticed during early childhood, adults taking a tolerant and permissive attitude toward all sexual behavior at least until the age of puberty. Among the Kazak, adults who are playing with small children, especially boys, excite the young one's genitals by rubbing and playing with

[5] Alorese, Chewa, Copper Eskimo, Crow (boys), Easter Islanders, Hopi, Ifugao, Ila, Kazak, Kwakiutl, Lepcha, Lesu, Mangarevans (formerly), Maori, Marquesans, Marshallese, Masai, Nama, Ojibwa, Palauans, Ponapeans, Pukapukans, Samoans, Seniang, Siriono, Tikopia, Trobrianders, Walapai, Wogeo, Yapese, Yaruro, Zulu.

them. In this society autogenital stimulation on the part of young children is accepted as a normal practice. Mothers in Alorese society occasionally fondle the genitals of their infant while nursing it. During early childhood Alorese boys masturbate freely and occasionally they imitate intercourse with a little girl. As the children grow older, however, sexual activity is frowned upon and during late childhood such behavior is forbidden to both boy and girl. Actually, however, they continue their sexual behavior, but in secret.

Among the Pukapukans of Polynesia where parents simply ignore the sexual activities of young children, boys and girls masturbate freely and openly in public. Among the Nama Hottentot no secret is made of auto-genital stimulation in early childhood. Young Trobriand children engage in a variety of sexual activities. In the absence of adult control, typical forms of amusement for Trobriand girls and boys include manual and oral stimulation of the genitals and simulated coitus. Young Seniang children publicly simulate adult copulation without being reproved; older boys masturbate freely and play sexual games with little girls, but the boys are warned not to copulate on the grounds that this behavior would weaken them. Lesu children playing on the beach give imitations of adult sexual intercourse, and adults in this society regard this to be a natural and normal game. On Tikopia small boys induce erections in themselves through manual manipulation, and this is ignored or at most mildly reproved by adults. Little girls also may masturbate in this society without being punished for such behavior.

Most of the societies that permit children free sex play (and some that are semirestrictive) also allow them opportunity to observe adult sexual behavior and to participate in discussions of sexual matters.[6] Among the Alorese sex knowledge is completely accessible to young children and by the age of five they are well informed on all details of the entire reproductive act. All members of the Pukapukan household sleep in the same room under one mosquito net; and although some parents wait until they think the children are asleep, there are frequent opportunities for youngsters to observe adult sexual activities and sexual matters are often talked about. Lesu children are free to observe adults copulate, with the specific exception that they may not watch their own mothers having intercourse. On Ponape children are given careful instruction in sexual intercourse from the fourth or fifth year. Trukese children receive no formal tutelage, but they learn a great deal by watching adults at night and by asking their elders about sexual matters. Among the Wogeo sexual matters are freely discussed by adults in the presence of children. In this society, however, parents take some precautions against their own children observing them in intercourse.

In the societies where they are permitted to do so, children gradually increase their sexual activities both as they approach puberty and during

---

[6] Alorese, Copper Eskimo, Cree, Dusun, Easter Islanders, Flathead, Ganda, Hopi, Ifugao, Lesu, Marquesans, Ojibwa, Ponapeans, Pukapukans, Samoans, Tikopia, Tinguian, Trobrianders, Trukese, Wogeo, Yapese.

adolescence. There are, indeed, some societies in which enforcement of the prevailing incest regulations is the only major restriction on sexual activity among adolescents.[7] As in the case of very young children, their sex play first includes autogenital stimulation and mutual masturbation with the same and opposite sex, but with increasing age it is characterized more and more by attempts at heterosexual copulation. By the time of puberty in most of these societies expressions of sexuality on the part of older children consist predominantly of the accepted adult form of heterosexual intercourse, the pattern which they will continue to follow throughout their sexually active years of life.

Among the Chewa of Africa parents believe that unless children begin to exercise themselves sexually early in life they will never beget offspring. Older children build little huts some distance from the village, and there, with the complete approval of their parents, boys and girls play at being husband and wife. Such trial matings may extend well into adolescence, with periodic exchanges of partners until marriage occurs. The Ifugao headhunters of the Philippines maintain a similar attitude toward the sex play of older children and adolescents. In this society unmarried individuals live in separate dormitories from early childhood. It is customary for each boy to sleep with a girl every night. The only check on promiscuity is that imposed by the girls themselves. Usually a girl is unwilling to form too prolonged an attachment to one boy until she is ready to be married. Boys are urged by their fathers to begin sexual activities early, and a man may shame his son if the latter is backward in this respect. Even after puberty there seem to be relatively few instances of conception resulting from this free sexual activity. Pregnancies do occasionally occur, however, and in that event one of the girl's lovers must marry her.

The Lepcha of India believe that girls will not mature without benefit of sexual intercourse. Early sex play among boys and girls characteristically involves many forms of mutual masturbation and usually ends in attempted copulation. By the time they are 11 or 12 years old, most girls regularly engage in full intercourse. Older men occasionally copulate with girls as young as 8 years of age. Instead of being regarded as a criminal offense, such behavior is considered amusing by the Lepcha. Sexual life begins in earnest among the Trobrianders at 6 to 8 years for girls, 10 to 12 for boys. Both sexes receive explicit instruction from older companions whom they imitate in sex activities. Sex play includes masturbation, oral stimulation of the genitals of the same and opposite sex, and heterosexual copulation. At any time a couple may retire to the bush, the bachelor's hut, an isolated yam house, or any other convenient place and there engage in prolonged sexual play with full approval of their parents. No marriage is consummated

---

[7] Ainu, Aymara, Balinese, Barama, Chewa, Copper Eskimo, Crow (boys), Dobuans, Easter Islanders, Futunans, Gilyak, Goajiro, Gond, Ifugao, Ila, Lapps, Lepcha, Lesu, Macusi, Mangarevans (formerly), Maori, Marquesans, Marshallese, Mongols, Nandi, Naskapi, Natchez, Nauruans (commoners), Palauans, Palaung, Ponapeans, Pukapukans, Seniang, Siriono (boys), Taos, Tarahumara, Thonga (girls), Toda, Tongans (boys), Trobrianders, Trukese, Tuareg, Walapai, Wogeo, Yapese, Yakut, Yaruro, Yukaghir.

in Trobriand society without a protracted preliminary period of sexual intimacy during which both sincerity of affection and sexual compatibility are tested. Premarital pregnancy is said to be rare in this society, despite postpuberal sexual intercourse over a period of three years or more before marriage. This experience has led the Trobrianders to doubt a causal relationship between coitus and conception. Instead they consider supernatural influences to be far more significant in causing a child to be conceived.

In this instance, as in other cases of frequent but infertile coitus among postpubescent males and females, the phenomenon of adolescent sterility would appear to be particularly pertinent. It may well be that although they have passed the menarche, the girls involved in this activity are not yet ovulating, or at least are incapable of carrying a fetus to term. Any such interpretation must remain speculative, however, until there is more satisfactory proof for the absence of any form of contraception.

An interesting attitude toward the sexual activity of adolescents is taken by the Ila-speaking peoples of Africa. Childhood is regarded as a time of preparation for adult life and mature sexual functions. At harvest time each girl is given a house to which she takes a boy of her choice, and there they play as man and wife. It is reported that there are no virgins among these people after the age of 10. On Easter Island children from the age of 6 on imitate the sexual behavior of adults without censure; and young people among the Maori play together at being husband and wife at night in the bush. Full copulation frequently occurs before puberty. Lesu adults regard as natural the attempts at intercourse in which children engage, and they give full approval to free sexual activity on the part of adolescents.

Eugene J. Kanin

An Examination of Sexual Aggression
As a Response to Sexual Frustration

The sexually aggressive adolescent male is usually portrayed as more experienced and successful in consummating erotic behavior than the nonaggressive. Kanin shows below, however, that a predatory youth actually is relatively dissatisfied. The aggressive male indeed is more exploitative and resourceful in developing disarming techniques in the sexual realm than the nonaggressive, but the latter appears to assess his sexual needs less extravagantly. Kanin suggests that the frustration of a sexually aggressive boy may be a function of relative deprivation—a deprivation which is enhanced by associating with peers who champion high expectations for exploitation.

INTRODUCTION

It has frequently been implied with varying degrees of elaboration that the resortment to deviant sex behavior can be accounted for by an absence of legitimate sexual outlets. Indeed, probably the most frequently verbalized popular justification for legalized prostitution centers about its ability to curtail rape. Trained observers, however, also convey comparable notions. Bonger,[1] for example, related rape to unemployment and the resultant inability to marry. Anderson [2] portrayed the hobo's association with prostitutes and his homosexual involvements as consequences of his non-marital existence. Cohen [3] reports that Jamaican girls are known to turn to homosexuality when deprived of heterosexual intercourse for long periods. These prolonged periods of heterosexual continence are viewed as a result of the proscription against the female assuming the initiative in sexual relationships. Others have described deviant sexual adaptations in sex-segregated

FROM *Journal of Marriage and the Family*, XXIX (1967), 428–433. Reprinted by permission of the author and the publisher.

[1] William A. Bonger, *Criminality and Economic Conditions* (Boston: Little, Brown and Company, 1916).

[2] Nels Anderson, *The Hobo* (Chicago: University of Chicago Press, 1923), pp. 137–149.

[3] Yehudi A. Cohen, *Social Structure and Personality* (New York: Holt, Rinehart and Winston, 1961), p. 171.

penal institutions [4] and in locales characterized by distorted sex ratios.[5] All of the above accounts imply deviant sexuality to be the consequence of a social structure that frustrates the acquisition of more legitimate sexual outlets.

In this paper an effort will be made to examine only one type of deviant heterosexual response, male sex aggression, to determine whether it tends to be a response of frustrated males unable to obtain heterosexual outlets by more sanctioned means which do not involve the application of physical force. No assumptions are made here concerning the reasons for these males lacking sexual activity. Our objective, then, is to examine the sexual histories of sexually aggressive and nonaggressive men and determine if, in fact, the former are the sexually deprived.

In this study sex aggression will refer to the male's quest for coital access of a rejecting female during the course of which physical coercion is utilized to the degree that offended responses are elicited from the female. In our sample, without exception, these acts are found to be restricted to pairings engaged in some form of dating-courtship activity, i.e., ranging from "pick-up" to regular date, and do not include attempted sexual assault of strangers. Furthermore, these dyads, regardless of whether they are casual and superficial or relatively involved and committed in terms of dating stage, are sexually quite active. For example, the majority of our cases (71 per cent) are characterized by having engaged in a relatively advanced level of consented sexual intimacy, genital "petting" of the female, prior to the aggressive act. These aggressive acts, then, represent a sex-conduct norm violation not ordinarily anticipated during the course of heterosexual interaction to be considered "normal" or expected, and yet the expression of physical aggression manifested in trying to gain the erotic goal, coitus, is usually not so extreme that these acts could be labeled carnal assault or attempted rape.[6] The majority of the aggressive episodes involve such behaviors as forceful attempts at removing clothing and forceful maneuvering of the female into a physically advantageous position for gaining complete sexual accessibility. In spite of the attempt to obtain a relative homogeneity of acts, it is acknowledged that these aggressive episodes actually represent a fairly wide range of behavior, both with respect to the degree of force utilized and the conscious intent to apply force.

---

[4] Donald Clemmer, *The Prison Community* (New York: Rinehart and Company, 1958), pp. 249–273; Joseph F. Fishman, *Sex in Prison* (New York: Podell Book Company, 1934); Arthur V. Huffman, "Sex Deviation in a Prison Community," *The Journal of Social Therapy*, 6 (1960), n. p.; Gresham Sykes, *The Society of Captives* (Princeton: Princeton University Press, 1958), pp. 70–72.

[5] Stanton Wheeler, "Sex Offenses: A Sociological Critique," *Law and Contemporary Problems*, 25 (Spring, 1960), 277.

[6] For a view of the varieties of offensive sexual behavior encountered by college and high-school girls, see Clifford Kirkpatrick and Eugene Kanin, "Male Sex Aggression on a University Campus," *American Sociological Review*, 22 (February, 1957), 52–58; Eugene J. Kanin, "Male Aggression in Dating-Courtship Relations," *American Journal of Sociology*, 63 (September, 1957), 197–204.

METHOD

Two criteria and usually three were utilized to determine whether the reported episode was to be accepted as offensively aggressive. First, the male respondent had to affirm that he made a forceful attempt for intercourse to the extent that he perceived it to be disagreeable and offensive to the girl involved. Secondly, he had to indicate that the female responded to his aggressive conduct with offended reactions, e.g., fighting, crying, screaming, pleading, etc. Both of the foregoing were necessary for the episode to be accepted as aggressively offensive. Lastly, the respondents were given the opportunity to describe the aggressive acts. Nine of the respondents offered insufficient description of the episode, and, consequently, this evidence was not utilized as a required criterion for inclusion in the count of aggressive-offensive episodes. For the remaining 78 cases, however, these descriptive offerings appear to validate their acknowledged sexual aggressions.

The sample for this study constitutes a random selection of 400 full-time, undergraduate, unmarried males at a large, coeducational Midwestern university. Of the 400 males selected, contact was established with 381 by telephone or by personal visit; 19 respondents could not be located. Everyone of the 381 males contacted agreed to cooperate to complete the research schedule. Upon appearance for their appointment, they were briefly instructed as to the nature of the study, were guaranteed anonymity, and were given the opportunity to refuse participation. None refused. Of the 381 schedules obtained, 40 were rejected as incomplete and were not utilized. The remaining 341 completed schedules were analyzed and constitute the statistical data for this study.[7] Case material was also obtained via direct interview or anonymous autobiography from approximately 60 university males.

RESULTS AND DISCUSSION

An examination of the sexual and dating histories of this sample of college males strongly suggests that offensive sexual aggression is but one facet of a wide range of erotic activity engaged in by the aggressive males. The evidence indicates that the aggressive male, in contrast to his nonaggressive peers, has not only had considerably more sexual experience but is more persistently seeking new sexual involvements and utilizing more surreptitious techniques with greater frequency in order to obtain sexual activity.

To illustrate, it is the aggressive male that tends to be sexually most successful and active. Contrasting the aggressive and nonaggressive populations

[7] Sex aggression since entering college was reported by 87 (25.5 per cent) of the 341 respondents. The episodes which designated them as sexually aggressive had to occur since their entrance into college. It was believed that aggressive episodes during the relatively immature heterosexual years would be more accidental due to a paucity of adequate communication and dating sophistication of males and females.

Table 1   Estimate of Frequency with Which Aggressive
and Nonaggressive Males Attempt to Neck and Pet While
Dating

	Nonaggressive Males		Aggressive Males	
	N	%	N	%
Most of the time	47	19.3	33	37.9
Quite often	81	33.2	35	40.2
Occasionally	101	41.4	18	20.7
Rarely or never	15	6.1	1	1.2
Total	244°	100.0	87	100.0

$X^2 = 23.23$; df = 3; p < .001.
° N = 244 rather than 254, since 10 men do not date.

finds 67.3 per cent of the aggressives as opposed to 37.9 per cent of the non-aggressives to have had sexual intercourse ($X^2 = 27.17$; df = 1; p < .001). That the aggressive male has more frequently achieved his goal is obvious. Although our statistical findings tell nothing of the females involved, the type of relationship involvement, or the approach utilized in acquiring these experiences, our case material strongly denies that these experiences were obtained by physically aggressive approaches or involved prostitutes. A more complete contrast of the sexual histories of these two groups would have to include genital petting, an activity that some investigators have designated as functionally equivalent to coition for adolescents. If we select out in these two groups those males who report either coitus or genital petting of the female, the nonaggressive male no longer appears to be so relatively devoid of sexual involvements. However, the greater experience of the aggressives is still marked. For the nonaggressive group, 66.1 per cent report a history of coitus or genital petting, while 89.4 per cent of the aggressives report such activity ($X^2 = 14.24$; df = 1; p < .001). These findings are significant in establishing that a considerable number of the non-aggressive males have been in situations where there was an opportunity for an aggressive attempt for coitus.

The data further indicate that the aggressive males also manifest a comparatively stronger desire to precipitate new sexual experience. Inquiring into the frequency with which these respondents attempt to initiate the more sanctioned superficial erotic activities while dating, "necking" and "petting," shows 37.9 per cent of the aggressive males reporting "most of the time" in contrast to 19.3 per cent of the nonaggressives. At the other end of the distribution, 47.5 per cent of the nonaggressive men and 21.9 per cent of the aggressives report they occasionally, rarely, or never try to initiate these erotic activities during the course of dating. The aggressive male appears to have more sexual experience and to be more eagerly seeking further experience. It is interesting to observe that the foregoing efforts meet with comparable success in both groups. Response to the question "Do you usually find that you have difficulty in getting your dates to 'neck' and 'pet'?" shows 16 per cent of the nonaggressives and 17 per cent of the aggressives answering affirmatively. There is some evidence, then, that the nonaggressive male's lack of erotic involvement is not due to his inability to precipitate erotic encounters.

A question could be raised concerning the exclusiveness of our measure of deviant means, namely, physical aggression. It seems appropriate to consider that nonaggressive males could utilize erotic-oriented approaches that would be deviant in that they would also be considered violations of the sex conduct norms. These approaches would be those embodying deception and intimidation. It was hypothesized, then, that sexual exploitation might be manifested in a segmental fashion contingent upon the personality of the male. That is, two males with strong erotic impulses might differentially implement their sexual aggressiveness; one perhaps finds expression in physical aggression while the other, lacking a capacity for physical aggression, might still be aggressive and exploitative by virtue of resorting to other techniques which could still be viewed as deviant. Feasibly, males who strive to gain sexual access by attempting to intoxicate the female, falsely professing love, falsely promising marriage, and threatening to dis-

Table 2 Incidence of Selected Sexual Exploitation Techniques Employed by 341 Aggressive and Nonaggressive Males While in High School and College

	High School		College	
	NONAGGRESSIVE MALES (N = 254) (PER CENT)*	AGGRESSIVE MALES (N = 87) (PER CENT)*C.R.	NONAGGRESSIVE MALES (N = 254) (PER CENT)*	AGGRESSIVE MALES (N = 87) (PER CENT)*C.R.
Attempted to get girl intoxicated	9.1	37.9 5.2	12.6	47.1 4.6
Falsely promised marriage	7.5	8.0 n.s.	4.3	11.5 n.s.
Falsely professed love	14.6	44.8 5.3	10.2	41.4 4.4
Threatened to terminate relationship	3.5	9.2 n.s.	2.8	20.7 3.2

* Per cents do not total 100, since some respondents indicated employing more than one technique and others indicated never utilizing such approaches.

solve the pair relationship unless the female renders herself sexually available, might not be the males who would resort to physical aggression. The reverse might be thought of as operative for the physically aggressive. These data, however, clearly fail to support such a hypothesis. On the contrary, it is found that not only did sexually exploitative behavior characterize the offensively aggressive male both during his high-school and college days, but he also utilized a greater variety of approaches. Table 2 shows, for example, in contrast to the nonaggressive males, the aggressives utilizing more "seductive" approaches than the nonaggressives, both in high school and in college. With the exception of the maneuver of falsely promising marriage—perhaps a too-incriminating approach even for aggressive males —the aggressive males were significantly more represented as engaging in surreptitious seductive behavior. An overall view of the incidence of this variety of exploitative behavior, considering high-school and college years collectively, shows that 80.5 per cent of the aggressive men but only 27.3 per cent of the nonaggressive men indicate having utilized at least one of the foregoing maneuvers in the quest for sexual intercourse ($X^2 = 70.05$; $df = 1$; $p < .001$). To further emphasize the history of such conduct, the writer notes that 64.4 per cent of the aggressives and 20.5 per cent of the nonaggressives reported employing these approaches while in high school. Sexual aggression, therefore, in the more covert form of deception and intimidation, is also characteristic of the physically aggressive male and apparently characterizes his heterosexual behavior shortly after he enters the dating arena. Exploitation of the female for erotic gratification permeates the entire approach of the aggressive male. The evidence unequivocally demonstrates that those who resort to deviant means are those who have been most successful in obtaining the goal of erotic experience.

The specific question may now be raised concerning the appropriateness of imputing sexual frustration solely on the basis of actual sexual experience. Up to this point it has been assumed on a priori grounds that the absence of heterosexual encounters can be translated into sexual frustration. However, to experience frustration one must first aspire for the elusive goal. Therefore, if these nonaggressive males should be found to demonstrate a comparatively lesser interest in sexual activity, it would indicate the erroneousness of imputing sexual frustration to those with less erotic experience and sexual satisfaction to those with more abundant experience. It is feasible that males without heterosexual experience can be quite content and, therefore, not in a state of sexual frustration. On the other hand, the erotically more successful males may be viewed as frustrated if their aspiration levels exceed their levels of achievement. Our data permit a partial testing of these assumptions. The respondents were asked to indicate the degree of satisfaction with which they view their sexual activities of the past year. The aggressive males, with their more extensive experience, are more apt to report dissatisfaction (50.6 per cent) than the nonaggressives, with their comparative paucity of experience (30.7 per cent), ($X^2 = 11.18$; $df = 1$; $p < .001$). These findings cogently suggest that satisfaction with one's premarital sexual state is not necessarily determined by one's degree of sexual experience. The omnipresent question, of course, is whether these nonaggressive males have a compensatory sexual outlet, e.g., masturbation, so that in spite of their fewer heterosexual involvements they may still be sexually quite active. A prior study of the same population of males found that subjective estimates of the number of orgasms per week that would bring sexual satisfaction was indeed significantly higher for the aggressive group. This means that these nonaggressives do, in fact, assess their sexual needs less extravagantly than do the aggressives.[8]

At this point it is found that aggressive males are sexually more successful than nonaggressive males, utilize a wider spectrum of approaches in order to gain sexual experience, more often attempt to engage in sexual play, and, in spite of their relative success, tend to be more dissatisfied with their sexual activity. These data appear to say that those with the greatest amount of sexual experience are the sexually most frustrated. Those most deficient in sexual accomplishment, on the other hand, tend to be the sexually most satisfied. It is suggested that the answer to this seeming contradiction is to be found in the differential levels of sexual aspirations entertained by these two groups. Evidence is available to suggest that this, in fact, is the case here.

Although constitutional factors are basic to the sex impulse, it would seem that the observed variations in sexual interest characterizing various human groupings are primarily due to social and psychological factors. Certainly the differential sexual orientations observed in cross-cultural and social class investigations cannot be rendered sensible by the consideration of biological factors. The problem now arises as to whether it can be demonstrated that these sexually aggressive males, in contrast to their nonaggressive peers, have been subjected to influences which could account for their more heightened erotic interests along with their greater dissatisfaction, in spite of comparatively greater experience. One such influence for the male would be his peer group of the same sex. Feasibly, a differential association with meaningful others of the same sex who champion, encourage, and offer status rewards for sexual activity might result in a differential experiencing of sexual pressures. In other words, those males involved in groupings that stress sexual activity and reward sexual accomplishment would also be the males who are most sensitive to their sexual tensions and who most desire sex activity. A collegiate male friendship group might be especially influential in this respect and serve as a reference group, considering the unusual significance these groups assume by virtue of living arrangements removed from familial and other former non-erotic-oriented primary group influences.

To assess the erotic orientation of these friendship groups, the schedule requested the respondents to indicate the degree their friends pressured one another to seek premarital sex experience. Table 3 indicates that the aggressive males demonstrate a significantly greater tendency than the nonaggressives to report their friends exerting a "great deal" and "considerable" pressure, 23.0 per cent and 6.0 per cent, respectively. Only 13.8 per cent of the aggressives indicate the absence of any degree of such pressure in contrast to 42.0 per cent of the nonaggressives.

Now if these aggressive males are immersed in friendship groups that encourage sexual activity, it could also be expected that male virginity

[8] Eugene J. Kanin, "Male Sex Aggression and Three Psychiatric Hypotheses," *Journal of Sex Research*, 1 (1965), 227–229.

Table 3　Degree of Pressure Exerted by Friends for New Sex Experience

	Nonaggressive Males		Aggressive Males	
	N	%	N	%
Great deal	6	2.4	4	4.6
Considerable	9	3.6	16	18.4
Moderate	52	20.5	26	29.9
Little	80	31.5	29	33.3
None	107	42.0	12	13.8
Total	254	100.0	87	100.0

$X^2 = 37.94$; df = 4; p < .001.

would be stigmatic. Inquiring into the possibility that one could admit to virginity to one's group of friends without some loss of status shows that this is more possible for the nonaggressive males. About one half (50.6 per cent) of the aggressive men, but 71.7 per cent of the nonaggressive men, report that the admittance of their virginity would not be accompanied by some loss of status ($X^2 = 12.96$; df = 1; p < .001). The evidence shows that these aggressive males do have a differential association with companions who encourage and socially reward premarital sexual experience.

Having established that these aggressive males are recipients of social pressures for erotic achievement, one may appropriately return to the finding that indicated these more experienced males to be more dissatisfied with their sex lives than the less experienced nonaggressives. As previously argued, greater sexual experience could readily be associated with greater dissatisfaction if one's peers place a high value on erotic accomplishment and offer prestige rewards. This means, in effect, that a high level of erotic aspiration is internalized from erotic-oriented significant others and, for the average unmarried college male, this level is almost impossible to achieve. At best his heterosexual outlets will be limited. As a result, these males are undergoing the experience of relative deprivation. They are dissatisfied only by virtue of their high aspirations. Supporting evidence for this argument can be presented by showing that the degree of sexual satisfaction reported by the aggressive respondents is rather strongly associated with the amount of pressure their friends exert for seeking sex experience. The aggressive male is more apt to indicate satisfaction when little or no peer group pressure is applied (63.4 per cent), while only 34.8 per cent of the recipients of great, considerable, and moderate pressure indicate satisfaction ($X^2 = 7.09$; df = 1; p < .01).

SUMMARY AND CONCLUSIONS

Sexually aggressive behavior, viewed here as a deviant sexual response, is examined as a possible consequence of sex frustration. The evidence, however, portrays these deviant males as significantly more experienced and successful in the erotic realm than their nonaggressive peers. Furthermore, these males are more persistently seeking additional sexual encounters. Indeed, their efforts may be characterized as predatory. In spite of their greater success, they tend—in contrast with nonaggressives—to report themselves sexually dissatisfied. Frustration, then, appears to be a quality more affiliated with the sexually active than with the sexually deprived. There is evidence here that the feeling of sexual deprivation is a state not necessarily dependent upon a given amount of sexual activity. In fact, these data suggest that sexual satisfaction, like feelings of economic security, rather than being associated with a specific number of sexual episodes or a given income —within certain limits, of course—has to be considered in the context of aspirations. It is noted that these aggressives have friends of the same sex who champion and encourage the acquisition of sexual experience. It is further observed that the males who are subjected to such pressures are also more apt to report sexual dissatisfaction. It is proposed that their erotic aspirations are exceeding their erotic accomplishments and that the ensuing frustration is due to a relative deprivation. In conclusion, it can be speculated from these limited data that the urgency with which unmarried males seek heterosexual erotic outlets is to a considerable degree a function of their peer group associations.

Anne McCreary-Juhasz

How Accurate Are Student Evaluations
of the Extent of Their Knowledge
# of Human Sexuality?

However much disagreement prevails on whether sexual promiscuity and premarital sexual indulgence are increasing among adolescents, the fact remains that sex is an exceedingly salient issue with youth. The extent and accuracy of their knowledge about human sexuality have been the subject of considerable speculation, but only limited data have provided bases for school policies on sex education. In this section, McCreary-Juhasz adds substantially to our understanding of adolescents' sexual behavior by providing information regarding the extent of their sex knowledge and the accuracy of their evaluation of it. The findings, based on a comparison between self-ratings and scores on a sex knowledge test taken by 893 males and females, suggest that little relationship exists between what they think they know and what they really know; both tend to either over- or underestimate their knowledge. Further, both sexes are fairly uninformed on all major sex topics. McCreary-Juhasz points to precise gaps in youths' understanding of sex and contributes crucial support for the growing clamor for formal programs in sex education.

THIS paper is a partial report of a comprehensive study of the adequacy and accuracy of the sex knowledge of university students. The study was designed to determine whether or not students entering universities know the basic facts about the physiology of sex and whether students preparing to be teachers are well enough informed to teach these facts. It was felt that the results of this survey would indicate the need (or lack of it) for (1) a program of sex education in schools and (2) teacher training for sex instruction, and that results from a carefully designed study would provide a basis for recommendations for sex education courses in schools. Results of a survey by the author in 1963 [1] indicated that teachers thought that they should give a course in sex instruction in the schools.

FROM *The Journal of School Health*, XXXVII (1967), 409–412. Reprinted by permission of the author and the American School Health Association.

[1] A. P. McCreary, "Sex Instruction for B. C. Schools," *The B. C. Teacher*, XLIII (1964), 163–166.

Many students have gaps in their knowledge of the various aspects of human sexuality. Research provides data on the incidence of this lack of knowledge. Cole and Hall [2] present a list of problems based on reported studies in which 10,000 high school and first-year university students participated. Thirty-five per cent of the students indicated that they needed correct information about sex. In addition, unknown numbers of students who believe they are well-informed, actually have inaccurate information. For example, Greenbank [3] found that half of the 1959 graduates of a Philadelphia medical school were under the misconception that mental illness is frequently caused by masturbation. (In the same study, 20 per cent of the faculty members also believed that this was true.) In a sociological study of 600 teenagers in New York City Social Hygiene Clinics [4] only 42 per cent had heard or read something about venereal disease. Of those, 14 per cent received information from the school. In the larger study of which this paper is a portion, 79 per cent of the graduate nurses working for either degrees or diplomas in Nursing at the University of British Columbia thought that masturbation was more common in young children than in teen-aged children. In the same group, 27 per cent thought that nocturnal emissions were a periodic discharge of male sex fluids similar to female menstruation. Thus, it is evident that university students, even in the fields of medicine and nursing do not have accurate information about sex.

This report provides information about the extent of sex knowledge and the accuracy of student evaluations of this knowledge. Eight hundred and ninety-three students answered a two-part questionnaire. Freshman students from all faculties at the university and education students in all years were in the sample. In the first part of the questionnaire students were asked (a) to refer to this list of topical headings:

1. Structure and function of the sexual organs.
2. Menstruation.
3. Puberty.
4. Conception.

5. Masturbation.
6. Venereal disease.
7. Wet dreams.
8. Menopause.
9. Contraceptives.

(b) to decide how well informed they were on each and (c) to circle the numbers 1, 2, or 3 to indicate their opinion as follows: 1. very well informed, 2. some information, 3. very little information.

The second part of the questionnaire was a sex knowledge test based on the nine topics presented in Part 1 and designed to check the accuracy of students' opinions regarding the extent of their knowledge. Items for the

[2] L. Cole and I. N. Hall, *Psychology of Adolescents*, 6th ed. (Toronto, Canada: Holt, Rinehart and Winston, 1965).

[3] R. K. Greenbank, "Are Medical Students Learning Psychiatry?" *Pennsylvania Medical Journal*, LXIV (1961), 989–992.

[4] *Teenagers and Venereal Disease* (Atlanta, Georgia: U.S. Dept. of Health, Education, and Welfare, Public Health Service Communicable Disease Center, General Disease Branch, 1961).

test were selected from the most frequent questions of teenagers attending a series of lectures on sex. The best answer was agreed upon by a team of three doctors. Possible scores for questions on each of the nine topics were ordered on a three-point scale with a perfect score on a topic rating 1, no correct answers on a topic rating 3, and all other scores rating 2.

For each topic, the per cent of the males, females and total sample obtaining each possible score was computed. In addition, for each self-rating category (1, 2 or 3) in each topic, the percentage of responses for male, female and total subjects, for each possible score was obtained. By means of the Cramér statistic,[5] contingency coefficients were obtained to test the significance of the relationship between the self-ratings and scores for each of the nine topics. These were practically negligible in all cases indicating that there was no relationship between the subjects' self-ratings on the adequacy of their sex knowledge and their actual scores on a sex knowledge test.

Studies quoted in the introduction to this paper indicate lack of adequate information about masturbation and nocturnal emissions specifically. In the present study, comparison of male-female ratings and scores on masturbation indicate that even though more than one third of the males had very little information they were much better informed than the females of whom more than two thirds had very little information. However, female self-ratings and scores for being well-informed on masturbation were quite similar. Possibly masturbation is more common and more widely discussed among males than among females. Although both males and females were better informed than they thought they were on nocturnal emissions or wet dreams the self-ratings by males were more accurate than those by females. In spite of this, between one third and one half of the subjects actually had very little information. Again, there was a higher percentage of well-informed males than of females. Since this is a normal physiological outlet for sexual tension in the male, these were the expected results.

On the other hand, 60 per cent of the females and only 50 per cent of the males were well-informed about menstruation. However, females did not rate as accurately as males. More than one quarter of the females who said they were well-informed had scores on the test which indicated only some information. Since films and printed material on menstruation are used widely in high schools one would expect students to be well-informed.

The figures for venereal disease indicated that, while less than 20 per cent of both males and females thought that they had inadequate information, over 80 per cent actually had very little information. The fact that the greatest discrepancy between self-rating and score was noted on this topic points to the need for accurate information on venereal disease. With the discovery of salvarsan, sulpha and penicillin for treatment, many people erroneously consider that venereal disease is no longer a problem.

On the topics of contraceptives and menopause over 80 per cent of all

---

[5] W. L. Harp, *Statistics for Psychologists* (Toronto, Canada: Holt, Rinehart and Winston, 1965), p. 604.

students were well-informed and for both males and females the scores exceeded the ratings. It is interesting that the percentage of males (23) having very little information on contraceptives exceeded that of females (16). The day when only males could procure contraceptives has passed. With the new outlook on birth control, females are expected to be more responsible and better equipped for contraception. This new morality together with the publicity on "the pill" may account for the female having more of this information.

One surprising finding was related to conception. Neither males nor females knew as much as they thought they knew, and about two thirds of the females had very little information. More than 30 per cent of the students overestimated their knowledge of the structure and function of the sexual organs. One could surmise that young people consider knowledge of contraception a satisfactory substitute for knowledge of conception, even though this seems to be putting the cart before the horse. Both males and females, (over 80 per cent of all students) were well-informed about puberty. Probably school health classes cover this topic.

SUMMARY AND RECOMMENDATIONS

On the basis of self-ratings and scores on a sex knowledge test from 893 students at the University of British Columbia the following conclusions can be drawn about the accuracy of students' evaluation of their knowledge of human sexuality:

(1) There was no relationship between the subjects' self-ratings on the adequacy of their sex knowledge and their actual scores on a sex knowledge test.

(2) Both males and females either over- or underestimated the extent of their knowledge with the greatest overestimation by males on structure and function and venereal disease and by females on venereal disease, conception and masturbation. The greatest underestimation by both males and females was on menopause and contraceptives.

(3) There was no topic on which all students were well-informed.

On the basis of this report it appears that university students are unable to evaluate realistically how much they know about the physiology of sex; and that "well-informed" means different things to different individuals. There appear to be great gaps in essential knowledge for a large majority of students. Many of them are obviously uninformed or misinformed about the structure and function of the sex organs. The lack of adequate information about venereal disease is especially serious. A basic course which would cover the essential topics thoroughly should be provided in schools, and teachers in training should receive preparation for such instruction. Such a program would insure a specified level of knowledge of human sexual development for all students and would serve as a basis for the discussion of related social and emotional problems which young people encounter.

Donald Weatherley

Self-Perceived Rate of
Physical Maturation and Personality
in Late Adolescence

The intensity and variability of physical growth during adolescence is such that at any specific age from approximately 11 to 18 some youths are nearly mature whereas others are relatively immature in respect to their ultimate physical stature. Longitudinal research at the Institute of Human Development, University of California, regarding the effects of early and late maturing upon personality dynamics has shown that, for boys, early physical maturation leads to certain advantages, including greater esteem from peers and adults, substantially more athletic prowess, and considerably enhanced heterosexual status. By and large, over-all psychological adjustment appears to be more satisfactory in the early- rather than the late-maturing boys. Research for girls has been more equivocal. Early physical acceleration may cause them to be conspicuously tall and stocky. In contrast to the boys' lot, neither of these attributes is an asset by contemporary standards of feminine pulchritude. Thus the general proposition is widely cited that early-maturing girls are at a disadvantage whereas late-maturing girls are at an advantage. However, contrary to expectations, recent research suggests that the early-maturing girls have "more favorable self-concepts" than those who are late maturing.

In an independent investigation, Weatherley categorizes college students, on the basis of their own reports of their rate of physical maturation, into groups of early, average, and late maturers. The results largely confirm the earlier Institute studies and help clarify the general assumptions. Late physical maturation represents an apparent handicap to boys' personality development, but average time of maturation is about as advantageous as early maturation. As the earlier studies showed, the effects of rate of maturation on personal adjustment are less salient for girls than for boys; further, in harmony with recent studies, Weatherley suggests both boys and girls benefit from the effects of early physical maturation.

I T has long been recognized that the timing of puberty and of the marked physical changes which herald its onset is subject to wide individual differences. It is relatively recently, however, that attention has been drawn to

FROM *Child Development,* XXXV (1964), 1197–1210. Reprinted by permission of the author and the Society for Research in Child Development.

the differential impact on personal and social adjustment of these individual differences in the rate of physical maturation. This issue has been brought into sharp focus by a recent series of reports stemming from the California Adolescent Growth Study, a project which involved the intensive observation and testing of a group of approximately 180 boys and girls over a seven-year period.[1] These reports were based on comparisons made with a variety of behavioral and personality measures of groups of extremely early and extremely late maturers (the upper and lower 20 per cent of the total Growth Study sample).

Clear-cut results were found for boys. Both trained adult observers and peers described the late-maturing boys' behavior in less favorable terms than that of the early maturers. For example, at age 16 the late maturers were rated by adults as significantly less attractive in physique, less well groomed, less moderate in their behavior, more affected, more tense appearing, and more eager. Peers described the late maturers as more restless, less reserved, less grown-up, and more bossy.[2] In brief, the tense, active, attention-seeking behavior of the late maturers contrasted sharply with the self-assured, well modulated, socially appropriate behavior manifested by the group of early maturers. Moreover, the late maturers were chosen much less frequently than early maturers for positions of leadership in their school and were much less prominent in extracurricular activities.[3]

An analysis of TAT protocols obtained when the boys were 17 years old revealed personality differences consistent with the behavior differences found between early and late maturers. These data indicated that accompanying the late maturers' less adaptive social behaviors were heightened feelings of inadequacy, negative self-conceptions, feelings of rejection and domination, and persistent dependency needs paradoxically coupled with a rebellious quest for autonomy and freedom from restraint.[4]

Finally, a follow-up study [5] provided evidence that the personality differences between the early- and late-maturing boys persisted into adulthood long after physical differences between the groups had disappeared. The male subjects of the Adolescent Growth Study were administered two objective tests of personality (the California Psychological Inventory and the Edwards Personal Preference Schedule) when they had reached an average age of 33. The test results indicated that as adults the late maturers were less capable of conveying a good impression, less self-controlled, less responsible, less dominant, and more inclined to turn to others for help than were the

[1] H. E. Jones, "The California Adolescent Growth Study," *J. Educ. Res.*, XXXI (1938), 561–567.
[2] M. C. Jones and N. Bayley, "Physical Maturing Among Boys as Related to Behavior," *J. Educ. Psych.*, XLI (1950), 129–148.
[3] M. C. Jones, "A Study of Socialization Patterns at the High School Level," *J. Genet. Psychol.*, XCIII (1958), 87–111.
[4] P. H. Mussen and M. C. Jones, "Self-Conceptions, Motivations, and Interpersonal Attitudes of Late- and Early-Maturing Boys," *Child Developm.*, XXVIII (1957), 243–256.
[5] M. C. Jones, "The Later Careers of Boys Who Were Early- or Late-Maturing," *Child Developm.*, XXVIII (1957), 113–128.

early maturers—a pattern of personality differences quite similar to the pattern that had emerged when the groups were compared in adolescence.

The results of this series of studies on males add up to a consistent picture which makes good theoretical sense. A large, strong stature is a central aspect of the ideal masculine model in our society. Thus, it is reasonable to assume that the early attainment of the physical attributes associated with maturity serves as a social stimulus which evokes from both peers and adults a reaction of respect, acceptance, and the expectation that the individual concerned will be capable of relatively mature social behavior. Such a reaction from others serves to support and reinforce adaptive, "grown-up" actions and contributes to feelings of confidence and security in the early-maturing boys. On the other hand, the late maturer must cope with the developmental demands of the junior high and high school period with the liability of a relatively small, immature appearing physical stature. His appearance is likely to call out in others at least mild reactions of derogation and the expectation that he is capable of only ineffectual, immature behavior. Such reactions constitute a kind of social environment which is conducive to feelings of inadequacy, insecurity and defensive, "small-boy" behavior. Such behavior once initiated may well be self-sustaining, since it is likely to only intensify the negative environmental reactions which gave rise to it in the first place. This interpretation, fully consistent with the evidence produced by the investigations of the Growth Study workers, implies that the late-maturing boy is likely to be involved in a circular psycho-social process in which reactions of others and his own reactions interact with unhappy consequences for his personal and social adjustment.

Does rate of physical maturation have the same effect on the personal-social development of girls? The early data obtained in the Adolescent Growth Study suggested that it does not—that an effect opposite to that found in boys occurs. H. E. Jones [6] reported that late-maturing girls were rated by adult judges significantly higher than early-maturing girls on a number of socially desirable traits such as sociability, leadership, cheerfulness, poise, and expressiveness. Peers also rated the late maturers in more positive terms than they did the early maturers. Moreover, the late-maturing girls were especially likely to participate in extracurricular activities at high school and hold positions of prestige in school clubs; early-maturing girls played a much less prominent role in school activities.[7]

These findings imply that in contrast to the situation with boys, late physical maturation is an asset and early maturation a liability to the social adjustment of girls. Why should this be true? Mary C. Jones and Mussen [8]

[6] H. E. Jones, "Adolescence in Our Society," *The Family in a Democratic Society: Anniversary Papers of the Community Service Society of New York* (Columbia University Press, 1949), pp. 70–82.

[7] M. C. Jones, "A Study of Socialization . . .," *op. cit.*

[8] M. C. Jones and P. H. Mussen, "Self-Conceptions, Motivations, and Interpersonal Attitudes of Early- and Late-Maturing Girls," *Child Developm.*, XXIX (1958), 491–501.

offered an explanation which focused upon the likely biosocial consequences of early physical maturation for girls. They pointed out that the early-maturing girl is inclined to acquire a stocky, muscular physique while the late maturer tends toward a slim, slight build, more in keeping with the feminine ideal in our society. Furthermore, the female early maturer is not only slightly out of step in physical development when compared with other girls her age, she is drastically different in physical status from her male péers of similar age, since boys in general lag about two years behind girls in manifesting puberal growth changes. H. E. Jones [9] also noted that the parents of early-maturing girls might well be unenthusiastic about their daughters' precocious interest in the opposite sex, an interest which is likely to draw them toward social contacts with boys much older than they.

This line of reasoning led Mary C. Jones and Mussen [10] to predict that the personality development of the early-maturing girls in the Adolescent Growth Study would reflect the ill effects of an accelerated rate of growth as did their social behavior, investigated earlier. This expectation, however, was not supported by TAT data obtained when the girls were 17 years old. Although the differences found for girls between early and late maturers were not nearly as striking as those found for boys on the TAT, the differences were generally in the same direction for both sexes. The implication of the projective test data was that early-maturing members of both sexes as opposed to late maturers tend to be characterized by more adequate thought processes, a more positive self-conception, and a more relaxed, secure view of themselves and their world.

Thus in the case of girls it is necessary to somehow account for the apparent inconsistency of findings indicating that early maturation leads to less adequate social adjustment in combination with other results indicating that early maturation is associated with a more "healthy" appearing personality picture. It is possible that the personality data were unreliable, that the differences found on the TAT were artifacts of sampling or measurement error; certainly this interpretation is more reasonable than one discounting the behavior rating measures and indices of social participation on similar grounds, as the findings on the latter sets of measures were more clear-cut than the TAT results. On the other hand, it may be as Mary C. Jones and Mussen [11] suggested, that early maturation is a social disadvantage early in the adolescent period, when the behavior ratings were made, but later in adolescence when physical differences due to different rates of maturation are less marked and environmental stress presumably associated with precocious growth is reduced, the early-maturing girls relax and manifest in their personality integration the beneficial effects of their earlier start toward the assumption of an adult status.

It is obvious that additional data bearing on the relation in late adoles-

[9] H. E. Jones, "Adolescence in Our Society," *op. cit.*
[10] Jones and Mussen, *op. cit.*
[11] *Ibid.*

cence between rate of physical maturation and personality attributes of girls would be helpful in choosing between these alternative explanations of the inconsistent appearing Adolescent Growth Study data. One purpose of the present study was to provide such additional data by assessing the relation between a measure of maturational rate and a variety of personality variables in girls in late adolescence. The design also permitted a between-sex comparison in order to determine whether or not rate of physical maturation had similar implications for the personality development of boys and of girls.

Another purpose of the present study was to assess once again the relation of maturational rate and personality characteristics for a group of males, considered apart from females. Although the California workers' findings for boys were generally clear-cut and consistent, the conclusions they generated rested, in one sense at least, on a quite narrow empirical base (as was also true for the less certain conclusions reached for girls). All the studies reviewed earlier involved the same small group of Ss, all of whom lived in the Berkeley, California, area. Furthermore, despite the fact that these reports have appeared relatively recently in the literature, all but the one concerning the follow-up study were based on data gathered more than two decades ago; the Growth Study Ss were, at the time the present study was undertaken, close to 40 years old—literally old enough to be the parents of today's adolescents.

It should be noted, however, that the present study was by no means a contemporary replication of earlier research; it differed in several important respects from the California investigations. The Ss in this study were on the average about two years older than were the Ss at the completion of the Adolescent Growth Study. A number of objective personality measures were used in the present study, only one of which (the Edwards Personal Preference Schedule) was used in the California research and then only in the follow-up study.[12] The most noteworthy distinction between the study reported here and the previous research in this area had to do with the nature of the measure of rate of physical maturation. The California studies used an objective skeletal-age index of physical maturation as a basis for identifying early and late maturers. In the present study a simple self-report measure of relative maturational rate was used. Its use involved the assumption that adolescents have a fairly accurate idea of the relative timing of their physical maturation and can reliably report this information.

Obviously, any one or more of the factors mentioned above could be responsible for differences found between results of the present study and the findings of the California series of investigations; such differences might not be easy to interpret. On the other hand, it was felt that if the present study yielded findings with implications convergent with those generated by previous research, especially that dealing with males where prior evidence was most definitive, the generality of the conclusions reached would be strongly supported.

[12] M. C. Jones, "The Later Careers . . .," *op. cit.*

METHOD

The Ss were 234 male and 202 female college students enrolled in the elementary psychology course at the University of Colorado. The mean age of the girls was 19.4 ($SD = 2.6$), the mean age of the boys, 19.9 ($SD = 1.9$).

Early in the semester the MMPI K scale [13] and the Taylor Manifest Anxiety Scale (TMAS) [14] were administered to the Ss in large group sessions. Approximately five weeks later 96 of the boys and 92 of the girls took the Edwards Personal Preference Schedule (EPPS).[15]

In order to obtain measures reflecting degree of identification with parents and peers, the Ss were asked in the initial testing sessions to give self-ratings of the degree to which they saw themselves as similar to each of the following individuals: their mother, father, same-sex best friend, and opposite-sex best friend. These self-ratings of perceived similarity were obtained for each of the following dimensions: overall personality, intelligence, warmth, orderliness, political views, and religious views. Seven-point rating scales were used, yielding scores which ranged from one (indicating the lowest degree of perceived similarity) to seven (indicating the highest degree of perceived similarity).

Rate of physical maturation was assessed by responses to the following multiple-choice question presented to the Ss during the initial testing sessions: "With regard to your physical maturation, you would say that you matured: (a) quite early, (b) somewhat early, (c) average, (d) somewhat late, (e) quite late." These alternatives were assigned weights from one (quite early) to five (quite late) so that the choice made by each S could be represented as a numerical score. In addition, each S was categorized into one of three groups on the basis of his response to the physical maturation question. Individuals who had chosen either the alternative "quite early" or "somewhat early" were considered early maturers. Those who had chosen the alternative "average," were considered average maturers. Those who had chosen the alternatives "somewhat late" or "quite late" were categorized as late maturers.

Means of these three groups for each of the personality measures were compared by *t* tests, with boys and girls treated separately. This analysis was considered more suitable than a correlational analysis as a basis for describing relations between maturational rate and personality variables within each sex group because it permitted the identification of nonlinear as well as linear relations in the data.

[13] J. C. McKinley, S. R. Hathaway, and P. E. Meehl, "The Minnesota Multiphasic Personality Inventory: VI. The K Scale," *J. Consult. Psychol.*, XII (1948), 20–31.

[14] J. A. Taylor, "A Personality Scale of Manifest Anxiety," *J. Abnorm. Soc. Psychol.*, XLVIII (1953), 285–290.

[15] A. L. Edwards, *Manual for the Edwards Personal Preference Schedule* (Psychological Corp., 1959).

Table 1   Distribution of Responses to Item Measuring Timing of Physical Maturation

	Males (N = 234)	Females (N = 202)
Very early	11.1%	15.8%
Somewhat early	21.4	21.8
Average	44.9	48.5
Somewhat late	19.6	12.9
Very late	3.0	1.0

RESULTS

In Table 1 are presented the distributions for boys and girls of responses to the item measuring perceived rate of physical maturation. The distributions for both sexes were skewed in a direction indicating that both boys and girls are more likely to see themselves as accelerated in development than retarded. For boys and girls combined, there was a significantly greater number of responses in the "somewhat early" and "very early" categories considered together than in the "somewhat late" and "very late" categories ($X^2 = 21.64$; $df = 1$, $p < .01$). While the skewness appeared slightly more marked in the distribution for girls than for boys, the distributions did not differ significantly from one another ($X^2 = 7.31$, $df = 4$, $p > .10$).

Mean scores obtained by early, average, and late maturers on the personality measures are shown in Table 2. This table includes only results for personality variables on which at least one inter-group comparison revealed a difference significant at the .10 level or less.

In general, the findings for boys were highly consistent with the California Adolescent Growth Study results. The most clear-cut differences found in the present study between early-maturing boys and those who described themselves as late maturers were on the same two EPPS variables—dominance and succorance—on which early- and late-maturing males differed when they were tested as adults in the Growth Study follow-up.[16] In the present study, late maturers as opposed to early maturers scored lower on the dominance scale ($p < .05$) and higher on the succorance scale ($p < .01$). They also differed in the same direction on these variables from the group of average maturers. Thus the late maturers revealed relatively weak tendencies to lead and control others and relatively strong tendencies to seek encouragement, sympathy, and understanding from others—characteristics found previously to be associated with late maturation not only in the follow-up study mentioned above,[17] but in two other investigations done as part of the California Growth Study.[18] It is also noteworthy that

[16] M. C. Jones, "Later Careers of Boys," *op. cit.*
[17] *Ibid.*
[18] Mussen and Jones, *op. cit.*; P. H. Mussen and M. C. Jones, "The Behavior-Inferred Motivations of Late- and Early-Maturing Boys," *Child Developm.*, XXIX (1958), 61–67.

Table 2 *Mean Scores on Personality Measures for Early, Average, and Late Maturers*

	Early Maturers	Average Maturers	Late Maturers	Early vs. Average	Average vs. Late	Early vs. Late
Males						
TMAS	6.84 (76)	6.44 (105)	8.09 (53)	ns	< .05	ns
EPPS:						
Achievement	15.40 (30)	17.44 (36)	16.96 (30)	< .10	ns	ns
Autonomy	15.17 (30)	15.69 (36)	17.17 (30)	ns	ns	< .06
Intraception	16.30 (30)	14.03 (36)	13.83 (30)	<.10	ns	< .10
Succorance	9.20 (30)	9.86 (36)	12.27 (30)	ns	< .05	< .01
Dominance	19.13 (30)	18.81 (36)	16.33 (30)	ns	< .10	< .05
Abasement	11.47 (30)	9.56 (36)	12.20 (30)	ns	< .05	ns
Endurance	10.17 (30)	13.42 (36)	10.50 (30)	< .05	< .05	ns
Perceived similarity to:						
Mother's political views	4.46 (76)	4.77 (105)	4.13 (53)	ns	< .05	ns
Mother's religious views	4.63 (76)	4.65 (105)	4.09 (53)	ns	< .10	ns
Father's political views	4.65 (68)	5.12 (100)	4.35 (51)	< .10	< .02	ns
Father's religious views	4.76 (68)	4.94 (100)	4.29 (51)	ns	< .10	ns
Boy friend's warmth	5.11 (76)	5.08 (105)	4.52 (52)	ns	< .05	< .05
Boy friend's political views	4.89 (76)	4.79 (105)	4.31 (52)	ns	< .10	< .05
Boy friend's intelligence	5.41 (76)	5.13 (105)	5.71 (52)	ns	< .05	ns
Females						
TMAS	6.91 (76)	7.46 (98)	9.54 (28)	ns	< .05	< .02
EPPS:						
Exhibition	16.38 (37)	14.96 (45)	17.00 (10)	< .05	< .10	ns
Nurturance	16.05 (37)	16.27 (45)	13.50 (10)	ns	< .10	< .10
Perceived similarity to:						
Mother's religious views	4.43 (76)	5.12 (98)	4.54 (28)	< .05	ns	ns
Father's political views	4.90 (68)	4.96 (92)	5.70 (23)	ns	< .05	< .10
Boy friend's orderliness	4.67 (76)	5.23 (97)	4.39 (28)	< .05	< .05	ns

Note: This table includes only those variables on which at least one between-group comparison was significant at the .10 level or less. The N for each cell is given in parentheses.

low scores on the EPPS dominance scale, and high scores on the succorance scale (i.e., the pattern characteristic of the late maturers) have been shown to be associated with scores on the Minnesota Multiphasic Personality Inventory indicative of maladjustment.[19]

[19] R. M. Merrill and L. B. Heathers, "The Relation of MMPI to the Edwards Personal Preference Schedule on a College Counseling Center Sample," *J. Consult. Psychol.*, XX (1956), 310–314.

The late-maturing boys also obtained higher EPPS autonomy scores than did the early maturers, a difference which just failed to reach significance at the .05 level. This may at first appear to be a finding inconsistent with the implications of previous research, since the term autonomy is one often included in conceptions of the "ideal" personality. Yet a consideration of the items included in the EPPS autonomy scale (e.g., "to do things that are unconventional," "to criticize those in positions of authority," "to avoid responsibilities and obligations") points up the anti-conventional, at least mildly rebellious trends tapped by this measure. Thus the late maturers' relatively high autonomy mean score, considered in combination with their high succorance but low dominance scores suggests a prolongation of the typically adolescent independence-dependence conflict in late-maturing boys. The previous research of Mussen and Mary C. Jones [20] led them to a similar conclusion for the group of boys they studied.

If late maturers are in fact caught between competing strivings for dependency and strivings for freedom from restraint we should expect to find in them evidence of less well resolved internal conflict in the form of heightened tension and subjective distress. Two measures used in the present study are most pertinent to this question, and on both the results confirmed expectations. On the TMAS and the EPPS abasement scale late-maturing boys scored higher than average or early maturers, differences which were statistically significant ($p < .05$) in the comparisons between late and average maturers. Scores on the TMAS reflect the degree of tension and manifest anxiety an individual acknowledges and have been shown to be highly correlated negatively with a measure of self-esteem.[21] The abasement scale items refer to feelings of guilt, inferiority, and depression; there is evidence that high scores on this scale are associated with maladjustment.[22] Of interest here also is the finding of the present study that the late-maturing males tended to score lower than the early maturers ($p < .10$) on the EPPS intraception scale (e.g., "to analyze one's motives and feelings," "to understand how others feel about problems"), suggesting that perhaps because the late maturer is, as indicated above, more likely than individuals maturing earlier to experience negative, presumably unpleasant feelings, he is less likely to develop a "psychological mindedness" in his orientation to himself and others.

On one EPPS variable—the endurance scale—a curvilinear relation with rate of maturation in boys was found; both the late and early maturers evidenced lower scores on the endurance scale (e.g., "to keep at a puzzle or problem until it is solved," "to put in long hours of work without distraction") than did the group of average maturers ($p < .05$). This is not an easy finding to interpret. The appreciable personality differences that set late and early maturers apart, however, suggest that a relative lack of per-

[20] Mussen and Jones, "Self-Conceptions, Motivations, . . .," *op. cit.*
[21] A. W. Siegman, "Cognitive, Affective, and Psychopathological Correlates of the Taylor Manifest Anxiety Scale," *J. Consult. Psychol.*, XX (1956), 137–141.
[22] Merrill and Heathers, *op. cit.*

sistence may have a different functional significance for early as opposed to late maturers. It may be, for example, that the late maturer as a corollary of his heightened tension and feelings of inferiority has less conviction that he will be able to succeed at tasks and thus is inclined to give up trying relatively quickly, while the early maturer is inclined to persist less than the average maturer because he is accustomed to success with less effort and seeks alternate routes to his goals when he meets a barrier. It must be recognized, however, that any such interpretation is, at this state in our knowledge, highly speculative.

The data for boys involving ratings of perceived similarity to parents and friends among various dimensions by no means revealed startling differences among the maturation groups (Table 2). Of the 72 comparisons made only 10 differences significant at the .10 level or less were found. Yet it is noteworthy that in eight of these ten instances, late maturers rated themselves less similar to parents or friends than did Ss who matured earlier. This at least suggests that late maturers are more inclined to see themselves as being different from others. A resulting sense of estrangement may contribute to the heightened subjective distress found in the late-maturing boys. This line of reasoning is consistent with the findings of previous studies which have shown that the tendency to view oneself as relatively dissimilar to others in personal characteristics is associated with relatively high anxiety.[23]

In previous research, no difference was found between groups of early- and late-maturing boys in degree of achievement motivation.[24] In the present study, boys classified as early maturers tended to obtain lower scores on the EPPS achievement scale (e.g., "to be able to do things better than others") than did the group of average maturers ($p < .10$). This may be a chance result. The high social prestige attained by the early-maturing boys who participated in the Adolescent Growth Study[25] certainly does not lead one to anticipate finding a less strong achievement need in early maturers. Also of pertinence here are data obtained in connection with a study of academic over- and under-achievement in which a number of the male Ss of the present study participated.[26] Thirteen of these Ss were identified as over-achievers (i.e., their academic performance appreciably exceeded that expected on the basis of aptitude scores) and compared in terms of their scores on the measure of perceived rate of maturation with 16 Ss classified as under-achievers (i.e., their academic performance was below that expected on the basis of aptitude scores). The results indicated a tendency for the over-achievers to report an earlier physical maturation

---

[23] J. E. Chance, "Adjustment and Prediction of Others' Behavior," *J. Consult. Psychol.*, XX (1958), 191–194; J. R. Davitz and D. J. Mason, "Manifest Anxiety and Social Perception," *J. Consult. Psychol.*, XXIV (1960), 554.

[24] Mussen and Jones, "Self-Conceptions, Motivations . . .," *op. cit.*; Mussen and Jones, "The Behavior-Inferred Motivations . . .," *op. cit.*

[25] Jones, "A Study of Socialization . . .," *op. cit.*; Jones and Bayley, *op. cit.*

[26] R. S. Wyer, D. Weatherley and G. Terrell, "Social Role, Aggression and Academic Achievement," *J. Abnorm. Soc. Psychol.* (in press).

than the under-achievers ($p < .10$). This suggestion of a link between academic over-achievement and early physical maturation in males also serves to raise a question concerning the reliability of the findings of a lesser degree of striving for achievement in the early maturers. It is, of course, possible that both findings are valid: early maturers may have less strong achievement needs but because of a more efficient and effective use of their personal resources manifest a relatively higher level of success in the academic as well as the social sphere.

Turning now to the results for girls, it can be seen in Table 2 that many fewer differences were found between the maturation groups than were found for boys. The most clear-cut result was obtained on the TMAS: late-maturing girls scored higher on this measure than either the average ($p < .05$) or early maturers ($p < .02$), indicating a higher level of manifest anxiety associated with late maturation. This finding, in the same direction as TMAS results for boys, is congruent with those data obtained in the Adolescent Growth Study that suggested a less adequate personality integration in late-maturing girls.[27]

Aside from these results on the TMAS, the implications of which appear to be quite meaningful, the infrequent differences among groups that were found on the EPPS and similarity rating measures do not suggest any specific personality pattern associated with either early or late maturation. The relatively few statistically significant differences which occurred in those data may well be the product of chance in view of the large total number of comparisons made. While failure to find definitive differences among groups under study may be due to a number of factors (e.g., in the present instance the relatively small number of late-maturing girls who took the EPPS reduced the probability of uncovering real differences on that measure which may exist in the population), it is pertinent to note that the previous research that attempted to trace the personality correlates of late and early maturation also produced much less clear-cut findings with girls than with boys.[28]

DISCUSSION

Whenever a research strategy involves the assessment of relations between a response-inferred independent variable or variables and a response-inferred dependent variable or variables, an important question arises which must be considered before the results can be taken seriously. To what extent is it likely that the relations found between the independent and dependent variables are the artifactual products of a response bias which similarly affects the measures used to define the independent variables on the one hand and the dependent variables on the other? This question is especially pertinent in connection with the present study since the distribution of scores on the measure of self-perceived maturation—the independent vari-

[27] Jones and Mussen, *op. cit.*
[28] *Ibid.*

able—was skewed in a direction indicating a greater tendency for Ss to see themselves as maturing relatively early than as maturing relatively late. Frazier and Lisonbee [29] reported a similar nonsymmetrical distribution of self-rated physical maturation in tenth-grade boys and girls.

It is possible that this skewness reflects a defensive inclination on the part of at least some of the Ss to describe themselves in what they regard as more favorable terms—i.e., as being relatively advanced in physical development. Conversely, the identification of oneself as retarded in maturation could stem in part from a response bias toward self-derogation. Certainly the retrospective report of so ambiguous a characteristic as maturational rate is potentially subject to such distortions. If in fact an appreciable portion of the variance in maturation scores is due to differences among individuals in their willingness to describe themselves in unfavorable terms, then serious doubt would be cast upon the validity of the relations found in the present study between the maturation measure and those dependent measures which are also subject to influence by this sort of response bias. While the EPPS was specifically designed to minimize the effect of a bias to respond in either a socially desirable or undesirable direction, the TMAS and the similarity ratings are dependent measures certainly susceptible to such influence.

Fortunately, in the present study data were gathered that made possible an assessment of the degree to which the maturation score involved variance attributable to individual differences in willingness to describe oneself unfavorably. An estimate of each S's defensiveness was obtained by use of the MMPI K scale that was administered to all Ss. An individual characteristically inclined to distort his self-description in a derogatory direction should obtain a very low K scale score; a very high K scale score is indicative of a defensive inclination to slant one's self-description in a favorable direction.

In the present study for neither boys nor girls were there found any differences in K scale scores approaching statistical significance when the groups of early, average, and late maturers were compared. When responses to the question concerning physical maturation were converted to numerical scores, the correlations found between these scores and scores on the K scale were essentially zero both for boys ($r = .024$) and for girls ($r = .047$). This finding fails to support an argument that scores on the maturation measure were contaminated by a personality-linked response bias. Thus it is not reasonable to discount the results found in this study as merely the product of a measurement artifact.

In the case of boys, the findings of the present study are clear-cut. They indicate that the late-maturing boy of college age is less likely than his earlier-maturing peers to have satisfactorily resolved the conflicts normally attending the transition from childhood to adulthood. He is more inclined to seek attention and affection from others and less inclined to assume a

[29] A. Frazier and L. K. Lisonbee, "Adolescent Concerns with Physique," *Sch. Rev.*, LVIII (1950), 397–405.

position of dominance and leadership over others. Yet he is not ready to accept the dictates of authority gracefully; he is inclined, rather, to defy authority and assert unconventional behavior in a rebellious vein. In view of the evidence of these potentially competing forces at work within him, it is not surprising that the late maturer also tends to acknowledge a heightened level of subjective tension and readiness to indulge in guilt-implying self-abasement. Nor is it surprising that he tends to see himself as being different from his peers and parents.

The foregoing portrait of the late-maturing boy is, of course, misleading in that it ignores the obviously large overlap among the groups studied and the obviously appreciable individual differences within the group of late maturers. It does, however, serve to bring into focus a central conclusion to be drawn from the results of the present study: late maturation is associated with less mature appearing, less "healthy" appearing personality characteristics. The high degree of congruence between the results of this study and the results of previous studies which involved quite different procedures, measures, and subjects, underscores the generality and importance of rate of physical maturation as a variable influencing personality development in boys.

A second conclusion which can be drawn from the results of the present study, a conclusion which involves a more precise description of the nature of the relation between rate of maturation and personality in boys, has no precedent in the earlier work done as part of the California Adolescent Growth Study. These earlier investigations used an extreme-groups design in which individuals who were extremely late in maturing were compared with individuals extremely early in maturation; no comparisons were made between either of these groups and a group of individuals whose rate of maturation was average. The inclusion in the present study of the group of average maturers made possible an inference concerning the relative impact upon personality characteristics of early versus late maturation when each extreme group was compared to an average group. As an inspection of Table 2 reveals, many fewer significant differences were found when the group of early-maturing boys was compared with the group of average maturers (of a total of 41 comparisons only 1 reached significance at the .05 level or less) than when late maturers were compared with the average maturers (9 of the 41 comparisons made were significant at the .05 level or less). The early- and average-maturing groups were quite similar to one another in the personality attributes they manifested, while the late maturers were set apart from both of these groups. Thus it is clear that the relations found between rate of physical maturation and the personality characteristics measured were not in general linear ones. The implication is that while late maturation is apparently a handicap to the personality development of boys, early maturation may not be an asset; it appears rather to have an effect on personality development no different from the effect of an average rate of physical maturation.

One of the questions that prompted the present study was whether late physical maturation was a liability or an asset to the personality development of girls. The results for girls, however, were much less striking than those for boys; they do not permit a definitive answer to the question. It is clear, nevertheless, that they offer absolutely no support for the proposition that the effect of rate of physical maturation on the adequacy of personality integration in girls is the reverse of that operating in boys. On the other hand, the fact that on the TMAS the results for girls paralleled those for boys lends limited support to the alternative proposition that late physical maturation has adverse effects on personal adjustment in both sexes in late adolescence. The very slim evidence on which it is based, however, makes it necessary to emphasize the tentative nature of this conclusion.

What is perhaps more noteworthy in the findings for girls is the very fact that they were so much less dramatic than those for boys. Since previous research [30] also produced less definitive results for girls than boys, one is drawn to the conclusion that for girls as opposed to boys rate of physical maturation is a much less influential variable mediating personality development. This is not surprising. In our society the cultural sex-role prescription for males is relatively unambiguous and is one which places a high value upon attributes associated with physical strength and athletic prowess, especially in the adolescent and young adulthood years. As Lynn [31] pointed out, however, the feminine sex-role prescription is much less definite and stereotyped; consequently it is less likely to be closely tied to any specific pattern of physical attributes.

A final word is in order regarding the measure of physical maturation used in the present study. An assumption involved in the use of this measure was that individuals are both aware of the relative rate of their physical maturation and are willing to report it with reasonable accuracy. The generally high degree of congruence between the results based on the simple self-report measure used in the present study and previous findings based on an objective skeletal-age measure of physical maturation is evidence bolstering this assumption. The veridicality of such self-ratings cannot be firmly established, of course, without directly comparing the ratings with an objective measure of physical growth. Nevertheless, the present results constitute sufficient indirect evidence of the validity of the self-report measure of physical maturation to encourage the use of a measure of this sort in situations where it is impractical to obtain objective indices of maturational rate.

The present study and those done earlier have clearly established the importance of rate of physical maturation as a variable influencing personality development at least in boys; this variable deserves further study. Especially interesting would be research bearing upon the interaction of the maturation variable and variables such as social class membership, parental child-rearing practices, or peer-group social structure.

[30] Jones and Mussen, *op. cit.*
[31] D. B. Lynn, "A Note on Sex Differences in the Development of Masculine and Feminine Identification," *Psychol. Rev.*, LXVI (1959), 126–135.

E. A. Peel

Intellectual Growth During Adolescence

Between childhood and adolescence, thinking processes become less bound to concrete experiences and more dependent upon abstract reasoning and manipulation of hypothetical relationships. In the paper presented below, Peel identifies one of the more fundamental aspects of cognitive growth during adolescence as a change from "describer" to "explainer" thinking. He sees three noticeable aspects of growth from partial and circumstantial observation to explanatory thought: (a) comprehensive judgments involving imagination and possibilities, (b) successful use of imagined hypotheses, and (c) spontaneous elimination of less applicable alternatives. He believes that adolescent intellectual growth may be enhanced by ensuring youth two kinds of experience: one, with "the properties of his environment, constructed by him," and the other, with "the properties of his actions, seen in mathematics and logic." Peel's discussion warrants the serious attention of students and teachers who are interested in the changes in cognitive behavior associated with adolescence.

ADOLESCENT THINKING

In every respect but one the adolescent has received unstinted attention concerning his development and its so-called problems. Furthermore he appears to thrive on it. Almost monthly he creates new values in a subculture which grows more self-determined and self-defined. The peripheral signs of this subculture, as seen in its sound and beat and clothes, assume an ascendancy that reaches into adult values. When I was young it was the late adolescent, nay the young adult, who gave the sartorial lead both to his juniors and seniors. But now it is the mid-adolescent who exercises such an influence on his elders. I'm not sure he always wishes it so—though what he wishes is often difficult to determine for his is a jealously guarded culture. It does not do for the adult to be a square but it is equally unwise to try to be too expert.

In their preoccupation with how he feels, plays, herds and adorns himself very few people have studied his intellectual growth systematically. This is not to say that educationists are insentive to the problem. The central

FROM *Educational Review*, XVII (1965), 169–180. Reprinted by permission of the author and the publisher.

theme of the Newsom report is the intellectual difference between primary and secondary school experience. The difference is more than a matter of attainment. There is a change of quality as well. Such nouns as *self-awareness, imagination, judgment, insight* crop up throughout the report. We are told that

> The work in a secondary school becomes secondary in character whenever it is concerned, first, with selfconscious thought and judgment; secondly, with the relation of school and the work done there to the world outside of which the pupils form a part and of which they are increasingly aware.

and that

> the quality of selfconscious judgment . . . describes a mental process that involves the use of reason and imagination to bring order into the world of things perceived.

Awareness, however, is not explanation.

There may be several reasons for this lack of information about adolescent thinking. On the surface young children's thinking changes more dramatically and is capable of examination by simpler material. There is also a widespread belief that by mid-adolescence, thinking is more a function of the particular school subject—say science, mathematics or history—than of more general thought processes and psychological changes. But thinking is an interaction between pupil and subject and the adolescent has not ceased to be a pupil.

In this neglect we tend to forget that there are many formative years between 11 and 20. The intellectual changes are indeed both complex and significant. Any problem in a school subject, provided it is not too technically difficult to be given to a wide age range of pupils, will bring out these qualities of the change. Here are a few.

> Suppose there are 32 entrants to a knock-out championship in table tennis. How many games must be played to find the winner? What if there are 24, 17? Is there a general rule? Can you prove it?

Most lower and mid secondary school pupils can produce the general induction—but only sixth formers, and not all of them, are able to prove the rule deductively from the essential structure of the problem—one winner and each losing individual being immediately eliminated.

Again if we give pupils a new number system, say to base 6 or 7, to learn and use, we find younger adolescents can learn the number system and use it by simple correlation of new symbols with decimal symbols, translation and retranslation, without ever giving a hint that the change of base is understood. Older pupils and students set about it quite differently by setting up possible rules, trying them out and accepting, modifying or rejecting as appropriate. In exercises they also give evidence of thinking in the novel system.

If you put colorless liquid samples of dilute acid, dilute alkali and pure water before a pupil and supply him with specimens of blue and red litmus paper after having shown him the reactions between the chemicals and indicator and then ask him to identify the three liquids you will find a failure before 13 to act purposefully according to hypotheses. The power to eliminate alternatives appears later.

Lastly, turning to social studies, if we ask pupils to define such terms as *laws*,[1] we are likely up to 13, to get such answers as *rules which should be obeyed, rules made for the good of the country* to 15 or 16 and a *system of rule imposed upon society in order to promote a freedom for the individual without encroaching on each other's freedom* from the most mature at 19.

These are pointers to what we may look for and how we may do it. Clearly the method of study requires a *guided* taxonomy, in which emphasis is laid on observing developmental changes as well as differences arising from learning various school subjects, followed by a more etiological analysis.

Our questions are

1. What is changing during adolescence?
2. What is common, what different in the modes of thinking required in different subjects?

I shall be concerned mainly with the former.

The method of experiment is to use simple contrived situations, purified from school problems or nearly similar. The material shall not demand too high a level of subject matter knowledge but is designed at producing a problem situation testing thinking rather than attainment.

DESCRIPTION AND EXPLANATION

What are the lines to guide our empirical studies? Over the period of adolescence the most fundamental is that between what I call describer and explainer thinking. Description, as I am using the term entails no more than a relating of the parts of a phenomenon with each other. Explanation involves referring the phenomenon to other previously experienced phenomena, and to generalisations and concepts independently formed. The familiar experiment from elementary physics of causing a tin to collapse by boiling a little water in it, stoppering it and immediately cooling it, illustrates well what I mean. A pupil may describe this sequence of events very adequately but he has not explained it unless he refers to the function of the steam in driving out the air, the subsequent cooling to condense the steam to produce a vacuum and the final collapse under atmospheric pressure. Here the concepts of boiling, gaseous state, condensation, vacuum and atmospheric pressure and strengths of material are all involved.

---

[1] D. M. Wood, "The Development of Some Concepts of Social Relations in Childhood and Adolescence Investigated by Means of the Analysis of their Definitions" (M. Ed. Thesis, University of Nottingham).

As in the case of the learners of the 6 base number system, who were able to apply their knowledge to simple tasks without understanding the base of the system, so the describer of the above phenomenon may well be able to predict what might happen in similar instances, but his power of prediction will be far more limited than that of the thinker who can explain the phenomenon. The latter would be able to predict outcomes in superficially quite different situations as, for example, to explain various physical and physiological phenomenon associated with going high into the atmosphere or deep into the sea.

Analogy clearly lies at the basis of explanation but there is a spectrum of predictive effectiveness ranging from the powerful models of physics at one extreme [2] to the tempting analogies at the other which so often ensnare the politicians and historians. The 100 days analogy was long used against the intentions of its originator.[3]

It is doubtful how far pure description is possible, that is, without any hint of explanation. We use the word *collapse* to account for the change in the shape of the tin. This implies analogy and explanation, which nevertheless are not very useful without the idea of air pressure.

If however we concede the point that pure description is at one end of an explanatory dimension, it would not invalidate the scheme of analysis to be outlined. The range of thought is wide during adolescent growth. The concession however does bear on naive positivistic assumptions in practical science and on the "unique event" theory of history teaching. According to it both would tend to be untenable.

THE IMAGINATION OF POSSIBLE EXPLANATIONS

The growth of explanatory thought involves several changes very noticeable in mid- and late adolescence. Let us look at three of them. First there is the growth from partial and circumstantial observations to comprehensive judgments involving the imagination and invocation of possibilities to explain the phenomenon.[4]

We may set a short anecdote with questions.

Only brave pilots are allowed to fly over high mountains. This summer a fighter pilot flying over the Alps collided with an aerial cable-way, and cut a main cable causing some cars to fall to the glacier below. Several people were killed and many others had to spend the night suspended above the glacier.

1. Was the pilot a careful airman? 2. Why do you think so? The questions evoke answers at four clearly marked levels:

[2] M. B. Hesse, *Models and Analogies in Science* (Sheed and Ward, 1963).

[3] See Cummings' Cartoon "The First Hundred Days," *Daily Express* (October 30, 1964).

[4] E. A. Peel, "A Study of Differences in the Judgements of Adolescent Pupils," *British Journal of Educational Psychology*, XXXVI (1966), 77–86.

1. Not sure. Maybe, involving or imagining extenuating possibilities, vision, weather, state of the plane.
2. No, because if he was careful, he would not have cut the cable.
3. No, because he hit the cable, etc.
4. Yes or No, with irrelevant comment or denial of the premise. E.g. Yes, he was brave; Yes, the cable shouldn't be there.

The ages associated with these levels are respectively 13½, 12½, 12, and 10½.

When instead of the above questions we posed the wholly nondirective question of:

What do you think about the happening in the story? We compel the child to identify his own problem and the replies indicate the level at which he is thinking.

At 14½ we got:

He was either not informed of the mountain railway on his route or he was flying too low also his flying compass may have been affected by something before or after take-off this setting him off course causing collision with the cable.

At 12:

I think that the pilot was not very good at flying and also not fit for doing it. He would have been far better off if he went on with fighting.

and at 11½:

The people must also be brave to stay the night suspended above the glacier. The pilot must be not only brave but a good driver.

From this and other test passages conducted with statistically respectable numbers, the genesis of the pupils' thinking-comprehension seems to proceed as follows:

First there is a capacity to think propositionally by pupils at least as young as 11–12. A proposition is produced linking that implied in the question with the salient feature of the story related circumstantially to the question. Other possibilities do not enter. To this extent the judgment is partial and circumstantial and is essentially descriptive since no outside concept is invoked.

followed next by

a transformation of this judgment by forming its complement with the addition of no new inferences from the material but a change of language form and emphasis. This phase appears at ages from a half year older than that associated with the first category answers.

followed finally by

recognition that there might have been other elements outside the pilot's control which made it not possible for him to see the cable etc. The answers at this stage shift to invoked explanations and suggestions to account for the incident. Their plausibility reveals that they have been related to the data of the problem. Chronological ages of 13+ and mental ages of 14+ years seem to be associated with this phase.

School subject matter confirms the appearance of *imagined* possibilities, comprehensively related to the data of the problem at 13+, but not frequently by younger pupils.

This was shown by Piaget and Inhelder [5] in their studies of pupils' understanding of fluid pressure and their discovery of Newton's First Law. The invocation of imagined causes does not appear to be marked before 13+.

INDUCTION AND DEDUCTION

Description turns on inductive methods, whereas explanation involves deduction from a basis of hypotheses. The contrasting roles of induction and deduction in mathematics need no underlining—we saw it in the table tennis problem. But a similar opposition is apparent between induction and hypothetico-deduction in material situations involving empirical data—such as those of science and geography. The successful use of imagined hypotheses to explain phenomena always contains a deductive element in the comparison of hypotheses with data to arrive at solutions or for the generalisations seen in so-called "thought experiments" in physics.[6]

When does the adolescent begin to show signs of using hypothetico-deductive methods spontaneously?

Here is an experiment aimed at obtaining an answer to this question.

The problem concerned crofter-farming in the Isle of Lewis. No text was used but two maps showed the essential geographical features: mountains, deer forest, rough grazing, common pasture and croft areas, and emphasised the generally poor nature of the land. Charts showed the proportion of crops and grass (good land) to common pasture (poor, ill-drained, rock strewn land), the composition of the crops and grass (grass, oats and potatoes) and the proportion of sheep (many) and cattle (few). Monthly rainfall and temperature charts were also provided.[7]

The central problem for the farmer lies in the natural restrictions placed on him by the poor quality of land and climate, even though there is plenty

[5] B. Inhelder and J. Piaget, *The Growth of Logical Thinking* (London: Routledge and Kegan Paul, 1958).

[6] F. Miller, *College Physics*, to "prove" the relativity of time with respect to the motion of the frame of reference (New York: Harcourt, Brace, 1959).

[7] W. T. Rhys, "The Development of Logical Thought in the Adolescent with Reference to the Teaching of Geography in the Secondary School" (Unpublished research: Birmingham University Education Department).

of land available. Only a minimum degree of geographical expertise is required that is not evident from the maps and charts, namely that sheep will graze on rough land but cattle not.

Rhys then asked the question:

> Are they making sensible use of their land by only growing a few crops on a very small area?

This may arouse a conflict between (a) the visual evidence of the large amount of land apparently available and the large number of sheep and (b) the nature of the land and climate leading to a deductive process to arrive at a conclusion. Here are two answers, the first characteristic of 11–12 year olds:

> Yes. Because they only live in a small place and they only need a small number of crops. The rest of the land has to be kept to feed the animals.

and the second characteristic of older pupils of age 14½ +:

> The crofters are sensible in growing only a few crops over a little area because the ground is mainly mountains and very rough. It would be hard to get the necessary amount of crops needed to feed the crofters, the only crops which they cultivated with a little success are the hardier, tougher crops, oats and potatoes. The land can be made of better use by rough grazing with sheep on the hills and mountains.

The first shows some deduction but solely in terms of area of land and numbers of sheep. The second starts from the quality of the land and deduces consequences which relate to the area and number features.

ELIMINATING ALTERNATIVES

The testing of hypotheses and the elimination of those less effective make up severe tests of adolescent and adult thinking. People are usually too ready to infer a particular belief from evidence which would also support another. In one test [8] students had to find the concept of *three numbers in increasing order* by putting up sets of three numbers for judgment by the experimenter, who of course knew the concept. The most frequent responses were positive instances enumerated to illustrate the concept chosen. Relatively few sets were chosen to eliminate alternative concepts, and also few negative instances deliberately chosen to test the assumed concept.

> Wason concluded: very few intelligent young adults spontaneously test their beliefs in a situation which does not appear to be of a "scientific" nature.

[8] P. C. Wason, "On the Failure to Eliminate Hypotheses in a Conceptual Task," *Qu. F. Exp. Psy.*, XII (1960), 129.

These results found support from a research[9] on student nurses' ideas of correlation. They were presented with packs of cards, each card of which described a patient by giving a relationship between a *symptom* and a *diagnosis*. Suppose the symptom was spots on the chest and the diagnosis measles. Four types of card are possible:

Presence of spots (positive)—diagnosis of measles (positive)
·Presence of spots (positive)—measles *not* diagnosed (negative)
Absence of spots (negative)—diagnosis of measles (positive)
Absence of spots (negative)—measles *not* diagnosed (negative)

They thumbed through the packs and were asked to judge to what extent each pack revealed a correlation between symptom and diagnosis. The worker concluded that

Their strategies and inferences reveal a particularistic, nonstatistical approach, or an exclusive dependence on the frequency of + + instances.

When secondary school pupils are given simple chemical experiments requiring the identification of substances and the elimination of alternative possibilities, they are rarely capable spontaneously of successful elimination procedures until they are 14, 15 and older.

What are the main features of intellectual growth between 11 and 20?

In the growth from a largely descriptive type of thinking to explanation we see a change from particularistic perceptual, perceptual, circumstantial and largely inductive ways of thinking to modes of thought revealing the invocation of imagined possibilities which gradually become more articulate in form to warrant the use of the terms hypotheses and propositions. This articulateness is shown in the increased use of deduction and in the power to eliminate unsupported alternatives.

THE ETIOLOGY OF CHANGES IN THINKING

The generalisations about the ages at which significant changes take place are of course statistical and assume fairly normal conditions of schooling and intelligence. I have deliberately avoided any reference to the influence of schooling and instruction. We need, however, to raise these questions when we turn now to the etiology of the changes.

The factors which enter into the changes we have described are *maturation, experience, communication* and *instruction* and the urge in every individual *to come to intellectual terms* with his environment.

We may pass over maturation fairly quickly. If cognitive maturation means anything it must reflect neurological maturation. We know little about the latter after the first few years of life. But we know nothing about matura-

[9] J. Smedslund, "The Concept of Correlation in Adults," *Scand. J. Psy.*, IV (1963), 165.

tion during adolescence—it is likely that there is little neurological maturation over this period. Lastly, the statement that development is maturation is largely unfalsifiable, particularly over later years, as during adolescence.

Turning to the role of experience there appear to be two aspects which count for much in the child's intellectual development. First there is physical experience which "consists of acting upon objects and drawing some knowledge about the objects by abstraction from the objects." [10] This is concept formation, the kind of experience that everyone recognises and uses to shape his behavior. But there is also another kind of experience where knowledge is drawn from the *actions* effected by the persons. This knowledge consists of the discovery of the properties of the set of actions used by the person in abstracting from and ordering the physical phenomena of his environment and constitutes "logico-mathematical experience." The laws of mathematical operations, associativity and commutativity and the like, are examples, as are those of the logical structure of classes, relations and propositions.

We have then two fundamental kinds of experience leading to recognition of the properties (a) of objects and material, and (b) of the actions carried out on the objects.

The two experiences develop hand in hand and attempts to teach a person to carry out certain abstractions about his environment will be fruitless unless he possesses also the related "structure of action." The growth of thinking, in fact, consists of the movement from structure of prior and lower order to those at a higher plane.

The third factor concerns formal and informal teaching by the use of language. It is fundamental and necessary and is very powerful in adolescence, when language is well developed, but like the other elements not by itself sufficient. As will be appreciated from the comments of the previous paragraphs the child can receive real information by such means "only if he is in a state where he can understand this information." The state requires that the new information is presented in a form demanding not more than the structure of action which the child has already formed. The child will make of the information what he can by virtue of his particular level of development—but this may not be what the adult intends. Hence the so-called discrepancy between language and thought.

The urge to come to intellectual terms with one's world provides the mainspring of intellectual development. It involves the child in a combined process of assimilation of and accommodation to the material world and his fellow creatures.

In the act of knowing the person is faced with a need to resolve a discrepancy basically between him and his environment which constitutes to him an external disturbance. Consequently he seeks equilibrium by active resolution and compensation. The most obvious and general action of this kind in adolescence is the need for and the process of explanation. When a

[10] J. Piaget, *Piaget Rediscovered* (Conf. Cognit. Studies and Curric. Det.; Berkeley: University of California Press and Ithaca: Cornell University Press, 1964).

person explains a phenomena he effects an equilibrium. Such an equilibrium is not stable in that better explanations may be forthcoming with more knowledge etc., but explanation is far more stable than description, which is relatively unstable tending to pass into explanation. Description, as I have defined it, does not relate an event or phenomenon to the wider context of knowledge. The equilibrium of description will always lead to that of explanation.

The above refers to equilibrium between person and environment, but the process of finding equilibrium also refers to parts within the phenomenon. All natural and contrived situations involve the idea of equilibrium—disequilibrium. Behind this interaction there are the ideas of cancelling an operation or a state and compensating for such a change to re-establish equilibria.

The principle is seen operating in all the dynamic problems in science as in heat-energy change, and the law of moments. The geographical environment is in a continuously changing state of dynamic equilibrium where forces of climate, terrain, organic life and the intervention of men are constantly operating on each other.

When we give problems from geography in which the balance of nature is upset by farming, mining and building we find that an awareness of equilibrium as a combination of cancellation and compensation is only fully apparent in the mid and late adolescent. The same is true of his understanding of history. Most events in history seen in treaties, declarations of war, concessions to groups, etc., contain the same principles of balance. Such material may be used to test thinking [11] as I did by using extracts from medieval European history. Often a balanced judgment is not forthcoming until 14–15 years of age.

But our world does not only consist of equilibria and disequilibria patterns. There is both balance and change. Changes with time are important. The human adapts himself to these changes by a *sensitivity to sequential phenomena*. This shows itself in two types of concepts which are complementary to each other: (a) those of no change, of conservation and invariance seen in the invariants of physics: matter, weight, momentum, . . . mass energy, . . . nuclear properties, and (b) those of directional changes: order-chaos, development-degeneration, integration-disintegration, cause-effect.

The former have been well investigated but some of the latter particularly of order-disorder as seen in thermo-dynamic changes have yet to be investigated in the adolescent range of thinking.

If the idea of structure of thought finds its origin in the equilibria of the physical world of science, of the geographical environment, and of men's interactions as in history and the social sciences, the idea of sequential and temporal order springs from the change of phenomena with time.

I could hardly conclude this discussion of adolescent thinking and its in-

[11] E. A. Peel, *The Pupil's Thinking* (Oldbourne Press, 1960), pp. 122–125. Passage from *The Sicilian Vespers* by S. Runciman.

vestigation without saying something about its implications for education. This must have been apparent at several places. The main change in adolescent thinking is the use of imagined explanations, carrying with it the capacity to manipulate and eliminate possibilities and is to some extent educable. I gave a test similar to the Pilot passage to two groups of 11-year-olds, matched for conventional intelligence. One of the groups came from middle class academic homes where ideas would be tossed about, the other from working class homes. The first group was markedly superior in ideas and their manipulation.

But although teaching aids intellectual growth its effect is limited as we saw when we looked at the etiology of the process. The pupil and student can only take what he is ready for. If he is given too advanced material he'll make of it what he can. The key to progress is in insuring that he has had the two kinds of experience required, that is, of the properties of his environment, constructed by him, and of the properties of his actions, seen in mathematics and logic, used to define the material properties. These two go hand in glove, mathematics and logic need to be based on material experience but they then become necessities for further progress. Mathematics is often not well taught and symbolic logic scarcely at all in secondary schools. Just as mathematics forms the cognitive structure of science thinking so logic provides the structure of the humanities and the language subjects. A lot can be done by giving language teaching a new look and by teaching all pupils and students some logic, not necessarily over-symbolic but linked with use.

What we hope ensues from learning mathematics, physics or history, or any other subject is not merely data collection but the power to think in the way inherent in these disciplines, so that long later, although particular theorems, laws or changes are half or almost wholly forgotten, they can be resuscitated and used in the proper manner and the new circumstance, and fresh information and problems can be dealt with constructively. This is learning to think.

David Elkind

Egocentrism in Adolescence

Within the framework of cognitive growth as outlined by Jean Piaget, Elkind illustrates how cognitive structure peculiar to given levels of development may be related to affective experience and behavior. The different forms of egocentrism or "lack of differentiation in some area of subject-object interaction" are traced through infancy, early childhood, childhood, early adolescence, and adolescence. The process of cognitive growth alluded to here is analogous to that Peel describes in the preceding paper; however, Elkind focuses on cognitive problems particular to each stage, which presumably must be resolved before cognitive growth may continue. At each stage the characteristic egocentrism must break down and a new level of differentiation must be achieved. During adolescence the major problem is "the conflict of thought," which is said to give rise to two mental constructions, "the imaginary audience," and "the personal fable," the former being related to self-consciousness and the latter to personal feelings of uniqueness. In his provocative discussion, Elkind clarifies the link between the stages of mental development and the dynamics of personality development.

WITHIN the Piagetian theory of intellectual growth, the concept of egocentrism generally refers to a lack of differentiation in some area of subject-object interaction.[1] At each stage of mental development, this lack of differentiation takes a unique form and is manifested in a unique set of behaviors. The transition from one form of egocentrism to another takes place in a dialectic fashion such that the mental structures which free the child from a lower form of egocentrism are the same structures which ensnare him in a higher form of egocentrism. From the developmental point of view, therefore, egocentrism can be regarded as a negative by-product of any emergent mental system in the sense that it corresponds to the fresh cognitive problems engendered by that system.

Although in recent years Piaget has focused his attention more on the positive than on the negative products of mental structures, egocentrism

FROM *Child Development*, XXXVIII (1967), 1025–1034. Reprinted by permission of the author and the Society for Research in Child Development.

[1] J. Piaget, *Comments on Vygotsky's Critical Remarks Concerning "The Language and Thought of the Child" and "Judgement and Reasoning in the Child"* (Cambridge, Mass.: M.I.T. Press, 1962).

continues to be of interest because of its relation to the affective aspects of child thought and behavior. Indeed, it is possible that the study of egocentrism may provide a bridge between the study of cognitive structure, on the one hand, and the exploration of personality dynamics, on the other.[2] The purpose of the present paper is to describe, in greater detail than Inhelder and Piaget,[3] what seems to me to be the nature of egocentrism in adolescence and some of its behavioral and experiential correlates. Before doing that, however, it might be well to set the stage for the discussion with a brief review of the forms of egocentrism which precede this mode of thought in adolescence.

FORMS OF EGOCENTRISM IN INFANCY AND CHILDHOOD

In presenting the childhood forms of egocentrism, it is useful to treat each of Piaget's major stages as if it were primarily concerned with resolving one major cognitive task. The egocentrism of a particular stage can then be described with reference to this special problem of cognition. It must be stressed, however, that while the cognitive task characteristic of a particular stage seems to attract the major share of the child's mental energies, it is not the only cognitive problem with which the child is attempting to cope. In mental development there are major battles and minor skirmishes, and if I here ignore the lesser engagements it is for purposes of economy of presentation rather than because I assume that such engagements are insignificant.

Sensori-motor Egocentrism (0–2 Years)

The major cognitive task of infancy might be regarded as *the conquest of the object*. In the early months of life, the infant deals with objects as if their existence were dependent upon their being present in immediate perception.[4] The egocentrism of this stage corresponds, therefore, to a lack of differentiation between the object and the sense impressions occasioned by it. Toward the end of the first year, however, the infant begins to seek the object even when it is hidden, and thus shows that he can now differentiate between the object and the "experience of the object." This breakdown of egocentrism with respect to objects is brought about by mental representation of the absent object.[5] An internal representation of the absent object is the earliest manifestation of the symbolic function which develops gradually during the second year of life and whose activities dominate the next stage of mental growth.

[2] P. A. Cowan, "Cognitive Egocentrism and Social Interaction in Children," *American Psychologist*, XXI (1966), 623; V. Gourevitch and M. F. Feffer, "A Study of Motivational Development," *Journal of Genetic Psychology*, C (1962), 361–375.

[3] B. Inhelder and J. Piaget, *The Growth of Logical Thinking from Childhood to Adolescence* (New York: Basic Books, 1958).

[4] W. R. Charlesworth, "Development of the Object Concept in Infancy: Methodological Study," *American Psychologist*, XXI (1966), 623; J. Piaget, *The Construction of Reality in the Child* (New York: Basic Books, 1954).

[5] It is characteristic of the dialectic of mental growth that the capacity to represent internally the absent object also enables the infant to cognize the object as externally existent.

Pre-operational Egocentrism (2–6 Years)

During the preschool period, the child's major cognitive task can be regarded as *the conquest of the symbol.* It is during the preschool period that the symbolic function becomes fully active, as evidenced by the rapid growth in the acquisition and utilization of language, by the appearance of symbolic play, and by the first reports of dreams. Yet this new capacity for representation, which loosed the infant from his egocentrism with respect to objects, now ensnares the preschool children in a new egocentrism with regard to symbols. At the beginning of this period, the child fails to differentiate between words and their referents [6] and between his self-created play and dream symbols and reality.[7] Children at this stage believe that the name inheres in the thing and that an object cannot have more than one name.[8]

The egocentrism of this period is particularly evident in children's linguistic behavior. When explaining a piece of apparatus to another child, for example, the youngster at this stage uses many indefinite terms and leaves out important information.[9] Although this observation is sometimes explained by saying that the child fails to take the other person's point of view, it can also be explained by saying that the child assumes words carry much more information than they actually do. This results from his belief that even the indefinite "thing" somehow conveys the properties of the object which it is used to represent. In short, the egocentrism of this period consists in a lack of clear differentiation between symbols and their referents.

Toward the end of the preoperational period, the differentiation between symbols and their referents is gradually brought about by the emergence of concrete operations (internalized actions which are roughly comparable in their activity to the elementary operations of arithmetic). One consequence of concrete operational thought is that it enables the child to deal with two elements, properties, or relations at the same time. A child with concrete operations can, for example, take account of both the height and width of a glass colored liquid and recognize that, when the liquid is poured into a differently shaped container, the changes in height and width of the liquid compensate one another so that the total quantity of liquid is conserved.[10] This ability, to hold two dimensions in mind at the same time,

---

[6] J. Piaget, *The Language and Thought of the Child* (London: Routledge and Kegan Paul, 1952).

[7] L. Kohlberg, "Cognitive Stages and Preschool Education," *Human Development,* IX (1966), 5–17; J. Piaget, *The Child's Conception of the World* (London: Routledge and Kegan Paul, 1951).

[8] D. Elkind, "The Child's Conception of His Religious Denomination, I: The Jewish Child," *Journal of Genetic Psychology,* XCIX (1961), 209–225; D. Elkind, "The Child's Conception of His Religious Denomination, II: The Catholic Child," *Journal of Genetic Psychology,* CI (1962), 185–193; D. Elkind, "The Child's Conception of His Religious Denomination, III: The Protestant Child," *Journal of Genetic Psychology,* CIII (1963), 291–304.

[9] J. Piaget, *The Language......, op. cit.*

[10] D. Elkind, "The Development of Quantitative Thinking," *Journal of Genetic Psychology,* XCVIII (1961), 37–46; J. Piaget, *The Child's Conception of Number* (New York: Basic Books, 1951).

also enables the child to hold both symbol and referent in mind simultaneously, and thus distinguish between them. Concrete operations are, therefore, instrumental in overcoming the egocentrism of the preoperational stage.

Concrete Operational Egocentrism (7–11 Years)

With the emergence of concrete operations, the major cognitive task of the school-age child becomes that of *mastering classes, relations, and quantities*. While the preschool child forms global notions of classes, relations, and quantities, such notions are imprecise and cannot be combined one with the other. The child with concrete operations, on the other hand, can nest classes, seriate relations, and conserve quantities. In addition, concrete operations enable the school-age child to perform elementary syllogistic reasoning and to formulate hypotheses and explanations about concrete matters. This system of concrete operations, however, which lifts the school-age child to new heights of thought, nonetheless lowers him to new depths of egocentrism.

Operations are essentially mental tools whose products, series, class hierarchies, conservations, and so forth, are not directly derived from experience. At this stage, however, the child nonetheless regards these mental products as being on a par with perceptual phenomena. It is the inability to differentiate clearly between mental constructions and perceptual givens which constitutes the egocentrism of the school-age child. An example may help to clarify the form which egocentrism takes during the concrete operational stage.

In a study reported by Peel,[11] children and adolescents were read a passage about Stonehenge and then asked questions about it. One of the questions had to do with whether Stonehenge was a place for religious worship or a fort. The children (age 7–10) answered the question with flat statements, as if they were stating a fact. When they were given evidence that contradicted their statements, they rationalized the evidence to make it conform with their initial position. Adolescents, on the other hand, phrased their replies in probabilistic terms and supported their judgments with material gleaned from the passage. Similar differences between children and adolescents have been found by Elkind and Weir.[12]

What these studies show is that, when a child constructs a hypothesis or formulates a strategy, he assumes that this product is imposed by the data rather than derived from his own mental activity. When his position is challenged, he does not change his stance but, on the contrary, reinterprets the data to fit with his assumption. This observation, however, raises a puzzling question. Why, if the child regards both his thought products and the givens of perception as coming from the environment, does he nonetheless

---

[11] E. A. Peel, *The Pupil's Thinking* (London: Oldbourne, 1960).
[12] D. Elkind, "Conceptual Orientation Shifts in Children and Adolescents," *Child Development*, XXXVII (1966), 493–498; M. W. Weir, "Development Changes in Problem Solving Strategies," *Psychological Review*, LXXI (1964), 473–490.

give preference to his own mental constructions? The answer probably lies in the fact that the child's mental constructions are the product of reasoning, and hence are experienced as imbued with a (logical) necessity. This "felt" necessity is absent when the child experiences the products of perception. It is not surprising, then, that the child should give priority to what seems permanent and necessary in perception (the products of his own thought, such as conservation) rather than to what seems transitory and arbitrary in perception (products of environmental stimulation). Only in adolescence do young people differentiate between their own mental constructions and the givens of perception. For the child, there are no problems of epistemology.

Toward the end of childhood, the emergence of formal operational thought (which is analogous to propositional logic) gradually frees the child from his egocentrism with respect to his own mental constructions. As Inhelder and Piaget [13] have shown, formal operational thought enables the young person to deal with all of the possible combinations and permutations of elements within a given set. Provided with four differently colored pieces of plastic, for example, the adolescent can work out all the possible combinations of colors by taking the pieces one, two, three and four, and none, at a time. Children, on the other hand, cannot formulate these combinations in any systematic way. The ability to conceptualize all of the possible combinations in a system allows the adolescent to construct contrary-to-fact hypotheses and to reason about such propositions "as if" they were true. The adolescent, for example, can accept the statement, "Let's suppose coal is white," whereas the child would reply, "But coal is black." This ability to formulate contrary-to-fact hypotheses is crucial to the overcoming of the egocentrism of the concrete operational period. Through the formulation of such contrary-to-fact hypotheses, the young person discovers the arbitrariness of his own mental constructions and learns to differentiate them from perceptual reality.

ADOLESCENT EGOCENTRISM

From the strictly cognitive point of view (as opposed to the psychoanalytic point of view as represented by Blos and A. Freud [14] or the ego psychological point of view as represented by Erickson [15]), the major task of early adolescence can be regarded as having to do with *the conquest of thought*. Formal operations not only permit the young person to construct all the possibilities in a system and construct contrary-to-fact propositions; [16] they also enable him to conceptualize his own thought, to take his mental constructions as objects and reason about them. Only at about the ages of 11–12, for example, do children spontaneously introduce concepts of belief,

[13] Inhelder and Piaget, *op. cit.*

[14] P. Blos, *On Adolescence* (New York: The Free Press, 1962); A. Freud, *The Ego and Mechanisms of Defense* (New York: International Universities Press, 1946).

[15] E. H. Erikson, "Identity and the Life Cycle," *Psychological Issues*, I (No. I, New York: International Universities Press, 1959).

[16] Inhelder and Piaget, *op. cit.*

intelligence, and faith into their definitions of their religious denomination.[17] Once more, however, this new mental system which frees the young person from the egocentrism of childhood entangles him in a new form of egocentrism characteristic of adolescence.

Formal operational thought not only enables the adolescent to conceptualize his thought, it also permits him to conceptualize the thought of other people. It is this capacity to take account of other people's thought, however, which is the crux of adolescent egocentrism. This egocentrism emerges because, while the adolescent can now cognize the thoughts of others, he fails to differentiate between the objects toward which the thoughts of others are directed and those which are the focus of his own concern. Now, it is well known that the young adolescent, because of the physiological metamorphosis he is undergoing, is primarily concerned with himself. Accordingly, since he fails to differentiate between what others are thinking about and his own mental preoccupations, he assumes that other people are as obsessed with his behavior and appearance as he is himself. *It is this belief that others are preoccupied with his appearance and behavior that constitutes the egocentrism of the adolescent.*

One consequence of adolescent egocentrism is that, in actual or impending social situations, the young person anticipates the reactions of other people to himself. These anticipations, however, are based on the premise that others are as admiring or as critical of him as he is of himself. In a sense, then, the adolescent is continually constructing, or reacting to, *an imaginary audience.* It is an audience because the adolescent believes that he will be the focus of attention; and it is imaginary because, in actual social situations, this is not usually the case (unless he contrives to make it so). The construction of imaginary audiences would seem to account, in part at least, for a wide variety of typical adolescent behaviors and experiences.

The imaginary audience, for example, probably plays a role in the self-consciousness which is so characteristic of early adolescence. When the young person is feeling critical of himself, he anticipates that the audience— of which he is necessarily a part—will be critical too. And, since the audience is of his own construction and privy to his own knowledge of himself, it knows just what to look for in the way of cosmetic and behavioral sensitivities. The adolescent's wish for privacy and his reluctance to reveal himself may, to some extent, be a reaction to the feeling of being under the constant critical scrutiny of other people. The notion of an imaginary audience also helps to explain the observation that the affect which most concerns adolescents is not guilt but, rather, shame, that is, the reaction to an audience.[18]

While the adolescent is often self-critical, he is frequently self-admiring too. At such times, the audience takes on the same affective coloration. A

[17] Elkind, ". . . The Jewish Child," *op. cit.;* Elkind, ". . . The Catholic Child," *op. cit.;* Elkind, ". . . The Protestant Child," *op. cit.*

[18] H. M. Lynd, *On Shame and the Search for Identity* (New York: Science Editions, 1961).

good deal of adolescent boorishness, loudness, and faddish dress is probably provoked, partially in any case, by a failure to differentiate between what the young person believes to be attractive and what others admire. It is for this reason that the young person frequently fails to understand why adults disapprove of the way he dresses and behaves. The same sort of egocentrism is often seen in behavior directed toward the opposite sex. The boy who stands in front of the mirror for 2 hours combing his hair is probably imagining the swooning reactions he will produce in the girls. Likewise, the girl applying her makeup is more likely than not imagining the admiring glances that will come her way. When these young people actually meet, each is more concerned with being the observed than with being the observer. Gatherings of young adolescents are unique in the sense that each young person is simultaneously an actor to himself and an audience to others.

One of the most common admiring audience constructions, in the adolescent, is the anticipation of how others will react to his own demise. A certain bittersweet pleasure is derived from anticipating the belated recognition by others of his positive qualities. As often happens with such universal fantasies, the imaginary anticipation of one's own demise has been realized in fiction. Below, for example, is the passage in *Tom Sawyer* where Tom sneaks back to his home, after having run away with Joe and Huck, to discover that he and his friends are thought to have been drowned:

> But this memory was too much for the old lady, and she broke entirely down. Tom was snuffling, now, himself—and more in pity of himself than anybody else. He could hear Mary crying and putting in a kindly word for him from time to time. He began to have a nobler opinion of himself than ever before. Still, he was sufficiently touched by his aunt's grief to long to rush out from under the bed and overwhelm her with joy—and the theatrical gorgeousness of the thing appealed strongly to his nature too—but he resisted and lay still.

Corresponding to the imaginary audience is another mental construction which is its complement. While the adolescent fails to differentiate the concerns of his own thought from those of others, he at the same time over-differentiates his feelings. Perhaps because he believes he is of importance to so many people, the imaginary audience, he comes to regard himself, and particularly his feelings, as something special and unique. Only he can suffer with such agonized intensity, or experience such exquisite rapture. How many parents have been confronted with the typically adolescent phrase, "But you don't know how it feels. . . ." The emotional torments undergone by Goethe's young Werther and by Salinger's Holden Caulfield exemplify the adolescent's belief in the uniqueness of his own emotional experience. At a somewhat different level, this belief in personal uniqueness becomes a conviction that he will not die, that death will happen to others but not to him. This complex of beliefs in the uniqueness of his feelings and of his immortality might be called *a personal fable*, a story which he tells himself and which is not true.

Evidences of the personal fable are particularly prominent in adolescent diaries. Such diaries are often written for posterity in the conviction that the young person's experiences, crushes, and frustrations are of universal significance and importance. Another kind of evidence for the personal fable during this period is the tendency to confide in a personal God. The search for privacy and the belief in personal uniqueness leads to the establishment of an I-Thou relationship with God as a personal confident to whom one no longer looks for gifts but rather for guidance and support.[19]

The concepts of an imaginary audience and a personal fable have proved useful, at least to the writer, in the understanding and treatment of troubled adolescents. The imaginary audience, for example, seems often to play a role in middle-class delinquency.[20] As a case in point, one young man took $1,000 from a golf tournament purse, hid the money, and then promptly revealed himself. It turned out that much of the motivation for this act was derived from the anticipated response of "the audience" to the guttiness of his action. In a similar vein, many young girls become pregnant because, in part at least, their personal fable convinces them that pregnancy will happen to others but never to them and so they need not take precautions. Such examples could be multiplied but will perhaps suffice to illustrate how adolescent egocentrism, as manifested in the imaginary audience and in the personal fable, can help provide a rationale for some adolescent behavior. These concepts can, moreover, be utilized in the treatment of adolescent offenders. It is often helpful to these young people if they can learn to differentiate between the real and the imaginary audience, which often boils down to a discrimination between the real and the imaginary parents.

THE PASSING OF ADOLESCENT EGOCENTRISM

After the appearance of formal operational thought, no new mental systems develop and the mental structures of adolescence must serve for the rest of the life span. The egocentrism of early adolescence nonetheless tends to diminish by the age of 15 or 16, the age at which formal operations become firmly established. What appears to happen is that the imaginary audience, which is primarily an anticipatory audience, is progressively modified in the direction of the reactions of the real audience. In a way, the imaginary audience can be regarded as hypothesis—or better, as a series of hypotheses —which the young person tests against reality. As a consequence of this testing, he gradually comes to recognize the difference between his own preoccupations and the interests and concerns of others.

The personal fable, on the other hand, is probably overcome (although probably never in its entirety) by the gradual establishment of what Erik-

---

[19] D. Long, D. Elkind, and B. Spilka, "The Child's Conception of Prayer," *Journal for the Scientific Study of Religion*, VI (1967). 101–109.

[20] D. Elkind, "Middle Class Delinquency," *Mental Hygiene*, LI (1967), 80–81.

son [21] has called "intimacy." Once the young person sees himself in a more realistic light as a function of having adjusted his imaginary audience to the real one, he can establish true rather than self-interested interpersonal relations. Once relations of mutuality are established and confidences are shared, the young person discovers that others have feelings similar to his own and have suffered and been enraptured in the same way.

Adolescent egocentrism is thus overcome by a twofold transformation. On the cognitive plane, it is overcome by the gradual differentiation between his own preoccupations and the thoughts of others; while on the plane of affectivity, it is overcome by a gradual integration of the feelings of others with his own emotions.

SUMMARY AND CONCLUSIONS

In this paper I have tried to describe the forms which egocentrism takes and the mechanisms by which it is overcome, in the course of mental development. In infancy, egocentrism corresponds to the impression that objects are identical with the perception of them, and this form of egocentrism is overcome with the appearance of representation. During the preschool period, egocentrism appears in the guise of a belief that symbols contain the same information as is provided by the objects which they represent. With the emergence of concrete operations, the child is able to discriminate between symbol and referent, and so overcome this type of egocentrism. The egocentrism of the school-age period can be characterized as the belief that one's own mental constructions correspond to a superior form of perceptual reality. With the advent of formal operations and the ability to construct contrary-to-fact hypotheses, this kind of egocentrism is dissolved because the young person can now recognize the arbitrariness of his own mental constructions. Finally, during early adolescence, egocentrism appears as the belief that the thoughts of others are directed toward the self. This variety of egocentrism is overcome as a consequence of the conflict between the reactions which the young person anticipates and those which actually occur.

Although egocentrism corresponds to a negative product of mental growth, its usefulness would seem to lie in the light which it throws upon the affective reactions characteristic of any particular stage of mental development. In this paper I have dealt primarily with the affective reactions associated with the egocentrism of adolescence. Much of the material, particularly the discussion of the *imaginary audience* and the *personal fable* is speculative in the sense that it is based as much upon my clinical experience with young people as it is upon research data. These constructs are offered, not as the final word on adolescent egocentrism, but rather to illustrate how the cognitive structures peculiar to a particular level of development can be related to the affective experience and behavior characteristic of that stage.

[21] Erikson, *op. cit.*

Although I have here only considered the correspondence between mental structure and affect in adolescence, it is possible that similar correspondences can be found at the earlier levels of development as well. A consideration of egocentrism, then, would seem to be a useful starting point for any attempt to reconcile cognitive structure and the dynamics of personality.

Stephen L. Klineberg

Changes in Outlook on the Future
Between Childhood and Adolescence

The following study offers theoretical and empirical analyses of relations between child and adolescent personality adjustment and orientation toward time. Klineberg investigates the specific assumption that "images of the distant future are available for the projection of wish-fulfilling fantasies in childhood, but become increasingly constrained by realistic considerations with the attainment of adolescence." Ninety French boys, divided into four groups, including both normal and maladjusted children and adolescents, were individually interviewed to assess six different aspects of future orientation. He reports that maladjusted rather than normal children between the ages of 10 and 12 manifest greater concern for future events. On the other hand, "by middle adolescence, maladjustment, poor school performance, and little involvement in present experiences come to be associated with a more restricted outlook on the distant future." Among normal youth, the relationship is shown to be reversed; as adolescents become increasingly concerned with their future adult responsibilities, a realistic perspective on the future emerges.

FRAISSE [1] asserted that "there is no future without at the same time a desire for something else and an awareness of the possibility of realizing it." The crucial dimension in this equation is the nature of the individual's concept of "realizability." Several writers [2] have suggested that a primary difference between the child and the adult is the relative lack of differentiation in the child's thought between unattainable wishes and realizable expectations. The process of bringing one's aspirations into line with reality is a continuous one, but there are compelling reasons to expect that it is

FROM *Journal of Personality and Social Psychology*, VII (1967), 185–193. Reprinted by permission of the author and the American Psychological Association.

[1] P. Fraisse, *The Psychology of Time*, trans. J. Leith (New York: Harper and Row, 1963) p. 174.

[2] E. Bleuler, "Autistic Thinking," *Organization and Pathology of Thought*, ed. and trans. D. Rapaport (New York: Columbia Univ. Press, 1951), pp. 399–437; P. Blos, *On Adolescence: A Psychoanalytic Interpretation* (Glencoe: The Free Press, 1962); K. Lewin, "Time Perspective and Morale," *Civilian Morale*, ed. G. Watson (Boston: Houghton Mifflin Co., 1942), pp. 48–70; K. Lewin, "Collected Writings," *Field Theory in Social Science: Selected Papers by Kurt Lewin*, ed. D. Cartwright (New York: Harper and Row, 1951).

during the period of adolescence that the individual's images of the relatively distant future undergo the most fundamental and far-reaching reevaluation.

Preadolescence has been described as the stage for the development of a "sense of industry," [3] for the concrete exploration of the surrounding environment,[4] for immersion in the concerns of childhood.[5] It seems that for the 10- or 11-year-old child, the sense of the relatively near future is well developed, for the ability to delay gratification is established; [6] but the awareness of a future beyond childhood is likely to be endowed with little sense of reality, and thus images of the relatively distant future may be largely free from the constraints of realistic considerations and available for the projection of wish-fulfilling fantasies. Ginzberg, Ginzberg, Axelrad, and Herma [7] argued that children "have been forced to accept the frustrations that are theirs by virtue of the fact that they are children. However, they have a possibility of escape: they can fantasy about the future." The more frustrated and unhappy the child feels in the present, the more likely he is to use this possibility of "escape" afforded by fantasies of the distant future of adulthood. Accordingly, Hypothesis 1 states that, among children between the ages of 10 and 12, there is a positive relationship between indexes of present maladjustment and measures of the degree of orientation toward the distant future.

In theory, at least, the attainment of adolescence in Western society brings important changes on three fronts. New role expectations tend to focus the individual's attention on the implications of the present for his future role as an adult in society. Thus, Jersild [8] noted that "many of an adolescent's labors, especially at school, are geared to the future"; and parents are likely for the first time to take seriously their child's thoughts regarding his future vocation.[9]

Furthermore, the ability to envision the distant future realistically may require a level of intellectual capacity which does not emerge until the advent of adolescence. According to Piaget, until the age of 11 or 12 the child is developing "concrete operations," which become the means for structuring immediately present reality. At this stage, "the role of *possibility*

[3] E. H. Erikson, *Childhood and Society* (New York: W. W. Norton and Co., 1950).

[4] B. Inhelder and J. Piaget, *The Growth of Logical Thinking from Childhood to Adolescence*, trans. A. Parsons and S. Milgram (New York: Basic Books, 1958).

[5] L. S. Stone and J. Church, *Childhood and Adolescence; A Psychology of the Growing Person* (New York: Random House, Inc., 1957).

[6] L. Melikan, "Preference for Delayed Reinforcement: An Experimental Study Among Palestinian Arab Refugee Children," *Journal of Social Psychology*, L (1959), 81–86; W. Mischel and R. Metzner, "Preference for Delayed Reward as a Function of Age, Intelligence, and Length of Delay Interval," *Journal of Abnormal and Social Psychology*, LXIV (1962), 425–431.

[7] E. Ginzberg, S. W. Ginzberg, S. Axelrad, and J. L. Herma, *Occupational Choice: An Approach to a General Theory* (New York: Columbia University Press, 1951), p. 62.

[8] A. T. Jersild, *The Psychology of Adolescence* (2nd ed.; New York: The Macmillan Co., 1963), p. 11.

[9] P. H. Mussen, J. J. Conger, and J. Kagan, *Child Development and Personality* (2nd ed.; New York: Harper and Row, 1963), p. 563.

is reduced to a simple potential prolongation of the actions or operations applied to the given content," [10] and the child "is not yet readily able to deal with possibilities not directly before him or not already experienced." [11] It is apparently not until the advent of "formal operations" in early adolescence that the individual becomes able to bring the verbal elements which comprise his anticipations of the future under the constraint of logical thought, linking a required logical consequence to an assertion whose truth is merely a possibility. As Brown [12] noted, "the social role of the adolescent requires him to deal in possibilities, to entertain alternatives and envision consequences. Formally operational intelligence enables him to do so."

Finally, personality theorists have argued that, in adolescence, the problem of self-definition or "ego-identity" [13] becomes critical, and brings an awareness, for the first time, of the entire life span,[14] as well as a new concern with evaluating the limitations and potentialities in oneself and one's present situation in terms of their implications for the future.

> The young person, in order to experience wholeness, must feel a progressive continuity between that which he has come to be during the long years of childhood and that which he promises to become in the anticipated future.[15]

Consequently, as Davis [16] noted, in adolescence "the lower status individual begins to feel the stigmas of lower status much more keenly."

In sum, there is good reason to expect that not until middle adolescence will the individual's anticipations of the relatively distant future come to be largely restricted to realizable objectives, to events which can be envisioned without a sense of incongruity with a now far clearer understanding of the nature of reality. Only then is it likely that the unsuccessful, pessimistic individual will come to restrict his perspective to the more immediate rewards offered by his present situation, as a protection against the negative affect engendered by anticipations of an unpropitious future. Foreshortened outlooks on the future have been reported among adolescents and adults of low socioeconomic status,[17] students doing poorly in school,[18] and

---

10 Inhelder and Piaget, *op. cit.*, p. 249.

11 J. S. Bruner, *The Process of Education* (New York: Vintage Books, 1960), p. 37.

12 R. W. Brown, *Social Psychology* (New York: The Free Press, 1965), p. 232.

13 Erikson, *op. cit.*

14 C. Bühler, "The Human Course of Life in Its Goal Aspects," *Journal of Humanistic Psychology*, IV (1964), 1–18.

15 E. H. Erikson, *Insight and Responsibility* (New York: W. W. Norton and Co., 1964), p. 91.

16 A. Davis, "Socialization and Adolescent Personality," *The Forty-third Yearbook of the National Society for the Study of Education. Part 1: Adolescence*, N. B. Henry, ed. (Chicago: University of Chicago Press, 1944), p. 208.

17 K. W. Back and K. J. Gergen, "Apocalyptic and Serial Time Orientations and the Structure of Opinion," *Public Opinion Quarterly*, XXVII (1963), 427–442; O. G. Brim and R. Forer, "A Note on the Relation of Values and Social Structure to Life Planning," *Sociometry*, XIX (1956), 54–60; L. Schneider and S. Lysgaard, "The Deferred Gratification Pattern: A Preliminary Study," *American Sociological Review*, XVIII (1953), 142–149.

18 A. Davids and J. Sidman, "A Pilot Study—Impulsivity, Time Orientation, and De-

persons suffering from anxiety [19] or depression.[20]

Accordingly, Hypothesis 2 states that, among adolescents aged 14 to 16, there is a negative relationship between indexes of present maladjustment and measures of the degree of orientation toward future events. Correlatively, a progressive increase in the degree of realism with which the future is envisioned by the individual is assumed to occur as he matures into adolescence: Hypothesis 3 states that maladjusted children are more oriented toward the relatively distant future than are maladjusted adolescents. Finally, the theoretical arguments reviewed above suggest that, in normal development from childhood to adolescence, there is a progressive increase in the individual's general concern with his future role as an adult in society. Hypothesis 4 states that normal children are less future oriented than are normal adolescents.

Davids and Parenti [21] found suggestive support for some of these notions, and an analysis of Brock and Del Giudice's [22] data revealed a progressive decrease in the frequency with which the word "tomorrow" was chosen as one to be used in telling a story, among lower class children between Grades 2 and 8. The present study was designed to offer a more direct and systematic empirical test of these hypotheses.

METHOD

Subjects

Ninety boys attending private institutions near Paris, France, participated in the present study. Group MC (maladjusted children) consisted of 24 subjects, aged 10 years, 4 months to 12 years, 7 months (mean age: 11 years, 3 months), selected from two *instituts médico-pédagogiques*. These institutions provide elementary school instruction, along with some treatment programs, for children whose personality or behavioral problems led to serious disruption in the public schools, but still allowed them to live and work closely with other children under adult supervision. Ten subjects were in the French equivalent of fourth grade, 13 in the fifth grade, and 1 in the

---

layed Gratification in Future Scientists and in Underachieving High School Students," *Exceptional Children*, XXIX (1962), 170–174; J. E. Teahan, "Future Time Perspective, Optimism, and Academic Achievement," *Journal of Abnormal and Social Psychology*, LVIII (1958), 379–380.

[19] D. Epley and D. R. Ricks, "Foresight and Hindsight in the TAT," *Journal of Projective Techniques*, XXVII (1963), 51–59.

[20] L. Binswanger, "The Case of Ellen West; An Anthropological-Clinical Study," *Existence: A New Dimension in Psychiatry and Psychology*, trans. W. M. Mendel and J. Lyons, eds. R. May, E. Angel, and H. F. Ellenberger (New York: Basic Books, 1958), pp. 37–91; E. W. Strauss, "Disorders of Personal Time in Depressive States," *Southern Medical Journal*, XL (1947), 243–258.

[21] A. Davids and A. N. Parenti, "Time Orientation and Interpersonal Relations of Emotionally Disturbed and Normal Children," *Journal of Abnormal and Social Psychology*, LVII (1958), 299–305.

[22] T. C. Brock and C. Del Giudice, "Stealing and Temporal Orientation," *Journal of Abnormal and Social Psychology*, LXVIII (1963), 91–94.

sixth grade. Unlike the other three groups, socioeconomic backgrounds among these subjects were generally quite low. Group NC (normal children) comprised 23 boys, aged 10 years, 3 months to 12 years, 8 months (mean age: 11 years, 3 months), of whom 8 were in the fourth grade, 13 in the fifth grade, and 2 in the sixth grade at one of two private boarding schools in the Paris area.

These two groups of children were thus equated for age and comparable in scholastic attainment. The normal subjects, however, were of higher socio-economic status, probably somewhat higher in tested intelligence, and free from any seriously debilitating problems. The comparison between these subjects and the maladjusted children in Group MC is well suited to reveal whether advantages such as these are, in fact, associated with a more restricted orientation toward the distant future before the attainment of adolescence.

Group MA (maladjusted adolescents) consisted of 21 subjects aged 13 years, 6 months to 16 years, 10 months (mean age: 14 years, 10 months), from a private school for scholastic rehabilitation, which offers intensive remedial work along with some therapeutic counseling for adolescent boys of high IQ, who nevertheless have had a great deal of academic difficulty in the public schools. Fourteen of the subjects in this group were in the ninth grade and 7 in tenth grade at the time of testing. Group NA (normal adolescents) comprised 22 boys, aged 13 years, 3 months to 16 years, 11 months (mean age: 14 years, 9 months), attending a nearby Catholic boarding school. Fifteen of these subjects were in the ninth grade, and 7 in the tenth grade.

While the two groups of adolescents were thus comparable in age and scholastic attainment, the maladjusted subjects were slightly higher in both socio-economic status and tested intelligence; in addition, they were more likely to be nominal Catholics or Protestants, while the subjects in Group NA were uniformly of the Catholic faith, and this religion was a salient aspect of their daily lives. To the extent that these differences have an effect on the present data, previous research would suggest that the result in all cases will be to decrease the likelihood that the normal adolescents in Group NA are, in fact, more oriented toward the distant future than the subjects in Group MA.

Each of the 90 subjects was individually interviewed by the experimenter, between January and March of 1963, using a pretested questionnaire designed to measure six different aspects of his outlook on the future. Subjects were told that the experimenter was working for "the association of authors of books for young people," and that his questions were part of an inquiry "into the kinds of stories which boys of your age might enjoy, and the interests of the young people of today."

Measures of Future Time Perspective

In the first question, the subject was asked to make up a story to TAT Cards 1 (boy with violin) and 14 (silhouette in window). The standard instructions calling for antecedents and consequences were omitted. At the completion of each story, he was asked to estimate the span of time encompassed by the action he described. This estimate, called "action time span" (ATS), reflects the subject's spontaneous tendency to extend his thoughts beyond the present, to consider the longer range outcomes of the situation depicted on the TAT card, before declaring that the story is over.

In the second question, the subject was asked to describe 10 different things which he had thought or spoken about during the preceding week or two, and was questioned about each event until it was possible to determine unambiguously its temporal focus at the time he had thought or spoken about it. The proportion of references to events in the past, present, and future was determined for each subject, as a measure of what Teahan [23] has labeled "Predominance," or the degree of everyday concern with future events. A pilot study with 20 children and adolescents in a French public school revealed two important attributes of this time perspective measure: (a) The time span encompassed by the vast majority of past and future events reported was found to extend less than a week in either temporal direction, suggesting that this cannot be taken as a measure of the degree of orientation toward the distant future; and (b) in the comparison between children and adolescents, the older subjects were far more likely to mention items which could only be classified as "present" (e.g., classical music, the quality of teaching at the school, sports, girls), with the result that a smaller proportion of the 10 events referred to the past or the future. With regard to the present study, then, it was predicted that both groups of adolescents would list a significantly greater proportion of present events and a smaller proportion of future events among 10 things they reported having recently thought or spoken about, than would either group of children.

In the third question, the subject was asked to list as many different events as possible which he thought might happen to him in the course of his life, and for each event, to specify his probable age when it was expected to occur. "Density" is the label given by Kastenbaum [24] to the total number of events which the subject is able to envision in answer to this question. "Spontaneous extension" is defined as the greatest distance into the future that he extends his imagination in listing these anticipations.

In the fourth question, the subject was presented, in random order, with 14 personal future events which happen to most people at some point in their lives (e.g., "you get married," "you can say that you have most of the things in life that you've always wanted," "you buy your first car," "you become a grandfather"); and he was asked to guess the age when each of these events would occur in his life. "Constrained extension" is defined as the median of the ages the subject predicts for each of the 14 events, as an indication of his readiness to envision the distant future.

The fifth question on the interview schedule was concerned with the

[23] Teahan, *op. cit.*
[24] R. Kastenbaum, "The Dimensions of Future Time Perspective: An Experimental Analysis," *Journal of General Psychology*, LXV (1961), 203–218.

temporal nature of parental discipline, which is only tangentially relevant to the present report. Following this item, 14 cards were randomly spread out in front of the subject, each card containing one of the events named in Question 4, and the subject was asked to arrange them in their probable order of occurrence in his own life. "Coherence" [25] is defined as the rank-order correlation between the subject's arrangement of the events on the basis of the earlier anticipated ages associated with each, and their ordering in his answer to this later question. This measure is likely to reflect the degree to which the subject conceives of the future as an orderly unfolding of events in a logical and predictable succession. The individual for whom the distant future is endowed with little sense of reality is less likely to be consistent in his guesses as to when these events will occur. It was therefore predicted that both groups of children would score lower on coherence than would either group of adolescents.

The intercorrelations among these six different measures of future time perspective were computed. None of them was consistently significant across the four groups of subjects.

Results

Maladjustment and Time Perspective in Childhood

The first hypothesis stated that, among preadolescents, there is a positive relationship between maladjustment and future orientation, that subjects

Table 1   Differences in Time Perspective between Maladjusted and Normal Children

Measures	Group MC ($N = 24$)		Group NC ($N = 23$)		z	p
	MEDIAN	SUM OF RANKS	MEDIAN	SUM OF RANKS		
1. Density	5.80	604.0	5.30	525.0	0.58	ns
2. Spontaneous extension	19.75	561.5	20.00	566.5	0.03	ns
3. Constrained extension	30.6	671.0	27.5	457.0	2.01	.0222
4. Coherence	.890	543.5	.904	584.5	0.68	ns
5. Predominance:						
% present	20.0%	552.5	18.6%	528.5	0.25	ns
% future	58.3%	521.0	60.0%	560.0	0.44	ns
% past	20.0%	559.0	18.0%	522.0	0.40	ns
6. Time span in:						
TAT No. 1	4 yrs.	685.5	6 days	442.5	2.31	.0104
TAT No. 14	6 days	697.0	2 hrs.	431.0	2.56	.0052

in Group MC would evidence a greater concern with distant personal future events than would the normal children in Group NC. Table 1 presents the results of the comparison between the two groups of children on the six

[25] M. Wallace, "Future Time Perspective in Schizophrenia," *Journal of Abnormal and Social Psychology,* LII (1956), 240–245.

Table 2 Differences in Time Perspective between Maladjusted and Normal Adolescents

| | Group MA (N = 21) | | Group NA (N = 22) | | | |
Measures	MEDIAN	SUM OF RANKS	MEDIAN	SUM OF RANKS	z	p
1. Density	3.95	388.0	5.75	558.0	1.79	.0365
2. Spontaneous extension	13.50	420.5	15.75	525.5	1.30	ns
3. Constrained extension	31.5	397.0	33.0	549.0	1.56	.0594
4. Coherence	.9515	452.5	.9465	493.5	0.22	ns
5. Predominance:						
% present	31.8%	356.0	46.7%	590.0	2.56	.0054°
% future	43.3%	514.0	33.0%	432.0	1.25	ns
% past	29.2%	546.0	15.0%	400.0	2.03	.0202°
6. Time span in:						
TAT No. 1	15 days	430.0	14 mos.	516.0	0.77	ns
TAT No. 14	11 hrs.	413.0	13 days	533.0	1.18	ns

° Two-tailed test of significance.

time-perspective variables. Since the observed distributions of response made the assumption of normality questionable, the nonparametric Mann-Whitney U test was used throughout; where these were directional hypotheses, only one tail of the distribution was considered.

There were no differences between the two groups of children in the number of events they spontaneously envisioned in their future (density), or with regard to the distance into the future that they extended their imagination in listing these anticipations (spontaneous extension). Furthermore, the two groups were equally consistent in their ordering of personal future events (coherence), and there were no differences in the proportion of events they reported having recently thought or spoken about which referred to the past, present, or future (predominance). The differences were significant, however, on the central measures of orientation toward the distant future. The maladjusted children made median estimates of their age when the same 14 personal events would occur in their lives which extended further into the future (constrained extension); and, to both TAT cards, they told stories which encompassed a greater span of time, in comparison with the normal children of the same age.

An examination of the TAT protocols revealed no differences between the two groups in their tendency to over- or underestimate the span of time covered by the action described, but significant differences in the nature of the outcomes depicted in their stories: subjects in Group MC were more likely to tell optimistic stories to both TAT cards ($p < .02$ on TAT Card 1; $p < .05$ on TAT Card 14), while the normal children were more likely to tell stories with no discernible outcome at all, merely describing the situation depicted on the card ($p < .02$ on TAT Card 14). These results are consistent with the hypothesis that images of the distant future are available during childhood for the projection of wish-fulfilling (therefore optimistic) fantasies, and that the likelihood of using them for this purpose is enhanced by maladjustment in the present.

Within-group analyses of the data lent further support to this hypothesis. The maladjusted children in Group MC came from a wide range of socio-economic backgrounds, with a general level of social status considerably lower than that of the other three groups. Based on criteria suggested by Warner, Meeker, and Eells,[26] three indexes were used to estimate the social class backgrounds of these subjects: (a) parent's occupation (ranging from engineer to waitress), (b) family income, and (c) adequacy of family dwelling (ranging from five rooms for four people to one room for five people). It was found that, among the subjects in Group MC, those in the upper half of the social status distribution told stories to TAT Card 14 which encompassed a significantly shorter span of time ($z = 1.78$, $p = .038$), while still showing greater action time span than did the stories told by the normal children in Group NC, who were of similarly high socio-economic status ($z = 2.28$, $p = .011$). The data are clear in their suggestion that, among these preadolescent children, low social status and general maladjustment are each independently associated with the tendency to tell stories encompassing a relatively long span of time, and that their effects on this measure of orientation toward the distant future are additive.

Furthermore, among the total group of 47 children, it was found that those who had been in the upper half of their class during the preceding semester were able to name fewer events which they thought might occur in the course of their lives than were children of the same age who had been doing poorly in school (medians on density: 4.9 and 6.8, respectively; $z = 1.74$, $p = .041$).

Maladjustment and Time Perspective in Adolescence

Hypothesis 2 stated that, in contrast to the younger subjects, there is a negative relationship among adolescents between indexes of maladjustment and future orientation. Table 2 presents the results of the comparison between subjects in Group MA and the normal adolescents (Group NA) on the six different time perspective measures.

Contrary to the hypothesis, the differences between these two groups were not significant in the span of time encompassed by the action described in their two TAT stories. However, it was found that the maladjusted adolescents in Group MA, compared with the normal subjects of the same age, envisioned significantly fewer different events in their future (density), and predicted that identical future events would happen to them at an earlier median age (constrained extension). Furthermore, in direct contrast to the findings with the younger subjects, the relationship between density and school performance was now reversed: among the 43 adolescents, those who

[26] W. L. Warner, M. Meeker, and K. Eells, *Social Class in America: A Manual of Procedure for the Measurement of Social Status* (Chicago: Science Research Associates, 1949).

had been in the upper half of their class during the preceding semester envisioned a median of 6.0 events in their future, compared to a median of 4.0 events listed by subjects doing poorly in school ($z = 1.48$, $p = .069$).

The finding that differences between these two groups of adolescents were more decisive with regard to the direct measure of verbalized anticipations of the future (density) than in the more indirect and covert dimension of action time span in TAT protocols suggests that this less overt aspect of future orientation may continue to reflect a degree of relatively unrealistic, wish-fulfilling fantasy until the changes (outlined above) which accompany adolescence are well on their way toward completion. Accordingly, the stories told by the youngest third of the maladjusted adolescents in Group MA (aged 13 years, 4 months to 14 years, 5 months) were compared with the TAT protocols of the older subjects in the same group. In stories told to both TAT cards, the younger subjects scored higher in ATS than did the older adolescents, significant in both cases at better than the .03 level. Among subjects in Group NA, no age differences were found. Furthermore, the hypothesized relationship between maladjustment and ATS was confirmed among the adolescents aged 14.5 and older: to both TAT cards, the 14 older subjects in Group MA told stories encompassing a significantly shorter span of time than did the 14 normal adolescents of the same age ($p = .019$ on TAT Card 1, and .066 on TAT Card 14).

Maladjustment and Time Perspective from Childhood to Adolescence

Hypothesis 3, which stated that maladjusted children are more oriented toward the distant future than are maladjusted adolescents, was also sup-

Table 3 *Differences in Time Perspective between Maladajusted Children and Adolescents*

Measures	Group MC (N = 24)		Group MA (N = 21)			
	MEDIAN	SUM OF RANKS	MEDIAN	SUM OF RANKS	z	p
1. Density	5.80	685.5	3.95	349.5	3.02	.0013
2. Spontaneous extension	19.75	668.5	13.50	366.5	2.64	.0041
3. Constrained extension	30.6	554.0	31.5	481.0	0.34	ns
4. Coherence	.890	416.0	.9515	619.0	3.08	.0010
5. Predominance:						
% present	20.0%	446.0	31.8%	544.0	1.67	.0475
% future	58.3%	608.5	43.3%	381.5	2.10	.0179
% past	20.0%	463.0	29.2%	527.0	1.27	ns
6. Time span in:						
TAT No. 1	4 yrs.	625.5	15 days	411.0	1.60	.0548
TAT No. 14	6 days	626.5	11 hrs.	408.5	1.68	.0465

ported. Table 3 shows the results of the comparison between subjects in Group MC and those in Group MA.

The adolescents envisioned significantly fewer events in their future (density), and those which they named extended to a shorter distance into the future (spontaneous extension). To both TAT cards, their stories encompassed a shorter span of time than did those told by the children in Group MC. Furthermore, as predicted, they scored significantly higher on coherence, evidencing a more consistent ordering of personal future events, and suggesting that images of the distant future are endowed with a greater sense of reality among adolescents than is the case for children.

The notion that developmental changes occur earlier with regard to verbalized anticipations of the future (density) than in the more covert dimension of the action time span in TAT stories was further confirmed by comparing the oldest third of the maladjusted children with the youngest third of the maladjusted adolescents on these two measures. Subjects in Group MA aged 13 years, 4 months to 14 years, 5 months who, as noted above, scored significantly higher in ATS than did the older adolescents in the same group, told stories to both TAT cards which encompassed a span of time equal to that of the maladjusted children. With regard to the density measure, however, the discrepancy between childhood and adolescence was complete: there were no clear developmental changes within either Group MC or MA, but a significant difference (Mann-Whitney $U = 5.0$, $p = .002$) between the oldest children and the youngest adolescents.

Time Perspective in Normal Development from Childhood to Adolescence

Hypothesis 4 stated that normal adolescents are more oriented toward the distant future than are normal children. Table 4 presents the differences between Groups NC and NA on the time perspective variables.

Table 4 Differences in Time Perspective between Normal Children and Adolescents

Measures	Group NC ($N = 23$)		Group NA ($N = 22$)		z	p
	MEDIAN	SUM OF RANKS	MEDIAN	SUM OF RANKS		
1. Density	5.30	524.0	5.75	511.0	0.10	ns
2. Spontaneous extension	20.00	571.0	15.75	464.0	0.95	ns
3. Constrained extension	27.5	384.5	33.0	650.5	3.27	.0006
4. Coherence	.904	425.0	.9465	611.0	2.38	.0087
5. Predominance:						
% present	18.6%	359.5	46.7%	675.5	3.84	.00006
% future	60.0%	669.0	33.0%	482.0	3.17	.0008
% past	18.0%	539.0	15.0%	496.0	0.23	ns
6. Time span in:						
TAT No. 1	6 days	471.5	14 mos.	563.5	1.30	ns
TAT No. 14	2 hrs.	473.0	13 days	562.0	1.26	ns

There were no differences between the two groups in the number of events they envisioned in the future, or in the temporary distance to which these anticipated events extended. However, in predicting the age when the same 14 events would occur in their lives (constrained extension), the adolescents made median predictions which extended significantly further into the future, suggesting that, as the individual matures, he becomes w.lling to envision increasingly distant future events. While the differences in ATS between these two groups did not reach appropriate levels of significance using the Mann-Whitney, the median test indicated that the adolescents were, in fact, more likely than the younger subjects to tell stories to TAT Card 1 in which the action covered a week or more ($X^2 = 2.78$, $p < .05$), and to Card 14 a day or more ($X^2 = 3.74$, $p < .03$). As predicted, subjects in Group NA also evidenced a significantly greater degree of consistency in their ordering of future events (coherence) than did the children in Group NC.

It was further predicted that adolescents would list a greater proportion of present events and (thus) a smaller proportion of references to future events among the ten things which they reported having recently thought or spoken about (predominance), and this, too, was supported by the data presented in Table 4, as well as by the evidence from the maladjusted subjects shown in Table 3. When subjects within each of these two age groups are considered separately, however, the proportion of present references which each reports seems less likely to reflect the maturity of his interests as it is the degree of his involvement in present experiences. To the extent that this is true, the theoretical considerations outlined earlier would suggest that the relationship between the percentage of present references among the subject's report of recent thoughts or conversations and measures of his orientation toward the distant future should be *negative* in childhood, when concern with the distant future is primarily motivated by the desire to "escape" from the present, but *positive* in adolescence, when images of the future now arise out of the experiences of the present and reflect the implications of present experiences for the future. Suggestive in this latter regard are the data presented in Table 2, showing both greater future orientation and a greater proportion of present references on the predominance measure among the normal adolescents, in comparison with the subjects in Group MA. Table 5 presents the rank-order correlations

Table 5   Correlations (rho) among Normal Children and Adolescents between Future Orientation and the Proportion of Present References on the Predominance Measure

Measures of Future Orientation	Group NC (N = 23)	Group NA (N = 22)
1. Spontaneous extension	−.631°°	+.405°
2. Constrained extension	−.063	+.272
3. Action time span in:		
TAT No. 1	−.441°	+.223
TAT No. 14	−.224	+.231

   ° $p < .05$.
  °° $p < .01$.

between the percentage of references to present events among the subject's report of recent thoughts or conversations and each of the four measures of orientation toward the distant future in each of the two groups of normal subjects. In all cases, the direction of the relationship was reversed between the children in Group NC and the adolescents in Group NA, significantly so in the case of spontaneous extension.

The developmental curves for ATS and density were also examined for the normal subjects, by dividing the 45 individuals into six consecutive age groups, each with an *N* of 7 or 8: there were no significant differences on either measure between any two adjacent groups. The abrupt changes which, in contrast to these findings, were seen in the developmental curves of the maladjusted subjects lend further support to the notion that the underlying nature of the individual's anticipations of the distant future undergoes a decisive transformation between the ages of 10 and 16, a transformation which affects conscious, verbalized anticipations of the future (density) somewhat earlier than the more covert dimension of the span of time encompassed in TAT stories.

DISCUSSION

The notion that images of the distant future are available for the projection of wish-fulfilling fantasies in childhood, but become increasingly constrained by realistic considerations during adolescence, was supported by the evidence from the present study. Among children between the ages of 10.5 and 12.5, maladjustment, poor school performance, low social status, and little involvement with present experiences were all found to be associated with a *greater* orientation toward the distant future. With the attainment of adolescence, a clear change begins to occur. Moving gradually from conscious to more preconscious levels, the subjective future seems to become constrained to an increasingly clearer understanding of the nature of reality, until, by middle adolescence, maladjustment, poor school performance, and little involvement in present experiences come to be associated with a more restricted outlook on the distant future. While among normal individuals the years from childhood to adolescence are characterized by an increasing concern with distant future events, the data indicate a decreasing orientation toward the future among maladjusted boys during this same period.

Three processes were assumed, on theoretical grounds, to be centrally involved in the change in outlook on the distant future which was found to accompany the attainment of adolescence: (a) new role expectations, (b) the acquisition of formal operations, and (c) the formation of a positive ego-identity. The degree to which each of these processes is, in fact, involved in the adolescent's creation of his images of the future must await the clarification of further research. One intriguing issue is the extent to which modern testing and anxious parents can succeed in forcing a more sober and realistic view of the future on children at an increasingly early age, before the levels of intellectual and personality development usually associated with the stage of adolescence have been attained.

Joseph Adelson

Robert P. O'Neil

Growth of Political Ideas in Adolescence:
The Sense of Community

The following selection continues the basic theme of the preceding three papers: in cognitive growth there is a fundamental shift from reliance on concrete reality to dependence on comprehension of symbolic and hypothetical relationships. Adelson and O'Neil trace children's growth in terms of a sense of community, a concept involving forms of government and "the social and political collectivity more generally, as in 'society' or 'the people.'" Adolescents, ranging from 11 to 18 were asked to describe the advantages and disadvantages of various forms of government, "the scope and limits of political authority, the reciprocal obligations of citizens and state, utopian views of man and society, conceptions of law and justice, [and] the nature of the political process." The findings regarding the growth of political ideas substantiate the more general assumptions about those of cognitive growth from childhood to adolescence. Younger adolescents apparently find it difficult to transcend personalized modes of discourse, to conceive of the community as a whole, to anticipate the long-range effects of political action, and to be sensitive to individual liberties. Fortunately, however, growth in cognitive capacity at least endows older adolescents with the capacity to use philosophical and abstract principles for making political judgments.

D
URING adolescence the youngster gropes, stumbles, and leaps towards political understanding. Prior to these years the child's sense of the political order is erratic and incomplete—a curious array of sentiments and dogmas, personalized ideas, randomly remembered names and party labels, half-understood platitudes. By the time adolescence has come to an end, the child's mind, much of the time, moves easily within and among the categories of political discourse. The aim of our research was to achieve some grasp of how this transition is made.

We were interested in political ideas or concepts—in political philosophy —rather than political loyalties per se. Only during the last few years has research begun to appear on this topic. Earlier research on political socializa-

FROM *Journal of Personality and Social Psychology*, IV (1966), 295–306. Reprinted by permission of the authors and the American Psychological Association.

tion, so ably summarized by Hyman,[1] concentrated on the acquisition of affiliations and attitudes. More recently, political scientists and some psychologists have explored developmental trends in political knowledge and concepts, especially during childhood and the early years of adolescence; the studies of Greenstein [2] and of Easton and Hess [3] are particularly apposite.

Our early, informal conversations with adolescents suggested the importance of keeping our inquiry at some distance from current political issues; otherwise the underlying structure of the political is obscured by the clichés and catchphrases of partisan politics. To this end, we devised an interview schedule springing from the following premise: Imagine that a thousand men and women, dissatisfied with the way things are going in their country, decide to purchase and move to an island in the Pacific; once there, they must devise laws and modes of government.

Having established this premise, the interview schedule continued by offering questions on a number of hypothetical issues. For example, the subject was asked to choose among several forms of government and to argue the merits and difficulties of each. Proposed laws were suggested to him; he was asked to weigh their advantages and liabilities and answer arguments from opposing positions. The interview leaned heavily on dilemma items, wherein traditional issues in political theory are actualized in specific instances of political conflict, with the subject asked to choose and justify a solution. The content of our inquiry ranged widely to include, among others, the following topics: the scope and limits of political authority, the reciprocal obligations of citizens and state, utopian views of man and society, conceptions of law and justice, the nature of the political process.

This paper reports our findings on the development, in adolescence, of *the sense of community*. The term is deliberately comprehensive, for we mean to encompass not only government in its organized forms, but also the social and political collectivity more generally, as in "society" or "the people." This concept is of course central to the structure of political thought; few if any issues in political theory do not advert, however tacitly, to some conception of the community. Hence the quality of that conception, whether dim, incomplete, and primitive, or clear, complex, and articulated, cannot fail to dominate or temper the child's formulation of all things political.

The very ubiquity of the concept determined our strategy in exploring it. We felt that the dimensions of community would emerge indirectly, in the course of inquiry focused elsewhere. Our pretesting had taught us that direct questions on such large and solemn issues, though at times very useful, tended to evoke simple incoherence from the cognitively unready,

[1] H. H. Hyman, *Political Socialization* (Glencoe, Ill.: The Free Press, 1959).

[2] F. Greenstein, *Children and Politics* (New Haven: Yale University Press, 1965).

[3] D. Easton and R. D. Hess, "Youth and the Political System," *Culture and Social Character*, eds. S. M. Lipset and L. Lowenthal (New York: The Free Press, 1961), pp. 226–251; D. Easton and R. D. Hess, "The Child's Political World," *Midwest Journal of Political Science*, VI (1962), 229–246.

and schoolboy stock responses from the facile. We also learned that (whatever the ostensible topic) most of our questions informed us of the child's view of the social order, not only through what he is prepared to tell us, but also through what he does not know, knows falsely, cannot state, fumbles in stating, or takes for granted. Consequently we approached this topic through a survey of questions from several different areas of the schedule, chosen to illuminate different sides of the sense of community.

METHOD

Sample

The sample was comprised of 120 youngsters, equally divided by sex, with 30 subjects at each of 4 age-grade levels—fifth grade (average age, 10.9), seventh (12.6), ninth (14.7), and twelfth (17.7). The sample was further divided by intelligence: At each grade level, two thirds of the subjects were of average intelligence (95–110) and one third of superior intelligence (125 and over), as measured by the California Test of Mental Maturity. Table 1 shows the distribution by grade, intelligence, and sex. For

Table 1   Distribution of Sample by Grade, Sex, and Intelligence

	Boys		Girls	
	AVERAGE IQ	SUPERIOR IQ	AVERAGE IQ	SUPERIOR IQ
5th grade: *N*	10	5	10	5
Mean IQ	106.1	127.8	105.1	128.4
7th grade: *N*	10	5	10	5
Mean IQ	104.1	140.0	104.5	134.4
9th grade: *N*	10	5	10	5
Mean IQ	106.6	133.2	105.1	134.0
12th grade: *N*	10	5	10	5
Mean IQ	106.1	140.8	103.8	134.8

each grade, school records were used to establish a pool of subjects meeting our criteria for age, sex, and IQ; within each of the subgroups so selected, names were chosen randomly until the desired sample size was achieved. Children more than 6 months older or younger than the average for their grade were excluded, as were two otherwise eligible subjects reported by their counselor to have a history of severe psychological disturbance.

This paper will report findings by age alone (to the next nearest age) and without regard to sex or intelligence. We were unable to discover sex differences nor—to our continuing surprise—differences associated with intelligence. The brighter children were certainly more fluent, and there is some reason to feel that they use a drier, more impersonal, more intellectualized approach in dealing with certain questions, but up to this time we have not found that they attain political concepts earlier than subjects of average intelligence.

The interviews were taken in Ann Arbor, Michigan. We were able to use schools representative of the community, in the sense that they do not draw students from socio-economically extreme neighborhoods. The children of average IQ were preponderantly lower-middle and working class in background; those of high intelligence were largely from professional and managerial families. Academic families made up 13 per cent of the sample, concentrated in the high IQ group; 5 per cent of the "average" children and somewhat over one quarter of the "brights" had fathers with a professional connection to the University of Michigan. In these respects—socio-economic status and parental education—the sample, which combined both IQ groups, was by no means representative of the American adolescent population at large. Yet our inability to find differences between the IQ groups, who derive from sharply different social milieux, makes us hesitate to assume that social status is closely associated with the growth of political ideas as we have measured them, or that the findings deviate markedly from what we would find in other middle-class suburbs.

Interview

The aims, scope, and form of the interview schedule have already been described. In developing the schedule we were most concerned to find a tone and level of discourse sufficiently simple to allow our youngest subjects to understand and respond to the problems posed, yet sufficiently advanced to keep our older interviewees challenged and engaged. Another aim was to strike a balance between the focused interview—to ease scoring—and a looser, more discursive approach—to allow a greater depth of inquiry and spontaneity of response. Our interviewers were permitted, once they had covered the basic questions of a topic, to explore it more thoroughly.

The interviews were conducted at the school. There were six interviewers, all with at least some graduate training in clinical psychology. The interviews were tape-recorded and transcribed verbatim. Those conducted with younger subjects were completed in about 1 hour, with older subjects in about 1½ hours.

Reliability

In order to appraise the lower limits of reliability, only the more difficult items were examined, those in which responses were complex or ambiguous. For five items of this type, intercoder reliabilities ranged from .79 to .84.

RESULTS

When we examine the interviews of 11-year-olds, we are immediately struck by the common, pervasive incapacity to speak from a coherent view of the political order. Looking more closely, we find that this failure has two clear sources: First, these children are, in Piaget's sense, egocentric, in that they cannot transcend a purely personal approach to matters which require a sociocentric perspective. Second, they treat political issues in a concrete fashion and cannot manage the requisite abstractness of attitude. These tendencies, singly and together, dominate the discourse of the interview, so much so that a few sample sentences can often distinguish 11-year-old protocols from those given by only slightly older children.

The following are some interview excerpts to illustrate the differences: These are chosen randomly from the interviews of 11- and 13-year-old boys of average intelligence. They have been asked: "What is the purpose of government?"

11A. To handle the state or whatever it is so it won't get out of hand, because if it gets out of hand you might have to . . . people might get mad or something.

11B. Well . . . buildings, they have to look over buildings that would be . . . um, that wouldn't be any use of the land if they had crops on it or something like that. And when they have highways the government would have to inspect it, certain details. I guess that's about all.

11C. So everything won't go wrong in the country. They want to have a government because they respect him and they think he's a good man.

Now the 13-year-olds:

13A. So the people have rights and freedom of speech. Also so the civilization will balance.

13B. To keep law and order and talk to the people to make new ideas.

13C. Well, I think it is to keep the country happy or keep it going properly. If you didn't have it, then it would just be chaos with stealing and things like this. It runs the country better and more efficiently.

These extracts are sufficiently representative to direct us to some of the major developmental patterns in adolescent thinking on politics.

Personalism

Under *personalism* we include two related tendencies: first, the child's disposition to treat institutions and social processes upon the model of persons and personal relationships; second, his inability to achieve a sociocentric orientation, that is, his failure to understand that political decisions have social as well as personal consequences, and that the political realm encompasses not merely the individual citizen, but the community as a whole.

1. "Government," "community," "society" are abstract ideas; they connote those invisible networks of obligation and purpose which link people to each other in organized social interaction. These concepts are beyond the effective reach of 11-year-olds; in failing to grasp them they fall back to persons and actions of persons, which are the nearest equivalent of the intangible agencies and ephemeral processes they are trying to imagine.

Hence, Subject 11A seems to glimpse that an abstract answer is needed, tries to find it, then despairs and retreats to the personalized "people might get mad or something." A more extreme example is found in 11C's statement, which refers to government as a "he," apparently confusing it with "governor." Gross personalizations of "government" and similar terms are not uncommon at 11 and diminish markedly after that. We counted the number of times the personal pronouns "he" and "she" were used in three questions dealing with government. There were instances involving six subjects among the 11-year-olds (or 20 per cent of the sample) and none among 13-year-olds. (The most striking example is the following sentence by an 11-year-old: "Well, I don't think she should forbid it, but if they, if he did, well most people would want to put up an argument about it.")

Although personalizations as bald as these diminish sharply after 11, more subtle or tacit ones continue well into adolescence (and in all likelihood, into adulthood)—the use of "they," for example, when "it" is appropriate. It is our impression that we see a revival of personalization among older subjects under two conditions: when the topic being discussed is too advanced or difficult for the youngster to follow or when it exposes an area of ignorance or uncertainty, and when the subject's beliefs and resentments are engaged to the point of passion or bitterness. In both these cases the emergence of affects (anxiety, anger) seems to produce a momentary cognitive regression, expressing itself in a loss of abstractness and a reversion to personalized modes of discourse.

2. The second side of personalism is the failure to attain a sociocentric perspective. The preadolescent subject does not usually appraise political events in the light of their collective consequences. Since he finds it hard to conceive the social order as a whole, he is frequently unable to understand those actions which aim to serve communal ends and so tends to interpret them parochially, as serving only the needs of individuals. We have an illustration of this in the data given in Table 2. Table 2 reports the answers

Table 2   Purpose of Vaccination

	Age			
	11	*13*	*15*	*18*
Social consequences (prevention of epidemics, etc.)	.23	.67	1.00	.90
Individual consequences (prevention of individual illness)	.70	.33	.00	.10

Note.—$x^2(3) = 46.53$, $p < .001$. In this table and all that follow $N = 30$ for each age group. When proportions in a column do not total 1.00, certain responses are not included in the response categories shown. When proportions total more than 1.00, responses have been included in more than one category of the table. The p level refers to the total table except when asterisks indicate significance levels for a designated row.

to the following item: "Another law was suggested which required all children to be vaccinated against smallpox and polio. What would be the purpose of that law?"

A substantial majority—about three quarters—of the 11-year-olds see the law serving an individual end—personal protection from disease. By 13 there has been a decisive shift in emphasis, these children stressing the protection of the community. At 15 and after, an understanding of the wider purposes of vaccination has become nearly universal.

Parts and Wholes

Another reflection of the concreteness of younger adolescents can be found in their tendency to treat the total functioning institutions in terms of specific, discrete activities. If we return to the interview excerpts, we find a good example in the answer given by Subject 11B on the purpose of government. He can do no more than mention some specific governmental functions, in this case, the inspecting of buildings and highways. This answer exemplifies a pattern we find frequently among our younger subjects, one which appears in many content areas. Adolescents only gradually perceive institutions (and their processes) as wholes; until they can imagine the institution abstractly, as a total idea, they are limited to the concrete and the visible.

Table 3 is one of several which demonstrates this. The subjects were

Table 3   Purpose of Income Tax

	Age			
	11	13	15	18
General support of government	.23	.33	.47	1.00*
Specific services only	.23	.17	.23	.00
Do not know	.43	.50	.30	.00

Note.—p level refers to row designated by asterisk.
* $X^2(3) = 9.54$, $p < .05$.

asked the purpose of the income tax. The responses were coded to distinguish those who answered in terms of general government support from those who mentioned only specific government services. (In most cases the services referred to are both local and visible—police, firefighting, etc.) We observe that the percentage of those referring to the government in a general sense rises slowly and steadily; all of the high school seniors do so.

Negatives and Positives

Before we leave this set of interview excerpts, we want to note one more important difference between the 11- and 13-year-olds. Two of the former emphasize the negative or coercive functions of government ("To handle the state . . . so it won't get out of hand"; "So everything won't go wrong . . ."). The 13-year-olds, on the other hand, stress the positive functions of the government—keeping the country happy or working properly. This difference is so important and extensive that we will treat it in depth in a later publication, but it should be discussed at least briefly here. Younger subjects adhere to a Hobbesian view of political man: The citizenry is seen as willful and potentially dangerous, and society, therefore, as rightfully, needfully coercive and authoritarian. Although this view of the political never quite loses its appeal for a certain proportion of individuals at all ages, it nevertheless diminishes both in frequency and centrality, to be replaced, in time, by more complex views of political arrangements, views which stress the administrative sides of government (keeping the machinery oiled and in repair) or which emphasize melioristic ends (enhancing the human condition).

The Future

The adolescent years see a considerable extension of time perspective. On the one hand, a sense of history emerges, as the youngster is able to link past and present and to understand the present as having been influenced or determined by the past. On the other, the child begins to imagine the future and, what may be more important, to ponder alternative futures. Thus the present is connected to the future not merely because the future unfolds from the present, but also because the future is *tractable;* its shape depends upon choices made in the present.

This idea of the future asserts itself with increasing effect as the child advances through adolescence. In making political judgments, the youngster can anticipate the consequences of a choice taken here and now for the long-range future of the community and can weigh the probable effects of alternatives choices on the future. The community is now seen to be temporal, that is, as an organism which persists beyond the life of its current members; thus judgments in the present must take into account the needs of the young and of the unborn. Further, the adolescent becomes able to envision not only the communal future, but himself (and others) in possible statuses in that future as well.

The items which most clearly expose the changing meaning of the future are those dealing with education. When we reflect on it, this is not surprising: Education is the public enterprise which most directly links the generations to each other; it is the communal activity through which one generation orients another toward the future. Several questions of public policy toward education were asked; in the answer to each the needs of the communal future weigh more heavily with increasing age. One item runs: "Some people suggested a law which would require children to go to school until they were 16-years-old. What would be the purpose of such a law?" One type of answer to this question was coded "Continuity of community"; these responses stress the community's need to sustain and perpetuate itself by educating a new generation of citizens and leaders. Typical answers were: "So children will grow up to be leaders," and "To educate people so they can carry on the government." Looking at this answer alone (analysis of the entire table would carry us beyond this topic), we find the following distribution by age (see Table 4).

Table 4   Purpose of Minimum Education Law

	Age			
	11	13	15	18
Continuity of community	.00	.27	.33	.43

Note.—X²(3) = 11.95, $p < .01$.

Another item later in the interview poses this problem: "The people who did not have children thought it was unfair they would have to pay taxes to support the school system. What do you think of that argument?" Again the same category, which stresses the community's continuity and its future needs, rises sharply with age as shown in Table 5.

Table 5   Should People without Children Pay School Taxes?

	Age			
	11	13	15	18
Continuity of community	.10	.10	.47	.60

Note.—X²(3) = 18.61, $p < .001$.

Finally, we want to examine another education item in some detail, since it offers a more complex view of the sense of the future in adolescent political thought, allowing us to observe changes in the child's view of the personal future. The question was the last of a series on the minimum education law. After the subject was asked to discuss its purpose (see above), he was asked whether he supports it. Almost all of our subjects did. He was then asked: "Suppose you have a parent who says 'My son is going to go into my business anyway and he doesn't need much schooling for that.' Do you think his son should be required to go to school anyway? Why?"

Table 6 shows that as children advance into adolescence, they stress in-

Table 6   Should Son Be Required to Attend School though Father Wants Him to Enter Business?

	Age			
	11	13	15	18
Yes, education needed to function in community	.00	.23	.43	.72***
Yes, education good in itself	.03	.23	.20	.27
Yes, education needed in business	.40	.47	.23	.13
Yes, prevents parental coercion	.57	.47	.43	.23

Note.—p level refers to row designated by asterisk.
*** X²(3) = 25.54, $p < .001$.

creasingly the communal function of education. Younger subjects respond more to the father's arbitrariness or to the economic consequences of the father's position. They are less likely to grasp the more remote, more general effects of a curtailed education—that it hinders the attainment of citizenship. Representative answers by 11-year-olds were: "Well, maybe he wants some other desire and if he does maybe his father is forcing him"; and ". . . let's say he doesn't like the business and maybe he'd want to start something new." These children stress the practical and familial aspects of the issue.

Older subjects, those 15 and 18, all but ignored both the struggle with the father and the purely pragmatic advantages of remaining in school. They discoursed, sometimes eloquently, on the child's need to know about society as a whole, to function as a citizen, and to understand the perspectives of others. Here is how one 18-year-old put it:

> . . . a person should have a perspective and know a little bit about as much as he can rather than just one thing throughout his whole life and anything of others, because he'd have to know different things about different aspects of life and education and just how things are in order to get along with them, because if not then they'd be prejudiced toward their own feelings and what *they* wanted and they wouldn't be able to understand any people's needs.

Older subjects see education as the opportunity to become *cosmopolitan,* to transcend the insularities of job and kinship. For the older adolescent, leaving school early endangers the future in two ways. On the personal side, it threatens one's capacity to assume the perspective of the other and to attain an adequate breadth of outlook; thus, it imperils one's future place in the community. On the societal side, it endangers the integrity of the social order itself, by depriving the community of a cosmopolitan citizenry.

Claims of the Community

We have already seen that as adolescence advances the youngster is increasingly sensitive to the fact of community and its claims upon the citizen. What are the limits of these claims, the limits of political authority? To what point, and under what conditions can the state, acting in the common good, trespass upon the autonomy of the citizen? When do the community's demands violate the privacy and liberty of the individual? The clash of these principles—individual freedom versus the public welfare and safety—is one of the enduring themes of Western political theory. Many, perhaps most, discussions in political life in one way or another turn on this issue; indeed, the fact that these principles are so often used purely rhetorically (as when the cant of liberty or of the public good is employed to mask pecuniary and other motives) testifies to their salience in our political thinking.

A number of questions in the interview touched upon this topic tangentially, and some were designed to approach it directly. In these latter we asked the subject to adjudicate and comment upon a conflict between public and private interests, each of these supported by a general political principle—usually the individual's right to be free of compulsion, on the one hand, and the common good, on the other. We tried to find issues which would be tangled enough to engage the most complex modes of political reasoning. A major effort in this direction was made through a series of three connected questions on eminent domain. The series began with this question:

> Here is another problem the Council faced. They decided to build a road to connect one side of the island to the other. For the most part they had no trouble buying the land on which to build the road, but one man refused to sell his land to the government. He was offered a fair price for his land but he refused, saying that he didn't want to move, that he was attached to his land, and that the Council could buy another piece of land and change the direction of the road. Many people thought he was selfish, but others thought he was in the right. What do you think?

Somewhat to our surprise, there are no strong developmental patterns visible, though we do see a moderate tendency (not significant statistically, however) for the younger subjects to side with the landowner (see Table 7).

Table 7   Which Party Is Right in Eminent-Domain Conflict?

	Age			
	11	13	15	18
Individual should sell; community needs come first	.30	.20	.30	.40
Detour should be made; individual rights come first	.60	.47	.27	.37
Emphasis on social responsibility; individual should be appealed to, but not forced	.10	.17	.17	.07
Ambivalance; individual is right in some ways, wrong in others	.00	.13	.27	.17

The next question in the series sharpened the issue somewhat between the Council and the reluctant landowner:

> The Council met and after long discussion voted that if the landowner would not agree to give up his land for the road, he should be forced to, because the rights of all the people on the island were more important than his. Do you think this was a fair decision?

The phrasing of the second question does not alter the objective facts of the conflict; yet Table 8 shows decisive shifts in position. It is hard to be sure why: perhaps because the second question states that the Council has considered the matter at length, perhaps because the Council's decision is justified by advancing the idea of "the people's rights." Whatever the reason, we now see a marked polarization of attitude. The younger subjects—those 11 and 13—continue to side with the landowner; those 15 and

Table 8 *Should Landowner Be Forced to Sell His Land?*

	Age			
	11	13	15	18
Yes, rights of others come first	.40	.37	.63	.70
No, individual rights come first	.57	.50	.33	.07**
No, social responsibility should suffice	.03	.10	.00	.23

Note.—*p* level refers to row designated by asterisk.
** $X^2(3) = 12.17$, $p < .01$.

18 almost completely abandon him, although about one quarter of the latter want to avoid coercion and suggest an appeal to his sense of social responsibility.

The final question in the series tightened the screws:

The landowner was very sure that he was right. He said that the law was unjust and he would not obey it. He had a shotgun and would shoot anyone who tried to make him get off his land. He seemed to mean business. What should the government do?

The landowner's threat startled some of the subjects, though in very different ways depending on age, as Table 9 shows: The younger subjects

Table 9 *What Should Government Do if Landowner Threatens Violence?*

	Age			
	11	13	15	18
Detour	.60	.63	.37	.10
Government coercion justified	.23	.27	.57	.83

Note.—$X^2(3) = 29.21$, $p < .001$.

in these cases did not quite know what to do about it and suggested that he be mollified at all costs; the older subjects, if they were taken aback, were amused or disdainful, saw him as a lunatic or a hothead, and rather matter-of-factly suggested force or guile to deal with him. Nevertheless, this question did not produce any essential change in position for the sample as a whole. Those older subjects who had hoped to appeal to the landowner's social conscience despaired of this and sided with the Council. Otherwise, the earlier pattern persisted, the two younger groups continuing to support the citizen, the older ones favoring the government, and overwhelmingly so among the oldest subjects.

These findings seem to confirm the idea that older adolescents are more responsive to communal than to individual needs. Yet it would be incorrect to infer that these subjects favor the community willy-nilly. A close look at the interview protocols suggests that older adolescents choose differently because they reason differently.

Most younger children—those 13 and below—can offer no justification for their choices. Either they are content with a simple statement of preference, for example: "I think he was in the right"; or they do no more than paraphrase the question: "Well, there is really two sides to it. One is that he is attached and he shouldn't give it up, but again he should give it up for the country." These youngsters do not or cannot rationalize their decisions, neither through appeal to a determining principle, nor through a comparative analysis of each side's position. If there is an internal argument going on within the mind of the 11- or 13-year-old, he is unable to make it public; instead, he seems to choose by an intuitive ethical leap, averring that one or the other position is "fair," "in the right," or "selfish." He usually favors the landowner, because his side of the matter is concrete, personal, psychologically immediate, while the Council's position hinges on an idea of the public welfare which is too remote and abstract for these youngsters to absorb. Even those few children who try to reason from knowledge or experience more often than not flounder and end in confusion. A 13-year-old:

> Like this girl in my class. Her uncle had a huge house in _____, and they tore it down and they put the new city hall there. I think they should have moved it to another place. I think they should have torn it down like they did, because they had a law that if there was something paid for, then they should give that man a different price. But then I would force him out, but I don't know how I'd do it.

What we miss in these interviews are two styles of reasoning which begin to make their appearance in 15-year-olds: first, the capacity to reason consequently, to trace out the long-range implications of various courses of action; second, a readiness to deduce specific choices from general principles. The following excerpt from a 15-year-old's interview illustrates both of these approaches:

> Well, maybe he owned only a little land if he was a farmer and even if they did give him a fair price maybe all the land was already bought on the island that was good for farming or something and he couldn't get another start in life if he did buy it. Then maybe in a sense he was selfish because if they had to buy other land and change the direction of the road why of course then maybe they'd raise taxes on things so they could get more money cause it would cost more to change directions from what they already have planned. [Fair to force him off?] Yes, really, just because one person doesn't want to sell his land that don't mean that, well the other 999 or the rest of the people on the island should go without this road because of one.

In the first part of the statement, the subject utilizes a cost-effectiveness approach; he estimates the costs (economic, social, moral) of one decision against another. He begins by examining the effects on the landowner. Can he obtain equivalent land elsewhere? He then considers the long-range economic consequences for the community. Will the purchase of other land be more expensive and thus entail a tax increase? Though he does not go on to solve these implicit equations—he could hardly do so, since he does not have sufficient information—he does state the variables he deems necessary to solve them.

The second common strategy at this age, seen in the last part of the statement, is to imply or formulate a general principle, usually ethico-political in nature, which subsumes the instance. Most adolescents using this approach will for this item advert to the community's total welfare, but some of our older adolescents suggest some other governing principle—the sanctity of property rights or the individual's right to privacy and autonomy. In either instance, the style of reasoning is the same; a general principle is sought which contains the specific issue.

Once a principle is accepted, the youngster attempts to apply it consistently. If the principle is valid, it should fall with equal weight on all; consequently, exceptions are resisted:

> I think that man should be forced to move with a good sum of money because I imagine it would be the people, it said the rights of the whole, the whole government and the whole community, why should one man change the whole idea?

And to the question of the landowner's threatening violence: "They shouldn't let him have his own way, because he would be an example. Other people would think that if they used his way, they could do what they wanted to." Even a child who bitterly opposes the Council's position on this issue agrees that once a policy has been established, exceptions should be resisted:

> Well, if the government is going to back down when he offers armed resistance, it will offer ideas to people who don't like, say, the medical idea [see below]. They'll just haul out a shotgun if you come to study them. The government should go through with the action.

The Force of Principle

Once principles and ideals are firmly established, the child's approach to political discourse is decisively altered. When he ponders a political choice, he takes into account not only *personal* consequences (What will this mean, practically speaking, for the individuals involved?) and pragmatic *social* consequences (What effect will this have on the community at large?), but also its consequences in the realm of *value* (Does this law or decision enhance or endanger such ideals as liberty, justice, and so on?). There is of course no sharp distinction among these types of consequences; values are contained, however tacitly, in the most "practical" of decisions. Nevertheless, these ideals, once they develop, have a life, an autonomy of

their own. We reasoned that as the adolescent grew older, political principles and ideals would be increasingly significant, and indeed would loom
large enough to overcome the appeal of personal and social utility in the
narrow sense.

To test this belief we wanted an item which would pit a "good" against
a "value." We devised a question proposing a law which, while achieving a
personal and communal good, would at the same time violate a political
ideal—in this case, the value of a personal autonomy. The item ran: "One
[proposed law] was a suggestion that men over 45 be required to have a
yearly medical checkup. What do you think of that suggestion?" The answer
was to be probed if necessary: "Would you be in favor of that? Why (or
why not)?" Table 10 shows the distribution of responses.

*Table 10   Should Men over 45 Be Required to Have a Yearly Medical
Checkup?*

	Age			
	11	*13*	*15*	*18*
Yes, otherwise they would not do it	.50	.07	.00	.03***
Yes, good for person and/or community	.50	.80	.70	.60
No, infringement on liberties	.00	.13	.27	.37**

Note.—*p* level refers to rows designated by asterisk.
** $X^2(3) = 11.95$, $p < .01$.
*** $X^2(3) = 33.10$, $p < .001$.

The findings are interesting on several counts, aside from offering testimony on the degree to which good health is viewed as a summum bonum.
The 11-year-olds, here as elsewhere, interpret the issue along familial and
authoritarian lines. The government is seen in loco parentis; its function is
to make its citizens do the sensible things they would otherwise neglect to
do. But our primary interest is in the steady growth of opposition to the
proposal. The basis for opposition, though it is phrased variously, is that
the government has no business exercising compulsion in this domain. These
youngsters look past the utilitarian appeal of the law and sense its conflict
with a value that the question itself does not state. These data, then, offer
some support to our suggestion that older adolescents can more easily bring
abstract principles to bear in the appraisal of political issues. Strictly speaking, the findings are not definitive, for we cannot infer that all of those
supporting the law do so without respect to principle. Some of the older
adolescents do, in fact, recognize the conflict implicit in the question, but
argue that the public and personal benefits are so clear as to override the
issue of personal liberties. But there are very few signs of this among the
younger subjects. Even when pressed, as they were in a following question,
they cannot grasp the meaning and significance of the conflict; they see
only the tangible good.

DISCUSSION

These findings suggest that the adolescent's sense of community is determined not by a single factor, but by the interaction of several related developmental parameters. We should now be in a position to consider what some of these are.

1. *The decline of authoritarianism.* Younger subjects are more likely to approve of coercion in public affairs. Themselves subject to the authority of adults, they more readily accept the fact of hierarchy. They find it hard to imagine that authority may be irrational, presumptuous, or whimsical; thus they bend easily to the collective will.

2. With advancing age there is an increasing grasp of the *nature and needs of the community.* As the youngster begins to understand the structure and functioning of the social order as a whole, he begins to understand too the specific social institutions within it and their relations to the whole. He comes to comprehend the autonomy of institutions, their need to remain viable, to sustain and enhance themselves. Thus the demands of the social order and its constituent institutions, as well as the needs of the public, become matters to be appraised in formulating political choices.

3. *The absorption of knowledge and consensus.* This paper has taken for granted, and hence neglected, the adolescent's increasing knowingness. The adolescent years see a vast growth in the acquisition of political information, in which we include not only knowledge in the ordinary substantive sense, but also the apprehension of consensus, a feeling for the common and prevailing ways of looking at political issues. The child acquires these from formal teaching, as well as through a heightened cathexis of the political, which in turn reflects the generally amplified interest in the adult world. Thus, quite apart from the growth of cognitive capacity, the older adolescent's views are more "mature" in that they reflect internalization of adult perspectives.

4. We must remember that it is not enough to be exposed to mature knowledge and opinion; their absorption in turn depends on the growth of *cognitive capacities.* Some of the younger subjects knew the fact of eminent domain, knew it to be an accepted practice, yet, unable to grasp the principles involved, could not apply their knowledge effectively to the question. This paper has stressed the growth of those cognitive capacities which underlie the particular intellectual achievements of the period: the adolescent's increasing ability to weigh the relative consequences of actions, the attainment of deductive reasoning. The achievement of these capacities— the leap to "formal operations," in Piaget's term—allows him to escape that compulsion toward the immediate, the tangible, the narrowly pragmatic which so limits the political discourse of younger adolescents.

5. In turn the growth of cognitive capacity allows *the birth of ideology.* Ideology may not be quite the right word here, for it suggests a degree of coherence and articulation that few of our subjects, even the oldest and brightest, come close to achieving. Nevertheless there is an impressive dif-

ference between the younger and older adolescents in the orderliness and internal consistency of their political perspectives. What passes for ideology in the younger respondents is a raggle-taggle array of sentiments: "People ought to be nice to each other"; "There are a lot of wise guys around, so you have to have the strict laws." In time these sentiments may mature (or harden) into ideologies or ideological dispositions, but they are still too erratic, too inconsistent. They are not yet principled or generalized and so tend to be self-contradictory, or loosely held and hence easily abandoned. When younger subjects are cross-questioned, however gently, they are ready to reverse themselves even on issues they seem to feel strongly about. When older subjects are challenged, however sharply, they refute, debate, and counterchallenge. In some part their resistance to easy change reflects a greater degree of poise and their greater experience in colloquy and argument, but it also bespeaks the fact that their views are more firmly founded. The older adolescents, most conspicuously those at 18, aim for an inner concordance of political belief.

These then are the variables our study has suggested as directing the growth of political concepts. We must not lean too heavily on any one of them: The development of political thought is not simply or even largely a function of cognitive maturation or of increased knowledge or of the growth of ideology when these are taken alone. This paper has stressed the cognitive parameters because they seem to be so influential at the younger ages. The early adolescent's political thought is constrained by personalized, concrete, present-oriented modes of approach. Once these limits are transcended, the adolescent is open to influence by knowledge, by the absorption of consensus, and by the principles he adopts from others or develops on his own.

A Developmental Synopsis

We are now in a position to summarize the developmental patterns which have emerged in this study. It is our impression that the most substantial advance is to be found in the period between 11 and 13 years, where we discern a marked shift in the cognitive basis of political discourse. Our observations support the Inhelder and Piaget [4] findings on a change from concrete to formal operations at this stage. To overstate the case somewhat, we might say that the *11-year-old* has not achieved the capacity for formal operations. His thinking is concrete, egocentric, tied to the present; he is unable to envision long-range social consequences; he cannot comfortably reason from premises; he has not attained hypothetico-deductive modes of analysis. The 13-year-old has achieved these capacities some (much?) of the time, but is unable to display them with any consistent effectiveness. The *13-year-olds* seem to be the most labile of our subjects. Depending on the item, they may respond like those older or younger than themselves. In a sense they are on the threshold of mature modes of reasoning, just

[4] B. Inhelder and J. Piaget, *The Growth of Logical Thinking from Childhood to Adolescence* (New York: Basic Books, 1958).

holding on, and capable of slipping back easily. Their answers are the most difficult to code, since they often involve an uneasy mixture of the concrete and the formal.

The *15-year-old* has an assured grasp of formal thought. He neither hesitates nor falters in dealing with the abstract; when he seems to falter; it is more likely due to a lack of information or from a weakness in knowing and using general principles. His failures are likely to be in content and in fluency, rather than in abstract quality per se. Taking our data as a whole we usually find only moderate differences between 15 and 18. We do find concepts that appear suddenly between 11 and 13, and between 13 and 15, but only rarely do we find an idea substantially represented at 18 which is not also available to a fair number of 15-year-olds.

The *18-year-old* is, in other words, the 15-year-old, only more so. He knows more; he speaks from a more extended apperceptive mass; he is more facile; he can elaborate his ideas more fluently. Above all, he is more philosophical, more ideological in his perspective on the political order. At times he is consciously, deliberately an ideologue. He holds forth.

Gary A. Davis

Training Creativity in Adolescence:
A Discussion of Strategy

Contemporary psychologists are beginning to do more than identify those traits characteristic of creative adolescents, for, although a trait approach to creativity is indeed informative, it fails to suggest precisely how creativity may be enhanced. In the following paper, Davis suggests that creativity may be profitably conceptualized as consisting mainly of three trainable components, (1) appropriate creative attitudes, the most critical of which is a favorable attitude toward highly imaginative problem solutions, (2) various cognitive abilities which facilitate whatever mental abstracting, combining, perceiving, associating, filling in gaps, and so forth, contribute to the fluent production of original ideas, and (3) techniques for the conscious and systematic production of new combinations of ideas. Further, by incorporating many concepts and principles from this three-part model, Davis describes a novel program for developing creativity in adolescents.

PSYCHOLOGICAL studies of the personalities and histories of artistic adolescents and of individuals scoring high or low on "creativity" tests have been successfully used to define numerous characteristics common to creative adolescents.[1] Typically independent, confident, and self-assertive, adolescents often involve themselves in radical, nonconforming and imaginative situations. Their curiosity, which draws them toward the complex and ambiguous, extends both inward, rendering them introspective and fantasy-prone, and outward, making them energetic and persistent.

Identification of these traits, however, is not sufficient; adolescents must

Written especially for this volume. This report was prepared pursuant to contract OE 5-10-154 with the United States Office of Education, Department of Health, Education, and Welfare, under the provisions of the Cooperative Research Program. Comments and suggestions on the manuscript by Susan E. Houtman and Mary L. Stelly are gratefully acknowledged.

[1] Jacob W. Getzels and Philip W. Jackson, *Creativity and Intelligence* (New York: John Wiley and Sons, 1962); E. F. Hammer, *Creativity* (New York Random House, 1961); E. Paul Torrance, *Guiding Creative Talent* (Englewood Cliffs, N.J.: Prentice-Hall, 1962); see also Frank Barron, "The Psychology of Imagination," *Scientific American,* CXCIX (1958), 151–166; Donald W. MacKinnon, "The Nature and Nurture of Creative Talent," *American Psychologist,* XVII (1962), 484–495.

be trained to be creative in order to approach their education, interpersonal relations, and ultimately their careers from broader, more flexible perspectives. The following discussion, therefore, aims to clarify three major dimensions or parameters of creativity, i.e., attitudes, abilities, and creative-thinking techniques, to emphasize the training strategies underlying each, and to show how these parameters may be integrated into a coherent, plausible classroom program useful for developing adolescent creative potential.

CREATIVE ATTITUDES

Attitudes may be defined as learned, emotionally toned predispositions to react consistently, favorably or unfavorably, toward persons, objects, or ideas.[2] The most important attitudes contributing specifically to creative development are those that predispose individuals to react favorably to new and innovative ideas and that stimulate them to engage in imaginative behavior.[3]

In recognizing the importance of these concepts, researchers have devised strategies designed to shape attitudes conducive to spontaneous, creative productivity. Osborn's brainstorming, for example, suggests the necessity of favorable attitudes toward both one's own and others' wild, new ideas.[4] Effective brainstormers must be instructed never to criticize even the most far-fetched problem solutions; rather, they are encouraged and reinforced for uninhibited idea production. The Covington, Crutchfield, and Davies *Productive Thinking Program,* which has been shown to improve problem-solving and creativity scores of fifth- and sixth-grade students, reveals the importance of positive attitudes towards open-mindedness, perseverance, and self-confidence in problem solving.[5] Covington, *et al.,* repeatedly remind students that their "ideas can be as good as other people's," and that they should not "jump to conclusions" or "give up too easily." Also successfully used to improve creativity, the Myers and Torrance *Idea Books* seek to foster favorable attitudes toward novel combinations of ideas by reinforcing imaginative responses to such nonsense questions as "Does the Sun sound tired today?"[6]

2 Herbert J. Klausmeier and William Goodwin, *Learning and Human Abilities* (New York: Harper and Row, 1966), p. 343.

3 e.g., Sidney J. Parnes, *Workbook for Creative Problem Solving Institutes and Courses* (Buffalo: Creative Education Foundation, 1966).

4 Alex F. Osborn, *Applied Imagination* (New York: Scribner's, 1963).

5 Martin V. Covington, Richard S. Crutchfield, and Lillian B. Davies, *The Productive Thinking Program* (Berkeley: Brazelton Printing Co., 1966).

6 Only two of these booklets might be suitable for young adolescents, R. E. Myers and E. Paul Torrance, *Invitations to Speaking and Writing Creatively* (Boston: Ginn & Co., 1965); R. E. Myers and E. Paul Torrance, *Plots, Puzzles, and Ploys* (Boston: Ginn & Co., 1966). The remaining three Idea Books are clearly for elementary level students: R. E. Myers and E. Paul Torrance, *Invitations to Thinking and Doing* (Boston: Ginn & Co., 1964); R. E. Myers and E. Paul Torrance, *Can You Imagine* (Boston: Ginn & Co., 1965); R. E. Myers and E. Paul Torrance, *For Those Who Wonder* (Boston: Ginn & Co., 1966).

CREATIVE ABILITIES

Despite the intrinsic complexity of the problem, psychologists have sought to distinguish various relatively unlearned mental abilities.[7] One of the most plausible analyses of abilities that may contribute specifically to creative behavior is that of Guilford, who identified the abilities of *fluency*, the total number of ideas which can be produced in a given period of time, *flexibility*, the number of distinctly different categories of solutions to a problem, and *originality*, the uniqueness of the solutions.[8] When asked to think of unusual uses for a brick, for example, more creative individuals not only list larger numbers of unusual brick uses, but their ideas tend to be of different types, e.g., make a doorstop, drown a cat, build a barbecue, hold test tubes. In addition to specifying these creative abilities, Guilford has suggested also that they may in fact be strengthened by giving students exercises similar to the tests measuring the particular abilities. For example, he assumed that if the number of responses to such tests as "List things which are solid, white, and edible" or "Name synonyms for the word *dark*" is a good indicator of the *fluency* ability, then the use of these tests as exercises might strengthen this ability.

Consistent with Guilford's suggestion of increasing abilities through exercise, Myers and Torrance attempt to both identify and strengthen a broad spectrum of simple and complex creative abilities.[9] Children or adolescents, for example, are given exercises in remembering, free-associating, discerning problems, perceiving relationships, imagining and elaborating on wild ideas, predicting or making up consequences of unusual events, filling in information gaps, pretending, and being more aware of sights and sounds. They also are trained to use descriptive adjectives, to find unusual uses for common objects, and to make up story plots, puzzles, punch lines, mysteries, and even more exercises.

CREATIVE THINKING TECHNIQUES

Creative-thinking techniques are conscious and deliberate procedures for producing new combinations of ideas. A major contribution of existing, professional level creativity programs has been to suggest techniques that may be readily adopted for classroom use. Osborn's brainstorming, operating on the principle of deferred judgment, is the best known. It encourages students to produce freely a large number of wild ideas, since the greater the number, the greater the likelihood of finding useful ones. In addition to contributing ideas of their own, students are encouraged to suggest how two or more ideas may be combined into still others.

[7] L. L. Thurstone, "Primary Mental Abilities," *Psychometric Monographs* (1938), No. 1.

[8] J. P. Guilford, "Creativity: Its Measurement and Development," *A Source Book for Creative Thinking*, ed., S. J. Parnes and H. F. Harding (New York: Charles Scribner's Sons, 1962), pp. 151–168.

[9] See footnote 6.

While brainstorming may be effective, it is a relatively broad, unstructured approach to group or individual problem solving which mainly provides an atmosphere conducive to unrestrained imagination. There are, however, a number of more specific creative-thinking techniques that teach students precisely how to produce new and potentially valuable combinations of ideas. Let us consider, in order, the methods of (1) attribute listing, (2) morphological synthesis, (3) checklisting, and (4) synectics.

1. The *attribute-listing* technique is a simple and effective method for generating creative ideas to improve or change virtually anything.[10] Using this method, teachers might ask students to itemize important attributes (or parts) of a product and then consider each attribute as a source of potential change or improvement. For example, with an object as simple as classroom chalk, students might learn to identify the attributes of size, shape, color, and material. Then, by considering changes for each of these individual attributes, ideas for a large variety of chalk may be quickly produced. While the usefulness of the attribute-listing procedure is limited to problems whose important attributes are identifiable, its scope is still wide: "Objects" in art, literature, science, business, and industry, for example, can be improved with this method. New ideas for writing short stories may be found by identifying and systematically changing such important attributes as the *setting, characters,* and *plot.* Or, in studying industry, students may learn to identify and improve the attributes of material, cost, market, and production processes. Attribute listing both sensitizes students to various properties of objects and equips them with a simple yet very productive means of innovation.

2. The *morphological-synthesis* technique,[11] which is fairly similar to that of attribute listing, may be used to produce more idea combinations than any other. Students first identify two or more important characteristics or dimensions (e.g., color, shape) of a problem and list specific values (e.g., red, blue, green; square, round, triangular) for each. They then examine all possible combinations, utilizing one value of each characteristic. For example, if students are asked to "invent" a new line of pop-up toasters, all combinations of 15 shapes, 20 different colors and color patterns, and 5 sizes would instantly produce 1500 possible products. It is possible, however, that a rigid application of the morphological analysis procedure conceivably might prevent a thinker from approaching a problem from different, more imaginative perspectives. For example, students intent on examining the 1500 combinations of ideas for pop-up toasters may fail to detect entirely new means of toasting bread. But the morphological-synthesis technique

[10] Robert P. Crawford, *The Techniques of Creative Thinking* (New York: Hawthorn, 1954); see also Gary A. Davis, Mary E. Manske, and Alice J. Train, "Training Creative Thinking," Occasional Paper No. 6, Wisconsin Research and Development Center for Cognitive Learning, University of Wisconsin, 1967.

[11] Myron S. Allen, *Psycho-Dynamic Synthesis* (West Nyack, N.Y.: Parker, 1966); Gary A. Davis, William E. Roweton, Alice J. Train, Thomas F. Warren, and Susan E. Houtman, "Laboratory Studies of Creative Thinking Techniques: The Checklist and Morphological Synthesis Methods," Technical Report, Wisconsin Research and Development Center for Cognitive Learning, University of Wisconsin (in press).

invariably produces an enormous quantity of idea combinations in a very short time and thus guarantees the production of idea combinations never before considered, some of which may prove to be surprisingly valuable.

3. With the *checklist* procedure, students consider each item on a prepared list as a possible source of innovation in respect to a given problem.[12] In the classroom, for example, they may be taught to consult a history book as a "checklist" of ideas for writing themes or short stories. Faced with the problem of selecting a career, they might consult the Yellow Pages, a checklist containing thousands of vocational suggestions. Likewise, a department store catalogue would provide ideas for solving a gift-giving problem.

A recently developed checklist, intended to stimulate ideas for changing a product, includes just seven items: [13] (1) add and/or subtract something; (2) change color; (3) vary materials; (4) rearrange parts; (5) vary shape; (6) change size; (7) modify design or style. Compared with the performance of control subjects, college students using this checklist produced a significantly larger number of creative ideas for changing or improving a *thumbtack* and a *kitchen sink*. For example, students improved a kitchen sink by adding a soap or hand lotion dispenser, by thinking of such unusual sink colors as orange or silver, by constructing the sink of such materials as nylon, plastic, or copper, by making it extra large or small in size, or by designing it in an Oriental or Scandinavian mode. The checklist essentially provides students with general categories of problem solutions which stimulated a large number of specific ideas.

One might argue that this technique could make students dependent on checklists, thus preventing them from "thinking for themselves." However, idea checklists mainly serve to stimulate original thinking. Thus, they are intended to supplement, not to replace, more intuitive forms of creative behavior.

4. The *synectic* method mainly emphasizes the use of metaphors and similes, especially those drawn from nature.[14] After posing a problem, teachers encourage students to ask how animals, insects, or even plants have solved similar problems. Solutions for a parking problem, for example, may be found by considering how bees or ants "store things." Proposing *ideal* but apparently ridiculous problem solutions, such as having insects work on command to solve a transportation problem, is another synetic method for stimulating new viewpoints on a problem. "Playing with" or free-associating word meanings may lead to still more new ideas. For example, speculating on the meaning of the word "opening" (cutting, prying, unfolding, etc.) may suggest new designs for a can opener. Ideas stimulated by using the synectic methods may seem "silly" and inappropriate for solving serious problems. However, it is exactly the wild, far-fetched, per-

---

[12] Osborn, *op. cit.;* Davis, Roweton, Train, Warren, and Houtman, *op. cit.*

[13] Davis, Roweton, Train, Warren and Houtman, *op. cit.*

[14] William J. J. Gordon, *Synectics* (New York: Harper and Brothers, 1961); George M. Prince, "The Operational Mechanisms of Synectics," *Journal of Creative Behavior,* II (1968), 1–13.

haps "silly" ideas which are sought, since these often lead to the most creative and workable problem solutions. For instance, when faced with the problem of inventing a vapor proof closure for space suits, one synectic group imagined insects running up and down the closure manipulating little latches—a far-fetched idea which led to a workable air-tight zipper.[15]

The above parameters of creativity—attitudes, abilities, and creative-thinking techniques—contribute to our understanding of creativity, and the strategies for training each possess some proven merit for fostering creative potential. Creative attitudes, mainly a prerequisite to creative behavior, may be altered in a more flexible, imaginative direction. Innate creative abilities, likewise, may be strengthened through exercise. Finally, relying less on "intuitive" creativity, instructors may teach techniques for producing new combinations of ideas.

Although these strategies have been employed in many existing college and industrial level creative-thinking courses,[16] an integrated attempt to incorporate them into a coherent and interesting program has been lacking. Such an effort, however, aimed at developing creative potential in adolescents, is presented below.

A WORKING CLASSROOM STRATEGY FOR TRAINING CREATIVE THINKING IN ADOLESCENTS

Thinking Creatively: A Guide to Training Imagination represents an effort to consolidate the various strategies for stimulating creativity in a meaningful, yet deliberately free and even humorous fashion.[17] The program is in the form of dialogue among four characters. Mr. I is a backyard scientist-inventor who tries to teach the other three characters creative attitudes and various problem-solving techniques. He often engages in activities consistent with a permissive, creative atmosphere, such as regularly making a carrot sandwich, pumpkin cake, or some other surprising delight. Dudley Bond, a distant relative of a very famous secret spy, is an eager young male character. While a bit awkward at times, Dudley displays a fine sense of humor and often enjoys the fascination and challenge of finding ideas for solving problems. Maybelle is Dudley's friend who needs help in learning to find ideas. Last, but hardly least, is Max, a professional bear who, being the clown of the program, rarely understands anything very clearly. He often displays his uncreative mean streak and freely criticizes some of the "nutty" ideas, thus allowing the others frequent opportunity to repeat the important creative attitudes. Throughout the program, the four friends attack numerous simple and complex problems. Mr. I explains the creative problem-solving procedures and attitudes likely to aid in solving a given

[15] Gordon, *op. cit.*, pp. 48–51.

[16] M. O. Edwards, "A Survey of Problem Solving Courses," *Journal of Creative Behavior*, II (1968), 33–51.

[17] Gary A. Davis and Susan E. Houtman, *Thinking Creatively: A Guide to Training Imagination*, Wisconsin Research and Development Center for Cognitive Learning, University of Wisconsin, 1968.

problem, and Dudley, Maybelle, and sometimes Max use the principles to produce specific problem solutions.

The program is based on several assumptions. First, supposing that most adolescents are largely unaware of or unconcerned with creative innovation, the importance of new ideas in all aspects of our fast-changing society is emphasized. Perhaps more directly relevant to students is the discovery that their capacity to produce new ideas will tremendously aid their own future occupations, whether they are in business, the arts, or professional sports.

The program assumes that appropriate attitudes are essential for creative productivity. Thus, by reading of the favorable problem-solving attitudes of the story characters, students learn to value unusual, new ideas in their own problem solving and to be receptive to those of others. They are taught an attitude of "constructive discontent"—the notion that virtually anything can be changed for the better. The story characters, for example, demonstrate this principle by finding improvements for a dull pocketknife, a wad of paper, a lost key, and a broken pencil, all of which Dudley happened to find in his pockets. Above all, adolescents learn that they themselves are capable of becoming more creative individuals. After having Mr. I continually remind them that they can become better "idea finders," students do exercises which allow them to see their developing creative capabilities.

A further assumption is that students' creative potential would be greatly enhanced if they understood creative-thinking procedures used by others to produce new combinations of ideas. Therefore, Mr. I, the scientist-inventor, teaches the other three characters a repertoire of techniques which closely parallel those described above. With the *part-changing* method, another name for the *attribute-listing* procedure, students learn to identify and improve the main parts or qualities of objects. With the *checkerboard* or *morphological-synthesis* method, they list specific ideas for changing one part along one axis of a two-dimensional diagram, list specific ideas for another part along the other axis, and then examine all possible idea combinations for potentially valuable problem solutions. Using the *checklist* procedure, students find they can be more efficient in producing a large number of potentially good ideas. The *synectic* methods are the source of some idea-finding techniques which focus on the use of analogies. Students learn to find problem solutions by studying how other people, animals, insects, and plants have solved similar problems, by "playing with" or free-associating word meanings, and by looking for perfect or ideal problem solutions—such as having the problem solve itself.

As a final main assumption, the training program recognizes that strong pressures exist which inhibit a free flow of ideas that might be judged non-conforming or perhaps "silly." However, judging from transcripts of comical and enjoyable brainstorming and synectic group sessions, there is reason to assume that a good sense of humor is very important for an uninhibited imagination. Therefore, to create an atmosphere conducive to relaxed spontaneity, in which the wildest ideas may be freely suggested, the program deliberately uses *humor*. The story characters readily propose "funny" problem solutions and, at the same time, engage in slapstick comedy.

Of course, there may be unforeseen difficulties with the present interpretation of creativity and its training. It would be unfortunate, for example, if the "intuitive" creativity of able students were adversely affected by teaching specific idea-generating techniques. Also, the humor in the program conceivably may not function as intended; for example, the students may be excessively entertained and thus distracted from the "serious" program content. Validation studies currently underway will answer these and other questions and therefore provide a suitable basis for modification.

Despite these possible shortcomings, the program may be used effectively. One major asset is its versatility. It might serve as a primary text for a creative-thinking course or as material for an independent-study project in creativity, thereby becoming a new subject area in the school curricula. Alternatively, it may be incorporated into any of several traditional subject matter areas, especially those clearly dealing with new ideas. Any writing, art, or industrial arts class requires ideas for its literary, artistic, or commercial products, while science and history courses frequently focus on innovation in society.

Since it is largely self-explanatory, students and teachers may read the program together or students may study it at home without assistance. In either setting, they may work on the problems presented at the end of most chapters. These simultaneously provide practice with the creative-thinking techniques and exercise in some important creative abilities.

Students in a wide range of ages, socio-economic levels, and abilities may benefit from the program. Younger, lower economic level, and less able students seem to enjoy particularly the "unacademic" humor; older, higher economic level, and more capable students may like having their abilities challenged and substantiated. For all students, the concepts, exercises, reading level, drawings, and humor are intended to be meaningful and interesting.

In sum, *Thinking Creatively: A Guide to Training Imagination* represents a new effort to combine the main components of the various strategies for stimulating creativity into a package which is both interesting and informative for adolescents. It attempts to increase students' awareness of and appreciation for novel ideas, to teach techniques for producing new idea combinations, to provide exercise for some creative abilities, and, through humor, to create a free atmosphere encouraging spontaneity and imagination.

Index